'This is a most welcome bringing-together of the w[...]
admired and influential thinkers and doers in the wo[...]
language education in the second half of t[...]

**Professor Ronald Carter, School of English, Univ[...]
Cambridge Language Sciences, University of Cambridge**

'John Richmond has done readers a service in compiling this book. It is a tonic to read not only Harold Rosen's academic work but his stories and poems, too. Those of us who knew Harold will enjoy hearing his voice again; those who have not yet met him will relish the wit, incisiveness and principle of this remarkable man. He is captured here reminiscing about his childhood, telling stories, showing fierce commitment to diversity and equity in his academic writings, and wisely thoughtful about narrative and life in his later years. This collection brings honour to the word "troublesome", reminding readers that challenge and critique are essential to ensure a fair and equitable education for all our children – and all our sakes.'

Eve Bearne, United Kingdom Literacy Association

'It is marvellous that John Richmond has assembled this fine collection of the writings of Harold Rosen. As a founder member of the London Association for the Teaching of English, and professor at the Institute of Education, University of London, Harold had an enormous influence on our understanding of the relationship between language and learning. We can see here that he was also a talented poet and story writer. A reader of this collection will appreciate the great contribution Harold Rosen made to education, language and literature.'

Professor Neil Mercer, University of Cambridge

Harold Rosen

Harold Rosen

Writings on life, language and learning, 1958–2008

Edited with an introduction by John Richmond

IOE Press

First published in 2017 by the UCL Institute of Education Press, University College London,
20 Bedford Way, London WC1H 0AL

www.ucl-ioe-press.com

British Library Cataloguing in Publication Data:
A catalogue record for this publication is available from the British Library

ISBNs
978-1-78277-189-0 (paperback)
978-1-78277-201-9 (PDF eBook)
978-1-78277-202-6 (ePub eBook)
978-1-78277-203-3 (Kindle eBook)

Typeset by Quadrant Infotech (India) Pvt Ltd
Printed by CPI Group (UK) Ltd, Croydon, CR0 4YY

Contents

Second Interlude

Part 2: The Role of Language in Learning

Third Interlude

Part 3: Story

Ending

Acknowledgements

The editor and publisher gratefully acknowledge the following copyright permissions:

- 'For Beatrice Hastings', 'The Dinosaur and the Professor', 'The Politics of Writing', 'The Autobiographical Impulse' and 'We are our Stories' were originally published by The English and Media Centre in *Troublesome Boy* (1993).
- 'The Autobiographical Impulse' is also republished with permission of ABC-CLIO Inc, from *Linguistics in Context: Connecting observation and understanding: lectures from the 1985 LSA/TESOL and NEH institutes*, Tannen, D. (ed.), Volume XXIX, 1st edn, 1988; permission conveyed through Copyright Clearance Center, Inc.
- 'The Politics of Writing' was originally published in Kimberley, K., Meek, M. and Miller, J. (1992) (eds.) *New Readings: Contributions to an Understanding of Literacy*. © A & C Black, an imprint of Bloomsbury Publishing Plc.
- The following works, all Copyright © the Editors of *Changing English*, reprinted by permission of Taylor & Francis Ltd, www.tandfonline.com on behalf of the Editors of *Changing English*:
  - 'A Necessary Myth: Cable Street revisited' in *Changing English* (1998), 5 (1), 27–34.
  - 'Autobiographical Memory' in *Changing English* (1996), 3 (1), 21–34.
  - 'Isaak Babel and the Bird' and 'Barn Owl' from 'Four Recent Poems' in *Changing English* (2003), 10 (2), 155–158.
  - 'Maginot Line' in *Changing English* (2004), 11 (2), 243–245.
- The following works, originally published by the National Association for the Teaching of English (NATE):
  - 'Messages and Message-Makers' in *English in Education* (1971), 5 (2).
  - *Stories and Meanings* (1985).
  - 'Out There or Where the Masons Went' in *English in Education* (1975), 9 (1).
- 'Stories of Stories: Footnotes on sly gossipy practices' in Lightfoot, M. and Martin, N. (eds.) (1988) *The Word for Teaching is Learning*. London: Heinemann Educational Books. © National Association for the Teaching of English (NATE).
- 'Multicultural Education and the English Teacher' in Eagleson, R.D. (ed.) (1982) *English in the Eighties*. Originally published by the Australian Association for the Teaching of English (AATE).
- 'The Voices of Communities and Language in Classrooms: A review of Shirley Brice Heath's *Ways with Words*' in *Harvard Educational Review* (December 1985), 55 (4), 448–57.
- 'The Nationalisation of English' in *International Journal of Applied Linguistics*, (1991) 1 (1). © John Wiley and Sons.

- 'Towards a Language Policy Across the Curriculum' and 'A Language Policy Across the Curriculum' in Barnes, D., Britton, J., Rosen, H. and the LATE (1969 [1971]) *Language, the Learner and the School*. Reprinted with permission from the London Association for the Teaching of English (LATE).
- 'Language across the Curriculum' in Hickman, J. and Kimberley, K. (eds.) *Teachers, Language and Learning*. Copyright © (1988) the editors and Routledge. Reproduced with permission of Taylor & Francis Books UK.
- 'The Importance of Story' in *Language Arts* (1986), 63 (3), March. Copyright 1986 by the National Council of Teachers of English. Reprinted with permission.
- 'Narrative in Intercultural Education' in *European Journal of Intercultural Studies* (1999), 10 (3), 343–53. Reprinted by permission of the publisher, Taylor & Francis Ltd, www.tandfonline.com.

About the Editor

In his early career, John Richmond was a classroom English teacher in two London secondary schools. Later, he was advisory teacher for English in the Inner London Education Authority; he helped to run two national curriculum development projects – the National Writing Project and the Language in the National Curriculum Project; and he was adviser for English and drama in Shropshire. During this period, he published books and articles on English teaching and the role of language in learning, and ran courses and gave lectures throughout the UK and internationally. He has been a Visiting Professor in the School of English at the University of Nottingham. Between 1992 and 2011, he worked in educational television at Channel 4 and Teachers TV in the UK, and at Teaching Channel in the USA. He is the principal author of *Curriculum and Assessment in English 3 to 11: A better plan* and *Curriculum and Assessment in English 11 to 19: A better plan*, both published in 2017 by Routledge.

Introduction

Harold Rosen was a leader of thought in the world of English teaching in the second half of the twentieth century. He and his colleagues forged and sustained a new understanding of the purpose and possibilities of the subject English within the school curriculum. Beyond the constituency of English teachers – people teaching that subject in secondary schools – Harold's teachings, writings and activities illuminated many more people's understanding of the relationship between language and learning in any context, whatever the age of the learner and the content of the learning.

Harold was born in 1919 in Brockton, Massachusetts to Jewish parents. At the age of two, he came to the East End of London with his mother, an active communist and inspirational woman whose influence remained with him all his life. He attended local elementary and grammar schools. In 1935, he joined the Young Communist League, where he met Connie Isakofsky. Their emotional partnership, marriage and intellectual collaboration lasted 41 years, until Connie's early death from cancer. It was the urgent clarity of the needs of those years – to defeat fascism and to liberate working-class people from every sort of poverty – which formed Harold politically.

In 1937, Harold went to University College, London to study English. He was a college rugby player, middle-distance runner and political activist. He graduated in 1940. He took a one-year postgraduate teaching qualification at the Institute of Education, University of London (IOE). From 1941 to 1943 he taught English at the Gateway School, Leicester. He moved to Harrow Weald County Grammar School in 1943, working there for another two years. Having been born in the USA, he was officially an American citizen (and remained so throughout his life), so it was the US army he joined when called up in 1945. He served in the infantry for a year. He then joined the Education Corps, first as an instructor at the US army university at Shrivenham in Oxfordshire, then as information and education officer in the Office of the American Military Government in Germany. Returning to civilian life in 1947, it was clear to him, as to so many people politically committed on the left, that the defeat of fascism must be only the necessary beginning of a shift towards more open and egalitarian societies in the victorious as well as the defeated nations.

When Harold left the army, he worked at Greenford County Grammar School and then Kingsbury County Grammar School, both in Middlesex. His career was impeded by the blacklisting of communists then practised in some circles of that

Local Authority. When the London County Council made its pioneering move towards comprehensive education, with the setting up of pilot comprehensives, Harold went to one of them, Walworth School, as head of English in 1956.

The work of the Walworth English department from the mid-1950s to the early 1960s has filtered through countless channels into the theory and practice of progressive English teaching in the UK and the English-speaking world. Briefly put, this theory and practice insists that the content of the curriculum which the teacher brings to the class must respect the culture and experience which the learner brings there. It sees the making of meaning in and through language as the essential act in which learners engage and which teachers help to bring about. It says that the best learning is a collaboration between teacher and learner, and between learner and learner. It was the effort to make this theory and to put it into practice which Harold joined and helped to lead for 40 years.

Harold was a founder member (in 1947) of the London Association for the Teaching of English (LATE), the first local organization dedicated to the improvement of English teaching by practitioners. LATE was the spur to the setting up of other local English teachers' associations, and to the establishment of the National Association for the Teaching of English (NATE). During the late 1960s, LATE broadened its attention beyond English teaching to the idea that all teachers have a responsibility to see that the relationship between language and learning in their classrooms (their own language as well as their pupils') is one which enhances, not diminishes, the effectiveness of pupils' learning. It was at LATE that the idea of 'language across the curriculum' (and the phrase itself) were born.

When he left Walworth, Harold began his long career in teacher education, first at Borough Road Teacher Training College in Isleworth, and then in the English department of the IOE, where he had trained. James Britton and Nancy Martin were the senior figures there at that time. Beginning under their leadership, and later when he rose to become head of the department and a professor of the university, Harold and his colleagues made the department a place of national and international fame and impact in the professional education of English teachers, and a centre of thought about language and learning.

In 1976, Harold and his colleagues proposed that the IOE should host twice-yearly conferences for teachers, which would be opportunities for the exchange of research, theory and practice in language education. These conferences came to be known as 'Language in Inner-City Schools'. They were organized by a group of people inside and outside the IOE, of whom I was one. They turned into very large affairs; at their peak, around 500 people attended, every January and June. They ran for more than ten years, and were a significant gathering and exchanging point of ideas and practices for teachers (many of whose homes and schools extended well beyond the inner city).

Harold had the intellectual apparatus necessary for a conventional academic career of great distinction. This wasn't the choice he made. His output of educational publications is large, as readers who persist to the end of this compilation will notice, but he put his greatest efforts into collaborations with colleagues, always addressing the needs and concerns of practitioners: for example, *The Development of Writing Abilities 11–18*, with James Britton and others; *Language, the Learner and the School*, with James Britton, Douglas Barnes and LATE; *The Language of Primary School Children*, with Connie Rosen, herself an inspiring figure in progressive primary education; and *Languages and Dialects of London School Children*, with Tony Burgess. In the later stages of his career, his attention turned more and more to narrative (or, as he preferred to call it, 'story'), and he published one single-handed full-length work on the topic: *Speaking from Memory: The study of autobiographical discourse.*

Harold wrote autobiographical stories about his childhood in the East End of London and about his own education. They are gathered (and some are repeated) in two volumes: *Troublesome Boy* and *Are you still Circumcised?* The stories are by turns shocking, funny, poignant and loving, and questions of language hover within all of them. (To me, they are often a reminder of the sheer brutality of teachers' behaviour which was accepted in the schools, particularly elementary schools, in the early part of the last century.) There is one story about an experience in Berlin in 1945 when he was a soldier in the US Army. Seven of the stories, including the Berlin story, are republished here.

Harold also wrote poetry; a selection of his published poems reappears here. One poem appears for the first time.

Harold left the British Communist Party in 1957, having decided that the party was no longer likely to help bring about the social change he desired in Britain. Its Stalinism was increasingly at odds with the direction and tenor of his educational activities and beliefs. He remained all his life a socialist, as fiercely critical of the evils which Western imperialism and unchecked market capitalism have brought upon the world as he was sorrowful at the dashing of the hopes of his youth with regard to the Soviet Union and the Eastern bloc.

In the politics of education, Harold fiercely resented – and, when he was still working, fought – the attacks on progressivism from within the Thatcher, Major and Blair governments. In fact, within the parabola of Harold's writing, thought and activity can be seen a change – often an angry change, expressed in defiant terms – from the essentially forward-looking, ground-gaining, progress-making tone of his early work, which saw clearly what was wrong with the territory into which he had come, and what needed changing, to the bitter but never defeated realisation that ground gained is not ground won for ever; that the forces of ignorant, retrospective reaction can and will take that ground back, given that they have the power to do so.

But there is always the official story and the unofficial story. Harold was as impatient with voices on the extreme left which said that nothing can be done, that teachers and schools are the helpless dupes of an oppressive system designed to replicate existing power relations, as he was active in opposing the increasingly detailed and reactionary control of teachers' working lives that some governments, especially that in England, were taking. His own life was an example of the unofficial story.

Harold's second wife Betty was, until her retirement, also an English teacher. She is the author of books on narrative and storytelling, and it was partly under her influence that Harold's later educational writing focused on the nature and role of story in our ability to conceptualize and communicate. It was Betty's idea that this compilation should be made.

Harold died in 2008. I knew him for the last 32 years of his life. I was never formally his student, and yet he was – as I told him not long before he died – one of my great teachers, for this reason: he showed how to combine intellectual effort with political purpose. Harold knew that a person's achievement is only meaningful to the extent that it changes the lives of other people, the lives of organizations (like schools) and the life of society as a whole, for the better: a principle which holds for even as great a talent and as significant a contribution as his own. I never met anyone who more completely lived the idea that the point is not simply to interpret the world, but to change it. Harold's life in education exemplified his conviction that theory and practice, thinking and doing, are interpenetrating. He understood and taught that education is a supremely practical business, not a 'pure' science. He was constant in his insistence that those whose job it is to help teachers teach better should apply their mental effort to that task, and not go off on academic frolics of their own.

This lived principle – that those who have been raised up within any social structure, in his case the structure of the British education system, must use their advancement to support the efforts of those who work within the structure – came from his socialist understanding of a possible just society, and his work towards that goal. One of his favourite poems was Brecht's 'Questions from a Worker who Reads'. (There is an oblique reference to the poem in the title of one of the pieces in Part One of this compilation.) Here are the first few lines:

Who built Thebes of the seven gates?
In the books you will find the names of kings.
Did the kings haul up the lumps of rock?

And Babylon, so many times demolished,
who raised it up again so many times?

> In what houses of gold-glittering Lima
> did the builders live?
> Where, the evening that the Wall of China
> was finished, did the masons go?

Harold validated, challenged and empowered the working lives of thousands of teachers, the builders of the structure of which he was a master mason. I was – and still am – one of those builders myself.

A book to which Harold contributed begins with the sentence 'We classify at our peril'. (The chapter Harold wrote is reprinted in Part Two of this compilation as 'Sense of Audience', although his contribution to the thinking and research which led to the book in question extended well beyond that chapter.) *At our peril.* And yet, with all the dangers inherent in classification, there is always an urge to group things – to find a shape. So it is here. The writings of a thinker as bold, as transgressive (I mean in the sense of crossing boundaries, elbowing against constraints) as Harold Rosen are not easily marshalled or corralled. An easy option would have been to arrange the writings in chronological order of their publication and let the reader infer for herself or himself the overall structures, the patterns of developing thought in the body of work as a whole. I have decided against that. Harold's educational writings are here grouped under three broad, loose headings:

* Part One: The politics of language and English teaching
* Part Two: The role of language in learning
* Part Three: Story

Within each heading, the pieces *do* appear chronologically. But of course their concerns very often – in fact, more often than not – chafe against the boundaries, bleed across them. That is the nature of the thinker and doer he was. And I hope that readers will appreciate another kind of transgression: the generic mixing whereby some of Harold's stories and poems are interspersed among the educational writing, in three Interludes, within Part Three, and in the Ending. Not many full-scale scholars of language, literature and culture have dared actually to do the thing they write so authoritatively about.

John Richmond
London, June 2016

First Interlude

The Children

A Young Communists Mayday march, c.1928. Harold carries the big banner.

On the Road

At ten he took to the granite-cobbled road
Which led from Whitechapel to the wide world.
He might have encountered
Mountebanks, footpads, vagabonds, pedlars,
Travelling players, or even highwaymen. But he didn't.

There was an off-chance of sighting
A dreadful figure in a hooded white robe
Tolling his leper's bell, crying, 'Unclean! Unclean!'
Or a tall long-bearded biblical fellow
Who blocked his way, raised his palm,
And peremptorily demanded his business,
Or a pilgrim perhaps returned from Compostella
Blissfully adorned with a cockleshell in his cap.
But he didn't see any such folk.

He might have reached finger-posted villages
Set in damp fields or clustered on river banks
Or a walled town, its chimneys smoking,
Its castle glowering over the peasantry
Or a turreted mansion whose chatelaine
Awaited her marauding knight.
But he didn't.

He didn't
Because he turned left instead at Aldgate Pump
To the Portland-stone banks and shipping offices
And immaculate expensive models of ocean liners
Ten feet long
To the black bowlers and the important striding legs
And eyes front.
Always the newsboys hollering the latest misfortune.

He found the river and the waterside,
Watched little ragamuffins from Stepney and Shadwell
Straddling old black cannons and squat mortars like toads
Emblazoned with alien heraldry and distant dates.
They wrestled each other off the barrels
Or shouted 'Boom, boom' across the water.
Over there, the tide out, he stood in the mud
Right under the giant hull of a merchant ship.
He saw brown faces from high, high up
Lining the rail grinning and waving.
A few thin ropes held all this tonnage back
From toppling on him.
Mudlarks bent over their work did not straighten up
To watch him stumble back to the wet green river-steps.
Made his way up to the miracle double bridge.
Where he saw the roadway split in two and rise into the air,
Horse dung and fag ends rolling towards the barrier.
The *Royal Sovereign* making its way from The Pool to Southend,
Crammed with Londoners on a day out to different air,
Swigging their beer and shouting up to the pedestrians.
Such a small boat to set in motion
All that hidden machinery
And make a street stand on end.

Afterwards an old man in a tatty overcoat, his back to the river,
Came forward to block his path.
'Here, here. Ever stood on the crack?
Just put a leg on each side and wait for a lorry.
You'll see.'
Astride he braced himself until the whole world trembled
Through his spine and his head rumbled.
'You see, you see. Thousands of tons of masonry but it always moves.'
A wonder of the world.

'Where have you been?' they asked. 'Where have you been?'
'Out in the world,' he might have said.
Very unlikely.
And after all, this was only a beginning.

Comrade Rosie Rosen

I was eleven, sitting on a hard chair, looking at the man across the desk. He looked weary, perhaps even cross. My mother was sitting on a chair next to me. She too was looking across the desk at the man. I thought I could detect the glint of battle in her eye, but the man hadn't noticed. He wasn't looking at either of us but down at the buff-coloured folder which he frowned at while opening it.

We had ended up in this room after crossing Westminster Bridge. From the north side you gaze across the river at County Hall. I had seen it from there several times – a very important building, very governmental, solid, expensive, closed. I had never wondered what went on in it. I don't think I knew that they governed London from there and I certainly didn't know that somewhere in there they governed my education. As we crossed the bridge County Hall expanded, spreading its long facade right along the South Bank of the river. There seemed to be no way into its white coldness. How did anybody get in? Was there a special side door for nobodies? This was not going to be easy. But my mother was not touched by doubt. I could tell by her walk and the hold of her head. She led me round to the back without hesitation. Had she been here before? We went up wide steps into a high entrance hall. Uniformed men asked her business and one gave her directions like a policeman. We trekked up wide staircases into a labyrinth of expensive wood, along panelled corridors, our shoes clacking on polished parquet. We were, I felt sure, in enemy territory. County

Hall men and women passed us about their business, intent, silent. I found them sinister.

My mother found the room we wanted. Its ordinariness came as a surprise – drab walls, well-worn lino, a few stacks of files on the floor, books and pamphlets leaning crazily on a set of shelves. A tray of papers on the desk was overspilling a little. I would have liked to be away from there, back on my side of the river, walking freely along the Embankment, taking in boats, bridges, public gardens and saunterers.

The man across the desk looked up and gazed at my mother without saying a word. Teachers do that, I thought. It's how they get on top of you from the word go. My mother wore for the occasion her best black gloves, a newish grey hat and a fox fur. Gloves, hat, fur – she was putting on the style. The man began talking in a rusty voice, affecting infinite patience and civility, cultivated in dealing with the lower orders, especially those from the East End. I heard heavy condescension and controlled insolence. I worried desperately. My scholarship to the grammar school was at stake.

'Before I hear what you have to say, Mrs Rosen, and I shall do, rest assured, you simply must understand I have noted all the details. I have read your letter most carefully. I see from the form you've filled out that you and your husband became U.S. citizens in 1913. I am very sorry to tell you that makes the boy an alien. You won't have read the regulations, of course. Oh, so sorry, you have? Well, they are very clear, aren't they? We are obliged to see that all conditions are met before we can ... '

'Just a minute, just a minute. No one has asked me about what happened to my citizenship after I came back to England in 1922. You certainly haven't, have you? I reclaimed my British citizenship in 1924 after they changed the law. There's quite a few things which concern this scholarship which I've not been asked about.'

'Mrs Rosen, we have checked the details very thoroughly.'

'You haven't got all the details so how can you have checked them?'

At this point she took out of her bag a little sheaf of papers. I marvelled at her composure. The desk-man made an attempt to speak but my mother, certain she had the initiative, cut him off.

'No, no, don't rush me. Are you in a hurry? Let's go through these papers one by one. And you should know that my local councillor, Mr Silver, will be coming to see you and my MP, Mr John Scurr, tells me he'll be writing to you.'

The official's manner was changing. Not that he became affable, but he was no longer dismissive and patronising. I had by now shed all my discomfort and sat revelling in my mother's aplomb. I was sure I'd get that scholarship.

I had heard my mother confronting officialdom before – across desks and counters and on our own doorstep. I loved the ways in which she could hold her own with the best of them, just as I winced when I heard nervous old folk struggling for English words to cope with men and their pens and papers and well-timed ways of looking over the tops of their glasses. I admit fully that I thought my mother was something special for all sorts of reasons, some of which don't look very good now. Yes, I know too that mothers are special to their children who are loved by them, defended by them and who are always there. But that's not what I mean at all. I was, I suppose, what I can only call a mother snob, inflated ridiculously by all the ways in which she was different from the Jewish mums who surrounded me. First of all she was born in England, right there in Stepney, not in Minsk, Vilna or Odessa. It followed that she'd been to school in England and after getting a job as a cashier in a large grocer's shop in Aldgate she took extra classes at the People's Palace so she spoke Real English. In the family it sounded Jewish. After all, you can't speak of Passover, a *barmitzvah* or how to make cheese *blintzes* without throwing in a few Yiddish words and phrases and direct translations from Yiddish. But my mother could drop all that very easily and posh up her English when the occasion demanded it. When she sometimes overdid it and made her lips look different my pride went sour on me. Usually I took great pleasure in her sounding so English, believing that it was mostly this which gave her the confidence to cross the frontiers of the ghetto to go to theatres and meetings and to take us on trips into the country. I was pleased she didn't speak to me in Yiddish and I indecently discarded it totally as soon as I could. To me her English made her a cut above, several cuts.

At eight I knew she was the cleverest woman in the world. If not in the world then at least between Gardiners Corner and Burdett Road. I knew, too, that she'd read millions of books – Whitechapel Library was one of her haunts. She had quite a few old books on the shelves of a small battered bookcase in her bedroom, bought, I suppose, for pence from market stalls or in fundraising bazaars. Once I could read I used to puzzle over the titles. So many of them seemed perversely opaque – *Hypatia*, *Quo Vadis*, *Pygmalion*, *Erewhon*, *Anti-Duhring*, *The Ragged Trousered Philanthropists* and *King of the Schnorrers*. I had gradually come to the conclusion that she knew every word in the English language. I used to sit on the floor and read when she was in bed in the morning. Once I was struggling through *Robinson Crusoe* because someone had given it to me as a birthday present and because it was brand new with a brilliant red cover, in the middle of which was pasted a picture of Robinson himself bare foot and thatched all over. But inside the print was too small, the black and white illustrations murky and the language elusive. The compensation was that if there was a word I couldn't understand I'd ask my encyclopaedic mother.

'Mum, what's an ague?' (I pronounced it to rhyme with plague.)
'A what? Something wrong there. Read the sentence out to me.'
'"I was stricken with an ague."'
'Ah, I see, you should say ay-goo. It means a fever.'

****

I was seven. I was sitting for the umpteenth time in a large seedy room in Cable Street. A crowd of men and women were sitting on an assortment of battered old chairs under a blue-grey swirl of reeking cigarette and pipe smoke. Against one flaking wall was propped the red banner with a yellow hammer and sickle in the middle of it. Down one end Milly was making lemon tea on an old black stove and serving portions of cheesecake. I was reading *Film Fun* and getting impatient for my mother to get me some of that cheesecake. These were The Comrades at a meeting of The Party in what were always called The Premises. That evening we'd struggled through the damp of Cable Street, across the puddles of the smelly yard and joined The Comrades. I knew in a half-truculent way that there was not going to be much in this for me. From time to time I looked up from my comic and tried to listen to the very serious men and women. Not easy. Each speaker took a long time and there was very little I could understand. Out there, nobody else talked like this, pointing didactic fingers and punching the air. I knew some of them very well for they often came to the house to deliver 'literature' (I had trouble with that word for a long time). When they did, they talked like everyone else – mostly. A few of them gave me their time and joked and told me stories and one of them sang Yiddish songs. Tobias, whom I had heard speaking like an avenging angel, gave me a copy of William Morris's *News from Nowhere* and wrote in it, 'The fault, dear Brutus, lies not in our stars but in ourselves that we are underlings'. I couldn't make much of that at the time. Keep it till later, he had said. One day he arrived with a cardboard box full of volumes of an out-of-date encyclopaedia – I think it was Harmsworth's. Volume Seven was missing but we sat together looking at the pictures and he kept up an instructive patter.

'You'll see. Some day this will help you with your studies. It's all in here.'

They were shoved higgledy-piggledy in the cupboard on the landing outside my bedroom and I often pulled out a volume and turned the pages. I liked Tobias, even when he was orating at The Premises.

This evening, as usual, the argot which so bewitched them was rolling out. They spoke of the dictatorship of the proletariat, surplus value, the balance of class forces, the crimes of the bourgeoisie. There were dark denunciations of class traitors and deviationists. My mother could speak this language, too. She was at a table at the front of the meeting as Branch Secretary with four other Comrades. After the meeting, long after I had finished my cheesecake and some lemonade, she stayed behind to plan leafleting, a poster parade, canvassing – activities which I'd sometimes be drawn into and be given a placard to hold or a tin to shake. Before The Comrades left The Premises they stopped to take some pamphlets from the piles on the trestle table. My mother took some too. They were as baffling to me as the speeches. They were called things like 'The Final Crisis of Capitalism', 'The Ninth Plenum of the Comintern', 'The Soviet Path to Peace'. I used to look for the ones with pictures in. There were always pictures of men in jail – The Twelve Class War Prisoners (in England), The Meerut Prisoners (in India), Tom Mooney (in the U.S.), marchers with slogan banners, strikers outside their factories and confrontations with police. They became the dominant icons of my childhood and my mother was in the thick of all this. Look at her speaking and them listening. What a woman!

My friends' mothers were not like that, loveable though I found them, plumply installed in their kitchens with their magic recipes, overflowing with affection. They were always good to me, stroked my hair and found me noshy tit-bits. They clearly thought life must be hard for a little boy whose mother was always *schlepping* him to meetings. All the same, if there was trouble with a landlord they were round to our house like a shot.

****

I was eight and it was May Day, Tuesday morning. My sister and I were standing in a municipal dust-cart. It was a brand new one, gleaming buff paint and the splendour of Stepney's coat of arms on the side. The gleaming cart-horses were perfectly groomed and their brasses were gleaming. For this day they were decked out with red and yellow ribbons plaited into their manes and tails. Large rosettes bloomed by their ears. There were thirty or so other little children in the cart with us. I looked over the side at the horses' huge bums and twitching ears. How did they know that they must stand still? Why didn't they lumber off down the road? When would the driver come? I couldn't wait. I had a little ache of anxiety about how we were going to find my mother in the milling thousands in Hyde Park. 'Silly,' said my sister. 'Don't you remember last year? We always find her. She comes to get us.' So we concentrated on cheering the contingents, passing us with their banners, placards and bands. A fairground was flowing along the street. We were in the dustcart because we were too small to march all the way and our Labour Council, like others, had provided their new carts for the kids and perhaps to add a brave dash of fresh paint for the parade. This was not yet another bitter taking to the streets calling for the release of somebody or hands off something or the end of cuts. This was a street festival, a non-stop party. I was just old enough to know that the tradition then was that you took the May Day holiday, no matter what day it fell on. Workers for Labour Councils were given the day off. I knew too that this was a school day and that we were absentees, a cartload of us. My sister and I started getting at our wurst sandwiches and someone was handing out bottles of pop. The cart moved off and we wore our arms out waving at the folk lining the Whitechapel Road. We sang that we were going to hang somebody or other (Joynson-Hicks, was it?) on the sour apple tree when the revolution comes and hurrah for the Bolshie Boys who didn't care a little bit. Then we entered the hostile silence of the City where gents stood staring stonily. Occasionally one of them raged and shook an umbrella like a man in a cartoon. Safe in our cart we laughed and booed and laughed and jumped up and down.

I knew all about May Day. How could I not know? My mother had instructed me over the years.

'They've got their days, plenty of them. Alexandra Day, Armistice Day, Empire Day. And we've got our day, just one, but it's ours. All theirs are for wars, for charity, for showing off with soldiers. They've stuck up their monuments all over the place. Generals and conquerors with soldiers dying like flies all round them and lists of all those poor young men, *nebbich*, killed in their wars. And they always trot out a priest or parson or rabbi to show how holy it all is. We've got our day, our festival, the workers' holiday. It's all ours and nothing to do with them.'

She could go on like this for a long time till it became an incantation. In a sort of trance I knew she had to be right. The trouble was I was dazzled by the Lord Mayor's Show and its tableaux and that golden coach. As for soldiers, I wouldn't ever have dared to admit to her that I tingled when they marched by with their shining bands and I didn't know who 'they' were who set up all those days. All the same, May Day in the cart was best, I was sure of that.

The next day I took an absence note to school, nothing very elaborate. 'My son, Harold, was absent from school yesterday because it was May Day, the workers' holiday.' Not a word was said about it and I knew why. The first time my mother had kept me away on a May Day my teacher had grilled me about it. Where had I been? I couldn't bring myself to tell the truth so I became shifty and mumbled nonsense. She lost patience with me and sent me to the Head. It didn't take him long to extract from me that I had been on the May Day demonstration. His eyes bulged and he poked me in the shoulder. He was shouting very close to my face. What could my mother be thinking of? Did I realise that she could be taken to court? Did she think she could keep me away whenever it took her fancy? As soon as I got home I spilled it all out, especially the poking in the shoulder and being taken to court.

'Court? We'll see about that. And I can tell you he'd better keep his hands off you.'

The next day she was up at the school. I wanted to hear every word of what had happened.

'I don't think we'll have any more *mishegas* about May Day again.'

'What did he say? What did he say? What about going to court?'

'Court! Don't make me laugh. It wasn't mentioned.'

My guess was that Mr Margolis got an earful of Them and Their Days and Us and Our Days. According to her, it all ended up very amicably and by the end she was taking coffee with him like a distinguished visitor. I heard her telling my *zeider* about it amidst laughter.

'We had a nice long talk. Mind you, he nearly took the wind out of my sails. So polite, butter wouldn't melt in his mouth. He says, "Mrs Rosen, I think there has been a little misunderstanding." So I think to myself, I know how to manage this. Mustn't push the little man too hard. Best to give a bit of ground for starters. So I say, "Well, you know, Mr Margolis, maybe I should have dropped you a line beforehand but I thought to myself, a man like you was bound to know it was May Day and, how shall I say, put two and two together." "Mrs Rosen," he says, "I don't mind saying this to you. I can tell you what it's really about. Truancy in this area is a problem. You've got to watch it like a hawk – helping in the shop, minding the baby, went to my auntie's – you can guess the sort of thing." Then I tell him why May Day is a different matter altogether. "Of course," he says, "of course." And this you won't believe, he ends up with, "Well, we're all socialists nowadays, Mrs Rosen."' My grandfather slapped his leg, pushed back his glasses and roared. I wondered why they found that so funny. It became part of the family lore, though, and was cited when anyone mentioned Mr Margolis. I knew now I'd have no trouble on future May Days. On these occasions my mother's brief note was meant as a tactful reminder of the negotiations over the coffee cups. As I got older I began to be troubled by the fact that as far as I could tell I was the only one in the school who stayed away. What were the other parents doing about Our Day? You could say that I'm still asking that question.

****

I was eight still and making my way to school filled with a sick fatalism. There was misery ahead and nothing I could do would stave it off. I was going to Empire Day which the school turned into an all-day jamboree with prayers, hymns, dancing, playlets, readings and above all the grand parade in the playground at the start of the day, to get us in the right frame of mind. We all stomped round in our idea of military marching, a strange little parody, swinging arms, knees up high and feet thumping hard on the asphalt, heads rigid. Small boys and girls in the newest clothes their parents could manage paraded in front of the dull red barrack which towered over them. The five-year-olds, somewhat bemused, got out of step, tripped over each other, and revelled in every second. The tedium and dangers of a routine school day had been declared null and void. All the joy was spiced with competition. Every child brought a Union Jack as they'd been told to do. For days the flags had been on sale in every little sweetshop where they flowered in little tubs next to the front door. If you were really poor you had to be satisfied with a ha'penny one, a pathetic rectangle of thin card glued to a stick with the thickness of a knitting needle. It wasn't going to stand up to a day's waving and jousting but while it was brightly new it could join the colour of the carnival in the morning sunshine. There it would have to stand comparison with those brought by youngsters whose parents could do much better. They arrived with real bunting ones which fluttered properly. There were a few which were taller that the children who held them, with golden spikes on top like Prussian helmets. Ostentatious declarations of loyalty, they belonged with the prayers for the Royal Family on the synagogue walls.

On this fine summer's morning I turned grumpily into Myrdle Street, passing the other children flaunting their finery and flags at each other. Not me. I was in my usual old jersey and scuffed shoes and no flag. My mother was not going to have me tainted with the iniquity of Empire and at least one person was going to crack the enamelled surface of unanimity – me. Carefully she had lectured me about what she thought Empire really meant. She had lots of pamphlets on the subject with appalling pictures in them of floggings, shootings and hangings presided over by men in pith helmets. They haunt me to this post-holocaust day. As ever, I only partly understood what she was saying but I approved of all of it. It was my mother saying all this and she knew. She knew the truth about Empire as she knew about everything else, schooled as she was by those Cable Street conclaves. Which was all very well but she had made quite clear that there was going to be no flag for me and no poshing up. It was one thing to be dazzled by her inside knowledge but quite another to be selected as the representative of her principles, defying the British Empire all by myself.

I'd had a taste of this before. Young as I was, I had learned to grit my teeth and stay seated next to my mother in the cinema when, at the end of the show, they played the National Anthem and a picture of King George V was flashed on the screen. All around me seats banged, people jumped up and stiffened their backs. I studied my feet. As they left they glowered and swore at us and sometimes jostled us a bit. I was frightened certainly of being hurt, but the real pain was the sense of isolation and difference. Only my mother, facing them all without a flicker of doubt, stopped me from rushing out in tears.

The martyrdom of Empire Day was going to be quite another thing. I was going to have to bear it all on my own, in broad daylight, amongst my friends, in front of all the teachers, for a long, long day. The anonymous rigid backs in the cinema were nowhere near as fearsome as the prospect of angry, shocked faces in the school yard. I was a small boy approaching the school gate, wanting to turn tail before retribution overtook me. I caught sight of Solly waving a big flag. His father owned an embroidery shop. Lily Kravitz, in a blue velvet dress with a big bow at the back, came running towards me, all friendly as usual.

'My mum says they're going to give us all sweets and an apple each.'

Then she took a close look at me, my flaglessness, my old jersey and my sulky face and ran off to her friends. And there was Monty whose father was always talking to my *zeider* about the affairs of the Tailors and Garment Workers' Union. He had his *shabbas* clothes on all right and he had a flag.

I sneaked into my classroom. My teacher at the time was Miss Waters who was a leg smacker and finger poker. I hadn't been in the room more than a minute or two when I felt her eyeing me strangely. She knew nothing of my mother's little chat with the Head on the subject of May Day. I huddled in my desk amidst the excited children but I couldn't hide from Miss Waters. She made her way towards me and asked me to come to the front of the class. I steeled myself. She whispered in my ear in an unfamiliar, kind voice.

'Harold, didn't you have a ha'penny to buy a flag?'

She had taken one look at my clothes and my misery face and assumed I was too poor to buy even the cheapest flag.

'Here's a ha'penny,' she said. 'The late bell hasn't gone yet. Nip over the road and buy yourself a flag. For goodness' sake look sharp or we'll be starting without you.'

It was a warm, understanding, untypical thing for her to do. That made it harder for me. If I had been given a dressing down or threatened or made to stand in the corner, I might have dug out of myself a little bravado, though I doubt it. I was far too demoralised by now. That sympathetic voice was irresistible. The severe Miss Waters, I felt, understood all my trials and my self-pitying torment. I looked up at her, ready to commit a monstrous betrayal. There was my principled mother quite deliberately sending me to school so that I could make my stand and begin my apprenticeship. And here was I on the brink of betraying her, actually rejoicing at having this hump of anxiety taken off my back. I took Miss Waters' ha'penny. She was gently pushing me out of the classroom.

'Hurry,' she said. 'We'll be waiting for you.'

I was away, out of the gates, down the street, across the road and into the sweetshop with its last few ha'penny flags. Mrs Abrams was baffled at my popping up like this. She gave me an old-fashioned look and sold me a flag. I was back at the school and into the classroom like a flash. I imagined the whole class was relieved that I was back in the fold and they no longer had to be sorry for me and Miss Waters smiled at me. She was soon marshalling us out of the building and into the playground. There we were lined up and we peeled off class by class into the march. Someone had managed to get a piano into the playground and Mr Margolis standing at the keyboard thumped out a military tune. He was surrounded by the staff who looked happy and approving. As we passed the piano party we waved our flags as we'd been told. Three times round, no less, we went. The relief I had felt soon seeped out of me. And by the time I had done my third renegade waving of that flag I was more downcast than I had been, struggling to do without one. Disconsolate when we finally came to a halt, I did not join in singing 'Land of Hope and Glory', as though I could buy my way back to a clear conscience with this gesture.

I suffered the rest of the day's endless festivities. From time to time Miss Waters took a long look at me, perhaps wondering why her ha'penny hadn't done as much for me as she had hoped. I ate my sweets and apple at playtime, though. I walked home slowly, still holding the accursed flag. I pulled it from its stick and tore it into little pieces and pushed them down a grating in Commercial Road. Then I broke up the stick too, and dropped it into a basement in New Road. I sneaked into our house, trying to avoid my mother – not an easy thing to do at the best of times. Soon enough we were in the kitchen together. She scrutinised me with a quick look and said, 'What's the matter, son? It was a bit hard, eh?'

She knew what she had let me in for and her voice told me she had had her qualms.

'It sometimes costs to stick up for what you believe in but it's the only way. All the same it was hard for you, wasn't it? I can tell. All day without a flag. That hurt a bit, didn't it?'

Then I did the worst thing possible, the very worst thing.

'Yes,' I said, 'it did.'

Chickens

One day she let it slip
Amongst the anecdotes.
'Hens. I used to keep hens,' she said,
Her gaze leaving us
For the distance of memory.
Later: ' … before you were born.'
That unreal time after history
And before me.
That must have been
The low white house
With the verandah.
'Rhode Island Reds, they were.'

But still. This woman keeping hens?
Not her. My mother on a sunny day
In the American countryside,
Barefooted, holding out an apron
Full of grain, the Rhode Island Reds
Excited, clucking around her.
Was that how it was?
Had she ever belonged
In a children's picture book?

Never. This same woman
With her avant-garde Eton crop
Demo-hardened
Singer of bizarre translated songs
(*Whirlwinds of danger are raging around us* …),
Soviet-style red kerchief round her head.
Addicted to meetings and street oratory,
Never short of a slogan or a cause,
Frequenter of Whitechapel library,
Canvasser on hostile doorsteps,
Total Eastender and utterly metropolitan.

Harold Rosen

'Rhode Island Reds,' she said,
'Lovely birds. You get very fond of them.'
It was nearly an obscure joke.

> The last line of this poem was a mystery to the editor until Harold's son Michael pointed out that the phrase 'Rhode Island Reds' might have more than one meaning in the life of a communist woman who had lived for a time on the east coast of the USA.

Part One

The Politics of Language and English Teaching

1

Harold's inaugural lecture as Professor of Education at the Institute of Education, University of London

Language and Class

A critical look at the theories of Basil Bernstein

Throughout the 1960s and into the 1970s, the theories about language and class developed by the sociologist Basil Bernstein and his colleagues, and the implications of these theories for education, had gained widespread attention and commanded widespread acceptance. In previous decades, the relative failure of working-class children to succeed in conventional educational terms had been ascribed to their limited intelligence. This idea, and in particular the notion of IQ (intelligence quotient), had by the 1960s been first questioned, then discredited.

The question, however, still remained: why do more working-class children fail or only modestly succeed in schools than do children from middle-class or upper-class backgrounds? Bernstein's theories seemed to provide an answer. The problem was nothing to do with intelligence; nor was it to do with working-class children's accents and dialects (though these had come under sustained attack from educational authorities more or less since the introduction of compulsory state education in the nineteenth century – see the Newbolt Report [1921], for example). The problem was to do with the relationship between the language of working-class children (or, at least, the children of what Bernstein called the unskilled working class) and cognition. The language which these children inherited from their families and their upbringing equipped them badly for dealing with the abstractions, the conceptualizations, the generalizations and the distinctions which were the stock in trade of the conventional curriculum. The theory emerged from academia into wider educational consciousness as a simple dualism: working-class children operated a 'restricted code' of language; middle-class children operated an 'elaborated code'. Hence the difference in achievement.

Bernstein and his colleagues, as Harold's paper showed, shifted their precise position within their overall theory almost constantly as one publication followed another. But the simple dualism stuck, and was even accepted by some on the left in politics who saw the imposition of restricted code on working-class families as another example of their oppression. At one point, Bernstein attempted to praise the many strengths of restricted code, as if the common meaning of 'restricted' could somehow be put aside. Despite the attempt, the powerful value judgements implicit in the two terms had a big influence on the attitudes and expectations of many teachers teaching working-class children.

Harold's paper robustly challenged Bernstein's theory. This is the text of the third edition (1974) of a booklet first published by Falling Wall Press in 1972, itself an extended version of a paper delivered at History Workshop No. 6, held at Ruskin College, Oxford on 5 May 1972.

... lower-lower class parental patterns, compared to middle class ones, tend to be antithetical to a child's positive mental health ... With generally less ego strength (lower self-esteem), the very poor individual is apt to have greater need than his middle class counterpart for security-giving psychological defences ... The subcultural patterns of this group ... suggest that their life style ... might be termed (within the middle class frame of reference), as immature in a number of respects, such as their greater tendency toward impulsivity, lack of goal commitment, magical thinking, physical learning and behavioral styles, low frustration tolerance, concrete attitudes, and so on.

(from Chilman, *Growing up Poor*, quoted in Ryan, 1971)

The jargon is contemporary but the matter familiar. For well over a century there has been an uninterrupted flow of scholars, philanthropists, politicians and others who contemplated the working class and were far from pleased with what they saw. There are innumerable accounts of fecklessness, improvidence, laziness, immorality, violence and tendencies to mob behaviour and riot. More recently, a considerable body of scholars, particularly in the United States, has exercised its expensive skills to show amongst other things that compared with the middle class (its own class), the working class bring up their children in an unsatisfactory manner with dire consequences for their subsequent success at school. By these means we are offered the central explanation of why the working class (or, as the jargon has it, the 'culturally deprived', the 'disadvantaged', the 'underprivileged') fail to learn in our schools in spite of our tireless efforts to educate them. As the scholarly scrutiny of the life-habits of the working class proceeds, more and more attention has focused upon their language (which as everyone knows distinguishes them from others much more effectively than, say, horny hands and overalls). In a wide range of publications and researches psychologists, linguists and sociologists have in a short space of time turned their attention to a subject which, in spite of its ready accessibility, they had been content to leave to such marginal characters as folklorists (dismissed as romantics), dialectologists (dismissed as mere linguistic cartographers) and novelists (not accepted as sources of evidence). Around this theme a debate has finally emerged precisely because on the one hand there are honest and devoted people who are trying to answer the question, 'Why do so many working-class children fail in school and how can we change things so that they do not?'; and on the other hand because there are people who, in the effort to guard their privileges and power within the educational system, seek tirelessly for new and better theoretical justifications – if need be, adapting and vulgarizing in the process. At the storm centre of the debate stands the work of Basil Bernstein, which advances theories that claim to lay bare critical relationships between class, language and educability. It would be difficult to exaggerate the extent to which Bernstein's ideas have received acceptance throughout the educational world and well beyond it, so much so that they are always referred to with deference at the level of professorial debate, and the terms 'restricted' and 'elaborated' codes have entered the folklore of classroom teachers.

There are two interesting features to the almost unanimous acceptance of these ideas (there are a few notable exceptions, one of which I shall refer to later). The first is that both right and left in educational politics have seen in these ideas support for their views. Thus Bantock (1965) on the right justifies separate education for working-class children and cites Bernstein in support, and Brian Jackson (1968) on the left accepts the main thesis. Jensen (1968) cites Bernstein in the very same paragraph in which he makes the outrageous statement that 'much of working-class language consists of a kind of "emotional" accompaniment to action here and now'.

This support from two opposed sides (many other examples could be cited) must mean that either someone (or everyone) has got it wrong, or that there are central ambiguities and unresolved contradictions in Bernstein's papers, so that like the Scriptures they can be quoted by the Devil, red or black.

Secondly, and more importantly, the way in which Bernstein's theories have permeated contemporary educational thinking and have been used to justify educational practices is a rare phenomenon in English education and calls for some explanation. Educational academics can weave theories and publish researches to their heart's content, and these can accumulate over decades, without affecting practice one iota or causing a ripple in staffroom discussion. But there are notable and significant exceptions.

In the fifties the one theory, with its practical application, which touched the lives of every child and teacher in the public system was the prevailing theory of intelligence and the concept of the Intelligence Quotient. It was, above all, educational academics who disseminated the ideas, developed the tests and even at times administered their application to secondary-school selection in the 11-plus tests (Vernon, 1957). However, by the end of the decade both the operation of the system and its underlying theory had been seriously challenged and, in the eyes of many, totally discredited. This opposition came in the main from teachers and from the political left, and was closely connected with the campaign for comprehensive schools (Simon, 1953). Opponents of the theory of fixed levels of intelligence were alerted to the need to challenge it when they saw how it offered an apparently cast-iron scientific case for an elitism which could in the political climate of the fifties no longer be taken as self-evident.

It was just when this theory was looking sadly tattered and when the high-priest of the psychometric ideology himself, Professor Vernon, felt obliged to publish a self-critical restatement of his position (Vernon, 1960), that the theories of Bernstein began to be available. These early papers, which Bernstein himself now says 'were conceptually weak and … horrifyingly coarse' (Bernstein, 1971, p. 11) and which were the only ones available for several years, were readily seized upon, not only because of the great upsurge of interest in linguistics, but also because they seemed to offer theoretical respectability to the widespread notion among teachers and others that an intrinsic feature of working-class language, rooted in their way of life, disqualified working-class children educationally and, by the same token, justified the notion of the superior educational potential of the middle class. Whereas in the fifties children had their IQs branded on their forehead, in the sixties more and more of them had the brand changed to 'restricted' or 'elaborated'. The ideology vacuum had been filled. Moreover, it had been filled at the very moment when the traditional denigration of working-class language was totally demolished by much of the work in linguistics which was coming to fruition at this time. No serious writer could go on asserting that working-class speech was ungrammatical, lazy, debased and so forth. Bernstein's theories made it possible to bypass all that and to suggest a much more profound and intractable deficiency. The language of the working class was 'restricted', not in the sense that it was 'non-standard', but in the sense that it could not reach out to certain kinds of meanings and limited the power of speakers to understand their environment. The theories pointed to a basic cognitive defect.

Bernstein protests that his work has been misunderstood, misused and vulgarized, just as the psychometrists did before him. And he is absolutely right. However, as he also tells us that his papers are 'obscure, lack precision and probably abound in ambiguities' (Bernstein, 1971, p. 19), this is scarcely to be wondered at.

I shall, therefore, in advancing certain criticisms, concentrate on the most recent of the papers selected for publication together last year – those papers, in fact, which present the most developed version of the work that has been going on for over a decade. These are: 'A socio-linguistic approach to socialization with some reference to educability' (1971), 'Social class, language and socialization' (1971), and 'A critique of the concept of compensatory education' (1969) – now available as Chapters 8, 9 and 10 of *Class, Codes and Control, Vol. 1* (Bernstein, 1971).

Let me now attempt to explain those concepts on which most of the discussion focuses, namely elaborated and restricted codes. I must admit before I set about it that I do not find the task an easy one. These concepts and the theoretical apparatus in which they find a place have been constantly reworked, redefined and explicated. Some have been totally abandoned, others disappear and reappear, so that it is difficult to know what is essential and what is marginal. (For example, in the early work the definition of codes is linked to predictability. The Introduction to *Class, Codes and Control* states that this notion of predictability was abandoned because it 'can be given little statistical significance'. It reappears in a very recent paper [1971], in that same volume.)

Moreover, the level of unrelieved abstraction at which the work is pitched makes it difficult to be certain at times to what reality the concepts and the theoretical apparatus refer. Nevertheless, in spite of all the shifts of emphasis, redefinitions and qualifications, the central concepts of the codes and the main supporting rationale have been sufficiently consistent to permit a summary.

The Bernstein theory

The thesis states that there is a fundamental qualitative difference between working-class (or at least unskilled working-class) speech (Bernstein says that the unskilled working class are 29% of the population) and middle-class speech; and that this is not a matter of underlying grammar, dialect or slang, but rather of the different use of the grammatical system and vocabulary. The difference will arise from different relationships to the social structure. The two classes can be said to be using different codes because there are differences in the principles which underlie the particular choices they make in speech. The differences arise because there are two different kinds of socialization involved, which find their expression in different kinds of language. Children thus acquire different kinds of cultural identity and different responses to that identity. Thus they come to perceive different orders of relevance and relation, of understanding of themselves, others and the world. The class basis of these differences lies in differences in the main socializing agencies, the relationships to family, peer-group, school and work. In practice, Bernstein focuses his attention on the family, which he discusses at some length, since it is seen as the microcosm of the operation of class. In neither his theoretical papers nor his research is there an attempt to examine or analyse the role of language in the other spheres – though, as we shall see, he does make statements about them from time to time. Because of the different ways in which the language codes are used, the middle-class families are given a sense that the world is permeable and are introduced to the principles of intellectual change, whereas the working-class families are not.

How are the two codes that give rise to such dramatic differences described?

First, the restricted code is highly predictable since it draws on narrow resources of language. Thus it is rigid, whereas the elaborated code is flexible.

Secondly, in the restricted code the speaker has difficulty in verbalizing his intent, while the middle-class speaker finds it easier to verbalize his subjectivity, sociologically, intellectually and affectively.

Thirdly, the codes give access to different orders of meaning: the restricted code to *particularistic* meanings rooted in the here and now, in which principles are never made explicit and therefore not made available to inspection and change; the elaborated code, by contrast, to *universalistic* meanings which make principles and operations explicit and thus give individuals access to the grounds of their experience – grounds which, therefore, they can change. Unlike the restricted code, the elaborated code makes possible 'the liberation of speech from its evoking structure and it can take on an autonomy'.

Fourthly, the concepts, *universalistic* and *particularistic*, are linked to two others, *context-free* and *context-bound*. The speaker of the restricted code is tied to the immediate situation, with the result that his speech can be understood only by the participants. On the other hand, the elaborated code, freed from this limitation, makes meaning available to all.

Fifthly, the restricted code operates through *metaphor* and condensed symbols; whereas in the elaborated code, condensed symbol gives way to rationality.

All these differences are connected with a family typology so that we find the restricted code in the *positional* working-class family, and the elaborated code in the middle-class *personal* family. (The family typology is much more complicated than this, but no evidence is offered for it. See Bernstein, 1971, p. 152.) The former has a clear-cut authority structure and its members are treated according to their status; the latter is based on genuine differences between persons with their unique attributes.

The concept of class in Bernstein

Bernstein concludes a recent paper, in which most of the ideas I have just peremptorily summarized are expounded, with these words:

> I have tried to show how the class system acts upon the deep structure of communication in the process of socialization.
>
> (Bernstein, 1971, p. 187)

Whatever else he has done, he has not done that – for the simple reason that he never examines the class system. By implication only, we are provided with a system consisting of two classes, called the working class and the middle class. The working class in his discussion are for the most part the unskilled working class. No further attempt is made at differentiation, whether in terms of history, traditions, job experience, ethnic origins, residential patterns, level of organization or class-consciousness. (In Brandis and Henderson, 1970, there is a complex statistical discussion [p. 130] of how an 'index of social class' was worked out for some of Bernstein's research. The statement of 'the problem' at the outset is limited entirely to 'occupational status' and 'educational status'. There is no discussion of the class system.) As a sociologist, Bernstein is content with the popular term 'middle class' to cover the varied strata whose relationship to the class system varies widely and whose class position certainly has important and different influences on their language. Hence the difference between the language of professors of sociology and that of minor civil servants. But, strangest of all in this system, the ruling class do not figure at all. When Bernstein talks of social control he is not talking of the ways in which one class controls or is controlled by another, but only of the ways in which members of the same class control each other.

Much of the language which the working class encounter in their daily lives is transmitted to them through a variety of agencies not under their control, which deploy a language designed to mystify, to intimidate and to create a sense that the present arrangement of society is immutable. Certain strata of the bureaucracy acquire this language as a vital part of their formation. There is nothing universalistic or person-oriented about it. Nobody knows exactly what part their family upbringing and education play in the acquisition of this highly marketable commodity.

A thorough attempt to analyse the relationship between class and language would require us to examine the relationship of the dominant culture of our society to the culture of the dominated. This would inevitably involve an examination of the part played by language in the operation of this relationship. No one so far as I know has attempted to do this. I believe that one thing which would emerge from such an undertaking would be that the linguistic capital of the dominant culture is persistently over-valued and that of the dominated culture persistently undervalued.

What effect does Bernstein's approach to class have on his analysis? He is aware that to describe certain characteristics of working-class speech explains nothing. His explanation lies in the socializing agencies, which are listed as: family, school, peer-group and work. Before we look more closely at that, we should notice that it omits two powerful agencies of socialization. First, it omits the media of communication, which – though they are largely in the hands of the ruling class – also have included since the beginning of the nineteenth century the published writings, pamphleteering, propaganda and theorizing of the working class. Secondly, and much more important, it omits the organizations created by and maintained by the working class themselves. I mean everything from political parties, trade unions and nonconformist chapels to brass bands and pigeon-racing clubs.

To return to the socializing agencies, it is a feature of the analysis that they remain a list, and that no attempt is made to attribute to any one a key role. However, no reader could be blamed for assuming that key role to be played by the family, since no effort is made to examine the others. All attention is directed towards the home. No attention is paid to that vast area of critical working-class experience, the encounter with exploitation at the place of work and the response to it; nor to the ways which take workers beyond the 'particularistic' circumstances of day-to-day work experience and move them on to explore the theory and practice of how to change society. Thus the working-class child, marooned in the family with his authoritarian father and status-oriented mother, appears by omission to be denied for ever access to an elaborated code and its benefits, since he is alienated from the only agency which could give it to him: school.

It would not be true to say that Bernstein pays no attention at all to the experience of work and how it relates to his theory. He devotes one highly significant paragraph to it:

If a social group by virtue of its class relation, that is as a result of its common occupational function and social status, has developed strong communal bonds; if the work relation of this group offers little variety or little exercise in decision-making; if assertion, if it is to be successful, must be a collective rather than an individual act; if the work task requires physical manipulation and control rather than symbolic organisation and control; if the diminished authority of the man at work is transformed into an authority of power at home; if the home is over-crowded and limits the variety of situations it can offer; if the children socialize each other in an environment offering little intellectual stimuli; if all these attributes are found in one setting, then it is plausible to assume that such a social setting will generate a particular form of communication which will shape the intellectual, social and affective orientation of the children.

(Bernstein, 1971, p. 143)

This telling passage gives us no indication of the source of the information and understanding offered to us. Or to put it more bluntly, how does the writer know about these features of working-class life? Do his ideas derive from a study of workers in industry? Which industry? Where? Or are we being offered a stereotype of the unskilled worker assembled from the descriptive literature of sociology? We are given seven and a half conditions for the existence of the restricted code – and notice that all must be present before the 'plausible assumption' about communication can be made. Are we to assume that they are all of equal importance? If they are, we are entitled to assume that they will become criteria for Bernstein's subsequent assertions and in the research that he cites. They are certainly not criteria for his research samples (see the reference to Brandis and Henderson above), and some of the criteria are never mentioned again, while others are simply asserted in other forms. Let us look at them more closely.

Common occupational function and social status: I assume that what Bernstein means is that all workers have to sell their labour power, and that the ones he is talking about have to do so relatively cheaply – though he does not say so. However, this primary characteristic conceals the fact that different sections of the working class differ in very important secondary characteristics, which in turn will affect how they use language. These characteristics should make us hesitate before we accept the invitation to join in the 'plausible assumption'. This is no simple matter of dividing the working class into 'skilled' and 'unskilled', nor of the niceties of the Halls-Jones scale. (The classification of workers into 'skilled' and 'unskilled' seems to bear little relation to the level of skill required in their jobs, and to have more to do with their power to win that grading from their employers. Agricultural labourers would be a case in point.) We must distinguish between those who are quiescent and defeated and those who are articulate, highly verbal, between those who are submerged in what Freire (1971) calls 'the culture of silence' and others who are capable of being quite explicit about principles and operations in those areas of experience which have been their universities. As the American sociologist Labov has pointed out, our knowledge of the relationship of language and work is based on 'meager anecdotal evidence or on lexical lists which have little social significance' (Labov, 1971).

What distinguishes the language of Liverpool dockers from that of Durham miners or Clydeside shipbuilders or London railwaymen or Coventry car workers? Or for that matter, what distinguishes the language of Liverpool dockers from that of London dockers? If questions of this kind are not asked, then we take away from people their history, be they working-class or middle-class. Though we have nobody who has done the kind of work in language that Hobsbawm (1964) and Thompson (1963) have done in history, we have no right to assume a linguistic uniformity based on general 'occupational function and status'. Indeed, in Hobsbawm's and Thompson's pages we can hear snatches of working-class language which might prove to be a guide. A History Workshop publication like Douglass's *Pit Life in Co. Durham* (1972) shows just how much there is to be learnt. In the absence of any serious study, I would suggest that the most articulate workers are those who have actively participated in the creation and maintenance of their own organizations, and amongst those the most articulate would be those who in that process had encountered and helped to formulate theories about society and how to change it. (There is a political geography to that. It is more likely to happen in Fife than in Cheltenham.) There are other strands which need teasing out, like the tradition of certain kinds of nonconformity and the persistence of an oral tradition amongst Irish workers. It takes a Ewan MacColl or Charles Parker to have an ear for such things. (See, for example, Parker, 1972.)

Little exercise in decision-making: This essentially is an outsider's view, and the studies of the History Workshop on job control show just how little the outsider knows about such matters. In addition, of course, as I have suggested, there are areas of decision which are not directly related to the actual performance of the job.

Assertion is a collective rather than an individual act: Since this theme runs right through Bernstein's thesis, it is worth dwelling on. I am not sure what exactly is meant by 'assertion'. Utterances through a spokesman, or asserting themselves in other ways – collective bargaining, demonstrations, strikes and so on? But in either case this notion is totally untenable and even pernicious. What this kind of formulation does, especially for certain kinds of reader, is to conflate the concept of solidarity with mindless conformity and a sheep-like response to undercurrents in the herd. It implies that since the outcome of the experience of a group is the decision to act together, it has not been preceded either by what Bernstein calls 'the exploration of individual differences' or, we can add, by prolonged formal and informal debate about alternative courses of action. These activities can occur only if language is available which is adequate to the task. What kind of people imagine that the 1972 miners' strike, for example, was made possible merely by the incantation of a few rabble-rousing slogans?

The home and the peer-group: I lump these together because there is already enough work in the United States to show that the assertions which have been made repeatedly about working-class family life and the peer-group have very little substance. I have in mind work such as Ginsburg's *The Myth of the Deprived Child* (1972), Ryan's *Blaming the Victim* (1971) and Labov's work, which I shall turn to shortly. Above all, these writers show how such assertions are rarely based on observation of life as it is lived, much less on participation in it. Bernstein's own research suffers from a similar limitation.

The general drift of what I have had to say so far is that the relationship of the theory to the texture of reality is at best tenuous. There are some occasions when the argument does attempt to bring the two closer together, but in a particular way that I want to examine; at the same time this will provide the opportunity to say a little about the elaborated code and the middle class.

> Imagine a husband and wife have just come out of the cinema, and are talking about the film: 'What do you think?' 'It had a lot to say.' 'Yes, I thought so too – let's go to the Millers, there may be something going on there.' They arrive at the Millers, who ask about the film. An hour is spent in the complex, moral, political, aesthetic subtleties of the film and its place in the contemporary scene. Here we have an elaborated variant; the meanings now have to be made public to others who have not seen the film. The speech shows careful editing, at both the grammatical and lexical levels. It is no longer context-tied. The meanings are explicit, elaborated and individualized. Whilst expressive channels are clearly relevant, the burden of meaning inheres predominantly in the verbal channel. The experience of the listeners cannot be taken for granted. Thus each member of the group is on his own as he offers his interpretation. Elaborated variants of this kind involve the speakers in particular role relationships, and if you cannot manage the role, you can't produce the appropriate speech. For as the speaker proceeds to individualize his meanings, he is differentiated from others like a figure from its ground.
>
> (Bernstein, 1971, p. 177)

This is strange indeed. We are presented with a hypothetical case in which the content of a conversation is summarized. That non-existent conversation is then commented on as though the actual text were in front of us ('The speech shows careful editing', etc.). We are in no position to agree or disagree. After a decade of research we are entitled to expect something better than this for our scrutiny, something which would permit alternative explanations. Let us, however, accept the example at its face value and write the missing paragraphs from the fiction for ourselves.

It then becomes impossible to take it seriously as a contribution to the argument. For after all we have here Hampstead Man, not Orpington Man, and remember the elaborated code is supposed to be characteristic of the whole middle class. It is only when we return to the explanation of universalistic meanings and the high-level intellectualism it implies that we appreciate the reasons for the example. But we are given no reason for believing that this kind of discussion is diffused throughout the various strata of the middle class. Now it is quite true that earlier in the same paper (p. 175) we are told that only 'a tiny handful are given access to the principles of intellectual change', but we are not told who they are. Yet if this is true, then the whole of the argument about educability can be dismissed, for no explanation would be left of why middle-class children *in general* succeed in school.

Of course, sections of the middle class differ from the working class in what they talk about and in their linguistic style. It is also true that many occupy posts in which their capacity to manipulate language in certain ways is what they sell to their employers. Consider all those working in clerical-administrative posts who in their working lives do no more than re-shuffle prefabricated verbal formulae or are the transmitters of the messages of others from above to below. Nothing universalistic about that. Certain sections of the middle class are intensely aware of language but in a particular way: they are concerned to express not so much difference from other individuals but conformity; the differences to which they give the closest attention are those verbal tokens which separate them from the working class. Hence the unwavering vigilance they maintain over the language of their children, guarding them even against such threats as 'grammar school cockney'. As Bourdieu puts it:

> The 'realism of the structure' which is inherent in such a sociology of language [i.e. Bernstein's] tends to exclude from the field of research the social conditions from which that system of attitudes arises which orders, among other things, the structure of language. To take only one example, the distinctive traits of middle-class language such as hyper-correction of errors and the proliferation of signs of grammatical control are indices – among others – of a language characterised by anxious reference to norms legitimised by academic correction – for example, the concern for good manners, manners at the table or manners of speech which betray the language habits of the petit bourgeois. This sort of worry is expressed even more clearly by the avid search to acquire techniques of social behaviour shown by aspiring classes in manuals of etiquette or guides to the proper usage of language. One can see that this relationship to language is the integrating part of a system of attitudes to culture which rests upon the simple desire to respect a cultural rule which is recognised rather than understood, and upon the rigorous attention paid to the rule. This desire

in the last analysis expresses the objective characteristics of the condition and position of the middle strata of the class structure.

(Bourdieu and Passeron, 1970, p. 146, H.R.'s translation)

This does not mean that many middle-class speakers do not use some, but not all, of the resources of language more freely and confidently than many, but not all, working-class speakers. *How* they use those resources is another matter – and it cannot be automatically elevated by calling it 'universalistic'.

Enough of the Millers and their friends. After discussing them, the same text leaps to five-year-olds in order to demonstrate the difference between context-bound and context-free. Here is the passage:

> Consider the two following stories which Peter Hawkins, Assistant Research Officer in the Sociological Research Unit, University of London Institute of Education, constructed as a result of his analysis of the speech of middle-class and working-class five-year-old children. The children were given a series of four pictures which told a story and they were invited to tell the story.
>
> Here are the stories:
>
> 1. Three boys are playing football and one boy kicks the ball and it goes through the window the ball breaks the window and the boys are looking at it and a man comes out and shouts at them because they've broken the window so they run away and then that lady looks out of her window and she tells the boys off.
> 2. They're playing football and he kicks it and it goes through there it breaks the window and they're looking at it and he comes out and shouts at them because they've broken it so they run away and then she looks out and she tells them off.
>
> With the first story the reader does not have to have the four pictures which were used as the basis for the story, whereas in the case of the second story the reader would require the initial pictures in order to make sense of the story.

(Bernstein, 1971, p. 178)

You will notice these are not stories told by actual children, but are constructed by Hawkins who, in his own research report, calls them 'slightly exaggerated' (Hawkins, 1969), and who nevertheless had several hundreds of the original stories to choose from. Once again, let us take them at their face value – archetypes, if you will. The middle-class child tells his story in a way that enables us to follow it without the pictures, the working-class child does not. In grammatical terms the middle-class child uses a more differentiated noun-phrase. Thus, we are told, he generates universalistic meanings. So this is what those giants have dwindled to. If there is a route from these bare little stories, elicited on demand and not from a genuine wish to tell anyone a real story, to the Millers' universalistic flights, then we are given no description of it. There is a vast lacuna to be filled in. And there is another interesting point here. The argument runs that the working-class child takes up a communalized role as against an individualized one. Yet in this instance, bearing in mind that the researcher and the child are both looking at the same set of pictures, it is clear that it is the working-class child who is responding to the person. What needs to be explained is why the middle-class child ignores him. Now it seems that in another experiment the children were left much more free in their construction of stories (they were invited to tell stories about dolls), and in this instance the working-class children's stories were 'freer, longer, more imaginative', while those of the middle-class children were 'dominated by the form of the narrative' (p. 180). The route to universalistic meanings cannot be through attention to form rather than content.

I have tried to make the following criticisms of Bernstein's work:

1. It is based on an inadequate concept of class which lacks theoretical support.
2. Arising from that, he presents a stereotyped view of working-class life in general and its language in particular.
3. Further, he attributes to middle-class speakers in general certain rare and remarkable intellectual virtues, but there is an inadequate examination of the way in which their language is affected by their class position.

Educability

My own interest in this matter relates to educability. On this subject there is an ambiguity in Bernstein's stance, or at least a tension between some of his ideas and others. Without any question there can be found throughout his work a persistent concern that education should be reshaped to accommodate the working-class child by embodying *his* values and *his* culture. It is probably this fact more than any other which has made the rest of his work acceptable to so many educational progressives, though no doubt some are dazzled by the terminology which has a radical and even Marxist flavour. (In the most recent papers, Marx is cited by Bernstein as a formative influence.) This concern is tied to giving working-class children access to the elaborated code, a concept which is explained in such a way that it furnishes no guide to possible strategies and can be made to justify quite contradictory practices.

Commentators frequently draw attention to the fact that the restricted code is never denigrated by Bernstein, but that on the contrary he holds it up for admiration and respect. There is indeed an almost obligatory paragraph which appears in the papers. Here it is:

One of the difficulties of the approach is to avoid implicit value judgments about the relative worth of speech systems and the cultures which they symbolize. Let it be said immediately that a restricted code gives access to a vast potential of meanings, of delicacy, subtlety and diversity of cultural forms, to a unique aesthetic the basis of which in condensed symbols may influence the form of the imagining. Yet, in complex industrialized societies its differently focused experience may be disvalued and humiliated within schools, or seen, at best, to be irrelevant to the educational endeavour. For the schools are predicated upon elaborated code and its system of social relationships. Although an elaborated code does not entail any specific value system, the value system of the middle class penetrates the texture of the very learning context itself.

(Bernstein, 1971, p. 186)

It must be acknowledged without reserve that these remarks constitute a powerful recognition of the potentialities of working-class speech. At the same time it must be said that remarks of this sort are always essentially *parenthetic*, in the sense that they are never explored and they are made in a context which explores tirelessly and intricately what the restricted code cannot do. What is this 'vast potential of meanings', and why have they not been subject to the same intensive investigation and research as the other ideas in the theory? Elsewhere, some of us have argued (Barnes, Britton, Rosen and the LATE, 1971) that expressive language is persistently outlawed in schools, especially in those areas of the curriculum which supposedly demand the elaborated code – history, science, etc. – in which school pupils are obliged to undergo a strange linguistic apprenticeship. In any case, the respect accorded to the restricted code has a hollow ring when 'rationality' is excluded from it ('restricted codes draw upon metaphor, whereas elaborated codes draw upon rationality'). How can this be free from value judgements? As Blackburn (1969) has pointed out:

Once theories are thoroughly cleansed of all 'value judgements' it is believed that they will be governed only by the wholesome discipline of objective facts. The predictable consequence of this attempted purge of values is to orient theory and research towards certain crude, over-abstracted value notions masquerading as scientific concepts: e.g. 'utility', 'efficiency', 'productivity', 'equilibrium', 'rationality', etc.

It cannot be repeated too often that, for all Bernstein's work, we know little about working-class language. For me the parenthesis is more important than the rest of the text.

There is one Bernstein paper which more than any other is seen by educational progressives as a successful answer to criticisms and, significantly, it is a paper to be found in left-wing company, in the reply to the Black Papers, *Education for Democracy*

(Rubinstein and Stoneman, 1970). This paper shows all the signs of being an attempt by Bernstein to align himself unambiguously in educational politics. In his stated attitudes he most certainly does so; but the attempt to fit these attitudes to the theory is less convincing, for as the Jewish proverb has it, he is trying to dance at two weddings at the same time.

The paper begins with an attack on the concept of compensatory education, for directing attention away from the inadequacies of the schools to the inadequacies of families:

> The concept 'compensatory education' serves to direct attention away from the internal organization and the educational context of the school, and focus our attention upon the families and children. The concept 'compensatory education' implies that something is lacking in the family, and so in the child. As a result the children are unable to benefit from schools. It follows then that the school has to 'compensate' for the something which is missing in the family and the children become little deficit systems. If only the parents were interested in the goodies we offer; if only they were like middle-class parents, then we could do our job. Once the problem is seen even implicitly in this way, then it becomes appropriate to coin the terms 'cultural deprivation', 'linguistic deprivation' etc. And then these labels do their own sad work.
>
> (Bernstein, 1971, p. 192)

Anyone who takes the trouble to read from end to end the papers written over the last decade will find that what Bernstein is criticizing is almost an exact description of his own work. Time and time again we are given an analysis of the positional and personal families, the family is said to be the microcosm of the social macrocosm, mothers are asked questions about how they would speak to their children, answer their questions, etc. As we have seen, Bernstein's theory, too, has it that there is 'something lacking' in working-class language: it is called elaborated code and the very same paper goes on to say so. You cannot protest very convincingly against the harm done by the label 'linguistic deprivation', when your own theory points to a deficit, indeed when you have actually stated elsewhere that 'the normal linguistic environment of the working class is one of relative deprivation' (Bernstein, 1971, p. 66) and that the codes 'are highly resistant to change' (*ibid.*, p. 91). The labels 'restricted' and 'elaborated' also 'do their own sad work'. It is true that this paper puts most trenchantly the dilemma of the working-class child in the middle-class school, but it did not require the codes theory to do any of this.

Anyone looking for a published scholarly viewpoint which is the opposite to Bernstein's should study William Labov's powerful and committed account of black working-class language. You will look in vain in this country for a similar sociolinguistic account of Cockney, Geordie or other working-class dialects. It is impossible to do justice to it here. But I must attempt some indication. Labov sets out to show that the concept of verbal deprivation has no basis in social reality:

> ... in fact, Negro children in the urban ghettos receive a great deal of verbal stimulation, hear more well-formed sentences than middle-class children, and participate fully in a highly verbal culture. They have the same basic vocabulary, possess the same capacity for conceptual learning, and use the same logic as anyone else who learns to speak and understand English.
>
> The notion of verbal deprivation is part of the modern mythology of educational psychology, typical of the unfounded notions which tend to expand rapidly in our educational system. In past decades linguists have been as guilty as others in promoting such intellectual fashions at the expense of both teachers and children. But the myth of verbal deprivation is particularly dangerous, because it diverts attention from real defects of our educational system to imaginary defects of the child.
>
> (Labov, 1972, p. 179)

Labov studies the language of those totally alienated from the school who 'participate fully in the vernacular culture of the street'. He shows in quite precise terms, examining stretches of recorded conversation, how the usual research situation reduces working-class language almost to zero, and how by changing that situation, by allowing a hitherto 'non-verbal' child to bring a friend, by introducing a taboo topic and by having the interviewer sit on the floor, etc., the same child becomes highly articulate – because, he argues, the culture from which he comes is a highly verbal one. He then turns his attention to middle-class speech:

> There are undoubtedly many verbal skills which children from ghetto areas must learn in order to do well in the school situation, and some of these are indeed characteristic of middle-class verbal behaviour. Precision in spelling, practice in handling abstract symbols, the ability to state explicitly the meaning of words and a richer knowledge of the Latinate vocabulary, may all be useful acquisitions. But is it true that all of the middle class verbal habits are functional and desirable in the school situation? Before we impose middle class verbal style upon children from other cultural groups, we should find out how much of this is useful for the main work of analyzing and generalizing, and how much is merely stylistic – or even dysfunctional. In high school and college middle class children spontaneously complicate their syntax to the point that instructors despair of getting them to make their language simpler and clearer. In every learned journal one can find examples of jargon and empty elaboration – and complaints about it. Is the 'elaborated code' of Bernstein really so 'flexible, detailed and subtle' as some psychologists believe (Jensen, 1968,

p. 119)? Isn't it also turgid, redundant, and empty? Is it not simply an elaborated style, rather than a superior code or system?

(Labov, 1972, p. 192)

Labov supports this with a detailed analysis of two texts, one from Larry, a fifteen-year-old, the roughest and loudest member of a Harlem gang, on the subject of belief in Heaven and Hell; and the other from Charles M, an upper middle class, college-educated Negro, on the subject of witchcraft. He comes to the conclusion that Larry is undoubtedly a skilled speaker with verbal presence of mind, who can use the English language for many purposes; but that Charles M is merely an educated speaker.

> The initial impression of him as a good speaker is simply our long-conditioned reaction to middle class verbosity. We know that people who use these stylistic devices are educated people, and we are inclined to credit them with saying something intelligent. Our reactions are accurate in one sense. Charles M is more educated than Larry. But is he more rational, more logical, more intelligent? Is he any better at thinking out a problem to its solution? Does he deal more easily with abstractions? There is no reason to think so. Charles M succeeds in letting us know that he is educated, but in the end we do not know what he is trying to say, and neither does he.
>
> (*ibid.*, p. 169)

Labov also poses a problem which he says nobody has yet tackled:

> When Bernstein (e.g. 1966) describes his elaborated code in general terms, it emerges as a subtle and sophisticated mode of planning utterances, where the speaker is achieving structural variety, taking the other person's knowledge into account, and so on. But when it comes to describing the actual difference between middle class and working class speakers (Bernstein 1966) we are presented with a proliferation of 'think', of the passive, of modals and auxiliaries, of the first-person pronoun, of uncommon words, and so on. But these are the benchmarks of hemming and hawing, backing and filling, that are used by Charles M, the devices which so often obscure whatever positive contribution education can make to our use of language. When we have discovered how much of middle class style is a matter of fashion and how much actually helps us express ideas clearly, we will have done ourselves a great service. We will then be in a position to say what standard grammatical rules must be taught to nonstandard speakers in the early grades.
>
> (*ibid.*, p. 171)

Labov enters the linguistic deprivation battle boldly selecting his targets (Jensen, Bereiter and Englemann, *et al.*) and produces the detailed linguistic analysis to support his argument. Why is there no English Labov?

A final point on educability. We are informed repeatedly by Bernstein that 'schools are predicated upon the elaborated code' (Bernstein, 1971, p. 186). No attempt is made, in fact, to examine how language is really used in schools most of the time. Some of us who have been studying tapes of language in school would say that very frequently, especially in the secondary system, there is an actual reduction in the range of pupils' language in many school lessons. There are many other things one would want to say about the way in which language is used and unused in school, but one thing is certain – Bernstein's alluring descriptions of the elaborated code do not fit it.

What evidence is presented for the validity of Bernstein's theories? Over the last two years some five volumes (Brandis and Henderson, 1970; Gahagan and Gahagan, 1970; Turner and Mohan, 1970; Robinson and Rackshaw, 1972) have appeared in rapid succession, and more are promised. I cannot at this stage do more than make some general comments on this work. Before I do so, let me stress that I am not concerned to examine details of research methodology or, with hindsight, to tut-tut over the limitations of what was or was not discovered. I would readily agree that any investigator would have been bound to stumble and grope in the thickets of design and execution.

The theory, remember, claims to be a vast overarching structure, linking the class structure of society to language, socialization, cultural transmission and cognitive development. The evidence of the research is based on studies of the family and young children. We must further limit this by adding that the mother's language is represented not by what she says and does, but by what she says she would say or do. And the child, not by observation of the free flow of his language, but in the 'laboratory' situation. The hazards of this kind of work are well known. As we have seen, Labov has shown the part played by eliciting techniques in giving a totally false picture of working-class language.

Thus, at its best, the research can shed light on only one small area of the vast territory covered by the theory. In that small area we discover, sometimes in grammatical terms, sometimes in semantic terms, that there are differences between working-class speech and middle-class speech and these are interpreted in terms of the theory. They do not strengthen it. For example, if a middle-class child uses more expressions signifying uncertainty it does not necessarily mean that he is able to tolerate the state of uncertainty any more than the child who does not.

I tried to indicate earlier that a sensitive awareness of working-class life and middle-class life would direct our enquiries elsewhere. To acquire this awareness we would need the active, informed help of the very people whose language is being studied, and this presupposes a very different approach to research altogether.

Conclusion

In all that I have said I may possibly have given the impression that I believe that working-class speech is as fine an instrument as could be devised for communication and thinking, and that middle-class speech is pretentious verbiage. That would be absurd romanticism. I *am* saying that the relationship between class and speech cannot be described or understood by the usual sociological methods. Working-class speech has its own strengths which the normal linguistic terminology has not been able to catch. There is no sharp dividing line between it and any other kind of speech, but infinite variations in the deployment of the resources of language. I do think there are aspects of language usually acquired through education which, given favourable circumstances, give access to more powerful ways of thinking; but given the conditions of life of many strata of the middle class, the language acquired through education can conceal deserts of ignorance. Moreover, the middle class have often to pay a price for the acquisition of certain kinds of transactional language, and that is loss of vitality and expressiveness, and obsession with proprieties.

Those are very vague alternatives to the theoretical elegances which I have criticized, and this points to a profound weakness in all I have said. I have at several points noted that we do not know much about the relationship between language and class. It is time to find out.

Appendix

School is concerned with the making explicit and elaborating through language principles and operations.

(Bernstein, 1971, p. 196)

The following quotations might be a starting point for re-examining that statement.

1. Extract from a tape transcript of a secondary school maths lesson

(I am indebted to Angela Williams for this extract from her research material.)

Teacher: Now then, if I say er … (writes on board). Simplify that. Simplify that. 3x + 2x + x. (Background – Miss, Miss.) How can you say that in a simpler way? (Miss, Miss) (P offers answer, indecipherable). Tina, you're not listening. No, that's not the answer. Bill, (Background – P shouts, Five).

Pupil: 5x.

Teacher: Oh, you're listening to … (P shouts, Six). 6x. You're listening to daft Alex Tripp again.

Pupil: Oh no. Miss.

Teacher: Oh yes, keep your mouth shut if you're not sure. Now then Alan (writes on board). 4x – 2x Alan. 4x take away 2x. Come on, it's easy, 4 take away 2.

2. Extract from a tape transcript of a secondary school geography lesson

Teacher: Look at page 206. Where would you find Portugal? (Several children gave the boundaries of Portugal and the countries that lie nearest to it. All the children were talking at once.)

Teacher: Now find Switzerland. Where is Switzerland, Essie?

Essie: Kind of north of Italy.

Teacher: All right. Now where is Denmark?

Girl: Sticking out into the North Sea.

Teacher: Genevieve Wells. What is Denmark that Switzerland and Portugal are not?

Genevieve: A seaport.

Teacher: Oh, no! (Disappointedly) Lisbon is one of the largest seaports in the world.

Children: It's a peninsula.

Teacher: That's right. What is a peninsula? (He calls on several children who do not give the right answer. Then he calls on Bob, Susan, Phillip. Melvin's hand is waving among others. Teacher calls on him.)

Melvin: A peninsula is a piece of land surrounded on three sides by water.

Teacher: (Very enthusiastically) Yes, that's right; a peninsula! A peninsula is a piece of land surrounded on three sides by water.

Teacher: What do these three countries (Portugal, Switzerland, Denmark) have in common? (Linda and Melvin have their hands up.)

Teacher: Linda.

Linda: They're small.

Teacher: Yes, they're all small. Now look at the picture on page 215. What are the women doing? (The children look at the picture and a girl answers that they are drawing water.)

Teacher: Yes. In many of these countries there is no plumbing. Why do you think they have no plumbing? (Several hands are up. Teacher calls on Essie.)

Essie: It's too expensive.

Teacher: Yes, it's too expensive. (Linda's hand is up. Teacher calls on her by name.)

Linda: It's a backward country.

Teacher: Yes. It's a backward country. (The picture shows a number of women with earthenware vessels drawing water from a well that seems to be in a central place.) (Henry, 1971)

3. Strandberg and Griffith (1968) gave four- and five-year-old children in a university laboratory school cameras loaded with color film. Later, they elicited conversations about the (remarkably successful) pictures the children took. The children talked more spontaneously (i.e. required fewer adult probes) and talked in longer and more complex utterances about the pictures they took at home of personally significant objects (e.g. a favorite climbing tree or a closeup of Mother's mouth) than they did about pictures taken under adult direction during the period of orientation to the camera. Since the pictures taken at home were also frequently of only one object, the authors conclude that the difference lies in the degree of personal involvement. Although topic is confounded with order in this study (since all the children told stories about the preselected objects first), it seems unlikely that this accounts for all the difference. Following are examples of one five-year-old's stories, first about an assigned picture and then about one of his choice:

That's a horse. You can ride it. I don't know any more about it. It's brown, black and red. I don't know my story about the horse.

There's a picture of my tree that I climb in. There's – there's where it grows at and there's where I climb up – and sit up there – down there and that's where I look out at. First I get on this one and then I get on that other one. And then I put my foot under that big branch that are strong. And then I pull my face up and then I get ahold of a branch up at that place – and then I look around. (Strandberg and Griffith, personal communication, 1969, quoted in Cazden, 1970)

> *A university is a place organized round talk.*
>
> (Bernstein, 1971, p. 176)

4. Academic language:

… the charismatic kinds of prowess, like verbal acrobatics, incomprehensible allusions, impenetrable obscurity as well as technical recipes which serve as support or substitute, like the concealment of sources, the introduction of pleasantries or the avoidance of compromising formulations ... (Bourdieu and Passeron, 1970)

CONCLUDING NOTE

The main part of the paper ends: 'we do not know much about the relationship between language and class. It is time to find out.' Harold was the principal member of a group which in 1974 privately published two booklets, *Language and Class Workshop 1* and *2* (Rosen, 1974a and 1974b). These brought together examples of the speech of working-class people from across the UK. The examples demonstrated that working-class speech is diverse and is easily capable of great delicacy and richness: evidence to challenge Bernstein's theoretical generalisations.

References

Bantock, G. (1965) *Education and Social Values.* London: Faber and Faber.

Barnes, D., Britton, J., Rosen, H. and the LATE (1971) *Language, the Learner and the School, revised edition.* Harmondsworth: Penguin.

Bernstein, B. (1971) *Class, Codes and Control, Vol. 1.* London: Routledge and Kegan Paul.

Blackburn, R. (1969) 'A brief guide to bourgeois ideology', in A. Cockburn and R. Blackburn (eds.), *Student Power.* Harmondsworth: Penguin.

Bourdieu, P. and Passeron, J. (1970) *La Reproduction.* Paris: Éditions Minuit.

Brandis, W. and Henderson, D. (1970) *Social Class, Language and Communication.* London: Routledge and Kegan Paul.

Cazden, C. (1970) 'The neglected situations in child language', in F. Williams (ed.), *Language and Poverty.* Chicago: Markham.

Douglass, D. (1972) *Pit Life in Co. Durham. History Workshop Pamphlet No.6.* Oxford: Ruskin College.

Freire, P. (1971) *Pedagogy of the Oppressed.* Freiburg: Herder and Herder.

Gahagan, D. and Gahagan, G. (1970) *Talk Reform.* Routledge and Kegan Paul.

Ginsburg, H. (1972) *The Myth of the Deprived Child.* Englewood Cliffs, NJ: Prentice-Hall.

Hawkins, P.R. (1969) 'Social class, the nominal group and reference'. *Language and Speech,* 12: 2.

Henry, J. (1971) *Essays in Education.* Harmondsworth: Penguin.

Hobsbawm, E. (1964) *Labouring Men.* London: Weidenfeld and Nicolson.

Jackson, B. (1968) *Working-class Community.* Harmondsworth: Penguin.

Jensen, A.R. (1968) 'Social class and verbal learning', in M. Deutch, I. Katz and A. Jensen (eds.), *Social Class, Race and Psychological Development.* New York: Holt, Reinhart and Winston.

Labov, W. (1971) 'Variation in language', in C. Reed (ed.), *The Learning of Language.* New York: Appleton-Century-Crofts.

Labov, W. (1972) 'The logic of non-standard English', in P. Giglioli (ed.), *Language and Social Context.* Harmondsworth: Penguin.

The Newbolt Committee (1921) *The Teaching of English in England* (The Newbolt Report). London: HMSO.

Parker, C. (1972) *Towards a People's Culture, Tract No. 3.* Brechfa, Ilanon, Cardiganshire: The Gryphon Press.

Robinson, W. and Rackshaw, S. (1972) *A Question of Answers.* London: Routledge and Kegan Paul.

Rosen, H. (ed.) (1974a) *Language and Class Workshop 1.* London: Language and Class Workshop.

Rosen, H. (ed.) (1974b) *Language and Class Workshop 2.* London: Language and Class Workshop.

Rubinstein, D. and Stoneman, C. (1970) *Education for Democracy.* Harmondsworth: Penguin.

Ryan, W. (1971) *Blaming the Victim.* New York: Pantheon.

Simon, B. (1953) *Intelligence Testing and the Comprehensive School.* London: Lawrence and Wishart.

Thompson, E. (1963) *The Making of the English Working Class.* Harmondsworth: Penguin.

Turner, G. and Mohan, B. (1970) *A Linguistic Description and Computer Program for Children's Speech.* London: Routledge and Kegan Paul.

Vernon, P. (1957) *Secondary School Selection.* London: Methuen.

Vernon, P. (I960) *Intelligence and Attainment Tests.* London: University of London Press.

A Social View of Language in School

Harold gave this paper at a conference on language in the middle years of secondary education, organized by the Centre for Information on Language Teaching and Research and held at the Manchester Teachers' Centre from 20 to 22 November 1973. The paper was published by the Centre for Information on Language Teaching and Research in May 1974 in the booklet *The Space Between ... English and Foreign Languages at School.*

It would be easy to begin in an innocuous, even bland kind of way. For in the last two or three years we have had a succession of books and papers, some more readily accessible than others, which have elaborated in different ways that language, in spite of Chomsky, is a social act intimately interacting with the culture in which it is located or, as we have come to say, that we must consider language in its social context. I am thinking particularly of the collections by Gumperz and Hymes (1972), Fishman (1971), Giglioli (1972), Pride and Holmes (1972), and, more specifically related to education, Cazden, John and Hymes (1972), and various publications of the Open University.

From Chomsky we learned the cheerful view of language development which has now become very familiar, namely that virtually any child irrespective of its culture, its mother tongue, its class, is 'born with the ability to master any language with almost miraculous ease and speed ... ' and is 'not merely moulded by conditioning and reinforcement but actively proceeds with the unconscious theoretical interpretation of the speech which comes his way'.

This powerful optimistic view was enormously helpful because it gave us an interpretation of language acquisition which was an antidote to the effects of other views which asserted that certain kinds of children were specially deprived in learning the basic grammar of their mother tongue. The more extreme of these views (and they are still vociferous) expressed the notion that young children from 'the lowest classes' could do little more than make animal noises. One should add that Chomsky's elaboration of his ideas also pointed to the probability that we learn our mother tongue almost entirely by listening to it and using it, and not by direct instruction or intervention.

The sociolinguists brought a new point of view into the discussion; not so much new, perhaps, as newly systematised, re-asserted, researched and developed theoretically. However enlightening Chomsky's thesis might be, it is, the argument runs, based on too limited a view of language, for it omits from consideration an essential quality of language and what it means to learn one's mother tongue.

> Recall that one is concerned to explain how a child comes rapidly to be able to produce and understand (in principle) any and all of the grammatical sentences of a language. Consider now a child with just that ability. A child who might produce any sentence whatever – such a child would be likely to be institutionalized: even more so if not only sentences, but also speech or silence was random, unpredictable ...
>
> We have then to account for the fact that a normal child acquires know-ledge of sentences, not only as grammatical, but also as appropriate. He or she acquires competence as to when to speak, when not, and as to what to talk about with whom, when, where, in what manner. In short, a child becomes able to accomplish a repertoire of speech acts, to take part in speech events, and to evaluate their accomplishment by others. This competence, moreover, is integral with attitudes, values, and motivations concerning language, its features and uses, and integral with competence for, and attitudes toward, the interrelation of language with the other code of communicative conduct.
>
> (Hymes, 1972)

In other words, we now have a view not simply of *competence* (i.e. an internalised grammar) but of *communicative competence* which attempts to restore socio-cultural significance to learning the mother tongue. Indeed, it is a more comprehensive view of the essential nature of speech. Once again this seems a very positive advance for us. We are offered a theory which concerns itself with the very stuff of language actuality, of real people speaking to one another, rather than one which concerns itself with the 'ideal speaker-listener' and with sentences concocted by grammarians. It is a view of language which attempts to incorporate all dimensions of variety – social and geographical dialects, degrees of formality, written and spoken forms, expressive and referential elements, etc. Above all, it accommodates interaction, the patterning of dialogue.

In education the benefits of this broader view would seem to be obvious. It discourages a simplistic and monolithic view of language as good, correct, standard, etc., and asks us to look at any particular use of language as being the outcome of a set of always changing forces and evolved from a complete set of speaking rules based on setting, participants, ends or goals, form and content of message, key (manner), channel, code, norms, genres. In these terms the goal of language learning in school emerges not as simply 'getting better at English' but rather as increasing the repertoire of appropriate and acceptable ways of speaking and writing. In fact, it would be no exaggeration to say that 'appropriate' has been sewn onto the banner of the avant-garde in defiance of the old word 'correct'.

Productive as these ideas are I want to suggest that from an educational point of view they are seriously deficient. At this point, I hope, some of the blandness will disappear, as indeed it should. For it is the social aspect of language which touches us most quickly and directly. After all, we ourselves are part of the social network. We are located in the system. If a theory tells us we are the speakers of elaborated code, it might give us a warm glow; if a research finding points to us as the group most afflicted by linguistic anxiety, our hackles rise.

To return to communicative competence. What are the limitations of the theory as it has recently been developed ?

1. In its apparently innocuous descriptiveness it would appear to be value-free. There sits the repertoire ready to be taken over item by item. But what value do we place on the separate items in the repertoire? What priorities do we accord them? This takes us back firmly to where we were in the old disputes. Do we give priority to the writing of business letters or of stories? Do we foster the competence required for formal debating speeches or informal small group discussion? Matters of this kind cannot be resolved by a set of sociolinguistic rules – and how we resolve them will depend on who we are, what we believe and what we cherish.

2. The idea of communicative competence is as yet almost entirely programmatic. It does not describe the complete repertoire or even basic repertoire required by a speaker of English. When items in the repertoire are carefully described, they demonstrate the theory as an instrument, but to the educator they are relatively trivial and frequently esoteric, e.g. how to ask for a drink in Subanum, or the opening gambits of a telephone conversation. This is not to deny that some studies do have much wider significance even when their focus seems narrow, e.g. Brown's and Gilman's 'The pronouns of power and solidarity' (1972).

3. The terms *appropriate* and *acceptable* can all too easily be used as new disguises for the old 'correct' label. Hymes argues that there are 'rules for speaking' as well as 'rules of grammar', e.g. rules for opening a conversation and breaking off a conversation. But these are different in different social groups and in many schools there is at least the likelihood that two different systems will confront each other hostilely. The pupils' domestically and communally acquired rules for speaking may be frowned on or declared null and void. Once again we are confronted with values. Is the language of advertising appropriate? Or indeed all the language of unscrupulous manipulation? I am only arguing that communicative competence can easily turn into a brutal linguistic pragmatism – whatever in language is 'successful' is good.

4. What about the aesthetics of language? Here we have an inheritance which cannot be ignored. People have been concerned for centuries to analyse what constitutes

powerful language, eloquent, moving, witty, comic language. Unfortunately this legacy is strong for the written language (more particularly for written *literary* language) and very weak for the spoken. Yet we all have our sense of the fluent speaker, the boring speaker, the person whose speech is full of vitality and the person whose speech is drab and lifeless. Yet both the eloquent and the insipid may be conforming fully to 'the rules of speaking'.

5. The theory leaves unresolved controversial educational issues, the most contentious of which arises from sociolinguistic theory, namely that there are certain kinds of communicative competence, associated with a social class, which cannot or do not carry certain kinds of message, the very kinds which are prized in education.

In spite of the limitations I have outlined, it is worth stressing that some of the basic ideas connected with communicative competence can be built on and developed. They point towards a consideration of different kinds of communicative competence within the national community, expressing different social relations. Distinct social groups may draw on a national system but will also have rules of speaking of their own.

That is not, however, as everyone sees it. For the ideas in their present form can tolerate two quite opposed interpretations in the educational context: one which holds that many children (and their parents) have little or no communicative competence and that it is the task of the school to provide it; and the other which holds that inevitably, as part of their socialisation, all normal children do have a highly developed system which like everyone else's can be extended.

All that seems very theoretical and speculative but it has at least taken me towards the sociolinguistic problem which people really have in mind when, in the educational setting, they talk of such things as the social roots of language. What they have in mind is working-class pupils in schools, or at least certain working-class pupils, usually euphemised as disadvantaged, deprived or inner-city children. For there is a profound belief that it is above all the language of these children which is a huge barrier to their learning in school. No less a person than Philip Vernon (1969) is now telling us that the mother tongue of such children 'is an ineffective medium for advanced education, communication and thinking', and dozens of other instances could be cited. Significantly, no similar concern is shown in educational circles for Labov's finding that the lower middle class scored highest on his Linguistic Insecurity Index (Labov, 1966). I see no signs that funded projects are going to proliferate around this problem.

So we can turn now to the overriding anxiety of teachers, administrators, government ministers and even shadow ministers. This anxiety has a long history, though it is only comparatively recently that one could make an academic living out of it.

When the Newbolt Committee made its report on the teaching of English half a century ago, it was generally regarded as a great achievement of liberal thinking. But look at this:

> The great difficulty of teachers in Elementary Schools in many districts is that they have to fight against the powerful influences of evil habits of speech contracted in home and street. The teachers' struggle is thus not with ignorance but perverted power. That makes their work the harder but it must also make their zeal the fiercer ... [This kind of speech] may be a negative quantity requiring great pains on the teachers' part to cancel out before any positive progress can be made.

and

> Teachers of English sometimes complain that when the children come to school they can scarcely speak a word at all. They should regard this as an advantage.
>
> (The Newbolt Committee, 1921)

That will strike many as an outmoded viewpoint, perhaps held by a few backwoodsmen. It is not. We might note in passing that, unlike many contemporary statements, it does at least acknowledge the 'power', albeit 'evil', of vernacular speech. However, in 1963, the Newsom Report put the issue like this:

> Because the forms of speech which are all they require for daily use in their homes and the neighbourhood in which they live are restricted, some boys and girls may never acquire the basic means of learning.

and

> There is a gulf between those who have and the many who have not sufficient command of words to be able to listen and discuss rationally, to express ideas and feelings clearly; and even to have any ideas at all. We simply do not know how many people are frustrated in their lives by inability to express themselves adequately; or how many never develop intellectually because they lack words to think and reason.
>
> (The Newsom Committee, 1963)

These extraordinarily offensive remarks ('and even to have any ideas at all'!) go much further than those of the Newbolt Committee, which at least recognised, while at the same time it feared, the power of working-class language. They suggest a deep-seated inadequacy implanted by inadequate lives. Moreover, we know that an official document of this kind does not emerge from the views of one or two individuals, but from a serious literature and a serious consensus. There is indeed a consensus and only a few dissident voices are to be heard. It cannot be too often stressed that in viewing the language of the working class, most investigators are peering through the lens of their own language and culture. Anthropologists have known the hazards of this approach for a long time. We should have been warned. Thus working-class life and culture is seen as a distortion of investigators' norms, deviation from their standards, deformation of what is right and good. Thus, too, the talk is always of deficit not difference.

More than this, the whole literature of deprivation, including linguistic deprivation, springs not from sympathetic participation in the life being described, nor from informed awareness and insight, but from special researches which set out to find out what has gone wrong, not what has gone right. The academic literature is of course esoteric and couched in suitably abstract terms, but when it is translated into everyday educational literature, it becomes fairly crude and blunt. It must be very comforting to some people to discover that the social and economic inferiority of millions is not due to anything inherently wrong with our society but to the way they talk to each other. Lest you think I exaggerate the typical posture, let me take one example from sociological literature, Sugarman writing on 'Social class, values and behaviour in school':

> He [i.e. 'the lower status child'] is unable to express meanings of any complexity or subtlety, to indicate how one event depends on others, results from others, precipitates others; to convey intentions, motives or feelings other than the most obvious. He cannot express these shades of meaning and in his social milieu he does not hear them expressed by others.
>
> (Sugarman, 1971)

One has to read the whole paper to see just how consistently it shows every feature of working-class life to be negative and disabling. There are now a few studies, invariably and sadly always from the United States, which do attempt to get inside the situation, from which a very different picture emerges (see for example Claudia Mitchell-Kernan, 'Signifying and marking: Two Afro-American speech acts', in Gumperz and Hymes [eds.], 1972; and Horner and Gussow, 'John and Mary: A pilot study in linguistic ecology' in Cazden, John and Hymes [eds.], 1972).

I assume that it is now generally agreed that we are not concerned with dialect, at least in this particular controversy, and that the old abuse thrown at dialect speech – namely that it is debased, corrupt, lazy, ugly, ungrammatical and so forth – does not need to be taken very seriously. Those linguists who were prone to call urban dialects sub-standard have recently become more careful. In general there is a more widespread, tolerant attitude to dialect than there used to be, even a sneaking admiration for it. Perhaps there is wider recognition that dialect as such has nothing to do with the capacity to learn. Side by side with growing tolerance and understanding, there is the ever-powerful drive to teach standard English and Received Pronunciation, usually on the benevolent grounds of wider communicative intelligibility. This is presented innocuously as 'adding to the repertoire', 'making a child bilingual', etc. But there are enormous difficulties which cannot be evaded.

If you are going to replace, for certain purposes, one set of forms with another and give yourself to it single-mindedly, there is a good chance that you will teach children to be silent. You run the risk that they will lose confidence in the old without gaining confidence in the new. Alternatively they may end up with a grammar which you find more acceptable but with which they have little or nothing to say. In any case it should be borne in mind that the process has nothing to do with using language well.

But there is a greater difficulty, which far transcends these, which turns on how the mother tongue relates to personal and social identity. Dialects are not isomorphic. What can be said in one dialect cannot be simply translated into another. To invite the dialect speaker to become a speaker of standard English, complete with RP, is to invite him into a terrain where he will always be at a disadvantage in the face of those born to it (the conversion syndrome). He will always be playing in an away match.

The exercise is doomed to failure, in any case, for most children. But we can succeed in making them despise their own speech, thus reinforcing a lesson which so many agencies ram home every day. We can create areas of doubt and confusion where none existed before. But as long as their own linguistic community continues to be the one in which they live, it will win. Only if education lures them away from their own community can the operation begin to succeed.

As I have indicated, dialect is not the main line of attack on working-class speech these days. It is not so much the formal properties of their speech which are being criticised as the purposes for which they use speech. Broadly speaking it is argued that precisely those kinds of uses of language which schools are dependent on – rationality, universalistic meanings, the verbalising of principles – are absent from 'the restricted code'. Many people in education are now very familiar with the main thesis, or with some version of it. I have attempted to show what I think is wrong with it (Rosen, 1972) and do not propose to repeat all that but I would like to stress a few points.

Like most theories of deprivation, it turns on the effect of home and, in particular, the mother, though some attention is paid to the peer-group and work situation. It is puzzling, to say the least, to account for the disappearance of fathers, let alone grandparents and others. The assertions about the influence of the work situation (no power of decision-making, acting only on consensus views, etc.) do not derive from observation, let alone participation. Even Hoggart's sensitivity to working-class life does not encompass the realm of work (Hoggart, 1957). Yet this is probably the most difficult experience for middle-class people, including most teachers, to penetrate and understand. And it is a major question: how does directly productive labour affect the consciousness of those engaged in it? This is not solely a question of physical activity of certain kinds but also a question of the social relations set up in the course of that activity. It is difficult to exaggerate how ignored this question is.

Moreover, the working class or one large section of it is treated as an undifferentiated mass without a past, bereft of significant history. When I have transcribed, as I have just recently, tapes of a Welsh miner, a London docker, a Scottish shipyard worker, a lock-keeper and others, I am amazed that people can go on talking in the way that they do about working-class language as though they are dealing with a single identifiable object. The cultural history of the working class in this country often realises itself in language. It is, as yet, relatively unreported and unstudied, its richness and its poetry relatively unknown and neglected, in spite of all the studies which claim to tell us about working-class speech. It is the strength of working-class speech which remains unexamined, usually because it is assumed not to exist. This is all the more depressing because teachers do not have to be impressed by the inadequacies (supposed or real) of working-class speech. Everything they have ever been taught predisposes them to be aware of them, exaggerate them or invent them. What we have to learn now is how to make ourselves sensitive to what is positive, to shift from the censorious and superior stance to an appreciative and responsive one; in fact, to do what we so often say our pupils should do, listen. And we have to do all this without losing ambition for our pupils, without abdicating from our task of increasing their power to use language more effectively, confidently and comprehensively.

I believe that vernacular speech offers to its speakers particular resources which, when used, render their speech uniquely eloquent and powerful. But this is almost entirely an intuition which I share with others. Little is known about it for the obvious reason that very few have cared to know. Much of education has been concerned with gentling the masses, teaching them obedience, a kind of decorum, respect for authority and all that. The old model is being seriously eroded these days, if for no other reason than that it does not work. It is not often enough recognised that an essential feature of that model was the toning down of vernacular speech. Control their language, control them. If there are to be new models they must include a radically changed attitude to language.

References

Brown, R. and Gilman, A. (1972) 'The pronouns of power and solidarity', in P. Giglioli (ed.), *Language and Social Context*. Harmondsworth: Penguin.

Cazden, C., John, V. and Hymes, D. (eds.) (1972) *Functions of Language in the Classroom*. New York: Teachers College Press.

Fishman, J. (ed.) (1971) *Advances in the Sociology of Language*. The Hague: Mouton.

Giglioli, P. (ed.) (1972) *Language and Social Context*. Harmondsworth: Penguin.

Gumperz, J. and Hymes, D. (eds.) (1972) *Directions in Sociolinguistics*. New York: Holt, Reinhart and Winston.

Hoggart, R. (1957) *The Uses of Literacy*. London: Chatto and Windus.

Horner, V. and Gussow, J. (1972) 'John and Mary: A pilot study in linguistic ecology', in C. Cazden, V. John and D. Hymes (eds.) (1972).

Hymes, D. (1972) 'On communicative competence', in J. Pride and J. Holmes (eds.), *Sociolinguistics*. Harmondsworth: Penguin.

Labov, W. (1966) *The Social Stratification of English in New York City*. Washington D.C.: Center for Applied Linguistics.

Mitchell-Kiernan, C. (1972) 'Signifying and marking: Two Afro-American speech acts', in J. Gumperz and D. Hymes (eds.), *Directions in Sociolinguistics*. New York: Holt, Reinhart and Winston.

The Newbolt Committee (1921) *The Teaching of English in England* (the Newbolt Report). London: HMSO.

The Newsom Committee (1963) *Half our Future* (the Newsom Report). London: HMSO.

Pride, J. and Holmes, J. (eds.) (1972) *Sociolinguistics*. Harmondsworth: Penguin.

Rosen, H. (1972) *Language and Class: A critical look at the theories of Basil Bernstein*. Bristol: Falling Wall Press.

Sugarman, B. (1971) 'Social class, values and behaviour in school', in M. Craft (ed.), *Family, Class and Education*. London: Longman.

Vernon, P. (1969) *Intelligence and Cultural Environment*. London: Methuen.

Out There or Where the Masons Went

This article appeared in *English in Education*, the research journal of the National Association for the Teaching of English, *Volume 9, No. 1, Spring 1975.* In the words of Mike Torbe, who wrote the editorial for this issue of the journal, 'The articles in this issue attempt to broaden the debate about the social context of education.'

> *Not knowing the people, they are like heroes without a battlefield …*
> *What do they not understand? The language.*
>
> (Mao-Tse-Tung, 1950)

So we are going to talk about the social context? And a good thing too. But strange. The tidy abstraction of it: a non-combative, dusted-down, orderly little phrase. What does it stand for? The little world we can look at through the window, go shopping in, take buses from, play truant in? The invisible hinterland of this morning's *Times* where I read of 'the magnification of state benefits as the major source of subsistence for unproductive members of society'? It cannot be the ramshackle edifice of institutions, pronouncements, channels of communication, labelled strata, laws and doctrines cobbled together by history for us to scuttle about in. The social context, as we call it, is not an arena in which we perform our dramas. It is the dramas themselves; people in action with each other and against each other improvising the text as they proceed.

> Thus it is not language which generates what people say. Language does not possess this magical power or possesses it only fitfully and dubiously. What people say derives from praxis – from the performance of tasks, from the division of labour – arises out of real actions, real struggles in the world. What they actually do, however, enters consciousness only by way of language, by being said.
>
> (Lefebvre, 1968)

Therefore, if I am a little bit needled by the phrase 'the social context', it is because, cropping up like this, it announces that we are moving on to our next interesting theme and in due course we shall proceed to others. But that isn't it at all. Essentially, *there is nothing else to talk about.*

And we have talked about it. When we have, it has turned out not to be a fastidious excursion into the streets, not an awestruck promenade around our minds, not a jolly linguistic field trip (though it often starts in these ways) but a battlefield on which the lines are being more or less clearly delineated. It is becoming increasingly difficult to refuse to take sides. We have to choose between theories of cultural deprivation and assertions of a popular culture; between descriptions of an impoverished restricted code and the unearthing of a living oral tradition; between visions of schools as civilized and well-ordered islands in a sea of barbarism and anomie and the aspiration that they that they should be reincarnated through the nourishment of the neighbourhood and community; between reading schemes and literacy through critical consciousness (Freire, 1974). Indeed, all the choices we make, minute, urgent, even trivial, are more and more seen as taking sides. English teaching has become overtly a political matter. Chris Searle (1973) can be heard demanding passionately 'reciprocity, *comradeship*, shared experience' against the amplified phantasmagoria of Sir Keith Joseph, making our flesh creep with the teeming illegitimates spawned by the plebs, calling for a return to the old orderly ways.

It is out of assumptions about the nature of our society that the new ways of English teaching have grown and changed. One old new way is for teachers to open the eyes of their gullible pupils to the seductions of mass media and advertising. Themselves immune (by what process of inoculation?), they will give immunity to others. They assume that all around them the most baleful cultural forces of our society work fully and effectively and that only their critically trained perceptions pick up the nuances of the non-stop confidence trick. Yet Raymond Williams showed us years ago the great difference between what people *make* of television and what they are expected to make of it. The banner-bearers of the High Culture have been telling us for so long that 'mass' culture is debased and fraudulent and sterile. Nevertheless the cankers have got at their own confidence.

> Our dried voices, when
> We whisper together
> Are quiet and meaningless
> As wind in dry grass
> Or rats' feet over broken glass
> In our dry cellar.
>
> (Eliot, 1936)

Our voices? Take this one, which Connie Rosen (Rosen and Rosen, 1973) collected from a school in Birmingham, an ordinary voice.

> This ordinary woman
> Works in the factory up the road
> Putting bolts in the drill

She presses the pedal that starts the drill working
The clashing and the grinding
The clicking and the shuttling
Are soothing to her ears
Filling her arms with rhythm
Her head with daydreams.
The siren sound
And my mother faces the world again.

The doleful litany chanting endlessly is that children and young people in schools are totally submerged by powerful manipulative forces outside their control which brutalize and stupefy them. If that message strikes home then it is small wonder if teachers who step forward to expose, analyse and demolish, feel in their hearts that they are puny in the face of giants who can spend more on one advertisement than one of them will spend on school books in the whole of a teaching career. Of course it is right to see and understand how such things work but the mistake is to believe that all around us are nothing but sad and spiritless victims. There are other forces at work. The miracle is not that we are all deformed by the dominant culture of our society but how much grows in the teeth of it, how our humanity asserts itself, how it asserts itself in the world of our pupils. We should not see the tabloids and commercials as the only emblems of their world, just as we should refuse to let a sanctified canon of literary works be the only alternative voice.

For there is that other assumption about society which corrodes our thinking, that the great working class of this country, with its largely unwritten history, its heroism, its self-transforming engagement with life, its stubborn refusal to be put down, is nothing but a deprived inarticulate herd. Even the new radical teacher, sensitive to the language of working-class pupils and armed with political theory, can be corroded by the social assumptions which abound in current educational and sociological literature. We are told that working-class children cannot learn to read because they have no books in the home and their parents do not read. Transmitted deprivation, I believe they call it now. Yet millions of people throughout Europe in the late nineteenth and early twentieth centuries won their way to literacy from homes which were totally illiterate. Theories about the cycle of deprivation, glibly cited by politicians, have lurking beneath their surface an unhistorical notion that generations passively reproduce cultural attitudes; long before the 1870 Act, Engels (1845) showed that, from amidst conditions of appalling squalor and exploitation, workers were producing a literary culture of their own:

They have translated the French materialists, Helvetius, Holback, Diderot, etc. and disseminated them, with the best English works, in cheap editions. Strauss' *Life of Jesus* and Proudhon's *Property* circulate among working men only. Shelley, the genius, the prophet Shelley, and Byron, with his glowing sensuality and his bitter satire upon our existing society, find most of their readers in the proletariat; the bourgeoisie owns only castrated editions …

Turn to David Craig's magnificent book *The Real Foundations: Literature and Social Change* (1973), which is so much more than literary criticism, and you will find the careful documentation and interpretation of changes in working-class consciousness, imagination and culture over more than a century and a half.

Teachers who have peered over the school wall and are intensely aware of 'out there' find themselves caught in a tormenting paradox and heart-breaking decisions. They see that most of their pupils are bound for jobs which are destructive of the spirit, that they will be working in conditions which are a denial of initiative, imagination and participation. And yet all their teaching has been designed to foster personal sensitivity, personal response and self-exploration. Thus there are only intolerable choices. Prepare them for boredom and docility (euphemized into 'preparing them for society') or have them jettison all the work of the school years as soon as they perceive its irrelevance to their situation. But there are several flaws in the picture. Our own location in society and our own formation lead us to see only three forces at work – the grinding and destructive power of brutalizing jobs, the downward pull of bookless homes and philistine communities ranged against our informed wisdom. Whatever we have gained from our education, what it is least likely to have given us is a confident belief that there is any nourishing resource and vigour in the pupils' homes and community and that we have much to learn from that community. Perhaps, in the necessary emphasis we have given to *personal* growth, language for *personal* development and literature as an intensely *personal* exploration we have made English sound like the greatest ego-trip ever invented and we have forgotten that when working-class children have responded to our teaching then it is either because we have lured them into a world of private experience and cushioned individualism or because we have seen them as socially constituted human beings who can draw sustenance for the imagination from their own world and its values, from parents, grandparents and neighbours. Ken Worpole (1974) has shown through the work of Centerprise and *A People's Autobiography of Hackney* what kinds of responses are nurtured and evoked in places which seem from the outside either silent and subdued or centres of degrading violence.

Few of us have seen English as a training in conducting inaccessible dialogues with the self. We have sensed the health in uninterrupted transactions between private experience and social experience but we have lacked a sufficient understanding of the social consciousness of our pupils. So much has already been achieved by pioneering English teaching, but if it is to take, to bite deep, then we must engage with working-class life and learn to apply our educated ears to its voice, with the same respect, awareness of nuances and human warmth we have applied so readily elsewhere. This is really the next bold step for English teaching. And it takes a lot of courage; for it means shifting our centre of gravity away from the usual sources of confirmation and approval. This is the shift that Chris Searle (1973) has made. He quotes Mazine, aged 13:

> All living in one community
> Thinking for each other
> Helping each other
> No betrayals …

and comments:

> The English teacher in the schools is probably in the best position to give back to the child his own world and identity in education, to re-affirm it, to share it himself, support it and strengthen it.

Chris Searle is concerned with working-class identity, not with how to create an individual awareness so frail is will melt in the heat of the production line.

One of the most deeply rooted ideas among us is that working-class life is a miserable and squalid affair unredeemed by delicate joys and sorrow, devoid of deep understanding and bold aspirations. I am not speaking of that suburban squeamishness which fears and hates every form of working-class assertion from the bold, shameless voices and noisy laughter to the nasty tendency to act together in defiance of established power. Nor am I speaking of the way in which the ruling class knows its enemy and manages to despise it, fear it and attack it. What I am speaking about is that tendency in progressive opinion of all kinds, including all kinds of socialists, to see working-class life as a horrifying ulcer springing from the unwholesomeness of capitalist society, a deforming disease which a new and better society would purge and cleanse.

> Ever since industrialism took over, writers in the vein of Ruskin and Morris have either argued from the physical ugliness, the blight of spoiled ground and sprawl of unplanned jerry-building, to the feelings of the people themselves, not seeing that human beings have extraordinary powers of resistance and enjoyment; or else they have taken a disgusted line about modern human nature itself and supposed that our actual capacity for experience has been weakened since the good old days (whenever they were).
>
> (Craig, 1973)

The alternative view amounts to this, that out there in the 'social context' there is a culture which is alive and kicking. Just as we have discovered that children do not come to school to be given language but arrive with it as a going concern, we need to discover that children come with culture as a going concern too. Indeed, their language, the despised vernacular of great cities and industrial towns, is part of their culture.

I do not think this means a sentimental, vicarious and undiscriminating adoration of everything which takes root in working-class communities, any more than I believe that it means the rejection of everything our own education has taught us. But the disentangling and sorting still has to be done. This is one of the huge tasks ahead of us – a vast re-learning and an application of responses refined in the study of poetry and novels to everyday speech.

I might have begun in another place. Let me spend a little time there. Suppose I tell you that there is a little-known story by D.H. Lawrence which contains this:

> Well, when my pore ole pot and pan were working, were working at Tickleton Main – ooh it were a deep pit you know. They used to come out wringing wet, their trammin' drawers you know. I've seen him slosh it on floor and it's sloshed down like a dirty old floor cloth. I've had to swill em out, swill em, swill coal dust off them and dry them before he went to work next day. His pocket which he brought his tramming drawers home in and his belt which used to fasten his trammin' drawers to 'im when he was trammin – he weren't in good health and I know he was on nights – I had nightmares occasionally.
>
> When aught depresses me I always have a nice little nightmare to myself and I know this night I didn't – I had Leonard's mother with me, you know, for twenty years – after dad died, after her husband died and she were bedridden five. And she were in t'other room and she said, 'Amy, what couldn't you sleep through t'night?'

> I says, 'Eh, why?'
> She says, 'You did sing.'
> I says, 'Did I?'
> 'I heard somebody singing,' she says. 'Well, you were singing.'
> She said, 'A' for what you're singing?'
> 'Well,' I says, 'it weren't me, Gran, it weren't me.'
> 'It were you what were singing.'
> I tell you and I felt – and I said, 'Were it this?'
> (Sings)
>> 'For he toils down that mine, down that dark dreary pit,
>> So that folks like us round the fireside will cheer.
>> And he toils down below far from heaven's glorious light
>> And his face may be black but his big heart is white.'
> I says, 'Was that it?'
> 'Aye,' she says. 'That were it.'

> I says, 'Oh my God.' I said, 'No it's never come to that.
> I'm singing in my sleep because I'm upset about his work.'
> But it must have been me because she said, 'That were t'song.
> That were it I heard you singing.'

How did you read that? What kind of careful, reverent attention did you give to it? What can you say about its dialogue, its shaped utterance, its sense of felt life and so on? But now read it again but bear in mind that it is in fact not by D.H. Lawrence but is the spontaneous speech of a Yorkshire miner's wife which appears in *Language and Class Workshop 2* (Rosen, 1974 [ed.]). Charles Parker recorded it and it came *not* in response to a request for a story or autobiography but to his request for old songs. I might have chosen other items from the collection: West Indian children telling traditional stories, miners' jokes, political fables, working women from Manchester and Liverpool finding fluent and powerful language as they become involved in controlling their own lives,, and working men and women giving their complex views about language. Give material like this the same loving attention you have lavished on literature and you will extend your humanity. It is not a matter of asserting that working-class culture is infinitely superior – who suggested that anyway? where? when? – but rather of demonstrating that is there at all, that it is pertinent to our concerns, that we build on it or build nothing.

> In the evening when the Chinese wall was finished
> Where did the masons go?
>
> Bertolt Brecht

References

Craig, D. (1973) *The Real Foundations: Literature and social change.* London: Chatto and Windus.

Eliot, T. (1936) *Collected Poems 1909–1935.* London: Faber and Faber.

Engels, F. (1845) *The Condition of the Working Class in England in 1844.* Available at http://www.gutenberg.org/files/17306/17306-h/17306-h.htm

Freire, P. (1974) *Education for Critical Consciousness.* London: Sheed and Ward.

Lefebvre, H. (1968) *The Sociology of Marx.* London: Allen Lane.

Mao-Tse-Tung (1950) *Problems of Art and Literature.* New York: International Publishers.

Rosen, H. (ed.) (1974) *Language and Class Workshop 2.* London: Language and Class Workshop.

Rosen, C. and Rosen, H. (1973) *The Language of Primary School Children.* Harmondsworth: Penguin.

Searle, C. (1973) *This New Season.* London: Calder and Boyars.

Worpole, K. (1974) 'The school and the community', in D. Holly (ed.), *Education or Domination.* London: Arrow Books.

Multicultural Education and the English Teacher

Harold first gave this paper at the third conference of the International Federation for the Teaching of English, held in Sydney in 1980. The paper was published in 1982, along with the other papers given at the conference, in *English in the Eighties*, edited by Robert Eagleson.

This is not the kind of conference at which we take notes and pass resolutions. Nevertheless, heterogeneous as we appear to be, divergent though our views may be in our discussions, we should perhaps acknowledge that we are the kind of international coterie, pedagogical mafia, which shares, or tends to share, a wide range of beliefs, aspirations, and assumptions which go far beyond the teaching of English and which has fitted itself out with a rudimentary communication network along which the avant-garde whispers are amplified.

Were we to take votes, it is predictable that there would be thumping majorities against corporal punishment, racial discrimination, sexism, child abuse, pollution and the killing of whales – and there would be thumping majorities for liberty, equality and fraternity and, perhaps, macrobiotic food. Therefore, there is also little doubt about how we would vote on multicultural education. We are in favour of it, of course. That consensus dissolves rapidly when we attempt to discover what we mean by multicultural education; why it is that, compared with the resounding declarations of intent, the manifestos and slogans, the ready assent, *in practice* it remains a project, a policy, a programme rather than an informing idea permeating the life of our schools; and why those very English teachers who were the champions of the validity of the pupils' own language and experience were so tardy and reluctant to acknowledge that language and experience in our schools had to be glossed in a new and radically different way.

The background

Let me illustrate. In a short space of time it has become an obligatory clause in the multicultural charter to say something like this:

> For the curriculum to have meaning and relevance for all pupils now in our
> schools, its content, emphasis and the values and assumptions contained

in it must reflect the wide range of cultures, histories and life-styles in our multicultural society.

(*The West Indian Community: Observations on the
report of the Select Committee on Race Relations and Immigration.*
Home Office, 1978)

Which, translated into Australian – or, more exactly, Queenslandish – is:

The curriculum (the total learning experiences provided through the school) should be multicultural in choice of content and global in perspective.

(*Education for a multicultural society. A discussion
paper based on the report to the Council of Directors of the
Queensland Department of Education.*
Queensland Department of Education, 1979)

The teacher of physics to seventeen-year-olds or the teacher of arithmetic to seven-year-olds might well be dismayed at such a revision of their ancient and respected crafts, but the teacher of English, whose syllabus – it is often said – is quite simply life itself, should not baulk at the prospect.

It is 'English for the Eighties' we are talking about. In the last year two books have appeared on the teaching of English. As unlike as they are, they share a sharply critical attitude to current developments in the teaching of English and a sense that they are speaking to our current condition, i.e. in 1980, a year after Blair Peach, a devoted teacher of English, was killed protesting against racism. The first is Allen's (1980) *English Teaching since 1965: How much growth?* You will search in vain in that work for a thoroughgoing response to the demand for a multicultural curriculum. In fact you will search for *any* response except for one bizarre, brief passage which occurs in a paragraph which expresses hostility to attempts to politicise English teaching:

The final culmination of the increasing political bent is shown when the extrinsic claims come to override all other considerations; thus … [there follow several examples] … literature must reflect 'the multicultural society in which we all live'. Such inverted judgments are those of a minority, to be sure, but they do, even in their extremes, have their breeding in the interplay of political sociology and English teaching.

For the moment let us note that, having dismissed with disdain the minority view, Allen – aesthete turned head-counter – does not tell us how we *should* respond to our multicultural society.

Similarly, Holbrook (1979) in *English for Meaning*, castigating the Bullock Report and telling us that English had lost its way, is silent about the impact on schools of thousands and thousands of children from ethnic groups with different cultures, different languages, different histories. He too has a single paragraph:

> I have visited schools where there is a rich atmosphere of creative living, even in grim areas; where young teachers work happily and enthusiastically with negro, Japanese, Greek and Indian children, as well as children of working-class parents on the one hand and TV producers on the other ... The best training for such work is good reading and good writing.

It would seem, then, that nothing need change. The tried recipe, good reading and good writing, makes unnecessary any concessions to multicultural education. What is this good writing and good reading which can be conjured out of processes which have nothing to do with the lived culture of the children?

But the organisers of this conference have clearly decided that it should be one of the major themes, and that is itself a step forward. Having taken it, we had better admit to ourselves that the concept bristles with all those difficulties which we know so well from similar educational pronouncements ('equality of opportunity', 'developing the full potential of every child', etc.), which are so broad and abstract in their formulation that in the first place they can win easy allegiance, and in the second they often turn out to be disguised versions of other less palatable meanings. The honeyed pieties of educational rhetoric are very seductive, and we need to be put on our guard. Therefore I shall begin by taking a look, all too hasty, at questions of cultural difference in our kind of diverse and stratified societies.

Here is a passage from *The Teaching of English in Multicultural Britain* (no date), a recent discussion document produced by the UK's National Association for the Teaching of English:

> We have to develop a classroom culture implicit in which is an understanding and appreciation of differences within the class and a willingness to be and to work together ... In building this sort of classroom culture we can create conditions which can give pupils a vital experience of living and playing a part in a harmonious, multicultural society.

In spite of the fact that I believe the document as a whole will serve as a valuable initiation of discussion and action, the oasis of a harmonious classroom in the midst of the cacophony of conflict and oppression all over the world does not seem the best of images to guide our practice. However, contrast that with:

> Based upon liberal, humanistic notions of the individual experience of other cultures, multiculturalism proposes the classroom as the locus in which the cultures of racial minorities in contemporary Britain should be shared. The greater understanding achieved at this level is then meant

to flow outwards to create a more harmonious society. In this account, schools are expected to affect wider social relations but are paradoxically granted autonomy from the effects of society … *Multiculturalism assumes that it is only the material taught that is problematic.*

(Carby, 1980, my italics)

I cite these two documents simply to show that, although the harmonious multicultural society is a reiterated theme of official and quasi-official statements, when the debate reaches classroom teachers there is division and conflict, much of which has its source in very different views of the cultures which are to be the sources of this new-style education. A few comments – three longish points – on this.

There has been a prolonged and fruitful discussion in Britain for several decades on the nature of culture, from Hoggart's *The Uses of Literacy* (1957) through the work of Raymond Williams, Stuart Hall and the Centre for Contemporary Cultural Studies at the University of Birmingham, E.P. Thompson and others. Scarcely any of the discussion of multicultural education is informed by that endeavour. I cannot pursue its intricacies here. Out of that sustained endeavour let me select, as a reminder of the vast scope of the idea of culture, E.P. Thompson's way of putting it (1961):

> Any theory of culture must include the concept of the real dialectical interaction between culture and something that is not culture. We must suppose the raw material of human experience to be at one pole, and all the infinitely complex human disciplines and systems, articulate and inarticulate, formalised in institutions or dispersed in the least formal ways, which 'handle', transmit or distort the raw material, to be the other. It is the active *process* – which is at the same time the process of change.

So, first, it is unhelpful to talk about *a* culture, whatever we mean by that word. We certainly need to go beyond that mindless chauvinistic use of the term which suggests that in our complex, class-divided societies there is something which we all share called a national (British, English, Australian, etc.) culture, a notion which can itself be used as a symbol, an ideological rallying cry with which to stir or alarm, as when we are warned in Britain of alien tidal waves which will overwhelm *our culture*. But this notion lingers on when, in the context of multicultural education, we set out induction into the 'national' (or 'mainstream') culture as a goal for minorities, or when we speak of children being between two cultures as though they were shuttling to and fro between two clearly defined sets of meanings, values and practices. And yet we know that in matters of language the idea is absurd. The Italian brick-makers of Bedford, as Arturo Tosi's careful sociolinguistic study (1979) has shown, do not speak standard Italian: in fact they speak an Italian that is no longer the language of the younger generations in the southern Italian villages from which they originally came. [Tosi developed his observations further in a 1984 publication.]

Culture then is not a monolithic entity, an integrated diversity of significant meanings and practices, nor a common core of democratically shared life. There is dominant culture and dominated culture both in the countries which have received new minority groups and in the countries from which they come. It would be more appropriate to ask: which stratum of their society do they come from and which stratum do they encounter? The English-as-a-Foreign-Language/English-as-a-Second-Language tradition talks of a target language. What is the target language of Jamaicans or Bengalis installed in the decaying areas of inner London: Cockney or Standard English? What I am saying is: the forms of cultural expression are related to power. As Raymond Williams put it in 'The idea of a common culture' (1968):

> … if it is at all true that the creation of meanings is an activity which engages all men, then, one is bound to be shocked by any society which, in its most explicit culture, either suppresses the meanings and values of whole groups and the possibility of articulating and communicating these meanings.

Why then should we treat culture as a universally benevolent, hygienic force dispensing life-giving power to all its consumers in all situations? If ethnic minorities are to be called upon to share in the new cultural wealth of their recently adopted land, shall we offer our own exquisite variety of sexism so thoroughly realised in all forms and at all levels of cultural activity? Or does the pluralism of multicultural education mean that with all-embracing tolerance we say, 'You keep your kind of sexism and we'll keep ours'? No one can seriously believe that the intention should be to cultivate everything on the grounds that your culture is good for you, whatever it is and whatever it embraces. Schools have never taken that view of their cultural diet. The trouble has not been that they have selected but the criteria they have used for selection. Nowhere has this been more evident than in the English curriculum.

Secondly, our kind of culture is certainly not monolithic, for it not only contains within itself diversity but also confrontation and hostility. A monolith is motionless stone, but cultures are mobile and dynamic and forged by people who do not merely gratefully receive the established meanings of the past but also reshape and develop some and abandon some. I recollect Marx's little outburst: 'the tradition of all the dead generations weighs like a nightmare on the brain of the living'. Therefore we cannot talk about minorities as though they are enclaves of a culture which truly belongs somewhere else, transplanted bits of the Caribbean, Bangladesh, Hong Kong, etc., which must either survive as intact museum pieces or crumble away as eroded antiquities. Under our very eyes we can see cultures changing as they embody new orders of experience. In London the most striking example is a West Indian culture which grows out of black experience in Britain. The change is often mirrored in dramatic generational differences. A culture which finds its way into school may embody something of the grandparents' version, or of the parents' version, but will certainly be the pupils' own version.

Thirdly, the difficulties abound. We often speak as though we have merely to divest ourselves of our prejudices, our so-called mono-cultural outlook, and invite all cultures to cross the school threshold and they will come trooping joyously in to occupy their rightful places. As the Bullock Report (1975) put it:

> No child should be expected to cast off the language and culture of the home as he crosses the school threshold, nor to live and act as though school and home represent two totally separate and different cultures.

The report makes this comment in the context of what it calls 'children from families of overseas origin'. But it is possible, following this rubric, for schools to be the arbiters of what constitutes the culture of the home, to trivialise it in paternalistic fashion, seizing upon obvious differences of food, custom and ceremonies. The culture of the pupils arises from lived understandings, and its meanings are not simply to be had for the asking. Bland and uncontroversial selections are likely to omit all those cultural practices which embody resistance and fracture the desired harmony. And behind all this is the danger of using multicultural education as a device for containment and control.

Again, there are radical qualitative differences between cultures which mean that we cannot place them in an array which makes them all in some sense equal. Whatever may or may not be done in school, cultures vary in their acceptability to the 'host' culture. We know, or think we know, the markers of culture. We know how to recognise the markers of acceptable institutionalised religions (places of worship, a priesthood, prayer, reverence). We know the markers of cultures which are permeated by literacy and institutionalised art forms – classical literature, song and dance. But oral cultures are more inaccessible because we have not developed the capacity to read them. They are likely to be partly invisible and at the same time to stir antipathy, for the oral cultures belong to the most oppressed people whose cultures have been oppressed in their country of origin. Small wonder if an attempt to incorporate them encounters ambivalence, distrust and reluctance. Schools which have ignored indigenous oral cultures are not likely to be highly responsive to oral cultures of more recently arrived groups, of which they have at best a tenuous awareness. The grand design of multicultural education can easily dissolve in justified reticence and suspicion, summed up by the black students who wrote on the blackboard, 'Sir is nosey about our language'.

We, for our part, must resist the temptation to forget the effects of transplanted colonialism: colonialism come home to roost. No consideration of the language and culture of West Indian pupils can omit the central fact that it is a black culture. The experience of racism makes the new growth of black culture an oppositional culture. It is a straight lie to claim that with steel bands and calypsos in the school concert we can produce racial harmony. A concept of education which does not look racism in the eye is a mockery and, what is more, is an obstacle to deepening our own understanding.

These are some, but by no means all, of the reasons why the multicultural enterprise needs closer scrutiny and why it calls for much more than a vote for pluralism. This is not an excuse for inertia or despair but only a sober appraisal of the fact that our national school systems have been special filtering devices transmitting particular versions of culture. It is the attempt to change that process which makes multicultural education a daunting enterprise and understandably makes honest sceptics out of those who have worked most closely with minority groups. A French colleague, Zavier Coulliard, puts these matters better than I have done. Preferring the word 'intercultural' to 'multicultural', he warns against the schools 'teaching' cultures to children in the typical academic manner so that the very bearers of these cultures cannot recognise themselves, and also against the dangers of 'folklorisation', the ransacking of cultures under the voyeuristic gaze of the dominant (I winced).

Intercultural education, by contrast, must be based on the active expression and exploration by the pupils of their sense of their lives in the here and now, of their intercultural experience. In the absence of real equality we need to give scope to the expression of tension and conflict, not to muffle its discordant and strident notes.

Let me compress in one citation all I have been saying. How would this young girl's poem fit into most of the multicultural manifestos we have read in the last few years?

Cry for Me

Cry for me
You son-of-a-bitch white man.
Cry for your brother who has
No work
No love
No mother
No father
No nothing.

Cry for me.
While you sit on your big white ass
In a nice warm room
I walk the cold streets,
Hunger burning in my belly
No warmth
No comfort
No thing.

> Cry for me
> You white bastard
> You took my identity
> SHIT … You don't even know what I'm talking about!
>
> Now you're going to lock me away
> In some dark place for many years.
> Can't you even shed one God-damn tear?
>
> You are the ones who are dumb.
> You are the ones who make us all go mad.
> Can't you find it in your heart to cry a little?
> Why don't you leave us alone?
> Can't you see what you have done to us?
> Cry nah!

Sandra Agard (from Talking Blues, 1976)

The teaching of English

Within the context I've sketched, we can turn now to the pupils in the English class, the English teacher and the teaching of English. The invisible foundation stone for the teaching of English has inscribed upon it these articles of faith:

1. English is the mother tongue of our pupils
2. The task of the teacher is to make pupils literate in that mother tongue
3. The pupils' use of the mother tongue must be extended or improved or modified because the spontaneous use of language in the community could not achieve this goal.

Mother-tongue English was always a fiction, but a fiction with considerable credibility for a long time. That fiction has slowly but surely been torn apart in the last twenty to twenty-five years as the demographic processes, with which you are all familiar, expressed themselves in the mother-tongue classroom – speakers for whom English was a first language but who spoke another, speakers whose dialect or language was a Creole or somewhere on the Creole continuum or who spoke a UK vernacular but could switch into a new form of Creole. Linguistic diversity, some of it inaudible, was the most manifest expression of cultural diversity.

The credible fiction of mother-tongue teaching which preceded this linguistic diversity is worth returning to, if only because the fierce exchanges we now hear centre on issues which were all there – albeit unrecognised, or stifled, or in embryonic form – long before the post-war immigrations began. They are now writ large, so large that almost everyone must make some kind of response. Mass education in 19th-century Europe was never designed to teach the mother tongue (there are remarkable exceptions like Norway). Indeed in some instances it involved the explicit suppression of mother tongues (Catalan, Breton, Welsh, Gaelic, etc.), patois and vernaculars of all kinds. The British version was an attempt to impose standard English, which was as like the English vernacular as consommé is to pea soup.

So we have had a century of rich experience of *refusing* to teach the mother tongue, and made no bones about it. Even the Newbolt Report of 1921, that extraordinary monument to claims for *the* central place in the curriculum to be occupied by English, said without blinking:

> The great difficulty of teachers in elementary schools in many districts is that they have to fight against the powerful influence of evil powers of speech contracted in home and street. The teachers' struggle is thus not with ignorance but with perverted power.

The report called for systematic training in the speaking of standard English and demanded that the elementary school should 'teach all its pupils who either speak a definite dialect or whose speech is disfigured by vulgarisms, to speak standard English, and to speak it clearly, and with expression'. No nonsense about mother tongue there. Indeed, with a naïve linguistic determinism the authors believed that the promotion of one favoured kind of English would resolve all class differences. (The word is 'harmony' again!) Half a century later there were voices insisting that the only language goal of education for immigrants was mastery of English, to ensure their peaceful and rapid integration.

As the great waves of post-war immigration brought new pupils into the classrooms of teachers of English, those teachers were caught in a paradoxical posture. On the one hand, they were in the midst of sharp and raging controversy about working-class language and culture. (Notice that the British form of this debate was concerned with the working-class and not, as in the U.S.A., 'the poor'; and concerned with the vernaculars of the majority, not with black English.) On the other hand, while some were struggling to analyse popular speech and the submerged cultural legacy, they were confronted with dramatically novel linguistic-cultural phenomena which they were ill-equipped, perhaps reluctant, to understand. That these two matters were in essence different facets of the same question took a long time to emerge, if indeed it has yet emerged. To add to my earlier formulation, language and cultural diversity is language and class writ large.

For much more than a decade in the world of English teaching we were reluctant to engage fully with these questions and, as I indicated at the outset, some are so still. We do not emerge honourably from that refusal. It expressed itself plausibly in terms of a division of labour. Those with special expertise in English as a second language or West Indian dialects should be left to do their work and deliver the successfully converted pupils to us. Yet the signs were there to be read. In very guarded phrasing, the Bullock Report (1975) spoke of immigrant families facing 'grave problems':

> Many immigrant children come from stable supportive families in which
> the relative affluence of the parents is evident; others face grave problems
> of insecurity and hardship, and in many respects resemble some of the
> indigenous families in the same inner city area.

Earlier official documents had more explicitly spoken of linguistic deficit in immigrant
children. Many English teachers were familiar with the long argument about
elaborated and restricted codes but were unaware that these terms were haunting the
discussion of so-called immigrant languages. The language of West Indian children
was creating special difficulties. They were, so to speak, compounding their felony.
The restricted code they brought with them was merging with the restricted code
of the inner city. Jamaican plus Cockney was producing a new kind of hyper-deficit.
Yet the truth was that the really transforming encounter was with the experience of
being assigned a special role in the economy and being the target of the dominant
ideology: it was out of this encounter that a new culture and a new dialect grew, a
culture and language of resistance – ('we speak a "livalect" not a dialect', they say) –
already embodied in a flourishing literature.

English teachers, ill-equipped as most were, have had to start on the arduous
business of reshaping their programmes in the light of an adaptation of their principles.
I say 'ill-equipped' since we know only too well that just as their formation, basically
literary-critical, had not prepared them for the urban comprehensive school, so had
its essentially mono-lingual Englishness not prepared them for linguistic-cultural
diversity. As I have tried to indicate, in other ways some of them were prepared. They
needed only to rotate some of their basic principles to engage with the new situation.

That, I think, was more or less where we stood in the English Department
of the University of London Institute of Education when we embarked on a small-
scale study of linguistic diversity in inner-London schools. The 'we', it should be
said, included some of our Australian colleagues studying with us at the time, in
particular John Snodgrass. I will spare you the history and most of the findings of that
research (Rosen and Burgess, 1980) [see 'Language Diversity as Part of the Language
Curriculum' in Part Two of this collection], but I would like to select one feature of it
and let it ripple outwards to illustrate some of the complexities which confront us all.

I have selected the language of West Indian pupils, as we awkwardly call them
in our schools. I might easily have chosen the preoccupations around 'inter-language'
or the disputes about 'semi-lingualism', starting with a text like this by a boy whose
mother tongue is Cantonese.

> Once there was a man, He was draw very well and keep the Old thing but
> there are No people to buy because they are so pool … [and so on]

I prefer to start with West Indian pupils because in several senses they are the most
visible minority. (It is an interesting fact that the Irish, who are by far and away our

largest minority, rarely figure in discussions of multicultural education in spite of their long and violent relationship with British life and despite the fact that we now have some excellent sociolinguistic studies of their speech.)

The case of West Indian speech stands out for several reasons:

1. West Indians are the focus of almost neurotic anxiety in political and educational circles. As I write this paper, I read in *The Times* that the government is considering a proposal to carry out national testing of West Indian children's performance in school.
2. It is nearly impossible to say exactly what West Indian speech in Britain is.
3. There has been a unique and dramatic development in West Indian speech which can only be understood in terms of Halliday's 'anti-language' (1976/1978), oppositional language.
4. The case is the perfect example of the dangers of taking a monolithic view of language and culture.
5. The case demonstrates the disastrous limitations of looking at culture as something 'over there', rather than a new but connected growth 'over here'.

In other words, West Indian language presents a perfect instance of the new kind of understanding required of English teachers.

Let's start with the apparently straightforward question we asked ourselves in undertaking our survey: 'What do our West Indian pupils speak?' In the first place many of them speak an English which is no different from the language of white Londoners (and we can complicate life by asking, 'What do *they* speak?). But that is not true of those of them who have what Gumperz (1968) calls 'fluid repertoires'; that is, 'when there are transitions between adjoining vernaculars or when one speech style merges into another in such a way that it is difficult to draw clear borderlines'. That is a familiar enough concept in sociolinguistics and in personal experience, often taking the form of a continuum from a vernacular dialect to standard. Individual speakers are located on the continuum and slide along it in various ways and to differing extents. But West Indian speech in London presents a much more complex picture, for two reasons.

First, it emerges from the interaction of two quite different continua. There is the Creole continuum (ranging from one of the West Indian Creoles to a West Indian standard). And there is the London continuum (ranging from a full Cockney to standard British English). These two continua are in dynamic interaction. Thus the range of possibilities is enormous. We have tried to synthesise these in our report. But the central fact is that most West Indian pupils – very roughly 95% of them – now speak like working-class Londoners, but almost all display some features of black dialect, and these features will be intensified in certain contexts.

This might suggest that we are making a fuss about nothing or at any rate assuming that what, to a sociolinguist, is a fascinating set of phenomena, must ipso facto be equally compelling to a teacher. But we shall have to ask when and why the slide towards the Creole end of the continuum takes place and what this signifies. And then inevitably we have to take a stand on so-called dialect 'interference' and the claims that it affects learning to read and infects written composition.

However, the second reason for selecting West Indian language for attention is much more important, since it is not only dramatic by any standards but also provides the starkest and most unambiguous example of the relationship between language and identity and of the response to our unharmonious multicultural society. I must put it briefly. The West Indian community in London has developed its own Creole, basically Jamaican but different from it. It exerts a centripetal force on black Londoners, especially teenagers in our schools, who learn to speak this dialect (not, you should notice, their first language) with a speed and success which any teacher of French or, for that matter, would-be teachers of standard English would envy. Nobody, as far as we know, predicted the emergence of this dialect in the black community, much less the eagerness with which black youngsters would undertake learning it. What a remarkable thing! The supposed carriers of linguistic deficit mastering without benefit of schools or the normal processes of infant language acquisition a second dialect into which they can switch at will. Their Cockney-speaking counterparts can do no such thing.

It is worth mentioning at this point that we asked a question in our survey which ran like this: 'Would you welcome the opportunity to read and write sometimes in your dialect, out of interest in it?' The question itself would have seemed to some people nothing short of scandalous. In the event, 26% of the bi-dialectal pupils (overwhelmingly West Indian in origin) said, 'Yes.' The figure is the more remarkable if we bear in mind:

1. It would be unrealistic to many pupils, for whom such a possibility did not exist.
2. Our sample consisted of first-year secondary pupils, 11 and 12 years of age, who had not reached the age when black identity really asserts itself.

What are we to make of this? We must surely go beyond the now often expressed view that all dialects are equal, and assert that, functionally, the speaking of dialects may constitute different kinds of acts for different speakers. There is now a considerable body of work which demonstrates that there is no foundation to the assertion that speakers of 'low-status varieties' inevitably succumb to the pressures of standardisation. The latest study of this kind, of somewhat unusual design (Milroy, 1980), an investigation of vernacular speech in Belfast, came to the conclusion that it is essentially linked to *loyalty* and *solidarity* and is often perceived by its speakers as opposed to institutionalised values. The harmony view of culture and language cannot accommodate *that* very easily.

I have already mentioned one of Halliday's most remarkable and ambitious speculative papers (1976/1978), in which he discusses what he calls 'anti-languages'. He begins with an examination of prison language and criminals' language, and argues that they are an attempt to establish an alternative social reality. He proceeds to the proposal that they throw some light on dialects which can be seen in some sense as anti-language.

> A non-standard dialect that is consciously used for strategic purposes, defensively to maintain a particular social reality or offensively for resistance and protest, lies further in the direction of anti-language; this is what we know as 'ghetto language' … A social dialect is the embodiment of a widely but distinctly different world view – one which is therefore potentially threatening, if it does not coincide with one's one.

How well this applies to black dialect in London! The act of talking black, of making a sharp discontinuity between your first dialect and this second one, code-switching, as we say, is to go on the offensive, perhaps in both senses. To us black dialect in this way is to declare an opposition.

I have come a long way round. By detaching one strand from the huge linguistic diversity in our classrooms it may seem that I am suggesting an impossible task for the English teacher. Not impossible, but demanding, delicate and exploratory. In inner-city schools what most pupils share is frustration and often anger, expressed, as we know, in anything from surliness to overt rebelliousness. They are not to be placated by token gestures towards their language or attempts to confiscate it and annexe it. It will not be enough to allow them to use their dialect in school; they will need to be convinced that they can use it to say the most important things they have to say in writing as well as speech.

I believe the best English teaching in recent years has been an attempt to tear down all those barriers which made the pupils invisible – invisible to themselves, to each other and ultimately to the world; an attempt to call a halt to all those verbal exchanges in English classrooms in which what was *not* said was more important than what was said. Until now it has been a minority attempt but one of enormous significance. As Chris Searle discovered as far back as the publication of his pupils' fierce poems, *Stepney Words* (1971), when the attempt is made, the sparks fly. To broaden that attempt to include all the minority children in our schools must mean that there will be sparks galore. Are we prepared for that?

References

Agard, S. (1976) 'Cry for Me', in *Talking Blues*. London: Centerprise.

Allen, D. (1980) *English Teaching since 1965: How much growth?* London: Heinemann Educational.

The Bullock Committee (1975) *A Language for Life* (The Bullock Report). London: HMSO.

Carby, H. (1980) 'Multiculture'. *Screen Education, 34.*

Eagleson, R. (ed.) (1982) *English in the Eighties.* Adelaide: Australian Association for the Teaching of English and Urbana, IL: National Council of Teachers of English.

Gumperz, J. (1968) 'The speech community', in D. Sills (ed.), *International Encyclopaedia of Social Sciences.* New York: Macmillan.

Halliday, M. (1976) *Antilanguages. UEA papers in linguistics 1.* Norwich: University of East Anglia. Reprinted in Halliday (1978).

Halliday, M. (1978) *Language as Social Semiotic: The social interpretation of language and meaning.* London: Edward Arnold.

Hoggart, R. (1957) *The Uses of Literacy: Aspects of working-class life.* Harmondsworth: Penguin.

Holbrook, D. (1979) *English for Meaning.* Windsor: NFER.

Home Office (1978) *The West Indian Community: Observations on the report of the Select Committee on Race Relations and Immigration.* London: HMSO.

Milroy, L. (1980) *Language and Social Networks.* Oxford: Basil Blackwell.

National Association for the Teaching of English (no date) *The Teaching of English in Multicultural Britain.* Sheffield: National Association for the Teaching of English.

The Newbolt Committee (1921) *The Teaching of English in England* (The Newbolt Report). London: HMSO.

Queensland Working Party on Multicultural Education (1979) *Education for a Multicultural Society: A discussion paper based on the report to the Council of Directors of the Queensland Department of Education.* Brisbane: Queensland Department of Education.

Rosen, H. and Burgess, T. (1980) *Languages and Dialects of London School Children.* London: Ward Lock Educational.

Thompson, E. (1961) '*The Long Revolution* 1'. *New Left Review,* 9.

Tosi, A. (1979) 'Semilingualism, diglossia and bilingualism: Some observations on the sociolinguistic features of a community of Southern Italians in Britain'. *Lingua e Contesto,* 4.

Tosi, A. (1984) *Immigration and Bilingual Education: A case study of movement of population, language change and education within the EEC.* Oxford: Pergamon Press.

Williams, R. (1968) 'The idea of a common culture', in R. Gable (ed.), *Resources of Hope: Culture, democracy, socialism.* London: Verso.

Neither Bleak House nor Liberty Hall

English in the curriculum

This was Harold's inaugural lecture as Professor of Education with special reference to the teaching of English in education. He delivered it at the Institute of Education, University of London on 4 March 1981.

The subject we call English is the giant of the curriculum devouring the largest share of the timetabled space. Yet, as has often been pointed out, it is the least subject-like of subjects, the least susceptible to definition by reference to the accumulation of wisdom within a single academic discipline. No single set of informing ideas dominates its heartland. No one can confidently map its frontiers; it colonizes and is colonized. When we inspect the practices which cluster together uncomfortably under its banner, they appear so diverse, contradictory, arbitrary and random as to defy analysis and explanation. If, however, we interrogate and scrutinize this 'chaos illumined by flashes of lightning', particularly though not exclusively from the point of view of teachers and pupils in inner-London schools, we may perceive more meaning than at first meets the eye. For it is they who must live out the victories and defeats in the attempts to make the English language a more potent force in their lives. It is in the inner-city that the most ferocious tensions and dilemmas are set up between the languages of the community and what the Bullock Report (1975) called with deceptive neutrality 'the linguistic demands of the school'.

In hard times it is Gradgrind and Squeers who cast the longest shadows and all the schemes which in the past confined, stultified and inhibited the language learning of school students are being dusted down, refurbished; old discredited practices come with modern labels. Cross out *Graded English Exercises* and call it *Graded Language Development* but keep the same programme. At the same time there are persuasive voices telling us that after all that is what schools are for. They were meant to be Bleak Houses sustaining a bleak capitalist system. It can only be a delusion to seek out space in a carefully patrolled system. There is no room for a view of English teaching which sees it as a potential force in enabling pupils to make sense of their lives. All that and a bit more besides will be ruthlessly crushed by the I.S.A. – for non-initiates, the Ideological State Apparatus. At the same time there are others who continue to behave as though all is possible. The political realities of schools do not have to be confronted. In Holbrook's latest book we find a conflict-free Utopia:

> Many a primary school seems a little Athens, because there is no conflict
> about its main purposes; everyone there enjoys learning in the fullest and
> truest sense, in kindness and orderliness.
>
> (Holbrook, 1979)

Not even racism, sexism, class and diversity of languages and culture disturb this
harmonious picture.

> I have visited schools where there is a rich atmosphere of creative living,
> even in grim areas; where young teachers work happily and enthusiastically,
> with negro, Japanese, Greek and Italian children, as well as children of
> working-class parents on the one hand and TV producers on the other
> (in NW1).
>
> (*ibid.*)

No need to change anything. The tried formula holds good: 'The best training for
such work is good reading and good writing' (*ibid.*). English, we are told, has 'lost its
way' (Allen, 1980); it has been seduced by sociology, linguistics, politics, multicultural
education.

But English teaching is not simply a matter of what anybody wants it to be.
We have also to confront its history, a task the Bullock Report did not undertake.
Firstly, let's look at what view of English-the-language, rather than English-the-
subject, has been adopted in schools. It has its own history almost impervious to
linguistic scholarship, but that history is a short one if we exclude initiation into
literacy which has been going on for millennia and was initially the prime concern,
albeit in very circumscribed terms, of the schools for working-class children after
the 1870 Act. But in the Public Schools and grammar schools, cowering in the
shadow of the Classics, the English language was treated exactly as though it were
a dead language, idealized, codified, monolithic, written not spoken. Access to it
was to be gained above all by the prolonged study of a certain kind of grammar,
certain diluted principles of rhetoric ('figures of speech and devices of style') and
a narrow selection of 'good' models. What emerges as the English language comes
in various guises, good English, correct English, Queen's English and finally and
triumphantly Standard English – all presumed to be clearly identifiable and leaving
only questions of style to be resolved. The text-books were crammed, and still are
for all their changes of presentation, with precepts about what English *should* be,
not with discussion of what English actually is. I cannot trace here the additions and
deletions to this programme over a century, though they are indeed extraordinary
and characteristically reveal a loss of nerve and a disintegrative plunder of the
manuals. Certainly the teaching of English was shaped by the class divisions of
the educational system, proposing nothing less than the abolition of working-class
language. But it would be a typical over-simplification to imagine that different

strata have been hermetically sealed off from each other. Some major features move down through the system, often modified to the point of caricature but sometimes totally unchanged, rather like the speech days in certain comprehensive schools.

I have in my possession a little book called *Notes of Lessons and How to Write Them* addressed explicitly and exclusively to elementary-school teachers, dated 1911 and written by an anonymous 'Head Master under the London School Board'. It includes among many lesson notes for the teaching of grammar (it has none on any other aspect of English) one set on the subjunctive mood, a sub-section of which goes to work on a single sentence, which no doubt the children of the day might have bandied about in the London streets: *If he were to have anything he would give it.* Here are the notes.

> Write the words 'expressed' and 'understood' on the Blackboard and explain their meaning to the Class. 'What mood takes a Plural when the Nominative is Singular,' 'How do you know the Subjunctive from the Indicative Mood,' ('By uncertainty and futurity.') 'Does the speaker in this sentence know whether he has anything or not,' 'No.' Then we call this form of the Subjunctive Mood 'complete uncertainty'. [original punctuation!]

Complete uncertainty! What better phrase with which to conclude? We have no record of what those London elementary-school pupils made of it, though we can make some good guesses. Meanwhile we can see how it illustrates the downward transmission of a certain view of English which can still be traced in changed realizations in classrooms and examinations to this very day.

This is not a matter of teaching of grammar but of certain critical underlying features rarely totally absent from English teaching. What are they?

1. The English language is essentially *opaque* in the sense that it is governed by sets of rules only mastered with difficulty, if at all. Thus there is interposed between learners and their active use and exploration of English the screen of a mystifying, closed legal system.

2. More important, ideologically, this English is based on *an authority,* whose credentials of linguistic power are not on display. They are not made available for reflection, criticism or rejection. The procedures, the criteria, the very grounds of authority's legitimation are invisible.

3. For the majority of pupils, this has meant that their language is essentially something to be cured, cleansed, purged of deformities rather than extended, enriched, developed. The consequent loss of confidence can only in the end contribute to a process of *subordination,* since the true sources of the powerful uses of language are withheld.

4. The machinery through which this kind of learning of language functions is an apparatus of disconnected drills and exercises on vocabulary, sentence completion, errors, pseudo-comprehension, etc., etc., reinforced by tests and examinations. This apparatus creates a sharp discontinuity between those language activities which arise from social relationships outside school and those which are demanded within school, without any meaningful connection between the two. This is the most thorough-going strategy of *control,* an elaborated methodology which leaves huge oppressive silences, a muffling and gagging of all those disturbing voices which might otherwise be heard in classrooms.

Mystification, oppressiveness, subordination, control? What happened to the 'mainstream culture', the promised land into which the barbarians, white, black, brown and yellow, were supposed to be led? More of that later. If I have seemed to have exaggerated or sensationalized I remain unapologetic. One of the most successful myths of the educational right is that a great tide of anarchic progressiveness or, worse still, subversive radicalism has swept through the schools and that English teachers are at the centre of it. On the contrary the sheer pervasiveness, in many different forms, of what I have described is there for all to see. That is why alternatives, which most certainly exist, from partial to total, are more than alternatives: they can make headway only as opposition, whether it is about the choice of literature, the significance of West Indian dialect, how children learn to read, the learning of English as a second language, the significance of spelling, English for industry and commerce, or anything else. That is why it is in inner-city schools above all that the most productive re-thinking of English teaching has taken place and is taking place. It is there that English teachers are more likely to perceive the collision between the time-honoured practice and the needs of their pupils; the need to use language to articulate significant and urgent meanings, the need to use language to formulate in new ways their experience and understanding, the need to find in literature an illumination (not a reflection) of their lives.

Whatever else has been in doubt, no one has seriously questioned the claim that literature should be a central preoccupation of English teaching, though in practice it is often simply abandoned. Even the most impoverished versions of mass-education soon after their inception made some concessions, perhaps no more than 'recitation', to the belief that in some way it would contribute to the training of the lower orders. Some kind of literary bookshelf has been nailed to a wall in Bleak House. There would be little point here in reciting the grandiose claims for literature in education, from Matthew Arnold to Leavis and his disciples; their passionate work deserves and has received attention enough. What runs through that history is the claim that literature is a *privileged* transmitter of a single set of cultural values, of *the* tradition. But it is more to my present purpose to consider how literature is actually institutionalized within the educational system. Here we can find processes analogous to those I have already presented, with this important difference, that they have been more noticeably influenced by the practices of universities, where the study of language has either been linguistic archaeology or been kept firmly at the periphery. The formation of specialist English teachers has been overwhelmingly literary. It is in the universities that an industry has been constructed around the reading of books and where it is determined what knowledge is required so that they may be handled properly and, of course, what kinds of examinations are best suited to testing this knowledge. Literary texts have been enmeshed in layer after layer of scholarship, sources, textual variants, biographies, alternative readings, 'background', literary history, glossaries and analyses of plot, character and, dare I say it, structure. Central to this formidable institution is the establishment of a canon of major works. More recently, as the newspapers have told us, we have had stylistics, semiotics and structuralism, theories about the nature of literary texts and, most ambitious of all, a 'science of literature' (Eagleton, 1978).

A missing ghost from this irresistible banquet is the reader whose actual processes in engaging with text are either assumed (they are, or should be the same as those of the scholar-critic) or ignored (the text exists in its own autonomous world independently of both reader and author). In the translation and adaptation of this world of literary scholarship to school we find the study of literature operating its own kind of tyranny. Just as we saw with language, literature is made arcane by an interposed screen of interrogation and privileged interpretation. In this inquisitorial court certain texts have been halo-ed or, the obverse of the same coin, abandoned as being inaccessible to certain kinds of pupil. There is hermeneutic challenge, not of the teacher but of the text, and it is present even in nursery rhyme and certainly in the popular ballad (it is the text which asks: what *are* the relationships amongst that terrifying trio Lord Randall, his mother and his true love?). 'The pleasure of the text' is appropriated and turned to ashes. Like so many other things, children are not to be trusted with it. As Barthes (1976) wrote:

> No sooner has a word been said, somewhere, about the pleasure of the text, than two policemen are ready to jump on you: the political policeman and the psychological policeman. Futility and/or guilt, pleasure is either idle or vain, a class notion or an illusion.

Literature in school cannot be seen solely in terms of itself but of how it is selected, policed and mediated. I am not arguing, as I hope will emerge, that literature in school can avoid selection and value, still less, thank goodness, that it has never meant more than that. But I am arguing that all those engaged in interesting new developments in the study of literature in universities never acknowledge the deep and prolonged pre-analytic *immersion* in all kinds of literature, an immersion which alone makes their activities possible or conceivable, which occurred during all those long years which finally led them to the conviction that the making and receiving of literature was indeed an essential and significant activity of human beings. It is precisely with those years and with that kind of reader that schools have to be concerned. It is a huge and grim irony that Dr MacCabe of all people is calling for the study of grammar in schools so that his handful of Cambridge students may more diligently pursue their structuralist studies.

Paradoxically, though English is without a clearly demarcated inter-subject frontier, it has usually a very clear partition within its own territory, a sharp disjuncture between language and literature, as every O-level entrant knows. Attempts have, of course, been made to bring different brands of linguistic scholarship to bear on the study of literature (accompanied by screams of protest). I mean rather that literature has been treated as an activity pursued by a special select group called authors or writers and quite unlike any uses of language which pupils or ordinary mortals pursue. This in school practice has meant a disjuncture between reading and writing, even more between normal speech and literature, and between oral and written literature. Consequently, literature has been set apart from universal human uses of language. Very rarely do scholars pursue these mutually nourishing resources. Eagleton (1978) notes that we find literature:

> … entwining itself with the stuff of spontaneous experience and the roots of language and gesture …

while for Raymond Williams (1977):

> … This whole range of conscious, half-conscious, and often apparently instinctive shaping … is the activation of a social semiotic and communicative process, more deliberate, more complex, and more subtle in literary creation than in everyday expression but in continuity with it.

The roots of literature reach down into the soil of the everyday uses of language, narratives, dialogues, rhythms, inventiveness, verbal play, improvised rhetoric and spontaneous drama. In this broad sense everyone produces literature. In a more specific sense all pupils who can write can also, however fitfully or hesitantly, but often very powerfully, activate the 'social semiotic and communicative process' to produce in the same mode as great writers and to share the medium. The wrenching apart of language and literature has always contributed towards hiding this indissoluble unity.

Jerome Bruner, in a lecture (1979) which dealt with early language development, commented that once the young child has possession of the basic language system then the curriculum is anything. He was unwittingly highlighting a central dilemma of English teaching. The use of language, as Halliday constantly reminds us, is the making of meaning and language development is the process of learning how to mean. But then, what special order of meanings is the unique preserve of the English teacher? The answer, it is often implied, is that anything will do so long as it arouses interest. Thus we can inveigle pupils into conspiring in their own language development without their noticing it. Interest is the bait, language development the fish. Totally to espouse that view is to make English all medium and no message. Its effect is to trivialize the pupils' communications and either to banish significant and compelling exchanges or more elusively to have an agenda which is hidden from the pupil and possibly the teacher too. English becomes an endless rehearsal for the real thing due to happen in a dimly perceived future and in another place. Master language first, then do something with it. In the effort to change anything-English into something-English, teachers have engaged in a serious attempt to gather together significant themes. It has not been a fruitless or mean-spirited search. It is easy to mock this enterprise only if we forget that there is no smooth, clearly sign-posted road away from the old oppressiveness; if there is stumbling, fearful hesitation it is because the road is haunted by desperation and fear of ambush. Yet the difficulties must be faced. There is nothing intrinsically emancipating about themes; they can operate a kind of containment as easily as anything else. In a penetrating discussion Peter Medway (1980) writes:

> Assemblages of topics, particularly for the lower secondary years (Whales, Weddings, September 1939, Australia, Creation, Witches, Cats, Fishing …), linked by nothing except a hope that they will stimulate language, induce the same sort of numbness and disorientation as watching a whole evening's television or reading a colour supplement from cover to cover; the important is introduced along with the lightweight, the intimate with the macrocosmic, the near-to-home with the far away … If American Indians come up in the slot previously occupied by Eccentric People I Know and Fairgrounds, they were better not appearing at all.

There are themes which are more than those to be unearthed in the interstices of the curriculum, the unclassified and uncolonized terrain of Fairgrounds and Fishing (neither of which is in itself trivial) but they cannot be assembled like a shopping list, nor by *a priori* social, political, aesthetic commitment; they are not tabulations but elusive discoveries to be made by teachers and pupils because they are buried or just beginning to appear. Just how formidable that undertaking is can be measured in the setting, let us say, of white teachers with black pupils or male teachers of girls. The truly compelling themes are not to be turned on as though turning on water from the tap.

I have been highly selective of the issues through which I have tried to inspect some deep-seated causes of the bleakness which contaminates so much English teaching. I might have chosen others, deprivation folklore, the monolingual and monocultural forms of racism, the service view of English, etc. I have had my say on these issues elsewhere. Up to this point I might have seemed to be joining a long line of Cassandras. After all, bleakness in our educational system has never been hard to find; it has even, as the Cockerton Judgment showed in 1901, been legally provided for. Bleakness in English teaching has been demonstrated, documented and denounced in reports and studies, novels and autobiographies, by commissioners, inspectors and writers of all kinds. For a century the critics with their disquieting exposures (Matthew Arnold, the Newbolt Report [1921], George Sampson [1925], Leavis [1967], Leavis and Thompson [1933]) have wrung their hands; and under our very eyes Her Majesty's Inspectors have joined that long line (Department of Education and Science, 1979). From quite different standpoints, the critics have denounced the mean view of English teaching and issued their remedies, sometimes not noticing that they were reiterating almost verbatim the strictures of their predecessors, that the mean view had nothing to do with an active, purposeful, creative use of language, that the typical encounter with literature could produce only distaste and bewilderment, that a narrow focus on grammar, drills and spelling was self-defeating.

One of the most dramatic displays of the Cassandra role was the work of Sir Philip Hartog. As early as 1907 he was insisting that children had the right to use written composition to express ideas and opinions of their own and that one of the greatest denials of this right was the examination system with its debilitating implicit rubric, 'Write anything about something for anybody'. Forty years later, yes *forty*, in 1947 he was obliged to come to the conclusion that nothing had changed.

In the thirty years or so since then things *have* changed. The high-level debate by visionaries and reformers could not make any major impact until the objective conditions in schools changed and until English teachers themselves could radically reshape the considerable insights lying embalmed for so long. The palpable failure of all those years, all those books, those stormy calls to arms, those extravagant pronouncements – 'English for the English', 'Sweetness and light', 'No form of knowledge can take precedence of a knowledge of English' – was partly due to the fact that these great spokesmen were not really addressing themselves to teachers: their idiom was fashioned to persuade those vested with power to do something before it was too late, culture *or* anarchy. They never confronted the political realities and decisive mechanisms which shaped the daily existence of teachers, nor were they equipped to do so. The best of their ideas were contaminated at their heart. The great Matthew Arnold himself, scourge of the Philistines, could almost in the same breath claim on the one hand that literary culture 'seeks to do away with classes' and 'men of culture are true apostles of equality' and on the other that each class must have a carefully differentiated cultural programme, a sentiment to be echoed later by T.S. Eliot and G.H. Bantock. Leavis's 'great tradition' was to be handed on by a chosen few. The Newbolt Report, which claimed that English could abolish divisions between classes, recommended drills in the speaking of Standard English for working-class pupils, whose language had an 'evil power'. Therefore, none of them could explain the abiding strength of the citadel they stormed unsuccessfully again and again, its armament too powerful to have much need of sustained and fervent intellectual advocacy. Six hundred pages of the Bullock Report against three-and-a-half tucked away in Stuart Froome's 'Note of Dissent':

> It is doubtful if children's talk in school does much to improve their knowledge, for free discussion as a learning procedure at any age is notoriously unproductive.
>
> (The Bullock Committee, 1975)

Only a sentence or two is needed to alert the troops, for 'free discussion … at any age' is after all a self-evident heresy. Sergeant Rhodes Boyson will know his duty.

> It is significant that most of the 'group of extremist teachers, a dozen or twenty', at that school came from the English Department.
>
> (cited in Grace, 1978)

Not quite the apostles and missionaries Matthew Arnold had in mind.

It is now time to ask how far the bleakness I have presented is incurably endemic in the system. Is there any space within the system for genuine alternatives? Were the apparent gains of the Sixties all illusion and deception? In London in particular English teachers have through certain organs and agencies been able to articulate, elaborate and collaborate, in what they believe is a measured challenge to entrenched orthodoxies. Has all that devoted energy been futile, or – worse still – been a camouflage, a typical manoeuvre of liberalism disguising the real nature of bourgeois hegemony? That last sentence obliges me to say that in order to answer these questions we shall, for a short while at least, have to re-lexicalize ourselves. For we must digress into that world of hegemony, interpellation, false consciousness, dominant ideology and, above all, I.S.A. (Ideological State Apparatus) which I alerted you to some half-an-hour ago. If you object that you'd prefer not to be involved in the irrelevant blood-letting forays of the academic left, I can only reply that these are not only serious ideas but also that in various forms they exert an influence on just those English teachers to whom one would look for commitment, that very important minority who keep alive and actively create the most convincing alternatives. Moreover, these ideas deal in very direct fashion with education and language. They address themselves to all those of us who believe in an alternative socialist society and for whom, therefore, alternatives *now* must have a special meaning. This is by no means the remote and esoteric business it might on the surface appear to be, for in one publication after another we can trace the lineaments of this austere determinist stance. With undisguised glee academics installed comfortably in the Ideological State Apparatus celebrate the end of all those very different hopes and programmes of the Sixties which they lump together as 'social democracy' or 'progressive-ism'.

There is nothing for it, then. We must visit briefly the bleakest of all Bleak Houses, or to be more exact an architect's model, designed by Louis Althusser (1971), a prototype which has inspired similar constructions (there are British and

American models). Over the doorway of this Bleak House school is inscribed the awful legend 'Ideological State Apparatus', for schools, we are given to understand, have the dominant role in the transmission of capitalist ideology, not only because they deliver in readily recognizable form explicit sets of ideas demonstrably designed to persuade, exhort and cajole, but because through every nuance of their functioning, their 'silent music', we absorb a taken-for-granted world, the stuff of thought itself, ensuring the continuance of the social order. We are continuously beckoned by ideology (called 'interpellation') and, it seems, never refuse to counter its solicitation. The result is that we have an imaginary relationship to our real conditions of existence.

We can now inspect the architect's model, the intriguing feature of which is that though it is in reality a kind of high security prison it is designed to look like Liberty Hall. How does it work?

1. It takes all children and 'drums into them, whether it uses new or old methods, a certain amount of know-how wrapped in ruling ideology … or simply ruling ideology in its pure state.' Note in passing that 'know-how' includes, along with such things as arithmetic, both the national language and literature.
2. It ejects at intervals an appropriate quota to fill particular roles in a class society, each quota being 'provided with the ideology which suits the role it has to fulfil'.
3. It works to perfection because the mechanism is concealed beneath an illusory ideology-free neutrality.

Language and literature in this reductive scheme of things are reduced to 'know-how'. Elsewhere it suits Althusser's purpose to drop his sarcastic reference to 'good books' and explain that literature is not ideology and to make the conventional distinction between the 'authentic' and the 'mediocre'.

In one extraordinary passage Althusser seems to become aware that his functionalist Bleak House, the perfect bourgeois learning edifice, might give offence. Here it is.

> I ask the pardon of those teachers who, in dreadful conditions, attempt to turn the few weapons they can find in the history and learning they 'teach' against the ideology, the systems and the practices in which they are trapped. They are a kind of hero. But they are rare and how many (the majority) do not even suspect the 'work' the system (which is bigger than they are and crushes them) forces them to do, or worse, put all their heart and ingenuity into performing it with the most advanced awareness (the famous new methods!).

> (*ibid.*)

So it turns out there is a little back door we hadn't noticed through which rare heroes enter Bleak House. The abstractness of the model forbids us to discover the processes by which such heroes are made. So, then, the rigorous intellectual procedures permit the unexplained entrance of heroes without provenance whose practice is not examined (that way abhorred 'empiricism' lies, and perhaps even obnoxious 'moralism'). Moreover, they are doomed heroes: they teach in quotation marks and are trapped in the practices of the apparatus. This eruption of Romantic tragedy in such a context is necessary because there has to be some minimal recognition, caricatured and distorted though it is, that the system is not impermeable. Millions of pupils, half-a-million teachers, thousands of schools with differences of history, different experiences of pressures and possibilities, daily encounters and choices, and in English teaching the unending struggle to engage with ideas and feelings at this moment in history: all this cannot be encompassed by one stereotyped formula, an oversimplified view of ideology which turns people into unwitting dupes. 'New methods' cannot be brushed aside in a contemptuous parenthesis. They must be ruthlessly scrutinized and discriminations made. It matters how reading is taught and how it should be taught. The hundreds of committed teachers who came to our conference, 'Achieving Literacy', a few weeks ago were addressing themselves to nothing less than the great qualitative leap in learning. The ferocious disagreements about the politics of literacy, about reading ages, phonics, screening, etc., are matters of substance, not irrelevant twitches of the Ideological State Apparatus. Presumably, those who believe in that improbable machinery learned to read within its embrace, and learned some of their confident and fluent use of language too. It matters that 'new methods' should replace the arid and oppressive imposition of literature, that the attempt should be made to realize its unique meaning-potential, to rescue the immediacy of its always-present provocation and juxtaposition of values. It matters that we should reflect upon such matters as the meaning of the creation of a London black dialect and what schools should do about it, upon how English as a second language can best be learned, upon how sexism in language invades the classroom.

The pseudo-apology to trapped heroes is a gross insult to the reflective and critical consciousness of many, many English teachers who throw enormous energy into winning spaces in Bleak House, where honest dialogue can happen and communicative power be extended. There are indeed heroes in schools. I am speaking, remember, of my friends and colleagues. They surface in public awareness when they stubbornly refuse to accept censorship of books or defiantly publish children's poems against official fiat. They would be embarrassed to be called heroes, aware as they are that they, like the rest of us in learning institutions, must become involved in shabby compromises, the set books and marking schemes. Yet in a way, that is beside the point: such heroes would not be possible if there were not repeatedly enacted little heroisms by teachers who would not for one moment espouse a radical view of society. Just as there are many teachers of quite differing philosophies who to their credit are against corporal punishment, so there are just as many who are opposed to the intellectual and cultural punishment of English-for-working-class-dunces. There is nothing mysterious about this. It happens because Bleak House (not the architect's model), for all its high walls, cannot shut out messages from outside which will be loud or muted according to the strength or weakness of the forces for change in the community. In English teaching we have been able to register this pulse in very specific ways. Put side by side two volumes, *Writing* (Worker Writers and Community Publishers, 1978) and *Our Lives* (ILEA English Centre, 1979), the first a collection of writing from a dozen or more community groups from all over the country, the second a selection of school pupils' autobiographies: the family resemblance, the shared assumptions, are unmistakable. They are in fact spelled out in the introduction to *Our Lives*. There are similar sympathetic vibrations between ventures in popular theatre and drama in schools, between new black literature and the writing of dialect stories and poetry in schools, between a revitalized interest in the oral tradition and the classroom extension of this tradition.

None of this should obscure the fact that all these initiatives run against the grain of most, but not all, schools, that they must always run the gauntlet of hostility and threat, that they are constantly policed by zealots with their own definitions of the appropriate language for meeting the needs of society and considerable power for enforcing those definitions. We can take some heart from this. A compliant teaching force surrounded by compliant pupils backed by compliant parents would require no such nervous vigilance. For the most part, schools are not battlegrounds where major collisions between alternative views are fought out and a few trapped heroes go to their doom. In most there is a never-ending series of small but important skirmishes and incursions. They arise because so many teachers cannot fail, to some extent at least, 'to suspect the work the system asks them to do' and to confront its contradictions and tensions.

In contrast to the distant and disdainful pronouncements about how schools work, we can look at the careful study carried out by Gerald Grace in sixteen urban comprehensive schools. In contrast to the fiction of teachers who, all imbued with the dominant ideology, do not suspect how the system works, he found that

> English teachers represented a complete spectrum of ideological positions in education, from the Arnoldian stance to the Marxist. If they differed significantly from other groups of teachers it was not in respect of a thorough-going radicalism designed to subvert the conventions of English usage, but as a group they contained more teachers who exhibited 'radical doubt' and critical reflection about the curriculum ... in certain schools their members showed *a distinctive awareness of recent theoretical criticisms of the assumptions of traditional curricula and of the dilemmas and possibilities which these posed* [my italics].
>
> (Grace, 1978)

He also found that, for whatever reasons, teachers in inner-city schools enjoyed 'a real and considerable freedom in their work situation' in relation to curriculum content, pedagogy and (to some extent) evaluation. In one school he found innovations taking place against 'wider institutional disapproval'. Since Grace is fully conversant with the debate over ideology he is at pains to point out just how vulnerable this partial freedom is. Similarly Willis (1977), studying a group of alienated working-class boys for three years and examining with sympathy their self-defeating counter-culture, faces up to the question of 'Monday morning' (i.e. what do you do in school):

> To contract out of the messy business of day to day problems is to deny the active, contested nature of social and cultural reproduction: to condemn real people to the status of passive zombies, and actually cancel the future by default … the necessary tension between short term actions taken in good faith in relation to barely understood laws of growth and their unpredictable long term outcomes is a common feature of life for all social agents.

I am sorry to have detained you so long over this digression, which has taken longer than I had intended. Let me try to see where it has taken us. I share this much ground with the Althusserian view. Schools do not offer infinite space for manoeuvre, limited only by the supposed abilities of the pupils and the extent to which teachers are prepared to espouse up-to-date ideas. Schools are sorting mechanisms which in a very rough and ready way supply different kinds of cohorts to the work force. They are also inevitably one powerful agency which in visible and invisible ways transmits the dominant ideas, values and attitudes of our society. I tried to show earlier how this has operated in English teaching. But I have argued that it is insufficient to subscribe to such ideas without placing side by side how the system is *supposed* to work as against how it *actually* works and how people actually respond to it. Finally, within schools there is movement, conflict, imperfect control which make it possible, inside limits which are always shifting and need therefore to be discovered in practice, to contest the terrain. For English teachers who have wanted to engage in this contest there have been certain specific possibilities created by the fact that the last pathetic residue of the mediaeval trivium of Grammar, Rhetoric and Logic could be seen in manifest disarray, and by the repeated failure of the established model to meet anyone's demands for working-class children, a failure made more blatant in multi-ethnic, multi-cultural, multi-lingual schools. But the mistake which many have made – and we must certainly accept a fair share of the blame – was to behave as though the contested space were solely a matter of persuasion, the sheer force of better ideas. Thus the tendency towards a euphoric rhetoric which took little account of the institutionalized obstacles and snares. The mirage of Liberty Hall shimmered for too long on the horizon. A dramatic reckoning came at the international conference on the teaching of English in 1971 after which Liberty Hall never recovered its hallucinatory power, though it still has its devotees (Abbs, 1976, pp. 187–188).

Spaces do not simply exist in the system; they have to be won, defended and extended. Peter Medway's recent minutely documented book, *Finding a Language* (1980) is the biography of such an attempt. He sets out to make English like this:

> Under the guise of just another curriculum subject, it has come to enact nothing less than a different model of education: knowledge to be made not given; knowledge comprising more than can be discursively stated; learning as a diverse range of processes, including affective ones; educational processes to be embarked upon with outcomes unpredictable; students' perceptions, experiences, imaginings and unsystematically acquired knowledge admitted as legitimate curricular content.

The account scrupulously inspects those ambitions at work. But there is a chilling conclusion. In Medway's words, 'our institutional base was eroded' and 'there was informal pressure'; so all came to an end. Victory and defeat. Yet I could point to several schools in inner London alone which have sustained similar attempts over years and still do: but they work with a stronger support system – the ILEA English Centre and its superb *English Magazine,* the London Association for the Teaching of English and, let me say it, the English Department here at the Institute. Very few of those involved are unaware of the fragility of their gains.

I have up to this point been content to leave markers as I have proceeded to indicate the grounds on which the spaces in the system are best contended for. I shall not now attempt to gather them together. You will not at this point suppose (or if you do I am done for!) that as a grand finale I will suddenly conjure up a vision of the great alternative. I want instead to select two themes and let them serve as a touchstone for the rest.

Look for a single phrase to answer the question 'What do you want space for?' and the answer is likely to be 'The experience of pupils'. It has become a kind of talisman for English teachers, perhaps too much so since it gives rise to so many misunderstandings. Their argument is familiar enough these days. There is validity in the pupils' lives and purposes, they have competences we give them no credit for, the thin gruel we administer with Bumble's spoon excludes a different but vital verbal culture outside. Stuart Hall (1977) puts it like this:

> The fact is, however, that this legitimation of certain kinds of language has had the effect of de-legitimating the natural speech, language and modes of expression in which that majority speaks: a language which has been formed in and by a real connectedness to life-situation and experience, and without which the working class boy is literally speechless (that is he has no language for his own experience of the world) … There is more

than one kind of speaking: and it is not by chance that education favours some varieties and degrades others.

Others have said it in different ways, but always it revolves round 'life-situation and experience'. To shift the focus of English teaching in this way is a huge step which carries with it certain consequences. Both logically and practically it suggests that teachers must abandon their role as unique suppliers of knowledge, being in no privileged position to recount and interpret experiences they have never had. They must therefore relinquish some of their authority. However, experience has never been more than a working term and is therefore open to attack from those who wish wilfully to misunderstand it. If teachers have turned to their pupils' experience it is not because they believe in some modern version of the Noble Savage, nor that all that needed to happen was that experience should be verbalized and they could stand back and admire it in middle-class humility. Of course, experience is not innocent. The very act of turning language upon it robs it of innocence, conceptually, affectively and ideologically in one fell swoop. It is nevertheless where the interaction of language, thought and society is passionately lived out. It is much more than a passive mirror image of dominant ideology realized as messy and impotent 'common sense'. It is not motionless and inert: it incites ideas, speculations and questions, often in the form of stories and poems. The experience of pupils in the inner city and elsewhere leads them to doubt and question in language saturated with thought and feeling. In any case, once real dialogue starts there is no way of keeping experience out.

That is why for so many English teachers the word 'experience' has so much resonance. There has been some cynical tittering over creative writing (and creative talking for that matter). In spite of all the ways it has gone wrong, at its best it has unleashed in classrooms stories, poems, autobiographies and drama of a kind never seen before in schools, a huge demonstration of the ability of children and young people to speak with authenticity, quite unlike the bogus, half-strangled essays and perfunctory compositions which have filled mountains of grimy exercise books. This is hard-won space amidst the resounding discouragement of the deprivation discourse which has been at pains to explain that it was precisely the experience of pupils which was the teacher's cross, above all in matters of language. The working term 'experience' cannot be the be-all and end-all but there is no other begin-all.

But who wants to settle for beginnings? So, we must go beyond experience; it is too turbulent, anarchic and fortuitous to allow for more than hasty reflection, notoriously unsystematised and unreliable. Social consciousness is not all it's cracked up to be. Contradictions, illusions and superstitions run in its blood stream. No matter: we have the perfect therapy for all that, called the curriculum, supposedly designed to put all in order with system and structure. Yet it is a platitude that the curriculum is itself in need of therapy because, among other reasons, it can neither make convincing links with pupils' experience nor accommodate the substantial understanding they have derived from it. Before English teachers can cope with that dislocation they must solve a conundrum.

> *'Ah,' said the King, hoping to catch out the Princess's suitor, 'how do you take something with you only by leaving it behind?' And the Prince, himself a reader of fairy tales, replied, 'Literature.' 'How so?' 'Because literature takes us beyond our own experience, but it only works if we bring our experience to bear on it.'*

Literature, alone of all modes of discourse, comes disguised as lived experience in all its immediacy and unpredictability. It handles ideas in everyday fashion; we suppose ourselves to be reacting to it much as we might to what happened just now on the street corner. It 'entwines itself with the stuff of spontaneous experience and the roots of language and gesture'. Its rhythms are physically experienced; its ways of meaning are plucked from spontaneous speech. Every genre can be heard in embryo in unrehearsed interaction. Because literature has this experiential feel it is suffused with feeling and provokes in us, as raw experience does, thoughts, charged with anger, guilt, delight, gloom, submission, content. Just as many new experiences cannot have meaning outside the relevant experiences which preceded them and the ones we expect are yet to come, so the 'experience' offered by literature can only have meaning if it interlocks with the reader's past and future.

> *'Just a minute,' said the King. 'I said, "… only by leaving it behind". You haven't left experience behind at all. You haven't dealt with that.' 'Ah, no. I was coming to that.'*

If experience is not innocent, neither is literature. For while it entices the reader's experience (more, colludes and conspires with it), at the very same time it disrupts it, disturbs it and fractures it, urgently demanding a meaning which could never have arisen simply from the reality it appears to offer. The text beckons us from several directions, juxtaposing conflicting values. Because it interrogates us, we must for our part interrogate it, at every twist and turn, every moment of doubt or bewilderment. It is at the very end of a Brecht play that comes the line, 'There must, there must, be some end that would fit.'

> *'Sounds very strenuous,' said the King. 'And I once read a book. It wasn't like that at all. It was, I'm glad to say, about a wise and good king and, well, he just lived happy ever after.' 'Try* King Lear*', said the Prince. 'Er – on second thoughts, you'd better start with* The Emperor's New Clothes*.'*

There are many texts which require not even a minimally strenuous encounter, which do not attempt to disrupt the reader's experience: they confirm it, they praise it, soothe it or merely console it. That means a tireless search for those texts which in the classroom are strenuous, not in the crude sense of being difficult, but in the sense that they ask for new meanings and values. That is only feasible in classrooms where there is space for the collaborative production of meaning, where the pupils' experience is acknowledged to be necessary and relevant. How else can it go beyond itself?

'How did you get on with The Emperor's New Clothes?' *asked the Prince. The King drew his fur robe tightly around him. 'A ridiculous and useless tale,' said the King. 'And no one else must be allowed to read it.' 'But surely … ' said the Prince. 'Silence!' shouted the King. 'Where do you think you are? Liberty Hall?' The Prince bowed himself out.*

Leaving the Palace, he passed the door of the servants' quarters. He could hear loud laughter and the voice of a storyteller saying, ' … and then the little boy said, "But he hasn't got any clothes on at all." '

References

Abbs, P. (1976) *Root and Blossom.* London: Heinemann.

Allen, D. (1980) *English Teaching since 1965: How much growth?* London: Heinemann.

Althusser, L. (1971) 'Ideology and Ideological State Apparatuses', in B. Cosin (ed.), *Education, Structure and Society.* Harmondsworth: Penguin.

Barthes, R. (1976) *The Pleasure of the Text* (R. Miller, trans.). London: Jonathan Cape.

Bruner, J. (1979) In a lecture given to the Association for the Study of the Curriculum, April 1979.

The Bullock Committee (1975) *A Language for Life* (The Bullock Report). London: HMSO.

Department of Education and Science (1979) *Aspects of Secondary Education in England: A survey by HM Inspectors of Schools.* London: HMSO.

Eagleton, T. (1978) *Criticism and Ideology.* London: Verso.

Grace, G. (1978) *Teachers, Ideology and Control.* London: Routledge and Kegan Paul.

Hall, S. (1977) 'Education and the crisis of the urban school', in J. Raynor and E. Harris (eds.), *Schooling in the City.* London: Ward Lock.

Holbrook, D. (1979) *English for Meaning.* Windsor: National Foundation for Educational Research.

Leavis, F. (1967) *Literature in our Time and the University.* Cambridge: Cambridge University Press.

Leavis, F. and Thompson, D. (1933) *Culture and Environment.* London: Chatto and Windus.

Medway, P. (1980) *Finding a Language.* London: Chameleon Books.

The Newbolt Committee (1921) *English for the English* (The Newbolt Report). London: HMSO.

Williams, R. (1977) *Marxism and Literature.* Oxford: Oxford University Press.

Willis, P. (1977) *Learning to Labour.* Farnborough: Saxon House.

The Language Monitors

A critique of the Assessment of Performance Unit's primary survey report *Language Performance in Schools*

In this paper, published in 1982, one of a series of occasional papers published by the Institute of Education, University of London, and known as the Bedford Way Papers, Harold criticizes aspects of the work of the Assessment of Performance Unit (APU), and one of its publications in particular. The APU was set up by the government in response to a recommendation in the Bullock Report (1975) that there should be a more effective method of measuring children's and young people's progress and performance in language in schools than had been devised hitherto.

The critique itself is preceded by an introduction derived from a full-scale report on the APU by Caroline Gipps and Harvey Goldstein, members of the Evaluation of Testing in Schools Project based at the London Institute. The report was published the following year as *Monitoring Children: An evaluation of the Assessment of Performance Unit* (Gipps and Goldstein, 1983).

Introduction

The following notes, which describe the origin, history to date, and objectives of the Assessment of Performance Unit (APU), are provided as a background to Harold Rosen's critique. They are derived from an introduction to a full-scale report on the APU which is being prepared by Dr Caroline Gipps and Professor Harvey Goldstein, members of the Evaluation of Testing in Schools Project. This project, which is based at the University of London Institute of Education, is funded by the Social Science Research Council and forms the major part of the Council's accountability research programme. [The report was published by Heinemann Educational Books and included an abridged version of the critique.]

The context in which the APU was set up

The APU was announced in 1974 and began to come to the attention of educationalists in 1975, with the publication of a paper 'Monitoring Pupils' Performance' (1975) by Brian Kay, who was the first head of the Unit. In order to throw light on how the APU was set up, it is important to consider the educational and political climate in Britain in the early to mid-1970s. The prime reason for the emergence of the so-called Great Debate and the accountability movement in the seventies was an increasingly questioning attitude among commentators, and sections of the general public too, towards the outcomes of the maintained education system.

The reorganization of secondary education in the sixties and early seventies resulted in the decline of the 11-plus test, which signified to some the end of quality control in primary education. For over forty years, the 11-plus had had a powerful effect on primary schools, focusing attention on mathematics, English and reading, the basic skills covered in the tests. With the introduction of comprehensive schools, the need for the 11-plus diminished and the primary schools were freed from its constraints. This liberation and the impact of the Plowden Report on primary education, *Children and their Primary Schools* (1967), gave a boost to the child-centred approach and widened the curriculum for this age group. The move towards progressive primary education resulted in a good deal of popular concern about falling standards. Critics of the progressive movement were not slow to suggest that children were entering secondary school with poorer attainment in mathematics and English. There was no conclusive evidence to substantiate this, but the ending of the 11-plus served to strengthen the hand of those who advocated a system of regular national assessment.

This is not to say that there had not been surveys of attainment in the past; the National Foundation for Educational Research (NFER) had carried out regular reading surveys for the Department of Education and Science from 1948 to 1964. These showed that during the sixteen years of the surveys there had been an advance of seventeen months in the reading age of 11-year-olds and of twenty to thirty months in that of 15-year-olds. Though there was much argument over the significance of this advance, the reading surveys had the effect of reassuring the public and the teaching profession that reading standards were not falling. The next NFER reading survey was not carried out until 1970, and it was unsatisfactory for a number of reasons, including a poor response rate and unsatisfactory tests. The findings were, however, interpreted as meaning that although standards had not actually fallen they had ceased to rise. This was greeted by critics of progressive education as evidence of deterioration in the maintained sector.

Following this reading survey, the criticisms surrounding it and general concern over standards of literacy, a committee was set up in 1972 under the chairmanship of Sir Alan Bullock. Its role was to consider all aspects of the teaching of English and how arrangements for monitoring the general level of attainment in this area could be introduced or improved; its report, *A Language for Life* (The Bullock Committee, 1975), gave fuel to the argument for better regular testing. The prime recommendation was for a system of monitoring, employing new instruments to assess a wider range of attainments. The committee supported the idea of a continuous programme of 'light sampling' which would enable standards to be kept under review without excessive testing, thus minimizing the likelihood of the tests influencing the curriculum. It was at the time that this report was being written and published that the APU was set up.

Primary education took on a higher profile in 1975 with the William Tyndale affair. Parents of children in the William Tyndale Junior School in Islington (part of the Inner London Education Authority) complained about the quality of education their children were receiving under the progressive regime of the head and his deputy. An enquiry, headed by a QC, was set up and as a result the head and several staff were sacked, an unprecedented step in this country. The shock waves following this decision spread throughout the education system, and many a chief education officer and education committee member wondered whether this could happen in their authority. Many LEAs interpreted the William Tyndale affair and the Bullock Report as providing clear signals to start thinking about setting up their own local testing programmes to provide information on standards in the basic skills, which they felt had been missing since the end of the 11-plus.

As the rapid growth of the education system in the sixties and early seventies started to slow down, more consideration began to be given to questions of quality both within and outside education. In 1976 Prime Minister James Callaghan, in a speech at Ruskin College, Oxford, suggested that education ought to be more accountable to society and that consideration of educational issues should be opened up to give the non-professionals a chance to have their say. 'We spend £6 billion a year on education,' he noted, 'so there will be discussion.' There was a feeling that education had fallen too much into the hands of the professionals, and behind the invitation to discuss lay more than a hint that the professionals had some explaining to do. Callaghan's call met with approval from much of industry and the general public and the ensuing discussion, including a series of semi-public meetings organized by the Department of Education and Science, was termed the Great Debate. Much of the response from the world of education was hostile, based partly on a genuine fear that the Great Debate would lead to something like the American version of accountability through testing, and partly on opposition to 'education for industry'.

The concept of accountability in education became prominent in the United States in the late 1960s when cuts in Government spending (due to the expense of the Vietnam War) resulted in the adoption of procedures to allocate the remaining slender resources. Accountability procedures had their roots in the 'scientific management' movement in which testing had played a central role by providing the data by which efficiency could be judged. This linking of the testing of pupils with accountability also became the practice in Britain. The DES in its 1977 Green Paper *Education in Schools* linked the APU into the growing accountability framework:

> Growing recognition of the need for schools to demonstrate their accountability to the society which they serve requires a coherent and

soundly based means of assessment for the education system as a whole, for schools and for individual pupils.

Thus the APU can be seen as a response to general concern over standards and also to the specific recommendations of the Bullock Report. Although the APU was not the direct result of pressure for accountability, since it came into being before the Great Debate got off the ground, it did start coming to the public's attention at a time when accountability was becoming an issue.

It should not be forgotten that in the early 1970s there was also within the Government a concern with underachievement and with the performance of ethnic groups, though this was overshadowed by concern over falling standards and accountability in education generally. In 1974 the DES produced a White Paper in response to a report on education by a House of Commons Select Committee on Race Relations. It was in this White Paper that the APU was formally announced. Given the climate at the time, any proposal to monitor standards nationally would have been strongly resisted by the teaching profession, which was feeling under attack. However, assessing the needs of disadvantaged children is less questionable professionally, and so the announcement of the APU, presented as part of a programme for dealing with disadvantage and underachievement, created little dissent among educationalists.

Attitudes to the APU

Why then did dissent appear later? What led up to the publication in 1979 and 1980 of several articles criticising the APU and its likely effects? These are interesting questions for, as sociologists like Broadfoot (1979) have argued, in the past the efficiency of assessment has been the main area of concern, not its purpose and effects. With the advent of the APU, however, this has changed, for the criticisms have centred on its wider effects (although the efficiency of the programme has been questioned too).

The first reason is that by 1975 it became clear that the APU was not assessing underachievement and disadvantage as originally announced, but was going to become a full-scale national assessment programme concerned with standards. Why was a national assessment programme considered to be dangerous? Though few observers believed that the more extreme aspects of the American accountability through testing model – such as basing teacher dismissals or school closure on test scores – would come into play in this country, when the APU showed that it aimed to monitor standards there was some concern that it was intended as an instrument to force accountability on schools, and therefore on teachers. Though ostensibly concerned with children's standards, this task was interpreted as dealing with teachers' competencies. By adhering to the principle of light sampling, however, the APU has gone a long way towards allaying fears over its intentions. Also, because only a small number of children are tested at any time and the names of children are not known to researchers, there is no way in which the results can be used to judge individual schools or teachers.

The second worry that has been expressed about the APU is its effect on the curriculum. Is it possible to have a national system of assessment and not to affect the curriculum in some way? In order to develop test items it is necessary to take a model of the curriculum. Will this model then become the dominant model for the curriculum? There was indeed some concern in the early days that the APU was an attempt by the DES to bring in an assessment-led curriculum. The way that it was thought this might come about is essentially an indirect one, by which the APU's curriculum model would provide a framework for a local-authority assessment and thereby a means for introducing a core curriculum (Pring, 1980). Pressure on LEAs to monitor their standards was anticipated, and an additional envisaged danger lay in the possibility that through 'item banking' procedures and, in particular, the LEA and Schools Item Bank (LEASIB) project at the NFER it would be possible to link local testing programmes to the APU's national monitoring programme. APU findings would provide a baseline of performance and a core of items from which LEAs would be able to develop their own tests and examine the performance of their pupils. The range of APU items would then provide the common core of a national curriculum. As it happens, there are technical problems associated with item banking and it is now apparent that LEAs will not have access to APU tests via LEASIB. The use by LEAs of APU test items is currently being discussed and while it is still some way off, this link is considered by some observers to be potentially highly dangerous.

There have been other more general concerns expressed about the curriculum. These are along the lines that any official testing encourages teaching to the test. Thus it is important that the tests themselves reflect good curriculum thinking, for what is tested today may become the curriculum of tomorrow.

These concerns can all be linked to one central criticism: the failure of the APU to clarify publicly its objectives. To quote one critic:

> Unless the objectives of monitoring are made very clear the objectives of both the monitoring and the total work of the Unit will remain something of a mystery. Under these circumstances mistrust easily becomes exaggerated, and commentators will inevitably speculate over the supposed real purpose of the Unit.
>
> (Dennison, 1978)

Objectives of the APU

There has been little public discussion of the APU's specific objectives. True, there are the terms of reference and associated tasks, but these are vague and give little idea of what the monitoring is actually for.

The Unit's terms of reference as laid out in the White Paper (DES, 1974) are:

To promote the development of methods of assessing and monitoring the achievement of children at school, and to seek to identify the incidence of under-achievement.

The tasks laid down are:

1. To identify and appraise existing instruments and methods of assessment which may be relevant for these purposes.
2. To sponsor the creation of new instruments and techniques for assessment, having due regard to statistical and sampling methods.
3. To promote the conduct of assessments in co-operation with local education authorities and teachers.
4. To identify significant differences of achievement related to the circumstances in which children learn, including the incidence of under-achievement, and to make findings available to all those concerned with resource allocation within the Department, local education authorities and schools.

What did public statements say about the Unit's aims? Brian Kay (1975) made no mention of under-achievement or disadvantage. The emphasis instead was on standards and their changes over time. In 1976 the Yellow Book (a confidential DES memo – see Lawton, 1980) referred to the Unit as dealing with the first task by setting up a monitoring system in mathematics (following on from development work at the NFER), in reading and the use of language (following on from the Bullock Report) and making a start in science. There was again no mention of disadvantage or what the monitoring might be for. Kay (1977) wrote a programme of work in January of that year which discussed each of the tasks in turn. Here the intention to look at trends in performance levels was put forward, as well as the possibility that the APU would make assessment materials available to LEAs. The DES documents *Educating our Children* and *Education in Schools*, both published in 1977, mentioned briefly the APU. Both referred to its role in developing a national monitoring system to provide information on standards. There was some mention of policy makers but no discussion of what policy questions might be answered by the APU's work. Publicity material produced by the APU between 1977 and 1980 continued in much the same vein: the APU's role was to monitor in order to provide information on standards and how these change over time. In-depth studies were mentioned as a way of pursuing interesting findings from the national surveys, and though these are the studies which would be most useful in terms of policy making, no discussion or elucidation of which policy questions might be answered has been forthcoming.

There is no evidence that the DES produced a clear statement about which policy questions they wished the APU to address. The aims seems to have been simply to develop a national system of assessment that functioned and was acceptable – with little thought as to what specific questions it might answer. Why did the Department or the Unit not list more clearly at the outset the policy questions to which they wanted answers? Was it that the APU is intended solely as a monitoring exercise to give information on overall standards and nothing else? Is the story of the APU just an example of lack of forward planning? Or is it a more deliberate policy of leaving all options open in order to gain maximum co-operation from interested professionals and lay people? Where do matters now stand in relation to fears of the introduction of a 'core curriculum'?

The forthcoming study of the APU will set out to answer, or at least throw light on, these and related questions. Professor Rosen's critique concerns itself with the Unit's attempts to monitor language performance in schools. He demonstrates that worries about the effects of the APU's monitoring work rest upon even more fundamental principles than the general concerns mentioned in this introduction. They have to do with basic assumptions about the nature of language and its use.

Critique

The Assessment of Performance Unit's Primary Survey Report, *Language Performance in Schools* (HMSO, 1981), is not about language performance in schools. It is about performance in a series of tests of reading and writing, or a 'battery' as it is more appropriately called. It would be too much to expect that the Report would attempt to justify, in general, testing procedures in education, though the authors must know that testing of this kind is surrounded by bitter controversy and that the activities of the APU are the focus of suspicions, doubts and anxieties by some, and enthusiastic, insistent promotion by others. This is certainly true of the APU's testing programme (see Holt, 1981, and Carter, 1980). The compilers of this Report keep their heads down and do not meddle with the politics of their own existence. They do not place the whole Report in a relevant context. We may contrast it with the opening of a document produced by the National Association for the Teaching of English (NATE), *Assessing Children's Language* (Stibbs, 1979):

> At a time of cultural insecurity, there is a special unease about language, because language reflects social values. There are pressures on teachers – often from the least informed about language and education – to teach a narrow set of language skills and uses, and to accept teacher-free assessments which seem to measure, more accurately than teachers can, the performance of children and schools.

There is no discussion in this document of the main purposes of this huge, ever-expanding exercise, though we are promised many further developments at various points in the text. Nowhere is there a calm appraisal of what are intended to be the consequences for pupils' language development, teachers' practices in language education and the political uses of their findings. To have done so would have invited a different kind of reading of this text.

As it stands it tempts the reader to become embroiled in the testers' problems rather than his own. What, in brief, is the relevance of this exercise? Ambitious claims are made in passing, but this is a very different matter from an open discussion of these claims.

We can, however, recover a little of the provenance of this particular Report by reference to another better-known one. The progenitor of the APU Report is acknowledged in the Preface by the Joint Heads of the APU:

> The Bullock Report expressed the belief that 'a monitoring system … must present a comprehensive picture of the various skills that constitute literacy'. The Language Steering Group of the APU was guided by this principle in devising a framework for monitoring language performances.

If that were so, then the unfortunate Steering Group would have selected a guiding principle which could only have postponed the actual testing procedures to a distant date. In the event no such 'comprehensive picture' of literacy skills emerges from this Report, nor for that matter any novel contribution to that extraordinarily ambitious goal. There is no indication in the Report that 'skills' is an inadequate concept for handling the complexities of what readers do or might do with texts, nor how a writer constructs or might construct a written text. These matters have had considerable attention in recent years and the theoretical studies all point to the difficulty of building a coherent theory of literacy which encompasses the psycho-social processes involved. Such a theory would have to be linked to an understanding of the ways in which children's responses to literacy tests are embedded in the meaning of literacy in contemporary society. In spite of all this, which would not be news to some members of the Steering Committee, the Report declares its uncritical allegiance to the Bullock Committee's Utopian guiding principle – as indeed, we must suppose, it was bound to do. There are contexts within contexts. Everyone knows that the Bullock Report (1975) itself was commissioned at a time when 'allegations about lower standards' were appearing on the national political agenda. Small wonder that the Bullock Committee devoted a whole chapter (chapter 3) to 'Monitoring'. It is to that chapter we should return if we wish to understand fully the promptings which lay behind the principles and procedures of the National Foundation for Educational Research, the body to which the APU farmed out the design and implementation of the tests. Somewhat surprisingly, the Report under review does not take us back to the moment of its birth. Certain oddities emerge at once. The Bullock Report did much more than ask for a 'comprehensive picture … (etc.)'. It elaborated with uncharacteristic, meticulous detail the precise features of the proposed tests and they are almost entirely adopted by the APU. The whole thrust of these recommendations can be brought under the rubric of *standards*:

> ... we think it appropriate to complete this section on standards by setting out our conclusions on how they can be more effectively monitored.
>
> (p. 36)

and

> It seems to us beyond question that standards should be monitored and this should be done on a scale which will allow confidence in the accuracy and value of the findings.
>
> (p. 44)

The concern that a sophisticated view of language skills should be the launching pad for the tests was linked to this other concern about the credibility of the findings, which needed to satisfy not only the hungry demands of the more-tests lobby but also the demands of those who might criticize the tests on the grounds that they were based on naive views of what language is and how children use it. How much that hope was justified we shall examine in due course. Meanwhile, let us repeat that the unambiguous central intention was to monitor standards, an intention which receives very muted acknowledgement in the final sentence of the Report's Preface:

> We hope this Report will help to inform the debate about standards of literacy.

It does no such thing, especially if we recall that the debate has not been about what children can do with language, but about whether they are getting better or worse at doing it. It does contribute a few marginal statistical items, but nowhere does it enter the debate nor suggest how its findings might contribute to it. Its authors must have known that more was expected of them.

****

Indeed, when we return to the body of the Report, as distinct from the preface, we find pretensions to something much more grandiose and yet at the same time what appears to be a retreat from expectations. There is an opening fanfare of aspirations, followed by a muted requiem. The fanfare first: the aim, we are told, is nothing less than to offer to the public the first APU contribution to '*a national picture of language development*' (our italics). That is followed by a disclaimer: the aim is 'not ... to pronounce on whether the standards revealed by the survey are higher or lower than they should be'.

It is curious that, having espoused the Bullock Report, these should be announced as the goals of the APU Report. But even more curious when we attempt to judge whether these goals have been attained.

When did language development become part of the APU's terms of reference or, rather, its main object? The clear intention, we repeat, had always been to monitor standards. Had the huge, exciting investigation of language development been the aim, then, in first place, the entire operation would have had to be conducted in quite a different manner; secondly, it would have meant ignoring why the APU was set up. The language task of the APU would have become so different as to be unrecognizable. Anyone concerned with the study of language development knows what a vast and complicated operation would have to be planned. Even the study of the process of early language acquisition has proved to be more exacting than the first grammar-based studies proposed (compare, for example, Brown, Cazden and Bellugi, 1969, with Halliday, 1975, and Wells, 1981) and is far from completed; and that early stage is more amenable to observation and collection of data. No reputable researcher would take seriously the proposal that language development could be studied by using the results of an annual series of tests. When we bear in mind that the development of language beyond the early years (almost unknown territory) is complicated by functional variety, cultural diversity and literacy, we know that a proposal of that kind would be dismissed as absurd irrelevance. A serious study of language development would require, at the very least, numerous detailed and longitudinal case studies of the language of children being used for genuine purposes. Needless to say, nothing faintly like that appears in the Report, not even a few in-depth case studies of some of the children who figure only as statistics or disembodied 'answers'. It is true, of course, that this Report is the first in a series, but it does not provide even a credible foundation for a language development study, especially as that would have to be based on the interaction of the different modalities of language: speaking, listening, reading and writing, the former two of which await the development of yet more tests. The truth is that the reader will search in vain for any clear statement in which the findings are pointed in the direction of language development: how, for example, they might in due course make a contribution to development during the years of secondary schooling. For that matter they will search in vain for any discussion of language development. A glance at the tepid Conclusion (pp. 133–4) will show how the pretentions of the opening statement dwindle to:

> it will be possible to relate and, in some cases, to amalgamate information in successive surveys.

A somewhat opaque promise. It is such a far cry from the earlier one that we can only conclude that the latter was no more than a genuflection to an idea which is currently in favour. Between the alpha and omega of this Report is the more familiar and humdrum business of test manufacture and administration into which the energies of the authors have been poured with no nonsense about language development.

We can now turn to the equally surprising opening statement that the Report has nothing to say about rising or falling standards. Perhaps it was intended to convey no more than that, since this was the first Report in the projected series, we must await the others for pronouncements about standards. Such a straightforward statement is easily composed in the English language. Why then did the authors not choose to make it? Why else all the huge concern with the application of the Rasch model to the language tests (elaborated with full technical detail in Appendix 2)? The model, we are told, is used solely to establish 'comparability of success rates' obtained in different phases of testing. It is, to say the least, disingenuous to leave the matter in the way the Report does and leave it to us to track through the pages to discover whether (a) they will be getting round to standards in due course, or (b) rising and falling standards are no longer within their purview at all. We might pass over this confusion and put it down to infelicitous language performance by the authors. However, if we turn to an earlier APU publication, *Language Performance* (APU, 1978), we find, without cautious ifs and buts:

> The substantial quantity of rich information that would be made available would serve not only to monitor change in standards but also to provide the kind of detail on which appropriate action could be based.

> (p. 3)

Very clear. Those were the marching orders given to the NFER and, as far as we can tell from the outside, they were never withdrawn.

****

The final insight into this matter, which can help us decide the cloudy intentions of the Report, is supplied by the mystery of NS6. NS6 is National Survey Form 6 and was developed in 1954 as a silent reading test of the incomplete sentence type. It was used for national testing of eleven- and fifteen-year-olds from 1955 onwards (Start and Wells, 1973). The use of this instrument is first announced in the Summary of the Report.

> In order to relate results obtained in the 1979 Survey with those of national surveys of reading carried out since 1955, a comparison of results achieved in National Survey 6 and in the APU survey is provided in the final section of Chapter 2.

> (p. 10)

This is unduly modest, as we shall see, but beyond doubt it is very different from the opening disclaimer about standards. The intention here is emphatic, '*to relate results*' (our italics). The only kind of relationship which can be intended must be a comparison of standards. It emerges on close inspection that this is no mere technicality, but rather one important example of the unfortunate tendency of this Report to run with the hare and hunt with the hounds. Its compilers are repeatedly caught on the horns of a desperate dilemma. On the one hand they show considerable awareness of serious issues in language education and language testing: on the other hand they are obliged to carry the burden of their terms of reference. In fact, they inherit this dilemma from the Bullock Report itself which says with emphasis (the words are italicized in the text):

> *We do not regard these tests* [i.e. Watts-Vernon and NS6] *as adequate measures of reading ability.*

> (p.16)

The Bullock Report spells out the inadequacy of the NS6 test in some detail. Nevertheless, when it comes to make its proposals for monitoring, it proposes that 'as a temporary expedient the NS6 test should remain in operation to ensure a continuing baseline until a new datum can be established' (p.38). To continue to use an instrument which you know to be profoundly unsatisfactory is not a good practice at any time, but to do so and publish the results at a time when they invite misinterpretation is nothing less than irresponsible. The APU's *Language Performance* (1978) gives no hint that the proposed procedures for language testing will include NS6. It simply repeats the Bullock Report's comment on its limitations.

When we turn to *Language Performance in Schools* (HMSO, 1981), the Report with which we are principally concerned here, we find the original dilemma revived. Painstakingly and powerfully, this Report lays bare the inadequacy of NS6, so much so that we might be forgiven for assuming that the function of this analysis is to justify its final burial. We are told that NS6 'bears no direct relation to the reading activities that pupils are characteristically asked to undertake in the classroom or outside of it'; it has 'low content validity'; the content is dated and 'it cannot easily be updated without invalidating the tests as a device for measuring changes in performance over time'; its assumptions of what constitutes reading are no longer generally accepted. The Report then turns its attention, quite properly, to its own view of tests. And here, we might think, the matter would rest, with NS6 unceremoniously interred in its own limitations. But, of course, as the Summary had forewarned us on p.36, NS6 is resuscitated under the heading of 'A link with previous national surveys'. Quite simply, 'it is desirable' to establish that link. Why? The inescapable conclusion is that the paymasters have called the tune, possibly against the better judgment of the research team. Having once become entangled in this predicament, they must follow its own logic and compare the new NS6 scores with those obtained by the survey conducted by HM Inspectors in 1976/77 (DES/HMI, 1978). All this is passed over relatively quickly. Yet here the APU must be inviting conclusions, though it offers none. The relevant passage is given below; no other comment is made.

> The mean score for pupils as measured by the NS6 test in the 1979 survey (adjusted to 11 years 2 months) was 30.25. The mean score of pupils who took the same test in the survey conducted by HM Inspectors in 1976/77, adjusted to the same age level, was 31.13 with a standard error of 0.33.

> A t-test of the difference between mean scores indicates that the differences are not statistically significant.

> (p. 36)

Why are we having brandished in front of us these figures? Obviously, we are being left to draw our own conclusions. They can only be that the standards of reading for this age group (as measured, remember, by admittedly defective tests) have over more than two years marked time. Having said that 'a link is desirable', the authors wash their hands of the whole business and leave the consequences of their 'desirable' action to take their own course. Strange. But something stranger and more disturbing is yet to come in the story of NS6.

The APU carried out two comparisons with NS6. We have tried to suggest how they might have been reluctantly jockeyed into administering NS6, but nothing in the run-up to this Report suggested that they should make comparisons between NS6 scores and their own qualitatively different set of results from the survey. On the contrary, it is emphasized repeatedly that we are being presented with innovative procedures based on different principles giving rise to figures with new meanings. These are intended to establish a new baseline. It might have been supposed that the comparison of the two NS6 scores (1976/77 and 1979) was simply a holding operation until the new baseline could be used in the forthcoming reports. Not at all. In the same section of the Report (paragraphs 2.84 and 2.85) a bizarre and unheralded initiative is taken. Statistics are produced comparing the NS6 (1979) results to the results of the APU tests. How is this possible? We are confronted with *global* scores for the latter which have been specially produced by statistical manipulation.

The statistical legitimacy of this procedure can be left to those best qualified to judge, though we should remember that the Report is addressed to the laity. However, there are basic objections to producing a global score for reading when children have been asked to carry out very diverse activities. Such arithmetical simplicity cannot deliver meaning to anyone. The only way to understand a score which is of any use is to back-track through the labyrinth of statistical procedures until you arrive at the separate scores. To offer a global score for the ability to read is as futile as offering a global score for personality. There are different kinds of readers as well as different kinds of reading. At best the results of the APU could be produced as profiles, but then it would not be possible to carry out the simple correlation manoeuvre so dear to the hearts of psychometrists.

The table 2.1 (p. 37) displays percentile points for both NS6 and global scores of the new tests. The meaning of this table is expressed as a correlation of 0.77. An explanation of this high correlation is put forward which proposes that the two tests, though conceptually very different, nevertheless test fundamentally similar abilities. This comes as something of a shock. What has been the whole point of the APU's testing of reading in an entirely new way? Why were the criticisms of NS6 set out so carefully for us? Are they now being withdrawn? It certainly looks like it, because we are now told that the only thing really wrong with NS6 is that it lacks 'face validity' or, in layman's language, it does not have credibility. Does that mean that the APU can now help to give it more credibility? The Report's authors might have mentioned that there is at least one other possibility, that the two kinds of tests suffer from very similar deficiencies in spite of their apparent differences.

As it turns out, the attempt to link the survey's work with NS6 is a muddle and its silences on the implications are fraught with danger.

****

We have traced at length just one aspect of the Report. In the comments which follow, we shall be pursuing what seems to us a difficulty which surrounds all testing of this kind. The demand for testing, vociferous and importunate, lures some people genuinely concerned with matters of educational principle to run ahead of their own competence. Having once agreed to participate in this hazardous programme, they must in the end either let pragmatism triumph over principle or simply down tools. We have already seen how the authors, having scrupulously set out the glaring deficiencies of a language testing procedure, then proceed to commit themselves to its use. There is no reason to assume that our understanding of the processes of reading and writing is so advanced that a team of testers can confidently set about monitoring standards on a national basis. Nor can we assume that there is some kind of consensus about English teaching and language education which can be used to justify one procedure rather than another.

It is the headlong drive for the production of simple figures which stands in the way of sober and sensitive concern for progress in children's use and reception of language. The pyrotechnics of statistical discussion are the inevitable concomitant of that kind of commitment and divert us from a consideration of what the tests are actually doing to pupils and teachers. One abiding difficulty for readers of a Report of this kind is that it tends to make them accept the agenda on which it is based rather than an alternative of their own. The use of language is indivisible. We have the Bullock Committee's word for it. Speaking, listening, reading and writing all interact, feed each other in contexts which arouse not mere compliance (docile acceptance of tests, for example) but active engagement. In the best primary schools they are all orchestrated to play a part in learning. There's the rub. We are not dealing with the best primary practice.

Out of 115 head teachers who responded to the suggestion that they should comment on the test materials, 101 commented favourably on the style and presentation of the materials and on the positive reaction of the pupils.

(p. 23)

103

There is more in the same vein. Such a seal of approval tells us nothing except what a considerable number of head teachers think is suitable work in language and the willingness of children to accept busywork. Thus by circularity the tests give confirmation to widespread practices. The head teachers' approval looks much less reassuring when it is seen against what has been reported about prevailing practices in primary and secondary schools by HM Inspectors.

> Primary: English exercises featured strongly in almost every 9 and 11 year olds class and there was excessive copying from reference books. (DES/ HMI, 1978, 5.35)

> Secondary: Over nearly 400 schools the lasting impression was of a general uniformity of demand … But the pattern most frequently found could be described as essentially one of 'notes' and 'essays', interspersed with the practice of answering examination questions alongside the exercises and tests.

> (DES/HMI, 1979, 3.7)

Small wonder then if a majority of head teachers found the APU tests congenial. If the tests had constituted a genuine departure from the prevailing practices condemned in the two documents cited above, the head teachers would have objected to them.

The APU has adopted the practice of claiming that its exercise is concerned with language performance. But this is not correct, as its research workers themselves know. They have until now whittled down their concerns to reading and writing, and offer their explanations. However, giving priority to literacy tests can only confirm the deep-rooted assumption within the educational system that what is written and printed has no essential connection with speaking and listening and that 'back to basics' means back to pens and books. For many years there has been a determined attempt to make the spoken language an intrinsic part of school learning (Wilkinson, 1965 and Barnes *et al.*, 1971). It is unlikely to receive encouragement from the priorities established in this Report. Whatever we are promised for some indefinite future, there is no concession that a productive way of exploring a topic, such as that in the booklets *Whales* (two of the booklets used to test reading, and included with the Report), is to talk about it.

The APU was certainly uneasy about this. *Language Performance* (1978), picking up once again from the Bullock Report and acknowledging that 'talking and listening occupy more time than either of these [i.e. reading and writing] in the life of most human beings' asks whether these activities should also be monitored (p.3). Two objections are raised: (a) subjectivity would be too great; (b) 'it would be difficult to establish comparability across time'. However, the Report suggests that 'suitable monitoring instruments and economical procedures' should be developed by research. All the contradictions of national testing are concentrated in these few lines. Oral performance is of critical significance but it is difficult, if not impossible, to test in the approved 'objective' manner. Postpone the endeavour but assume a solution to be possible. Meanwhile proceed with the supposedly less subjective business of testing the testable.

Subjectivity, which includes making principled value judgments on argued criteria, is perceived as an obstacle, an impediment which testers abhor. Since comparability over time is the goal, learning activities, however important, which cannot be reliably stored and compared must either be rejected or somehow or other (not forgetting 'economical procedures') be coaxed into testable format. More significantly, no indication is given of the hazards of isolating oral language from written language: it is simply taken for granted that each kind of language use must be separately assessed. Can we expect that, when the full testing programme goes into action, statistical procedures will be devised for an even more global score? But, then, speaking is an essentially collaborative activity and collaboration in learning, to which we so often pay lip service, is the very last thing to which test constructors, steeped in individualistic ideology, give attention. And all this in spite of the fact that there is impressive evidence of what children can achieve by collaboration in learning, unembarrassed of course by the problems they are creating for anyone wishing to record individual scores. Thus talking and listening become jam tomorrow. The backwash implications are obvious.

In the concluding Chapter 7 of the Report, we are promised that the APU will 'extend the scope of the monitoring programme to encompass the skills involved in listening and speaking' and, more positively, that this will link reading and discussion as well as writing and listening. But why are these two forms of interaction chosen? Why not, for example, discussion of first drafts of writing, or dozens of other possibilities? Somewhere or other there must be a record of the proceedings which led to these decisions. However, if we are tempted to welcome this further proliferation of the programme, we should try to imagine what this promised addition will look like compared with the committed talk of children which has emerged from a continuous context of learning and, at its best, is a serious engagement with the 'grammar of motives'.

It might seem that there is a paradox here. On the one hand we have argued that the omission of talking and listening will have a backwash effect and on the other that its inclusion will be disastrous. The paradox is, of course, only resolved by refusing to be lured into 'improving' the language performance tests and rejecting the whole operation. On the other hand, there are important studies of the performance of pupils engaged in different kinds of talk (see, for example, Barnes and Todd, 1977). What emerges from them, as we have noted for language development in general, are the theoretical difficulties of analysis and interpretation (Adelman, 1981) and deep awareness of how much more remains to be done. One thing is certain: what we need now is more observation and analysis, not commando raids for the collection of monitoring samples. The APU work is a diversion of resources and attention from this kind of task.

****

We can now turn to the assessment of reading, which is where the whole of the language performance operation began in the distant days of the setting up of the Bullock Committee. As we have already noted, the Report is nothing if not frank when it stares soberly at the task confronting it in the assessment of reading.

> … no model of the reading process is generally accepted to be an adequate representation of the processes by which readers comprehend what they read; and as such comprehension is as complex as thinking itself, this lack of consensus is to be expected.
>
> (p. 19)

Consensus is beside the point. What should be paramount is an appraisal of the explanatory power and limitations of rival representations of the reading process. Anything less is abdication. It is nevertheless true that we do not have a perfect understanding of reading.

> The process of reading is not very well understood. Researchers do not yet know enough about the developed skills of the fluent reader, the end product of the instructional process, let alone the process of acquiring these skills. But researchers are beginning to realize that reading will not be completely understood until there is an understanding of all the perceptual, cognitive, linguistic and motivational aspects not just of reading, but of living and learning in general.
>
> (Smith, 1971)

That should not unduly dismay those teachers who succeed in teaching thousands of children to read, but it should be chastening to anyone seeking how to compile comprehensive tests of the extent to which those teachers have been successful. Nothing daunted by the lack of adequate theoretical equipment, the APU has pressed on. We are offered an examination of the research literature, but it is the literature of reading assessment. An appraisal of theories and studies of the reading process would have been a much more arduous task. The one principle the APU has clearly enumerated for reading is the theory of context:

> … there is always a context about which we can ask, 'Who is saying (or writing) what, to whom and why?'.

and

> In schools, the importance of trying to provide a context within which pupils can use language with a real purpose is not, perhaps, sufficiently recognized.
>
> (APU, 1978, pp. 5 and 6)

Context is a more complicated matter than this, but we would agree whole-heartedly with the principle. Here, as so often in the Report, the logical consequences of this principle are not frankly confronted. The context in which a child might want to seek out a book about whales (a book, not a booklet of heterogeneous snippets) is utterly different from a context of responding to being tested. There is a context, no question of that, but it is a bad one. There is a 'real purpose' but it has little to do with the child's purposes.

The reading tests are based on short booklets containing passages 'selected or adapted from text-books, works of reference and works of literature of a kind likely to be employed or referred to by teachers'. It is claimed that the selection of themes and the design of the booklets were 'likely to engage the interest of most of the children in the age group'. Two specimen booklets are included with the Report. No doubt they are being scrutinized eagerly by publishers. Of the test questions this ambitious claim is made:

> In developing the questions, the guiding principle was that they should be questions that an experienced teacher would be likely to ask pupils.

All very reassuring, until we examine these comments more closely. As Carter (1980) has pointed out, the snippets in the booklets bear a dismal resemblance to 'the force feeding of facts and a language curriculum which demands that young children work mechanically through endless comprehension and other "English exercises"'. As for the 'experienced teacher' and his or her 'likely' questions, that person is a figment of the testers' imagination. They must be very distant from schools to try to foist on us the notion that all experienced teachers share a common way of asking children questions or, indeed, that they would choose to ask a set of questions at all, let alone printed ones calling for written answers.

In order to pass judgment on the booklets (*Whales 1* and *2*), the questions based on them and the comments in the Report, a reader must cope with the section called 'Examples of Pupils' Reading Performance' (2.37–2.68). There is no space here to show how difficult it is to make sense of this section. Suffice it to say that it requires many readings and dartings to and fro in the text for the reader to be confident of grasping the principles and procedures. There are three matters with which a reader will be concerned: (a) the reading booklets themselves; (b) the questions on them; (c) the pupils' responses. Some of his or her difficulties will arise from the fact that national testing has inevitably to be surrounded with a security operation. We cannot therefore be given all the facts and we have to take on trust that we have been given representative examples. So it is that we are given two of the booklets (both on the same theme!) but not even the titles of the others, and that we are given only a selection of the questions asked. The selection does not include all the questions discussed in the text.

Many teachers reading this Report will be keenly interested in the way in which literature was handled in the tests. Their interest will be cooled when they learn that 'it is not possible to reveal in detail in this Report the range of pupils' responses to the literary works or passages … without releasing materials needed for use in future surveys'. A test of the kind of detective work expected of a reader would be for him or her to attempt to answer this central question, 'What exactly would any individual pupil have to do in completing the reading tests?' The reader will never discover, for example, how many questions a pupil was asked, nor how long he or she would be given to answer them.

Of the passages in the booklets, this much should be said. They are in many respects typical of the 'information books' which have flooded into primary classrooms. With the exception of the 'literary passages' they consist of very limited selections of items of information strung together under titles like 'Three species of toothed whale' or 'Two centuries of whale hunting' (20 lines!). Format is varied, so that 'Some uses of whale products' is a list which names the products and gives their uses. It would be true to say that many pupils would be familiar with the kinds of prose represented here, because fact-hunting, detecting and copying are unfortunately common practices, as are worksheets with 'comprehension' questions on them. Yet in a way that is beside the point. It is not the intrinsic quality of the material which matters, but the reasons why it is put in front of pupils, why they are answering the questions, why they are searching for the 'right' answer, why they are seeking out bits of information. It is conceivable that a pupil might have sought out a book containing any one of these bits of information and found it useful because he or she had an authentic purpose, an active social purpose. That is quite a different matter from being confronted with a booklet on whales and told to answer a set of questions about it which requires you to go skimming to and fro for someone else's remote, perhaps incomprehensible, reasons. And why whales? If the pupil is lucky, the topic may be of riveting interest, but if not? As for the questions themselves, as we might have guessed, they are multiple-choice. Recollect that these are supposed to be questions which, typically, a teacher might ask. So we have (p. 45):

Having read this passage, which of these words do you think best describes dolphins?

1. Foolish
2. Beautiful
3. Hideous
4. Infectious
5. Friendly

It has all been said before. Questions of this sort do not work with the grain of the reader who constructs his or her idea of what dolphins are like without thinking whether they are infectious or not or by running through lists in his head. It may well be that what the passage most impresses on the young is that dolphins are intelligent, but then that is not one of the choices. Any one of the alternatives could be plausibly supported.

We might illustrate the arbitrary and subjective underlying basis of the tests by the questions designed to test whether the pupil can use an index efficiently. Note that the question does not ask the pupil to find anything in the text, only to give the number of the extract set against the entry! (Thus 'Blubber 2'. Correct answer '2'!) Now being able to use an index is a desirable skill, though at 11 years of age there are good readers who have not mastered it. Finding your way about a book calls for many supportive skills of this kind, especially when the book has an 'apparatus' (prefaces, glossaries, tables of contents, footnotes, etc.). Why was this particular skill selected? There may be good reasons but there is nothing objective in the choice.

A departure from the multiple-choice question was an open-ended question. This very different kind of question is not susceptible to the scoring system of the other items. In fact, only a hundred answers were analysed, and presumably (we are not told) were not included in the scoring statistics. The analysis consists of nothing more than a sorting of answers under categories derived by the authors and expressed as percentages. (11 per cent 'stressed that the extinction of whales would be a loss to the world and future generations'.) Anyone may make guesses as to why this was included in the Report and what it contributed to the outcomes. The selected responses of the children certainly stand in stark contrast to the constraints imposed on them.

It would be tedious to trace in detail the shortcomings of those questions we are permitted to see and the discussion of them. It is, however, worth lingering on the way in which literature is handled. There are teachers who regard the reading of literature as central not only to reading development but to the whole development of a child. Literary passages are included in the tests and some perfunctory statements made (p. 31) about how a reader 'certainly interprets the meaning of what is written'. To be sure, 'all literate pupils are capable of understanding and appreciating some aspects of works or passages of literature, provided an appropriate selection of such passages is made'. These rather patronizing statements settle nothing. Of course children can respond in delicate and perceptive ways to what they read. What is at issue is whether it is possible to test this in the style we are presented with here, and whether any useful statements about the *national* significance of their responses can be made.

There is too another cause for concern, namely, the selection of 'appropriate' passages. Nowhere in this Report do the authors make an attempt to come to terms with cultural diversity. This is the more surprising since during the period of the preparation of this Report all the controversial and difficult issues surrounding multi-cultural education have been highlighted in public discussion, and official statements have urged all those involved in education to take account of cultural diversity in our schools and our society. Nowhere in the testing of reading is this likely to be so salient as in the choice of literature (though it is also true of themes like whales). Of this kind of appropriateness, not a word anywhere in the Report. It is as though the right hand of the DES does not know what the left hand is doing. It would be interesting to know what the Swann Committee [a government-commissioned committee engaged in producing the Swann Report, published in 1985 under the title *Education for All*, and concerned with ethnic diversity in education] would make of it all. 'Appropriate' assumes some kind of shared culture and patterns of feeling and meaning. It is precisely those feelings and shared meanings with which literature engages, and with which the reader negotiates with the writer.

The multiple-choice question does not begin to tap this many-faceted negotiation. Much is made of handling words in context, especially metaphorical uses. The example is given of 'the line *snaked* through our hands' and 66 per cent 'recognized that the implication was that the line could be said to be more like a snake'. Many of those children could have chosen that meaning when supplied with nothing more than the isolated phrase. It is difficult to judge from this 18-line passage, but the choice of 'snaked' is likely to have been made because it adds to the sinister aspect of the whale-killing. There is more to metaphor than the discovery of a literal translation. But then what a reader responds to in a text, and how, is very different from what he or she can make explicit about the means by which that response was elicited. This does not deter the APU. We find on page 32 this startling information:

> … pupils were asked to consider the stylistic effect of the last four sentences used in the account.

Needless to say, the pupils were asked to do nothing of the sort, nor should they be if the assumption is that there is one correct answer.

Here is the actual question (p. 51):

> 34. What effect do the last four sentences have on the story?
> 1. They make the mood calmer
> 2. They show the sailors were happy
> 3. They give us a shock
> 4. They introduce a new mystery
> 5. They make it more amusing

The Report tells us that 41 per cent recognized that their effect was to make the 'mood' of the story calmer. 'Recognized' is a euphemism for 'selected that form of words to have put in their mouths'. The comment in the Report seems to suggest that this method can produce initial evidence that 'some 11 year olds are capable of appreciating stylistic effects of considerable subtlety'. The evidence is crude and unsatisfactory compared with what a discussion could produce when children have been moved by a work of literature. In the context, it strains credulity to ask us to believe that the APU thinks it has made a discovery.

The reading performance tests, like the writing tests, are scored on the basis of percentage of correct answers. What use can anyone make of these data when only certain questions and scores are presented to us? Firstly, distributed through the text are the percentages relating to particular questions. So we learn what percentages of pupils can identify 'the main idea or gist of a paragraph' or 'locate information' and so forth. There is no discussion of what all this fragmented and partial information might add up to, nor how it might be used by teachers or parents. Two brief paragraphs summarize the findings.

It is difficult to imagine who could cite them and expect them to be taken seriously. They run like this (a selection) on page 36:

(a) As is to be expected, pupils had least difficulty in answering questions about matters that were clearly asserted and easy to locate in the text ... There were a number of items which were answered correctly by between 90 and 77 per cent of the pupils involved.

(b) With reference to Whales (booklet 1) approximately three-quarters of the pupils were able to answer correctly one or more questions that involved comparing information given in different passages ...

(c) Over two-thirds of the pupils who read the booklet gave evidence of being able to use an index efficiently ...

We shall pass over briefly the study of pupils' attitudes to reading. Those who have some faith in attitude testing are hardly likely to be persuaded in so short a space to change their views. The chief difficulty is that people have attitudes to their attitudes and to those who are enquiring about them. With children the difficulties are even greater, for they must find some verbal formulation of unformulated feelings and ideas which are undergoing change, and therefore fraught with contradiction and tentativeness. All attitudes are potentially dynamic, but since we are here concerned with attitudes to a construct (myself as reader) which is in a formative and highly plastic state, the chances of trapping this elusive creature by the well-known tests are very small. Yet here again the APU show itself well aware of some of the shortcomings of attitude tests. On page 54 (para. 3.11) we have them set out for us: attitude tests are dependent on self-knowledge; they are affected by the desire to please (or, we might add, the desire to offend); they are dependent on memory; 'a response attitude can develop'. Yet a few lines above that succinct critical statement we can find this one:

Such scales [i.e. attitude scales] have the advantage of yielding objective, reliable data.

Attitude scales are duly adopted, but with reservations and supplementary procedures. What is more, preparations are in hand to extend this investigation of attitudes to reading by the fuller use of 'indirect measures of attitude measurement'. The contortions of the APU at this point arise solely from its pursuit of measurement in an area where what we need most is depth investigation. Indirect measurement ('where behaviour is interpreted for pertinent information', e.g. observation in classrooms and libraries) has from the testers' point of view certain disadvantages: cost in time and expense and,

> ... if the purpose of the exercise involves comparison, the need to standardise situations or isolate differing influential factors creates major problems. Therefore, the validity of relevant evidence has to be weighed against economy of research procedure and the purposes of the observations.

Yes, of course, the purposes of the observations. We had almost forgotten about them! In the opening paragraph of the 'attitudes' chapter (Ch. 7, p. 52) we find:

> Of particular concern to teachers are pupils 'who have the ability to read books, but choose not to do so'.

To meet this concern we need to know not only about the children's views and perceptions, but also about the reading policy of the school, how books are made available, what use is made of books in the classroom, the principles of selection of books and, of course, the teachers' and parents' attitudes. There is no reason why we should restrict ourselves to a child's eye view of these matters. But that is a different kind of research. If the money spent, and still to be spent, on developing measuring instruments were devoted to a study over time of the development of groups of young readers, it would involve far fewer children but would be of far greater value to all concerned. But the APU must follow inexorably its own logic. So we must contemplate for the future additional indirect instruments. But here researchers are trapped.

> Pilot work is therefore planned on an instrument that *simulates* [our italics] a situation in which pupils select books from a representative variety of fiction and non-fiction.

It is not clear how this simulation will help us to discover why some readers don't read.

We are not suggesting that the findings in this section of the Report are worthless, but rather that, where they do shed light on expressed views which are of interest, invariably they are only the beginning of what we need to know and do no more than propose by implication the kind of study we have suggested above.

> Talking about books was by far the most popular activity as a follow-up to reading. In contrast, two-thirds of the sample expressed their dislike for writing about a book after reading it.

(p. 81)

It is just possible that there are some who are not aware that children feel that way and may be moved towards a change of view should they chance to light on this finding. But for others it is only a spur to understanding why talking is popular and writing disliked. At best the attitude tests give us tantalizing glimpses of the answer.

One child, responding to the attitude test on reading, completed the sentence, 'The place I like to be when I am reading is ... ' with 'a very quiet corner in the classroom'. We all know how difficult it is to probe that invisible dialogue of the child with the book. We start asking questions on the assumption that we know what is to be understood and how it is to be understood; what, in other words, should be the nature of that dialogue, right down to what the child should be feeling. Writing is in some respects quite another matter. The very motive for writing is that it should produce a removable product. We may not know much about how a mind behaved in order to produce it, but we can analyse what is in front of us in great detail.

****

The research team's task in studying the response to their writing tests was therefore less inevitable than for the reading tests. This section of their Report is by far the most interesting and the team's discussion of the scripts could form a better basis for discussion than any other. However, as we shall see, it is the tester's needs which cause the greatest problems. Let us begin by setting the investigation of children's writing in its daunting research context. Vygotsky, writing in the Thirties (Vygotsky, 1978) put it like this.

> The developmental history of written language, however, poses enormous difficulties for research. As far as we can judge from the available material, it does not follow in a single direct line in which something like a clear continuity of forms is maintained. Instead, it offers the most unexpected metamorphoses, that is, transformations of particular forms of written language into others ... it is as much involution as evolution. This means, together with the processes of development, forward motion, and appearance of new forms, we can discern processes of curtailment, disappearance, and reverse development of old forms at each step.
>
> ... But only a naive view of development as a purely evolutionary process involving nothing but the gradual accumulation of small changes and the gradual conversion of one form into another can conceal from us the true nature of these processes.

The question then is, 'How can this development be investigated?' The APU had to administer its entry into schools with all the usual complicated protocol and ultimately confront children with specially designed writing tasks based on certain assumptions about the nature of writing. The most surprising assumption is that at 11 years of age most pupils are able 'to adjust what is written to different audiences and social relationships' and, judging by the eight activities (p. 85), to produce 'different types of writing'. The development of this capacity to differentiate writing according to function and to audience is very slow and many reasonably competent adult writers never achieve it fully and have little or no need to do so. Moreover, the chances of discovering the extent to which embryonic forms of these kinds of writing occur are small when performance is linked to separate tasks. In pre-adolescent children they are more likely to be observed embedded in kinds of writing which they find both easier and more congenial.

Bedevilled as usual by the constricting conditions of the investigation, the APU is aware that the actual context for the writing scarcely provides genuine audience or genuine communication: i.e. to whom am I writing this and for what acceptable reasons? We are given the possibilities A 'traditional test conditions'; B 'specific task' given by the normal teacher; and C normal class coursework. Inevitably, in practice, the choice imposed by the imperatives of comparability and cost of administration dictates the choice of A. It is just possible that for some, even many, pupils the design of A might permit the pupils to treat the writing task more like B or C. Certainly the most unpromising and inappropriate stimulus can be taken up enthusiastically by someone. This can hardly be depended on to produce valid responses. There is an attempt to reassure us that there is 'evidence' and 'close analysis has revealed …️ (etc.)'. Since we are not permitted to inspect the evidence nor appraise the analysis, we must take this on trust, and readers will have to judge from the rest of the Report how far they are prepared to do this.

The problem emerges very sharply when we inspect the items on the list of activities. They include an informal and a formal letter. Every child will be aware that the task is a bogus one and that the only meaning he or she can put on it is that he or she is being tested. Thus the informal 'letter to a friend' is not going to be judged by the true recipient for appropriateness. The same is true for other activities, e.g. to report (a) 'a verifiable account of an event', and (b) 'an account of something learned'. Why? We know it to be true that vast quantities of writing demanded in schools are not genuine communications. That many pupils submit to this unceasing demand to produce does not justify the replication of the practice in a prestigious series of tests. The most likely consequence is that this list will spawn thousands of composition titles calling for responses in conditions not dissimilar to those set up by the APU.

The decision was taken to use two types of marking for the compositions, impression marking and analytic marking, and this decision is supported by an experimental study. Tediously, we must again draw attention to the fact that this experiment, on which such a crucial matter turns, is not reported. We hear – what by now is a refrain in the Report – that 'it would not be appropriate to summarize the findings' (not even summarize?). Indeed, this whole section on marking is confusing. The analytic marking is not related to background variables since only a sub-sample was marked in this way. If these are really valid procedures their use becomes very limited. We learn, too, that the marking schemes could be applied by teachers who had undergone a period of training, but we discover nothing about the training programme.

The analytic marking uses four sets of criteria (p. 90):

1. Content and organisation
2. Appropriateness and style
3. Grammatical conventions
4. Orthographic conventions

These are put before us as self-evident components of the written system, which should be subjected to analytic marking. There is a common-sense rationale here but there is nothing objective in the selection. 1 and 2 are global characteristics, requiring the same order of judgement as impression marking, where both 3 and 4 examine highly specific features of the writing system. There are enormous difficulties here and they cannot be enlarged upon, but the paragraphs relating to 1 and 2 (p. 90) are far too sparse to reassure us that these have been satisfactorily resolved. 'Appropriateness and style', for example, were marked on the first twenty lines of the scripts. The paragraphs (4.35–4.37) dealing with these yoked criteria reveal both a vagueness and over-specificity.

> The term 'style' … is used to refer to the writer's choice and purposeful use of vocabulary and sentence structure and the general appropriateness of such expression with regard to the writer's subject matter, audience and purpose, insofar as these can be determined.
>
> (para. 4.35)

The criteria here, avowedly somewhat inapplicable, cover so much of what is essential to writing that it would be impossible for any marker to separate them from other criteria. There is a strong sense that the team is both laying down dubious laws in a dogmatic manner and at the same time leaving loopholes in the laws. So, dealing with colloquial language, they tell us:

> While such usage might be judged appropriate in a personal letter it would not necessarily be appropriate in other contexts.

A few lines below, we find the Report speaking of 'stylistic errors' as though they had provided grounds for confident allocation of language to outer darkness. 'It would not necessarily … ' hardly constitutes a useful guideline to a marker and, even less, does it enable a reader to perceive how this criterion would be applied.

There is no avoiding the fact that written discourse is governed by an interaction of cognitive demand and social conventions, but the conventional aspects of writing (including stylistic choices) are constantly being renegotiated by writers because their style cannot be separated from their social, ethical and ideological stance, which leads them not only to be concerned with their ideas but also with the medium. The point here is to ask what kind of model of writing is in the minds of the APU team. Each one of their common-sense categories for analytic marking suggests that prior analysis of them is at a very superficial level. We might take, for example, what would seem at first blush to be an uncontroversial category, namely 'content'. This is construed, we must conjecture, as a set of propositions evaluated for their aptness. There is no way, however, of judging the aptness of content without being able to specify what the writer was supposed to transmit for his or her own purposes and by what criteria what kinds of writer need what selection of information. The focus must always be on the writer's meaning. As Dillon (1981) puts it:

> If this finding and expression of meaning involves constructive activity by human subjects … then quantifying the content and measuring the efficiency of its transmission by various sentence forms becomes an impossible and futile undertaking.

(p. 163)

Grammatical and orthographic matters are in some ways, but certainly not all, much more straightforward for the observer, but how a marker decides on where to place a script on a five-point scale on the basis of twenty or ten lines of writing (why lines and not number of words?) is another matter. To put it at its simplest, how does one compare one pupil's errors, which are due to ambitiousness in vocabulary and sentence structure, with those another who, by writing with caution, makes himself or herself less accident prone? The fact that orthography and grammar were weaker in the story task than the report task is related to this difference. The Report mentions (4.91) that different tasks produce different tendencies to error but does not acknowledge that within-task differences can be significant.

****

We can now examine how the APU discusses the application of its procedures and comments on the pupils' performance in three of the tasks: 'reporting, narration, and writing to change the reader's state of mind'; more specifically (a) a report on the sighting of a UFO, (b) a story based on some suggestions, and (c) a letter to cheer up an absent friend (a formal letter is also discussed at this point). We shall examine these topics in the order given above, in which they appear in the text of the Report.

(a) The UFO report

The pupil is presented with a first-person narrative of the UFO sighting, a sketch map and a formal document setting out the items which should be included in a report to the Ministry of Defence on a UFO sighting. The task is then to read the documents and '*Imagine you are the person in the story … write a report of what you saw*' (i.e. to the Ministry of Defence).

Once again, there is a test behind the test. Once again, a fiction is created, for the pupil did not write the narrative, the pupil did not undergo the experience, and, most important of all, is not writing to the Ministry of Defence. And yet this mock report is to be judged by all the criteria which should be applied to a genuine report. Since we were given to understand that the language tests were all considered to be eminently suitable for eleven-year-olds, we must be left wondering how a bogus report to the Ministry of Defence fits that description. A genuine formal written report is not likely to be within the experience of most eleven-year-olds, nor does there seem to be any good reason why it should be, unless some natural compelling occasion arose. The task is ingeniously devised but can only be applauded if we accept its assumptions. It is an excellent example of the kind of exercise which has been in English text books for decades, since, in fact, the arrival of 'social' English in the Thirties.

A further difficulty is commented on in the Report.

> Mainly, any writing task based on a written source will be assessing both reading and writing skills, difficult though it is to pin-point the interaction.
>
> (p. 95)

There follows the usual indigestible detailed information about percentages of pupils who correctly reported such items of information and some thin speculation to account for the figures. But there is no return to the very point being raised. It is left floating in mid-air, as though the recognition of a difficulty in some way resolves it. We ourselves have suggested that linking reading and writing would be no bad thing, but this kind of assessment creates its own difficulties. In due course (chapter 6) we are going to encounter mean scores for writing performance. Yet we are told here that this exercise assesses both reading and writing in a way which makes one inextricable from the other. What then is the meaning of these scores, with all their air of numerical precision?

(b) A story based on some suggestions

It turned out that the majority of pupils responded to the request for a report in (a) by a first-person narrative and in this section (4.66) the Report comments: 'there seems to be a general belief that children are likely to enjoy and profit from this mode of writing'. Beautifully non-committal. Do they or don't they? And if the team did not know the answer, they should either have attempted to find out or found some justification for choosing a fiction narrative as one of their tasks. It rather looks as though they are saying that there is a folk-belief that it is so, and that it is so strong that they were obliged to go along with it. There is a rapidly developing literature on narrative in general and to a lesser extent on the development of narrative in children. We have no way of knowing whether the APU team consulted it but the phrase 'there seems to be a general belief' hardly inspires confidence.

The task proposed to the children 'was intended to be supportive'. It not only set a dramatic scene but proposed four questions relating to the 'character' and 'plot' as a basis for the story. Now it might be imagined that here is an activity that the children could take to like ducks to water, and that optimum performance looks like a realizable goal. As always, the APU is sadly fettered by its own task. Just for a moment let us consider what is happening and what might happen. Here is an eleven-year-old confronting a piece of paper which says 'Write a story', not any story, not one you remember, not one which has been incubating, but one which must accept the setting, the personae and the mood proposed by some unknown other. That is not all: if the setting, etc. have by good chance fired your imagination and set your mind racing towards possibilities, then wait a moment. The invisible story-demander is also setting out some possibilities in the form of questions which your story can answer 'if you like'. (Is that how children compose stories, by answering questions?) So the child's capacity to tell stories is constrained by the tester's needs.

Once we accept the premises of the APU's rationale, what else can the unfortunate tester do? Yet what are stories for? They are for all, but especially at this age, a complex way of understanding and interpreting the world. They are indeed a form of *thinking* and of *communicating thought*. How do you do that on demand? Because that is obviously unreasonable, the APU turns to the only humane alternative, supportive material, only to be caught up in the contradiction that while this helps the child to write something, it means that there is little likelihood that the writing will draw on anything more than a competence with the conventions and story formulae. On the other hand the APU's scene-setting and questions are in themselves a possible starting point if they are placed in the context of a classroom negotiation, exploration and sharing. They then undergo a qualitative change and potentially at least the imagination is liberated. Even then there should be alternatives. What then becomes possible is that the initial impetus can be taken in any direction and the tester's unspecified 'anticipations' are not allowed to hamper the line of thought.

Drearily and predictably the Report's comments follow. The stories tapped a 'familiar source … melodramatic tales of murder, treachery, natural disasters, etc'. The testers could breathe a sigh of relief: the children found 'sufficient content for the story', but the price had to be paid in 'stereotypic denouements' and

> … pupils tended to link their stories to them [i.e. the leading questions, and the opening description], to an extent which detracted from the independent status of the finished piece.

> (4.71)

There were other hazards which, we suggest, derived from the instructions. No conclusions are drawn for the future about the suitability of the team's procedures and their expectations. We are told that the children provided little evidence of 'revisions' or 'advance planning'. Is this because the team expected them, or is it merely the occupational hazard of testers, a tendency to be both perfectionist and censorious? One example of this tendency is the comment on 'the management of information', where story-writing skill is linked to the ability to vary syntactic structures. If the researchers were to take a look at the paragraph presented as the stimulus they might see one possible cause of lack of syntactic variety.

Imagine this scene:

> A tall ragged man is trudging up a steep, muddy lane. A little girl and an old woman are hurrying after him. It is pouring with rain. The man looks grim and determined. The little girl and the old woman look frightened.

The role of the dialogue in story-telling is of great interest. How do children manage it? What do they make it do for them? The Report dwells on dialogue in the stories, but not to answer questions of this order. It limits itself instead to the safer territory of the punctuation of dialogue. The comments within those limits are eminently sensible, if somewhat familiar.

(c) A letter to cheer up an absent friend

The importance given to letter-writing in schools might lead one to think that it had some unique significance as a form of writing. The reasons for this emphasis we need not go into, except to say that they are not unrelated to the kinds of criticisms which led to the setting up of the Bullock Committee. Accordingly, we may expect letter-writing to be given a place amongst the writing tasks. And, of course, the fictional procedure appears once again, an imaginary situation into which the pupil must project a fictive communication. A few comments on the pupils' performance are stitched together at this point, but they carry little conviction and certainly shed little light. As we noted above, the writing of an informal and intimate letter relieves the writer of almost all conformist obligations short of comprehensibility. The last thing a letter need have is organization, paragraph structure and the like. The analytic markers took the view that 'the ability to show that the reader was kept constantly in mind' was important, and yet they were being asked to comment on organization. It is difficult to see how they could carry out this task. A brief citation from one letter is characterized as being 'perfunctory' and 'the writer falls victim to her recollections'. This gives us some indication of just how subjective this part of assessment has become.

We might have guessed, in view of the letter-writing obsession, that the APU could not settle for an informal letter where, they must admit, standards cannot be regimentalized. And sure enough, in addition to the informal letter, they asked for a formal letter, thus conferring the APU seal of approval. Even here the by-now familiar contortions are prominent. Addresses of sender and recipient are dictated to the pupil (without reference to layout, etc). But the pupil letter-writer has to use a false address 'in the interests of anonymity'. How, we wonder, did the less literate or confident children cope with the contrivances and distractions? The never-ending simulation game played in these tests is taken a stage further by providing the pupils with 'simulated writing paper and envelope'! The task is described so vaguely ('a letter of request to an adult ... whose name and departmental address were given') that unlike the report of the UFO incident we cannot know exactly what the children were expected to do. It remains only to say that the Report at this point drops an extremely significant comment.

> It is important to note that the analysis of pupils' performance on this task exists as a description of what was or was not achieved rather than a prescription for what should be achieved.

Thus, in the midst of the text, a key point of principle is dropped casually in our path. In practice, however, it is impossible through the discussion in the Report to detect any difference of presentation between this section and any other, and the usual ritual of juggling with 'facility values' is gone through. We have commented at the outset on the double vision of this Report. The authors could well claim that they have not been, in the main, prescriptive. The comment seems superfluous except insofar as it anticipates possible criticism. In any case, a casual comment of this kind does not absolve the APU from responsibility. It would have us believe there is no more to all this than description. Then why select this task for presentation and analysis when others are not reported on? Shades of accountability.

The chapter closes with a pyrotechnic display of a selection of statistics. Since all the niceties are derived from the value judgment we have already discussed, we shall make no comment on them. A summary statement at the end of the chapter gives as much attention to the development of testing methodology as to any meaning which may be attached to the results. It includes the unjustified claim that it has obtained information about writing for different audiences. Not until we have a thorough theoretical analysis from a sociolinguistic point of view of what the written system of English consists of, can we do more than scratch the surface of children's development as writers. Meanwhile, in judging performance and progress, we need to examine writing produced in different kinds of school contexts and not performance on tests, however artfully contrived.

The two remaining chapters (5 and 6) of research findings deal with the relationship between 'background variables' and the reading and writing results. Before we plunge into these pages of statistics, we must remind ourselves what we are looking at. As we have pointed out, we are looking at global scores for reading and writing which have been derived from diverse activities each scored separately for its 'facility value' (level of difficulty). As we have shown, standing a long way back from these figures are the procedures which give rise to specific items. In some cases, decisions have been made about what constitutes a 'correct' answer and in others (e.g. analytic marking of writing) abstract qualities in a written text have given rise to hard figures of dubious validity.

Once we move away from the initial processes of children's performance and testers' assumptions and practices, the whole operation consists of deriving statistics from other statistics. When we bear in mind that all these subsequent manipulations are based on the Rasch model, which has been seriously criticized, we can make some estimate of how much reliance we can place on this final statistical flurry. It is not, therefore, our intention to allow ourselves to be enticed by these tables and statistics into considering their implications. It is more important to signal that when these figures are cited in public debate they should not be treated as gospel. Some observations are, however, in order.

On page 121 we note the sudden attention to speakers of English as a second language. This is a matter of most serious concern. In all the lengthy description and analysis which precedes these figures, no reference has been made to such groups of pupils. Now we have thrust before us a handful of generalized statistics. It seems clear that concern for these pupils is perfunctory. It is ironical that the Report which in general transmits an air of high statistical expertise should base its figures on incredibly shaky foundations. To put the matter briefly, speakers of English as a second language are treated as a homogeneous group, in spite of the fact that even a passing interest in bilingualism teaches us that it exists in many different forms and, more obviously, competence in the second language ranges from zero to highly fluent use. (See, for example, Simoes, 1976 or Rosen and Burgess, 1980.) Furthermore, the information on numbers of second-language speakers 'was obtained from head teachers' and we have good reason to know that this is not necessarily a reliable source. Pupils who have a native-speaker fluency in English do not necessarily make known their first language, nor do some head teachers make it their business to find out.

Given the coarse data by means of which this background variable is investigated, it cannot be wondered at if the APU arrives at findings which are already commonplaces among those concerned with bilingualism. This group of pupils has lower mean scores than first-language speakers. Those who were literate in their first language did better than those who were not. It must be emphasized that the language performance of second-language speakers needs delicate and sophisticated study, such as that being pursued at the University of London Institute of Education by Josie Levine and teacher colleagues. Whereas the APU makes frequent references to ambitious plans for expanding its work in many directions, no indication is given that it has the intention of refining this crude and very limited undertaking.

Perhaps the best comment on these sections of the Report is to be found in the text:

The information provided about relationship between performance and background variables should be interpreted with caution.

(p. 31)

We are promised that the pattern will become clearer when more information is made available.

****

It will no doubt seem to some that this lengthy appraisal is hypercritical, carping and ungenerous. Certainly, a general impression which comes from a reading of the Report is of huge energies conscientiously devoted to a monstrous task. More than that, it is apparent that the team has wrestled heroically with ever-increasing problems as it has attempted to work with the grain of educational practice and also to stay close to the interests of the children. But a close reading of the Report is a frustrating experience requiring no little concentration if one is to penetrate its mysteries. It is, after all, only the tip of the iceberg which we are permitted to inspect. Repeatedly we are told or have to infer that more has gone on than is reported. The text has been carefully policed.

There will be many who quite properly will be envious of the resources allocated to an endeavour which has produced so little and the effects of which can so easily be harmful. For it would not be difficult to propose a study of school pupils' language development, one which we so desperately need and which could be conducted in a manner which would constitute a unique form of in-service education for teachers. We may well sympathise with the research team, but that sympathy must be tempered by a scepticism about the whole strategy in which they became involved, its political background, its long-term intentions and the use to which it will be put. Though we may see the team locked in an heroic struggle with the tiger of assessment, we must also see that they should not have ventured on the jungle safari in the first place.

We said at the outset that nothing can obscure the fact that this Report is linked to a preoccupation with standards. It may make some teachers nervous; it may make some teachers shift their practices in ways which will not be helpful to children; but it is unlikely to raise standards of performance. There is an alternative; it is the active participation of teachers in assessment, teachers who are close to the children being assessed. The possibilities have already been sketched out. Stibbs (1979) calls it 'in-service training through collaborative marking':

To join other teachers, perhaps more experienced than ourselves in the coursework of many pupils, helps to get a sense of what represents progress and excellence in language use, while reminding us that different pupils progress in different ways.

(p. 36)

The constraints imposed on the research team by the grand design of the APU could not have permitted them to carry out the kind of investigation of children's language which could give us deep insight into language development. Language development is nevertheless inscribed boldly on the Report's programme. Here is the alternative proposed so long ago by Vygotsky (1978):

> Any investigation explores some sphere of reality. An aim of the psychological analysis of development is to describe the internal relations of the intellectual processes awakened by school learning. In this respect, such analysis will be directed inward and is analogous to the use of x-rays. If successful, it should reveal to the teacher how developmental processes stimulated by the course of school learning are carried through inside the head of each individual child. The revelation of this internal, subterranean developmental network of school subjects is a task of primary importance for psychological and educational analysis.

The APU report does not give us x-rays but rather fuzzy aerial photographs.

References

Adelman, C. (1981) *Uttering, Muttering: Collecting, using and reporting talk for social and educational research.* London: Grant McIntyre.

Assessment of Performance Unit (APU) (1978) *Language Performance.* London: Department of Education and Science.

Assesment of Performance Unit (APU) (1981) *Language Performance in Schools: Primary survey report No. 1.* London: HMSO.

Barnes, D., Britton, J., Rosen, H. and the LATE (1971) *Language, the Learner and the School* (revised edition). Harmondsworth: Penguin.

Barnes, D. and Todd, F. (1977) *Communication and Learning in Small Groups.* London: Routledge and Kegan Paul.

Blackstone, T. and Wood, R. (1981) 'Making schools more accountable'. *New Society*, 24/31 December.

Britton, J., Martin, N. and Rosen, H. (1966) *The Multiple Marking of English Compositions.* London: HMSO.

Broadfoot, P. (1979) *Assessment, Schools and Society.* London: Methuen.

Brown, R., Cazden, C. and Bellugi, U. (1969) 'The Child's Grammar from I to III', in J. Hill (ed.), *Minnesota Symposia on Child Psychology, vol. II.* Minneapolis: University of Minnesota Press.

The Bullock Committee (1975) *A Language for Life* (The Bullock Report). London: HMSO.

Callaghan. J. (1976) 'A rational debate based on the facts', speech delivered at Ruskin College, Oxford, 18 October.

Carter, D. (1980) 'APU Tests a Mistake'. *The Times Educational Supplement*, 27 June.

Carter, D. (1981) 'Bogus Objectivity'. *The Times Educational Supplement*, 2 October.

Chatman, S. (1978) *Story and Discourse.* Ithaca, NY: Cornell University Press.

Dennison, W. (1978) 'The APU – Where is it leading?' *Durham and Newcastle Research Review*, 8: 40.

Department of Education and Science (DES) (1974) *Educational Disadvantage and the Educational Needs of Immigrants. Cmnd 5720.* London: HMSO.

Department of Education and Science (DES) (1977) *Education in Schools: A consultative document. Cmnd 6869.* London: HMSO.

Department of Education and Science (DES) (1978) *Assessment in Schools. Reports on education 93.* London: HMSO.

Department of Education and Science/HM Inspectorate (DES/HMI) (1978) *Primary Education in England: A survey by HM Inspectors.* London: HMSO.

Department of Education and Science/HM Inspectorate (DES/HMI) (1979) *Aspects of Secondary Education in England: A survey by HM Inspectors.* London: HMSO.

Dillon, G.L. (1981) *Constructing Texts.* Bloomington: Indiana University Press.

Genette, G. (1980) *Narrative Discourse.* Oxford: Basil Blackwell.

Gipps, C. and Goldstein, H. (1983) *Monitoring Children: An evaluation of the Assessment of Performance Unit.* London: Heinemann Education.

Halliday, M. (1975) *Learning How to Mean.* London: Edward Arnold.

Holt, M. (1981) *Evaluating the Evaluators.* London: Hodder and Stoughton.

Kay, B. (1975) 'Monitoring pupils' performance'. *Trends in Education*, 2.

Kay, B. (1977) *A Programme of Work for the APU.* London: Department of Education and Science (quoted in Lawton, D. [1980])

Lawton, D. (1980) *The Politics of the School Curriculum.* London: Routledge and Kegan Paul.

Meek, M. with Armstrong, A., Austerfield, V., Graham, J. and Plackett, E. (1983) *Achieving Literacy: A kind of evidence.* London: Routledge and Kegan Paul.

Meek, M., Warlow, A. and Barton, G. (eds.) (1977) *The Cool Web: The pattern of children's reading.* London: The Bodley Head.

Peaker, G.F. (1966) *Progress in Reading, 1948–1964. Education pamphlet 50.* London: HMSO.

The Plowden Committee (1967) *Children and their Primary Schools* (The Plowden Report). London: HMSO.

Pring, R. (1980) *APU and the Core Curriculum.* Exeter: Curriculum and Resources Centre, University of Exeter School of Education.

Rosen, H. and Burgess, T. (1980) *Languages and Dialects of London School Children.* London: Ward Lock.

Schools Council Language for Learning Project (1981) *Investigating Talk.* London: English Department, Institute of Education, University of London.

Simoes, A. (1976) *The Bilingual Child.* New York: Academic Press.

Smith, F. (1971) *Understanding Reading.* New York: Holt, Reinhart and Winston.

Start, K.B. and Wells, B.K. (1972) *The Trend of Reading Standards.* Windsor: NFER-Nelson.

Stibbs, A. (1979) *Assessing Children's Language Performance.* Ward Lock/National Association for the Teaching of English.

Vygotsky, L. (1978) *Mind in Society: Development of higher psychological processes* (M. Cole, V. John-Steiner, S. Scribner and E. Souberman, eds.). Cambridge, MA: Harvard University Press.

Wells, G. (1981) *Learning through Interaction.* Cambridge: Cambridge University Press.

Wilkinson, A. (1965) *Spoken English. Educational Review, Occasional Publications*, 2.

Language and the Education of the Working Class

This essay first appeared in 1982 as 'Language in the Education of the Working Class', in *Languages for Life, University of Sussex Education Area Occasional Paper 10*, edited by Trevor Pateman. Under its present, slightly different title, it appeared in 1986 in *Education and Social Class*, edited by Rick Rogers, published by The Falmer Press.

As I contemplate my own title I am highly conscious of the fact that no less a person than Dell Hymes (1979) has urged us to entertain a possibility about the relationship of schools to language:

> We must consider the possibility that schools, along with other institutions, have as a latent function the maintenance and reproduction of the present social order on the apparently impartial ground of language.

'The apparently impartial ground of language' I accept must be part of my undertaking. No sooner have I said that than I become aware of the risk involved in handling such weighty coinage as 'latent function' and 'reproduction of the social order'. For, whatever is said about working-class children's language and what is done to it, for it and against it in schools, it is enacted in classrooms where social processes become multidimensional, spontaneous and simultaneous events (Hammersley, 1980).

I want to avoid, if possible, some of the seductions of my theme. I do not propose to be lured by it into a relatively amateurish and most certainly derivative analysis of the nature of the working class in contemporary Britain, nor into a consideration of the general issue of the education of the working class. I want as far as I am able to keep the focus on language in education. At the same time I am well aware that neither of these two issues can be ignored. I shall, therefore, state my position briefly rather than argue it.

I do so because the working class, its supposed composition and characteristics, have won themselves a generous acreage of space in educational literature. Then, too, educational and sociolinguistic analysis is rarely based on a sober analysis of the realities of class in our society. We might be encouraged to expect just that when Halliday (1978) informs us that:

> The social structure is not just an ornamental background to linguistics as it has tended to become in sociolinguistic discussions. It is an essential element in the evolution of semantic systems and semantic processes.

That sounds like a promising programme. What then is this critical social structure? Schooled by Bernstein, Halliday tells us that it is:

> … typically the social hierarchy acting through the distribution of family types having different familial role-systems.

But why should the social structure be typified by familial role-systems? Typically, I would prefer to say, the worker sells his or her labour power, and arising from this primary fact the social order is adapted and shaped, an order in which, in addition to the family, there are government and its civil service, the police force, the armed forces, organized industry and commerce, the communication system and, needless to say, the educational system. I should say, in passing, that Halliday (*ibid.*) knows better than this, when he refers, for example, to dialect becoming 'a means of expression of class consciousness and political awareness', though this idea is not pursued to its logical conclusion or developed.

I select Halliday as one of the most powerful sociolinguists in the Anglophone world (and perhaps beyond) who is also deeply involved in a very practical way with language in schools (see Halliday, 1981). In contrast to the family focus of so much educational discussion of working-class children, I would want quite simply to assert that those children are powerfully affected not only by the shared economic position of their parents but also by the lengthy history of education and the varied location of their parents in the social system; by the different histories they inherit, their degree of class consciousness, their ethnicity and their sex. Working-class children are not an undifferentiated cohort.

If we look at schools placed in the network of social relations at the intersections of specific expectations and obligations (discipline them, skill them, acculturate them, test them, certificate them, keep them off the streets) it becomes an urgent matter to consider what the possibilities are within schools for working-class children. It has become a commonplace of the radical critique of the schools that they are perfectly engineered institutions for reproducing the existing social order. This is supposed to hold true for the structure of the educational system, the internal organization of schools, the special version of culture they disseminate and their hidden curricula. There are other radicals who regard this critique as a betrayal of socialist endeavours to change education under capitalism. Entwistle (1981) for instance, dazzled by some of Gramsci's more dubious pronouncements, laments the abandonment of

> Traditional socialist initiatives towards the reform of schooling aimed at creating universal access to mainstream culture.

It will be a premise of what follows that schools are neither totally efficient mechanical devices for ensuring the continuation of capitalism nor neutral purveyors of mainstream culture. If I believed the former then this present exercise would be an irrelevance. If I believed the latter, then I would be ignoring the waning of the educational optimism of the sixties and the cause for the relatively sudden interest in working-class language in the sixties enshrined in that notorious dictum 'educational failure is linguistic failure'. Because schools in our society are so diverse, because they are never controlled in total fashion, because teachers themselves are not uniform, mindless zombies nor uncritical transmitters of the dominant ideology, because pupils are beginning to exert powerful pressures within the system, because politics in the community can break into sealed institutions, schools themselves are the arenas where genuine battles over contending practices are fought out. To turn our backs on them, to write them off as parts of the controlling apparatus and no more, is to refuse to participate in life itself.

With that preamble, I can now turn to what may be more narrowly construed as language issues. It feels as though it is only a short while ago that a discussion of working-class children and language in school would have made obligatory and exclusive preoccupation with theories of verbal deficit and the taking of sides in the debate about Bernstein's restricted and elaborated codes. That is no longer necessary for two reasons. Firstly, the two sides have become clearly demarcated. Whereas, let us say, in 1970 the theory of codes or some now repudiated versions of it held sway, there has appeared since then a sequence of critiques which lay bare the areas of disagreement. Notably Dittmar (1976) and Edwards (1976) and most sociolinguists. Only recently there was published *Verbal Deficit: A critique* by Gordon (1981), which not only brings together and synthesizes the ideas of the anti-Bernstein school but also traces the history of verbal deficit theory and adds its own arguments. It is no longer possible with any intellectual honesty to treat elaborated and restricted codes as though we were dealing with uncontentious objective aspects of language use. As long ago as 1963 the Newsom Report (The Newsom Committee, 1963) was able to present its own crass and scandalous version of verbal deficit:

> There is a gulf between those who have, and the many who have not, sufficient command of words to be able to listen and discuss rationally; to express ideas and feelings clearly; and *even to have any ideas at all.*
>
> (para. 49, my emphasis)

The origin of these extraordinary assertions is made clear when the report refers to 'the evidence of research' as showing that these many idea-less have-nots have forms of speech which are restricted. The authors of the Bullock Report (1975), who were well placed to know about the serious criticisms of the verbal deficit thesis, simply accepted it and dismissed Labov's work (1972) with a condescending nod. Their way of putting it was:

> There is an indisputable gap between the language experiences some
> families provide and the linguistic demands of school education.
>
> (para. 5.9)

They left in no doubt who was expected to jump the gap. The careful documentation
in the HMI survey, conducted for the Bullock Committee, of the empty drudgery
which constituted the typical linguistic demands of a school scarcely makes the
educational leap across the gap seem a feat worth undertaking. As for concepts of
verbal deficit (some adherents of the theory of codes, including Halliday, claim that it
is not a deficit theory, though how this can be true when it rests on a demonstration of
what some children do not possess remains a mystery to me), they continue to exert
an influence through both further refinement and dissemination (see, for example,
Open University, 1981). But the notions of verbal deficit long preceded academic
debate. Enough of that: the opposed positions are there for all to see.

My second reason for not wishing to go over that ground again is that the
intensity of focus on that issue alone has distracted attention from other matters and
narrowed down the discussion of language and class in education.

It is a limitation in much of the literature on language and class that the
language (or sociolect) of each class is treated as though it exists in isolation from
that of other classes and independent of class relationships. In fact it is an important
feature of our society that workers encounter the language of other social strata in
certain significant contexts – in their place of work, in the media, in their necessary
negotiations with bureaucracy. Children encounter a sociolect different from their
own in school, though that contact is full of social and linguistic ambiguities. But as
Edward Thompson (1963) says:

> We cannot have two distinct classes, each with its independent being.
> We cannot have love without lovers, nor deference without squires and
> labourers.

It does not take working-class children very long to discover that their speech is
disapproved of, if not actually despised, and to perceive that these criticisms come
from above. In most schools for most of the time there is continuous pressure on
them to use what Labov called careful rather than spontaneous speech. What this
amounts to is nothing less than a drastic reduction in the linguistic resources which
working class children can call upon to express their own ideas and opinions and
to come to grips with the intellectual demands made upon them. On the other
hand, for older pupils in particular, it is in school that the lesson is learnt that their
language can be used as an oppositional weapon, the most striking example of which
is the adoption by West Indian pupils of Black English as a second dialect. The
dialect of the pupils and the dialect of the teacher do not glare at each other over the
barricades. It is rather that the pupils are expected to express novel meanings when

the very language in which they could best negotiate those meanings is, for the most part covertly, ruled out or attenuated. Thus legitimizing the language of working-class children and, more importantly, creating the conditions for its spontaneous use, become an important matter for contention.

Noëlle Bisseret (1970) has argued that language practices are not only a fundamental part of class identity (the nuances and ambivalence behind the phrase 'talking posh' would be a highly concentrated example) but also that the dominant ideology attempts to win, and largely succeeds in winning, acceptance of the idea that the language of the dominant is in some state of perfection and that any difference of system of meaning in the working class is only seen as an absence of meaning. The argument is complex but suffice it to say that it is not difficult to find examples of what she means. Olson (1977), in a well known paper 'From utterance to text', which contrasts the power of vernacular speech with the power of the written word, claims that the essay form is the ultimate high cognitive achievement of Western civilization. Dell Hymes (1979), on the other hand, attacks some of the language ideals adopted by our dominant culture:

> For a time the pinnacle of knowledge appeared to many to be a single logical language to which all science and legitimate knowledge might be reduced.

In discussing what he calls 'admissible styles' Hymes draws attention to the undervaluing of the interpersonal, expressive uses of language:

> Increasingly, we are concerned to have a place for things that cannot be said without distortion, or even said at all, in the idioms of elaborated, formal, purportedly rational and referential speech … There are things we know and need to be that have no standing there. A sense of this is a reflection of the central problem of the role of language in modern society, namely what the balance is to be between modes of use of language.

So it comes about that the entrance money to be paid for advancement in the educational system creates a sharp dilemma for working-class children. They may accept the class-based judgment passed on their language and strive to adapt and adopt the meaning system which school presses upon them. If they do so, they sever themselves from their own meaning system or even develop a contempt for it. If they reject the language the school offers they retain the class identifying power of their own language but lose the opportunity of mastering much of the understanding which enables them more effectively to change their condition. The dilemma becomes the more painful when we remember that there exists in the working class both an awed reverence for the language of the educated and a deep and justified suspicion that it is used to mystify and exploit them especially in its written form: laws, contracts, missives from employers and landlords, communications from the government and local authorities, etc. It requires no allegiance to the concept of hegemony to appreciate that educated language, even when delivering potent meanings, has its own pathology which derives from the social relations of communicator and audience.

In general, the language of members of the dominating class and its agents may appear in all respects superior, especially to themselves, solely by virtue of its dominance. It is an additional and significant step when measures are taken actively and specifically against the language of the dominated. Teachers and pupils alike are caught in an intricate knot of power relationships, but they need not merely register those relationships. The Bullock Report (1975) may with apparent innocence speak of the 'linguistic demands' of the schools but this conceals both the oppressive linguistic policy of many schools and at the same time the determined efforts of many teachers that the language of working-class children shall not be put down. One reason why we should be grateful for the presence of West Indian pupils in our schools is that they have brought this issue to a head.

If the phrase the 'linguistic demands of the school' means anything, it means the acquisition of standard English, which is firmly counterposed to dialect. Indeed, the Bullock Report made this very clear when it spoke of 'assisting children to master standard English which is in effect the dialect of the school'. The issue of standard English and dialect becomes one of major emphasis in language policy. Linguists have not been reluctant to enter the fray, lending their academic authority to very familiar pronouncements which are political and social rather than linguistic. Thus Crystal (1976):

> We have to be realistic. Whatever we think of the ideal of total dialect or stylistic tolerance, in all circumstances it is at present and in the foreseeable future only an ideal. The children being taught now are having to grow up in a society where the formal standard language, in its various varieties, retains considerable prestige.

And the role of the teacher is to provide the child 'with as much command of the standard form of language as possible'. There is nothing linguistic in this argument and Crystal has no privileged right to lay down the law. His views are no more cogent than the familiar common-sense ones like 'You can't change human nature' and 'Don't bang your head against a brick wall'. However, notice how surreptitiously 'standard' has become 'formal standard' and its acquisition by working-class pupils amounts to 'as much command as possible'. As in most discussion, certain critical aspects of standard and dialect remain unexplored.

Firstly, it is always necessary to distinguish between written standard and spoken standard and their distinct social roles. Secondly, the mistaken impression is given that standard of either modality is so tightly uniform that it does not include a very wide range of variety within itself, including its degree of closeness to spoken forms, which can include an incorporation of dialect. Thirdly, and it is here where the most confusion occurs, it is the mastery of a written system, not of written standard, which is the crucial attainment. That it happens to be in standard does not mean its central characteristics derive from standard.

The major difficulty for children consists in learning a form of the language which has developed its own cognitive and aesthetic strategies. To write a novel means centrally to know and understand what novels are and could be, and only in trivial sense (if at all) to know how to write standard English. And the same is true of sustained written argument and exposition. Even spelling and punctuation are requirements of a written system rather than of standard. The main problem for working-class children is not that their writing is non-standard, but that they have not acquired the idiom and cadences of written language and the historically developed devices for coping with and compensating for loss of face-to-face interaction. My colleague Tony Burgess has been observing how many working-class children reach a plateau where for the most part they have acquired written standard but are only minimally at home with the written system. It has not become a genuine medium for expression.

It must be said that most linguists, at least those who concern themselves with language variety, espouse a very liberal doctrine towards dialect and this (where it has been able to penetrate) has had considerable influence among teachers. Trudgill (1975) in the United Kingdom is an outstanding example. He, like others, has called down upon himself the wrath of all those who cannot perceive dialect speech as anything other than the debased, deformed lingo of the ignorant. Urban dialect, in particular, is seen as a failed attempt to speak standard. And to class bias we must add racist bias when Creole is the focus of attention. The linguists have been at pains to show, since they proscribed the label 'sub-standard', that all dialects are equal, that the vernacular speech of every society or social group is a full language in the sense that it has ordered phonology, syntax, lexis and limitless meaning potential. This point of view, which we might call egalitarian dialectology, commendably democratic though it is, leaves out what dialect means to the dialect user for whom it cannot be equal to other dialects. It has been the tradition of dialect study to note certain differences in structures, sounds and vocabulary, but differences are more profound than that: they relate to ways of speaking, ways of conversing, shared idiom and shared verbal culture. This is just as true of urban dialects like Cockney, Scouse, Geordie etc., as of rural dialects.

I would like briefly to expand on that. The standard spoken dialect is a far from clearly designated territory. Whereas much ink has been spilled over the absence of the copula in Creole, it is not often noticed that in standard it is perfectly possible to say 'That your car?' or 'She your sister?'. Nevertheless, since it is often referred to as the prestige dialect or the language of the dominant, we need to examine standard more closely. Whereas it is the language of the dominant culture, it is for obvious reasons also the language of a huge support army of the system which in order to carry out its duties needs also to be highly literate – clerical and administrative workers of all kinds and, of course, teachers. Unlike the speakers of other dialects the labour power they sell to their employers includes the ability to speak standard and write it. These mostly monodialectal speakers act as a kind of linguistic buffer state between the working class and the ruling class; at the frontier of this buffer state inter-dialect communications are most dense. It is characteristic of these speakers of standard to patrol their linguistic borders with anxious surveillance, to mark themselves from the working class. Thus the prestige dialect for many of its speakers produces an anxious monitoring of their own speech and a powerful urge to put conformity before all else. This is all well documented in Labov (1972), who shows lower-middle-class speakers to be highest on his index of linguistic anxiety. Many, but thank goodness not all, teachers are prey to these very anxieties. Thus in schools there is so much obsession with certain markers of class dialect.

Non-standard dialect speech is essentially part of an oral culture. However, most of its speakers are consumers of standard not producers of it; they read it but very rarely write it. The most important and intimate exchanges of their lives are conducted through their vernacular. Perhaps we should say that it is as dialect speakers that they come closest to being free negotiators of meaning. Oral cultures are always rich with their own stories, jokes and songs. Most dialect speakers operate on a continuum and it might be supposed that the powerful pull of standard is the only dynamic force at work. Why then do 'low-prestige' varieties persist, especially as there is strong research evidence to show that speakers of low-prestige varieties rate their own speech as inferior, even unintelligent (Lambert and Tucker, 1972)? Against this there is the work of Giles and his colleagues (Giles and Powesland, 1975). In resisting the treatment of a speaker as a 'sociolinguistic automaton' they assert that moods, feelings and loyalties figure prominently as influences on people's language. Very briefly stated, their ideas are simple in the extreme. When two people talk there is a tendency for their speech to converge on several dimensions (speech rate, volume etc.). But this only holds true in symmetrical cooperative exchange. Where there is hostility and conflict, speakers will diverge. This work suggests that where a group or class identity is threatened in interaction, then solidarity will lead to a defence of the speech which identifies the group. Once again there could be no better example of this process at work than the use of a Creole by black Londoners. It is the more remarkable in that it is a variety which attracts more stigma than any other dialect both from outside and inside the speech community which uses it. The very act of speaking a dialect can be a way of saying something. In James Baldwin's words (1979):

> People evolve a language in order to describe and thus control their circumstances, or in order not to be submerged by a reality that they cannot articulate. (And if they cannot articulate it, they are submerged.)

We can now turn to the educational aspect of spoken language. It has been demonstrated again and again that the classroom paradigm is one which departs radically from extra-school interaction. The teacher speaks for most of the time, controls who may speak and what they may speak and channels all utterances through his or her control. In this way the verbal resources for learning become attenuated and stylized. The work of Barnes (1976) and others has shown how the verbal resources for learning can be released more effectively in groups of pupils working without the teacher. The substance of the claim has rested on verbal interaction as a powerful learning medium. It is necessary in the light of what I have been saying about working-class speech to add that the claim becomes more telling since it is only in small-group interaction that spontaneous vernacular speech can be realized in classroom conditions. I cannot develop the argument fully here but only want to point to the fact that the growing body of work on classroom interaction has not to my knowledge given any attention to this matter. We might add improvised drama to take the discussion still further. And to add the oral culture of the pupils is to go further still. Some groups of teachers have already done so (Rosen, 1979).

I want now to return to the question of literacy. As we have seen, the issue of standard is something of a diversion. However, with certain significant exceptions, the printed language in our culture is standard and has been for a long time, in spite of Burns and the nineteenth-century Lancashire poets. Literacy exists as two complementary activities, but from the point of view of the learner, especially the working-class child, they are two distinct activities. Reading obliges *all of us* to enter a world which is different from our speech. It is there for the meaning to be extracted. Writing demands that we make the meaning. This involves either censoring out or adapting spoken forms. Allowing for this universal difficulty facing all children, there may well be special difficulties for working-class children.

First, there is the question of linguistic distance. The standard-speaking child is in many respects closer to the written form, especially that which he finds in most primers. This may not be critical but it might be more critical for some dialects than others, since the linguistic distance might be greater. But there is another aspect to this, which has not to my knowledge been fully explored. The standard-speaking child experiences receptive literacy before he or she starts to learn to read and write. His or her parents are more likely to be literacy-saturated, and consequently literacy feeds back into their speech. It is an interesting question in its own right to consider not only what literacy does to our consciousness but also what it does to our everyday speech. It is possible that some children do get a flying start in learning to read for those reasons. But that is merely speculative. What is certain is that literacy almost by itself is at the centre of current controversy in education. Many critical questions are brushed aside as it takes the centre of the stage. And the notorious fact is paraded again and again that it is above all working-class children who fail at reading and writing. Usually it is reading rather than writing which is placed at the centre, for there is much more concern about the ability to receive messages than to deliver them.

We should never forget that most working-class children do learn to read and write (as any tube journey would show us). Nevertheless, it should be a concern that many do not or do so at such a low level that there is justified concern about it having more than minimal effectiveness. It has been suggested (Postman, 1973) that reading for working-class children is so organized that it ensures that they become obedient citizens, but of course there is no shortage of reading which does something very different or even would make them disobedient citizens. There may be all sorts of conflicting motives for wanting to teach children to read but I am in no doubt that working-class children have particular cause to need literacy. They need it so that they shall not be manipulated by the printed word; they need it so that they become confident users of the written language for their own purposes; they need it so that they can seek out those books and writings which best speak to their experience and aspirations. Paul Willis (1977), in spite of his devastatingly critical analysis of how schools fail working-class children, concludes:

> … it is a condition for working class development that working class kids do develop certain disciplined skills in expression and symbolic manipulation.

There can be no single explanation for reading failure but it is imperative that we look for ways to eliminate failure amongst working-class children. We have some clear pointers.

First, dialect is not a barrier in learning to read, as Goodman and Buck (1973) demonstrated so clearly:

> The only disadvantage which speakers of low-status dialects suffer in learning to read is imposed by teachers and schools. Rejection of their dialects and educators' confusion of linguistic differences with linguistic deficiency interferes with the natural process by which language is acquired and undermines the linguistic confidence of divergent speakers.

Secondly, Labov suggests that failure in reading is not a rejection of literacy but a rejection of the school culture in which reading (we could add, conceived of in a particular way) plays a central and symbolic role.

Thirdly, the healthiest sign we have had is the involvement of working-class parents in the teaching of reading, including the making of books. This entry into schools could have much deeper and richer consequences for the schooling of their children. It also cuts through the mystique of the reading industry.

But to launch children into literacy is only the beginning of the process which could make them into confident, critical readers and powerful effective writers. For this to happen the whole context of the use of language must be one which confirms and extends their experience, which makes room for their ways of speaking. And that is a long way from what we have in the past conceived of as the well-ordered school dispensing a certain kind of nerveless language, free from risks and obsessed with proprieties.

I have not forgotten Dell Hymes' warning with which I began: 'the maintenance and reproduction of the present social order on the apparently impartial grounds of language'. We have to unveil the impartiality of language, not only for ourselves but also for our pupils. This can mean creating a language curriculum in which the mysteries of linguistic judgment are laid open to the active investigation by the pupils themselves of how language works in our society. The vacuum left by the abandonment of traditional grammar teaching can be filled by inviting working-class pupils to study their own language, the diversity which surrounds them, and the linguistic myths which have helped to keep them in their place. Here at last we can say that the work is in hand; the ILEA English Centre's *The Languages Book* (Raleigh, 1981) [a classroom resource helping pupils and teachers to do these things] is already widely in use in London schools.

I am not so blithe about our schools as to believe that major shifts can occur without struggle and with more than limited possibilities for success, but where there is success, and we can point to it, it becomes more important than its limitations would suggest. For this is the way we begin to work out, not in grand schemes and dreams but in lived experience, an alternative society.

Meanwhile there is much to do. I have had no time to consider the implications of bilingualism in our schools, what it means to be a learner of English as a second language, nor huge changes we need in the literature programme. There is exciting work to be done. Consider narrative in the widest and deepest sense of the word. What do we do with it in schools compared with its role in cognition and its pervasiveness in working-class culture? Consider it as a form of explication, persuasion, and exploration of the possible.

Let me practise what I preach with a borrowed story to set all I have had to say in proportion. I borrow it from Geneva Smitherman's *Black English and the Education of Black Children and Youth* (1981). The story is told by Reginald Wilson.

> I'm standing by the shores of a swiftly flowing river. I hear the cry of a drowning man. So I jump into the river, pull him to the shore and apply artificial respiration. Then just as he begins to breathe, there's another cry for help. So I jump into the river, reach him, pull him to the shore and apply artificial respiration. Then just as he begins to breathe, another cry for help. So back into the river again. Reaching, pulling, applying, breathing and then another yell. Again and again, without end goes the sequence. I'm so busy jumping in, pulling them to the shore and applying artificial respiration that I have no time to see who is upstream pushing them in.

References

Baldwin, J. (1979) 'If Black English isn't a language then tell me what is'. *The New York Times*, 29 July.

Barnes, D. (1976) *From Communication to Curriculum*. Harmondsworth: Penguin.

Bisseret, N. (1979) *Education, Class Language and Ideology*. London: Routledge and Kegan Paul.

The Bullock Committee (1975) *A Language for Life* (the Bullock Report). London: HMSO.

Crystal, D. (1976) *Child Learning, Language and Linguistics*. London: Edward Arnold.

Dittmar, N. (1976) *Sociolinguistics*. London: Edward Arnold.

Edwards, A. (1976) *Language in Culture and Class*. London: Heinemann Educational.

Entwistle, H. (1981) 'Sense and nonsense in radical pedagogy'. *Working Teacher*, 3: 3.

Giles, H. and Powesland, P. (1975) *Speech Style and Social Evaluation*. London: Academic Press.

Goodman, K. and Buck, C. (1973) 'Dialect barriers to reading comprehension revisited'. *The Reading Teacher*, 27 (1).

Gordon, J. (1981) *Verbal Deficit: A critique*. London: Croom Helm.

Halliday, M. (1978) *Language as Social Semiotic*. London: Edward Arnold.

Halliday, M. (1981) Contribution to the symposium 'Mark these Linguists'. *The English Magazine No. 7*. London: ILEA English Centre.

Hammersley, M. (1980) 'Classroom ethnography'. *Educational Analysis*, 2 (2).

Hymes, D. (1979) 'Forward to fundamentals', in O. Garnica and M. King (eds.), *Language, Children and Society*. Oxford: Pergamon Press.

Labov, W. (1972) 'The logic of non-standard English', in P. Goglioli (ed.), *Language and Social Context*. Harmondsworth: Penguin.

Lambert, W. and Tucker, G. (1972) *Bilingual Education of Children: The St. Lambert Experiment*. Rowley, MA: Newbury House.

The Newsom Committee (1963) *Half our Future* (The Newsom Report). London: HMSO.

Olson, D. (1977) 'From utterance to text'. *Harvard Educational Review*, 47 (3).

Open University (1981) *Language in Use (module E263)*. Milton Keynes: Open University.

Postman, N. (1973) 'The politics of reading', in N. Keddie (ed.), *Tinker, Tailor …* Harmondsworth: Penguin.

Raleigh, M. (1981) *The Languages Book*. London: ILEA English Centre.

Rosen, H. (1979) 'Dialect diversity and education', in Venås, Kjell (ed.), *Dialekt og riksspråk i skulen: rapport frå eit nordisk symposium på Lysebu 2–5 April 1979*. Oslo: Nordisk Ministerråd, Sekretariatet for nordisk kulturelt samarbeid.

Smitherman, G. (ed.) (1981) *Black English and the Education of Black Children and Youth*. Detroit: Wayne State University Press.

Thompson. E. (1963) *The Making of the English Working Class*. London: Gollancz.

Trudgill, P. (1975) *Accent, Dialect and the School*. London: Edward Arnold.

Willis, P. (1977) *Learning to Labour*. Farnborough: Saxon House.

The Voices of Communities and Language in Classrooms

A review of Shirley Brice Heath's *Ways with Words*

This is the only example in this collection of a review by Harold of another person's writing. The review appeared in the *Harvard Educational Review,* volume 55, number 4, in November 1985. The reason for its inclusion here is that Harold enormously (but not uncritically – see below) admired Shirley Brice Heath's *Ways with Words* (1983), seeing the book as representing the kind of achievement whose absence in the United Kingdom he often publicly regretted: the careful, detailed, collaborative and broadly positive study of the language of working-class communities. For Harold, the book stood in magnificent contrast to the shelves and shelves of 'studies' which, often on the basis of rapidly collected 'data' or even on the basis of no actual evidence at all, generalized about what particular groups in society could – or, more often in the case of working-class groups – could not do. The review also highlights the educational lessons which Shirley Brice Heath draws from the work of the teachers in the schools in the communities her book describes: Roadville and Trackton in the Piedmont Carolinas.

The reputation of Shirley Brice Heath's book will have marched triumphantly ahead of this review, not, I hasten to add, because of a voguish novelty in its content, not because it is ethnography-on-the-doorstep, but rather because it represents a unique blend of cultural-linguistic analysis with a resolute intention to intervene positively in the world she describes. We have not been short of analyses in the human sciences which purport to offer, and on occasion actually provide, illumination to teachers. Heath's huge endeavour to present the texture and meaning of the daily goings-on and of the talk, as we say, of 'ordinary folk' is complemented by a readiness, notoriously rare, to work alongside teachers in the construction of programmes and practices. These are then informed by an awareness of the language and culture she has come to know as 'ethnographer learning'. For all her expertise she stays a learner, offering the teachers and students ways of understanding but also learning from them.

Trackton and Roadville are the two small communities at the heart of Heath's study. They are, you might say, exotic little places as remote – culturally speaking – from the lives of most contemporary city dwellers or farming communities as the

Trobriand Islands described by Bronislaw Malinowski (1935). Why, then, should we follow with the closest attention the inhabitants' daily doings on porches or in the plaza, and eavesdrop on their chatter? We must admit that we often have a voyeuristic taste for scenes from the lives of those who in space, time, or culture seem distantly bizarre. There are academic studies which pander, wittingly or unwittingly, to these desires in peeping-Tom mainstreamers. Heath's book, however, is never in danger of being one. Heath proposes that (a) there are more Roadvilles and Tracktons than we recognise and know about, even if they are a stone's throw away, and (b) that schools which address themselves to formulating a culture-sensitive curriculum must be, in a sense, ethnographic centres. Her book, then, is no travelogue for the fireside but a sharp challenge to everyone concerned with schooling, teachers in particular.

Heath is a rare figure, an academic who does not see her role as a chastener of the ignorant. We do not have to hear yet again how teachers have got it all wrong, are victims of their cultural prejudices, and are irredeemably class-bound, linguistically naïve, and politically impotent. She operates amongst them as a colleague who shares their dilemmas and strategies. It can be put very simply: she is not seeking the accolades of the academy but intends, when her ethnography is put to work, to help students to learn.

Back then to Roadville and Trackton in the Piedmont Carolinas. We might have called these two tiny collections of houses industrial villages. Almost – for they lack the communal amenities we associate with the term 'village', except for churches, which are shown to play a major role in the people's lives.

Trackton is black and Roadville is white. They are both dependencies of the textile mill, the major source of employment for these working-class people. They are both off the beaten track and some way from Gateway, a small town which Heath sees as the embodiment of mainstream values. Until she takes us fully into their lives, the people and their towns seem fragile, marginalized in a society which has passed them by. Vulnerable encampments, micro-ghettos. It is here – in these towns and in Gateway – that Heath installs herself with the solid advantage that she grew up in Piedmont and has personal acquaintances in both Roadville and Trackton. *And she pursues her work for ten years*: watching infants grow up and enter school and get jobs; witnessing marriages, departures, deaths. Ten years, I say again, from 1969 to 1978.

In an uncompromising prologue, Heath lays out the context and theoretical starting-points of her study. The context was the concern felt by 'black and white teachers, parents, and mill personnel', about communication, the 'effects of the preschool home and community environment on the learning of those language structures and uses which were needed in classrooms and job settings' (p. 2). At this point, let me pause to say that the citation of the 'concern' felt by certain significant people does not make clear whether Heath subscribed to that view or is merely tendering it for the record. I had the same difficulty at certain critical points in the text. The concern of mill owners baffles me, too, for right down at the end of the book we are told that the mill offers 'almost no opportunities to write, few chances to read, and almost no occasions when their uses of oral language are critical for success' (p. 365).

Heath sets out, nevertheless, to satisfy a 'need for a full description of the primary face-to-face interactions of children from community cultures other than [the] mainstream one' (p. 3) which would meet the above concerns and in the end 'help working-class black and white children learn more effectively' (p. 4). At this stage in the text certain terms begin to glow provocatively. I take it that here 'working-class' is being contrasted with 'mainstream'. What then does 'mainstream' imply? Middle-class? There is the suggestion here of a norm. Sure enough, tucked away in the notes to a later chapter is an attempt to face up to the difficulty (p. 391, n. 2), but it raises more questions than it answers: what are the fundamental determinants of class? how do the practices of everyday life relate to them? who are the 'middle class' and to what extent is it a homogeneous stratum? Yet her allegiance is clear and explains how it was that she became, through her collaboration with teachers, an 'associate, colleague, aide, and sometime co-author of curricular materials' (p. 4).

The aspirations are familiar enough – more effective learning by students through deeper understanding of the culture by teachers – yet we know these aspirations have been repeatedly challenged; mainstream school culture has been criticized as promoting shoddy or even pernicious values; it has been contended that schools are class institutions which internally regulate their diet for different clients; it has been said that mainstream culture does not exist, for there is no such homogeneous thing in our society, and so on. The relationship between schools and jobs is never a simple one, and the proposition that certification and high test scores will lead into the Promised Land is a plain and painful delusion. I think Heath knows all this and is content at the outset to pretend a certain innocence. The key lies in her tart and brief rejection of certain bleak, radical views at the very end of the book:

> It is easy to claim that a radical restructuring of society or the system of education is needed for the kind of cultural bridging reported in this book to be large scale and continuous. I have chosen to focus on the information and bridging skills needed for teachers and students as individuals to make changes which were for them radical, and to point to ways these cultural brokers between communities and classrooms can perhaps be the beginning of larger changes.
>
> (p. 369)

Heath is no political innocent: she has read her Bowles and Gintis (1976) (see p. 369, n. 5), and much more besides; and she may be reassured, because at a period of intense attack from the Right on the best hopes of schools, teachers, and students (recorded in a moving section of the epilogue), it no longer looks so radical to join in the attack. (See, for instance, Henry Giroux's *Theory and Resistance in Education* [1983].)

Moreover, Heath makes clear that she has rejected totally the well-known scientific model of 'experiments' and research design. Instead she offers a record of 'the natural flow of community and classroom life over nearly a decade ... actual processes, activities, and attitudes involved in the enculturation of children in Roadville and Trackton' (p. 8). It should be noted that Gateway gets nothing like the 'thick description' which is lovingly devoted to Trackton and Roadville (the ratio is approximately seven to one, the townspeople getting one chapter of twenty-six pages). Perhaps the assumption is that her most likely readers all swim in the mainstream one way or another, or have at least gazed at it long enough from the bank, but the assumption does raise some problems. More of that later. For the moment let us emphasize that she is content to let her case rest in the hands of her readers, who must be the judges of how scientific her work is.

This reviewer-reader's assessment is that, if anything, she might have probed further, in her own chosen manner, certain aspects of the lives of the communities which for me remain shrouded in mystery. But before pursuing that, I have to say without equivocation that I applaud her stance. Whether the research watchdogs bark or not, I cannot imagine anyone honestly concerned with the complex interpretation of community, language, and schooling who would not choose to become caught up in the fates of the infants, young people, and old folk who are brought to life with deep but unsentimental respect in her text. No research training of any type could by itself produce her eye and her voice. These must emerge from values which we are left to deduce less from explicit intellectual propositions than from our perceptions of her conduct. I defy any reader to exorcise Heath from her account, to distinguish the dancer from the dance. The result is not an egocentric display but a subtle refusal to disappear behind the foliage of research lingo. She openly acknowledges a role, openly intervenes, and finally goes for total immersion in a bold collaboration with teachers and students. The 'neutral observer' becomes a sorry figure in comparison. Listen to the infants of Trackton talking to Heath about some wooden blocks she had brought for them to play with and we get a glimpse of how involved they are with her: '"Dese Shannon's blocks?" "You buy dese?" "Can I keep dese?" "What you do wid 'em?" "How'd dat git dere/*pointing to the glue/*?"' (p. 107).

One more insistence: the book represents an unwavering case for looking at the social and cultural context in a particular kind of way rather than constructing an edifice of discrete data ('input', as she says witheringly). We know about context these days. A lot of people vote for it. We know too the acrimonious battles fought in the field of linguistics (compare Halliday [1978] to Chomsky [1979]). It seems almost strange that Heath should have to underline its importance. However, her warm acknowledgement of Dell Hymes as her teacher should remind us that, as he has so persuasively argued, only a profound awareness of who and what our students are and the accommodation of that awareness in the ways schools conduct themselves can take us forward. (See, for example, Hymes 1980 and 1982.) But there are those who bitterly dispute this idea. Here in Britain there are those who argue that it is none of our business. Schools must deliver the national culture, whatever that is, to students, whoever they are. For Heath, culture includes history. Obvious again? Not at all. There are sociological studies, including sociolinguistic studies, which assume that the working class has no history, that it is no more than 'the murmur of societies', 'a multitude of qualified heroes who lose their names and faces while becoming the mobile language of calculations and rationalities' (de Certeau, 1980). Teachers, schools, curricula have histories too. Heath is as good as her word. Her book begins with a history of workers in the mills of Piedmont. Yet this readiness to inscribe history into ethnography creates its own vulnerability.

Rich and intimate as it is, Heath's description cannot be total; telling how it is means telling how it seems through a prism which foregrounds the significant and does not register what seems insignificant. Consider this: 'Any reader who tries to explain the community contrast in this book on the basis of race will miss the central point of the focus on culture as learned behaviour and on language habits as part of that shared learning. Children in Roadville and Trackton came to have different ways of communicating, because their communities had different social legacies' (p. 11).

I was distressed by this evasion, especially as it runs counter to some of the deepest implicit awarenesses of the book. A second reading (my first was almost uncritically rapturous) revealed a persistent refusal to confront the issue of race. I do not trust Heath's apparent *naïveté*; at best it is an astute calculation of political possibilities. Throughout the text we are made aware that Roadville is white and Trackton is black. Why bother? Yes, indeed, communities have different social legacies. A major component of this legacy must be the experience of racism and *its continued existence*. Why has Heath chosen to warn us off? Black English is the expression and negotiation of black experience. Racism does no more than lurk in the shadows of this text raising questions which are not posed by Heath. The historical chapter firmly announces, 'The Civil Rights Movement forced the breaking of the colour barrier on hiring, and blacks began to assume production line jobs in the mills' (p. 27). In the rest of the book there is scarcely a whiff of the continuation of that struggle. Are Trackton people so 'lumpen' that none of their 'ways with words' are affected? One way of cleansing the book of such awkward considerations is to avoid (a) analyzing talk in black and white encounters and (b) probing further the implications of what momentarily pops up in the text. From the description of Gateway, homogeneously 'mainstream', there peeps out the existence of black suburbs. Suddenly we hear someone in Roadville declaring, 'When the niggers (pause) uh, the blacks, you know, started comin' in, I knew that wasn't for me. I wasn't ever gonna work for no nigger' (p. 39). These almost subliminal moments make one aware of a kind of self-denying ordinance or self-censorship operating in the ethnography.

By the same token, Heath's history tells how 'workers began to show signs of an independent and unbiddable spirit when strikes claimed the lives of some of their leaders' (p. 25). Does nothing of that remain in either Roadville or Trackton? Apparently not. In speaking of Trackton, Heath writes that 'they do not themselves take part in any aspect of the political process … ' (p. 62). Of white Roadville no such comment is made, though it seems to apply equally. For them 'the sun shines on the chimneys of the mill' (p. 47). On the job in both Roadville and Trackton, 'workers look for no reasons for the task, nor do they give their opinion of the role of their task in the whole … The topics of their talk rarely include their work' (p. 365). I find it odd, but it is perhaps true. Are they unionized or not? Do they never talk about their working conditions and attempt to change them? Is it all harmony, or resignation? Do blacks and whites occupy the same kinds of posts, and is this never a theme of anyone's conversation? What is the significance of the fact that 'most households [in Trackton] have a double portrait of Coretta and Martin Luther King' (p. 55)?

Gateway's townspeople, we are told, are mainstreamers divided into two groups – 'old-timers' and 'newcomers'. From thousands of miles away I remain skeptical. I cannot believe they are all economically and professionally successful, that there are no sharp divisions and clashes based on ethnicity and class. Nor can I envisage a town of 50,000 inhabitants without its 'lower orders' – garage mechanics, truck drivers, workers in small enterprises, street cleaners, hospital employees, school ancillary staff, minor government employees, and so forth.

I have a feeling that there is a calculated strategy behind this, for, as I have indicated, Heath is highly conscious of these matters and how they have been debated. Yet she treads very warily round them. The reason eludes me. The book is far, far richer ethnographically than, for example, Paul Willis's *Learning to Labour* (1977), but far weaker politically. However, nothing I have said would lead anyone to be in doubt about the unique qualities of this book. Indeed, I suspect that it is constructed in order to provoke my kind of response.

Let us now see how Heath imposed order on what must have been one of the most daunting piles of accumulated material ever to have confronted a researcher at the moment of writing-up. Part 1 begins by taking us into the two communities, sampling their day-to-day living and their notions of 'getting on'. Armed with this awareness, we are led into a presentation of 'learning how to talk' in Trackton and 'teaching how to talk' in Roadville, which simultaneously compares early language development in the two communities and enlarges our view of how life is conducted. It is a credit to Heath that there is no way of summarizing the density of her descriptions. All is alive and enacted. But at carefully selected moments a very legible signpost appears. In black Trackton, for example, 'babies are in the midst of nearly constant human communication … which flows about them' (pp. 74, 75). In white Roadville: 'At both individual and group levels, the belief in and practice of using "the right word" help structure the cognitive patterns which children draw of the world, i.e. what they come to know, and their notion of how to show what they know. Rigidly prescribed oral performance ... is the way to prove learning' (p. 144).

Yet it is the voices, scenes, and episodes which command our attention and stir our thinking. In what for me is the most memorable transcript in the book, Annie Mae of Trackton, 'the community cultural broker', delivers her sociolinguistic analysis and language development curriculum:

> He gotta learn to know 'bout dis world, can't nobody tell 'im. Now just how crazy is dat? White folks uh hear dey kids say sump'n, dey say it back to 'em, dey aks 'em 'gain 'n 'gain 'bout things, like dey 'posed to be born knowin'. You think I kin tell Teegie all he gotta know to get along? He just gotta be keen, keep his eyes open, don't he be sorry. Gotta watch hisself by watchin' other folks. Ain't no use me tellin' 'im: 'Learn dis, learn dat. What's dis? What's dat?' He just gotta learn, gotta know; he see one thing one place one time, he know how it go, see sump'n like it again, maybe it be de same, maybe it won't. He hafta try it out. If he don't he be in real trouble; he get lef out. Gotta keep yo' eyes open, gotta feel to know.
>
> (p. 84)

> Whatcha call it ain't so important as whatcha do with it. That's what things 'n people are for, ain't it?
>
> (p. 112)

I can see myself and others interpreting that text, knowing that in the process I am telling Annie Mae what she means, and in the stiff cadences, our stock-in-trade, losing its nuances and fervour.

Compare the do-it-yourself Headstart program of white Roadville as Peggy sees it.

> I figure it's up to me to give 'im a good start. I reckon there's just some things I know he's gotta learn, you know, what things are, and all that, 'n you just don't happen onto doin' all that right. Now, you take Danny 'n Bobby, we, Betty 'n me, we talk to them kids all the time, like they was grown-up or something, 'n we try to tell 'em bout things, 'n books, 'n we buy those educational toys for 'em.
>
> (pp. 127–128)

Always, Heath by her uncanny ear makes her choices jump from the page at you, and the invitation is to understand before we rush to deliver verdicts or pigeonhole complex utterances in neatly polarized concepts (restricted/elaborated; universalistic/particularistic).

The story continues. We move on to consider oral traditions in Roadville and Trackton and then literate traditions. I shall single out one central aspect of oral traditions – narrative – and let it stand as a paradigm for all that is best in this book. Since I hold that narrative is a touchstone of oral tradition, I believe that Heath's account should become a point of reference for all discussion of spontaneous story telling. (See Rosen, *Stories and Meanings*, 1985 [reprinted here in Part Three].) Moreover, Heath's work on literacy in the community was being cited widely before the appearance of this book. (See, for example, her 'Protean shapes in literacy events' [1982].)

In Roadville there are criteria for story-telling which establish a clear framework, firmly excluding some possibilities and making very clear the principles of inclusion. Stories must be accounts of actual events, free from hyperbole, 'an expression of social unity, a commitment to maintenance of the norms of the church and of the roles within the mill community's life' (p. 150). Above all, they require a moral or summary message. The induction of children into story-telling constitutes a dramatic apprenticeship to this tradition: 'Children in Roadville are not allowed to tell stories, unless an adult announces that something which happened to a child makes a good story and invites a retelling. When children are asked to retell such events, they are expected to tell non-fictive stories which "stick to the truth"' (p. 158).

Fictive stories are lies. Roadville stories are moral episodes, and the monitoring of their narrations ensures that the model is thoroughly learned.

> Sue: Why did you drop your eggs? What did Aunt Sue tell you 'bout climbing on that thing?
>
> Wendy: We better be careful.
>
> Sue: No, 'bout eggs 'n climbing?
>
> Wendy: We better not climb with our eggs, else 'n we'd drop 'em.
>
> (p. 158)

To turn to Trackton's stories is to enter another narrative universe. In Trackton, 'Good story-tellers … may base their stories on an actual event, but they creatively fictionalize the details surrounding the real event, and the outcome of the story may not even resemble what indeed happened' (p. 166).

Stories do not contain didactic highlighting to guide or control moral conduct. The stories must be dramatic, and therefore storytellers frequently resort to dialogue, which in itself opens up a source of mimicry, humour, narrative point. The free expression of feeling generates word-play and word-artistry which Heath is quick to pounce on (see twelve-year-old Terry's tale on p. 181 in which fantasy and reality are inextricably intertwined). She sums up her detailed examination and comparison with a bold contrast: 'In short, for Roadville, Trackton's stories would be lies; for Trackton, Roadville's stories would not even count as stories' (p. 189). All this is laid out beautifully and delicately for us: the participants, the settings, the microdramas of the tellings and their subtexts. To this are added some very detailed inspections of the storyteller's art in both communities, rounded off with a more general and distanced view. However, to demur a little again, there is no attempt to tell us why such divergent cultural practices have arisen, nor to see their roots in the social and economic experience of the narrator. Black and white again?

Part 2 is the knight's move, for it contains an account of the collaboration between the author and the schools, a manoeuvre of high risk not only in its execution but even more in its being recorded here in cold print. The project, as I have indicated, is 'to make accessible to teachers an understanding of the differences in language and culture their students bring to their classrooms' (p. 265) and then to engage in the development of programmes and practices in the light of that understanding. The goal is success in school for everyone. Heath recounts in detail the endeavours of the teachers.

It would be easy to dismiss much of what the teachers do as familiar curriculum practice – familiar, that is, to anyone conversant with the curriculum reforms of the last twenty years: for example, what came to be regarded as 'good practice' before the current fierce dismantling process got under way. Mrs. Gardner, having been allocated a class of nineteen black first-grade students designated potential failures, opens up her classroom and engages in her now-despised 'activity methods'. Her children tell stories and there is lots of talk. That old standby, the grocery store, is set up in another class. In a fifth-grade science class, consisting again of black boys with a low reading level, an ethnographic project on local agricultural practices is mounted, involving the youngsters in work in the community.

To say we've heard all this before is to miss the point. It is the nature and consequences of the process of change which are significant, and if they include reinventing the wheel (a much maligned practice!), so be it. The contrast is between, on the one hand, teachers and students actively engaged in changing their ways of learning and teaching and, on the other, uniform programmes emanating from above which presume that teachers are mere docile transmitters and that learners are uniform and culture-free in their needs. I feel it both irrelevant and impertinent, therefore, to scrutinize closely the language teaching described in this section. In any case, there are better things to do than snigger at one teacher's enthusiasm for topic sentences or another's insistence on 'a school-accepted format' (p. 320) for written work. But, of course, this puts Heath in a difficult position. She too rejects the role of judge and jury, but her respect for the teachers and children leaves us to guess, though not without clues and nudging, where her preferences lie. The science-cum-ethnography project is described with scarcely concealed delight, but it includes amongst its goals the mastery of 'the language of science' and making 'acceptable scientific statements' (p. 325). It would appear that this includes 'avoid telling stories about their knowledge: be able to discuss an item or event for its own sake, not in terms of their direct experiences with it' (p. 325). Do those suspect goals receive Heath's imprimatur? I give her the benefit of the doubt, for she must know the philosophical and linguistic debate on these matters. I never understand what it means to do something for 'its own sake'. And what has Heath been doing for the previous three hundred pages but telling stories about her knowledge, and not for their own sake but for ours?

Picking her way judiciously through the innovations, Heath makes very clear that the teachers did not see themselves as launching basic changes in content, nor abandoning established classroom methods (basal readers, for example). The criteria for 'school success' in the end remain unchanged, and the core of mainstream values is not tampered with: 'students learned to share the goals and methods of the classroom' (p. 340). There is not a hint that black and white students in the Carolinas studying in the same classrooms might raise some tricky issues in history and social studies and in the job-getting aspects of some of their work. What Heath has chosen to do is to present all that seems most positive in the teachers' work and to imply that ethnicity did not affect the basic processes. Yet, the introduction of teachers – and, later, students – to ethnographic ways of studying surreptitiously their own and their community's practices does in fact erode the old curriculum. New *ways* of learning constitute new learning. How else can one begin? As Heath observes, 'Students now provided information for the teacher to question – the reverse of the usual classroom practice of the teacher presenting the information and questioning students on their knowledge' (p. 342). Furthermore, she offers: 'Critical in the thinking of these teachers was that their approach was not a remedial one designed for poor learners. Instead, they felt that the attention given to different ways of talking and knowing, and the manipulation of contexts and language benefited all students' (p. 355).

The principles do not in themselves constitute a complete apparatus for changing the role of language in the curriculum, but they have a huge potential if pushed to their logical conclusion. They could be extended into a critical examination of the language of textbooks or the ways in which communities are linked to and shaped by influential forces in society, including the ways in which language is used in the media, by politicians and others, to affect daily lives. Finally, there is the question of how Roadville and Trackton students are to develop their own voices so that they can articulate a critical view of society and act more powerfully in it. Ethnography cannot by itself achieve these ends. To assert this is not to diminish the courageous work of the teachers; it is only to sketch out its essentially initiatory character and its vulnerability.

And vulnerable it proved to be. In a sad but all too familiar phrase, we learn that 'in the Piedmont of today, the methods used by these teachers have all but disappeared' (p. 356). The bureaucracy of tests has taken over and, as one teacher says, 'there's no joy left in teaching now' (p. 359). This defeat is known on both sides of the Atlantic. To reverse it requires acting outside the classroom.

Heath writes in her last pages of 'a recognition and a drive to use language as a source of power', but an indication of limits she sets herself is registered in the way that the sentence tails off into a circumscribed notion of power and its source: 'for access to and maintenance of expanded types and places of work' (p. 363). The source of the power is much more than the job market.

In the end, teachers can defend successfully the enclaves they have constructed only if they have won the parents and community to their methods and can invoke their support in sustaining them. And those are 'ways with words' which have to be learned too. They constitute the language of political participation. If all of us do not learn this way with words, we shall go on placing wreaths on the tombstones of projects all over the world, overcome with sadness and impotence.

Whatever we do or fail to do in resisting the conversion of our schools into brutally frank machines for social control, in the end thousands of teachers must encounter millions of students daily in classrooms. Heath's book suggests to us a new way of looking at that encounter. Ethnographers are the heroes of her text. There are other kinds of heroes whom we need to acknowledge, but that should not prevent us from saluting the ethnographers – and Shirley Brice Heath in particular.

References

Bowles, S. and Gintis, H. (1976) *Schooling in Capitalist America: Educational reform and the contradictions of economic life*. New York: Basic Books.

de Certeau, M. (1980) 'On the oppositional practices of everyday life'. *Social Text*, 1.

Chomsky, N. (1979) *Language and Responsibility*. Brighton: Harvester Press.

Giroux, H. (1983) *Theory and Resistance in Education*. Portsmouth, NH: Heinemann.

Halliday. M. (1978) *Language as Social Semiotic*. London: Edward Arnold.

Heath, S. (1982) 'Protean shapes in literacy events', in D. Tannen (ed.), *Spoken and Written Language: Exploring orality and literacy*. Norwood, NJ: Ablex.

Heath, S. (1983) *Ways with Words*. Cambridge: Cambridge University Press.

Hymes, D. (1980) *Language in Education: Ethnolinguistic essays*. Washington, DC: Center for Applied Linguistics.

Hymes, D. (1982) *Ethnolinguistic Study of Classroom Discourse. Final report to the National Institute for Education*. Philadelphia: University of Pennsylvania Graduate School of Education.

Malinowski, B. (1935) *Coral Gardens and their Magic, vol. 2*. London: Allen and Unwin.

Rosen, H. (1985) *Stories and Meanings*. Sheffield: National Association for the Teaching of English (and reprinted here).

Willis, P. (1977) *Learning to Labour*. New York: Columbia University Press.

Struck by a Particular Gap

In 1984, Her Majesty's Inspectorate published a slim booklet called *English from 5 to 16*. Unexceptionably, the booklet proposed that teachers should be promoting pupils' development as speakers and listeners, readers and writers. It then said that teachers should 'teach pupils about language, so that they achieve a working knowledge of its structure and of the variety of ways in which meaning is made, so that they have a vocabulary for discussing it, so that they can use it with greater awareness and because it is interesting.' (Her Majesty's Inspectorate, 1984, p. 3)

From today's perspective, this proposal, quoted in isolation from the rest of the booklet, sounds perfectly reasonable. But at the time many English teachers perceived an underlying meaning beneath the surface code. Reading the booklet as a whole, weighing up what its authors might really have in mind as the more important things to teach pupils about language, and putting these thoughts next to worries about other aspects of the booklet (the detail in its proposals for age-related objectives for pupils at 7, 11 and 16, and its narrow, muddled and often backward-looking collection of statements about what a language or English curriculum should contain), readers came to the conclusion that the booklet was once again proposing something which had been vigorously debated for the previous 20 years, and rejected: the tempting idea that learners, in order to get better at using an element of their first language, need a set of rules, definitions and distinctions about that element in advance.

Decoded, the part of *English from 5 to 16* quoted above was returning to a dispute over whether English teachers needed to reinstate old-fashioned grammar teaching as a major element of the curriculum. Overwhelmingly, those who wrote down their responses to the booklet and sent them in to HMI said, 'No.'

When HMI published *English from 5 to 16: the Responses to Curriculum Matters 1* in 1986, it acknowledged the degree of dissent from the original booklet on this and other topics. It suggested setting up an enquiry, 'with the ultimate object of drawing up recommendations as to what might be taught [about language] to intending teachers, to those in post and to pupils in schools.' (Her Majesty's Inspectorate, 1986, p. 40)

The government accepted the idea of an enquiry, and convened the Kingman Committee to discuss the matter. While the Committee was debating, Harold wrote the introductory article to a volume entitled *Learning Me Your Language*, edited by Michael Jones and Alastair West. It was published in 1988, the same year as the Kingman Report. As will be seen, Harold was highly critical of the government's real motive in setting up the Kingman Committee, the qualifications of those chosen to form its membership, and its notion of 'a model' – a single, unambiguous paradigm – of the English language, which teachers would be invited, and perhaps required, to accept.

> *I am working towards national agreement on the aims and objectives of English teaching in schools in order to improve standards, but I have been struck by a particular gap. Pupils need to know about the workings of the English language if they are to use it effectively.*
> Kenneth Baker, Secretary of State for Education and Science
>
> (DES press release, 16.1.87)

Let us disregard the cynical laughter back there triggered by the idea that Kenneth Baker is interested in working towards national agreement. We must not be diverted by unpleasant memories of how teachers woke up one morning to discover that Mr Baker had been struck by the particular idea of taking away teachers' negotiating rights. We should by now be so inured to attacks upon teachers and schools in the public system that we should have become impervious to shock or surprise. We have come to expect the worst. Indeed we may have cajoled ourselves into believing that we had seen the worst. The Secretary of State has shown us that the unthinkable is being thought and said and may soon be done. Yet when the Kingman Committee was set up and we learned of its terms of reference and its bizarre composition, we still found reserves of incredulity and dismay. There will be more to come unless we find ways in print, in talk and in the classroom to resist, counter and challenge. This book is one such effort.

The terms of reference and official pronouncements about the committee revealed a significant change from the discourse of *English from 5 to 16: Responses to Curriculum Matters 1* (Her Majesty's Inspectorate, 1986).

> The responses to *English from 5 to 16* [Her Majesty's Inspectorate, 1984] … make clear that a prerequisite to a national policy statement about the teaching of English is agreement about what all our children should be taught about the English language and how it works. [The assumption is made] that it is possible for the profession to agree broad categories of language experience which should be offered to pupils.

Agreement, agreement? More of that later and of *English from 5 to 16*. Meanwhile we should all take note that the Kingman Committee did not come into being as a result of an irresistible popular demand. It did not emerge from a ferment of discussion, it was not a response to a profession crying out for a definitive and authoritative statement from a collection of clandestinely nominated individuals and its topic was not selected for priority after a thorough canvass.

Let us take a look at the committee itself. It is not, of course, my intention to deal in personalities. My guess is that it would be a pleasure to sit down with most of the members of the committee and discuss the teaching of English, the English language and language more generally. But wearing their Kingman hats they must accept that they have been caught up in a political process. Mr Kenneth Baker tells us 'there is disquiet'. But we do not see committees of inquiry set up every time a Secretary of State notices there is disquiet. Politicians are in business to create disquiet where none exists, to amplify disquiet when it suits their political purposes and to ignore disquiet, however vociferous, when it is critical of their policies. Committees of inquiry are the continuation of politics by other means.

However, time was when it was necessary that such committees should establish their credibility by some semblance of a comprehensive representation of differing standpoints including those known to be opposed to the very thinking which led to their formation. Compare Kingman to Bullock and Swann. The government is not noted for its readiness to consult with those who do not toe the line. Professor Randolph Quirk, who those in the know confidently predicted would head the committee, went into print to declare his views. He dropped out of the running in spite of his acknowledged eminence in linguistic scholarship and his interest in language education. We can leave aside the virtues of those who finally survived what must have been a fascinating screening process. Who were the delicately tuned folk at the DES who were able to declare of some contenders, 'Lo! with a spot I damn him thus'? The result was a committee which left people agape with incredulity. The collective credentials of the members revealed shocking and obvious omissions. Had you asked those who played an active part in the field of English teaching, they would have come up with a list of those who were *not* asked. The list of members constitutes a calculated insult to the English teaching fraternity. There are reasons to believe that there are members of Her Majesty's Inspectorate who were unhappy with the final outcome, but they are suspect anyway, coming under hostile scrutiny for their stubborn refusal to act as the ideological arm of the party in power.

In sum, we are entitled to ask whether the committee contains a single member who can lay claim to having made a major contribution to the theory and practice of English teaching in the last quarter of a century. You will, however, find in this volume contributors who would easily satisfy that criterion and there are others not represented here. The committee does not contain anyone who can speak with the authority of recent experience and recognised achievement in the teaching of English in the comprehensive school, especially in inner cities. Ethnic minorities are not represented by those who have direct experience of multicultural education and linguistic diversity and are known for their creative contribution. It must have taken very adroit fixing to have by-passed so many obvious candidates. Why should English teachers respect the findings of such a rigged committee and embrace with enthusiasm its exhortations? It may be said in reply that the committee, as is customary, has called for written evidence from anyone who cares to respond. There are three examples of such responses in this book from organisations which were under an obligation to express the collective opinion of their members. We do not know what notice will be taken of their contributions, though I think it unlikely they will be treated seriously.

We can deduce that there was a certain sensitivity and (who knows?) bad conscience being felt in certain quarters. After all, criticisms and hostility were being expressed very early on and we should take some encouragement from the fact that it evoked a conciliatory gesture. It justifies the publication of this book. Out of the blue, in addition to the general invitation for the submission of written evidence, certain selected individuals were written to in these terms:

> The Committee recently issued a general invitation for written evidence from anyone with views on the teaching of English in schools. I am writing to you now, in recognition of the distinguished contribution you have made to English teaching, to invite you to submit written evidence, relevant to the terms of reference.

I do not know who else received this flattering invitation but I certainly did. I went through some prolonged and somewhat absurd agonizing about how to respond. It was not, to be sure, a matter of doubt about what I wanted to say but quite simply whether the very act of writing to a committee whose authority I did not recognise would be a kind of betrayal. It was about this time that the plan for this book emerged from the energetic and competent activities of Michael Jones and Alastair West. That settled it. All doubts banished, I wrote the following reply.

Dear Peter Gannon

Thank you for your invitation to me to submit my views to the Kingman Committee. I am afraid I cannot accept it in spite of my great interest in the matters it is discussing. The committee was set up in a political context by a government with clear political and educational intentions in mind. That would not have mattered if the constitution of the committee itself had not made it abundantly clear that the intention was to keep off the committee anyone who had made a major contribution to the teaching of English and, more generally, language education over the last quarter of a century or more. The list of members reads like a calculated insult and a planned attempt to exclude the vigorous and sustained presentation of certain points of view. It hardly meets the case at this very late stage in the day to invite submissions from those who have made, as you write, 'an outstanding contribution'. Warm invitations of this kind confer no power whatsoever on those invited and their contribution can be completely ignored. You must surely be aware that you are inviting an obvious question. If these people have made such an outstanding contribution, why is it that not one of them is on the committee? Who struck them off the original lists and why? Or, if they were not on the original lists, there is an even more damning question to be asked.

Lest this letter be misinterpreted, I must make it clear that this is not a personal grievance. I am making a qualitative judgement about the committee.

I imagine your letter is a kind of 'amende honorable' in the face of many criticisms similar to my own which must have reached you. It will not serve. I have no knowledge of how any submission by me might be treated but I do have some unhappy past experience of the use of selective citation of my work. I do not want to risk being singled out in that way, however slight the risk. I much prefer to present my views, unfiltered, in a public forum and eventually in print.

I am sorry if this letter seems to you churlish and uncooperative. It is in fact a very moderated expression of the dismay I felt when I first read of the committee and its terms of reference. Since that time I have had the opportunity to learn that many colleagues of all kinds share that dismay.

I should be grateful if you would put this letter before your committee to keep the records straight.

Yours sincerely

Let me return to the context of the Kingman Committee's appearance. In the broadest terms I see it as one small tactical manoeuvre in the general strategy of bringing the teaching profession to heel, intimidating dissentient voices and closing down the options. To carry out its policy the government needs compliance, however sullen and grudging, by way of centralised control. There are two arms to this strategy: the first is brutal diktat, like the abolition of teachers' negotiating rights or the 'opting out' policy for schools; the second is the much more difficult business of trying to control what goes on in classrooms. Enter the Kingman Committee. The preparatory work had been done by *English from 5 to 16*, which sent up the signals with its notorious list of objectives. People reading this could not believe their eyes. They could not believe that in the 1980s it could be seriously proposed that children should be taught a handful of grammatical terms. Coming from any other source it would have been drowned in hoots of derision. I say nothing of the other objectives, which attracted their share of critical onslaught. But we had been warned. It does not matter whether what is being promoted is an obsolete and discredited practice or an up-to-the-minute 'model' of sentence structure from the linguistic manuals. The intention remains to stir up the feeling amongst the susceptible that English teachers have sold out and left their pupils in the mire of ignorance about how language works. Not like those golden days when school leavers could happily discuss your noun clauses in apposition or spot an example of prolepsis. For grammar and definitions speak, in this context, with the voice of authority, remote and invisible. Mysterious and impenetrable forces have worked out how it should be with words.

This is not to say that direct and conscious attention to language should not figure in the language curriculum in schools in various ways, always bearing in mind that it should take the form of active exploration and critical investigation. You would be hard put to it to discover from Mr Baker's 'disquiet' at the 'particular gap' which has come to his attention, that teachers, in collaboration with linguists, have for years been working on just this question: there have been conferences and publications. The National Congress for Languages in Education, for example, has brought together the very diverse activities in schools and colleges in *Language Awareness* (Donmall, 1985). I find no hint there of a search for a model of the English Language.

English from 5 to 16: Responses to Curriculum Matters 1 is a document which would make interesting study for an advanced course in language awareness. Presumably it is on the Kingman Committee's reading list. Despite some of its extraordinary contortions in its effort both to accommodate criticisms and justify the original *English from 5 to 16*, it showed beyond doubt the importance of sustained and informed challenge to official initiatives. The objectives were rewritten in the light of the critical comments and some criticisms were frankly accepted:

> … for most readers the objectives were misaligned and … accord might be possible with substantially realigned objectives cast in broader terms.
>
> (p. 18, para. 45)

Lovely words, 'misaligned' and 'realigned'! There was more realignment than this, on the subject of the 'age-related nature of the objectives', for instance. The force of many criticisms was acknowledged and accordingly

> … expectations might be redrawn in more general terms to accommodate the great diversity of children's abilities and rates of progress, as emphasised by respondents, while still providing teachers with indicators as to progression.
>
> (pp. 8 and 9, para. 22)

Now compare that to the Kingman Committee's terms of reference:

> To recommend what, in general terms, pupils need to know about how the English language works and in consequence what they should have been taught, and be expected to understand, on the workings of the language, at age 7, 11 and 16.

Apart from the vacuous reappearance of 'in general terms', the conciliatory tone of *Responses* is abandoned. For if the great diversity of children – not simply difference of ability – is to be accommodated and catered for creatively, what can be usefully said about what they can be expected to understand at specific ages apart from a few recommendations so vague as to be useless? More ominous by far is that, since the government has declared its intention of testing children at 7, 11 and 14 (diversity or no diversity), the Kingman Committee may be preparing, unwittingly perhaps, a blueprint for a set of gruesome tests.

The longest paragraph of *Responses* (p. 19, para. 45) is devoted to knowledge about language. Not a word is said about this in the objectives. Perhaps the Inspectorate knew what was afoot better than the rest of us. We should have read that paragraph with every ounce of our hermeneutic skill. We would certainly have concluded that there was no need for a few more conciliatory objectives since something much more portentous was on its way. Read this passage in the light of what happened subsequently:

> It may be that a concentrated and thorough public discussion of the issues is needed; *perhaps even a national inquiry* [my italics] is required to focus opinion and guide policy formation about what needs to be known by teachers and pupils.

(p. 19 para. 45)

All credit to the Inspectors for suggesting that what is needed is 'concentrated and thorough public discussion'. Now we do know a thing or two about how to conduct thorough public discussion. We know about the usefulness of a preliminary document, about kinds of conferences which promote full interchange, about the availability of teachers' centres, professional associations, in-service programmes, staffroom meetings and so on. No vetted audiences, no closed doors, no monologues, no calculated leaks, winks and nods. We do not lack the basic expertise in how to give a democratic airing to controversial questions in order 'to guide policy formation'. There are euphemisms and evasions here. What exactly is a national inquiry? And what's national about it? Look at the Kingman Committee and ask yourself in what sense it can be called national and ask further how it has earned the right to pronounce and guide policy. Many of its members could be seen as raw apprentices who will be relying on various forms of documentation to learn hastily the rudiments of the subject – (knowledge about language) – sometimes from those who have been effectively barred from participating in the debate. To submit evidence or offer a written outline of a standpoint is worlds away from the active role of participant in the day-to-day give and take of ideas and the active process of collectively shaping a final outcome. Expert witnesses have been effectively marginalised. They can be ignored or selectively quoted and at the same time be used to give legitimacy to a venture known to be shaky at the outset.

All the signs are that there is muddle and mystery about what the Kingman Committee will actually be talking about. The actual terms of reference are clear and concise. The focus is exactly that set out in the *Responses,* i.e. what should be taught about language. The task, sharply circumscribed even through the intention of setting out 'a model of the English language', will inevitably take the committee into some very deep and perilous waters. However, a press release from the DES on 18th February 1987 at a stroke seemed to broaden the inquiry to include absolutely everything which teachers of English would consider their province:

> Sir John Kingman said today the Committee's terms of reference gave broad indications of the issues to which evidence should relate, but it would be useful to receive comment on the following specific matters:
>
>> the needs of society in present day England as they relate to individuals' ability to communicate in speech and in writing;
>>
>> the needs of individuals, as they relate to skills of literacy and communication generally, in a rapidly changing world;
>>
>> the training – both initial and in-service – of this country's teachers in relation to those needs;
>>
>> English language teaching in primary, middle years and secondary phases of schooling.
>
> Sir John said the Committee would consider the evidence and might, at a later date, decide to invite oral evidence on the basis of the written material submitted.

It seems as though Sir John Kingman is proposing, in the short time available to him, to go over the ground covered by the Bullock Report, to which he makes no reference whatsoever. Is this a covert rejection of the Bullock Report? No one has enlightened us. It is difficult to take at its face value the intention to explore the specific matters listed by Sir John. One can only surmise that in its early days the committee members were fidgeting uneasily at the thought of having to isolate 'knowledge about language' from the practice of English teaching in general. Good for them, if that is indeed so. I hope it does not slow them down too much; theirs will be a very hurried excursion across the terrain. Sir John has also told us that there will be visits to schools and colleges. They will be asking a question or two, I have no doubt. They might ask, but I doubt whether they will, what English teachers regard as the most burning issues in English teaching today. They would come away with a long list, but in the substratum would be an abiding concern with the relationship of language to the culture of the students and the culture of the school, though only a minority would put it in those terms. I am confident that of all the issues and problems confronting teachers, knowledge about language, as construed in the terms of reference, would not come very high on the list, thought it would certainly be there. How did it achieve top priority?

Language, as everyone keeps telling us these days, cannot be understood without relating use to context. And that must be true of learning about language too. It is a fatuous exercise to lay down a syllabus for all children irrespective of who they are, the state of affairs in a given school, the rest of the curriculum and the culture(s) in the community from which the children come. The classrooms I know well, in which many of the pupils are bilingual and often bi-literate, offer a different range of possibilities from those which are completely monolingual. Any convincing language awareness programme must grow out of the linguistic resources available in the classroom, which are never meagre but always different. All the illusions of a national curriculum haunt the aspiration of laying down in advance what all pupils need to know about language. That is why all the work already done on language awareness is notable for the diversity of courses it has already generated.

The record is impressive and this is no place to record the wealth of materials already available. I have already referred to the volume brought out by the National Congress for Languages in Education (Donmall, 1985). It contains three appendices: a classified bibliography, a map of language awareness activities and a list of schools carrying out language awareness work. So much for Mr Baker's gap-spotting. What the documentation reveals is that courses have started with different goals, under different auspices and are aimed at different groups of pupils. The list of schools is classified into broad categories.

1. A course for 11- to 13-year-olds, to create awareness of and interest in 'language' as a preparation for foreign language learning.
2. A language awareness or linguistics element in Humanities or English for 11- to 13-year-olds.
3. A course in language development of children as part of a child-care, preparation-for-parenthood and social-studies course in fourth or fifth years [today's Years 10 and 11].
4. Introduction to linguistics in the sixth form (possibly as part of General Studies).

No doubt all this will find its way to the Kingman Committee. When it does it will have to resolve a question which has not arisen so far: why language awareness should be a matter for English teachers alone. Some of the best initiatives have grown out of a collaboration amongst those with a designated commitment to language (English as mother tongue, English as a second language, languages other than English, both 'foreign' and 'community' languages) and also embraced teachers of history, geography, social studies, etc. Even the fertile brain of Mr Kenneth Baker is unlikely to come up with a proposal for a committee of inquiry into every branch of the curriculum that might engage in language study. Those who want a tidy curriculum laid out in an operator's manual, should have their attention drawn to Professor Sinclair's contribution to the NCLE volume:

> Language awareness is very much a 'grass roots' movement. ... I believe that the creative untidiness of the actual content of language awareness courses is in fact unrelated to the fuzziness of the cover term. They have different origins and it is a case of a useful concept happily meeting up with a spontaneous school-based perception of a need ... Language awareness courses arise in different schools for different reasons, are devised by different groups and are applied at different stages to different pupils in pursuit of different objectives. There is nothing in the day-to-day teaching that one can perceive as common to all.

> (p. 33)

I shall not go through the committee's terms of reference one by one. There is enough comment both explicit and implicit in the papers which we have gathered together in this book. I want rather to take a look at the opening fanfare which establishes the melody for all that follows.

> (To recommend) a model of the English language, whether spoken or written.

Not, we see, a model of language. A model for the English language only leaves high and dry the hopes of those of us who have seen language-awareness programmes as rooted in linguistic diversity, starting with the linguistic diversity of this country. The history of linguistics is littered with attempts to create one definitive model of language which would not only account for all languages but would also capture every aspect of language, no matter how rare or deviant. Saussure left us with an unfortunate legacy, for the emphasis of his model dispensed with everything that threatened good order and discipline. It was *language* on which we needed to concentrate; it was governed by an invisible social contract, an agreement to abide by the rule system of a language frozen at a given moment in time. All the rest was set aside as a matter of individual psychology which accounted for what people actually said, the way they spoke to one another, why they said this rather than that.

We have come a long way since then. As early as 1929, Volosinov (1973) launched an all-out assault on Saussure's ideas, demonstrating that actual living speech was essentially a social rather than psychological matter. So powerful was the influence of Saussure and other structuralists that we had to wait until the 1960s for all kinds of sociolinguists to insist that highly abstract models cannot account for systematic relationships between social structure and language structure. We owe a great debt to Halliday (1978) for elaborating and making concrete that generalisation. But we can see today that students of language have gone a stage further. They are insisting that language is so complex, that there are so many of the features which can be studied from different points of view, that no one model can hope to produce a scheme which will encompass all possibilities. Language resists being imprisoned in a model. Halliday himself, who has produced a complex 'map' (*ibid.*, p. 69) which the Kingman Committee may well find tempting, writes in a recent work (Halliday, 1985):

> It is unlikely that any one account will be appropriate for all purposes. A theory is a means of action and there are many different kinds of action one may want to take involving language. Some years ago one of the speakers at a conference began his paper with the words, 'I take it for granted that the goal of linguistics is to characterise the difference between the human brain and that of an animal'. That this should be one of a hundred goals one might readily accept; but that this – or anything else – should be 'the' goal of linguistics is hard to take seriously.
>
> (p. xxix)

Yet the Kingman Committee has been set the task of taking seriously that very goal. And Halliday is no lone figure. Wunderlich, the German linguist, offers a similar point of view.

> There are so many aspects to human language and their manifestations, their individual and social functions, their psychic and physical qualities, their acquisition and history, that it is difficult, if not hopeless, to establish connections between all of them.
>
> (Wunderlich, 1979)

The tradition emerging from Saussure set out with high optimism to reduce language to 'well-ordered', rule-governed structures and decades of assiduous industry were devoted to this end. But that kind of optimism is evaporating. Even the euphoria generated by Chomsky's concentration on syntactic structures is, as Bruner has noted, now dissipated. Linguists nowadays are much more disposed to take a modest view of their activities. Some spotted the dangers earlier than others. Hockett, in 1968, renouncing his earlier Chomskyan stance, argued that the trouble with orderly models was that they did not allow for disorderly aspects of language.

> I now believe that any approximation we can achieve on the assumption that language is well-defined is obtained by leaving out just those

properties of language that are most important. For at bottom the power and productivity of language – our casual ability to say new things – would seem to stem exactly from the fact that languages are not well-defined, but merely characterized by degrees and kinds of stability.

This position would elicit ready applause from those teachers of English who value in their pupils their 'casual ability to say new things' and who are rightly suspicious of those who want to foist on them a model which bails out the baby with the bathwater. Many of them know how long it took linguists to raise their eyes above the sentence level. For English teachers are centrally concerned with total texts, spoken or written, written composition, oral 'literature'. They know that the questions which come tumbling out are frequently ones which linguists would not claim to answer. A class is looking at or listening to a story:

- How do we know it is a story?
- What connection does it have with other stories? Other non-narrative texts?
- Does it have culture-specific features?
- What kind of cognitive processes enable us to produce and comprehend stories?
- Can we, do we, rely solely on the text in order to grasp its meaning?
- What are the differences between telling and writing a story? What are the features of oral narrative performance?
- How do events become transformed when they are narrated? Or, if you will, how does *histoire* become *récit*?
- Is there a special class of stories which we call literature? What are the criteria?
- If we know the author (fellow-student?) does that make a difference?
- What's a pseudo-author? A pseudo-audience?
- Do we accept that there is such a thing as a 'well-formed' story which, like the linguists' well-formed sentence, must conform to certain rules?
- How do we account for the universality of narrative? Is narrative transcultural, as Roland Barthes claimed?
- What do people mean when they say a story is racist or sexist?
- How do we hear the silences in stories?

And much, much more. It is just because, as we engage with language in the classroom, we become aware of a proliferation of possibilities and questions to which the answers must remain speculative. If we want help we must look to many different sources. All the indications are that the Kingman Committee will look for a model drawn from linguistics. If it did not look elsewhere that would be a mistake. For linguists have, in spite of imperial flourishes, no monopoly of language scholarship. We have millennia of the study of rhetoric which always looked at language in action and still does.

There is still no one who can hold a candle to that greatest of contemporary rhetoricians, Kenneth Burke (1950 and 1969). In semiotics and literary theory,

Harold Rosen

questions of language are always at the forefront. Bakhtin's remarkable essay 'Discourse in the novel' (1981) reaches into basic questions of language and offers a theoretical base for considering conformity and deviance in language, showing them both to be always there in language use. It was Wolfgang Iser (1978), a literary theorist, who offered us understanding of how a reader makes sense of a literary text. Speech act theory came from philosophers. Discourse analysis is seen by its most eminent exponent, Van Dijk (1985), as *par excellence* an interdisciplinary study. Readers can no doubt show how some of their profound insights into language came from diverse and surprising sources. Linguists, some of them at least, are much more ready now to acknowledge the need to collaborate with scholars in other fields and to abandon that peculiarly nasty form of academic terrorism which suggested that other perspectives were non-scientific and irrelevant. For us by contrast anything which helps us understand will be welcomed.

The brief excursion I have just made is intended to alert us to the danger of reductive models of language, which, though they may have strengths, are too limiting for our purposes. We can only hope that the Kingman Committee will not be too easily seduced and that some members will put on the table some of the work I have done no more than signpost. Language is not a well-oiled machine whose dictates we follow like zombies. It is a human creation shot through with conflict and tension. It is both a potential liberator and also what Frederic Jameson called a prison-house. Committees of inquiry must of necessity strive to be above the political battle. We cannot and must not. Jerome Bruner is uncompromising. In his recent book, *Actual Minds, Possible Worlds* (1986), he writes:

> I do not believe for one minute that one can teach even mathematics or physics without transmitting a sense of stance towards nature and the use of the mind ... the idea that any humanistic subject can be taught without revealing one's stance towards matters of human pith and substance is, of course, nonsense.

(p. 128)

I hope by now that the oh-so-eminently-reasonable first term of reference begins to look at least problematic, if not a kind of nonsense. I fear the Greeks bearing a model of language.

People have been saying to me, 'All the same, the committee may come up with some interesting stuff. You might, who knows, find yourself agreeing with it.' Quite true. It has been my intention to show that we must act through an interpretation of very sparse evidence. We must construct a subtext. We should certainly not sit on our hands and wait, hoping for the best. We have been given very little cause for optimism. Moreover, we should do our best to disseminate those views which are unlikely to find expression and support in the Kingman Committee. Should it turn out that a report appears which will have us cheering wildly or merely sighing with relief, I am persuaded that will be because even prior to this publication we have created a climate in which no less was possible. If our most pessimistic anticipations are fulfilled, then we need a book like this one (and others) for people to turn to, take heart from and learn in the fraught days which will follow. We are taking our stand, addressing the precise moment but in a form more durable than the hullabaloo around the committee. We reject marching orders from an authority without title.

A few words about this book as a whole. Needless to say it does not cover all the ground. There was no time for that. Nevertheless, the range of viewpoints and the different themes of these papers stand solidly at the heart of current English teaching. They will show a sturdy tradition, grounded in theory and forged in years of practice, almost all of it emerging in the first place from the base, the classroom. It was created by teachers who never needed to wait for the tablets from the mountain. Even a cursory reading will reveal they are not a monolithic group reiterating compulsively a party line. Readers will be quick to see differences of emphasis and divergences but they will also see the strength of commonly held principles. It was never our intention that our contributors should constitute a harmonious chorus. I have no doubt that my own introductory piece would not command the unconditional approval of the other contributors, though I hope they will not feel I have let them down. The breadth and variety of the contributions should demonstrate that those who have misgivings about the Kingman Committee are not a clique of malcontents to be airily dismissed by a suitable label, but a set of teachers who have earned their standing in the profession the hard way. But this is not a negative and destructive text. It is not limited to critique. It also sets out an exciting set of possibilities and achievements.

I do not believe teachers will jump to it because O'Grady says. They will not start working to the Kingman rule book the moment it arrives. They are much too canny for that. They will watch warily and manage things accordingly. Change in the classroom is a slow process and the wreckage of grand new schemes is strewn about the field or crammed into the darkest areas of stock rooms. To win assent for innovation means appealing to teachers' intellect and imagination and never flying in the face of their experience and commitment. Ruefully thumbing through tattered books, they will want to know what resources the government will throw into the ring. They already have considerable knowledge about language including the languages of government reports. So we offer them this book in the hope that it will give them views about language in schools which they can test in the same sceptical but receptive fashion with which they scrutinise all publications which purport to tell them how to do their jobs.

References

Bakhtin, M. (1981) 'Discourse in the novel', in *The Dialogic Imagination: Four Essays*. (C. Emerson and M. Holquist, trans.). Austin: University of Texas Press.

Bruner, J. (1986) *Actual Minds, Possible Worlds*. Cambridge, MA: Harvard University Press.

Burke, K. (1950) *A Grammar of Motives.* Berkeley, CA: University of California Press.

Burke, K. (1969) *A Rhetoric of Motives.* Berkeley, CA: University of California Press.

Donmall, B. (1985) *Language Awareness. NCLE Papers and Reports 6.* London: Centre for Information on Language Teaching and Research.

Halliday, M. (1978) *Language as Social Semiotic.* London: Edward Arnold.

Halliday, M. (1985) *An Introduction to Functional Grammar.* London: Edward Arnold.

Her Majesty's Inspectorate (1984) *English from 5 to 16.* London: HMSO.

Her Majesty's Inspectorate (1986) *English from 5 to 16: Responses to Curriculum Matters 1.* London: HMSO.

Hockett, C. (1968) *The State of the Art.* The Hague: Mouton.

Iser, W. (1978) *The Act of Reading.* Baltimore: Johns Hopkins University Press.

Van Dijk, T. (1985) *Handbook of Discourse Analysis, vol. 1.* New York: Academic Press.

Volosinov, V. (1973) *Marxism and the Philosophy of Language* (L. Matejka and I. Titunik, trans.). New York: Seminar Press.

Wunderlich, D. (1979) *Foundations of Linguistics.* Cambridge: Cambridge University Press.

Some Notes on the Idea of Culture

Harold wrote this essay in August 1989. It has not been previously published, and it is possible that, so far as he was concerned, it remained unfinished. But the main lines of its argument are clear.

We have been immersed in the multicultural or intercultural debate for many years. The debate has been dominated by two themes: (a) how to establish genuine and profound relationships between different cultures, especially between dominant cultures and those which have arrived in Europe relatively recently; and (b) how to create a multi- rather than a mono-culture. These well known intentions and aspirations, elaborated in a thousand discussions, rarely linger over the concept of culture itself. It has been as though this concept was not in the least problematic, one of those ideas whose meaning was comfortably settled so long ago that we could now take it for granted and concentrate on the political and educational issues which arise from cultures in contact. Of course European cultures never were mono-cultures, and contain within them the history of the most ruthless attempts to suppress a wide range of cultural expression.

The neglect of serious discussion of the idea of culture in those circles concerned with multicultural education is all the more strange since, at the very moment when their banner was nervously and variously hoisted, what came to be called cultural studies was developing rapidly (see for example Bourdieu in France, Raymond Williams and Edward Thompson in Britain, Carlo Ginsberg in Italy). In a short space of time a new set of labels emerged: youth culture, pop culture, popular culture, counter culture, high/low culture, sub-cultures, dominant/dominated cultures, working-class/middle-class culture, and so on. The old European idea of culture being the possession of those familiar with certain artistic achievements was being rapidly replaced by an anthropological notion of culture extended from studies of remote tribal societies to the heart of our own societies and their social practices.

The discussion of multicultural and intercultural education has been relatively untouched by these developments. The predominant note has been that culture is good for you. The liberal view is that many cultures are even better for you and the conservative view is that the national culture (whatever that is, for no serious attempt at analysis is made) must be defended against alien intruders, and the educational system must be used to promote and impose it upon all. The liberal view was expressed in a much quoted sentence of *A Language for Life*, an official report on the teaching of English in schools in England and Wales (The Bullock Committee, 1975):

> No child should be expected to cast off the language and culture of the home as he crosses the school threshold nor live and act as though school and home represent two totally separate and different cultures which have to be kept firmly apart.

But what exactly was this elusive commodity which the child was carrying invisibly to school? By what means was the school supposed to do something to or with it? How was it expected to survive in one of the great strongholds of the dominant culture? What the report fails to note is that in England from the introduction of universal education in 1870 schools had quite deliberately put at the forefront of their programmes not simply the ignoring of the culture of most children but an active extirpation of it.

The liberal assertions of *A Language for Life*, echoed in numerous documents since its publication, were perhaps a necessary stage amidst the prevalent assimilationist attitudes and practices of the times and the relative silence of minorities which had yet to become organised and publicly articulate. But we now need to go beyond simplicities or we shall leave the field to such exponents of cultural ideas as Professor Scruton (*The Times*, 17.1.84):

> [An educated person] is likely to reject ... the view that schools should become multicultural – where this means equal emphasis on Shakespeare and reggae music; inventing a 'multicultural history' for Britain; teaching children in their 'mother tongue' and not in English; being prepared to dismiss everything he knows to be worthwhile for a child to learn in the interest of an 'equality' which would be worth nothing even if we could achieve it. Above all, he would not assume that a teacher who endeavours to communicate the culture which is expressed in his language, and who is aware that there is no greater mental discipline than to understand the achievements and institutions of the civilization into which one was born, is a 'racist'.

This intellectualized version of cruder chauvinist assumptions pursues its theme by attributing to the exponents of multiculturalism ideas which they have never advanced. We should take note that Scruton refers to 'the' culture which is expressed in the teacher's language, brushing aside the manifest linguistic pluralism which exists even within the narrow confines of the Anglo-Saxon cultural world. And he refers to 'the civilization into which one was born', brandishing the word 'civilization' in much the same way as Europeans who have wished to subjugate others have used the word. As outrageous as these ideas are, they do touch some sensitive spots in multicultural rhetoric. For example, we do need to examine more closely how exactly culture is mediated in schools, while being conscious of the fact that this complex process consists of much more than a handing down of ideas and doctrines. We should also ask more insistently what place should be found for the millennia of European history, literature and ideas. For to be conscious of Eurocentrism in curricula cannot mean turning our backs on European culture, nor can it mean that by some almost automatic process we can derive programmes and pedagogy which find a proper place for it. Scruton is able to perpetrate his calumnies the more easily because accusations of racism are thrown about far too wildly. Further, multiculturalism is frequently predicated on the notion that no culture or cultural practice is superior or inferior to any other. This well known relativist position is often dishonest in the sense that many, perhaps most, of those who subscribe to it either do not believe it or, more significantly, do not live it.

One could cite many others who have produced attacks on multiculturalism. And it has to be said that in spite of their obvious prejudices, they do probe certain weaknesses. But what is typical of certain bombardments from both sides of the political spectrum is the rarity with which they explore the day-to-day realities of cultural practices in contemporary society. The word 'culture' is flourished like a talisman, a magic charm. Stuart Hall [various dates of publication, including 1996] has asked us to recognise the double hazard of cultural investigation and urged us to avoid

> the Scylla of a reductionism which must deny almost everything in order
> to explain something, and the Charybdis of a pluralism which is so
> mesmerized by 'everything' that it cannot explain anything.

So then, let me turn to the central concern of these notes – the nature of a culture – trusting that they will serve to illuminate questions of linguistic diversity. I take as my starting point Claude Lévi-Strauss's view of culture as a system of meanings through which people perceive their world. I would wish to elaborate that view with the addition of Edmund Leach's idea that culture is characterized by complexity and fluidity. Let me sketch out, rather schematically, how I think it would be helpful in the context of intercultural education to regard culture. Culture consists of all those social practices, modes of discourse, ways of conducting social life, bodily behaviours and social institutions which give form and meaning to our lives. It follows then that it is many layered, highly intricate and unlikely to be encompassed by monolithic explanations (e.g. cultural reproduction). Note, for example, how the concept of a single language has to be given full cultural meaning by consideration of the many aspects of grammatical, lexical and idiomatic diversity and the elusive phenomena of discourse patterns, or what Dell Hymes calls 'ways of speaking'. What are the major characteristics of culture perceived in this way?

Harold Rosen

1. In our kind of society, culture is powerfully *interactive* since diverse cultural forms encounter, clash and blend. The cultural lines of communication cross and recross. It has become impossible to live in cultural enclaves and ghettos. Culture is always a critical political matter. The history of the oppression of the Welsh language and the struggle for its survival illustrate this clearly. Schools are in our day a central part of the communication system.

2. Culture is *dynamic*; that is, it is not only in a constant process of change but also has to be made and remade in every generation for better or for worse. Thus everyone is an active maker of his or her culture, not a passive absorber of an unchanging legacy. Language change is typical, since it is brought about not by the decrees of linguistic scholars or pundits but by ordinary motivated language users. The dynamics of cultural practices are affected by what Raymond Williams called *residual, dominant* and *emergent* features. For at any given moment there are cultural phenomena in the process of becoming obsolete but still exerting power (e.g. feudal hangovers) and others which are at early stages of development (e.g. feminism), both existing in a context of prevailing norms.

3. Culture is *stratified* in various ways. It is stratified by class, gender and ethnicity and therefore by unequally distributed power. The weakness of pluralism is that it does not deal with power. Cultures are not equal, for this potent reason. An oppressed culture is lived differently from a dominant one, as we can observe in dialect speakers' ambivalence of attitude to their own speech.

4. Culture is *diversified by form*, i.e. by sharply defined, discrete activities and products which are clearly perceived by participants to be discrete: visual images, emblems, religious practices, songs, plays, styles of dress, etc. In language there are products of enormous variety, oral and written literature, verbally saturated ceremonies, religious rituals, adages, mottoes, slogans. At this level we have not only products but also means of production which have become in our day a cultural industry. This commercially mediated culture is central to the experience of all. It is the major form of visibly institutionalized culture, usurping the role of older institutions including the church. The control of the new institutions has become one of the major political issues of our day.

5. There is a less sharply defined middle ground, where meanings are being made and delivered and are seen to be doing so, but the delivery system is less clear, more informal and more fluid. These unofficial exchanges can be seen at work in social networks, the ways in which informal groups behave, typical gathering places (pubs, cafés, clubs), in the unwritten rules of public conduct.

6. Institutions are not only means of delivering culture, but in themselves come to constitute cultural messages. Thus a church is the arena for delivering and receiving religious doctrine, but the building itself becomes an elaborate icon. Schools, too, not only deliver verbal messages but have an architectural meaning; so do banks. We can see in institutions the distinction between culture actively

created by those who need it and use it and cultural products made by one group to be consumed by another.

7. Finally, there are the most invisible and most difficult-to-recover cultural phenomena: the ways we do and say things in everyday life. They are forms of behaviour so taken for granted that for the most part we do not perceive them as systematic: body language, ways of eating, ways of walking, the disposition of physical objects in a room, inter-generational formalities, etc. Here we have a vast signifying system at the very heart of our lives. It is at the opposite pole of that view of culture which consists of an appreciation of Beethoven, Shakespeare and Leonardo da Vinci.

This very sketchy description of the scope of culture is almost anthropologically neutral, and I have underemphasised the central role of language, which is at one and the same time both a transmitter and mediator of culture and also a manifestation of it. Thus we can note the difference between a parent instructing a child on acceptable eating behaviour and reading a poem to her or him. Language is the most detailed, fully elaborated and conventionalized meaning system we have. At the same time it carries a richness of resources which speakers can deploy in a creative fashion, and which they inherit through a process which is inseparable from their mastery of grammar and lexicon. It contains historically evolved forms: stories, songs, idioms, proverbs, wit, jokes, religious references. The political battles which have raged, sometimes bloodily, around language rights show how fiercely people are aware of the links between their language and their identity.

Bourdieu, like others, has attempted to show that schools are the consistent purveyors of the dominant culture and determine what has cultural value and what has not in matters such as knowledge, ways of speaking, ways of relating to the world, what it means to be educated. The curriculum is full of cultural silences, e.g. aspects of working-class and colonial history, the neglect of certain literary works, the ignoring of oral culture. However, there is a growing awareness that schools are not, and cannot be, a set of predictable reflexes to the dominant culture, and that the curriculum itself is a discourse in which there are emancipatory possibilities. Why? Because at the centre of cultural practice there is a paradox: on the one hand there is in most people at the very least the conservative submission to the dominant culture and subordination to its values and, on the other hand, a creative endeavour for change. Thus we have both the acceptance and active practice of sexism, side by side with the growth of feminism. Gramsci puts one side of this abstractly: hegemony is both coercive and consensual. Languages are often overtly oppressed and suppressed but the speakers of them may well come to accept the notion of their intrinsic inferiority.

Within the paradox there are possibilities. But when we are discussing the diverse minority cultures in Europe we need to recognise that much of their meaning systems is informal and elusive. We also need to avoid naïve and romantic views of culture, as though all culture is a manifestation of the invincible human spirit, for we know that all cultures carry within them some of the most appalling practices and beliefs. Intercultural aspirations have to come to terms with the fact that uncritical attitudes to cultural difference can be disabling and divisive, ignoring irreconcilable values. Against this we have to construct barrier-breaking activity and the ceaseless negotiation of meanings across the cultural frontiers.

We should never forget that it was from the cultural womb of Europe that the holocaust emerged, nor Walter Benjamin's grim warning (1968) that 'There is no document of civilization which is not at the same time a document of barbarism'. We need these reminders so that when we propose positive and creative intercultural linguistic programmes we do so with our eyes open.

References

Benjamin, W. (1968) 'Theses on the philosophy of history', in H. Arendt (ed.), *Illuminations* (H. Zohn, trans.). New York: Harcourt Brace Jovanovich.

The Bullock Committee (1975) *A Language for Life* (The Bullock Report). London: HMSO.

Hall, S. (1996) 'Race, articulation and societies structured in dominance', in H. Baker, M. Diawara and R. Lindeborg (eds.), *Black British Cultural Studies: A reader*. Chicago: University of Chicago Press.

The Nationalisation of English

A government-commissioned committee chaired by Brian Cox had produced the Cox Report (1989), which formed the basis of the first version of the National Curriculum for English. For the first time in the history of state education in England and Wales, the school curriculum was a matter of law. This paper is a critique in particular of one of the Cox Report's recommendations, which was adopted in the National Curriculum: that children and young people who did not already speak Standard English 'should be helped' to do so. The paper was first delivered at the annual conference of the National Association for the Teaching of English, held in Manchester in April 1990. It was later published in the *International Journal of Applied Linguistics*, 1 (1), in 1991.

It is a well-known fact that Standard English is the official dialect of the British state. Judging by the way some people speak of it, I think it must also be the chosen dialect of God. The English language in Britain has been nationalised at a moment in history when almost everything in sight either has been or is going to be privatised. To say that English has been nationalised is not quite correct, since it is one particular kind of English which has for the first time in British history become a matter for legislation and therefore compulsion and control. The adoption of the Cox Report (1989) as the National Curriculum for English means that one of its provisions (a whole chapter supplies the rationale) which in the old days might have been a recommendation now has the full force of law. Thus:

> All children … should be able to use Standard English when it is helpful to do so in speaking as well as in writing.

(para. 15.41)

> From level 7 pupils should be using Standard English, wherever appropriate, to meet the standards of attainment.

(para. 15.24)

If you track through the Cox Report picking up every reference to the teaching of spoken English, you will notice a certain shyness about coming straight out with the clear instruction, 'All pupils must be taught to speak Standard English' or ' … must be able to speak Standard English by the time they leave school'. The injunction is quite clear all the same. This should come as interesting news to the Scotsman who only the other day was told by a judge in court that he should go back to Scotland as he couldn't speak English. He had used, among other alien expressions, *aye* instead of *yes*.

Harold Rosen

The Cox Report is crammed with all kinds of commandments interwoven with suggestions, the latter toning down what would otherwise have seemed too peremptory and hectoring for the intended audience. The language of the report is worthy of study in its own right as an example of quangoese, but I want to concentrate on one provision amongst many, many others – the obligatory teaching of spoken Standard English. I do so because:

1. it could affect in a fundamental way the lives of millions of children;
2. it insists that teachers engage in an activity to which some have deep-rooted objections, shared in many cases by the students who are to be the targets for this treatment;
3. it is the kind of demand which can only be made by those who are at a great distance from the social and linguistic realities of the classroom;
4. it is slipped into a text which in many ways teachers might find acceptable;
5. it conjures up nightmares of the process of attainment testing: it is not difficult to imagine the grotesque humiliations and absurdities which might occur.

Since English teachers are now saddled with this legal obligation, I presume that if they failed to meet it they could face some dire sanction, dismissal, fine, or even prison. We have always had a language police, but they have been self-appointed arbiters: editors, manual writers, gate-keepers of different kinds, and, yes, teachers. However, if we were bold enough, or privileged enough, or defiant enough, we might ignore them, especially when they couldn't agree among themselves. Now the state itself is taking on the role. This is no mean thing. The element of statutory compulsion in education is worth some analysis, especially when it concerns what dialect children may speak. Note that if I am a parent, I am compelled to send my child to school; the child's teachers are compelled to deliver the National Curriculum to my child, no matter what nonsense it may contain. But strangely, as parents in the London borough of Tower Hamlets recently discovered, the authorities are not obliged to provide an institution where these compulsory activities should take place.

In practice, written Standard English has long been the national written language in the sense that it has been used for all official purposes and in commerce, education, etc. You can be sure that if you are being taxed, summoned to appear in court, or informed about the National Curriculum, you will learn about it in written Standard English. Such has been the history of the written language that there has been no credible alternative since Latin and French disappeared from the law courts. Thus, there can be no reasonable dispute about written Standard English being taught in schools. However, that leaves unresolved several tricky questions which the Cox Report does not seriously explore. What, for example, unambiguously defines what is and what is not Standard English? Since it is acknowledged that written Standard is in a constant process of change, often borrowing from the very dialects from which it is supposed to be sharply distinguished, it is clear that we do not have the tidy category which the name implies. Then, to say that written Standard should be taught does not tell us what we mean by the word *taught*. Does it mean an active interventionist process in which the hounding out of linguistic heresy is made salient? Or is it the more oblique process of relying on literacy to do most of the work? Finally, as Cox acknowledges, writing in dialect is used for stories, poems, dialogue, plays, etc. Some writers slip in and out of dialect as it suits them. All this is relatively familiar stuff. Spoken Standard is quite another matter.

On spoken Standard, the Cox proposals are, I believe, both wrong-headed and pernicious. I want to focus on this theme. Let me begin by summarising my standpoint. The proposals are for me a nonsense because:

1. the description of spoken Standard and non-Standard in Cox, in spite of its air of up-to-the-minute linguistic expertise, is seriously flawed;
2. the additive principle (i.e. adding spoken Standard to a non-Standard dialect) is socially naïve and does not confront honestly the consequences: note that Cox says 'the aim is to add Standard English to the repertoire, not to replace other dialects';
3. such suggestions as are made on the crucial matter of a pedagogy which will produce speakers of Standard have no credibility and do not rest on a body of successful practice;
4. there is no reference to the highly relevant and well-documented fact that in the matter of class dialects, prestige and stigma travel in both directions; the phenomenon is sufficiently well-known to be given a name in the sociolinguistic literature – 'covert prestige'.

I want now to elaborate on each of these points, but first let me stress that the best descriptions of Standard in the world, culled from the most impressive authorities, do not enable one to read off a curriculum and pedagogy from them. We should know this very well: elegant descriptions of sentences do not, between the lines, inscribe instructions for what we should do about sentences in the classroom, if anything. Similarly, describing Standard English is not the same as making out a case for teaching it in some way or another, nor for assuming that there is a kind of teaching which will render the whole process both painless and worthwhile.

But first a little history. The Cox Report has no time to linger over the history of its own proposals. If it had done so, what would have emerged is that its central proposal about spoken Standard has been around for a long time. Cox differs only insofar as it sets its aged idea in an apparently benign and tolerant context. In his recent book, *The Politics of Discourse: The standard language question in British cultural politics*, Tony Crowley (1989) traces with meticulous detail the rise of the concept of Standard English and the moves made to privilege it within the educational system. I borrow from his book in some of the details which follow.

As early as 1909, the linguist H.C. Wyld wrote: 'The best thing you can do, if you have a native provincial dialect, is to stick to it, and speak it in its proper place, but to learn also Standard English.' Not only is Wyld making, some eighty years earlier, exactly the same proposal as Cox, but he, unlike Cox, has the honesty to admit that there could be some disastrous consequences of following his recipe. For example, a speaker might end up with speech which is 'a tissue of affectations … We feel in listening to such speakers that they are uneasy, unsure of themselves, that they have no traditional or social background.'

In the Cox Report, there is not a breath of the fact that there is a price to be paid for following this proposal. Notice how vicious is Wyld's mockery of the *nouveau* Standard speaker. First you urge people to learn Standard and then ridicule them when they cannot pass themselves off as the genuine article. Perhaps Chapter 4 of the Cox Report should be entitled 'Invitation to linguistic insecurity and the joys of hypercorrection'!

In the report of the Newbolt Committee, *The Teaching of English in England* (1921), the old cry goes up again but, I believe, for the first time in an official document:

> It is emphatically the business of the Elementary School to teach all its pupils who either speak a definite dialect or whose speech is disfigured by vulgarisms to speak Standard English, and to speak it clearly, and with expression … They should learn to recognize every sound in Standard English, should observe for themselves how sounds are produced … and should practise producing them properly.

Newbolt says 'it is emphatically the business of the school', and this is virtually paraphrased in Cox: written and spoken Standard are 'unquestionably a responsibility of the English curriculum'. Could the Cox Committee have been unaware that someone has been there before them?

In 1925, no less a person than George Sampson in *English for the English* was writing:

> The language of all English schools should be standard English speech. It is not the job of teachers either to cherish or destroy a local dialect; they have simply to equip their pupils with normal national speech – as a sort of second language, if the grip of the patois is too strong.

Standard is here called 'normal national speech', apparently a quite straightforward phenomenon with no trouble about the word 'normal'. Nevertheless, Sampson found himself in some difficulty in defining it and attempted to extricate himself in this extraordinary manner:

> There is no need to define Standard English speech. We know what it is and there's an end to it … If anyone wants a definite example of Standard

English we can tell him that it is the kind of English spoken by a simple unaffected young man like the Prince of Wales.

Seen with this 80-year-old history in mind, Cox leaves us with a distinct sense of *déjà vu*, once you have taken out the class arrogance and substituted its gentler and more ingratiating tones:

> ... those who do not speak it [Standard English] as a native dialect should be helped to extend their language competence so that they can use Standard English with confidence.
>
> (para. 15.38)

The phrase 'should be helped' suggests a very benign, almost therapeutic process and masks the social coercion implicit in the statement that 'all pupils should be in a position to use Standard English speech'; it also leaves hovering in the air unanswered the question, 'What happened?'. Seventy years after Newbolt's unambiguous prescriptions, why is the Cox Committee setting out precisely the same goals? Don't they owe us an explanation and some account of how it is all going to be different? Is it that they feel with the majesty of the law behind them that some magical coercive powers will do the trick? Do they perhaps imagine Standardised Attainment Tasks will terrorise pupils and teachers alike into achieving the impossible? I don't believe it. But that does not mean that the attempt will not do untold damage.

Let me now return to the main criticisms which I made earlier and elaborate on each one of them. I do so because I believe there is a most serious battle to be fought on this issue, and we must equip ourselves accordingly.

Firstly, I said that the description of Standard and non-Standard English was seriously flawed. We are given the familiar statement that all dialects, including Standard, have their own distinctive grammar and vocabulary. But how separate and sharply demarcated are dialects in Britain? Or, to put it another way, how different in respect of grammar and lexicon does a speaker have to be before we say that he or she is speaking one dialect rather than another? Why ask the question? Because the discussion in Cox presents dialects as though they are quite discrete entities except at one point, when it suits the Committee's turn to suggest otherwise:

> Research shows that secondary pupils do use fewer non-standard forms in talk with teachers than in the playground.
>
> (para. 4.50)

So it would seem that it is not a matter of all-or-nothing, but usually a matter of partly-partly. The report does not draw on the implications of this aspect of language variation, though the phenomenon is well-known enough and lay persons are usually highly conscious of it. This is all the more strange since, when it comes to dealing with Creole, the report has this to say:

> Much more difficult problems of definition arise with creole varieties of English including Creoles of Caribbean origin.

(para. 4.15)

Why? Because:

> Speakers' use of Creole varieties lies along a continuum, from varieties of Creole which may well be incomprehensible to a speaker of Standard English to varieties much closer to Standard English.

Of course, exactly the same applies to many, if not most, dialect speakers of English. As Fasold (1975) says,

> ... to assume that each dialect has an autonomous existence; and that bidialectal speakers shut off one grammar and switch on another, is just not credible in a case where most of the rules in the supposedly autonomous grammars would be exact duplicates of each other.

Tony Burgess and I dealt with this matter in our research, reported in *Languages and Dialects of London School Children* (Rosen and Burgess, 1980), in which we argued that for London pupils it is much more common to find code-sliding than code-switching. We said of Cockney:

> Intuitively we recognize the Cockney speaker by his grammar, his accent and his lexicon but also by his use of voice quality, his discourse style and the kind of gestures integrated into the speech flow. He will have an abundance of idioms and expressions of his own. Even among such readily recognized speakers there are differences. It is typical of urban diversity that a Cockney can adopt features of Standard in certain contexts; he can be more Cockney or less. In educational circles it is often declared policy to foster bidialectalism ('the language of the playground and the language of the school'). But what we are discussing is not code-switching. There is usually no unambiguous cut-off point at which London pupils can be said to have switched from Cockney to Standard or vice versa. It would be better to talk of code-sliding along a continuum.

This fluidity exists not only amongst dialects (for Cockney you could substitute other dialects). There is also an interface between dialects, i.e. there are situations where regional or class dialects confront Standard dialect in active hostility. As the work of Giles and Powesland (1975) shows, two different consequences may flow from this: 'people are continually modifying their speech with others so as to reduce or accentuate the linguistic (hence social) differences between them.' Cox does not explore this matter and therefore does not weigh the possibility that the effects of the recommendation may be the opposite of those intended.

In common with the prevailing view, the Cox Committee is anxious to divorce spoken Standard from accent. You can, the argument runs, speak Standard with any accent you like. Indeed, the Committee is against tampering with accents, thus apparently toning down their championing of Standard with a liberal concession. So it seems that the much-vaunted benefits will still accrue if speakers retain the accents which will mark them out by class and/or region. This is both a gross over-simplification and a fraud. Let us try it out. Suppose someone says *'Enry says 'is farver's a right nutter.* Who amongst all those who are sticklers for such matters would regard that as Standard spoken English? Yet this utterance is simply *Henry says his father's a right nutter.* This is plainly Standard without the accent.

Wherever there are penalties to be paid for speaking non-Standard grammar or lexicon, they will also be paid for accents which belong with region and class. More importantly, perhaps, since great emphasis is placed upon acceptability (a slippery and dubious concept), the first utterance would be no more acceptable by the self-appointed arbiter of these matters than any dialect utterance. It is absurd to pretend that learning to speak Standard does not involve some changes in accent, especially when it is part of the curriculum. Accent is just as socially sensitive as the lexico-grammatical system. A couple of so-called dropped aitches will damn you in some people's eyes as surely as an *ain't* or a *we was.*

To sum up:

1. Failure to recognize dialect/Standard continua is a failure to acknowledge the flexibility of speakers and their competence in making choices both away and towards Standard.
2. The discussion of accent does not come to terms with the realities of how speakers are judged and offers an illusory view that learning Standard is only a matter of grammar and lexicon.
3. Chapter 4 of the Cox Report draws attention to what it calls non-Standard features of which people are very conscious (these people are not specified), like *they never saw nobody, he writes really quick, he ain't done it,* etc. Note the extraordinary comment on these features – suddenly the tolerant tone drops and we read: 'Many people are highly critical of such forms and they are undoubtedly a social irritant.' (para. 4.14)
4. Unwittingly, the writers reveal who is looking for such features, and whose linguistic prejudices are being articulated with approval, ignoring the fact that there are some features in the speech of some Standard speakers which others might regard as a 'social irritant' (*one* instead of *I,* for example).

My second starting point was a challenge to the additive principle, i.e. the proposal to bolt on another dialect. At first blush, it seems a straightforward idea. Yet it is clearly not problem-free; indeed the report specifies some of the difficulties:

Adding a new dialect to the repertoire has implications.

(para. 4.33)

The profound implications for the pupils' relations with their families and communities should be recognized.

(para. 4.36)

But it is far more difficult to teach a new spoken dialect because so many aspects of spoken production are automatic and below the level of consciousness.

(para. 4.44)

This is all true. But these problems begin to indicate just what kinds of social and psychological burdens are being thrust upon teachers. It would be only reasonable to expect that some credible solutions would be offered. I cannot find them, and will return to this point later. First let me stress that there are difficulties which are not even mentioned. I do not believe that it is possible to embark on a deliberate programme of adding Standard speech without giving pupils the idea that the speech they already use is in some way inferior or deficient. As Leith (1989) writes, 'the prestige of one dialect leads to the disparagement of the others'. Pupils may, and I am sure many will, in practice, reject the idea. Not that it requires the curriculum to deliver this idea. The most likely result of the whole venture, as Hymes (1972) pointed out a long time ago, is that pupils will lose confidence in their own code without having mastered another. What we need is a totally honest appraisal of what it means to take on board spoken Standard English and to understand why the effort to impose it meets with such resistance. Observe, for example, James Joyce speaking though Stephen Daedalus in *A Portrait of the Artist as a Young Man* (1916):

> He felt with a smart of rejection that the man to whom he was speaking was a countryman of Ben Johnson. He thought: the language in which he speaks is his before it is mine. How different are the words *home, Christ, ale, master* on his lips and on mine! I cannot speak or write these words without unrest of spirit. His language, so familiar and so foreign, will always be for me an acquired speech. I have not made or accepted its words. My voice holds them at bay. My soul frets in the shadow of his language.

Now, it is quite clear that many people do indeed switch from the language of their childhood to Standard spoken English, usually with an accent more or less like Received Pronunciation (RP). Many people, like me, have done just that. But lest anyone cite such people to justify the feasibility of the Cox proposal, let us consider why we are no more than marginally relevant to the present case. If we examine the processes by which these conversions take place, we shall find:

1. increasing distancing of a person from home and community, typically in the past through the route of grammar school and higher education and often involving the loss of the first dialect;
2. residential shift from a working-class to a middle-class area in childhood;
3. boarding school;
4. direct individual tuition with a necessary minimum of cooperation by the learner ('elocution').

To put this more generally, what we find is a crucial change in the life of the speaker which shifts him or her into a Standard-speaking milieu and which makes available the new models. An essential motivating factor is the desire to be accepted in the new peer group. With the exception of elocution lessons, the process is for many unconscious and imperceptible. The variations are too numerous and subtle to set out here.

That said, we ought to note that even in these propitious circumstances, there is usually a price to be paid for acquiring spoken Standard English. Converts usually lose their first dialect. Or perhaps it would be more accurate to say they bury it deep in the recesses of their psyches. They develop a special set of anxieties from the way they have to monitor their own speech, unlike a native speaker of Standard. They are par excellence victims of hypercorrection and linguistic anxiety (well documented in Labov, 1971). To become an occasional speaker of Standard is to become a nervous, anxious speaker at a disadvantage in the face of those for whom it is a mother tongue.

Cox says, quite rightly:

> … if people need to learn a language for some real purpose, they learn it. Furthermore the desire to join a group is often very strong indeed.
>
> (para. 4.50)

But what happens if they are not moved by a real purpose and are only under the pressure of someone else's purposes? 'The desire to join a group' is disingenuously expressed; after all, it is not just any group but a particular and unnamed group that the authors have in mind. Against this kind of blandness, let me place Halliday's view (1978):

> Most of the time what we find in real life are dialect hierarchies, patterns of dialectal variation in which a 'standard' (representing a power base in society) is opposed by non-standard varieties … The non-standard dialects may become languages of opposition and protest … Here dialect becomes a means of expression of class-consciousness and political awareness.

My third starting point was a concern about the kind of pedagogy which would inevitably be installed to carry out the operation of creating a nation of Standard speakers. A reading of the relevant section reveals very quickly that the writers cannot point to any successful body of practice, and their attempt to come up with suggestions is derisory:

> ... competence in Standard written English will enable pupils to convert their dialect into competence in spoken Standard English.
>
> (para. 4.50)

It may or may not. For we know that it is perfectly possible to be a highly competent reader and writer of written Standard and yet retain dialect speech. If that is the case, what does the teacher do then? Firstly, resort to role-play 'in which it is natural to use Standard English', and secondly, initiate activities which oblige pupils to speak to a wider audience. Finally, if 'pupils are motivated ... they will learn to speak it if they are given appropriate educational experiences and opportunities'. I repeat, the point is precisely that many will, reasonably enough, not be motivated. The scrabbling around for curriculum suggestions smacks of desperation, for it is exactly those 'experiences and opportunities' which the promoters of novel schemes are under an obligation to set out for us. The underlying idea seems to be that spoken Standard will be acquired by a relatively spontaneous and indirect process. Thus the unpleasant spectacle of direct intervention is kept from us, though it is never explicitly disavowed.

It is easy to see that teachers are to be left to do the dirty work. They must fulfil the statutory requirement and become the key implementers of the nationalisation of English. I am reminded of the fact that when Kenneth Baker, the then Secretary of State for Education, introduced the National Curriculum, he made it very clear that it was to be devised from above and proposed from above. He then had the breathtaking impudence to turn his well-known vacuous smile towards the teachers and tell them that he relied on their imagination and ingenuity to make the whole incredible scheme work, whether they agreed with it or not.

My fourth point was that we need to come to terms with somewhat paradoxical phenomena, in particular what has become known as covert prestige. The Cox Report does not make an attempt to do this. We know that working-class speakers often denigrate their own language and will say that Standard speech is superior and, what is more, that the speakers of it are superior people. Yet they also in practice will show hostility to Standard English and RP. It turns out that prestige and status (the usual terms) can be accorded to non-Standard speech and that stigma (another favourite word) can be attached to Standard English. It is an interesting question to ask why on one occasion in Parliament, Mrs Thatcher said to an opposition member, 'You're frit' (= frightened), obviously enjoying her excursion into demotic, and why Reagan during his last election campaign never tired of saying, 'You ain't seen nothing yet'.

Needless to say, for adolescent working-class girls and boys, it is the peer-group which exerts the strongest pull after the home. There are many contexts where the speaker of Standard is the odd man or woman out, inviting ridicule, mockery and downright hostility in such places as assembly lines, building sites, working men's clubs, pubs, etc. I've already mentioned that in sociolinguistic literature there's a technical term for it – 'covert prestige'. If the Cox Report followed its own logic, there should be programmes of study for mother-tongue speakers of Standard to learn the local non-Standard variety of English. On the other hand, I am haunted by the vision of classrooms in which teachers attempt to teach spoken Standard, and I can see the range of reactions from embarrassment to sullen silence and open rebellion.

Let me now return to a related matter. The report is almost obsessively concerned with the concept of appropriate language. The word *appropriate* itself is peppered over the document, just as it was throughout *English from 5 to 16* (H.M. Inspectorate, 1984). There are twenty-five uses in the summarizing yellow pages alone. Here are a few of them:

> ... making appropriate responses to increasingly complex instructions and questions
>
> (para. 15.16)

> ... act appropriately on information, explanations and instructions
>
> (para. 15.19)

> ... respond appropriately to a range of ... instructions given by the teacher
>
> (para. 15.24)

> ... talk about appropriateness in the use of the spoken language
>
> (para. 15.24)

> ... negotiating a consensus as appropriate
>
> (para. 15.29)

> ... pupils should consider the notion of appropriateness to situation, topic, purpose and language mode
>
> (para. 15.38)

We have lived with the notion of appropriateness for a long time. For me, at least, it goes back to my first reading of the paper by Hymes (1971) on communicative competence, a much-read and cited document in the '70s. It served as a basis for many of us to argue that rigid notions of correctness needed to be replaced by the more flexible and theoretically respectable idea of appropriateness. Hymes wrote:

> We have then to account for the fact that a normal child acquires knowledge of sentences, not only as grammatical, but also as appropriate. He or she acquires competence as to when to speak, when not, and as to what to talk about with whom, when, where, in what manner.

The elaboration of this approach by Hymes had a powerful liberating effect, just as other expositions of a context-based view of language did. But it left unanswered awkward questions. First, who decides? Who is the arbiter of whether something I have spoken or written is appropriate or not? If we do not resolve this question, we are likely to substitute for the monolithic view of correctness (i.e., something is right or wrong) a whole set of correctnesses, a more subtle tyranny (i.e., something is right or wrong in this context). Secondly, as we do not see in Cox, appropriateness can be negotiated, contested, defied, changed in the very process of interaction. Thirdly, the doctrine of appropriateness can easily become servile propaganda for submission to authority and force majeur. Fourthly, the doctrine of appropriateness implies that there is a fixed set of rules, whereas, in practice, situations vary from those in which protocol is very tight to those in which diversity is tolerated and the boundaries of acceptability are fuzzy; or, to put it differently, people are tolerant.

What must not be allowed to happen is the promotion of a kind of teaching which proposes to pupils a kind of linguistic determinism – i.e., given the context, audience, purpose, etc., there is an already-established discourse to which they must conform. Many contexts are sites of contestation which is pursued by the use of 'inappropriate' language. Of course, there are some genres which, in Kress's words (1982) are 'fixed, formalised, and codified'. But they are few and far between, for as Bakhtin (1986) says, compared with grammar, 'genres are much more flexible, plastic and free', they are 'subject to free creative reformulation', and 'one can deliberately mix genres'.

I have been talking about the nationalisation of English, meaning the imposition by law of Standard English, i.e. the language. However, I had in mind another meaning as well, namely the nationalisation of the curriculum subject English. We need to ponder well this huge shift and what it does to the possibilities for the subject and its relationship to the appraisal of teachers.

Moreover, we should not forget how a national curriculum might have been negotiated out in the open, how differences might have been accommodated, how objections might have been discussed. It is too late for that now. All the same, it was correctly pointed out that the National Association for the Teaching of English was far too tame in its response to Cox. We can make up for that now by adopting every feasible tactic to remove or alter all those provisions to which we are opposed and also to develop what has been left embryonic or omitted. We need to challenge every attempt to impose practices we do not support. Undoubtedly, the haste with which the Educational Reform Act has been pushed through and the fact that the current Secretary of State for Education is clearly trying to extricate himself from the previous incumbent's wilder lunacies mean that the conditions are quite propitious for us to draw up our first short list, leaving behind our lengthy analyses of the whole report, and to try out our strength in initiating change without waiting for invitations from the top. I have declared my own preferred items. To take a step of this kind is to become involved in some of the most profound linguistic processes in society. In Foucault's now almost proverbial words (1972):

> ... in every society the production of discourse is at once controlled, selected, organized and redistributed according to a number of procedures whose role is to avert its powers and dangers.

It is possible to read the Cox Report as precisely an exemplar of the process of controlling, selecting, organizing and redistributing discourse. It is also possible to read it as a vindication of what innovative teachers in general and the National Association for the Teaching of English in particular have been creating, providing and developing since 1950. Both readings make sense, and a careful reading of the text would show the tension which gives rise to the paradox, a tension between the desire to recruit the support of the most influential English teachers and the need to satisfy the demands of the instigators of the exercise. A Foucault reading needs a special gloss: the procedures of control are not irresistible. We have reached a stage where discourse itself is an area of conflict. If it were not, the Cox Committee would not have been conjured into being. We read the report against a background of shouts of 'bring back grammar' and 'defend our literary heritage'. The corollary to Foucault is that we should counter-control, counter-select, counter-organize by our own procedures which we should set in motion right now.

Our route is lucidly set out in Bakhtin (1981):

> The word in language is half someone else's. It becomes 'one's own' only when the speaker populates it with his own intentions, his own accent, when he appropriates the word, adapting it to his own semantic and expressive intention ... Language is not a neutral medium that passes freely and easily into the private property of the speaker's intentions; it is populated – overpopulated – with the intentions of others. Expropriating it, forcing it to submit to one's own intentions and accents, is a difficult and complicated process.

There is a whole lexicon of words in the Cox Report which must now be made to submit to teachers' intents and accents.

References

Bakhtin, M. (1981) *The Dialogic Imagination*. Austin: University of Texas Press.

Bakhtin, M. (1986) *Speech Genres and Other Late Essays*. Austin: University of Texas Press.

The Cox Committee (1989) *English for Ages 5 to 16* (The Cox Report). London: HMSO.

Crowley, T. (1989) *The Politics of Discourse: The standard language question in British cultural politics*. London: Macmillan.

Fasold, R.W. (1975) *How to Study Language Maintenance and Shift*. Baltimore: Linguistic Society of America.

Foucault, M. (1972) *The Archaeology of Knowledge.* London: Tavistock.

Giles, H. and Powesland, P. (1975) *Speech Style and Social Evaluation.* London: Academic Press.

Halliday, M. (1978) *Language as Social Semiotic.* London: Edward Arnold.

H.M. Inspectorate (1984) *English from 5 to 16.* London: HMSO.

Hymes, D. (1971) *On Communicative Competence.* Philadelphia: University of Pennsylvania Press.

Hymes, D. (1972) 'Introduction', in C. Cazden, V. John and D. Hymes (eds.), *Functions of Language in the Classroom.* New York: Teachers College Press.

Joyce, J. (1916) *A Portrait of the Artist as a Young Man.* London: Viking.

Kress, G. (1982) *Learning to Write.* London: Routledge and Kegan Paul.

Labov, W. (1971) 'The study of language in its social context', in J. Fishman (ed.), *Advances in the Sociology of Language.* The Hague: Mouton.

Leith, D. (1983) *A Social History of English.* London: Routledge and Kegan Paul.

The Newbolt Committee (1921) *The Teaching of English in England* (The Newbolt Report). London: HMSO.

Rosen, H. and Burgess, T. (1980) *Languages and Dialects of London School Children.* London: Ward Lock.

Sampson, G. (1925) *English for the English.* Cambridge: Cambridge University Press.

Wyld, H. (1909) *Elementary Lessons in English Grammar.* Oxford: Oxford University Press.

The Whole Story?

Harold gave this talk on 5 April 1994, at the annual conference of the National Association for the Teaching of English.

This piece is the clearest example of the difficulty of classifying his writings, as mentioned in the introduction. The second half of the piece, about autobiography, lays out some early ideas on the topic, later developed at full length in his book *Speaking from Memory*, published in 1998. Taken by itself, it obviously belongs in Part Three of this collection, 'Story'. However, the first half of the piece is clearly a political statement, as well as a description of an intellectual journey taken, as always, in collaboration and comradeship with others. Hence the decision, on balance, to include it in Part One.

Occasionally, dates of publications later than 1994 are given; these are of accessible modern editions of classics.

The title of this conference intrigues and teases me: 'Reading: the Whole Story'. I assume it was intended to have a provocative and teasing ambiguity. But we know there is never, never the whole story. Every story has its silences and, like all language, is governed by what must not be said, what perhaps may be said, what its author prefers not to say. What's more, a story is not whole unless it gives shape (and therefore meaning) to the events it presents. Thus in the very act of giving salience to *this* rather than *that* the raw wholeness of experience has to be managed, manoeuvred, cajoled into a form which obliges storytellers to jettison much more than they incorporate. They confer legitimacy in this context on that notorious phrase 'economical with the truth'. There are no whole stories, only versions, which are better value anyway. Michael Walzer (1987) writes:

> ... it is better to tell stories than to remain silent even though there is no definitive and best story ... no last story that, once told, would leave all future storytellers without employment.

Twenty-three years ago I first addressed a plenary session of NATE conference in a talk called 'Messages and Message-makers' [reprinted in Part Two of this collection]. I began by saying, 'The difficulty is, "How should we look at language for our purposes?"' By 'our' I meant English teachers and anyone else who might have been listening. What, I was asking, is the story of what happens when we talk to one another? Not, you will notice, the whole story, but the story which would do justice to the messages exchanged in classrooms, including the way messages travel in the diverse activities we call literacy. There had been, as I tried to show, very little in the work in linguistics which could provide a satisfactory answer. The story the linguists had to tell was for the most part about the inhabitants of sentences. The question I asked then remains a central one, and we should go on asking it. For that was the way back in 1971, which you have been informed by a string of Secretaries of State was the heyday of the Educational Establishment which, amongst its other nefarious achievements, had abandoned phonics, thrown out Shakespeare and left spelling and punctuation to look after themselves – all this on the basis of airy-fairy theory, fashionable fads and defiance of good order and discipline. I shall return to airy-fairy theory, for it is a critical term in the present confrontations.

The whole story according to midgets like John Patten [Secretary of State for Education from 1992 to 1994] is that the Educational Establishment, by some mysterious conspiratorial process, captured control of schools and battered all opposition into silence or subservience. Somehow they had defeated the greatest resources of the state machine and the darker powers that stand in the shadows behind it. That at any rate is the Tory story of recent times – the new revisionism. I think the time has come in the battle against the idiocies of the National Curriculum and the subject orders for English to say unequivocally that we are in contention with a government of unashamed lies, obscene secrets, shady fiddles, and impenetrable cabals. There is a clumsiness, an infantilism in almost all government rhetoric about education in general and English teaching in particular, but its use of the term 'Educational Establishment' was a blend of lying impudence and low cunning. If Raymond Williams were still alive he would add to his list of keywords an entry under 'establishment', noting that in *The Spectator* in 1957 the word meant 'those elements in society and politics which are self-satisfied and opposed to all change' or, in C.P. Snow, 'the people who have the real power, the rulers, the establishment'. It is precisely *that* establishment and its hold over legislation which means that my original question, when posed in 1994, has to be seen in the new context established by a linguistic expert like John Major. We now know, if we didn't know it before, that what language is, how it works, how we learn it and what is the meaning of literacy are all sites of the sharpest contention. If ten or fifteen years ago we could engage in open, honest debate about dialect, about working-class language, we now have to contend with a Prime Minister who can stand up in a conference and mock Cockney speakers with an insulting and travestied version of their language.

The truth about the Sixties and Seventies is not a story about lefty gurus, but a fulcrum in post-war history when the old ways, the old schools, the old methods, the old texts, the old text-books (remember them?) were manifestly moribund. In the new comprehensives it was change or perish. The pressure for change was irresistible. If radical voices of different tinges were listened to eagerly it was because there was no credible alternative on offer – which is why a book like *Language, the Learner and the School* (Barnes, Britton, Rosen and the LATE, 1971) was disseminated so widely. The Tory myth of the Sixties is densely populated with anonymous sinister figures, sustained by unspecified theories and perpetrators of unnamed crimes. Witch-hunts are always powered by such enigmas. No one tells us which theories are in question, let alone what might be wrong with them. For in all the denunciations and name-calling there is never a genuine engagement with the actual ideas; no one names the opposition. Public official discourse about language and literature has sunk to the level of playground abuse; its tirades are not directed against serious ideas but against people called 'nutters' and 'neanderthals'. [While he was Education Secretary, John Patten described Tim Brighouse, then Birmingham's Director of Education, as 'a madman ... wandering the streets, frightening the children'. Brighouse sued, and won substantial damages which were donated to educational charities.] In the light of such debased discourse even the notorious Black Papers can be seen as an almost decent way to conduct controversy. Before we sup with the devil on committees and on enquiries, we need to ask ourselves what these palpable strategies are about.

The desire to send armed expeditions into English teaching and colonize it springs firstly from an awareness that it occupies a key ideological position; as many have noted, the Newbolt Report of 1921 was quite open about this. English was going to stop class war. English is inevitably about cultural and intercultural meanings and, as the report's authors said, about Englishness. Secondly, the desire is about control. Armed with hundreds of new powers enshrined in regulations and orders, it is possible to carry out surveillance of materials, methods, practices. The time is past, the government believes, when the luxury of choice, variety, the clash of alternatives can be afforded. The old liberal boasts are dropped without ceremony. In the place of alternative narratives, the government wants the one whole story – On Her Majesty's Service; in Edward Said's words (1993), 'an official, forceful, coercive identity ... a strange mixture of invention, history and self-aggrandisement calling for unthinking assent'. I do not believe the government will succeed, because there are always dissenting stories. But where and how will they be told?

The bleating of the lamb excites the appetite of the tiger. Carefully judicious statements, the rhetoric of conciliation, a desperate anxiety to be seen as moderate, statesmanlike and open to supposedly reasonable compromise has its hazards. Some may see it as an advance when, after an era of blatantly rigged committees (the Kingman Committee, for example) and suppression of major documents (like the Language in the National Curriculum project materials), representatives of the English teaching constituency are recruited to offer their advice. It is a kind of victory, I must admit. However, as a terribly cautionary tale I invite you to read Urszula Clark's article in the current number of *English in Education*, 'Bringing English to order: A personal account of the NCC Evaluation Project' (1994). Here is the sad story of what it means to be caught in the coils of the government's system of consultation.

> From the beginning, working on the project commissioned by NCC [the National Curriculum Council] to evaluate the implementation of the

> English orders felt like working in a dark, ever-receding tunnel, stabbing
> around in the vague hope that something might penetrate the blind silence
> and wilful obstinacy that disregarded the voice of the English teaching
> profession … Trust, integrity, academic freedom: none of these appeared
> to be of any consequence.

I cannot give you the whole story (!) but let me add a little more. The project team, having been assured that the research was an opportunity for teachers to have their say, and having believed it, discovered that their channel of communication with the NCC 'became increasingly one-way, shrouded in mystery and secrecy' and their reports 'were sent off as if to a black hole'. And so on … Finally, Urszula Clark asked the crucial question:

> Why did I continue working on the project and complying with requests
> made of me by the NCC? Because the demanding and absorbing nature
> of the work made it difficult to step back. When I did, I believed each time
> that things couldn't get much worse; that, if I didn't continue, somebody
> else would – somebody not as sympathetic to the philosophy of English
> teaching I believed the NCC were set on destroying, somebody who might
> have allowed himself or herself to be manipulated by the NCC more than
> I allowed myself to be.

What could illustrate more powerfully and tragically the hazards and agonizing dilemmas of incorporation, and the wild extravagance with which the creative energies of teachers can be squandered? There is an alternative model. It is the brilliant way in which teachers defeated the government in the boycott of its SATs [standard assessment tasks – compulsory tests which the government had imposed on 14-year-olds] last year. I know how easy it is for me to speak from the well-upholstered armchair of retirement to urge policies which I do not have to implement. I am not saying that no involvement whatever with government machinery can be countenanced, but at least there should be some principles on which it should be based. First, clear, explicit, publicly available terms of participation. Second, written guarantees of openness and the right to make public matters of concern. Third, noisy withdrawal at the first signs of double-dealing. How far is it possible to conduct a dialogue with the deaf and duplicitous?

A few weeks ago, Jimmy Britton died. I knew him and worked closely with him for half a century. We were both founder members of NATE. He was by a long way the best teacher I ever had. We shall find a time to celebrate his memory richly and relevantly, the better to understand what is going on now. Now there was a man our enemies would put on their hit list. Let me single out one reason why they hate and fear an influence such as his. You will know that one of NATE's great achievements is that it has always looked for its intellectual resources in the spirit of what I might call post-Matthew-Arnoldism and post-Leavisism. Moreover, it has looked for them outside those boundaries which constricted an earlier generation to literary criticism and philology. It was, I believe, Jimmy Britton more than any other single person who taught us to conduct daring expeditions into philosophy, psychology, literary theory, discourse processes – and linguistics; to search out what could underpin our practices and point to new ones. His book *Language and Learning* (1970) is an explorer's manual which grew out of a unique seminar he ran at the Institute of Education where English teachers were at first baffled, wondering what Piaget's *Play, Dreams and Imitation in Childhood* (1945) could possibly have to do with them, or apparently unlikely texts like Cassirer's *An Essay on Man* (1944). Sooner or later they were profoundly changed by the experience. It was there that we encountered Suzanne Langer, Piaget (of course), Sapir, Polanyi, Vygotsky, Luria, Harding, Gusdorf, Firth and others, an international invisible college of scholars – British, American, French, Swiss, German, Russian. From that seminar we shaped our convictions – to be hospitable to the experiences and language of our students, to perceive literature as something not only received by students but as inevitably created by them, to consider the nature of expressive language, to understand why language is inextricably involved in learning. We learned to give central importance to *talk*, deliberately given that modest, everyday name, rather than 'oracy' or even 'speech'. We conducted the first investigations into classroom talk. One weekend, at a conference of the London Association, we 'invented' language across the curriculum. So we found ourselves scouring the libraries, immersed in journals, using the first widely available tape recorders, making our own discoveries. This was one of the laboratories where airy-fairy theory took shape.

The intellectual resources which in the Sixties and Seventies became currency for so many teachers never were Holy Writ and were never meant to be. Some of them became obsolete, some were returned to again and again (Vygotsky [1962 and 1978], for example). A new language was spoken, of class, of power, of politics. In the Britton tradition we found Freire, Raymond Williams, Terry Eagleton. There was Roland Barthes' *S/Z* (1975). We asked, with Stanley Fish (1980), whether there was a text in this class; from Bakhtin (1981) we came to understand that the imagination was in a constant state of dialogue. What Jimmy Britton launched us towards as the Seventies and Eighties put new items on the agenda was, in Walter Benjamin's brilliant phrase, that we must 'brush history against the grain'.

What we inherit from Jimmy is more than a set of seminal ideas. It is a kind of practice which insists that in the midst of burning preoccupations, indeed because of them, we must continue to enlarge on our understanding; we must pursue just those activities which so enrage the philistines. I want in the remainder of my time to conduct just such an exercise as my own sort of tribute to Jimmy Britton; the cheaply mocked theory is our great strength. The ideas we have championed and translated into practice are not whims and fads but are sustained by some of the most important ideas of our time. There is a whole territory which we now need to explore which is, I believe, unknown to most English teachers. Let me call it *autobiographical discourse*, to which as you will see I give a particular meaning. In a very short space of time there have appeared studies which in different ways and from the standpoints of different kinds of analysis have attempted to describe, discuss and assess the significance of life stories. As far as I can tell, no one has brought these interlocking works together, let alone attempted to appraise the full significance of autobiographical discourse. I hope to do just that in the work I am engaged upon which will in due course appear under the title *Speaking from Memory*. I did some ground-clearing for it in two papers, 'The Autobiographical Impulse' and 'Talk as Autobiography' (both of which you'll find in *Troublesome Boy* [1993]). [Both pieces appear in Part Three.]

A good place to begin is with the question, 'How did human beings become storytellers?' A nice speculation. It must be, surely, as soon as they could tell each other about their pasts. We can see the process at work with very young children. Bruner (1990) says: 'The formal structures of autobiography get laid down early in the discourse of family life and persist stubbornly'.

From that time on we are incorrigible autobiographers, for as soon as we can narrate the past, in a variety of ways, we tell one another stories of personal experience. They are woven into our system of verbal communication. Once you become aware of this you have to conclude that it is not an optional extra, a privileged adornment embroidered onto the homespun fabric of everyday discourse, but a serious requirement of everyday social life. To speak is, among other things, an effort and an offer to share each other's lives.

Lejeune, in his book *On Autobiography* (1989), says: 'Every person has within himself a rough draft perpetually reshaped of the story of his life.' That's a good place to start, but I would like to go further. I want to suggest that everyone, at the least, draws on that rough draft and turns episodes from it into speech and possibly into written language. That process may deliver anything from a rounded and shaped story or novel-length life to a few bare utterances. To understand autobiography we get beyond illustrious writers (Rousseau, Gorki, Gosse) and hundreds of lesser writers and try to perceive the essential processes which lie beneath their discourse. Then we will see that they are practising a common art which historically preceded them and which can be heard in the buzz of everyday talk. Lurking beneath the surface of anecdotes, the telling of moments of disaster or delight, recollections of childhood, crises, turning points are the great themes of *memory*, *identity* and the *making of meaning*. Life histories are archaeological expeditions into our memories. But we do not unearth ancient immobile artefacts. Through the very act of reporting memory a strange alchemy changes it. It is transformed by all that has intervened since and by the narrative frame around it.

Perhaps I have said enough to indicate that I am talking about a whole landscape, not a single feature on it. Let me offer a somewhat leaky definition which will at least indicate the wide scope of my subject.

Autobiographical discourse is to be found in all those texts or parts of texts, spoken or written, in which the speaker or author represents his or her own life, or parts of it, by a presentation of episodes in it (i.e. it is narrative in mode).

What that effort does not do is answer one of the great controversial questions about autobiographical acts. Do they represent the truth? Or only partly? To answer that we have to distinguish between the conscious insertion of fictions and the doing so unawares, in good faith. Then there is the opposite process: inserting into fictions materials drawn from life. In fact, we have come to speak of *autobiographical fiction*, either to mean that a novel or story can be a thinly disguised autobiography (*Sons and Lovers*) or that a novel or story can disguise itself as an autobiography (*Moll Flanders, Robinson Crusoe*). The matter is much more complex than I have time to deal with here. Mary McCarthy's *Memories of a Catholic Girlhood* (1957) shows very clearly some of the problems. The book brings together a set of stories which has appeared separately as fictional short stories. Mary McCarthy annotates them as autobiography in an introduction and with notes appended to each chapter. In the notes she is able to show how she now knows that some of the material written in good faith are fictions. There is an interesting discussion of these matters in Paul John Eakin's *Studies in the Art of Self-Invention: Fictions in Autobiography* (1985). He writes:

> Autobiographers no longer believe that autobiography can offer a faithful and unmediated reconstruction of a historically verifiable past; instead it expresses *the play of the autobiographical act itself* in which the materials of the past are shaped by memory and imagination to serve the needs of present consciousness.

I want to give some quick indication of where the new ideas about autobiography are coming from. It's a strange experience, reading these works. It's as though there is a treasure hoard stored in a huge chamber, and those who would inspect it, analyse it and reveal its secrets enter the chamber by different doors. Those coming through one door are so intent on their business that they don't even notice others entering by other doors. I have noticed four doors, and I shall give you an indication of them at breakneck speed by choosing representative figures, one or two for each door.

So then, through the first door, labelled *literary theory* and *literary criticism*. I choose Lejeune (1989), *On Autobiography*, already mentioned. The book consists of a selection from Lejeune's work published between 1975 and 1986, typically neglected until this English translation. Lejeune is not only a towering figure in the French study of autobiography; for a while he worked singlehandedly to amass an archive of all French written autobiographies. Though he began as a literary theorist concentrating exclusively on the accepted masterpieces, we can see his ideas developing so that he eventually discovers that what some do with their pens others do with their mouths. Eventually he arrived at the position where he began to commit himself to everyday manifestations of life stories. This is how he registers his new stance:

> I loved the immensity of the field that was opening up before me … Nothing about the field is narrow or limited. Around 1972 I was interested almost exclusively in masterpieces. Today I am involved in something quite different which surely I could not have foreseen. I had become democratised: it is the life of everyone which interests me; no longer sophisticated texts but the elementary, the most widely known, of autobiographical discourse and writing.

Now through the second door, labelled *ethnography* and *anthropology*. I select Richard Bauman's *Story, Performance and Event* (1987), straight from the school of Dell Hymes, whose ethnography of speaking and concept of performance provide the analytical base. With this text we make the crucial move from the written to the oral. Bauman offers us transcriptions of 30 stories told by Texan oral storytellers, collected over 15 years. They range from obvious fictions (tall stories and the like) to some which are tales of personal experience. His lively, original and intensely detailed analysis turns on his key concept of oral performance.

> … a mode of communication, a way of speaking, the essence of which resides in the assumption of responsibility to an audience for a display of communicative skill, highlighting the way in which a communication is carried out, above and beyond the referential context.

Bauman's work is a kind of manifesto. He not only studies oral narratives; he champions them, including stories of personal experience. Like others before him and since, he believes that narrative is a primary cognitive instrument for making experience comprehensible, though he is not unaware of the fact that it can be an instrument for obscuring, confusing or distorting what went on.

The third door is labelled *psychology*, one might say inevitably although until very recently mainstream psychology took very little notice of autobiography. As Rubin in *Autobiographical Memory* (1986) points out:

> The study of autobiographical memory is one of the least developed areas in the study of human memory.

That is no surprise when we recollect the powerful hold of the empiricist tradition, with its obsession with nonsense syllables and the like. In that tradition autobiography would be considered bizarre, irrelevant and, worst of all, mere anecdotage. However, things are changing and there is talk now of 'remembering in natural contexts'. Salaman (1970) unashamedly treats *her own* memories as valid psychological evidence, and also the memories of writers like Chateaubriand and De Quincey. Poor old Skinner would have a fit! But let me concentrate on my chosen figure coming through the third door: Jerome Bruner, and particularly his book *Acts of Meaning* (1990). In the Eighties he was more and more drawn to the study of autobiography and produced a rapid sequence of papers on the subject. There followed this book, and another in 1992, co-written with Susan Weisser, called *Autobiography and the Construction of Self.*

Acts of Meaning is a long argument for a culturally oriented psychology, too complex to be reduced to a few lines of summary here, but the book concludes with a fascinating project. Bruner and his collaborator elicit half-hour spoken autobiographies ('Tell us the story of your life'). It was not so much that they wanted to probe what autobiography is as that they wanted to observe the self in action, engaged in self-construction. A certain set of principles emerges. A life is created, not recorded, by autobiographical acts. It is a way of construing experience, and re-construing and reconstructing to the end. Most lives are accounted for in patches which are glimpses of a more general narrative about a life, a total narrative most of which is left implicit. It is through such accounts that the culture functions and people discover and make the central meanings of their lives. Note in passing that the study is based on oral narratives, though no explanation is given for this choice.

It is much more difficult to choose one scholar or one work for the fourth door, which I label *cultural history*. In the end I select *The Myths We Live By*, edited by Raphael Samuel and Paul Thompson (1990), which is a set of papers from the Sixth Annual Conference of Oral Historians, for through this door march a solid phalanx of oral historians. The practice of listening to and recording the life stories of those rendered silent and invisible by history is much older than we are inclined to think, going back as it does at least to Henry Mayhew and his most scrupulous and sympathetic methods. The editors of *The Myths We Live By* in their introduction show how far we have travelled from the earlier concerns of oral historians, obsessed as they were by reliability as historical evidence in their recordings. The new approach is the attempt to understand how to 'read and interpret life histories'.

> When we listen now to a life story, the manner of its telling seems to us as important as *what* is told.

The basic proposition to set oral history on its new course is that

> Life stories should be seen, not as blurred experience, as disorderly masses of fragments, but as shaped accounts in which some incidents were dramatized, others contextualised, yet others passed over in silence, through a process of narrative in which both conscious and unconscious, myth and reality, played significant parts.

What this new agenda means for oral historians can be seen dramatically in the papers that follow – accounts by children of a 'strike' against lack of heating in their school, an examination of Anzac legends via interviews with Australian veterans of the First World War, stories of survivors from Nazi extermination camps. The Popular Memory Group from Birmingham concludes:

> From the moment we experience an event we use the meanings of our culture to make sense of it. Over time we re-member our experience as those public meanings change. There is a constant negotiation between experience and sense, private and public memory.

Thus the life story is irresistibly drawn towards the fable.

That was, as the French say, a speedy tour of the horizon. I spoke earlier of the complex landscape which is constituted by the extraordinary range of autobiographical acts only some of which are acknowledged in the work I have been citing. Let me sketch out a kind of taxonomy of such acts, although I don't like the term, since it implies clear-cut boundaries which in fact are crossed and re-crossed. However, I believe no attempt has been made to do this before. Perhaps I should call it mapping. The matter is somewhat confused by what writers choose to call their work as distinct from what the work actually proves to be. This is, as Lejeune (1989) points out, as matter of history:

> ... since the middle of the seventeenth century a game of exchange between memoirs and the novel had little by little transformed narrative in the first person; until the end of the eighteenth century, when the word 'autobiography' was invented, memoirs and confessions were the most used terms.

I shall list first *written* forms of autobiographical acts.

(i) *Literary book-length works* which purport to tell a whole life. There is, of course, a whole library of such works and they are being added to every day (see, for example, Jung Chang's *Wild Swans* [1991]). Many were not published in the author's lifetime, like the remarkable *Christian Watt Papers* [2012] or the collections of working-class life stories in *Useful Toil* and *Destiny Obscure* (both 1994) edited by John Burnett.

(ii) *Memoirs.* The kind of writing in which an author gives an account of a public life, quite often by such notables as statesmen or generals. Gusdorf (1980) somewhat sarcastically noted:

> ... as they have the leisure of retirement or exile, the minister of state, the politician, the military leader write in order to celebrate their deeds ... providing a sort of posthumous propaganda for posterity that is otherwise in danger of forgetting them.

Memoirs are, adds Gusdorf, 'limited almost entirely to the public sector of existence'.

(iii) *Diaries, journals, collections of letters.* I place these together by virtue of their system of composition: a sequence of entries made close to the events and in principle quite independent of each other, although a general meaning may emerge from the juxtaposition of entries and the chronological order. Some of them, we know, were written with ultimate publication in mind, others not. Typical would be Pepys' *Diaries* [2003], Boswell's *Journals* [1994] and Cowper's *Letters* (1937).

(iv) *Autobiographical writings.* This seems a vague and loose term yet it covers many interesting and important works. They consist of groups of stories each of which is sufficiently self-contained to stand on its own feet, but they are also collages from which emerge larger meanings. We know Gorki's autobiographical trilogy but his *Fragments from My Diary* (1975) fits into this category for it consists of discrete stories of his encounters with people who made a deep impression on him. I would include here John Clare's *Autobiographical Writings* edited by Eric Robinson (1983), and the relevant section of Walter Benjamin's *Reflections: Essays, aphorisms and autobiographical writings* (1995). Mary McCarthy's *Memories of a Catholic Girlhood* (1957) I have already referred to.

(v) *Embedded autobiographical writing.* Personal stories are inserted into other kinds of texts, even the most improbable ones. They are of great importance because they constitute a way of eluding the genre police. My most recent exciting experience of this kind is Steven Rose's *The Making of Memory: From Molecules to Mind* (1992), which is not only a meticulous account of experimental work; it is interleaved with such writing as is prompted by another intention: 'I want to describe what it feels like to be a neuroscientist'. So we get an account of a day in the lab and the experience of an academic conference. A classic of the fusion of the scientific and the personal is Oliver Sacks' *The Man who Mistook his Wife for a Hat* (1985).

(vi) *Journalism and travel writing.* When journalists write of events as personal experience, unequivocally placing themselves and their feelings at the centre of their accounts, they enter autobiographical space. So do certain kinds of travel writers who do the same thing. My generation was brought up on Stevenson's *Travels with a Donkey* (1993) and Kinglake's *Eothen; or Traces of travel, Brought home from the East* (1997), indispensible items in the canon of the day.

(vii) *Testimony in writing.* We meet this in various forms such as written evidence for a court or accounts of accidents for insurance purposes. And, of course, in the CV, a classic instance of self-censorship and the peremptory demand for autobiography.

Now let me list spoken forms, the least examined material.

(i)   *Attempts to speak a whole life.* This is the large territory of the oral historian and community groups in which people gradually construct or reconstruct their personal-cum-social lives.

(ii)   *Framed episodes.* Autobiographical stories insert themselves into conversation when a speaker captures conversational space to tell a personal story on the assumption that its intrinsic interest will justify a larger than usual allocation of turn-taking.

(iii) *The embedded personal story.* A story can be told as a powerful way of participating in conversation and making a relevant contribution to an argument or other function of the talk.

(iv)   *In the audio-visual media.* Perhaps more than we realise, personal stories are told by non-professionals as, for example, eye-witness accounts and talk about their lives. There are also full-scale, 'face-to-face' accounts by well-known figures, some of which have become classics.

(v)   *Embryonic autobiographical acts.* These are very brief utterances about the speaker's past. The head of a possible story shows above the parapet but for one reason or another the conversation sweeps on and the full tale is never told.

(vi)   *Courtroom testimony and formal interviews.* This category is of great significance for it reminds us that autobiographical acts are not only examples of benign meaning-making discourse but also emerge from duress. They are often part of the oppressive action of the state and end up in dangerous dossiers.

The map I have outlined is not, of course, exhaustive. New forms are emerging and will go on doing so. There is, for example, a slide-audio trilogy called 'Serving the Status Quo: From Stories we Tell Ourselves, Stories we Tell Each Other', reported in Simon's *Teaching against the Grain* (1992).

I have had to cram in enough to indicate my present preoccupations; enough, that is, I hope, to constitute an invitation to you and NATE in general to join in. If you're asking what all this has to do with English teaching, that's another part of the story which I am ready to tell some other time. But I hope I have put enough markers to help you to tell the story too. Meanwhile two signposts. Jack Zipes said the other day that we must take notice of how stories of all kinds are now utterly commercialised, are on the market, and that we must find ways of eluding that market. There *are* ways. There is absolutely no area of the curriculum in which autobiography could not make itself heard, drawing its meaning from the lives of students and teachers. Storytelling, Jack Zipes went on to say, must be subversive. I believe is it a potentially oppositional strategy. It can be an act of reclamation, of rescue in the constructing of identity. A special place must be given to teachers telling their own stories, including those of their lives as teachers, a constructive starting point for curriculum reform.

Autobiography is the mode of discourse best equipped to stop others from telling our stories because, especially in its spoken form, it is the most resistant to surveillance and prescription. When E. P. Thompson died, many quoted his opening to *The Making of the English Working Class* (1965):

> I am seeking to rescue the poor stockinger, the Luddite cropper, the 'obsolete' hand-loom weaver, the utopian artisan ... from the enormous condescension of history.

The task for us now and for our students is to do our own rescue work, to counter the condescending powers with the assertion of who and what we are.

References

Bakhtin, M. (1981) *The Dialogic Imagination* (C. Emerson and M. Holquist, trans.). Austin: University of Texas Press.

Barnes, D., Britton, J., Rosen, H. and the LATE (1971) *Language, the Learner and the School* (revised edition). Harmondsworth: Penguin.

Barthes, R. (1975) *S/Z* (R. Miller, trans.). London: Jonathan Cape.

Bauman, R. (1986) *Story, Performance and Event.* Cambridge: Cambridge University Press.

Benjamin, W. (1995) *Reflections: Essays, aphorisms and autobiographical writings* (modern edition). New York: Random House.

Boswell, J. (1994) *The Journals of James Boswell: 1762–1795* (modern edition) (J. Wain, ed.). New Haven, CT: Yale University Press.

Britton, J. (1970) *Language and Learning.* London: Allen Lane.

Bruner, J. (1990) *Acts of Meaning.* Cambridge, MA: Harvard University Press.

Bruner, J. and Weisser, S. (1992) *Autobiography and the Construction of Self.* Cambridge, MA: Harvard University Press.

Burnett, J. (ed.) (1994) *Destiny Obscure: Autobiographies of childhood, education and family from the 1820s to the 1920s.* London: Routledge.

Burnett, J. (ed.) (1994) *Useful Toil: Autobiographies of working people from the 1820s to the 1920s.* London: Routledge.

Cassirer, E. (1944) *An Essay on Man.* New Haven, CT: Yale University Press.

Chang, J. (1991) *Wild Swans: Three daughters of China.* London: William Collins.

Clare, J. (1983) *Autobiographical Writings* (E. Robinson, ed.). Oxford: Oxford University Press.

Clark, U. (1994) 'Bringing English to order: A personal account of the NCC Evaluation Project'. *English in Education*, 20 (1).

Cowper, W. (1937) *William Cowper's Letters: A selection* (modern edition) (E. Lucas, ed.). Oxford: Oxford University Press.

Eakin, P. (1985) *Fictions in Autobiography: Studies in the art of self-invention.* Princeton, NJ: Princeton University Press.

Fish, S. (1980) *Is there a Text in this Class?* Cambridge, MA: Harvard University Press.

Gorki, M. (1975) *Fragments from My Diary* (M. Budberg, trans.). London: Penguin.

Gusdorf, G. (1980) 'Conditions and limits of autobiography', in J. Olney (ed.), *Autobiography: Essays theoretical and critical.* Princeton, NJ: Princeton University Press.

Kinglake, A. (1997) *Eothen: Or traces of travel brought home from the East* (modern edition). Evanston, IL: Northwestern University Press.

Lejeune, P. (1989) *On Autobiography* (K. Leary, trans.). Minneapolis: University of Minnesota Press.

McCarthy, M. (1957) *Memoirs of a Catholic Girlhood.* London: Heinemann.

The Newbolt Committee (1921) *The Teaching of English in England* (The Newbolt Report). London: HMSO.

Pepys, S. (2003) *The Diaries of Samuel Pepys – a selection* (modern edition) (R. Latham, ed.). London: Penguin.

Piaget, J. (1945*) Play, Dreams and Imitation in Childhood.* New York: Norton.

Rose, S. (1992) *The Making of Memory: From molecules to mind.* London: Bantam Press.

Rosen, H. (1993) *Troublesome Boy.* London: English and Media Centre.

Rubin, D. (1986) *Autobiographical Memory.* Cambridge: Cambridge University Press.

Sacks, O. (1985) *The Man who Mistook his Wife for a Hat.* London: Duckworth.

Said, E. (1993) *Culture and Imperialism.* London: Chatto and Windus.

Salaman, E. (1970) *A Collection of Moments: A study of involuntary memories.* London: Longman.

Samuels, R. and Thompson, P. (eds.) (1990) *The Myths We Live By.* London: Routledge.

Simon, R. (1992) *Teaching against the Grain: Texts for a pedagogy of possibility.* New York: Bergin and Garvey.

Stevenson, R. (1993) *Travels with a Donkey in the Cévennes and Selected Travel Writings* (modern edition). Oxford: Oxford University Press.

Thompson, E. (1965) *The Making of the English Working Class.* London: Gollancz.

Vygotsky, L. (1962) *Thought and Language* (E. Hanfmann, G. Vakar and N. Minnick, trans.). Cambridge, MA: MIT Press.

Vygotsky, L. (1978) *Mind in Society: Development of higher psychological processes* (M. Cole, V. John-Steiner, S. Scribner and E. Souberman, eds.). Cambridge, MA: Harvard University Press.

Walzer, M. (1987) *Interpretation and Social Criticism.* Cambridge, MA: Harvard University Press.

Watt, C. (2012) *The Christian Watt Papers* (modern edition) (D. Fraser, ed.). Edinburgh: Berlinn.

Second Interlude

St Bernard

Dilapidated mongrels
Arrived from nowhere
To fight and copulate and crap
In our dogless street.
Fearful we kept our distance.
But outside his surgery
Dr Sacks's St Bernard
Sat like a deity.
At his chosen moments
He eased off his haunches
Lolloped slowly along the pavement.
All the kids left
Their skipping ropes and tipcat
To greet this huge pacifist,
A thousand miles from his alp,
Took all the adoring pats and touchings
Benignly as his due.
A little girl reached up
To embrace his neck.
He adapted well to the odour
Of pickled herrings
And the *shtetl* cuisine.

Harold Rosen

Womenfolk at the windows:
'A miracle a miracle
Never barks never bites
A mouth like that
Could gobble her up
A miracle thank god.'

Dr Sacks too a large respected figure
Never walked his dog
Must have chatted with him indoors
Sealed their bonding
After their daily turns of duty.

As he left us for his sentry post
The everyday took over.

Haimishe **Fish**

Haimishe fish
My *booba* always called them
As some might say
Cuttlefish dog fish monk fish
Well … No not quite.

At the fishmonger's in Hessel Street
A long tank crammed with fish
Hundreds of them
Sluggish fins and tails
Resigned fatalistic grey
Carp and bream,
Haimishe fish
Just this side of death
Not in their element.

That's where *booba*
Had our fish
Plucked from the tank

Brought home
Lodged in the biggest saucepan
Left for an hour or so
For a last hopeless swim
Then dealt with for supper

Always called *haimishe* fish.
There were *haimishe* cucumbers too
Stubby with warts on.
Haimishe – from the home country
Where the old folks had come from.
Was this the nostalgia of exiles?
From Vilna Odessa Warsaw
The tastes of home
Pickled fishy fried in batter chopped.
No one ever said
Haimishe cossacks
Haimishe pogroms.

Haimishe fish
Freshwater fish
From back home
Which they had turned their backs on.

Music

I was never given the least chance to learn a musical instrument and assumed that this was because I couldn't … At the rag-collectors, the Sterns, round the corner on a Sunday evening you could sit on the sacks of rags and listen to the family playing string quartets, and at the Michaelsons you could listen to the old man playing the mandolin and the balalaika, and Solly Gilborsky over the road played the fiddle very seriously and devotedly at ten years of age, and the local tenth-rate grammar school I went to with a population of 150 boys had a magnificent orchestra though the only music taught in the school consisted of improbable lessons by the chemistry teacher who tried to teach us silly songs (the boys had all learned their instruments in the dirty back streets which the school was teaching us so successfully to reject) …

Around me in my childhood were dozens of sad violin players whom I regarded as being possessed at birth with virtuosity.

In a letter to Betty, January 1977

Penmanship

All Mr O'Carroll's teaching of writing skills rested on the one foundation principle – 'Up thin, down thick'. He was a methodical man and as a writing master his procedure was unvarying. He walked up and down the rows, cane in hand, to achieve a classful of impeccable calligraphers who no longer made aitches without loops, zeds and kays without their twiddly bits or mutated their Qs into gees. If you malformed a letter you put out your hand and got a stinger, delivered without mercy or malice. Up and down he went, swishing away for half an hour. This reign of terror may have worked well for some but it made my pen falter and the faint chance I had of turning out a page without blots and exotic shapes for letters vanished in my despair and resignation. Resigned I certainly was. On the day when I could see that my kay, the old enemy, had gone astray again, Mr O'Carroll was right over the other side of the room dispassionately dispensing just deserts. I realised I'd have a long wait before he got round to me. I put up my hand.

'Please, sir, my kay, I've done my kay wrong. Can I have the cane now?'

Mr O'Carroll obliged and, crossing the room, delivered a whack and coolly went back to where he had left off. Give him his due, he always caned the left hand. So I tucked my hand under my arm and took up again the deformed writer's crouch. I'm afraid Mr O'Carroll put the final touches on the making of an illegible handwriter and was the cause later on of all those infuriated teachers' cries of 'I'm not even going to try to read this scribble' and 'Fit for the waste-paper basket' and those sneery remarks at the bottom of my written work in the grammar school: 'This may be the work of a genius but no one will ever know.' I couldn't very well explain to them that it was all Mr O'Carroll's fault and about that cane doing overtime and up-thin-and-down-thick.

I had one last chance to reform and, who knows, to produce manuscripts I could feel good about instead of being embarrassed by their sheer ugliness. Much of my disgruntlement was due to the fact that my scrawl was exposed day after day to my teachers' grimaces. My classmates would take a peek, too.

'Didn't know you could write Yiddish.'

'A doctor, that's what you're going to be. You've got the writing for it.'

'It's a code, a secret code.'

I had this last chance, as I said, when I started in the grammar school. I knew we were going to do prestigious and snobby things like French, Latin and Physics, and go to a proper sports field and have a cap badge with a galleon and French motto on it, *Tel grain, Tel pain.* We were the elect, swept up into a rarefied air, laced with the scent of privilege. Then came a terrible blow that brought us down to earth. They told us we would be having a handwriting class. We were incredulous, insulted, humiliated. Kids' stuff. The ones whose penmanship was already as good as any adult's and whose hands raced and looped lightly across the page were sure it couldn't mean what it said. It was bound to be some kind of special writing.

'Special writing,' someone said, 'like you see on parchment. You do it with a feather pen. Lawyers have to do it.'

'It's like the way they write the Torah scrolls. You have to do it perfect. You have to do it perfect.'

'That's more what you call lettering, not handwriting. They said handwriting, not lettering.'

Though I joined in the outrage at being demoted in this way I secretly thought that there was just a chance that I might redeem myself and learn to write decently. So I hoped they were wrong about lettering, parchment and all that. They should be so lucky.

When the time came we were all taken by surprise. The teacher gave out something he called copybooks. We had never seen such things before. In fact even at that time most people would have regarded them as museum pieces. They looked like ordinary exercise books but they had 'Copybooks' printed on the cover and when you opened them you discovered that on each page there were printed in faultless copperplate four or five sentences like Procrastination is the thief of Time, Cleanliness is next to Godliness, The child is father to the man, Necessity is the mother of invention. Underneath each of these improving sentiments there were three lines, just like on our millboards in Miss Campbell's class when we were babies. We were expected to produce perfect replicas of the copperplate models. The class set to work, fizzing with resentment.

'If my poppa saw me doing this he'd have a fit,' said Barney. 'He thinks we spend all day showing how clever we are like *yeshiva bochers.*'

'Not my dad. Know what he'd say? "So what's wrong with learning to write nice? Those people know what they're doing, I'm telling you. A degree every one of them's got. Nothing wrong with learning to write like a *mensch.*"'

I don't know how a *mensch* writes but it was soon clear to me that even with the severe guidance of the model lines of copperplate my writing wasn't going to get any better. When we finally parted with the copybooks at the end of the term, everyone, myself included, reverted to the style they'd been using for years. No one's looked like copperplate. Not one of our teachers had handwriting that was faintly like copperplate. They made no comment about all this and the copybook exercise was treated as a ritual, the origin of which had been forgotten but which was kept up for good form's sake.

Between the First Year and the Fifth Year my writing got worse and worse, partly because we spent so many hours scribbling notes from the board and partly because I was always rushing my homework in the hope of leaving time to join the boys in the street. Mr Gunn, the History teacher, wrote beautifully on the board and very fast, too. If you didn't keep up with him he was wiping it off and starting on the next bit. Lazy Mr Powell sat on his desk, swinging his legs, fingering his little moustache and dictating at a speed nobody could keep up with. Too fast, too fast, some of us would shout. It made no difference. He swept on, caring no more about our protests than he cared about the geography he was supposed to be teaching. We prayed for a break when he would draw a map on the board, a diagrammatic one on which we could not distinguish between land and sea, rivers and boundaries. I decided in the end that the reason he'd taken to dictation was that his writing, too, was quite illegible. I had seen a page in the notebook he was dictating from when I went to the front to use the pencil sharpener. That didn't stop him crossing out my homework and writing, 'Hasty, sloppy and unreadable. Re-write. See me.' I saw him all right, at the end of the day. He'd obviously forgotten what it was all about.

'My work,' I said. 'The Amazon. You said I've got to rewrite it.'

'Got it with you? No? I might have guessed. I remember now. Well, I'm not having it, my boy. Do you really expect me to spend hours and hours trying to read your stuff?'

'No, sir.'

'Well, I can tell you this much. Anything you write in the exam which looks like your usual mess will not be marked. You'll get nought. Get this into your noddle. The examiners are told that they're not obliged to read your kind of writing. You'll get nought. The thing is that your writing – I mean it's so uneducated – not a peasant, are you?'

So he got The Amazon 'in best' as we used to say. Usually anything Mr Powell said didn't leave a lasting impression on me but we were getting very close to the Matric exams. In addition to the anxieties we all shared – do I know enough to pass? – I was now alarmed at the possibility that the examiners would not even read my work. Our teachers often invoked the examiners who gradually grew in our thoughts to become implacable, omniscient ogres who wouldn't give a second thought to brushing pages of desperate work into the waste paper basket. They would settle my hash at a glance. I was very rattled. The shadows of the ever-punitive examiners darkened my frenetic revision. Abe, who was revising with me in the evenings, lost his patience.

'Why do you let a pisher like Powell put the wind up you? *Er veist nisht fon der hant un der fis.* He doesn't know his arse from his elbow. Did you ever get nought for the end of year exams? For the mock exams? So leave off grizzling, will you?'

I remained inconsolable.

It takes some believing but only a month or two earlier my writing had been in demand. I wrote love letters for a sailor. I was in the Reading Room of the Whitechapel Library where some of us used to do our homework. A wiry little chap slid into the seat next to me and started muttering something or other. Eventually it turned out that he was a sailor whose ship had docked somewhere in the Thames nearby and that he needed to write to his beloved in Liverpool. He pushed a cheap little writing pad under my nose and asked me to do the job for him. It was obvious to me that he couldn't write but at first I assumed he'd dictate in whispers and I would simply be his scribe. (Me, his scribe!) But no, he wanted me to compose as well and it had to be a love letter. Somehow he made all this clear. I don't remember what I wrote though I could make a good guess. I'd not yet written any love letters myself but I had read a lot of novels and with shameless confidence I wrote a nice devoted piece to Agnes in Liverpool. My sailor watched my writing flowing out of my pen as though I were performing magic. He couldn't take his eyes off it. I whispered my text back to him and did the envelope. He took the letter and envelope and pushed sixpence across to me – the first money I earned by my writing in both senses of the word. I did the same job for him half a dozen times and then my sailor stopped coming to the Reading Room which was just as well because he never showed me replies from Agnes, if there were any, and I was running out of ideas. At the time I was grimly amused by the fact that I was earning money from my penmanship while my teachers waged an unceasing and ineffectual war against it. I wonder how Agnes managed.

There were ten days to go until the exams. We were at our sports field for athletics trials. Winners would represent the school and I hoped to be one of them. I'd run the half mile and was now doing the long jump. I was not what you'd call a brilliant long jumper but probably the best the school could come up with for the under-sixteens. It was a lean year. Facilities in those days were primitive: the long jump pit was far too narrow and the run up was on worn wet grass. My third jump. I made an over-anxious flailing effort to do a hitch-kick which I'd read about in a book. I landed awkwardly and hit my elbow, my left elbow, on the brass rule at the side of the pit. During the rest of the afternoon it became very painful and swollen. The teacher in charge advised me to go to the hospital when I got back – to be on the safe side, as he said. I could get straight off the tram from the sports field and into the London Hospital on the Whitechapel Road. At the hospital a sporty young doctor listened to my story and asked me how far I'd jumped on that third jump and I had to admit that it was such a bad jump I hadn't stopped to find out.

'I long jump for the Hospital. Hard on the ankle and the Achilles. But the elbow, that's a new one. Let's get it X- rayed.'

Harold Rosen

I wanted to ask him how you jumped for a hospital but didn't want to sound stupid. The upshot was that I had broken my elbow and went home with my arm in a sling and feeling shaky. My mother took one look at the sling and, for once forgetting to drown me in sympathy, clapped her hand to her face and said, 'Your exams! How are you going to do them? *Gottinue!* Were you out of your mind? Fooling around just before your exams! What were you thinking of? What did they say to you at the hospital? Broken! *Vey iz meine yahren,* broken! Such a fine time to do long jumping. You couldn't wait till after exams, so urgent it was. You're not studying long jumping. You don't do Matric in long jumping.'

She sat down and rocked to and fro as though there'd been a death in the family.

'Mum, it's my left arm. The doctor showed me the X-ray. It's just a little crack. Anyone would think it had been amputated.'

'God forbid. Don't even say such things. Such jokes he makes.'

The next morning my form master at registration was full of concern and wanted to know the whole story. As the exams grew near most of our teachers underwent a change of heart. Slowly they changed sides and joined us as confederates in efforts to outwit the implacable examiners. By subtle analysis of past papers they tried to forecast questions and suggested ingratiating little turns of phrase we might use. My form master was not quite as frantic as my mother but shared her anxiety.

'Your writing, Rosen. It's not a work of art at the best of times but with that arm … '

'It's my left arm, sir.'

'Yes, but you have to rest on it and that sling will throw you out of balance.'

He spoke as though he was trying to convince himself and me, rehearsing something.

'Leave this to me. I'll write to the University.'

Write to the University! To me that was like writing to God. What would he say? A few days later he beckoned to me. I went to the front of the room and he took out of an envelope a little wodge of papers.

'Read it,' he said. 'It'll cheer you up.'

I took the top sheet. It looked like a diploma with the University of London's crest at the top. It read:

This candidate 05774 has recently broken his arm. This has adversely affected his handwriting and examiners are required to take this into account when marking his papers.

My heart sang. I'd tried out my writing by then and it was the same old ugly scrawl. My arm in a sling had not made a scrap of difference. But They wouldn't know.

'There'll be one of those pinned to every paper,' said my form master. 'Should help a bit.'

Believe it or not, he winked, that old comrades-in-crime gesture from one of my teachers! Abe wanted to know all about it.

'Recently broken his arm,' I quoted. 'And it didn't say which one.'

'That's one thing you can stop moaning about then,' said Abe. 'Arm in a sling, everyone should have one. Mind you, that's what I call perfect timing.'

I was so ecstatic that I felt as though I had already passed my exams. Even the examiners' iron hearts would melt when they read those notices. I could hear them saying, 'Tough on the lad. And he's churned out a readable script.'

I imagined them giving me the benefit of several doubts, nudging me across a border or two and enjoying the feel of magnanimity in doing so. In each exam a slip from the University was placed on my desk and when things weren't going too well the sight of it consoled me. How could they fail a boy with a broken arm?

I passed. I got my Matric and went on to the Sixth Form. Well, you never know. Those beautiful slips may have just seen me through. Without them I might, like many of my friends, have ended up as a clerk in the City – if my writing had been good enough.

Millions of handwritten words later my writing doesn't seem to baffle anybody. In the Sixth Form I taught myself to write very small and not to swoop erratically across the page but lightly to push the pen up and down. It gradually became a sensual pleasure. It feels nice and I enjoy seeing a page of text unwinding from my pen. The word-processor, calling for eight fidgety fingers, cheats me of the pleasures it took so long to develop. My thoughts don't go tap-tap. They inscribe themselves in an idiosyncratic flow. So against all the odds I end up with Roland Barthes and celebrate the 'joyous physical experience' of the calligrapher.

Part Two

The Role of Language in Learning

The Walworth School
English Syllabus

In 1956, Harold went to Walworth School in south-east London as head of the English department. During the two years he was there, he and Guy Rogers (the previous head of English at Walworth, by now the head teacher there, and a founding secretary of the London Association for the Teaching of English) offered an evening course at the Institute of Education, University of London, entitled 'English in the comprehensive school'. The course was timely because, after the relative success of the 'interim comprehensives' like Walworth and Peckham Girls' School, formed in 1949, the London County Council had decided to open up four of its grammar schools to a comprehensive entry in 1955. John Dixon, Harold's successor as head of English at Walworth in 1958, was 'an ardent member' (his words) of the course. The discussions at the course helped Harold to formulate his seminal idea: that the English curriculum should be based on the language and culture of the neighbourhood. This he spelt out in detail in the syllabus he handed on to John Dixon. In 2009, Dixon and Simon Clements described in more detail the context in which they took on Harold's syllabus.

> [Harold] handed on [this syllabus] when he left Walworth and we two – with Leslie Stratta – first joined the English department. The fundamental principles he set forward, and the detailed advice and practices he added, offered us an exciting launch pad, the basis for committed joint work over the following five years. But you have to imagine a different world, so first a word about the context.

> It's fifty years ago. Imagine a time when roughly fifty comprehensive schools have opened to date, and Walworth – created by knocking down a wall between a Central and an Elementary school – is still without an allocation of 11+ 'successes', though it's got a handful of so-called 'failures' staying in the Sixth Form. So 99% of secondaries in England and Wales are still Grammar or recently-formed 'Moderns'. The prevailing assumption is that you test at 11+, select say 20% for a grammar-school curriculum and the established five-year course to GCE, leaving the rest to follow courses still being thrashed out, and ending after four years without a qualification. The idea of teaching them all together in the same school is hotly contested; the idea of a common syllabus for them all verges on the incredible.

Harold Rosen

> As for Walworth School, the main building is an 1880s three-decker
> and it's still surrounded by terraces of mid-nineteenth-century houses,
> the homes of a rather old-fashioned working class, with the first black
> workers from the Caribbean still to arrive in the area. Not an ideal
> place to choose for a pioneering experiment – or was it?

Walworth School – English syllabus

(Provisional, January 1958, to go into full operation School Year 58/59)

Introduction

The teaching of English at Walworth calls for a sympathetic understanding of the pupils' environment and temperament. Their language experience is acquired from their environment and from communication with the people who matter most to them. This highly localised language is likely to stand out in their own minds in strong contrast to the language experience being consciously presented in the framework of English lessons in particular, and school work in general. This contrast can all too easily become a conflict, 'aversion to poshness', and affectation can easily bedevil the teaching of English. Whatever language the pupils possess, it is this which must be built on rather than driven underground. However narrow the experience of our pupils may be (and it is often wider than we think), it is this experience alone which has given their language meaning. The starting point for English work must be the ability to handle effectively pupils' own experience. Oral work, written work and the discussion of literature must create an atmosphere in which the pupils become confident of the full acceptability of the material of their own experience. Only in this way can they advance to the next stage.

It is here that the greatest difficulty lies. Language needs to be communicated to a wider group than the class or the school or the area. It must be so used that it is intelligible to the widest sections of the community. This is where grammatical accuracy, punctuation and spelling find their proper place – within the framework of nationally accepted standards of speech and writing. They are only part of a complex form of speech and writing. The desire to use this form and understand it must be built up.

All normal children are interested in the life they live, in those who share it with them and their own part in it. These are our pupils' interests (children's interests are not just their hobbies!). This interest should be used in all aspects of English work. It should be the basis of preparation for written work and a basis for literary study. The teacher at Walworth will inevitably feel a conflict between the lively but often barbaric expression of the pupils and the need to inculcate standards of acceptability. The wish to say something and communicate it should always be seen as *basic*, and therefore sincerity is the first standard to apply. The less confident the pupils, the more they are convinced that they cannot write and have nothing to say, the more this standard should take precedence. Standards of acceptability should always follow it.

The syllabus which follows is in two parts: (a) an outline of methods of approach which will more or less apply to all classes in the school; (b) year-by-year syllabuses.

It is important to stress at the outset that above all the syllabuses must be treated with flexibility. Full allowance must be made for the difference between classes, which will be due not so much to differences of ability as to differences in previous training. Room must be left to bring into the classroom topical matters. Teachers will have special interests through which they can impart special flavour and interest to their lessons. It should, however, be added that any important departure from the syllabus should be discussed with the head of department.

I. Reading

Each class will have at least one prose reader. This should be regarded as the minimum reading to be done in the term. One period a week should be set aside for work aimed at fostering a desire to read and raising the standards of the pupils' tastes. The lesson should never consist simply of reading round the class. It should be a lesson in which varied activities take place. Some of the possibilities are listed below.

(a)   The teacher should from time to time bring along a book suitable for the class, read some of it and talk briefly about it. If possible it should be a book in the school library.
(b)   Pupils should be urged to bring their own books and similarly introduce them to the class.
(c)   A form reading record may be kept in which pupils enter books they have read with brief comments on them. It must be easily available (from teacher's desk?).
(d)   Silent reading, particularly of some chosen section of the class reader, followed by discussion.

It should be added that experience at Walworth shows that our pupils need a great deal of personal encouragement and treatment in developing their reading tastes. It is important that teachers should recommend books not only suitable to classes, but also to individuals. The range of taste in a class is amazingly wide. There are children who are voracious readers, but who lose the reading habit for lack of suitable material. If teachers find they are not in a position to help classes or pupils they should consult the head of department. No real help can be given to an English teacher unless he is prepared to read children's books from time to time.

Comprehension work should be seen as a part of the general drive to improve children's ability to read by deepening their response and increasing their ability to deal with more complex material. It must be done regularly.

(a) Material should be carefully chosen.
(b) The teacher should not rely on sets of questions in the books.
(c) As a general principle, questions should be directed towards a general understanding of the passage, and not as tests of 'hard words' or background material.
(d) It is almost impossible for a comprehension question to be too easy.
(e) Some work should be done on particular passages in books being read by the class.
(f) The Certificate of Attainment revealed a great weakness in written comprehension. More attention must be given to it.

II. Text books

Considerable difficulties will inevitably arise because many books in use in the school conflict in aims and methods with those outlined in the syllabus. This will be so if we could replace them all tomorrow. Most teachers feel very strongly the need of a good text book on which to base their work, but the best text book in the world will not help the teacher who places almost total dependence on it. It will be necessary to select material, modify it, amplify it and in many cases reject it. (How many text books deal adequately with figurative language?) Ideally teachers should duplicate material needed in class, but it is recognised that difficulties often prevent this.

III. Grammar

The place of Grammar in the secondary-school syllabus is a matter of violent controversy. This syllabus does not pretend to solve the problem. It represents an uneasy compromise between certain modern trends in the teaching of Grammar, and the demands of various public examinations. It is not included in the belief that it is a means of correcting common errors, which must be treated as they arise. The detailed syllabuses [which follow] contain for the most part simply the topic to be treated, but it should be remembered that different methods of treatment can lead to lessons so different that they will have only the syllabus topic in common.

The following points should be observed when those parts of the syllabus relating to Grammar are being dealt with.

(a) Grammar should be ignored when the general level of work is very low and the morale of the class needs to be improved and its English work made more lively.
(b) Lessons should not consist of the issuing of rules but rather of the observation of the way language works.

(c) Words should never be studied in isolation but always as parts of sentences, if possible in a context.

(d) An effort should always be made to link grammatical work with creative work and to stimulate thought about and an interest in language. E.g., nouns with a first form: what do we have names for? why do we have Christian names? why surnames? how are things named – churches, boats, racehorses?

(e) The work should never be *rushed*. Each stage should be mastered by the whole class and covered in a variety of ways before passing on.

(f) Very detailed suggestions for Grammar lessons will be found in Gurrey's *Grammar at work*, Parts I, II and III. An intelligent plea for a new approach to Grammar will be found in Hugh Skyes-Davies's *Grammar without tears*.

IV. Spelling

It can be said without doubt that the general level of spelling in the school is low, and while the English teacher should not feel that he alone is responsible for improving it, he should make some special effort to raise the standard.

(a) The English teacher might be able to arrange with the form teacher to use registration periods for writing up spelling lists. (Recent decisions on staff procedure at registration make this less likely than it was.)

(b) This syllabus includes the systematic treatment of spelling rules which are given in an Appendix. Only serious and regular treatment will lead to an improvement in spelling. The spelling rules should be copied out, learnt and tested. If possible, form rooms should have posted in them current work in spelling, i.e. rules and lists.

V. Speech training

No specific mention of Speech is made in the detailed syllabus. For teachers without special training (most of us!) it should be treated as an integral part of verse speaking, dramatic work and oral work. It should not be forgotten that pupils will modify their speech of their own accord when their desire for more education is aroused and they will unconsciously model themselves on teachers whom they admire and respect. Teachers with special qualifications may include speech training in the syllabus after consultation with the head of department.

If at any time the school acquires a tape-recorder a special appendix on its use will be added to the syllabus.

VI. Poetry

(a) The annual poetry competition in which every pupil takes part should be seen as an integral part of the syllabus. It should not be rushed through perfunctorily in class, but should be used to give serious consideration to the way in which poetry should be spoken and the relationship between reading, meaning and feeling.

(b)   The poetry lesson should not consist solely of lengthy consideration of single poems, though this may well be done from time to time, more frequently as the pupils go up the school.

(c)   Pupils should be given ample time to read through the anthology, select poems they like, want to read or have read. Good poems which have made an impact should be re-read.

(d)   The teacher should bring his own books to class and read from them, noting carefully any poems which the pupils respond to well. If possible the pupils should be encouraged to go beyond their anthology and explore books in the library.

(e)   A repertory of poems enjoyed by the class can thus be built up and repeated from time to time. In this way a much closer and deeper familiarity with the poems can be established.

(f)   Poetry should not always be dealt with in a single lesson, but can be linked with other work, or ten minutes can be spent at the beginning or end of a lesson.

(g)   In the upper part of the school an occasional concentration on the work of one poet may be well worth while: e.g. Clare, or selected reading from work just published.

(h)   Learning by heart. The following conditions must apply to carrying out this part of the syllabus:

   (1)   The poem to be learnt must be a poem which the teacher feels is well worth while learning.
   (2)   No learning by heart should be done unless the poem has been discussed fully in class and there is a sympathetic response to it.
   (3)   The teacher should always try to help the class to learn it.

All the emphasis should be placed on the way the poem is spoken rather than detailed accuracy or the ability to gallop through breathlessly to the end.

VII. Drama

(a)   Out-of-school dramatic work should provide a stimulus to work in class.

(b)   Plays worked on in class are not productions. The teacher should concentrate on stimulating dramatic imagination and the beginnings of dramatic study.

(c)   When dramatic work is being done in class, the whole class must be involved:

   1.   They must be kept alert by demands for suggestions and alternatives, and made to step in to try different parts.
   2.   Casting must embrace everyone, several teams being formed if necessary.

(d)   Many plays will need to be read through before being acted. The more difficult plays will also need to be discussed briefly and then more fully while being attempted.

(e)   The aim in the new building should be to get all classes into the hall at some time to do dramatic work.

(f)   Where a play has caught the imagination of a class it should be worked on more fully, and the class encouraged to give a floor reading to another class. Simple props and costume might be used.

VIII. Homework

The bulk of the homework should be set in connection with the composition scheme [see below]. Odd exercises from text books should be set very rarely and only when they tie up closely with work being done in class. The maximum effort should be made to return the work to the class in a lesson with comments and discussion. Work should be read out, both good and bad. A particular point might be chosen to show how different pupils have treated it. While praise and encouragement should be the keynote, this is a lesson in which our pupils can be taught to take criticism because the atmosphere is friendly and constructive. It is also part of the campaign to make public what children write.

IX. Marking

The following method should be used, but it should not be forgotten that personal comment, provocative and appreciative, is probably of more value.

(a)   All composition work should be given a general impression mark as follows:

A – Work of outstanding quality

B – Good work

C – Average work, which can be said to be satisfactory

D – Poor work

E – Completely unsatisfactory

+ and – to be used if the teacher wishes to do so.

(b)   A second mark using the same scale as above, but confined to *correctness*, may be used if the teacher wishes to do so. It may also be used for one particular point, say, punctuation, if prior warning has been given to the class.

(c)   Code for errors

1.   Spelling – *recieve* – word may be written in the margin

2.   Punctuation – [comma with a circle round it] – *wrong*; [full stop with a circle round it] – *omitted*

3.   Grammar, expression, etc. [vertical squiggle] in margin or [horizontal squiggle] underneath.

(d)   The marking code and correction code to be written out at the back of English books.

(e)   The above code may be considered a minimum, but teachers are warned against a proliferation of squiggles which can only be confusing.

X. *The backward pupil*

The syllabus will have to be modified for backward pupils, but the aim should be always to keep to as much of it as possible, varying the work more often within the lesson.

It should be remembered that many so-called backward pupils are perfectly capable of normal work if 'caught' in time, and that there is a tendency to accept their low attainments too readily. The best form of help for those who cannot read properly is specialised treatment in very small groups when staff is available. Experience has shown that even teachers with no special training can effect great improvements.

Raising the standard of English of backward pupils is a very responsible job, since no real progress can be made in other subjects until it is achieved. When the school acquires a teacher who has specialised in this work, we might be able to add more specific suggestions.

> There then follow detailed syllabus guidelines for the (then) four compulsory years of secondary education. Each of these sets of detailed guidelines begins with 'Composition', and refers to the 'Composition Scheme', which is Appendix I to the syllabus.

Composition scheme

1. All composition work up to and including the 4th year will be based on the compilation of magazines. The purpose will be to give every pupil the opportunity for individual development of composition work while at the same time giving the teacher ample opportunity for direction of the work. The magazine method should aim at the outset to increase pride in work and provide a stronger incentive for undertaking it. It should further give a practical basis for correction (above all self-correction) and enable the teacher taking over a class to pick up the threads of composition work with greater ease. While the syllabus lays down the general lines of approach, it should also leave ample room for variety and initiative on the part of both teacher and pupil.

2. Method

(i)   A theme is selected for a form and all written work centred around it (see suggestions below). The theme and its development should be preceded by discussion with the form and oral preparation for composition work should be regarded as crucial.

(ii) All work for inclusion in the magazine should be done as normal class work and homework and then written up, improved and illustrated for the magazine.

(This of course does not preclude the possibility of a pupil adding material on his own initiative.)

(iii) The duration of the work on one theme (i.e. one magazine) will depend on circumstances, but in general it is not expected that more than three magazines will be attempted in one year. A complete year's work on a magazine which had aroused sufficient interest is to be welcomed.

(iv) It is worth emphasising that the selection of the theme is vital. It must lend itself to varied treatment and to full development. Further, it should be borne in mind that a great deal of help is needed, particularly with classes unfamiliar with the work and undertaking it for the first time. Interest can easily flag, and the higher standards aimed at in the magazine version will not be achieved.

(v) The scheme does not exclude the possibility of other types of composition work which a teacher may feel necessary. In fact a special piece of composition work may be used to prepare the way for a magazine 'article'.

3. <u>Magazine themes</u>

Note: The themes given below, some with detailed suggestions, are only offered as an aid to the teacher. They can be modified or altered to suit different needs. When sufficient experience has been accumulated we should be able to suggest with more confidence which themes are suited to which years, and which appear to be the more successful. We hope to be able to add to them as ideas emerge from the work.

Out of School
The games we play
In the playground
My family
Out with the family
An evening found the fire
Doing homework
A story – e.g. Adventure in a Derelict Building
A dream
Sunday morning
Saturday shopping
Pets
Hobbies
A book review
Wireless, TV, film
Poems linked to the theme

Harold Rosen

The Travellers
Portrait gallery (of members of the party)
How it all began
Making plans
We run into difficulties
A piece of good luck
Fear!
A great disappointment
One of the party has an accident
Letters home
Letters received
We get into the papers
We broadcast
Homecoming

The Street
(One way of tackling this is for each member of the class to be a character in an imaginary street discussed and agreed on beforehand, but this is not necessary.)

Description of a street
General appearance
Further work possible on particular places – a shop, school, etc.
Some of the people
A wedding
A funeral
A festival
Morning in a shop
Evening in the pub
Our naughty boy
Our eccentric
The old folk
Someone moves in
The gossips at work
Neighbours lend a helping hand
Local boy makes good

The Reporter
My paper and my job
I cover a fire
I cover a crime
I check the facts
I interview a personality

I give Walworth a write-up
I do the book column/film column/TV and radio column
I nearly lose my job
I report on disastrous weather and its consequences
Abusive letter from reader and my reply

(Some of the best possibilities will be found in news of burning topical interest.)

Persons, Places, Things

Other people's jobs (precision)
People observed – a docker, a teacher, a conductress, etc.
Processes in school, hobbies, sport and work
Things which interest me
Objects
My bike
My record player

The District

Club
Church
Market
Particular shops
My barber
Local characters
The river
Morning and evening
History (for those who can take it)

(Non-GCE 5th form) *Souvenir of Walworth*

My first day
Great days
In trouble
If I had my time over again
Most enjoyable moments
Lessons I enjoy
Changes I would like to see

[Other possibilities]

Making and Doing, Black and White (a series of contrasts), Pages from my Diary, Documentary Film of Walworth School

Clements and Dixon (2009) describe Harold's concept of 'magazines'.

> Harold used the umbrella word 'magazines', which we interpreted as students' best work or cumulative folders … In effect, writing over a term or year was given a certain coherence, by following themes through, starting from local (personal) experiences in an early mag and building out towards wider horizons. Every week or two students added a new chapter or section, corrected, written out in their best and illustrated. As they gained confidence, it was something to pass round and treasure.

> Harold foresaw an elaborating progression from year one to four, including by the third year an extended story, often an adventure involving a group, chapter by chapter … We enjoyed developing that tradition.

> For the fourth year Harold left us a skeleton outline to build on: more adult themes, introducing discussion and argument, including controversial topics, and moving into more generalised thinking. But whereas he had been working largely on his own, Guy Rogers (our Head and Harold's old friend) set up departmental meetings for us in school time, culminating in our case in a two-day department conference: in was there that we two and Leslie Stratta were delegated the intractable job of preparing outline themes, materials and approaches for the Fourth and Fifth [today's Years 10 and 11] – out of which came *Reflections* and its *Teachers' Book* (Clements, Dixon and Stratta, 1963a and 1963b), with the investigative themes of Family, Community and Work; the Mass Media; and Questions of our Time …

> … we owe to Harold two central ideas: first, seeing our teaching as a medium for a progressive interaction between the language and culture of the neighbourhood and the enriching language and culture we might offer in response, having sensed the connections; and second, the fact that students' cumulative written projects over a term or a year could make a contribution to the school's cultural life. We feel that these were seminal.

The syllabus statement ends with Appendix II, on spelling rules: six rules for the first year, with examples; more examples of the six rules for the second year, with a further three rules added; and the instruction that all nine rules are to be revised in the third and fourth years, with additional spelling lists to be written out and learned.

References

Clements, S. and Dixon, J. (2009) 'Harold and Walworth'. *Changing English*, 16 (1).

Clements, S., Dixon, J. and Stratta, L. (1963a) *Reflections*. Oxford: Oxford University Press.

Clements, S., Dixon, J. and Stratta, L. (1963b) *Reflections: Teachers' book*. Oxford: Oxford University Press.

The Language of Textbooks

This essay appeared in *Talking and Writing: A handbook for English teachers*, published in 1967 and edited by James Britton. In his introduction, Britton writes: 'Mr Rosen's article on the language of the textbook … belongs here because its stress is upon the talking and writing that must establish connections between the personal experience of the child and the impersonal language of the textbook – the language that "looks at children across a chasm".'

'Concepts and the language that infuses and implements them give power and strategy to cognitive activity.'

(Bruner, 1962)

You are almost certainly having difficulty in making sense of that sentence. If you are not, you are fortunate and rare; if you are, then console yourself, your difficulty is useful. It should give you greater insight into the linguistic-intellectual bafflement which besets children in school, particularly in the secondary school and more particularly in 'subject' learning. Difficulties of this sort turn whole subjects into foggy mysteries and for many children the fog is so impenetrable that all higher levels of learning become unattainable. They permeate textbooks, are scattered indiscriminately throughout stodgy pages of dictated notes, and, less frequently, are part of the teacher's spoken instruction or exposition in the classroom.

Why does that opening quotation make us grope and fumble? First, it is a high-order abstraction, the components of which are themselves abstractions. It is language at the apex of a pyramid of experience, thought and verbalizing. All that was offered to you was this apex, but the vast range of human activities, details of which you could respond to with comfort and interest and which constitute the base of the pyramid, were hidden from you, as indeed were all the intervening tiers between base and apex. But there is more to it than that. The tone is highly formal, because the sentence avoids almost entirely that work-a-day language which we use to make contact with our fellows and which readily touches off responsive thought and experience. There are other difficulties to surmount. The sentence is highly compressed (three sets of yoked items, concepts-language, infuses-implements, power-strategy) and all the most important words are highly unpredictable.

We could add, more subjectively, that the sentence in some ways seems bloodless, lifeless because it does not take its vitality from any particular situation; it has no context of you and me and what we do. It provides no links with our personal world; any such links must be provided by us. It floats out there. It is a totally impersonal utterance as far away from spontaneous spoken utterance as the statutory provisions of the Education Act are from two boys having an argument in a school playground.

For all this, it is an utterance of great potential power.

> … words like 'cause' and 'effect' do not refer to things in the way words like 'table' and 'chair' do (still less do they call up definite pictures in the mind), but they have distinctive and important meanings, and their use is a mark of the high degree of order and systematization imposed by us on the world we live in. In the same way the use of words like 'right' and 'wrong', 'duty', 'crime' (and many others subsumed under them: 'property', 'theft', 'punishment,' 'reform', etc.), and of comparable words in other types of society presupposes a nexus of expected ways of behaviour.

> (Robins, 1964)

Order and systematization; what rewards for mere words! What temptations! Let's look at the problem another way. A pupil (fourth year in a secondary school) writes in his geography book:

> An erratic is quite an exciting result of glaciation as a large rock not geologically the same as its surroundings may be found perched incredibly precariously on smaller stones. This is an erratic.

His teacher has put a red ring round 'exciting' and written in the margin, 'No need to get excited. "Spectacular" a better word to use here.' Every need to get excited one would have thought; excitement about erratics cannot be so abundant that teachers can afford to dampen it. At least the teacher is showing some concern for language, for the language of his subject, even if his concern is misplaced. How far has his concern taken him? Has he really worked out the nature of definition and what kind of difficulty the pupil, using his own language, had in attempting the task? What is 'better' about 'spectacular' and worse about 'exciting'? Perhaps he is pedagogically wrong and linguistically right. He knows, at least intuitively, that in *adult* scientific use 'exciting' would find no place in the definition of an erratic; this is his intuitive linguistic criterion. 'Exciting' brings to the definition personal, idiosyncratic, subjective aspects of an erratic which the recording scientist sets out to eliminate. An erratic is an erratic whether you get excited about it or not. To grasp fully what an erratic is you may indeed need to get excited about it, however mildly, but when you have learnt to distinguish between your excitement and the objective properties of the erratic, you have reached a stage when you know something about your own thinking. Thus there is also a psychological criterion of linguistic difficulty.

As the study of linguistics has developed, it has increasingly drawn our attention away from older, and often obsessive, distinctions between kinds of language (correct – incorrect, good – bad, U – Non-U, etc.) and begun to develop new ones for us.

They help us to analyse and understand the linguistic differences between different utterances. The concept of 'register' analyses language in three dimensions: *field of discourse* (what is the subject-matter?); *mode of discourse* (is it spoken or written?); *tenor of discourse* (what is the relationship between speaker and hearer, reader and writer? Or, 'How formal is the utterance?'). Thus we might say of a passage in a physics textbook that its field of discourse is physics, magnetism; its mode of discourse is written-scientific; and its tenor of discourse highly formal. Of course each of these categories can be refined and all three of them are interacting and interrelated.

How does this help us? First, when a pupil enters the field of discourse of most school subjects he is often called upon to express himself in the written mode before he has tried to order his experience in the mode in which he operates most easily, the spoken. A group of pupils on a field trip, in a museum, or working in a laboratory sharing impressions, jointly evolving conclusions, would use very different language from the language of their subject textbooks. It would also be different from the language they would use in a written record, however free they were to express this in their own way. In the written scientific mode boys and girls are often cut off from the non-language events to which they must refer (handling of substances and apparatus, living specimens, features of the landscape, buildings, museum exhibits, etc.). Thus their written language must carry the whole burden.

Written-scientific language is, moreover, one very limited kind of English. How is the pupil to have access to experience of this mode? How is he to learn its distinctive features?

The tenor of this kind of discourse, i.e. highly formal, creates an even greater difficulty. The adult use of this tenor presumes, first, an enormous unknown audience about whom the only valid assumption is that they want access to the data and ideas without ambiguity and subjectivity and, secondly, a writer who wishes to make them available. This writer–reader relationship is the more sophisticated by virtue of its tenuousness. How unreal and remote this is for the ordinary pupil. It is even more unreal when one bears in mind that for him it is a mere pretence. He writes for no one; or for one person, who is not remote and unknown and who knows it all anyway.

An awareness of 'register' then can help us to see this special language-learning problem more clearly and even give us some more clearly defined goals for language learning.

> Productive teaching is designed not to alter patterns already acquired but to add to [the pupil's] resources; and to do so in such a way that he has the greatest range of the potentialities of the language available to him for appropriate use in all the varied situations in which he needs them.
>
> (Halliday, McIntosh and Strevens, 1964)

What linguistics does not tell us, however, is what kind of difficulties school learners have in mastering this 'range of potentialities' and becoming sensitive to 'appropriate use'. Are some registers more difficult to learn to use than others? If so, why? Do we learn them in an order which relates to psychological and social development? Every teacher could give the beginnings of an answer to these questions but they are only beginnings, crude ones at that. We know that pupils will handle comfortably fiction narrative long before they can cope with historical-argument (if they ever do!). We need to fill out a detailed picture of this process. We need to know more about the process of transition to new and less accessible registers and their relationship to those already under control. Nor have the linguists got much further than distinguishing the conventional features of different registers. We would be just as interested to know in non-impressionistic terms what constitutes an effective use of a register.

Thus for the linguist a good and a mediocre historical account may both be perfectly in register. What differentiates them? Not all registers are of equal educational importance, though which are the more important is a controversial issue (to some teachers the formalities of business letters obviously deserve high priority). All school subjects operate sub-languages which are encrusted with linguistic conventions, some of which still serve a useful purpose and some of which do not.

> The climate of more than half the continent is thus marked by the aridity and the high range of temperature experienced. The main sources of its rainfall are the Pacific and Indian Oceans, and therefore its rain-carrying winds are southerly and south-easterly. The near-approach of high land to these oceans limits the distribution of heavy rain to the peninsulas and islands of the south and south-east. Seasonally it is limited by the fact that such on-shore winds are experienced only in the summer season, hence giving rise to monsoonal rainfall.

This is an extract from the textbook *Geography for Today*, Book III, written by a committee. 'Aridity', 'on-shore winds', 'monsoonal rainfall', even 'experienced' all seem to be valuable, but what about 'near-approach of high land … limits the distribution … ', 'Seasonally it is limited by the fact that … hence giving rise to … '?

On the whole then we have a better apparatus for handling the linguistic aspects of textbook language than we have for the psychology of understanding and using it. We need a dimension which embraces both the linguistic and the psychological components. Until we know more about it let us call it the personal-impersonal dimension. Most subject learning comes to be expressed almost entirely in impersonal language; this becomes more and more true as our pupils progress through the secondary school. In English lessons they will continue to use personal written language; they may also do so in history and geography, though in these subjects a sort of ill-defined journalism is often the accepted medium. In the sciences, however, and on many occasions in other lessons, impersonal language is the order of the day (even in music, or English!). When used effectively this language is weighty, detached, highly respected and fulfils the special needs it has been evolved to meet. But it is also a product of people's mature experience through centuries. It is the language of educated adults; for pupils it is hard and remote. For them to formulate even elementary concepts within this language requires lengthy linguistic and social experience and the opportunity to experiment with it freely. Two assumptions about this kind of language seem to be prevalent. First, it is thought many pupils will never be able to acquire it so that no special steps need to be taken to help them to do so. They should be trained in the 'practical' uses of language. Secondly, when pupils are thought to be suitable subjects for advanced learning, it is assumed that such difficulties as they encounter will be of some pure intellectual kind and that language will look after itself. The problem does not exist.

> Science textbooks are only exceptionally written in prose of the highest quality, and more often they are written in prose that may be described in contrary terms, yet the students who use these books do not in fact find them difficult to understand. They may be strange, because they deal with unfamiliar matters; they may be voluminous, making great demands on the memory; but they are not as obscure, even to the inexperienced reader, as the so-called average man is led to believe.
>
> (Savory, 1953)

Yet this impersonal language is at the furthest pole from the pupils' own spontaneous language, which leaves them free to use language in any way which satisfies their personal purposes, permitting them to leave upon it the stamp of their own subjective view of the world. Impersonal language requires them to eliminate their subjectivity or at least to cover its traces. The deepest personal involvement may precede or even accompany their exploration of the new areas of experience but they have to learn how to eliminate its voice.

This impersonal language, which needs differentiating still further, has two distinct qualities to which we have already drawn attention. First, it submits to certain language habits which are the product of a complex history. These are linguistic conventions which could well be looked at critically and, like any other conventions, they can be broken by anyone who has weighed their worth and found them to be stultifying and irksome. (The change in the use of formal language is a case in point. See Sir Ernest Gowers's *Plain Words*.) Within these conventions, however, there is also language which has been perfected to embody rational thought, ultimately at its highest level. (Of course not all impersonal language is of this kind – 'Keep off the grass' for instance – but this is not the main object of our concern.) Little attempt has been made to study this dual quality of impersonal language; certainly teachers and textbook writers are not accustomed to looking at the language of their subjects from this point of view. There are times when they are more punctilious about the conventional rather than the linguistic-intellectual aspect of their subjects, as though one were to be more interested in the judge's wig than in justice.

(The word-by-word rote learning of laws, etc., is still very common. Is there only one way of expressing Boyle's Law? Compare the following versions.

> The volume of a given mass of gas at constant temperature is inversely proportional to the pressure to which it is subjected. [C. T. Smith, *Intermediate Physics*]

> The volume of a given mass of gas varies inversely as the pressure if the temperature remains constant. [W. Pearce, *School Physics*]

An interesting contrast is this lower level of abstraction:

> At the same temperature the rule is simple. By doubling the pressure, we halve the volume. By halving the pressure we double the volume. If we mean by matter what has mass, the amount of matter remains the same when we double or halve the space to contain it. (Lancelot Hogben, *Men, Missiles and Machines*))

The mother tongue is acquired almost entirely through linguistic experience and activity. There cannot be many teachers of English who delude themselves that their pupils learn English solely or even mainly in English lessons. The home is a teacher; the environment is a teacher; so is other school learning. The home and environment extend the use of day-to-day 'natural' language and English teaching derives strength from these spontaneous uses of language, providing the only occasions in which these uses can grow towards creative-imaginative writing and reading.

But school is the arena for other language learning. In other lessons there is the unique opportunity for access to new kinds of language. Here the pupil will be confronted with verbalized thought on a systematic and ordered basis. This will probably be his only chance, certainly his main chance, of acquiring the language and thought of impersonal observation and description, generalization and abstraction, theories, laws, the analysis of events remote in time or space, argument and speculation. The concepts which make all this possible are embodied in special languages and sub-languages. The more deeply a subject is penetrated and understood the further its language grows from the currency of everyday speech and from personal literature. In the effort to master it we lift our thinking towards it and as our thinking develops we use the language with greater confidence and purpose. Its potential is enormous and there are discoveries and fulfilments to be met in our struggles to master it.

Yet we know that many young people leave school afraid of this language, regarding it as alien and inaccessible; others mutter it like an incantation or, sheltering behind it, conceal their own ideas and doubts, hoping that the words themselves will work of their own accord. They cannot use this language flexibly, they are chained to its formulations. Some have so precarious a hold upon it that it slips away under stress. How can they be helped towards boldness and confidence and mastery? How can they be helped towards this language in such a way that it develops rather than retards their thinking?

A bridge needs to be built between personal, creative language and impersonal language. Children and young people should not be rushed into the use of the adult, mature language of a subject. Real learning means making knowledge personal, bringing to bear on it all of one's own experience that seems to be relevant. This is only possible when we express the new experience in our own language in our own way, taking over just so much of the new language of the subject as is right for us, trying it out and tasting it. The new language should be encountered in the most favourable circumstances, in lively books which have been produced by writers who have some kind of awareness of the problems we have been discussing. (A pioneer in this field is Amabel Williams-Ellis, who for a long time has been aware of the need for using rich source material. See for example *Men Who Found Out, Good Citizens*, etc.) In *100,000 Whys*, M. Ilin discusses the candle flame in this way:

> You only see the beams and nails and bricks when the house burns up. The same thing is true here: the water and coal are only visible when we make a small conflagration – light the candle.
>
> Very well. When the candle burns we get water and carbon. But what becomes of them? The water goes off in the form of steam. This is the steam which condensed on the spoon when we held it over the flame. But what becomes of the carbon? When the candle smokes the carbon goes off in the form of soot – tiny particles of carbon – and settles on the ceiling, walls and furniture of the room.
>
> But if the candle is burning well there is no soot, for the carbon is all burned up. Burned up? What do we mean by that? Now we have to begin at the beginning again. What becomes of the carbon when it burns up? One of two things: either it is lost, disappears entirely, or it is turned into some other substance which we simply don't see.
>
> Let's try to catch this ghost.

The creative-personal uses of language should not be seen as the exclusive affair of the English teacher inhabiting a shadowy and suspect world of 'self-expression'. New learning can and should be expressed in as personal a way as a young writer wants, side by side with his first efforts to move towards more impersonal treatment; this could well include poems and stories. The naked textbooks should always be supplemented with real documents and source material from real books, autobiographies, original works and novels. Any one class will contain pupils at very different stages of progress from the personal to the impersonal. If different ways of verbalizing new experience are left open to them, they can cross the bridges when they are ready to cross them. We need to make it possible for all the pupil's hard won achievements of imagination and thinking, all those concepts he has already mastered, to help him forward to new concepts, and conversely for these new concepts to make living contact with his imagination and thought. Some indication of this process can be seen in these entries from the history book made by an eleven-year-old:

1. *Death of a Viking King*
   King Rikki died at the break of day.
   I am Thor his son
   Today just before dusk
   He will be pushed,
   Pushed into the water,
   In a burning ship.

   The sun has just set
   The people are gathering on the beach
   A large Viking ship on rollers
   Waits,
   Waits to be pushed into the sea
   Priceless treasure is being unloaded
   On to the waiting ship,
   Golden goblets
   Plates, money,
   Jewels, swords,
   Shields and helmets,
   Food and Drink
   Suits of armour
   And precious brocade
   And then the body of the king
   Is laid in the boat with greatest care
   The oarsmen and servants start
   Pushing it towards the sea.
   It gathers speed,
   And now a burning torch is thrown on board!
   SPLASH!
   The boat is in,
   Burning
   Sailing out to sea
   Until at last a mass of flames
   It sinks.

2. As Edward had spent much of his life in Normandy, Norman ways pleased him more than english ones. He had been brought up by monks and was himself in many ways a monk. In those days monks were often called 'Confessors'. Thus Edwards nickname came about as Edward the Confessor.

3. SUTTON HOO TREASURE SHIP

   This is a helmet [a picture of it is pasted in the book] found in 500 pieces. It is made of iron covered bronze and then tin so that it looks white and shiny. However the eye brows and moustache are bronze. The dragons eyes are garnets (in beetween eye brows).

Who writes textbooks? What is a good one? Perhaps we should consider first whether, in our anxiety to leave behind the bad old days of elementary schools and the smatterings of knowledge which went with them, we have not been too eager to see the glossy new textbook as a visible guarantee of real secondary education. In English lessons texts are beginning to replace textbooks, and one historian (Abrams, 1964) has recently argued for the banishment of history textbooks from the history class. The best textbooks in existence have to assume a kind of evenness of development in any group of users. Many seem to be written by people who have only read other textbooks; they may have been bigger and more difficult but they were textbooks none the less. The authors or compilers handle a grubby second-hand or umpteenth-hand language which they have accepted as part of 'the content' of the subject. They show little awareness of what pupils will make or fail to make of their language beyond some crude notions of easy and difficult vocabulary and shorter sentences. (There have been attempts to deal with the problem of 'readability' of textbooks but they do not deal with the problems raised here.) Yet frequently it is in these books that pupils meet for the first time the written impersonal language of educated people.

Most school textbooks are written by teachers and an awareness of the language of their subject should be part of the equipment of all teachers. What kind of reality and personal meaning inheres in the concept 'revolution' for a class of fourteen-year-olds? Or in 'therefore', 'correlation', 'in direct proportion to'? How much is it convention and how much a necessity to say, 'let us assume'; 'limited the authority of the king'; 'ensure that seed dispersal takes place'? Clearly different subjects present different problems. The word 'power' will be used differently in geography, history, science and mathematics. The 'body' of the physics lesson is not the same as 'the body' of the biology lesson. The sciences can always be accompanied by observation, experiment and discussion (are they?) but history and geography have to deal with second-hand experience. History handles difficult social concepts of politics. Geography sometimes deals with social institutions and sometimes scientific concepts of weather, geology and map projections. We need to study more closely these language differences and how secondary pupils grapple with them.

Probably, for all their shortcomings, subject textbooks have for many pupils real value. However limited their use of impersonal language, it is from the textbook that they learn it. Having said so much we can then recognize that textbooks also do harm. If more of them are to come flooding into our schools, and the market seems insatiable, we should take an unflinching look at them. Any history book will contain pages and pages of sentences like this:

Monasteries had formed part of English life in a very real sense.

What is a monastery? How does it 'form part of English life'? What 'English life'? What senses are there other than 'very real' senses? Can 'English life' of a past period take on meaning before many institutions like monasteries have been looked at concretely?

Language like this looks at children across a chasm. The worst way to bridge this chasm is to encourage children to take over whole chunks of it as a kind of jargon (examinations have been the great excuse). For fluent children, such as moderately successful grammar-school pupils, this process is fatally easy. Probably few of us who have grown up in the system are free from some taint of this schooling. Instead of the new formulations representing hard-won victories of intellectual struggle or even partial victories, they are not even half-hearted skirmishes. Instead there is empty verbalism, sanctioned utterance and approved dogma; behind them is a void or a chaos. The personal view is made to seem irrelevant; it is outlawed. The conventions of this language are not taken over as are the conventions of other uses of language, at first experimentally and then with growing confidence, but unthinkingly, lock, stock and barrel. Language and experience have been torn asunder.

For other pupils, however, the gap between their own language and the textbook is so great that the textbook is mere noise. Their own language has not organized their thinking in such a way that they can be cognitively responsive in even a minimal sense. The textbook is alien both in its conventions and its strategies. The subject never begins to come through; it is another way of life. Though this is not a matter of language alone, language plays a big part. The willing bright pupil has sufficient language achievement behind him to enable him to mime the textbook, though his hold may be precarious and over-dependent on verbatim memory. At least his morale will be high when he is confronted with new verbal experience. He has done it before; he will do it again. At the other extreme is the pupil who receives nothing but scrambled messages. He has failed to decode them in the past; he will fail again.

But most boys and girls do not drop neatly into these extreme categories. Many pupils are very ready for new uses of language and very responsive to them; they sense the adult status of an impersonal form of language and glimpse its power. The beginnings can be clearly seen in the primary school. It crops up in unexpected places, in the midst of personal writing for example.

> ... The copse we entered had a silver birch wood at one end and a drainage lake at the other. All over the land were channels draining the earth. The end of the lake nearest the wood was actually a reed bed. We set off in good spirits to erect the first net. After a short reconnoitre we placed it in a gap between a bramble bush and the end of the wood. This, my friend told me, was a good trap for titmice. This net up, we proceeded towards the lake and placed two nets at the reeded end. Each net was sixty feet long and about ten feet high. They were supported at either end by a bamboo pole, which, when wanted to, pulled apart. We had to guy each pole because of the elastic pull of the net. The net itself, was of fine nylon mesh with four horizontal thick strands of elastic passing through the middle. The bird flew into the mesh, which stretched, and then dropped down behind one of the horizontal strands, thus falling into what may be termed a pocket.

But they may not yet be ready to handle the whole apparatus of the fully developed language of a subject. Again and again young pupils are asked to deploy the language of objective argument when their own thinking has only reached the stage of committed assertion and passionate partisanship. Mostly we are in too great a hurry, rushing children not to the concept which is just ahead and therefore challenging, but to one which is well beyond their reach, outside the range of their thought and completely severed from their experience.

This discussion both implicitly and explicitly has pointed to some practical applications of an understanding of impersonal language. Let us bring some of them together.

The language of education is historically evolved and fashioned, embodying generations of endeavour to understand the universe and society. It remains inaccessible until the learner has made it interact with his own experience and past learning. The first way he achieves this is through social speech. We need to bring out into the light of day all the pupils' thinking and feeling about a subject. Whatever the final form of recording may be, however much it may be finally distilled into the bare impersonal item, it must begin as personal spontaneous language.

> Science is not an impersonal construction. It is no less, and no more, personal than other forms of communicated thought. This book is not less scientific because my manner is personal, and I make no apology for it. Science searches the common experience of people; and it is made by people, and it has their style.
>
> (Bronowski, 1953)

Of course, there is talk and talk. 'What is the specific weight of mercury?' is very different from 'What were you trying to do?', 'How did you do it?', 'What did you find out?'. And that is different from spontaneous inquiry and observation. How often do genuine speculation and genuine argument enter into science lessons or geography or history? How much of the subterranean world of thought is brought to the surface?

The teacher's own talk plays a vital role. If he is only a glorified question-master and boiler-down of his own notes then his pupils will never catch sight of what happens to a subject when it becomes a real part of a person. They will never hear his doubts, nor his enthusiasm, nor hear the biography of an idea in the life of an individual.

Do we need textbooks? What exactly for? How can we help pupils to use them? How should a first-form book differ from a fifth-form book? Can textbooks be made more like real books without sacrificing system and objectivity? A part of the answer must surely be that we must stop thinking in terms of one subject, one textbook, one year, one pupil.

We should attach much less importance to the linguistic conventions of our subjects and begin to sort out what these are. It is possible that our pupils will find fresher, livelier language than the dated and jaded jargon of the textbooks. Dictated notes and summaries should disappear for ever. Language cannot be used as a gift or a dole. What are notes for? A class can only know how it wants to make them when it knows what use it wants to make of them. In any case notes are cryptic and we probably use them too soon. Always the emphasis should be on the individual and the group shaping their own awareness in their own language without their being denied access to more mature formulations. Creative, personal interpretation should be provided for and welcomed. Space-fiction can be the free-est mode of speculation about astronomy, physics and society. Poetry is hospitable to all experience.

We need more patience. We are so anxious that each endeavour should be a perfect fragment of the finished product. In our anxiety that the little area of chemistry or history which we are examining should look like the real thing, like *bona fide* history or *bona fide* chemistry, paradoxically we make it unreal, much farther away from the real thing.

A serious concern with the language of the textbook, the language of a subject, is a proper and central concern for all teachers, for it involves the vital participants in most learning – words.

References

Abrams, P. (1964) 'History without textbooks'. *Where?*, Autumn.

Bronowski, J. (1953) *The Common Sense of Science*. Cambridge, MA: Harvard University Press.

Bruner, J. (1962)' Introduction to L. Vygotsky', in Vygotsky, L., *Thought and Language*. Cambridge, MA: MIT Press.

Halliday, M., McIntosh, A. and Strevens, P. (1964) *The Linguistic Sciences and Language Teaching*. London: Longman.

Robins, R. (1964) *General Linguistics: An introductory survey*. London: Longman.

Savory, T. (1953) *The Language of Science*. London: Andre Deutsch.

Towards a Language Policy Across the Curriculum

At a weekend conference in May 1968, the London Association for the Teaching of English produced a document called 'A Language Policy Across the Curriculum'. It was more widely disseminated when it appeared at the end of the first edition of the paperback *Language, the Learner and the School* (Barnes, Britton, Rosen and the LATE, 1969). Douglas Barnes wrote the first part of the book: 'Language in the Secondary Classroom – A Study of Language Interactions in Twelve Lessons in the First Term of Secondary Education'. James Britton wrote the second part: 'Talking to Learn'. The third part was Harold's first version of what he called a 'discussion document', providing an intellectual context for the LATE document, and describing the evolution of the ideas which had led to the document's production.

As a whole, the book had an enormous and immediate influence in promoting two major ideas: that learners need to use their own language, especially their spoken language, in coming to grips with new knowledge which the school wishes them to take on; and that schools as whole institutions, and especially secondary schools, need to consider how the language through which they offer knowledge to learners is actually experienced by those learners. Implicit in the phrase 'language across the curriculum' was the judgement that learners very often experienced the language demands of the school as contradictory, or deadeningly repetitive, or simply mysterious.

The 1969 edition of *Language, the Learner and the School* sold about 35,000 copies in two years. A revised edition of the book, including an expanded version of Harold's discussion document, was published in 1971. That is the version which appears here. It is followed, as Harold explains, by a revised version of the original LATE document. The original version, as he says, 'we have rendered obsolete ... which is just as it should be'. The 1971 publication was timed to coincide with the National Association for the Teaching of English's annual conference in that year, the sole topic of which was 'language across the curriculum'.

Schools are language-saturated institutions. They are places where books are thumbed, summarized and 'revised', notes are dictated, made, kept and learnt, essays are prepared, written and marked, examination questions are composed and the attendant judgements made. Teachers explain, lecture, question, exhort, reprimand

and make jokes. Pupils listen, reply, make observations, call out, mutter, whisper and make jokes. Small knots gather round over books, lathes, easels and retorts, or over nothing, in classrooms, labs, workshops, craft rooms, corridors and toilets to chatter, discuss, argue, quarrel, plan, plot, teach each other, using words to stroke or strike. There are foundation-stones, notice-boards, blackboards, pin-up boards, circulars, full of injunctions, warnings, records of triumphs, mottoes, cuttings, compositions and graffiti. As the school day unfolds, law and lore become established, puzzled over or rejected.

In the penumbra of their attention most teachers have a kind of concern for language. It may be a desperate sense that their pupils' pitiful gropings for words and their botching together of a few tortured written sentences reduce their language to an absurd caricature. Or they may feel in a way which is rarely explicit that there are linguistic proprieties which belong with a subject for which they have a responsibility. More shadowy still is a sense that some kind of spoken contribution by pupils helps them to learn. How else can we explain that ubiquitous figure, the teacher as interrogator, who emerges so strongly from Douglas Barnes' study [in the first part of the book]? Finally, when they ask pupils to write, they feel that much greater constraints must be imposed and they become more vigilant, more censorious and more censuring.

Boundaries must be clearly established and a chemistry student should write chemistry not history, autobiography or journalism. Douglas Barnes' study also shows us how in some teachers' language there are more delicate perceptions than those I have so baldly outlined. His study suggests that in the substratum of instructions, anxieties and prescriptions lies the promise of much more formulated notions of how language is working in teachers' classrooms. In this attempt they are likely not only to make exciting discoveries about their own teaching but to discover something more general about language in education or how we use words to live. It is probably only through such a programme of patient self-education that so Utopian an undertaking as 'A Language Policy Across the Curriculum' can become a working reality. I shall return to that theme later.

Douglas Barnes displays the teacher's strategies – his questions, explanations, coaxings – under a magnifying lens, and that kind of exposure is bound to shed a somewhat ruthless light on any of us. Catch our most satisfying conversational moments on tape or in transcript and we wince. Yet somehow we must learn to wince, to take it, for the midwifery of new ideas insists on these pangs. What has been put under the lens is, of course, the teacher in his most institutionalized garb with, inevitably, language behaviour to match. There have been other ruthless studies of the teacher in this most formal posture which press us to ask whether the teacher must be both Chairman and Chief Speaker ('The Ringmaster' as Smith [1968] calls him). But we are interested in much more than the teacher's language. What is the pattern of interchange in many (most?) of those encapsulated curriculum units we call lessons? From his researches, Flanders (1962) produced his simple arithmetic answer, his Rule of Two-Thirds, 'In the average classroom someone is talking for two-thirds of the time, two-thirds of the talk is teacher-talk, and two-thirds of the teacher-talk is direct-influence.' Some teachers on encountering this fact may well feel that that is just how it should be; but to most it comes as something of a revelation which leads them to feel that they ought to make more space for pupil-talk and even that they should reduce their outflow of 'direct-influence'.

There is another study, little known as yet, by Bellack *et al.* (1966), which investigated 'the patterned processes of verbal interaction that characterize classrooms in action' and tried to find out who spoke about what, how much, when, under what conditions and with what effect. This study too caught the teachers in their 'Ringmaster' instructional posture, teaching a course on 'International Economic Problems' to adolescents. Bellack's analysis followed up Wittgenstein's approach, 'the *speaking* of language is part of an activity, or a form of life' and various human activities are essentially linguistic in nature. From this he evolved his metaphor of 'language games'. Linguistic activities have definite functions to perform and can be likened to games because they have 'rules' for all 'players' and only certain moves are possible. Players have to learn the language rules and how various parts of the game are related. Teaching-learning is one of the games.

Bellack worked out the four basic moves of the game: the *structuring move*, which sets the context for subsequent behaviour ('Today we begin our unit on trade ... etc.'); the *soliciting move*, which is intended to elicit a response, frequently verbal ('Now give me another reason' or 'Repeat that so that John can hear'); the *responding move*, which fulfils the expectation of the soliciting move, typically by an answer to a question ('Because they don't export very much'); the *reacting move*, which modifies or evaluates what has previously been said ('France. Right. And also Germany and Belgium' and 'Well, now that is not the question of course I asked'). These basic moves were then highly refined and the whole system much more elaborated. There is no space to outline it here but suffice to say that by using it the researchers were able to produce *The Rules of the Language Game of Teaching*, which turns out to be a very lengthy code. As a complement to Barnes' study I would make the following selection.

1. The teacher is the most active player in the game. He makes most moves; he speaks most frequently; his speeches are longest. The ratio of his speech to the speech of all other players is three to one.
2. The major part of the game is played with substantive meanings (i.e. the specific concepts of the lesson) specified by the teacher's structuring.
3. Fact-stating and explaining are used much more frequently than defining and interpreting. Opinions and the justification of them are relatively rare.
4. The teacher is primarily a solicitor and the pupil a respondent.

The picture which emerges from the work is one of enormous walls of constraint closing round the normal uses of language or, to use the terms of the study, the language games which are *not* played are just as significant as the one which is. A different or modified code would be needed to accommodate pupils talking to one another. Take this anecdotal chain from a small group of ten-year-olds in a primary class.

A We used to have races in our house for getting dressed and um eating our breakfast quickly you see and we have er I er once I woke up in the middle of the night and the curtains were closed and I'd probably turn my light on so that in the morning you see Mum used to turn the light on so er I got out of bed went and got dressed and went downstairs to have my breakfast came up and woke Mum and I said to Mum 'What are you doing in bed Mum?' and she said 'What are you doing out of bed it's eleven o'clock'. I had to go back to bed with my clothes on.

J Often when I wake up in the night I turn my light on and I can't make the effort to go and turn the landing light on I can't make the effort and I fall asleep with my light on and er once one Sunday morning I woke up … (inaudible) … What's the time? She said er, 'Eight o'clock' and I dashed out of bed and got ready as quick as I could … I said 'Mum, I'll be late for swimming can I have a towel please?' She said 'It's Sunday.'

C Oh my sisters never play chase with me I always go asking them but they're lazy they're all weaklings. I go outside and run around then Jean comes outside says 'Can I play?' I say 'No 'cos you know what for' and then she went inside and said 'Clare come out and play with me' and I went inside and said 'Can I play?' and they said 'No' and then yesterday Janine was after my ball and I threw it at her and it hit her wrist and then it went into Mrs Kidd's garden so I knocked on the door and er her daughter came and said 'What do you want ?' and I said 'Can I have my ball back?' and she said 'Where's that?' and I said 'Behind the car. I chased after the ball' I said and she got hold of me and pulled me right across the grass and she went inside brushed herself down and she went inside and watched television.

J When we were on holiday the week before last we were next door … and made our own knocking code. I would just bash my head on the wall behind. I'd just pretend I'd bash my head on the wall and we had this knocking code you see. One it meant you know we had certain things 'Is it er is it alright for me to come in? Urgent you must come in now, see you in the morning.'

These sustained individual contributions might be contrasted with a sequence which would fit Bellack's system perfectly.

> *T* Well, anytime you taste sweat and tears, why does it seem to taste about the same level of saltiness? (pause) Blood. (pause) Well, think back to before we could think back. Before we were and were able to think.
>
> *P* Came from the sea
>
> *T* Came where?
>
> *Ps* From the sea
>
> *T* What came from the sea?
>
> *P* Fish
>
> *T* All the … what?
>
> *Ps* Animals. Living things
>
> *T* All living things as far as we know. And everything happened in … what ?
>
> *P* In stages
>
> *T* In stages, yes. But everything happened, it happened in what?
>
> *Ps* In the sea. Evolution.
>
> *T* Yes, evolution originally happened in the sea. O.K. So all life originated in what sort of environment, surroundings … ?
>
> *P* Water
>
> *T* What sort of water?
>
> *Ps* Salt, salty
>
> *T* Salt water, yes. In fact, all the processes that go on in our bodies must go on in water. In … what's the word? Things in water … dissolved in water … all the reactions?
>
> *P* Saturated
>
> *T* Well that's if you get too much
>
> *P* Solution
>
> *T* Yes, good. In solution. All the, you might say … chemical rearranging that goes on inside our bodies must take place in a salty solution, because when life as we understand it started, it started in what? In a salty solution.

O.K.? And our blood is salty, and must be kept at the same level of saltiness, so we believe, as the sea was when we started, where our forbears started. O.K.? This is why the blood doesn't get any more or less salty. If we have got too little, when we sit down to dinner we somehow put a lot of salt on automatically, have you noticed that?

Walker (1969), in whose paper this transcript is quoted, says that *focusing* (his term) is a technique all teachers use, and that he has the impression that it occurs most often in the teaching of science. The features of focusing are the restriction of pupil participation to relevant, objective statements and the use of them to develop the idea on which the teacher intends to converge. He notes also the rejection of information and compression of knowledge. I feel he has selected a very recognizable example which probably we have all used some form of in our teaching, for better or worse, but I want to ask how he construes the words 'relevant' and 'statement'. What is here considered relevant is the effort on the part of the pupils to guess almost the very form of words the teacher has in mind and, one hopes, move towards his meaning. Bellack's system would have that neatly docketed in a flash, but it could scarcely lay bare the delicate, slow, often apparently circular process by which we and our pupils move towards each other's meanings, nor does it seem designed to evolve the rules of that other language game, the Working Group Game, in which players, unmistakably in earnest, seek to get things done together by observing, thinking, investigating, planning and solving. The teacher's carefully composed structuring and soliciting moves, whatever their advantages, have the disadvantage of tightly circumscribing the responses and consequently of circumscribing the extent to which a pupil can formulate and represent in words what he is thinking.

> The moment a conversation is started, whatever is said is a determining condition for what, in any reasonable expectation, may follow. What you say raises the threshold against most of the language of your companion and leaves open only a limited opening for a certain likely range of responses … Neither linguists nor psychologists have begun the study of conversation: but it is here we shall find the key to a better understanding of what language really is and how it works.
>
> (Firth, 1957)

If all conversation proceeds more or less on a single system in school classes then we have imposed the *same* limitation on all discourse, whereas in normal conversations the kind of limitation changes as our purposes change. Needless to say, when we play the Language Game of Teaching we have to assume that there is a minimal concern to keep to the rules. An occasional rare pupil can spoil the game not by rowdyism but by refusal to play. Postman and Weingartner (1969) tell this story.

There is a sad little joke about a fifth-grade teacher in a ghetto school who asked a grim Negro boy during the course of a 'science' lesson, 'How many legs does a grasshopper have?' 'Oh, man,' he replied, 'I sure wish I had *your* problems!'

There are sharper criticisms yet to make of the game we have been looking at. They arise from the limitation of thinking resources called into play by the limited language resources. It is through the enormous variety of dialogue with others that we gather together the linguistic resources to dialogue in our heads; there is nowhere else to get them from. Restrict the nature and quality of that dialogue and ultimately you restrict thinking capacity. Out of the vast repertoire which language offers us very few items are left available to the pupil as a speaker, though the teacher himself uses a wider selection. This is what Mead was trying to teach as far back as 1900 (see the posthumous collection of Mead's work, published in 1934). He argued that an organized personality could emerge only through a capacity to take up the role of 'the other' and, so to speak, carry it around with us. Language, he maintained, put the intelligence of the individual at his own disposal.

But the individual that has this ability is a social individual. He does not develop it by himself and then enter into society on the basis of this capacity. He becomes such a self and gets such control by being a social individual and it is only in society that he can attain this sort of self which will make it possible for him to turn back on himself and indicate to himself the different things he can do.

The quality of our words in the head, inner speech, must be closely tied to our experience of talking with others, which gives us resources for thinking and learning, for self-prompting and intellectual adventure. School could be a place where pupils enriched their resources, because it would be there that they encountered new verbal strategies and were inspired to more ambitious uses of language than those provided outside. James Britton shows in his section of this book [Part Two – 'Talking to Learn'] some of the possibilities when the pupils take up the dialogue and begin to make the language moves for themselves, keeping the flow going as easily as they would at home or in a coffee-bar. He documents the group effort at understanding, the collective solution of a specific problem, joint exploration through expressive talk, the struggle to organize thoughts and feelings and, finally, the growth of explicitness. His transcripts show how teachers can begin to escape from the grip of the classroom interrogation and exposition and how the word 'discussion' can take on new meaning.

The reader will not have been slow to notice that throughout this book up to this point language has been more or less synonymous with speech; frequently, indeed, with something more modest which we prefer to call talk. I hope that as the argument has unfolded the reader will have appreciated that this viewpoint has been central to it, implicitly and explicitly. We are saying that it is as talkers, questioners, arguers, gossips, chatterboxes, that our pupils do much of their most important learning. Their everyday talking voices are the most subtle and versatile means they possess for making sense of what they do and for making sense of others, including their teachers. School should be a place in which we can hear the full sound of 'the conversation of mankind' (in Michael Oakeshott's phrase). How much more rewarding for the teacher to join this conversation as an adult voice and as an adult listener. Some children need to discover their voices, find their tongues, and some teachers need to rediscover theirs. When pupils are free to talk, teachers are free to observe and to understand what kind of learning is going on. For in the end, the teacher can only make sense of his pupils making sense. He can only work with their meanings.

> As soon as students realize their lessons are about their meanings, then the entire psychological context of schools is different. Learning is no longer a contest between them and something outside of them, whether the problem be a poem, a historical conclusion, a scientific theory or anything else. There is, then, no need for the kinds of 'motivation' found in the conventional Trivia contest. There are few occasions for feelings of inadequacy, few threats to their sense of dignity, less reason to resist changing perceptions. In short, the meaning-maker metaphor puts the student at the centre of the learning process. It makes both possible and acceptable a plurality of meanings, for the environment does not exist only to impose standardized meanings but rather to help students improve their unique meaning-making capabilities. And this is the basis of the process of learning how to learn, how to deal with the otherwise 'meaningless', how to cope with change that requires new meanings to be made.
>
> (Postman and Weingartner, 1969)

Making new meanings. Exactly so, and we make them partly by talking our way towards them.

It may seem to some that under this dispensation schools would indeed become talking shops in which any sloppy, half-baked chatter was elevated to 'learning' and nothing ever got done. The versatility of language is such that exactly the opposite is true. A group of children go pond-dipping, or are working out the contour system from maps and models, or are investigating conditions in nineteenth-century factories, or are trying to design a tool to do a special job. Where does talk come in? Any or all of the following possibilities might be realized:

1. *Preparatory talk.* Some of this would be strictly practical planning – ways and means, some would be related to ideas, data, possibilities, some would be personal,

expressive, anticipatory and some interpersonal (i.e. related to the social life of the group, its harmony and tensions).

2. *Talk on the job.* Observations, questions, speculations, formulations. Practical instructions, requests and decisions. Expressive language again, both personal and interpersonal, especially related to shared interest.

3. *Retrospective talk.* Recalling and savouring, ordering, concluding, debating, theorizing, suggesting new possibilities and further plans.

4. *Talking in the head.* The younger the children the more likely it will be that much of their activity will be accompanied by speech intended for no one else, i.e. giving themselves instructions or supplying a running commentary which is meaningful only in the context of the activity (Luria's 'self-regulative' and 'synpraxic' speech). Older pupils will do all or much of this in their heads and, as I have already indicated, the quality and complexity of this speech will be highly dependent on the quality of their experience of speech with others.

If we examine the following entry from a mathematics teacher's log-book (it appears in the Crediton Mathematics Centre Report, 1966), we can see some of these possibilities emerging. The reader is invited to try sorting out this talk using the above system or his own.

> *What is a Point?*
>
> This first discussion about a point came rather by surprise. The class had made some punched cards on which they had recorded certain details of their form, e.g. boys travelling by bus, by train, boys who stay to school lunch, etc. We had talked for some time about boys who came by train and also stayed to lunch, etc., and had used the cards to demonstrate this idea of intersection. When the intersection of 'boys who came by train' and 'boys who came by bus' was suggested, the idea of an empty set came under discussion. It was during this that one boy likened it to a point!
>
> What is a point? *It is a mere flick of the pen ... It's a dot ... it could be round or square depending what shape pencil you had ...*
>
> How big is it? *As small as you can make it ... smaller than that ... you can't measure it ...*
>
> What happens if it is put under a microscope? *It will look bigger but will not be ... The measuring instrument would be bigger so it wouldn't help ... Really it's just an idea – something in the mind.*
>
> The discussion moved on to 'position'.
>
> How many positions in this room? *Unbelievable ... One in every 10^6 ... Can't count them ... The same as the number of points on a compass ... Depends on*

how many objects in the room … Many more than quadrillions … Don't be silly –
everything is made so quadrillions would mean it took 10^6 years … Depends on how
big a molecule is … Now he's bringing physics into it … You would die before you
finished … No matter what answer you give it depends where you are seeing it from.
If I stand in this corner there are millions over there and if I stand over there there
are millions here. It doesn't matter where you stand they are still there.

A few days later the class were asked to look at a white mark on the board
for a few seconds. They were told to close their eyes and think hard about
the point. Has anyone anything to say?

It's grown bigger …
Opening up into a lot of circles …
Mine's gone …
Getting bigger …
Looks like a cow …
Falling to pieces …
Two with a hole in the middle …
Two changing colour …
Growing legs …
Ball – like sun – bright shining orange …
Like flowers in a field …
Different colours all over the place …
To half yellow, bottom half red – I've lost it now …
It keeps disappearing – comes back yellow – comes back red and green …
Cylinder shape opens out at bottom into oval …
Like looking at a strong light – mauve …
Two about ⅛" apart (R.H.S. yellow – L.H.S. green) going darker – turning into a
ball about 3 times size …
Purple blob giving off green light …
Like a line 1" long – gone into circle ½" radius – green on yellow …
2 dots – big and little – big in foreground …
Breaking up – very bright background – spider's web – turning round …

Comments of this kind continued to come and more and more motion was
being experienced – the children seemed deeply involved with their dot
and were not at all interested in each other's comments. S's cow amused
nobody. At times I asked a boy who had commented to keep me in touch
with his point – this was done regularly and seemed to stimulate the 'dot'
activity. There was no indication that any of the 'stories' were made up
and I must admit to some fear at the excitement some children got from
this – on one occasion W was talking about the blackish-yellow background

eating up his dot. He became very excited as some sort of climax seemed imminent. I told him to open his eyes. He seemed relieved!

P suggested that children could not retain the image of a white dot on a black background with their eyes shut for a long period, which prompted me to do the following short activity. I made a special effort, by continuous repetition, to make the children think of a white dot on a blackboard. I told them not to allow it to move, change colour or shape. They were then told to close their eyes and think hard about the situation and not to allow any change. A minute later (absolute silence during the minute) they opened their eyes and reported changes of colour, shape, etc. The changes were much more restricted but only three boys managed to keep the situation.

The following paragraph was produced after the weekend by a boy – I suspect he put himself back into the situation to write this.

We drew a dot on the blackboard. We looked at it closely, then we shut our eyes. We tried to concentrate on the white dot. On my first go nothing interesting happened, but the opposite happened the second try. First of all there was just a black background but suddenly, a crooked line came in one half, blue the other half, red then a mustard colour Enkalon carpet came. Then it faded away and it went to a bluey black background and lots of little white specks like stars. When that faded a beautiful light green and a dark blue came in. These colours were like fluorescent. Then a pineapple came in, it was like one of the tinned slices. When the lines came, a few more came in. They were like the red and blue. There was one a mustard and yellow colour and lots more others. Then we opened our eyes and we started shutting and opening our eyes. We did this because we weren't used to the light. Then we had our milk and talked about what happened.

And talked about what happened. We can only guess at the details of that retrospective interchange round the milk bottles, but in those outer ripples of classroom interest the talk was highly motivated and partly shaped by the variety of talk-with-activity which preceded it. They might have gone further with their mathematical speculation or more widely theorized about perception or simply rehearsed their experience. And the teacher's language glimpsed here shows him entering the talk in different ways but always by feeder roads not at the stop lights. At first glance it seems as though he restricts himself to the inevitable questioning procedure. But he looks at his questions and what follows from them. 'Has anyone anything to say?' is a pseudo-question and really an open invitation. We enter a different world of communication with 'I asked a boy who had commented to keep me in touch with his point'. In touch with the boy's 'unique meaning-making capabilities'.

A further question arises. I imagine that most teachers would find acceptable the debate about 'What is a point ?' which opens the log-entry though some would raise an eyebrow at the fact that it 'came as rather a surprise' and wonder what kind of random syllabus is being followed. Nevertheless the debate seems recognizably mathematical, conceptual and cognitive, and could conceivably some time reach a pre-ordained conclusion. But what about all those performing dots? What irrelevance and wild self-indulgence! I imagine that the teacher himself might well answer that problems (the interesting ones) are best solved by viewing them in every possible way, even the most unlikely, fantastic and idiosyncratic. In this way more possibilities are brought under review in novel ways and the problem may be seen to be a different one. Its multi-faceted surface is revolved and inspected from improbable angles. I would add that an essential part of this procedure is carried out by language just as we see the boys in the maths class shaping their possibilities in words. Indeed the whole exercise is centred on the word 'point', taken from the interlocking lexicon of mathematics. (A useful curriculum discussion might well begin with the question, 'To what extent can we say that the language of a subject is the subject?'.) The boys are learning to trust the tips of their tongues, that 'blurting out the first answer that comes into your head' has its uses and is not resorted to only by the idle and stupid.

But I would want to go further than this. Most of the understanding which schools attempt to inculcate in a highly organized way is embodied in language. In the varied fields of the curriculum these ways of saying and writing about things have been evolved by the most advanced scholars in those fields and have been followed by students and teachers. Sometimes they are followed blindly without an understanding of their rationale or their flexibility. What are finely adjusted systems of discourse become all too easily verbal rituals clung to like talismans in every field from literary criticism to physics. A common characteristic of these ways of saying is their impersonality; their cold neutrality is uttered by a disembodied voice marshalling abstractions and generalizations. They keep their distance and shift discourse from its specific context to a very general one, from the world of you and me and him and her to the world of 'one' and the passive voice, from this to that, from here to there. But this kind of public discourse is not a record of the thinking and talking which brought it into being, of how the individual talked himself into sense. That personal hinterland is populated with memories, images, attitudes, feelings and fancies which colour all our thinking. If we restrict the expression of new experiences to the most public, the most general, the most disembodied utterances, we do so at our peril. Firstly, we price ourselves out of the market, for many children cannot talk this tongue. Secondly, as we have already suggested, we limit thinking. Thirdly, we repress a response which has value in its own right. We can go further yet. The acquisition of these forms of public discourse is a slow process. Personal expressive language is what springs easily to the lips of everyone, but mature specialized language can only be acquired by being differentiated out from other forms. The language in the textbook, on the blackboard and in the mouth of the teacher can be aped relatively easily, but this does not make it available for considered, appropriate, individual use.

I have perhaps made these points too cryptically. Let me expand on them a little. Let me take the last point first, namely the development of differentiated language. Everyone is aware, to a greater or lesser extent, of the differentiation of language; specialist writers on language with very varied viewpoints have given the question a great deal of attention. Laypeople are all well aware that when they look at a poem written, for example, by a fourth former and at the same pupil's physics notebook they are looking at language functioning in different ways, just as they know that a newspaper's report of the day's proceedings in parliament is functionally different from that same newspaper's advice on how to kill lawn weeds or get rid of pimples. To be sure it is all English, but we know that difference of function has, in ways which are often elusive, changed the language, so much so that after a sentence or two we know what kind of prose is likely to follow. Probably, if we go a stage further, we sense that the difference of function has meant a different stance on the part of the writer, a different psychological cast, if you like. He is about a different kind of business. We enter more difficult territory when we attempt to enumerate and categorize these differing functions into an orderly scheme or model. It is even more difficult if we attempt to do so in a way which is appropriate to the language of students of school age. Just such an attempt is being made by the Writing Research Unit at the University of London Institute of Education for the written language of secondary-school pupils. Only the sketchiest indication can be given here of the Unit's model of function categories. The following extract from one of its documents will serve to illustrate the underlying ideas.

There are in our scheme three main categories:

Transactional

This is language to get things done: to inform people (telling them what they need or want to know or what we think they ought to know), to advise or persuade or instruct people. Thus it is used for example to record facts, exchange opinions, explain and explore ideas, construct theories; to transact business, conduct campaigns, change public opinion. Where the transaction (whatever it is we want to do with language) demands accurate and specific reference to what is known about reality, this constitutes a demand for the use of language in the transactional category.

We shall need to subdivide this category in various ways, but before going into this we shall describe the other two main categories.

Expressive

Since 'expressive' covers a wider range of uses in speech than in the written language, we shall consider the spoken uses first:

(a)   Exclamations – expressions of fear, joy, pain, anger, surprise, etc. – made when there is no one there to hear them.

(b)   More extended remarks we may make to ourselves to express our feelings, put into words our immediate consciousness.

(c)   Exclamations (as in (a) above) spoken in the presence of a listener. (In these circumstances they will often be given and received as in part an appeal for help, sympathy, some kind of response. To interpret them fully the listener must know the speaker and see the predicament, e.g. the proper response to the boy who continually cried 'Wolf' would be to ignore it, unless we could see the beast.)

(d)   More extended speech addressed to a listener with whom the speaker has a common understanding (shares experiences in common: i.e. a listener whose context for the utterance will largely coincide with the speaker's) and constituting an expression of the speaker's feelings, mood, opinions, immediate preoccupations; thus, what is said reveals as much about the personality and state of mind of the speaker as it does about the events, etc., spoken about (e.g. 'Sometimes when I take my wife out in the car, I drive and she talks – expressively').

(e)   Interpersonal expressive. We have referred to a speaker and a listener: to complete the account we must extend this (1) to include more than two people and (2) to provide for the fact that any listener may in turn become a speaker.

Applying now similar criteria to writing:

(a)   The kind of writing that might be called 'thinking aloud on paper'. Intended for the writer's own use, it might be interpreted by a reader who had shared much of the earlier thinking, but it could not be understood by one who was not 'in the context'.

(b)   The kind of diary entry that attempts to record and explore the writer's feelings, mood, opinions, preoccupations of the moment.

(c)   Personal letters written to friends or relations for the purpose of maintaining contact with them (as a substitute, so to speak, for being with them). Where the writer deals with his own affairs and preoccupations, the letter may read very like the diary entry (and a close relationship with the reader is claimed or assumed by regarding him as a 'second self'), but the writer may at other times more actively invoke a close relationship with his reader by (1) importing references to shared experiences in highly *implicit* terms and (2) implying strongly held shared opinions and values in the way he refers to people and events in general.

(d) Some writing of the following kinds may also, on balance, be said to have an expressive function:

1. Writing addressed to a limited public audience assumed to share much of the writer's context and many of his values and opinions and interests (e.g. topical newspaper commentary in a conversational manner, some editorials, 'interest' articles in specialist journals, gossip columns).

2. Writing intended to be read by a public audience in which the writer chooses to approach his reader as though he were a personal friend, hence reveals much about himself by implication in the course of dealing with his topic (e.g. some autobiography).

From the examples of both speech and writing we can draw up the following *generalizations about the expressive function*:

(i) Expressive language is language close to the self. It has the functions of revealing the speaker, verbalizing his consciousness, displaying his close relation with a listener or reader.

(ii) Much is not made explicit in expressive language because the speaker (writer) relies upon the listener (reader) (a) interpreting what is said in the light of a common understanding (i.e. shared general context of the past) and (b) interpreting their immediate situation (what is happening around them) in a way similar to his own. It follows from (a) above that the meaning of an expressive utterance may vary in accordance with the situation. Compare the meaning of 'So, you're home at last' said by a wife in the small hours and by a mother at the airport.

(iii) Since expressive language submits itself to the free flow of ideas and feelings it is relatively unstructured.

Poetic

Poetic writing uses language as an art medium.

A piece of poetic writing is a verbal construct, an 'object' made out of language. The words themselves and all they refer to are selected to make an arrangement, a formal pattern.

(a) In all poetic writings the *phonic substance of language* itself is arranged (though the effect of the arrangement is generally more prominent, more sharply felt in a lyric than it is in a novel).

(b)   The writer's *feelings* (about himself, about his topic, towards his reader, about the human condition), expressed naturally or casually in a piece of expressive writing, are in poetic writing ordered, arranged to create a pattern.

(c)   Where there is a narrative, *the events* referred to make up or are part of a pattern.

(d)   A pattern of *ideas*, a formal 'movement of thought', adds a characteristically poetic dimension to the writer's thinking.

These are not independent systems of arrangement, of course, but elements in a single significant design. Consonance and dissonance between formal elements bind the writing into a complete whole, a single construct (whether it be a sonnet or a novel, an epic or a curtain-raiser).

The phonetic, syntactic, lexical and semantic aspects of the utterance itself are the objects of attention, by the writer and the reader, *in a way that does not hold for non-poetic writing*. (We might roughly compare the two response processes with those of 'taking in' a painting and studying a map.)

The function of a piece of poetic writing is to *be an object that pleases or satisfies the writer.* and the reader's response is to share that satisfaction. In this sense, it constitutes language that exists *for its own sake* and not as a means of achieving something else.

(Perhaps it should be added that the nature and degree of the author's satisfaction must vary very much from one piece to another. The more complex the construct, probably, the greater the area of his experience that is lit by this satisfaction.)

The demand for *transactional* writing in school is ceaseless but *expressive* language with all its vitality and richness is the only possible soil in which it can grow. But many teachers who readily take delight in it feel that its proper place is in the English period when something called 'creative writing' or 'self-expression' is afoot. It is likely that right up to the last stages of secondary education the unfettered and honest expression by pupils of the meanings they have derived from their learning will be highly expressive and that their modes of expressing themselves will be very different from, and often better than, the strangled paraphrases of the average textbook writer. I imagine many teachers would still insist that it is their function to teach the proper language of a subject. There can be no quarrel with that, but when? how? how much? And we need a further consideration of what that proper language is, when it is appropriate to use it and how pupils can be helped towards it. We can applaud every thoroughly absorbed feature which we notice in the pupil's work without feeling that we have also to censure unsuccessful efforts to use it or the absence of any effort at all. The time has come for all specialist teachers to discuss this subject and perhaps to codify their ways of using language. It would also be refreshing if specialist teaching included conscious attention to the language of their specialism. What, for example, is a 'proof', or a 'law' or a 'peasant'? Why do we not mention the broken test-tube or the colour of King Charles' hair? What are the problems in expressing in unilinear language non-unilinear processes ?

Attending to the language of a subject is one way of attending to the subject. In this way the growth towards the appropriate transactional form can be through an understanding by the pupil of when and why he should modify his language from the expressive to the transactional on some occasions and can please himself on others. Finally, if we are right about expressive language, all teachers should be hospitable towards it. Most teachers are so already, to some degree, particularly when they are talking to small groups and individuals. But when they call upon their pupils to write they are strongly affected by a kind of professional rigidity heightened by that conservatism which is inherent in the written word. Certainly many do not see the rewarding possibilities of the pupil's expressive view of their teaching and the insights it would give them into the responses they themselves have fostered – in expressive geology, for instance:

> *The Stone*
>
> It was formed, with the slates and shales, sandstones and clays, as a piece of hillside, long ago. Through the aeons, its limestone surface, mercilessly attacked by tropical storms and glacial nights, submerged in swamps and raised high on the heads of young mountains, has acquired the veins and wrinkles of human skin. Infinitely solid, and yet one can almost see through it to the heart of its being. It looks almost like a large, dull, irregular pearl, or a giant's tooth, with the grey-brown pits and streaks of sandstone bitten into it, like vast fillings. Underneath, where the brittle, eight sided pillar-nerves joined it to the gum, it has a crystalline glow when held to the light.
>
> It is not a fiery rock, forged in the heart of a volcano, like rugged granite or tough basalt. It is a cool, serene piece of matter, born of water and retaining some of water's sheen.
>
> – It is a piece of history, with a history of its own.

Stephen

I suggested that the expressive view had its own justification; this is particularly true when it moves towards the poetic function. This is scarcely the place to justify the writing of poems and stories but it is the place to suggest that, since all experience is the potential raw material of expressive/poetic language, the deeper the feelings which are stirred by what is being taught, the more likely it is that they will find their expression in poetic forms. It is unlikely, however, that a teacher will ever see such products unless his receptiveness to them is made apparent. A biology teacher could enjoy with a class this view of jellyfish, not because it neatly illustrated a point, but for its own sake and to share the writer's satisfaction with what he had made:

Jellyfish

I had learnt about it in Biology;
Yet now, as I toed it gently with my boot,
It seemed different,
Alien and strange.
I looked at it;
Pink and gleaming
It shone like a moonstone,
A quartz crystal,
Or an iridescent pearl.
Long tendrils splayed about
It had been abandoned by the sea,
Rejected by the tide,
To quietly melt and rot
On this lonely shingle beach.

Christopher

Even the pupil's view of boredom is to be preferred to simply witnessing it.

Geometry

Little arrows, following
each other round
a square.

Squares, within
squares, in different
colours.

Colours, distinguishing
lines, for which there are
many names.
Names, everlasting,
words, round which we wrap
our tongues.

Tongues, beginning
to talk, because we
are bored.

Yawns, like circles,
on our books, following
little arrows.

Bigger arrows, following
each other round
a square.

Leonie

It follows naturally that the variety of reading material the teacher puts before his class could be a happy complement to such an attitude. It should not seem far-fetched to picture a teacher of geography reading a passage from Alan Moorehead's *Cooper's Creek* or one of Henry Lawson's Australian stories, or a science teacher reading a science-fiction story or an extract from *Doctor Faustus*, or a history teacher from one of dozens of novels. Teachers in these fields could begin to compile for each other fascinating anthologies.

In discussing the functions of language I have inevitably included the written language. In spite of the fact that schools eat their way through mountains of blue-lined paper, very little is confidently known about the process of writing as distinct from the product. What actually happens when a school pupil or a mature adult writes? What difference does it make to him if he is writing an entry in a diary which he locks away carefully rather than an account of the discussion which went on at the Congress of Vienna? Something is known, of course, and it should be taken into account when pupils are asked to carry out the thousand and one assignments which keep their heads down during the school day and often in the evening. Firstly, no matter how much a writer wants to write, it is a hard and thorny business. We learn to talk almost effortlessly; almost everyone does everywhere and no special arrangements have to be made for us. But writing has to be taught in a more or less formal way. The writer is a lonely figure cut off from the stimulus and corrective of listeners. He must be a predictor of reactions and act on his predictions. He writes with one hand tied behind his back, being robbed of gesture. He is robbed too of the tone of his voice and the aid of the clues the environment provides. He is condemned to monologue; there is no one to help out, to fill the silences, put words in his mouth or make encouraging noises. His reader will be tyrannical in a way which listeners cannot be, for he will be able to take his time in scanning the text and move to and fro in it. Listeners are usually waiting their turn anyway and some of their attention goes to their own imminent performance. The writer is thus under some compulsion to organize his utterance into a whole. He can no longer be the improviser he was as a speaker. He must become instead both more elaborate and more complete. He is unlikely to be given a second chance. No school pupil can be expected to do all this without help. He needs a reader more sympathetic than most. To ease the transition from speaker to writer he needs the help of reader-listeners, his classmates. There are practices which are still very common which do not help or help very little. I do not propose to list them. I want instead to suggest some questions which a school staff might jointly consider.

1. Does much of the written work consist of the pupil, in order to show what he knows, telling the teacher what he already knows so that he may judge whether the pupil knows it? Is it in fact a pseudo-communication?
2. Does the preparation for written work give the pupil the confidence that he has something of his own to say and can say it in his own words? Has the writing a helpful context?
3. Is the pupil confined to the repetition of facts? How does he know how to select the relevant ones and interconnect them?
4. How much freedom is there for comment, doubt, opinion, puzzlement?
5. Is the teacher the only audience? Or other pupils? Or others? Or the writer himself?
6. Does the pupil know what the writing is for? To use for examination revision? For future references? To clarify his ideas? To publish them?
7. Is the writing not so much composing as copying? Verbatim?
8. Does any writing ever arise from the pupils' suggestions? Is the task identical for all pupils? If it is, can they modify it?
9. How is written work received? Is anything made of it or is it only marked? Are there times for discussion of reformulations and re-structuring? Does the writer believe anyone cares? About what?

Perhaps that is too much of a self-inflicted inquisition, though teachers almost anywhere would be happy to see a report of the joint attempt to supply answers.

Competent writers are readers, not consumers of textbooks. They become competent talkers by attending to the flow of varied speech around them. Similarly, alone with his bitten pen, the writer can go on scratching away largely because he knows how writers write and can select from the repertoire what suits his purposes. He will make mistakes; he will imitate one model too closely, fall in love with lurid phrases, concede too much to the reader or too little, but he will learn how to find his way about. Or will do so if he has access to a wide enough range of the written language so that he has some chance of noting differences of function and execution. If he meets the Factory Acts or the Thames Basin or the Balance of Payments only in one chapter in the class textbook, he is like a child who had learnt his mother tongue from a single speaker and a not very impressive one at that. There are written documents of all kinds other than books and a generous variety of books too. We have been shown the way very recently by the varied material published by the Humanities Curriculum Project and the Jackdaw Collections. Paperbacks are cheap enough for pupils and schools.

Harold Rosen

I have up to this point been trying to invite the reader to join me in a consideration of the ways in which language does and might enter school life. I have not been exhaustive, not have I, I hope, been too ready with conclusions, remedies and marching orders. The matters I have discussed raise numerous questions, many of which are unresolved. But I have been trying to insist that we have not given sufficient attention to these questions and that curriculum discussions, curriculum reform itself can only be strengthened if it includes considerations of language and learning; that teachers who embark on observation, exploration and experiment concerned with the role of language in learning will make a valuable contribution to education, particularly if they also take a not uncritical look at the relevant literature.

My intention has also been to give the reader some sense of the thinking behind the document 'A Language Policy Across the Curriculum' [which follows], produced by the London Association for the Teaching of English, for my own ideas and those of many others have been shaped by the hours and hours of work and talk which preceded and followed the appearance of that document. It is worth tracing the history of the document in various versions so that some sense of its potential can be appreciated.

In the Association we are all more or less specialist teachers of English and for many years we busied ourselves with our own fascinating specialist concerns, with what did or would happen in the two hundred minutes per class of curriculum space allocated to us by the timetable. Increasingly, however, we found ourselves being pushed beyond the boundaries we had come to accept or perhaps helped to create. We found ourselves discussing the relationship between language and thought, how language represented experience, the functions of language in society, different kinds of language and how they were acquired, the difference between talking and writing, the nature of discussion and group dynamics. Inevitably we started to trespass in areas marked 'Keep out', though some colleagues waved a welcome from the other side. There were others peering over fences, those engaged in integrated studies, group work, inquiry methods, environmental studies, social studies and innovations of all kinds. Some of them, though not many, were also concerned with questions of language. Soon we found ourselves talking about 'language in education', or 'language and learning', and finally about 'language across the curriculum'. We felt sure that language was a matter of concern for everybody, that if children were to make sense of their school experience, and in the process were to become confident users of language, then we needed to engage in a much closer scrutiny of the ways in which they encountered and used language throughout the school day. For this we needed all the help we could get from other subject teachers.

We started in May 1966, and we started – for reasons which have been made clear already in this book – we started with talk. At that time an emphasis on talk did not seem to be a radical idea: the word 'oracy' was already being used by educationalists alongside 'literacy' and 'numeracy'. We soon discovered, however, that the unanimity was a superficial one. The *Schools Council Examinations Bulletin No. 11*, for example, phrased the problem like this:

> ... they [the Steering Committee] recognize that 'the language of the coffee bar is not appropriate to school', and 'An idea of examiners deliberately coming down to the lowest teenage level was rejected, although the problem of contact was recognized'.

(p. 196)

By contrast, we were far from sure that we knew enough about the language of the coffee bar. We had certainly not settled what might be considered the appropriate language for school, though we knew quite well what was usually considered appropriate. It was largely for this reason that we began by looking closely at the language of children in various kinds of contexts and roles, both in the presence of adults and on their own. The questions we asked ourselves were:

> What are the different kinds of talk used by children and young people?
> What are their different functions?
> How does the size and nature of the group affect the quality of the talk?
> How do different kinds of talk develop in the school years?

We began making tapes of children talking in different situations. We discovered that what we believed to be reasonably skilled predictions – we are all experienced teachers – were in many cases very wide of the mark. We had imagined, for example, that a tape of children preparing a meal would show them engaged in discussion, and even argument and recrimination, about fair shares, about who does what and the organization of clearing away, about how much they should leave for the adults, and so on. Instead of which the eating of food was accompanied by talk addressed to no one in particular, which simply named the foods, and the organization was carried out quietly with only one or two subdued reminders – more in the nature of spoken memoranda than exhortation. We discovered more too about the effect of the presence of teachers – the way, for instance, the presence of a respected and appreciated teacher created a sort of psychological and social space in which less assertive children could make a contribution and all members of the group could engage in sustained talk. And most important – since it is the kind of pupil activity that most teachers by definition do not see much of – we learnt to sketch in the outlines of the folklore of jokes, reminiscences and attitudes which held the group together when there were no adults present. (Normal children spend a great deal of their time laughing.) In this way we became more certain that smaller groups were essential for certain activities and that only small groups of talkers could address themselves to problems in the way that so many children on the tapes had done. Almost without noticing it, we began to talk about language with scarcely a thought of school subjects.

Our next move, of which this section of the book is in a sense a part, was not only to be concerned that the talk of schoolchildren should be given new importance and attention, but also to scrutinize more closely all uses of language in school subjects. We had found ourselves concluding that if we were committed to this development of children's language in school, then we needed to take a practical step towards making some impact on the way in which language was used throughout all the processes of school learning. This in turn meant that in any given school there needed to be a common approach to the uses of language. This task was in one sense straightforward and in another bristling with difficulties. It was straightforward because we aimed at drawing up a brief document – a 'manifesto' was the first grandiose term we used – which set out in unadorned terms what we thought ought to be done. It was difficult because we wanted the 'manifesto' to present a view that was relevant to teachers of subjects other than English.

This was, broadly speaking, the function of the LATE conference in May 1968. At that conference we attempted to broaden the terms of the inquiry, to see how far the outlines of our work and thought on talk could be extended to other kinds of language activity, and to draw up the first draft of a statement which could be circulated to schools for discussion and amendment. It is worth stressing, however, that very little detailed study of language in operation in the classroom is available to us, and in most cases we have had to rely on our combined wisdom and our critical assessment of our own practices. Douglas Barnes' paper which forms Part One of this book was one piece of detailed study; Nancy Martin and Alex McLeod of the Writing Research Unit of the University of London Institute of Education presented some preliminary findings as a result of a survey of one week's written work in five London schools. But for the most part is it uncharted territory.

Parallel to our earlier questions about talk, we went on to face questions of this kind:

How much writing and of what kind do pupils ordinarily do in and out of school (continuous and non-continuous, notes, exercises, etc.)?
What kinds of writing do teachers expect of pupils in different contexts, and why?
How does the nature of the writing task affect what the pupils write and how. they write it?
What other influences (reading, conversation, etc.) might affect the way in which pupils write ?
How do different kinds of writing develop in the school years?

But to return to the original document. It was produced from the heat of our discussions, produced by five working groups in half a morning, typed and duplicated in a lunch hour, finally sewn together and edited by a small committee. It appeared in the first edition of this book. When we produced it we were highly conscious of the fact that, given more time, we could have refined it, that we could have consulted our colleagues more fully. But we were anxious to get started, for something to happen, to stir up wider participation, inquiry and collaboration. Probably this led us to phrase our policy in deliberately 'do this, do that' terms. We made too many assumptions and were too tempted to pithy slogans.

Many of those who encountered the document had no context to provide the thinking and experience behind it. We hope this book will go a long way towards remedying that, but it is clear to us that current ideas about the connexion between language and thought have not had wide dissemination. It would be one happy result of our work if it stimulated a growth of interest in such ideas. Other teachers felt that our tone was somewhat self-righteous or condescending. Perhaps we gave the impression to some teachers that most of what they are doing is wrong and that we know how to put it right. To this we can only plead that it is certainly not the case, though we did try to be fairly crisp and provocative in the hope that this would prove a better way of starting discussion. Others still expressed surprise that we should think our suggestions were in any way radical, while some have dismissed them as wildly impractical. About 'radicalness' we feel confident: our experience cannot be so far from the mark, and (as we have shown) we have a great deal of evidence to support us. The discussion document said at one point that 'the written language used by children must be their own expression of observation, ideas, conclusions', and we could fill warehouses with exercise books which do not even begin to meet that requirement. As for being impractical, we have been moved to undertake this work because, like many others, we have found that many of the old practices do not work. We are not unaware of the difficulties – examination syllabuses, the need to 'cover the ground', the wrong architecture and so on. But nothing we have suggested should make it more difficult for children to pass examinations, nor are any of our suggestions dependent on very desirable changes in school buildings.

A more intractable problem has been that some schools are not in the habit of organizing discussions about anything. They have neither the tradition nor the organization for formulating policies agreed on by the staff. It may turn out that we were wrong to assume that the best or the only way of starting was in the schools. Perhaps the powerful subject associations and the bodies which are undertaking curriculum experiments might be more effective initiators. However, we do not wish to be pessimistic. There are several schools which have taken up the idea of a 'language policy', and it may even be that schools not normally given to such procedures may have their first staff discussions on the issues we have presented. In so far as changes are needed, they are more likely to come about if teachers feel that they must remove obstacles which prevent them from teaching in the best possible way.

For all its faults the policy document has continued to produce encouraging results. In a number of schools, teachers' centres and colleges it has been a focus of discussion, and, more significantly, given rise to activities which we feel confident would not have occurred without it. Firstly, we have had critical comments and suggestions. What they reveal above all else is that teachers are beginning to examine for themselves the language of their pupils. Here is a report of one such examination. Its heading is worth quoting too, suggesting as it does a sustained interest in the questions raised by the document.

Language Across the Curriculum III

M (Chairman) said he could see four problems in this area.

1. Note taking.
2. Essay questions – Kids can't always handle the language required.
3. Most material had to be given in wodges of words.
4. The experiences to be handled are remote.

H presented us with the following extract from a third-year Geography exam.

Question: Write all you can about the early explorers of America.

About 100 years ago a few men came to America they wanted to explor America. They wanted to be early explorers so they went all over the high and low mountains to explor then they went through the villages and over the lakes. They found out quite a bit about America they found out the names of all the states of America and kept it all down in a Record book so that he cooldent forget anything he found out the names of streets and roads and of course the names of all the mountains. the rested on mountains and on the land they did not have a lot of money But they had enough to keep them alive after they found out all they wanted to know they went back to there own country and so that is what the early explorers done.

There was some discussion about this extract and some comparison with the extracts from the C.S.E. woodwork paper included in the last report. The fifth year boy had a better grasp of the facts than appeared in the Geography paper. Perhaps the Geography question could have been more precise. It would have helped had the third year writer been made to answer that question first orally in class.

J said that there were further problems here. If you ask a specific question then you get an answer which is just an enumeration of the facts. The children don't expand on the facts. It is very difficult to get exploratory communication.

M talked about a lesson he had had recently on the subject of lowering the voting age to eighteen. The class had not taken the problems far enough. Discussion could help here – kids could be pushed to question their own statements and see the implications.

P said this was a problem. The answers to a question tended to be all or nothing. J said we were asking for a very sophisticated level of activity when we asked for exploratory communication in History.

P gave an account of a piece of improvised drama with one of his classes. Columbus was asking Ferdinand for support for a voyage of exploration. The whole thing was over in ten seconds flat. There may have been a failure of imagination here but that was not the only failure.

M picked up one of the problems he had isolated at the start of the discussion. The experiences presented were remote, e.g. the vast majority of our kids have not seen a mountain. The same could be said to be true of many of the historical facts presented.

J felt that History should not be an isolated subject. The experience of History came mainly through the experience of words and this was an artificial extension of experience. D agreed. The pupils very often had not sufficient data to recreate the past in order to make this a real experience. Where we can give them sufficient data then they can project themselves into the situation. N added that concrete experience was needed.

Query by M.T. added while writing this up.

Can English teachers help here? I've just emerged from reading *The Railway Navvies*, and *The Great Hunger* and *Famine and Insurrection* by Liam O'Flaherty with the feeling that there is a lot in each of these books I would like to read with English classes. Would it help if this were timed to reinforce work done in History classes? If so, could this be extended?

We have, we believe, stimulated a great upsurge of interest in the making of tapes, transcripts and the setting up of listening groups which are beginning to develop the skills of analysis. The LATE has had functioning since its conference a Talk and Talkers Group which has accumulated an archive of tapes and transcripts which is ransacked regularly by those looking for discussion material. It has also kept in being a Language Across the Curriculum Group without whose activities this book could scarcely have been written, nor this section in particular. As far away as Evanston Township High School, Illinois, Miss Nancy Martin initiated discussions and a 'workshop' with teachers from all departments of the school, and the policy document was one of the main starting points.

Teachers of Science, Maths, Social Studies and Geography are becoming more and more involved not only in their own schools but also in their national organizations. The Association of Teachers of Mathematics has been the most prompt to join us in discussions and plan joint activities. Thus their members were able to read in their journal an article by one of our members, George Robertson, entitled 'Directions in English teaching', in which he says:

> I think the 'modern' Maths and English teachers have much in common. They have implicit in their method a responsibility to know and understand the pupil in all aspects of his life which affect learning; that is, *all* aspects.
>
> They commit themselves equally to re-examining from first principles the whole process of educational administration in its colossal effects on the crucial social interactions in learning of pupil and pupil, of pupil and teacher, and of teacher and teacher.
>
> They imply various articles of faith and inspiration about the beauty and satisfaction of order, about the ability of men to respond as individuals with a desire for order, and about the nature of social order, which are quite evidently bones of contention in our society today …
>
> English and Maths teachers equally stand in the position of not only unlocking their culture for our pupils, but of modifying the ways in which they will perceive it.
>
> (Robertson, 1969)

Close relations have been established with Science chiefly through the wholehearted participation from the outset of our venture of Mr Dick West who gave a science teacher's view of language at our conference. He has since then joined us frequently in planning and discussion and has put his views in print. In an article in *Forum* (1969) he writes:

> Nuffield has emphasized the 'personal' nature of the pupils' record of work, and I think we must push this one stage further and break once and for all with the traditional sterility of scientific report writing with its emphasis on the impersonal. What the child does and sees is unique to him at the time it occurs and his report should be a unique communication. The experiences can then be generalized with a sense of involvement on the part of the participants. Not only is the generalization of events essential to scientific thinking, but the ability to generalize and relate our own experiences is essential to communication. Effective communication should lead to effective learning. It would appear that freedom for the child to express his experiences *in his own language* must come first. The language used may not be in itself scientific but it will be used in the context of a scientific experience. Out of this can grow the true language of science. Words used can become clothed with meaning and the child can move forward to effective classification of his experiences.

The excitement of discovery need not be dampened by the problems of 'correct' verbalization.

Forum also found room in another issue (Spring 1970) for an article by Peter Griffiths on language policy.

At one meeting a group of English teachers found themselves persuaded by a geography teacher to play a geographical game in which they had to be members of the Board of Directors of Iron Manufacturing Company. The report gives some idea of the discussion which followed the game.

> Mr Hore pointed out that once the final decisions have been made the children are ready for the vital final stage, a comparison with the real situation (in this case it was a map of the present coal, iron and steel industries of England and Wales).

> All the time they have been discussing the possible location of steel plants, they have been sneaking up to reality. Now they can discuss the unique situation in the light of the general tendencies they have established in their discussions.

> Questions were asked about the amount of verbal information involved, and we looked at another more simple snakes and ladders type of game played on a stylized map using facts taught in advance. Writing produced during any game would range from private jotting to public and coherent statements. It was suggested that there might be different ways of looking at games. The English teacher would see the talk and discussion as being of first importance, but does a Geography teacher have to correct wrong assumptions? Mr Hore felt that he probably would, but that these could be pointed out when the real life situation is discussed and that on the whole there were no right answers. Answers as questions tend to be open-ended. It is the role of the teacher to compare the decision reached at the end of the game with the real-life situation.

> As to the need to supply additional sources of information to which the children can refer while making their decisions, this depends largely on how far the age group using the game is capable of absorbing more information.

> The question of patterns of speech and involvement was raised. Does conversation become complex and heated or does it tend to be at a low level? Mr Hore thought that it could be very lively and vigorous if the teacher was able to stand back and allow the children to really play out their roles. There was a possibility of the game becoming unscripted drama. This had happened when the postulated situation was a strike on a national newspaper and people had taken roles to resolve the strike.

We were hopeful that our bare suggestions would be filled out through the work of teacher groups and this is indeed beginning to happen. For example the peremptory dictum, 'Notes should never be dictated', which attracted some fire, has been constructively worked on by Miss Rosemary Leonard.

I refer to it not in order to demonstrate that agreement has been reached and the matter closed but because it shows how the debate can be carried a stage further. Only when our original document is amplified, modified and fortified with a thick batch of protocols will it really achieve its purpose.

Lastly, we are beginning to assemble a picture of how teachers see the language activities of their classrooms against the background of our suggested policy. Here are two submissions from the dossier.

Science Teacher: Secondary Modern

1. Encourage children to talk amongst themselves during experimental work. Constructive talk is always allowed and even a certain amount of 'social' chat, as long as children are predominantly concerned with the job in hand. Class discussion forms a large part of class activity. Usually I collect all kinds of opinions – both right and wrong – before attempting to arrive at a correct solution to a problem. I try to get children themselves to correct incorrect statements of others. I also encourage a very close teacher/pupil contact by chatting about almost anything.

2. In science, I always allow children to use their own familiar language in describing a situation. Scientific language is only suggested after they have been allowed free expression. They never copy work from a blackboard that may describe what or why or how something happens. Sometimes they will copy brief instructions, but where possible duplicated sheets are used. Spelling is corrected superficially only. I encourage children to describe accurately what they have observed.

3. School science journals are available in the lab.; charts, booklets and a science library are also present. Textbooks are mainly of the type giving experimental instructions, with a little 'padding'. Reference books are available in plenty and children are encouraged to use them.

4. Only C.S.E. candidates are encouraged to take notes. I find there is little enough timetable time for other classes and groups for them to be 'wasting' time other than doing and finding out.

Handicraft Teacher: Secondary Grammar

Comment Feel that language is important and must not be ignored in subjects such as woodwork and metalwork.

Talk Situations Boys managed to talk to me and discuss individual difficulties – these are then discussed with the group. Attempt to socialize the situation and discuss with boys other things in addition to problems connected with particular subject. Boys managed to express themselves in their own manner, no criticism of accent, dialect, etc. Students often take the 'role' of reader and suggest ways of changing the situation. Technical terms introduced when pupils are able to accept them.

Written Situations, Note-taking, etc. Note-taking used a great deal plus research work *but unfortunately* there is no co-operation with, or help from, other departments in the school. Examinations restrict experimentation in 'co-operative teaching'. Written work has to be highly technical in nature – when marking written work English is corrected as and when necessary. Again examination syllabi control a great deal, the attitudes towards what is 'handed in'.

Suggestions towards progress Closer liaison between departments and greater flexibility would assist in the development of Language Across the Curriculum. Grammar school teachers too often live in little 'boxes' with the examination results as ultimate goal.

I apologize in advance to the reader for this breathless Cook's tour of activities. I have had of necessity to keep the account brief but I have tried through quotation to give some flavour of the present state of the enterprise. I have not wanted to present an advertiser's picture of successful Treatment or Wonder Cure but rather to suggest to other teachers some of the varied ways in which the language policy might serve them. We were probably too optimistic in thinking that some schools would fairly rapidly produce a codified policy of their own and proceed to take steps to implement it. It is much more likely that the more modest and less dramatic activities of the kind I have reported on so briefly will constitute the preparatory phase, and they will have to become more widespread and influential. A first step towards this has been an expansion of activity from the London Association to the National Association for the Teaching of English. The Primary Committee has made a fine set of tapes of young children talking which will replay study wherever learning through talking is being discussed. Listen to this pair of infants (it is time we heard from them) examining a land-measuring tape:

Girl It's a tape measure ...

Boy It only goes up to nine and starts at one again ... Hey when you pull that out ...

Girl How do you put it back in?

Boy   Ah I know … When you pull it out the think – the thing goes round and round – it's a handle …

Girl   That goes up when you want it to if you turn it back …

Boy   Oh yes, you turn it back. When you want it to go back *in* then when – if you want it to come out …

Girl   Yes, you pull it out.

Boy   When you turn that round that goes round.

Girl   That goes round [Together]

Boy   And when you turn it that way that goes round. [Laugh] [Repeat with different emphasis] That goes round, press that.

Girl   What number does it go up to? Starts at one.

Boy   Starts at one … It comes what, it comes – first there's a red one, a red one. And then there's a black one, a black one.

Girl   Well now that's one foot then it starts on another foot.

Boy   Oh yea.

Girl   And when it's a red one it's two feet … [Bang] Whoops …

Organizationally the debate and study will now be taken to national level; the 1971 conference of NATE will be devoted exclusively to Language Across the Curriculum and its various commissions will consider talk and discussion, the book and the textbook, writing and kinds of writing, language and thought, and the role of the English teacher.

We have undoubtedly come a long way since we sat in small groups (less than two years since the time of writing these words) and tried to spell out what was meant to be a dramatic challenge. Since then we have rendered obsolete our own document, which is just as it should be. We have tried again with mark 2, which follows this final section of this book. Some readers will have copies of mark 1. They might derive some interest from comparing the two.

We have perhaps without realizing it been following the promptings of that great pioneer of language studies, J. R. Firth, who as long ago as 1935 was urging us to give our full attention to what he called 'the biographical study of speech'.

We are born into a vast potential cultural heritage, but we can only hope to succeed to a very small part of the total heritage and then only in stages. There would appear to be a need to emphasize that for each stage of childhood and youth, for each type of child, there are a relevant environment and relevant forms of language. There is a vast field of research here in what may be called the biographical study of speech. There is material for all the branches of linguistics in the study of all the various components of meaning in this linguistic life-history of the young person as an active member of his age-group as well as a pupil, in his seven ages of childhood and youth.

There is plenty for us to do. To that end we should talk to one another.

References

Barnes, D., Britton, J., Rosen, H. and the LATE (1969 and 1971 [revised edition]) *Language, the Learner and the School*. Harmondsworth: Penguin.

Bellack, A. *et al.* (1966) *The Language of the Classroom*. New York: Teachers College Press, Columbia University.

Crediton Mathematics Centre (1966) *Logbook, Report No. 3*.

Firth, J. (1957) 'The technique of semantics', in *Papers in Linguistics, 1934–1951*. Oxford: Oxford University Press.

Flanders, N. (1962) 'Using interaction analysis in the in-service training of teachers'. *Journal of Experimental Education*, 30 (4).

Griffiths, P. (1970) 'Language policy'. *Forum*, 12 (2).

Mead, G. (1934) *Mind, Self and Society*. Chicago: University of Chicago Press.

Postman, N. and Weingartner, C. (1969) *Teaching as a Subversive Activity*. New York: Delacorte Press.

Robertson, G. (1969) 'Directions in English teaching'. *Association of Teachers of Mathematics Supplement*, 13, November.

Schools Council (1966) *Schools Council Examination Bulletin*, 11. London: HMSO.

Smith, L. and Geoffrey, W. (1968) *The Complexities of an Urban Classroom*. New York: Holt, Rinehart and Winston.

Walker, R. (1969) 'A sociological language for the description of the stream of classroom behaviour' (unpublished paper). London: Centre for Science Education, Chelsea College of Science and Technology.

West, R. (1969) 'Reflections on curriculum reform'. *Forum*, 12 (1).

Acknowledgements

My thanks for help of various kinds are due to: my colleagues in the Writing Research Unit of the University of London Institute of Education; Stephen Harvey for 'The Stone'; Christopher Naylor for 'Jellyfish'; Leonie Richards for 'Geometry'; members of the staff of Walworth Secondary School for the minutes of their discussions on 'Language Policy Across the Curriculum III'; Peter Hore for the report of the geographical game; and the Primary School Sub-Committee of NATE for the tape produced by the 'Children Talking' group.

A Language Policy Across the Curriculum

Language and the teacher

Language permeates school life. Boys and girls in their attempts to master the school curriculum and in the process of growing up have to call upon their language resources. Moreover they are expected to increase these resources by making the language encountered in their school learning a living part of their thinking and communicating. We take the view that we have chosen a most promising moment to put before all teachers a document which will open discussion on the educational implications of these obvious facts. We think it is a promising moment because teachers of all subjects and in all kinds of schools are becoming aware that language is inextricably bound up with all the learning that goes on in school. They are becoming acquainted with the research on the relationship between language and thought, with theories on the acquisition of language and with work on the nature of language itself, for these ideas are finding their way into the most important educational debates of our day. Innovations in the curriculum and the discussions which surround them have helped to focus attention on language. We believe that many teachers are now prepared to go far beyond the older view that language was someone else's business, or, perhaps, that they were the guardians of linguistic proprieties. They are now prepared to consider what needs to be done to improve our procedures in schools in such a way that language becomes a facilitating force in learning rather than a barrier bristling with formidable difficulties.

For all the dissemination of new ideas, relatively little has been done to work out in detail just what needs to be modified or changed in our day-to-day practices in order to achieve solid advances. We still have ahead of us that crucial and demanding phase of realizing in classroom practice the theories which seem so promising. Therefore we want to move discussion to this stage.

We would like to see more teachers of all kinds and of all specialisms talking together about language, their pupils' and their own, in all its variety. We would like them to join us in studying how changing situations change the productivity and potentiality of talk. We would like them to join us in considering the differences between speech and writing and what it means to the young writer to compose in words his own observations, conclusions and attitudes. We would like them to observe with us the effects of giving scope to the full expression of the personal view in all new learning. We would like them to consider critically with us what we offer pupils to read in school books and to decide how pupils can best make sense of the printed word.

We want to go beyond wringing our hands at the low level of literacy, at shrinking from contemporary speech manners, at frustration in the face of inarticulacy and reticence. We want instead to evolve a realistic programme that could be implemented by any school which was convinced that a change was necessary and possible.

Language and the pupil

In children's encounters with the curriculum there is a confrontation between their comfortably acquired mother-tongue and the varieties of language which have grown up around institutionalized areas of learning. In many of these areas special demands are made on their thinking – they are expected to reason, speculate, plan, consider theories, make their own generalizations and hypotheses. These are in many respects language activities, that is, language is the means by which they are carried out, the means, therefore, by which children do much of their learning. The effort to formulate in the pupil's own words the appearance of something, or to draw conclusions from an experiment, or to express the significance of an historical document is an essential part of the learning process, for he will be using language to give meaning to his experience. But there are formal mature ways of expressing these things which have arisen in a different context, are designed to meet different expectations and are directed at more or less public audiences. The school pupil is remote from such a situation and its attendant language needs. His healthiest need is to make sense in his own terms of what he is learning. It will take many years of development before his situation begins to approach that of the scientist, historian, technologist, etc. This stage is likely to be reached towards the end of his secondary schooling.

Mature language is highly differentiated, modified to meet many differing and complex functions. Some of these functions require from the mature adult that he inhibit all those features of language which are the expression of personal and inter-personal feeling in the interests of dispassionate objectivity and undistracted communication. Since these are very sophisticated achievements we cannot expect to find them in school pupils. If such writing is to develop at all it must grow out of the confident use of personal expressive language and the thoughtful, conscious consideration of the new language the teacher has to offer.

Talking

The speaking voice precedes the writing pen and the reading eye in the life-history of every normal child. Given the opportunity and a favouring environment he can use it to do more things than he can do with the written word. Through improvised talk he can shape his ideas, modify them by listening to others, question, plan, express doubt, difficulty and confusion, experiment with new language and feel free to be tentative and incomplete.

It is through talk that he comes nearer to others and with them establishes a social unit in which learning can occur and in which he can shape for public use his private and personal view. Thus we think that school learning should be so organized that pupils may use to the full their language repertoire and also add to it. From our discussion and exchanges of experience we would make these suggestions.

1. Many school activities should be carried out by small groups which can use their talk to move towards understanding by means which are not present in the normal teacher-directed classroom.
2. Though much of this talk may seem uneconomic, tentative and inexplicit, it is often the only way in which genuine exploration can occur. Teachers can frequently help forward discussion at the crucial moment, but probably we need less intervention and more patience.
3. We need to find ways of helping pupils without putting words in their mouths. We could perhaps be less concerned to elicit from them verbatim repetitions of time-honoured formulations than to ensure that pupils engage in a struggle to formulate for themselves their present understanding. Discussion is an essential part of that process.
4. Teachers should encourage pupils to consider the language of the subject in ways which are appropriate to their development. Time spent in considering why reports, observations, theories, etc. are expressed in one way rather than another should be an essential part of intellectual development. We all need to learn more about the language of our subjects.
5. Room should be found for speculation and fantasy.
6. As teachers we might free ourselves much more from situations which confine our own language to the most formal exposition and most limiting kinds of questions. Talk with small groups and individuals gives the teacher greater linguistic scope and makes it possible for him to influence the pupils' language more profoundly. We need to experiment more with questioning so that it leads to fuller and more adventurous responses.

We acknowledge that more talk by pupils creates its own problems and that not all talk is productive. We need to identify these problems – and find ways of overcoming them.

Writing

The written language has the advantages of permanence, completeness and elaboration. It gives the writer the time and scope to examine his own language and fashion it more precisely to his purposes. Yet young writers are frequently at a loss when confronted with a typical school assignment or they are reduced to summaries and paraphrases from textbooks and notes. Some of their difficulties are an inevitable part of the transition from the spontaneous spoken word to the new and complex conventions of the written word. Other difficulties arise from special features of the school situation. Much they are asked to write is broadly speaking informative; yet no genuine informative act is taking place, i.e. no one is being informed. The tasks frequently seem to lack a clear function, nor do they seem to leave room for the expression of the writer's own ideas and his way of seeing things. All too rarely in school writing assignments is the writer expressing something he wants to say to others.

It is probably in the written work of pupils that the most stereotyped and uniform language is to be found. We do not believe that most teachers prefer it to be like this. How could it be changed?

1. By written work arising as a logical need from the learning in hand – the need to record, to report, to propose solutions, to weigh possibilities, to sort out ideas, etc. The ideal to aim at is the genuine need to communicate something to somebody. An exchange in talk beforehand is likely to help pupils discover this communicative need.
2. By greater tolerance for the pupil's own expression of his observations, ideas and conclusions, and the encouragement of very varied responses including personal imaginative ones.
3. By discussing with pupils the formalities and conventions of particular kinds of documents (e.g. laboratory records, notes, etc.) and allowing them to devise their own.
4. By avoiding stereotyped conventions irrespective of the function of the writing and by encouraging appropriateness of response. The impersonality of certain kinds of prose is appropriate only for certain purposes.
5. By encouraging self-initiated work and providing generous choices or at least the possibility of modifying the set task.
6. By attempting to develop a genuine sense of audience not only through a genuine message from pupil to teacher but also by widening the audience to other pupils in the class and school and people outside the school.
7. By breaking the bonds of the school 'exercise' designed to be completed in a standard homework stint or school period and written in a standard exercise book. More sustained efforts can be made with books, pamphlets, displays, etc., and may be the result of a successful collaboration.

It follows from these suggestions that written work asks for the teacher's attention and interest more than (perhaps, instead of) his marks. If prior and exclusive attention is given to spelling, punctuation and correctness (in its narrowest sense) then all too easily the writer feels that the message itself and his effort to communicate it are of less importance. If his writing is made more public then he is more likely to develop the incentive to become his own editor and to set himself higher standards of presentation.

Many hours are spent by pupils *copying* notes but many pupils never learn how to *make* them. This would not only be for many an investment in their educational future but would be for all part of the process of learning. They would be engaged in abstracting and verbalizing the essence of what they had learnt. Moreover, note-making could be their living experience of how writing needs to change as its function changes, for notes will be different in kind as the writer's purposes change. The co-operative composition of notes under the teacher's guidance; a set of notes made by pupils for each other's use; the study of extracts from the note-books of scientists and writers; these could all help to build up a notion of the varied criteria for the selection and presentation of material. The dictation or copying of notes may seem to be a quick and efficient method for accurate learning but in the long run it actually omits a vital process in teaching.

Reading

The books made readily accessible by teachers not only provide an inexhaustible supply of material by means of which pupils can teach themselves and supplement what has been taught, they also represent the chief means by which they can learn the varied adult forms of discourse and when they should be used. The standard textbook supplied to every member of a class can scarcely fulfil such ambitious requirements even if it is well written. Frequently it is not. Many textbooks seem to be addressed to the teacher rather than the pupil and their language shows little awareness of the kinds of linguistic difficulty confronting the pupils they purport to address. The excellent work already done by teachers and librarians has pointed the way to the following suggestions.

1. Pupils should have access to all types of reading material relevant to the topic they are studying: reference books, newspapers, periodicals, cuttings, documents, stories, biographies.
2. They should have the opportunity to observe the varied emphases, commitments, attitudes and presentation of different writers.
3. Textbooks should not be treated as sacred sources of irrefutable data but rather as one of many sources of handy reference. For the study of some topics the school textbook may well be dispensed with.
4. For children who have difficulty with reading, material should be taped and the tape made available with the text. Pupils might make some of these tapes.
5. There should be time for reading in class not only for specific assignments but also for reading of a more exploratory kind.
6. The teacher should read aloud material which is compelling and provocative.

The teacher

The teacher's role in schools is changing and much of what we have proposed is in line with this change. The more teachers work alongside their pupils the more likely it is that our suggestions will make sense. The more they foster the initiative of their pupils the more likely it is that their pupils will develop a confidence in their own use of language. The less they attempt to verbalize ideas for their pupils the less stereotyped will their pupils' language be.

How could the policy be implemented?

1. Teachers in schools, teachers' centres, etc. should pool their observations of language in use in school (including, of course, their own). They should examine in detail specific problems, e.g. teachers' and pupils' questions, the language of textbooks. Teachers with different specialisms should compare their problems, e.g. Is note-making in history different from note-making in chemistry?
2. Subject associations should devote conference time and meetings to language problems, e.g. the metaphors of biology.
3. Wherever possible teachers should attempt to make themselves familiar with relevant recent studies and researches on the nature of language, how it works and how it is acquired.
4. Small-scale investigations should be made by teachers to furnish documents, tape and videotape for their discussion, e.g. the use of language on a field trip, including the preparation and follow-up.
5. Arising from discussion and investigation it should be possible for some schools to put into operation a language policy which would act as a guide to all their teachers. Such a policy would, of course, be developed and modified in the light of the experience gathered from its formulation and application and would, therefore, be shaped to meet the needs of specific schools.

As a step towards implementing the last suggestion we put forward this document. It is not, we would emphasize, a blueprint but a starting-point. We would be disappointed if it were taken over lock, stock and barrel.

Messages and Message-makers

Harold gave this talk in 1971 at the annual conference of the National Association for the Teaching of English, held at the University of Reading in April of that year. It was printed later that year in *English in Education*, 5 (2), which was a report of the conference. As was explained in the introduction to 'Towards a Language Policy Across the Curriculum', language across the curriculum was the theme of the conference. That phrase, and the idea it expresses, had gained substantially in recognition since the first publication of *Language, the Learner and the School* in April 1969, because of the book's great popularity: a success which led to the preparation of a revised and expanded edition in time for the 1971 conference.

Author's note: In the context of the conference I decided not to dot the i's and cross the t's of its proceedings but rather to select several themes of general relevance which were not likely to have been fully explored by the various commissions. There were (a) the models of language use – message making, (b) the speaker and his messages, and (c) some social aspects of the writer and his messages. I also tried to refer to as much relevant work in the field as possible, not I hope in the vain attempt to display scholarly erudition, but because I know many teachers in the audience wished to follow up the work of the conference.

The difficulty is, 'How should we look at language for our purposes?' There is no shortage of approaches and, while each contributes its insights, linguistic, psychological, sociological, anthropological, literary-critical, philosophical and so on, teachers confronted by and contributing to the raw data which make such studies possible are bound to say, 'Yes, I see that. I can make something of that, but something vital has been lost. If I assembled all these truths they would not add up to living speech any more than psychology delivers to us living minds.'

It has been said that all grammars leak. All abstractions about language leak.

It is possible, for example, to make the messy phenomena of language more tractable by treating people as message-sending and message-receiving machines and thus to arrive at a relatively simple triadic model on which to work:

ENCODER — CODE — DECODER

It is also possible, as Chomsky has done, to regard those engaged in actual discourse as providing 'scattered and degenerate' data. Unfortunately, it would seem, we hesitate, we grope, we distort, forget where we started and get it all wrong. In a word, we don't put up a very good performance – and so it becomes necessary to look for the universal competence which underlies all that mess of performance, to lay bare the finite means by which human beings are potentially able to produce an infinite number of sentences. Chomsky put it like this:

> Linguistic theory is concerned with an ideal speaker-listener, in a completely homogeneous speech community, who knows its language perfectly and is unaffected by such grammatically irrelevant conditions as memory limitations, distractions, shifts of attention and interest, and errors (random or characteristic) in applying his knowledge of the language in actual performance.

> (Chomsky, 1965)

Now this programme may produce a powerful grammar and in turn lead on to important psychological speculations. But for our purposes it is not enough; it just will not do. For a start, we are very much concerned with, if not actually obsessed by, the heterogeneous nature of our speech community. People talk differently and they notice the fact. They write differently for different purposes and in obedience to consistent sets of conventions. In other words there is a social component in language which is of compelling interest to us. We must make the attempt to understand society, if we are to understand language.

What for certain purposes may be regarded as 'scattered and degenerate' for our purposes may turn out to be crucial. The slips of the tongue, hesitations, corrections, silences and all sorts of hummings and hawings need explanation and, if the grammarian does not attend to them, all listeners do, since they provide them with important signals. So often they are not the blemishes of inarticulacy but a reflection of the struggle to be articulate. Pauses in speech which were considered until the 1950s to be free-variants were shown by Goldman-Eisler to be systematically related to verbal planning. The grammatically irrelevant may be the psychologically significant. Therefore it concerns us. There is a world of language use marked and tainted by human beings and their society. Miller and his co-workers in *Plans and the structure of human behaviour* put it like this:

> How language is used for giving instructions, for descriptions, for asking questions, for making love, for solving problems, for making plans, or organizing images, raises so many different psychological problems, each unique and special for each unique and special use of language, that no single generalizations cover them all. The grammatical plan, as we have said before, specified only the legal moves in the social game of communication. The reasons for playing the game, however, cannot be deduced from its rules.

> (Miller, Galanter and Pribram, 1960)

So it is best to acknowledge that the simplest of communications has dimensions which demand our attention, even if they have not yet become amenable to systematic elucidation. We shall find in the literature

(i) those who are concerned with language as a self-contained system, that is the relationship of symbols to other symbols

(ii) those who are concerned with language as the relation of symbols to what is symbolized and

(iii) those who are concerned with language as the producer of behaviour in its user and others (I am referring only to the main contemporary trends). But we must take our illuminations wherever we can find them and in the end we must make our own educational synthesis.

For example, since psychotherapy has depended almost entirely on the dialogue between patient and therapist, some interesting discoveries have been made. There is an extraordinary little book called *The First Five Minutes: A sample of microscopic interview analysis* by Pittenger, Hockett and Danehy (1960), in which two psychiatrists and a linguist take 25,000 words to describe a 500-word interview! Here is a sample. The interchange consists of these four words:

> Patient: May I smoke?
> Therapist: Sure.

Patient: May I smoke? [The interview is transcribed phonetically in the book.]

> This is two questions at once. In words, it is the question it obviously seems to be. The other question is carried by the style of delivery: the slight breathiness, slight oversoft, second-degree overhigh tone, and the clipping on 'smoke' and its peculiar release. For some women this combination of features would be kittenish. For P [the patient], it seems to be rather a sort of pseudo-kittenishness, an out-of-character style adopted for the moment precisely to put the second question: 'What sort of situation is this? Do I have to ask your permission to smoke? What is our relative status? What things can I do on my own and what things must I get your permission for?'

> The timing of the double question is significant. T [the therapist] has just reassured P that there is no rush – so that time out for a question about smoking and to light a cigarette will not matter. The apparent need for a cigarette is also important. P's tension at the beginning of the interview has now decreased to the point that she can think of a cigarette. Yet possibly the need is itself an indication of continuing tension, which the activity of smoking may help to alleviate.

Therapist: Sure.

Just as P asks two questions, T answers two and comments on both. The choice of 'sure' rather than something like 'yes', the second-degree overhigh, and the intonation with its scoop to (3), are marks of surprise – but of a surprise as controlled and stylized as is the kittenishness of P. Thus T is saying (1) 'Yes, you may smoke'; (2) 'I know that you are asking another question too'; (3) 'The answer to your second question is that you don't have to ask permission here, and I'm surprised (officially and formally) that you should feel or suspect that you do'.

We do not have to subscribe to the conclusions of the authors to acknowledge that they are making articulate what we all have to do all the time to make language work, that 'simple' utterances have complex meanings, that every text has its sub-text which uncontaminated grammar can tell us little about (phonology may help, but not necessarily). Vygotsky (1962) puts it like this:

A thought may be compared to a cloud shedding a shower of words. Precisely because thought does not have its automatic counterpart in words, the transition from thought to word leads through meaning. In our speech, there is always the hidden thought, the subtext.

After illustrating how Stanislavsky trained his actors to create the sub-text of their roles, he goes on:

To understand another's speech, it is not sufficient to understand his words – we must understand his thought. But even that is not enough – we must also know its motivation. No psychological analysis of an utterance is complete until that plane is reached.

Gusdorf (1965), stressing motivation, makes a similar point: 'words are sedimentary deposits in which desires of expression are manifested'.

Language in school might be looked at critically in this way. This would amount to an examination of the extent to which the pupil is able to read the sub-text of the teacher's language and his books; and reciprocally the extent to which the teacher is able to read the sub-text of the pupil's speech and writing; and the extent to which pupils are able to read the sub-text of each other's speech and writing. Explicitness can never be total nor is it always desirable.

****

I want to return now to that triadic model which I mentioned at the outset:

ENCODER — CODE — DECODER

It can, of course, be re-expressed in a variety of ways such as

SPEAKER/MESSAGE/LISTENER

Harold Rosen

WHO-SAYS-WHAT-TO-WHOM?

STIMULATOR/STIMULUS/RESPONSE (in 'verbal behaviour').

and so on. The variants are instructive because they suggest to us very quickly that each triadic model is in some way inadequate and crude and yet that each version contains some essential aspect of language events. Any one of the versions implies that we cannot think of speakers simply as message-senders because there is a dynamic interaction with others, and also that no message floats 'out there', is hermetically sealed (though some messages seem to do so more than others, like 'Keep off the grass', Grimm's Law and proverbs).

So we have to start tinkering with the model. From classical rhetoric we inherit a more complicated model (though some people who ought to know better have not noticed). It is a model originally intended for persuasive oratory and eventually extended to cover all discourse. It contains six components:

THE SPEAKER/HIS DISCOURSE/HIS AUDIENCE (the familiar triad)

and also HIS SUBJECT or THEME, THE OCCASION, and the END-IN-VIEW.

Two of these additions we have come to know in a different tradition as *function* ('end-in-view') and *context of situation* ('occasion'). But the leakage from this model is still too great and of the most recent ones it is perhaps Dell Hymes, borrowing heavily from Jacobson, who offers one which is most suitable.

Hymes is an anthropologist concerned above all to understand the unwritten language of primitive peoples, but it happens that he actually related his model to language development in children. At a conference on the acquisition of language he commented on the design of a research project which concentrated exclusively on grammar and phonology. He was anxious to broaden the methods of the enquiry to include 'the acquisition of a complex of functions of speech'. In the process he gives his model.

> The end result of verbal development is a child who can produce utterances characterized not only by grammaticalness, but also by appropriateness. Put otherwise, the child not only knows the grammatical rules of its language, but also its speaking rules or some portion of them. Its conduct shows some knowledge of expectations as to when speech is obligatory, when prescribed, when informative as an act, by virtue of being optional. It shows some knowledge of a system of speaking, a system characterized partly by the fact that not all theoretically possible combinations of such various factors of speech events as senders and addressors, receivers and addressees, channels, settings, codes and subcodes, topics, message-forms can appropriately co-occur. It shows some knowledge of the hierarchy of functions which may characterize speech generally, or speech events

particularly, in its society. And such knowledge is necessary, for of course it is not enough for the child to be able to produce any grammatical utterance. It would have to remain speechless if it could not decide which grammatical utterance here and now, if it could not connect utterances with situations.

(Hymes, 1964)

We have tinkered sufficiently with the original model then to produce this:

1. addressor/addressee/topic/setting/(straightforward)
2. channel (speech or writing ? what special forms of them ?)
3. code and message-form (how particular linguistic resources are used to form the given message).

I do not want to pursue the question of the model much further. It has been my intention only to show how much we must attend to if we are to begin to understand language interchange in school. Such models can be productive. At the University of London Institute of Education Writing Research Unit we have been able to draw upon them and adapt them to the school situation. Professor Britton, in a forthcoming article in the *Education Review* entitled 'What's the use?: A schematic account of language functions' (1971), gives a full analysis of the function models, the starting point for which are ideas taken from Sapir's distinction between communicative and expressive functions and Lyons' definition of context. Models end up by looking like lists. It is only by an examination of the interaction of the various elements and the underlying theory that they begin to make sense. Not all the elements will exert equal influence at any given time – it might be the setting, it might be the addressee, etc. The setting, it should be remembered, must include what has already been said and possibly what has yet to be said, the *verbal* setting.

****

I propose by focussing on the speaker or addressor to try to show how much further we have to go once the model has given us an operational framework. What are the questions we want to ask about a speaker? These are some of them:

(i)   How does he stand in relation to his theme? This means both 'What does he know about it?' and 'What is his attitude towards it?'

(ii) How does he stand in relation to his audience? What is his relative status? What degree of intimacy is there between them? Are there shared or opposing attitudes? How aware are they of this?

(iii) How does he stand in relation to the situation? Is he on home territory? Is he at ease or daunted by it? Is it both familiar and alien at the same time?

(iv)   What linguistic resources are at his command? To what extent does he perceive the linguistic demands of the total situation? If he does, has he the resources to meet them? What are his linguistic allegiances ?

(v)   How far is he affected by his own attitudes to language and his attitude to his own language ?

(vi)   What is his motivation for talking?

You can no doubt add to the list or refine it or elaborate it, but some such set of curiosities should underlie our attempts to understand the speaker enmeshed in the school situation.

There is a much more difficult question, which very few are anywhere near competent to answer fully, which is simply 'How does he do it ?' What processes have gone on inside the speaker to make it possible for him to utter? John Laver, in an article called 'The production of speech' in *New Horizons in Linguistics* (1970) examines the problem and recent work on it. This is how he summarizes the process.

> There seem to be five chief functions: the ideation process, which initiates the approximate semantic content of any verbal message the speaker wishes to communicate; the permanent storage of linguistic information; the planning process, which constructs an appropriate neurolinguistic program for the expression of the idea; the execution of the neurolinguistic program by the articulatory muscle systems; and the monitoring function, which allows the detection and correction of errors. I shall refer to these functions as ideation, storage, program-planning, articulation and monitoring, respectively.

I must add that Laver stresses that the five functions are neither sequential nor independent.

The trouble with all I have said so far is that it must still leave us with the feeling which I mentioned at the outset that something is missing, that some vital force which animates real talk keeps escaping us. It does indeed. For although we have been looking at the way in which any utterance stands at the centre of a web of relationships and forces, the speaker is made to seem more like the fly than the spider. Real talkers are engaged in a reciprocal activity; they exchange words, as we say. Usually one speaker must give way to another, and he in his turn must give way until someone has the last word or the kettle boils. This dynamic process, which Douglas Barnes is studying in the school situation and the London Association for the Teaching of English 'Talk and Talkers Group' devotes itself to, has – in spite of the explosion in linguistics – been given very little attention by academics. An honourable exception is the work of Crystal and Davy, who study in their recent book (1969) the language of what they call 'informal conversation'. They draw these conclusions from a minute study of several short tapes. (I have omitted from the quotation line references to the tapes.)

> Semantically, the most important feature of this variety is the randomness of the subject matter, the lack of an overall contrived pattern, the absence of any conscious planning as conversation proceeds. Conversation does not take place in a series of coordinated blocks, but – especially as someone searches for the beginning of a topic – in a series of jumps … There is a general absence of linguistic or cultural pressures to make the conversation go in a particular direction, and there is a corresponding admission of all kinds of spontaneous effect, especially switches in modality. Many features are indicative of this: the simultaneous start given to an utterance, A supplying B's image, the occurrence of afterthoughts, the loose stringing together of ideas, the rough synonymy, the repetitive nature of certain parts of the discourse (such as multiple agreement), and the redundancy which allows omissions. Other important semantic points have already been mentioned: the freedom to introduce material of almost any kind (the limits depending on the sex, class, and intimacy of the participants), such as jokes, bathos, irony and accent- or dialect-switching; the importance of intimacy-signals, silence-fillers, 'rapport-makers', or whatever one calls them; and the importance of the context in which the utterance took place, so that omissions go unnoticed, speech which is obscure to the analyst is understood by the participants, and so on.

Now this description is based on a conversation between two middle-class housewives of similar educational background. How much of this description would have to be changed and how much would be duplicated in the informal and formal conversations in school – especially as spontaneous unguided talk is gradually shifted towards what the writers call 'monothematic discussion'?

There is also some danger of our concluding that the speaker is merely a passive victim of the linguistic forces operating upon him, that, once we settle what these forces are and how strong, we can predict his utterances. Of course, we can't. Every speaker has his own speech style. He makes his own personal choice from the possibilities open to him and often does so consciously. Here, too, though this fact has been recognized for a long time, there is no abundance of studies to turn to. We might contrast this with the mountains of literary-critical attempts to identify the 'personal style' of writers great and small. I can think of one study in 1942 by Sanford, which used a variety of measures to study the differences between two delightful chaps nicknamed Chatwell and Merritt, but little else. Their names suggest their conclusions.

> In summarizing Merritt's style of speech, the statistical evidence says that it is complex, perseverative, thorough, awkward, cautious, static, and highly definitive. He is cautious and indirect, but once he makes a judgement he explains it and presents all aspects of it, leaving little for the imagination and little to be questioned.

> What about Chatwell, the second subject? We could continue through the statistical picture of Chatwell's speech, presenting evidence that it is colorful, emphatic, direct, active, progressive, coordinated and confident. Chatwell uses speech not so much to describe the external world and its relations as to express his own individuality and to impress the auditor.

> (in Miller, 1963)

I have scratched around for these two studies partly to show how little has been done and partly to explain the frustrations of so many teachers who are collecting splendid material, settling down to study it, and finding that it is difficult to make their intuitions explicit. Such theoretical frameworks as are offered to them seem sterile and powerless to explain what they feel to be there.

Sanford's clinical but imaginative study (using obsolescent methods) is a reminder of the expressive function of language for the speaker. The speaker never totally separates his message about the world from messages about himself and his attitudes and feelings. This expressiveness insinuates into language not only clues about the speaker, who he is and what he is, but also his feelings about his theme, his feelings about his listener, his feelings about his listener's feelings and even his feelings about the language he is using. It can take the obvious form of passionate and bewildering outbursts of despair and ecstasy or more elusive signals, the faintest lexical shifts, almost imperceptible changes in sentence length, minute fidgets in pitch, intonation or audibility which the speaker himself may be totally unaware of or powerless to alter.

The positive aspect of this expressiveness is not that it is a useful safety valve, a special and separate means by which we make ourselves fit to carry on at some other time and in some other way the real business of the world. It is the way in which we define our individual relationship with the world and with other people. To censor it out, drive it underground, or, worse still, to inhibit its development is to inhibit our unceasing efforts to make the world a meaningful place. This is why making a special and separate category called 'creative writing' has its dangers, especially when there is a separate book, a separate subject and possibly a separate room, with teacher to match, within which creative writing can be safely locked away, a ghetto in which expressive messages are permitted. I leave the last word to Gusdorf (1965).

> Thus the function of expression consists in a movement of man outside himself in order to give meaning to the real. Expression is the act of man

establishing himself in the world, in other words adding himself to the world. It is the duty of each to so create his own balance, or to recover it, bringing his inner resources into play when the balance is upset. Language, by erupting toward the stars, thereby allows us to come down to earth. It has the power to re-establish us if we are abruptly cut off from our usual securities. Such is the function of the least elaborated speech in which expression takes place in a pure state independently of all discursive intelligibility. All the different kinds of cry, howl, exclamation, interjection, and oath are attempts to adapt the self to a world that is slipping away. Surprise, joy, fear, and terror give rise to purely emotional speech. Expression is condensed at its most intense, a catastrophic reaction, a desperate attempt to face the disordering of circumstances that strikes us with a radical disorientation. Faced with anguish, torture, or death, when a man no longer has anything human to affirm, his cry remains the only testimony of which he is still capable.

The speaker strives to make sense, to negotiate with others. In order to do so he must be able, in Mead's words, 'to take up the role of the other'. The other will be primarily his immediate audience but will at times include others beyond them both. In the literary-critical tradition this is called 'empathy' – the capacity to perceive the needs of the listener and how they interpenetrate with our own. If we are to speak to each other we must know something of each other's beliefs, intentions, opinions, intellectual capacities in general, linguistic capacity in particular. My knowledge will be necessary because it will tell me about your ability or willingness to accept my message and enable me to modify my message accordingly. It's a tall order and consequently a life-long task. (How much am I succeeding at this moment?) I suspect it rarely succeeds totally. How is this all-important capacity developed? Why does it develop so much more highly in some than others? Has literature a special role to play in fostering it?

Mead (1934), Piaget (Piaget and Inhelder, 1969) and Vygotsky (1962) all shed some light here. Piaget sees the development from egocentric to social language as 'seeking and finding in the other's mind some basis on which to build'. He mentions the inexperienced lecturer who is incomprehensible because he is talking to himself, though there's no need to be inexperienced to do that! Vygotsky sees it more as part of the process of converting inner speech to outer speech. I think we might say that all mature speech is affected by the effort to prevent our messages from drifting back to our private unedited codes. Some circumstances demand more editing than others and not all editing is benevolent. We can see around us all the time the editing process being used not to help the listener but to manipulate him. Assuming goodwill, however, we can say that the listener must carry out a similar activity. Much of ordinary conversation can be seen as an effort to make good the initial failures of speakers and listeners to take the role of the other. Successful talk often has behind it a growing reciprocity and that is why talk is itself educative.

There is a certain amount of experimental work, notably by Werner and Kaplan (1963) and by Flavell (1968), but it is very circumscribed. However, Flavell in a speculative passage asks whether schools propose to pupils role-taking tasks which are teacher-selected rather than self-selected and what are the consequences of this. We might well explore this further. Werner and Kaplan showed the ways in which messages become modified when they shift from being addressed to the self to being addressed to another, and Flavell conducted a series of experiments designed to reveal children's capacities and strategies in role-taking.

I need hardly say that I have not been talking about role-playing, which raises all sorts of conceptual difficulties. Nevertheless, once we consider the speaker as shaping his discourse under the influence of his awareness of the other, we must also be conscious of him as shaping his discourse because of an increasing awareness of his own changing roles. In this situation, here in this hall for example, we might say that my role implies that some language is forbidden, some is insisted upon and some is permitted; some language carries rewards of approval, some penalties of disapproval. In an audience of this size and kind the risks are that what incurs one judge's reward incurs another's penalty. Which is what makes some lecturers so twitchy.

Once again I do not want to suggest that role consciousness on the part of the speaker implies a simple determinism or that roles are sharply distinct entities – parts in a play all written out for us. If there are expectations, it is open to us to resist them; bans can be defied. It is not for us simply to describe the social constraints which hem in a speaker. Some of the social constraints of language are just as suspect as other social constraints. There are great educational possibilities in the critical evaluation of the linguistic expression of roles, greater possibilities than in the uncritical inculcation of linguistic table manners. The entrance fee to the house of the elect has for too long been a token with conformity written on it.

Let me take as an example a role which you are very familiar with – writer-in-the-role-of-scientist – in this case a psychologist. Those of you who have ventured into this field will be very aware of how the role pressures have shaped the language of the practitioners. Here is a passage from George Kelly (1970), which I am quoting at some length, firstly because it defies the pressures to take up the conventional language, secondly because it shows him on the contrary taking up the role of the reader. In order to do the second he must reject the first. Finally, I am quoting it because in many ways it goes to the heart of what I have been trying to say throughout this lecture.

Kelly is trying to compare the methods of those psychologists who treat man as a 'behaving organism' with his own approach. First then, his picture of the behaviourist approach:

Let me start by trying to differentiate two levels at which I may try to understand another person – say, my reader. It is not hard for me to imagine him – you, I mean – at this moment a figure bending over a book. It – the figure – is skimming the paragraphs with the right forefinger in a position to turn to the pages that follow. The eye movements zigzag down the page and quickly the next leaf is flipped, or perhaps a whole section – a chapter or more – is lifted with the left thumb and drawn horizontally aside.

Now Kelly's alternative:

But now let me say it quite another way. There you are, my reader, wondering, I fear, what on earth I am trying so hard to say, and smiling to yourself as the thought crosses your mind that it all might be put in a familiar phrase or two – as indeed it may. You are hunched uncomfortably over the book, impatiently scanning the paragraphs for a cogent expression or a poignant sentence that may make the experience worth the time you are stealing from more urgent duties. The right forefinger is restlessly poised to lift the page and go on to discover if perhaps something more sensible follows.

Let me confess that I feel at this moment like urging you not to try so hard. While it has taken me hours to write some of these paragraphs – the four preceding ones, for example – and I would like to think the outcome has been worth some of your time too, they were not meant to be hammered into your consciousness. They are intended, instead, to set off trains of thought. And, in following them, I earnestly hope we shall find ourselves walking along the same paths.

There now, isn't that the way it really is? It isn't? Then, tell me, what *are* you doing? And while we are at it, tell me also how my efforts strike you – I mean, what do you think I am trying to do, not merely whether I am making sense or not. Only please do not tell me that all I am really doing is pounding a typewriter in an effort to keep my wife awake; I have other psychoanalytically oriented friends who are only too happy to offer me that kind of 'interpretation'.

Although these two descriptions of my view of the reader both represent a wide departure from accepted literary style, I hope they will make clear the contrast between construing the construction processes of another person and construing his behaviour merely. In the first instance, I construed only your behaviour. There is nothing wrong with that, as far as it goes. In the second case I went further and placed a construction upon the way in which I imagined you might be thinking. The chances are that I was more or less mistaken in both instances, particularly in the second. But the point I want to make lies in the difference in my mode of construing you. In both formulations I was indeed concerned with your behaviour, but only in the second did I strive for some notion of the construction which might be giving your behaviour its form, or your future behaviour its form. If immediate accuracy is what I must preserve at all costs, then I had better stick to the first level of construction. But if I am to anticipate you, I must take some chances and try to sense what you are up to.

One does not have to be a psychologist to treat another person as an automaton, though training in 'experimental psychology' may help. Conversely, treating him that way does not make one into a scientist – though some of my colleagues may wish to dispute this. It is easy enough to treat persons we have never met as behaving organisms only, and many of us think that is the sophisticated way to go about secondary human relations. We may even treat our neighbours that way, especially if there are more of them than we care to know. I have even observed parents who go so far as to treat their children so, and they sometimes come to me for psychological advice on how to do it. I sometimes suspect it is because they have more children than they care to know. To be very frank about it, my construction of you while writing some of these passages has often lapsed into no more than that. And, if you are like me in this respect, there must have been moments when you regarded me as a disembodied typewriter, or as an Irish name on the title page of a book, or as a kind of animated sentence ejector.

Since we have been looking at the speaker transformed into writer, let's pursue this a little further, for the change is a profound one. I shall not examine this whole process. I have attempted to do so briefly in the new chapter of the revised edition of *Language, the Learner and the School* (Barnes, Britton, Rosen and the LATE, 1971) and there is no need either for me to catalogue the revolutionary advances which the invention of writing made possible. Instead I want to look at a less explored area – some social aspects of writing. I find it surprising that in his attempt to examine the relationship between social class and language Bernstein has given little attention to this matter. He makes a broad distinction between the language of social classes based on the social use those classes make of speech. I find his description of middle-class speech strangely idealized and his explanations seem to take no account of the fact that the elaborated code user is one whose speech has been profoundly affected by literacy. As Michael Young has pointed out, those activities which are mediated by writing and books are accorded special prestige, and no theory of the curriculum can escape this fact. We take little or no interest in the oral tradition. For, after all, writers and book-readers, you and me, have no privileged access to that tradition. Writing began as the monopoly of a privileged class, and in our own day books are written which surround their contents with all kinds of linguistic mystification. The world of books and writing is not a free-wheeling democratic teach-in.

When the speaker becomes the writer he is not simply given access to a medium of new expressive and communicative power. It is not simply a switch of channels posing certain technical transmission problems. It is a different kind of social act which is scarred by its history. The written message is partly shaped by the social forces which have used it, not simply as a medium for enlightenment but also as a means of wielding social power over others. It is the written language par excellence which can be shaped to keep people out as well as bring them in. The paradox of language is that part of its social nature lies in its anti-social use.

Of course a gathering of this kind is pre-disposed to see in writers, written messages and readers unique values – and you are right. I am only asking that we should not be blind to the fact that some of the resistance to books and writing in our schools arises from the fact that they are seen not only as alien but actually hostile, caballistic messages passing between those who wield power. Hans Enzenberger (1970) has urged us to look at writing in this way and, though he may set some teeth on edge, some of you will see the implication, that in our proper anxiety to make accessible the benefits of literacy we should not be starry-eyed.

> Nevertheless, almost everybody speaks better than he writes. (This also applies to authors.) Writing is a highly formalized technique which, in purely physiological terms, demands a peculiarly rigid bodily posture. To this there corresponds the high degree of social specialization that it demands. Professional writers have always tended to think in caste terms. The class character of their work is unquestionable, even in the age of universal compulsory education. The whole process is extraordinarily beset with taboos. Spelling mistakes, which are completely immaterial in terms of communication, are punished by the social disqualification of the writer. The rules that govern this technique have a normative power attributed to them for which there is no rational basis. Intimidation through the written word has remained a widespread and class-specific phenomenon even in advanced industrial societies.

> These alienating factors cannot be eradicated from written literature. They are reinforced by the methods by which society transmits its writing techniques. While people learn to speak very early, and mostly in psychologically favourable conditions, learning to write forms an important part of authoritarian socialization by the school ('good writing' as a kind of breaking-in). This sets its stamp for ever on written communication – on its tone, its syntax, and its whole style. (This also applies to the text on this page.)

The formalization of written language permits and encourages the repression of opposition. In speech, unresolved contradictions betray themselves by pauses, hesitations, slips of the tongue, repetitions, anacoluthons, quite apart from phrasing, mimicry, gesticulation, pace and volume. The aesthetic of written literature scorns such involuntary factors as 'mistakes'. It demands, explicitly or implicitly, the smoothing out of contradictions, rationalization, regularization of the spoken form irrespective of content. Even as a child, the writer is urged to hide his unresolved problems behind a protective screen of correctness.

Structurally, the printed book is a medium that operates as a monologue, isolating producer and reader. Feedback and interaction are extremely limited, demand procedures, and only in the rarest cases lead to corrections. Once an edition has been printed it cannot be corrected; at best it can be pulped. The control circuit in the case of literary criticism is extremely cumbersome and elitist. It excludes the public on principle.

The differentiated access to literacy is one way of looking at the problem of equality of opportunity, which is the central debate in education today. But who says we must take literacy as we find it? I believe that the written language will need to undergo considerable demystification before it is accessible to all.

The world we share is not a lump sum of the individuals in it but all kinds of communities and oppositions. It is customary for us to emphasize the communal element in language but we should set the balance right.

I wish there were time to put before you an exemplar of the demystification of written prose – Roland Barthes' (1970) analysis of the writing of history and his programme of change. He attempts to show how, through 'a radical censorship of the utterance', the fiction of objectivity is created. By removing all linguistic traces of himself, the historian tries to give the impression that the events are speaking for themselves. We cannot go on regarding specialized forms of written discourse as the perfectly fashioned instruments for carrying out their tasks. The modish way of doing this is to talk of 'registers' and, instead of undertaking the difficult task of subjecting every kind of professionalized writing to critical analysis, to itemize its features 'scientifically'. Every register becomes a kind of Holy Writ and we look to discourse to provide perfected models. The models are far from perfect and certainly susceptible to change.

If I am even nearly right about all this, then we should be able to see in quite a new light those messages by which the curriculum delivers in written form its 'subjects' and 'disciplines'. We can ask of every school subject, 'Why do you write yourself in this way, and then demand that pupils toe the line?'

At my most pessimistic moments I am tempted to believe that people are born to speak and everywhere we find them silenced, or croaking. Fortunately it is not like that. But we would do well to see who is silenced, and why, and put matters right.

References

Barnes, D., Britton, J., Rosen, H. and the LATE (1971) *Language, the Learner and the School* (revised edition). Harmondsworth: Penguin Books.

Barthes, R. (1970) in M. Lane, *Structuralism: A reader*. London: Jonathan Cape.

Britton, J. (1971) 'What's the use?: A schematic account of language functions'. *Educational Review*, 23 (3).

Chomsky, N. (1965) *Aspects of the Theory of Syntax*. Cambridge, MA: MIT Press.

Crystal, D. and Davy, D. (1969) *Investigating English Style*. London: Longman.

Enzenberger, H. (1970) 'The consciousness industry'. *New Left Review*, 64, November/December.

Flavell, J. (1968) *The Development of Role-taking and Communication Skills in Children*. New York: John Wiley.

Gusdorf, G. (1965) *Speaking*. Evanston, IL: Northwestern University.

Hymes, D. (1964) 'Formal discussion', *The Acquisition of Language, Monograph of the Society for Research in Child Development*, 21 (1).

Kelly, G. (1970) 'A brief introduction to personal construct theory', in D. Bannister (ed.), *Perspectives in Personal Construct Theory*. London: Academic Press.

Laver, J. (1970) 'The production of speech', in J. Lyons (ed.), *New Horizons in Linguistics*. Harmondsworth: Penguin.

Mead, G. (1934) *Mind, Self and Society*. Chicago: University of Chicago Press.

Miller, G. (1963) *Language and Communication*. New York: McGraw-Hill.

Miller, G., Galanter, E. and Pribram, K. (1960) *Plans and the Structure of Behaviour*. New York: Holt, Rinehart and Winston.

Piaget, J. and Inhelder, B. (1969) *The Psychology of the Child* (H. Weaver, trans.). New York: Basic Books.

Pittenger, R., Hockett, C. and Danehy. J (1960) *The First Five Minutes: A sample of microscopic interview analysis*. Ithaca, NY: Paul Martineau.

Sanford, F. (1942) 'Speech and personality: a comparative case study'. *Character and Personality*, 10.

Vygotsky, L. (1962) *Thought and Language* (E. Hanfmann, G. Vakar and N. Minnick, trans.). Cambridge, MA: MIT Press.

Werner, H. and Kaplan, B. (1963) *Symbol Formation: An organismic developmental approach to language and the expression of thought*. New York: John Wiley.

Young, M. (1971) 'An approach to the study of curricula as socially organized knowledge', in M. Young (ed.), *Knowledge and Control*. London: Collier Macmillan.

Thinking

Harold's first wife Connie was a major figure in language education in primary schools. She was director of the Schools Council project Language Development in the Primary School, which ran from 1969 to 1971. The work of the project is described in *The Language of Primary School Children*, which she wrote with Harold, and which was published in 1973. The book brings together a rich diversity of children's language, revealed in reading, writing, talk and drama. It is more than that, however, in that the classroom evidence is presented in such a way that a theory of learning emerges from it: a theory that sees true learning as the positive encounter between children's existing experience, their existing perspective on the world, and the experience, knowledge and understanding the school wishes them to take on. Successful teachers, the book shows, are those who can make the encounter positive by being interested in and respectful of that which the children bring to it.

This piece is only one section of the book's last chapter, offered so as to give a flavour of the interaction between theory and practice which the book as a whole exemplifies. In the book's introduction, the two authors, having described the sometimes robust nature of their collaboration, say:

> ... we ... ended up with a text some of which is written by one hand, some by the other and some which is quite literally by both of us. We think the reader would have some difficulty in distinguishing which is which ... We believe that if the book has one strength it is the sheer amount of personal observation it records. Only one of us carried out this observation, which is naturally written in the first person. We thought it best to retain this style even when the writing was in fact jointly undertaken.

Two hands are at work here: one in the foreground, one in the background.

Susan Isaacs (1930) many years ago commented on how easily children slip from 'reality-thinking' into fantasy and vice versa. The child constructor of an aeroplane encounters and solves real technical problems but he also takes it for a flight across a puddle which is 'the Atlantic' and this can reach beyond the technical limitations which he is obliged to accept as a constructor. The child then can experiment with life in two different but interrelated ways. His representations of reality must risk stubbing their toes against stubborn properties of matter. His fantasies elude these constraints, soar over them (often quite literally in fantasies of flight) to see what is beyond them as his imagination would wish it. The followers of George Kelly (1963 and 1968) would see this as 'tight' and 'loose' construing and suggest that neither way is good in itself but only movement between the two.

Children use language for the expression of this two-sided process and the language too slides with ease from reality to fantasy.

Triangles

> A triangle is a rigid shape. However much you move or wriggle it it still stays the same size and does not move. I made a triangle out of Meccano and found that it was true. You cannot move a triangle, making another shape out of it. Then using cardboard triangles I made and designed a space ship of the future. I made it by slotting the red and white triangles into each other. I called it the Flying Saucer Mark 100 from the year 2020. It looked like this ... This proves that triangles are rigid shapes and cannot be made into any other shape.
>
> Vanessa, 11 years

School gives Vanessa the chance to test out the reality of the shapes of triangles and to proceed to the generalized laws about such shapes, but when it comes to writing about it she is not only free to give her own account but also to move on to her fantasy game, the making and designing of the space ship. This is fantasy not so much because the space ship is an imaginary craft (it is, after all, a real model) but because 'the making and designing' are fictions. In a younger child the balance would be likely to be the other way round. In the course of fantasy he can show from time to time a concern with the realities of the physical world. By contrast Vanessa's attention is firmly focused on the shape of triangles but then goes on to play with spaceship building. This is not due to her being obliged to engage in both activities according to some pre-arranged pattern, an exercise in reality and fantasy with triangles. She writes and behaves in a context which has assured her that it is acceptable to think in both ways. We cannot set aside special times for children to think in special ways. If we do, then two results are likely to follow. Firstly, imagination and thinking are likely to be censored by the pupil as irrelevant. Secondly, fantasy becomes a special game to be played when teacher says so and played in the teacher's way with teacher's themes. Imagination is the free play of the mind or it is nothing. For fantasy to serve any purpose for children they must be motivated to use it and not obliged to switch it on when they have no need for it nor to switch it off when it is their way of building a bridge between the real nature of things and how they would like them to be. The form of the activity they undertake is also significant. Dramatic play may often be a much more flexible way of providing ample opportunity for the combination of symbolic fantasy and the understanding of real things and processes.

Harold Rosen

Some seven- to eight-year-old children in a West Riding junior school situated in a mining community had been looking at caterpillars and they collected together what they had written into a class book. Here are some of the pieces.

Caterpillars

The caterpillar has thirteen rings on it. He will hardly stay still. It is walking on the side of my word book. If you put your finger an inch above it, it will put its head up and try to cling on to it. It is trying to read my name and it is playing with Ian's caterpillar. I can see hairs on it. It has pale yellow on it.

It is very good at balancing. It is playing on the page of my word book.

Once upon a time there lived a caterpillar with lots of lovely colours on it. The colours were black, green and red. One day the little caterpillar made a chrysalis. When the butterfly hatched it had lovely wings. When had passed a week, the butterfly laid thirteen eggs and when it had laid its eggs it sat on the flowers and got all of the nectar out of the flower. Then it died.

Caterpillars have little feet their front feet are for eating with. It holds the leaf with them and eats the leaf. The caterpillar eats privet leaves.

The caterpillar will become a butterfly or moth. They eat leaves. They walk like this they put some of the body forward. Then they bring the back up. They are black and yellow on the back. There are little hairs on the body. It has a black head.

All of these children, having looked closely at caterpillars, reach a point of accepting them in their own rights as creatures 'out there' with their own qualities and ways of going on distinct from the writer's. Even the fiction story is rooted in an awareness of the life cycle of caterpillar and butterfly. And we know that the richer and more complex the child's awareness of the world the more effectively he can act in it. To formulate this awareness helps him to take possession of it. Therefore we want him to understand the caterpillar as a creature beyond his own yearnings and projections. Not everything significant about a caterpillar will yield to direct observation, or to put it differently, the significance of what is observed cannot be derived from the observation itself. To say that the caterpillar is trying to cling to your finger implies a view of what 'trying' means and that certain activity constitutes evidence of its existence. Inevitably the language of the children shows that when they refer to internal states they are inclined to invest the caterpillar with their own feelings and behaviour. So 'it is trying to read my name' and 'playing'. But in the third and fourth passages the children confine themselves to what they can see, thus avoiding the problems of interpretation of certain movements and also avoiding the fantasy of a caterpillar reading. There is no need for us to place a greater value on the one treatment rather than the other but only to ask ourselves whether the persistence or dominance of the fantasy way of treating caterpillars is not an indication of children either retreating to an earlier way of thinking or being encouraged to stay there rather than being helped towards what Piaget calls 'decentring'. It is important to provide experiences of this kind in school, to help children to examine and to observe carefully, but it is also necessary for the teacher to step out of the situation to allow the children choice in the way they deal with the experience.

I commented on this example to one group of teachers and said that in fact some of the children were interested in the caterpillar for itself but others had created a fantasy of their own about it. I thought that one certainly could not say that children by seven or eight had reached a position of neutrality and objectivity. One of the teachers commented that it would be different for different children and even different on different days for individual children.

But children are easily influenced one way or the other. A class of children, even seven- and eight-year-olds, can all be writing impersonal descriptions and accounts of the caterpillar, whereas, either by the request of the teacher or by a general understanding that that is what is required of them, you can just as easily find a class of seven- and eight-year-olds writing fantasy stories about the caterpillar. Surely some adjustment is required. When there is genuine choice, as the caterpillar pieces show, there are differences amongst children in how they treat experience. There is probably a great need in our schools for much more real first-hand experience and much more detailed and concentrated observation, but in those schools that do base a great deal of work on first-hand observation there is also a need for more choice, for the children's interpretation. The schools where children are constantly urged towards fantasy stories of all kinds, and where writing and reading dominate the school day, need to turn outwards towards reality and the verbalizing of it; and those schools where observation and experiment are major activities need very often to free children's language to express the truth of their experience. Observation and experiment should themselves help the decentring process.

In trying to take hold of this difficult theme, all of us find difficulty in relating *general* ideas about children's fantasy and thinking to the daily realities of schools. There are deep suspicions amongst some adults, including teachers, that fantasy is a childish thing, to be accommodated as long as better strategies are not available. There are others who, knowing full well that fantasy is a characteristic mode of thinking in children and despising the superficial realism of 'putting away childish things', allow themselves to resist the child's own drive to be a competent thoughtful experimenter in the real world. Even when we are not driven to such extremes we are still confronted with the dilemmas of decision. Are there occasions when the bubble of fantasy should be pricked? Should children be positively encouraged towards flights of fancy when they are dealing with realistic concerns? One student teacher expresses this dilemma very well, seeing it arise from his work with some children.

During this term these children had listened to a reading in the class of *Catweazle*. Many had seen it on TV; during the Epping visit they were specially hopeful of finding a toad because of this. Catweazle's toad is of course connected with magic. In the pub they asked whether there were any toads and were told that they would be unlikely to find any as the local heavy insecticide sprays tended to kill off the foodstuffs toads need. The children discussed this quite seriously with the local villager. There was neither sloppy sentimentalism nor any hint of destroyed interest. They were directed to the question of toads by the story but very concerned in fact to consider them as creatures with a real life, not the fantasy one they had been hearing about. They see, I suspect, natural things as natural.

Are we doing a great favour if, because of our interest as adults in imagery in writing, we block the fight of the growing child at that age to separate fact from fantasy, truth from myth? I sometimes feel quite uncomfortable about this when I hear 'expressive movement' teachers developing themes about 'witches, wizards, trolls, dark forests', etc. with children of this age. What adults want from creativity, and what children want from the creativity of thinking they are developing painfully, may well be two quite different things. It is all very well to be an expressionist like Munch when you are adult; it might well be that in growing to become adult, one needs above all to develop ability to think creatively in a thoroughly matter-of-fact way.

The student teacher voices the difficulty and shows clearly the need to question this aspect of the work. But is he not making things too difficult? He did after all read a story of magic in the first place and could scarcely have done so in the cheerful expectation that good sense would prevail and the quest for real toads begin. We magnify the problem if we set up one way of thinking *against* the other. All of us, adults too, move to and fro constantly between the dream and the reality confronting us all. The likelihood is that inside us the two are never separate but for good reasons we learn to separate them when we have things to say to each other. Separating them means that we do learn, as the student suggests, to distinguish between fact and fantasy, between it being so and wishing or fearing it to be so. But we go on needing to do both, and rationality can grow out of both. The teacher, nevertheless, cannot evade judgement and decision. He will have to make up his own mind that some children, or even an entire group of children, are locked in a world of fantasy from which he can help to release them, or that on the contrary they need to be given more trust in their own imaginations.

What we have been saying seems a far cry from current preoccupations with language and 'concept-formation'. Yet the process of mastering concepts, of separating out different classes of experience and seeing relationships between them, must take us back to how children interact as total human beings with their world. So much discussion of concepts (and teaching them!) reduces this major process to a matter of learning word-meanings in the narrowest sense, perpetuating the old illusion that every word corresponds to a bold, sharply defined little parcel of meaning. Once this meaning is grasped it is ready to go to work; it is in business. And since in a tacit way some kinds of business are seen to be more important than others, discussion of concepts soon turns on ideas about space, time, number and quantity. As so often happens, the feelings with which they are invested are frequently ignored or made to seem an unmanageable nuisance. Finally, in pursuit of educational shortcuts and aware of the need to teach the special concepts which school learning requires, the mastery of concepts is tackled head on and we begin with the concept and try to inflate its emptiness with meaning doled out by a teacher.

We have to remind ourselves again and again that concepts are classes of experience, and therefore to build a concept the individual must bring together a series of experiences which for him have certain similarities and which relate to others in particular ways (e.g. the concepts of 'up' and ' down'). Concepts live in people, grow more and more complex, and are in many respects highly personal. Thus they inevitably include an element of feeling which may be very strong.

Here, for example, is Toby, aged six, talking to his father and shedding some light for us on the concepts 'brother ' and 'dog'. (The pattern of the opening questions is borrowed from Piaget.)

F: How many brothers have you got, Toby?

T: Four.

F: Four brothers, who are they?

T: Jasper, Chris, Benjy and Tim.

F: But Jasper's a dog, is he your brother?

T: Yes, he's a boy like me.

F: So how many brothers has Timothy got?

T: Four.

F: Who are they?

T: Jasper, me and Benjy and Chris.

F: And how many brothers has Christopher got?

T: Four.

F: And how many brothers has Benjamin got?

T: Four.

F: And how many brothers has Jasper got?

T: Four.

F: I see.

Another voice: How many brothers have I got?

T: Four, five, I mean.

F: Do you think it would be better if you only had one, or none?

T: Better, if I had just Jasper.

F: Just Jasper, but he's a dog isn't he?

T: Well I like him – he's better than the whole lot.

F: He's better than the whole lot, why's that ?

T: Because he's a dog. He's got fur, hasn't he?

F: Would you like it if your brothers had fur then?

(A great deal of laughter)

T: No. No. I wouldn't like *all* of them to be dogs.

F: You like a mixture do you? Which of the brothers is it most useful to have?

T: Jasper.

Toby has no difficulty in knowing how many brothers he has or in including himself as one of the siblings, though some six-year-olds cannot do this. He stays consistent with that idea, except that from his experiences he can include Jasper, the dog, in the kinship relationship. He does know that dogs are dogs and human beings are human beings, but in six-year-old fashion he chooses to give elasticity to the idea of 'brother' to include Jasper, and in all the respects of caring for the animal – play, the constant presence of the dog at meals and play and bedtime, the companionship – all are used as qualifying factors for brotherliness. One might even concede that, if peacefulness, lack of competition, devotion were brotherly features, then Jasper might indeed score very highly. The six-year-old would have the world as he makes it. If it isn't, so much the worse for the world. He bends it a little to suit his convenience. In spite of his view of life, his family are interested in him and care for him a great deal. He is not exactly short of talk or of encounters with different members of the family. But ideas about the socially accepted concept of 'brother' do take a very long time to sort out. It takes children a very long time to know which features are generally accepted and which are rejected, what is excluded and what is included, how 'brother' relates to father, mother, sister, daughter, son, aunt, uncle, etc. and how to place the concept in a constellation of relationships. It takes a lot of living and listening to do that. We can accept the child's representation and yet know that maturity will enable him to leave his egocentric view of the world, and he will come to know that without abandoning any of his feeling for Jasper he can put him in his doggy place.

If all teachers were fully acquainted with theories of language development they would not necessarily be better teachers. Books provide insights for those whose thinking is already inclined towards what they are reading. Nevertheless, some of the misunderstandings and myths about language do need some careful investigation and discussion. One of these is that language and experience are two quite separate things. I have heard teachers say that children can't understand the experience until they have the language, and it's the business of the school to supply the language. Toby's reluctant concession that Jasper may not after all be a brother has to do with his understanding of his brothers and himself, which he does through talk and experience together. It's a long process of sorting, matching and organizing.

References

Isaacs, S. (1930) *The Intellectual Growth of Young Children.* London: Routledge and Kegan Paul.

Kelly, G. (1963) *A Theory of Personality.* New York: Norton.

Kelly, G. (1968) 'A brief introduction to personal construct theory', in D. Bannister (ed.), *Perspectives in Personal Construct Theory.* New York: Academic Press.

Sense of Audience

In 1975, James Britton and his colleagues at the Institute of Education, University of London (Tony Burgess, Nancy Martin, Alex McLeod and Harold Rosen), published *The Development of Writing Abilities (11–18)*. The book was the outcome of a major research project, funded by the Schools Council, investigating the writing done by students in secondary schools. It has been immensely influential.

In attempting to sort and classify 2,122 pieces of writing done by 500 pupils in the subjects English, geography, history, religious education and science, in the school years that we would today (in England) call Years 7, 9, 11 and 13, Britton and his colleagues propose two groups of categories.

Audience

The first category is that of *audience*. The researchers found that almost all (about 95%) of the writing pupils did was for the teacher, and that more than half of what they wrote for the teacher was writing from 'pupil to examiner'. ('Examiner' here refers to the teacher as assessor, marker, judge of pupils' work.)

Breaking these figures down further, it became clear that the great majority of writing in geography, history and science was for the 'teacher as examiner' – the percentages are 69%, 81% and 87% respectively; in English and religious education more of the writing was for the teacher as 'partner in dialogue' (65% and 64% respectively).

The disparity between the percentages quoted above for geography, history and science as against English and religious education (where the figures for 'teacher as examiner' were 18% and 22% respectively) was a finding which gave further impetus to the language across the curriculum movement: the simple-to-state but hard-to-achieve idea that schools, and secondary schools in particular (because of their departmental structure), need to find common approaches (though not identical behaviours) across the staff of a school in key areas of language and learning. The situation in many secondary schools in the 1960s and 1970s was not merely that there were differences of approach; it was that those differences were mutually incoherent and contradictory, and therefore deeply confusing to the learner.

Britton and his colleagues of course agree that teachers must assess. But they say that to confine children's writing almost exclusively to one audience, the teacher, and for that audience in three major curriculum subjects to act very largely in one role, that of examiner, is severely to constrain the role which writing should play in the learner's development.

Function

The second group of categories by which the researchers group pupils' school writing is that of *function*. What are the purposes for and kinds of writing that children and young people do?

Harold lays out the function categories elsewhere, in 'Towards a Policy for Language across the Curriculum' (see chapter in this collection). To repeat what he writes there, the three categories form a continuum, thus:

Transactional < > Expressive < > Poetic

Writing, the authors say, begins with the expressive. Expressive writing is the written form of 'language close to the self'. It is the stem from which other kinds of writing flow. It is personal. The writer feels free to speculate, to tell anecdotes, to admit to feelings, to try out thoughts and ideas in a tentative way.

Transactional writing is the written form of 'language to get things done: to inform people (telling them what they need or want to know or what we think they ought to know), to advise or persuade or instruct people'. Factual truth has a high value in transactional writing.

Poetic writing is not confined to poetry. 'Poetic writing uses language as an art medium.' It is any kind of writing where the imagination is active, for example in the writing of fictional stories.

The researchers found that the majority of the writing they had collected (about two thirds) was located towards the transactional end of the continuum.

Once this average proportion was broken down by subject, differences were sharp: 34% of writing in English was transactional, while the figures for geography, history, religious education and science were 88%, 88%, 57% and 92% respectively. The kinds of transactional writing students were required to do were overwhelmingly those of low-level factual report and the generalised re-presentation of previously given information. There was very little theorising or dialogue of ideas or advocacy or argument.

Britton and his colleagues are anxious to make it clear that they are not in any sense 'against' transactional writing. They are, however, concerned that the kinds of transactional writing young people were doing largely excluded those requiring a measure of independent thought. And when they combined their findings about the function of most pupils' writing with those about the audience for most pupils' writing, it became clear that what we might call 'low-level factual report and the generalised re-presentation of previously given information', written by the pupil for the teacher as examiner, was easily the commonest kind of writing that pupils were doing in school.

As Britton writes in the preface to *The Development of Writing Abilities (11– 18)*, 'We [the writing research team] have been at considerable pains to maintain our joint responsibility for the final text. Inevitably, however, the burden of first drafting the various chapters fell to various individuals … ' Harold drafted chapter 4, 'Sense of audience'. In modified form, the chapter had previously been published as 'Written Language and the Sense of Audience' in *Education Research,* 15 (3). The chapter first discusses the demands which an audience makes on writers of all kinds; then it discusses those demands with specific reference to writing done by pupils in schools; finally it lays out in some detail the categories and sub-categories of audience which the research team had used to assign the 2,122 pieces of writing they considered.

A young child will adapt his speech to his sense of the person he is addressing, either bowing to imposed constraints or recognizing and meeting some need in the other person. Thus he might refrain from addressing an uncle by his first name because it is explicitly forbidden to do so, or he might simplify his speech grammatically and lexically because his younger brother would otherwise not understand it. But when children begin to write, this process of adjusting to their audience presents them with new problems even though they may fail to recognize them. We want to suggest that one important dimension of development in writing ability is the growth of a sense of audience, the growth of the ability to make adjustments and choices in writing which take account of the audience for whom the writing is intended. This accommodation may be coarse or fine, highly calculated or totally intuitive, diffused through the text or explicit at particular points in it; but, whatever the form of its realization, a highly developed sense of audience must be one of the marks of the competent mature writer, for it is concerned with nothing less than the implementation of his concern to maintain or establish an appropriate relationship with his reader in order to achieve his full intent.

Before we proceed to an outline of the model which we propose for charting this development, we must undertake some exploration of the concept 'sense of audience'. After having done so we shall look at its operation in the specific context of school writing.

Writing may be looked upon as soliloquizing monologue. This way of looking at it seems reasonable enough. The 'others' are not there, they cannot interrupt, and who they are and what they are do not make themselves insistently felt at every turn. The writer need not retract, concede, bluff, cajole, placate, counter-attack, deny, nor acknowledge directions and fancies which are not his own. Writing, then, appears to emancipate the writer not only from the fragmentation or disruption of his discourse by the intrusion of others but also from the acknowledgement of the fact that he must accommodate to the needs of others.

Yet while we may perceive some truth in all this, we also know it to be an absurdly inadequate description of what writers do – indeed must do. In spite of the fact that a writer is physically isolated from his audience, the act of writing inserts itself into a network of social relationships which will make him say this rather than that – in this way rather than that – or perhaps suppress this and add that. An invisible audience will exert some degree of control on his writing, impelling him towards choices along every dimension of language. There are some circumstances in which this is so obvious that we need not linger on them. What we shall be referring to as conative writing would be a case in point: for when a writer is setting out to convince his readers to change their beliefs, attitudes or behaviour, he must represent to himself their present posture. A letter-writer will make choices which take into account not only his status/relationship with the addressee but also, so far as he is able, whatever conventionalized formulaic repertoire is available for expressing this relationship ('Dear Sir', or 'Mr Smith', or 'Smith', or 'Joe', or 'Joe Smith'). A scholar at home in the intricacies of his field will in a popularizing article be under considerable compulsion to simplify, to explain and to make certain assumptions explicit. And so on: these are all examples in which the writer will have a lively representation of his audience in mind – or, if he does not, he will fail in his intent, of which he is likely to be highly aware. In such cases it is a relatively easy matter to detect the influences that the audience has had on a particular piece of writing, or at least some of them. In the same way, in the conversation game one of the players can act with fully planned intent – having decided 'to butter someone up', or 'to keep someone in his place', or 'to create a good impression', or 'to show I'm not a snob'.

How does a writer enter into contact with an audience whom he may not know or not know very much about? Here we must face up to a difficulty which is relevant to the problem which we shall face later: the specifically educational aspect of the sense of audience. The bulk of writing in our society is of a professional or quasi-professional nature. The practitioners are, in part, aided by the conventions, practices and 'house-style' of the agency for which they write, and by their experience of public communication in general. This would also hold true for internal documents which circulate in large organizations like industrial enterprises, the civil service, etc. Writers in this situation need never have pondered the problem of audience: they have merely, so to speak, to serve their apprenticeship. They adjust themselves to the ground rules. On the other hand, it is true that in a single issue of a journal the contributors may display varying capacities or degrees of willingness to adjust to their common audience. All speakers go beyond the conventional devices provided by the language (levels of formality, politeness rituals, status-acknowledgement formulae, etc.) because of their sensitivity to the feelings, attitudes and knowledge of others and their ability to divine what has been thought rather than expressed. In the same way, writers may follow their own personal sense of audience and even ignore established conventions. We may say, then, that sense of audience is well provided for in the written language but that each writer must learn the system and must also learn how to make individual use of it.

Professional writing in general is addressed to a wide unknown audience, but there are kinds of writing which are addressed to very different kinds of audience which may be very limited in number, be personally known to the writer, and with whom he shares a special relationship. We therefore need to establish a set of writer–reader relationships which cover the whole possible range, even though only one of these relationships dominates published material.

Since the time of Aristotle, the studied adjustment of discourse to its audience has been a major concern in rhetoric. In 1776 Campbell elaborated this attention to audience in two chapters, the first entitled 'Of the Consideration which the Speaker ought to have of the Hearers, as men in general' and the second dealing with consideration for the hearers 'as such men in particular'; he proposed that the speaker should consider how to shape his language to allow for the level of understanding, the imagination, the memory and the passions of the audience. Rhetoric was an educational programme preoccupied with prescriptions of how speakers (and, later, writers) *should* take their audience into account, suggesting in the manuals what devices might be resorted to and what tactics should be adopted. However, much – perhaps most – discourse is not the product of manifest intent nor do its authors operate with a vast array of rules inculcated by an explicit specialist training. Although the rhetoricians taught us that the audience contributes to the discourse, we now have to go much further than them and observe that adjustment to the audience is inherent in the social contract of all language use. Thus we do not learn our mother tongue and then follow this basic training with a course on audience rhetoric: the two run concurrently and are central to socialization in general. In speech we can rely on society to make a fairly good job of teaching a sense of audience: there are immediate penalties for ignoring the audience. In particular, the speaker runs into serious trouble when he has to adjust to an audience with whose needs he is unfamiliar or whose demands he has not been taught by life to meet. Within his own linguistic community the speaker can develop a delicate sense of audience; outside it he can run into difficulty. As Gumperz (1962) points out, the linguistic community is 'held together by the frequency of social interaction patterns and set off from the surrounding areas by weaknesses in the lines of communication'.

A writer has options open to him. Seen as someone engaged in more than producing discourse which is intelligible and satisfying to himself, he becomes the performer of a social act in the arena of *context of situation.* (See Malinowski [1923], 'The problem of meaning in primitive languages'; Firth [1935], 'The technique of semantics'; and Halliday [1971], 'Language in a social perspective'. Firth gives the following description of context of situation:

> The central concept of the whole of semantics considered in this way is the context of situation. In that context are the human participant or participants, what they say, and what is going on. The phonetician can find his phonetic context and the grammarian and the lexicographer theirs. And if you want to bring in general cultural background, you have the contexts of experience of the participants. Every man carries his culture and much of his social reality about him wherever he goes. But even when phonetician, grammarian, and lexicographer have finished, there remains the bigger integration, making use of all their work, in semantic study. And it is for this situational and experimental study that I would reserve the term 'semantics'.)

The effect of context of situation on speakers is readily apparent. We can detect without difficulty some of the ways in which they are influenced by the circumstances of time, place and possibly accompanying activities. At the centre of the situation will be the other participant or participants also being affected by the other features of the context of situation. (We might think of the headmaster addressing a morning assembly, and construct for ourselves a model of how this general notion operates in a specific situation.)

To this we can add that the speaker and his listener(s) are not hermetically sealed in their context but operating within the whole culture of their society. In fact we have taken as the major premise of our work on function that for language to function effectively there must be 'tacit acceptance by both speaker and hearer of all the relevant conventions, beliefs and presuppositions' (Lyons, 1963).

But this picture is an idealized one and leaves out of account several features which loom large in the light of our preoccupations with writing rather than speech, and with one particular context, namely school. To the latter point we shall return. For the moment let us say that writers will differ greatly in the extent to which they are justified in making tacit assumptions and in their capacity to write in a way that accommodates these assumptions. In the speech context of situation the hearer is sharply in focus and indeed in most cases is likely to appear to the speaker as the major element, while for the writer this will not be true. The concept of context of situation has been shaped very much with speakers in mind and needs to be modified for writers. For the writer, it does not consist of the immediate environment, but rather of the universe of discourse he is entering (business letter, official document, short story) – the situation of writing this kind of thing in this sort of society for this sort of person. The writer, then, must construe his audience on the basis of clues which are harder to come by since they are on a more generalized plane. To put it another way, the writer does not, like the speaker, have the context of situation displayed before him, but must *represent to himself* a context of situation, and this includes his readers.

Dell Hymes (1971) has insisted that in considering the linguistic development of children we need a broader view of what he calls 'communicative competence', which includes a knowledge not only of grammatical rules but also of 'speaking rules'. Some of these rules relate to addressor–addressee relationships which, he points out, begin to develop very early. He starts with the basic facts of social relationships rather than the basic facts of language. The communicative act grows out of these relationships and entails 'the selection and creation of communicative means considered specific and appropriate to it by the participants'. He suggests several areas for closer attention which do shed some light on our present concern. Firstly, *self-identity* is crucial to the kind of differentiated linguistic competence required of the individual in contemporary industrial society. Thus he shows the paradox of audience adjustment revealed by a black mother who said: 'You know, I've noticed that when the children play "school" outside, they talk like they're supposed to in school; and when they stop playing school, they stop.'

Secondly, Hymes developed the notion of *sociolinguistic interference*. 'When a child from one background enters a situation in which the communicative expectations are defined in terms of another', misunderstandings and misanalysis follow. In terms of audience we might see this most clearly displayed when the child moves from speaking to writing and perhaps again in the shift from the school exercise to the genuine communicative act. The ghost of the former audience is likely to haunt the new situation. Finally, Hymes sees that schools ask for special forms of communicative conduct (including writing) which bring with them their own hazards.

> Indeed, since the beginnings of stratified society and the use of writing, it has been characteristic of the greater part of mankind that a desired or required communicative competence has confronted man as an alien thing, imposed by a power not within his control. In the complex circumstances of our own society it is hard to see how children can be expected to master a second system, complementing or replacing their own, if the process is not perceived as intrinsically relevant or enjoyable, preferably both.

What is it that the writer must do if he is to exercise 'communicative competence' in respect of his audience in the context of situation peculiar to the writer–

reader relationship? He must carry out a procedure of self-editing, of arresting, reorganizing and adjusting his message for his absent audience. He will be unable to do this unless he can *internalize* his audience. Mead (1934) suggested that this was an essential part of all thinking. The individual must be able to call out in himself the responses which his gestures evoke from others. He begins by being able to internalize individuals and finally internalizes a 'generalized other' who speaks for society at large. This must be close to what the mature writer has to do when he addresses a public audience. We may say, then, that a writer's capacity to adjust to his audience is dependent on the degree to which he can internalize that audience. Piaget showed how little the young child could do this because he 'has not like the adult the art of seeking and finding in the other's mind a basis on which to build anew' (Piaget and Inhelder, 1969). And building anew is exactly what the full exercise of writing ability demands.

This is no place to examine the whole of role theory, but inevitably, having considered the process of taking the role of the other, we must look at the role taken up by the writer. In so far as a writer considers his audience to be in one role, his own role must be a complementary one. If he sees them as interested but uninformed laymen, he becomes the obliging expert. If they are seen as equals sharing a community of interest or concern he speaks as a peer. Furthermore we cannot rule out an element of role-playing (as distinct from role-taking); for a writer (particularly a school pupil) might assume a role to which he has no acknowledged social claim, either for the purpose of practice, humour, or deceit or simply because it is demanded of him. He then sets up a fictitious top-stratum relationship with his audience beneath which there lies another. A schoolboy, for example, may set out to act the politician and treat his audience as citizen-voters when in fact they are his fellows.

Thus we conceive of the audience categories as a relationship between writer and reader.

The sense of audience in the school situation

Now let us look at the school situation and consider the application of our discussion to it. What is unique to this situation or more prevalent in it than is generally true?

The pupil operates within a context of culture which will exert an influence not only on the values he expresses but also on the ways in which he expresses them. It will also lead him to construe his audience (let us say, teachers) partly or wholly in the way in which his culture construes them. In some degree the pupil and teacher will share a common culture, but frequently there will be dramatic divergences – such as inner-urban working-class pupil with parents from overseas, and university trained, suburban middle-class teacher. (See Goodacre, *Teachers and their Pupils' Home Background*, 1968.) The messages which flow from pupil-writer to teacher-audience will be affected by the extent to which they share common cultural assumptions and also by the extent to which the pupil is aware of how matters stand. Thus the pupil-writer may construe his teacher-audience naively, crudely or with considerably astute sophistication. We need hardly add that the pupil's sense of audience in this situation will be strongly coloured by the teacher's attitude to cultural divergence. (See Becker, 'Social class variations in the teacher–pupil relationship', 1952.) The most vivid demonstration of the effect of 'context of culture' is the change which comes over adolescent pupils' writing when it is genuinely directed to a peer-audience. Our research has revealed how dramatic this change is. (See McLeod, 'This is what came out', 1969.)

If we look more closely at the context of situation we see that almost all the writing with which we are concerned is in the school domain. The act of written communication in this domain is in many ways unlike other similar acts even when they are apparently identical. For example, a pupil may be asked to 'account for the collapse of the Roman Empire' or to 'describe the transport system of France', both undertakings which we might expect mature adult writers to engage in. In school, however, the context is one in which this undertaking will be taken to be an 'exercise', one of hundreds the pupil will complete during his school career, the features of which he will learn as intimately as he learns the code of sanctions which his school operates. In this context he is likely to discriminate between a variety of tasks (note-taking, summarizing, 'essays', etc.), but, whatever the task, his audience will overwhelmingly be predetermined and sharply defined: the teacher, a known audience of one.

Ideally one of the goals of schools is that they should, wherever this is possible, produce writers who have developed the capacity to generate their own reasons for writing and to define their own audiences, which should include those which are large in number and unknown. In school, however, it is almost always the teacher who initiates the writing and who does so by defining a writing task with more or less explicitness. Not only does he define the task but also nominates himself as audience. He is not, however, simply a one-man audience but also the sole arbiter, appraiser, grader and judge of the performance. He becomes an audience on whom pupils must focus a special kind of scrutiny in order to detect what they must do to satisfy him. The peculiar feature of this relationship is that the pupil will see his teacher's response as a means by which his progress is being charted. It is part of a larger and more elaborate system of making judgements and not simply a question of the reader's pleasure or understanding or insight. Indeed the writer is frequently placed in the position of telling the reader what the latter already knows more fully and more deeply.

The fact that the pupil is subject to frequent demands for writing, some of which he finds distasteful or merely dull, may lead to his sense of audience taking on a particular complexion. His writing may be dominated by the sole consideration of meeting minimum requirements. In other words it may be shaped solely by the demands of his audience and not by the complementary pressure to formulate ideas in a way which satisfies the writer. The analogy here is hack-writing, and school becomes the writer's Grub Street. Readers will be aware that this sort of sense of audience can be finely tuned with arithmetic precision – the exact number of lines or pages.

We are well aware that other kinds of relationship exist between pupil and teacher, and also that pupils frequently are concerned to satisfy themselves as well as their teacher-audience. We try to accommodate these possibilities in our scheme. We are also aware that teachers often attempt to direct the sense of audience away from themselves by a variety of means. They may simply urge the pupil to *represent to himself* a general reader's difficulties of understanding or flow of sympathies or capacities for response. They may offer *stylistic advice* or *rhetorical precepts* which have a more general reader in mind, but this advice is not made explicit.

But whatever strategy the teacher adopts, it is difficult for him to elude the stubborn reality of himself as audience, and he is likely, in our experience, to continue dominant in that role. Thus many pupil-writers have to operate a double-audience system which may give rise to particular tensions. Behind one audience stands the spectre of another. This will not always be so, especially when the writer actually enjoys the language game being proposed to him. Moreover, a distinction should be made between the feigning required for some specific fictionalized audience, and the gradual development both of the desire to reach out beyond the teacher and an awareness of how to do so. In other words the development of the pupil may be seen in terms of the move from 'the internalized other' (the teacher) to 'the generalized other' (the writer's unknown public).

Another way of looking at the teacher-as-audience is in terms of status. Normally in school the hierarchically ordered system will lead the writer not only to regard the teacher's demands as paramount but also as requiring a writing decorum which expresses the inferior status of the writer. The writer may reject his status by defying the rules of decorum. Similarly, a teacher may create a relationship which renounces his status and makes possible a different audience role. Whatever happens, the relative status of writer and reader will be set in terms of school relationships. The teacher's superior status is not marked out boldly like the ranks in the army, and we can detect variations as between teachers, and in one and the same teacher on different occasions. Similarly, the role the teacher takes up will vary; he may be instructor, collaborator, tester, wise adult or punitive arm. The pupil-writer may subtly accommodate to these different roles. Once again his maturity may well be marked by the development of the ability to abandon his inferior status and speak to adult peers.

Throughout his school career the pupil is provided with another source of awareness, his reading. From this he can learn strategies by means of which writers accommodate to their audiences (usually either the public at large or the school learner). This learning can be applied to any school writing but would be more readily drawn upon when the teacher encourages the pupil to direct himself to a more general audience.

It has been our assumption so far that all writing will be influenced by the writer's sense of audience. There is, perhaps, one exception. When writing is seen as a mere task and the writer is indifferent to the demands of the teacher, or when in desperation he is merely stringing sentences together, he may produce a piece in which it is not possible to discern a hint of sense of audience.

Classifying the sense of audience in school writing

We have by now given sufficient indication of the considerations which led us to attribute importance to the writer's sense of audience, and of general application of audience to the school situation. We can now pass on to the model which we evolved by means of which we could allocate scripts to particular categories, and thus use this dimension in the classification of school writing. The model is displayed schematically below and followed by an explanatory text; a diagrammatic representation is given in Figure 1.

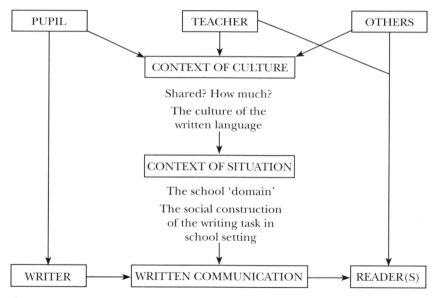

Fig. 1 Diagrammatic representation of the sense of audience in a teacher–pupil situation

Sense of audience: Category system

Definition: the sense of audience is revealed by the manner in which the *writer* expresses a *relationship* with the *reader* in respect to his (the writer's) *undertaking*. The main divisions are self, teacher, wider audience (known), unknown audience: a full list of categories is given below.

1. *Self*

Child (or adolescent) to self

2. *Teacher*

2.1   Child (or adolescent) to trusted adult
2.2   Pupil to teacher, general (teacher–learner dialogue)
2.3   Pupil to teacher, particular relationship
2.4   Pupil to examiner

3. *Wider audience (known)*

3.1   Expert to known laymen
3.2   Child (or adolescent) to peer group
3.3   Group member to working group (known audience which may include teacher)

4. *Unknown audience*

Writer to his readers (or his public)

5. *Additional categories*

5.1   Virtual named audience
5.2   No discernible audience

Note (a) We have attempted to cover the full range of possible writing in school, while at the same time introducing special distinctions relevant to school writing. Most of the work we examine is inevitably assigned by the teacher and we would therefore expect most writing to fall in one of the subdivisions of category 2.

Note (b) For reasons we have, we hope, made clear we wish to focus attention on the reader, but since it is a relationship which we are classifying we have expressed categories in terms of both writer and reader; see, for example, category 3.1, 'expert to known laymen'. However, it is the second term, which refers to the reader, which is systematically varied; the first term names the general or usual complementary role of the writer.

The classifications

1. Self

This is writing from one's own point of view without considering the intelligibility to others of that point of view; a written form of 'speech for oneself'. The writer himself must be the first-stage audience for any worthwhile writing; and some other reader must also be in mind except where:

(a)   what is set down or explored is considered by the writer to be of no concern to anyone else (it might be mnemonic like a shopping list, record a stage in his thinking, or be preparatory to further activity including writing – graphically it may be very different from conventional written language); or

(b) what is set down or explored is regarded as a private concern, e.g. an entry in an intimate diary; or

(c) the exploration is so difficult or tentative that the writer could not afford to have anybody else in mind (i.e. is unable to operate the internalized other): he is using writing to discover what he thinks.

Assigned tasks may sometimes move into this category, particularly in the circumstances of (c) above. Some notes are likely to move into this category, where they may appear in two forms: (i) a diary-form entry where the writer comments on something which has interested him, or (ii) preparatory notes for an assigned task. (Here the teacher conditions the task but is not in mind as an audience to this preparatory version.)

2.1 Child (or adolescent) to trusted adult

Only a mother understands the egocentric speech of the infant, and clearly the talking relationship with the mother is the general incentive that makes the infant talk. We transfer this to writing that can only go on because there is this teacher, this particular human being, who will understand what it is you are trying to say. It is writing that accepts an invitation because it comes from this particular person in whom there is confidence.

Because writing is a way of committing oneself, and because it is at first a difficult process, young children may rely upon the trusted adult reader in even the simplest piece of work. Later, the fact that this particular adult wants to hear anything you have to say may operate as a strong incentive, and a liberator, so that children who haven't written begin to do so simply because they now feel free to say what really matters. (See, for example, the black children's first pieces at thirteen or so in Kohl's *36 Children*, 1972.) And in more ordinary circumstances adolescents may rely on this relationship in order to write dispassionately or objectively or critically about their families, etc.

The shaping responses of the 'internalized other' can be less heeded (and hence less of a brake) when a writer relies on the understanding of a particular trusted reader: writing for a trusted adult has therefore some affinity with the previous category, writing for oneself. Mead's distinction, that between the internalized other and the generalized other, is relevant here.

Teachers are likely to vary very much in their understanding of this role and their willingness to assume it. (It has been suggested that where they have established such a relationship but betray it by reading work out to the whole class without prior permission, the writers lose some of their directness and begin to show off to the class. In our terms this would be a move from category 2 to one form of 3.2, 'child or adolescent to peer group'.) We might speculate that, among assigned tasks, examples of writing for oneself will crop up more frequently in classes where the teacher has established the 'trusted adult' relationship and tries to work within it a good deal.

A role for the English teacher only? Not at all. Speculation in even a specialized intellectual field may need to rely upon this relationship – though it may not be possible for a reader to discern the fact. Of course, writing about personal relations is more likely to rely on the trusted adult than is writing on impersonal matters, and this would favour work in English lessons.

Preparing to distinguish category 2.2, 'pupil to teacher' from this one, let us sum up the pupil's attitude to category 2.1 writing as follows: 'My relationship with this particular adult provides me with an area in which I am free to operate, and I operate as myself.'

2.2 Pupil to teacher, general (teacher–learner dialogue)

Here the adult represents an audience which is an object rather than an area of free operation and the object has its teacherly characteristics which affect the pupil as writer.

Children may like or dislike, trust or mistrust teachers in general: the stereotype 'teacher' may often be what is felt as audience in category 2.2. On the other hand, particular teachers may be liked or disliked, trusted or mistrusted – and also known or unknown (for example, if the teacher is new to the class). The particular teacher is likely to be there as an 'internalized other' in writing in this category. He may be a teacher who never takes the role described under category 2.1, or he may be a teacher who normally takes this role but on this occasion sets a task which is taken perhaps as rather more of a routine assignment, or more narrowly restricting as to area of concern. Thus the pupils may have a sense of audience which says 'We know what teachers in general expect of us, and to some extent how this particular representative embodies those expectations. This is our attempt to meet them.'

Distinguishing 'Pupil to teacher, general (teacher–learner dialogue)' (2.2), from 'Pupil to teacher, particular relationship' (2.3)

As a child in the secondary school comes to know his teachers he is likely to develop a personal relationship with one or more of them: a relationship that is fed by his growing interest in the subject taught. When this happens the pupil gains confidence both in the teacher as a person and in his own ability to operate within the subject field – and this will be reflected in his writing for this *particular* teacher. This category, 'teacher, particular relationship', is therefore, like 2.1, 'child to trusted adult', a personal relationship but also, unlike 2.1, a professional relationship based upon a shared interest and expertise, and an accumulating shared context.

In the course of teaching a class, a teacher is likely to build up a small group of pupils who hold such a relationship with him, and they may function as an elite group who form part of the audience felt by one of them in his writing (see also category 3.2, 'child or adolescent to peer group', but in 2.3 the role of the teacher is more central).

Harold Rosen

Distinguishing 'Pupil to teacher, general' (2.2) from 'Pupil to examiner' (2.4)

It is fairly widely assumed that, among the many things teachers do, their teaching function can be distinguished from their testing function. It is this distinction that we want to apply in defining 'pupil to teacher' as a different audience category from 'pupil to examiner'.

The basic difference seems to be that between, on the one hand, an ongoing process, an interaction between pupil and teacher, a continuing dialogue; and, on the other, a 'show-up', a demonstration, an endpoint. In the teaching situation, a pupil looks, in his writing, to the response of the teacher and beyond that to his own activity to follow. He writes for a response; a genuine question, therefore, may be as appropriate as a statement, and a suggestion that invites development may be as highly valued as a conclusion. The test piece, on the other hand, is a culminating point rather than a stage in a process of interaction. (If candidates in the test situation ask questions, it will be because they are demonstrating their ability to frame the *right* or *approved* questions, rather than because they are seeking answers.)

A test may set out to measure what a pupil *can do* as well as what he *knows*, and here the teacher/examiner distinction may be more difficult to make. Thus:

(a) Suppose a teacher asks a first-year class to write a ballad, not as a test but as a piece of teaching. The poor performer may nevertheless find this an impossible task and his writing will show this. He cannot regard it as an 'invitation to be accepted' but only as a 'demand to be met'. It seems to us logical to regard this not as teacher-directed (the teaching miscarried in this case) but as coming within the category 'pupil to examiner'.

(b) When a piece of writing seems to offer back what the pupil has received – a mirror to instruction – this would also suggest 'pupil to examiner'. Where the writer seems to be *actively operating* within a task area this would suggest either normally, (i) pupil to teacher – especially where the writer tries to interest the reader or to write from his own interest; or occasionally, (ii) pupil to examiner, in the sense 'See how well I can operate!' Where the pupil seems to be copying straight from a textbook, or reproducing notes which the teacher has given him, the writing would again suggest category 2.4 because the pupil has taken the 'teacher as examiner' as the audience for the task as a whole (though this may not further affect what he writes). Exercises in précis, too, are likely to be of the form 'See how well I can operate'.

(c) The best exams in English may set out to test a candidate's ability to use language in optimum conditions, i.e. perhaps in circumstances modelled on the teacher–learner dialogue. In such cases an actual exam may call forth writing which we should rightly classify as 'pupil to teacher'.

(d)   In an exam (unknown audience) the writer may take up the task as his own (a writer to his public) or may, availing himself of anonymity, use the situation as a confessional.

(e)   The 'mock exam' presents a special case: in this 'show-up', teaching is likely to concentrate upon improving performance. We suggest that only where the writing seems to be strongly influenced by the teaching relationship (the teacher–learner dialogue) should it be regarded as moving out of the 'pupil to examiner' category.

Every interaction with someone else tells us something about that person; but when the interaction is between teacher and pupil, what a teacher learns from it leads not to a verdict but to further interaction. We need to distinguish writing aimed at a verdict from writing that is a link in a chain of interaction. The distinction being made is clearly not an organizational one but an educational one. There are many teachers whose everyday teaching consists in leaping from test to test. Work produced in these circumstances, while not examination work in the formal sense, is nonetheless likely to go into category 2.4.

3.1 Expert to known laymen

There is probably no need here to distinguish the teacher as layman from any other layman or group of laymen.

Essentially the writer will have chosen his topic, or it will have been suggested to him as an individual, as an expert. The writing will be explicit down to the non-expert level: that is to say more of the context will be supplied and less implied than would have been the case where an expert wrote for fellow experts. (This will distinguish work in this category from work in the 'pupil to teacher' category, where, however expert the writer may feel himself to be, he will assume that the teacher is even more of an expert.)

We have probably met writing of this kind in form magazines – in a 'hobbies section', to use the language of the *Boy's Own Paper* era. When the teacher sets an individually chosen or appropriately assigned 'hobbies' task, the result is not substantially different.

Where a task of this kind has been misassigned, is inappropriate for an individual, or the child has nothing in which he feels he can operate as an expert, the writing is likely to fall either into the 'pupil to teacher' category (where the child does his best to interest the teacher) or (in more desperate cases) into the 'pupil to examiner' category. Where expertise is based on written sources, the writing tends to move into the writer-to-public category (for example, a piece on cosmetics takes up the manner of women's magazines, or technical know-how may derive from manuals).

3.2 Child (or adolescent) to peer group

One of the things that good teachers do is to make children responsive to each other's efforts. (Probably in the best teaching this aim is subordinate to that of establishing a child-to-adult channel – but that is a matter of opinion, and certainly teachers will vary in what they set out to do.)

Writing to the peer group is familiar to most of us from form magazines: here sometimes it suffers from a kind of precocity, a pseudo-journalistic style, sometimes from extreme banality. But the influence of the teacher can move it from this level without substituting himself for the peer group as audience. Or he may function rather as spectator and adviser, or he may identify himself with the form's point of view and remain a member of the audience. A lot depends on genuine sense of freedom from censoring surveillance.

Another situation will also produce writing in a related category: here the peer group is the 'hidden audience', aimed at via the teacher and despite him. The in-group joke will be a sign of it. But the effect of the hidden audience has to dominate the writing (at the expense of the ostensible audience, the teacher) for a piece of work to go into this category.

3.3 Group member to working group

For this category the teacher is likely to be regarded as a member of the group; the writing is likely to be a link in a chain of group activity the past phases of which will be taken for granted as a part of the initial context. The audience is seen in this respect to be a known audience. There may be other indications of this fact in the way the writer appears to take into account the views and attitudes of individuals in the group – perhaps anticipating their particular difficulties or objections. Sometimes, though not always, what is offered will be seen to be *material for the group to work upon* – a contribution to an ongoing activity.

This contribution to a joint undertaking is usually distinguishable from the 'expert to laymen' writing, but occasionally there can be a merging of the two – the joint undertaking may demand an expert's particular contribution.

4. Writer to his readers (unknown audience)

A writer who operates well in any of the categories will be, in the first instance, his own audience. Writing in which he functions as his own audience only at a minimum level is more likely to be in category 2.4 ('pupil to examiner') than in any other; and writing in this category is least likely to lead on to writing in category 4. On the other hand, pupils who operate well in categories 1 (child to self) and 2.1 (child to trusted adult) are likely to produce examples of category 4.

The move from any other category to this one is distinguished by the following characteristics:

(a)   the writer's sense of the general value or validity of what he has to say;

(b)   his sense of the need to supply a context wide enough to bring in readers whose sophistication, interests and experiences he can only estimate;

(c)   a readiness to conform with and contribute to some cultural norm or trend;

(d)   a desire to achieve an effect, or make an impression on readers in general;

(e)   a sense that the writer's audience is not one with which he identifies himself in a personal way;

(f))   a familiarity with adult writing of the kind he is attempting which seems a satisfactory model to the writer.

These characteristics are intended to be signposts, not the makings of a category definition. Other circumstances are likely to throw up poor work in category 4. Where there is a considerable gap between what a writer aims at and what he achieves, and where he is not aware of this gap, he may well produce naive or pretentious or tedious writing with a public audience in mind.

5.1 Virtual named audience

Sometimes children are asked to write a letter or address a piece of writing to a named person, or type of audience. In such cases, the writer may direct the piece towards the teacher, where it is likely to be a variety of category 2. But sometimes the writer may feel that the named person or audience is real to him, whereupon the writing may have an audience direction more akin to a personal letter than writing which has, as destination, the teacher. It would seem proper to distinguish these two cases.

5.2 No discernible audience

Occasionally there were scripts which could not be allocated to any category because there was no discernible audience. This category was not intended to be a dumping ground for cases where a decision was difficult. It was meant to include those cases where, for one reason or another, the writing had no audience direction. It should not be confused with category 1, 'Child (or adolescent) to self'.

References

Becker, H. (1952) 'Social class variations in the teacher–pupil relationship'. *Journal of Educational Sociology*, 25 (8).

Britton, J., Burgess, T., Martin, N., McLeod, A. and Rosen, H. *The Development of Writing Abilities (11–18)*. London: Macmillan Education.

Campbell, G. (1776) *The Philosophy of Rhetoric*. London: W. Strahan.

Firth, J. (1935) 'The technique of semantics'. *Transactions of the Philological Society*, 34 (1).

Goodacre, E. (1968) *Teachers and Their Pupils' Home Background*. Windsor: National Foundation for Educational Research.

Gumperz, J. (1962) 'Types of linguistic communities'. *Anthropological Linguistics*, 4 (1).

Halliday, M. (1971) 'Language in a social perspective'. *Educational Review*, 23 (3).

Hymes, D. (1971) 'Competence and performance in linguistic theory', in R. Huxley and E. Ingram (eds.), *Language Acquisition: Models and methods*. London: Academic Press.

Kohl, H. (1972) *36 Children*. Harmondsworth: Penguin.

Lyons, J. (1963) *Structural Semantics*. Oxford: Basil Blackwell.

Malinowski, B. (1923) 'The problem of meaning in primitive languages', Supplement 1 to C. Ogden and I. Richards, *The Meaning of Meaning*. New York: Harcourt, Brace and Co.

McLeod, A. (1969) 'This is what came out'. *English in Education*, 3 (3).

Mead, G. (1934) *Mind, Self and Society*. Chicago: University of Chicago Press.

Piaget, J. and Inhelder, B. (1969) *The Psychology of the Child* (H. Weaver, trans.). New York: Basic Books.

'Turn Research Upside Down'

This morning I told my Diploma students about our project 'Language in the Inner City', about the particular way it was developing and that it was above all founded on notions of teacher initiative. Did they want to join in? In what ways? The flood gates opened and new possibilities poured through, including using our workshop time to make a video of one multi-linguistic classroom incorporating each child as a linguistic cameo. The room was agog. It confirms our notion that we must turn research upside down. No more pirate raids for 'data'. We become facilitators, donkey-workers and learners instead of 'experts'. And the students, with a precious year off to study, not being located as blotting paper but getting a chance to do things they hadn't dreamed of. So even in this job [with adults] the authentic moments come and you can feel them in the air just as you might with eight-year-olds.

In a letter to Betty, autumn 1976

The Dramatic Mode

This essay appeared in 1980 in *Coming to Know*, a collection edited by Phillida Salmon. Salmon was by training a clinical psychologist. She became Senior Lecturer in Child Development at the Institute of Education, University of London. Throughout her career as a psychologist and academic, she was concerned to emphasize the personal in a discipline which had often ignored it. This concern she applied of course to the processes of learning. In her introduction to the part of the book where Harold's essay appears, Salmon writes: 'Rosen's case is that to equate drama with conventionalized theatrical forms is to miss seeing that spontaneous drama plays a major part in the human repertoire – a part that enables us to know and to represent our world with richness, depth and delicacy.'

Forgers, imitators, counterfeiters – we don't think much of them. 'Copy-cat!' children still cry in angry contempt. Aping our betters or anyone else never won admiration. Imitation is for the dull plodders devoid of originality and the creative spark. Imitation has had a bad press. Cassirer (1953), writing of the language of gestures and in particular the gestures of imitation, says, 'In imitation the *I* remains a prisoner of outward impression and its properties; the more accurately it repeats this impression, excluding all spontaneity of its own, the more fully the aim of imitation has been realised.'

For Chomsky (1959) the use of language is creative precisely because it cannot live off imitation. A speaker must actively apply his knowledge to create and understand novel sentences. Imitation, it seems, is humdrum; freshness, originality, invention are what we prize.

But imitation will not let itself be pigeon-holed quite so easily along with the most routine and unimpressive behaviour. What are theatres but temples of imitation? Willingly, eagerly we sit and watch these fellows imitating other fellows and, what is more, we know they are feigning ('They do but poison in jest'). They are licensed to imitate the rest of us and we have built elaborate places in which they may perform their esoteric, specialist antics. The covenant between actors and audience is known down to its last clause; no recital is necessary. And yet there is no need for us to go to theatres to see and hear such things. In any children's playground the actors will be at work. A few hours after men on the moon had shown us the weightless plod they needed to move across its surface, thousands of children were plodding across their playgrounds in similar manner. 'Who's been sitting in my chair?' they will repeat in three different voices, each of them different from their normal voices, each an imitation of an anthropomorphized bear. And it is not as though as adults we put away such childish things. Without our even noticing it, our speech and actions slip into imitation: we dip into our repertoire of other voices to present someone of another class, from another place, of a different age group, of the other sex. As an integral part of the performance there will be gestures, postures and actions. What immediately comes to mind is the comic performance, the caricaturing of acquaintances or public figures; but we also perform to make a serious point in a serious way, to report disturbing or disastrous events, for instance.

Why do we do this? Are our own bodies and voices not enough for us, that we must disguise and distort them? I was goaded into sorting this out for myself some years ago. I had been watching student teachers of drama. I grew increasingly dismayed as I watched them putting classes of children through their paces, carefully worked out dramatic 'exercises' which were in all respects inferior to what the children would have done spontaneously. I was reminded of some of the strangled exchanges which passed for oral discussion amongst pupils who in another setting were lively, fluent talkers. I started scribbling on a scrap of paper. What took shape on the paper was the first version of the model which appears in Figures 1 and 2. What I was trying to do was to understand the essence of dramatic behaviour or activity because it seemed to me that in their anxiety 'to develop skills' and fashion a respectable syllabus for themselves, the students had somewhere, somehow, lost the core, the heart of the matter. As I tried to sift my experience and observations, what emerged more and more clearly was that dramatic behaviour was ordinary, pervasive and universal. More than that, it was not an optional extra grafted on to human activity by the talented or exhibitionist but a common human resource intrinsic to language and bodily movement. It can and does exist independent of theatres, stages, drama classes and dramatic texts.

What we call play has received close attention for a long time (Bruner, Jolly and Sylva, [eds.], 1976) but mostly this has been part of the study of the early development of children. Play will change with maturation into games-with-rules (Piaget, 1951) or inner speech (Vygotsky, 1962), as though it has served its developmental turn and can be forgotten. Dramatic behaviour may be a form of play but there are many other non-dramatic forms. It may not, in any case, be play at all. A serious narration of a terrifying experience may include dramatic behaviour – replication of the threatening voice of an unknown assailant, his curious gait or posture. Nonetheless, some of the studies of play are relevant to my exploration. Then there are those who have concerned themselves with play-with-language (e.g. Cazden, 1976; Weir, 1962; Chukovsky, 1968). But play-with-language is not the same as play-through-language, though the distinction may be difficult to draw simply because it may be both at the same time or one may slide into the other. At 38 months Simon shows this very clearly (Boomer and Spender, 1976). The extracts are taken from a pre-sleep monologue made by his father Garth Boomer, 'inspired by the late Ruth Weir's study of the monologues of her son':

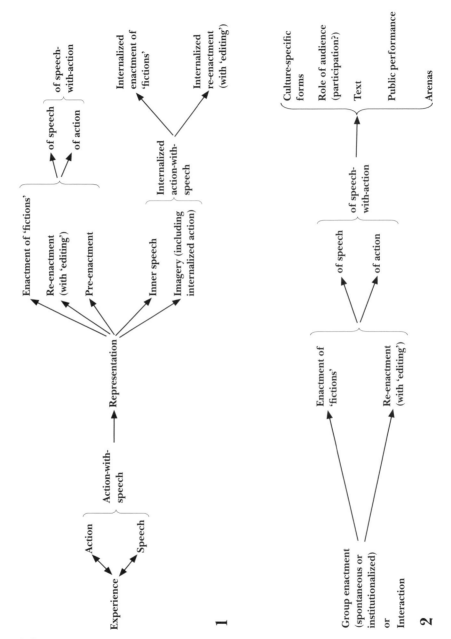

A theoretical model of the location of dramatic activities (very tentative): Figure 1, from experience to dramatized thought and externalized drama; Figure 2, from informal spontaneous improvisation to public spectacle.

First extract

I told yoi
A piggy nick
A piggy back
A piggy back on me
Right under there (chanting)
Right under here on my head
I don't know what to do
I don't know what to do
Pat her
(indistinct sounds)
Oh, no you can't
Oh, yes I can
(repeated three times)
Oh, yes I can
Oh, no I'm not
(repeated three times)
That's the slip
It is the slip to go in the water

That's the water down there
and you jump
jumpy, jumpy, jumpy (chant)
(sound like R, rrr ...)
A piggy nick
A piggy nick?
Oh, that's another good word

Anyone would be hard put to it to allocate with complete confidence all these utterances either to play-with-words or dramatic play-through-words, even with access to the tape. It is much clearer in the next two extracts. The authors explain that 'Earlier that day, Simon had fallen off a makeshift swing ... children from the flat downstairs comforted him.'

Second extract

That won't hurt
Look at that
P'yoopy, yoopy, yoopy, yoop
(indistinct whispering)
Sit down, sit down (dramatized)

> Why you crying
> Oh hosh hosh
>
> We don't mean to cry do we
> NO
> That's right

Third extract

> We have a swing
> O pee doodle
> Fell off the swing
> … clumsy
> Why you crying, don't cry, hush don't prosh will you don't cry

A whole literature has sprung up which deals with body language (Birdwhistell, 1952; Argyle, 1967; Goffman, 1959; Hall, 1959) and non-verbal communication, but it does not deal with our capacity to 'quote' from these 'silent languages' much less with our capacity to use our bodies to imitate machines, things and animals.

I was drawn into my speculations the more easily because I had lived a long time with the idea that poetry and fiction have their roots in everyday speech, that highly wrought, complex, intensely conventionalized written texts can be found in both embryonic and sometimes highly developed form in spontaneous speech. It was a short step to take to the idea that drama too was intrinsic to everyday social behaviour; perhaps since it was rooted in imitation it was even more fundamental than poetry or fiction.

Though it takes many different forms, can be momentary or sustained, can be dominant or merely contributory, I did not intend dramatic behaviour to be understood in the metaphoric sense of 'all the world's a stage', nor in the sense that we are acting out roles, nor as encapsulated little dramas which crop up in daily lives. What I was concerned with was almost the opposite: it occurred when we stepped out of role but paradoxically maintained a role in doing so. If we insist that all the world's a stage (I don't) then what I'm talking about is a play within a play. We do not merely speak and act but also speak the speech of another and intend to be understood as such. Our speech is peppered with invisible but detectable quotation marks. We also perform the actions of another and intend them to be perceived as such. This is imitation of quite a different kind from Cassirer's ('devoid of spontaneity') and from Chomsky's, which he dismissed to refute the Skinnerian behaviourist model. Chomsky was concerned to demonstrate that language could not be learned by imitation with reinforcement but that children needed to derive and internalize the grammatical system. For him imitation meant the straight copying of the language of others.

But there is a richer notion of imitation which was, in fact, explored by Cassirer himself in a passage which follows closely on the one I cited at the outset: 'If we consider only this factor of pantomimic imitation of given objects of sense perception, we do not seem to be on the road to *language* as a free and original activity of the human spirit.' He takes us back to the Aristotelian idea that all reproduction presupposes an internal productive process and is therefore more than a repetition of something outwardly given. Cassirer then proceeds to develop this view of 'apparently passive reproduction':

> For this reproduction never consists in retracing, line for line, a specific content of reality; but in selecting a pregnant motif in that content and so producing a characteristic 'outline' of its form. But with this, imitation itself is on its way to becoming *representation*, in which objects are no longer simply received in their finished structure, but built up by the consciousness according to their constitutive traits. To reproduce an object in this sense means not merely to compose it from its particular sensuous characteristics, but to apprehend it in its structural relations which can only be truly understood if the consciousness constructively produces them.
>
> (Cassirer, 1953)

This is to reinstate imitation as an active creative process, to accord honourable status even to trivial acts of impersonation, the use of special voices readily recognized as departures from normal speech, the altering of normal gesture to render a grotesque version of a type. Nevertheless, to reinstate imitation is not entirely to exonerate it. There is still affectation, which makes judgments difficult. We can deliver a meaning in a particular way by representing another. There are quotation marks around the performance. There is the other extreme at which the behaviour of another is imitated in order that the imitator may pass himself off as such a one. The two processes can come close to each other, so much so that no hard-and-fast line can be drawn. But dramatic behaviour, as I am presenting it, nearly always distinguishes itself by being embedded in other behaviour. This serves not only to signal it but also to affect its meaning. Put less abstractly, we might say that for drama to be effective we must know it for what it is. For affectation to achieve its goal we must fail to detect it.

There was for me another starting point. I had for several years been involved in the debate on linguistic deprivation, which still rages (Rosen, 1972). In essence this became an intellectual confrontation between those who argued that many working-class children failed in school because the language of their social milieu could not carry certain critical meanings, and those who argued that no such limitation had been demonstrated. There is no point in following the debate here. I mention it because in exploring the relevant literature I had been struck by the frequency with which people whose research work had been confined to studies of young children confidently made assertions about the language (and much more) of adult working-class people without anything more than anecdotal or second-hand or even conjectural 'evidence'. A group of us for several years collected tapes of adult working-class speakers and studied them. Of the many observations we made, two emerged clearly. The first was that working-class speakers had a very strong tendency to use narrative when they wished to make a theoretical point, to clarify an idea or exemplify a generalization. Second, in the course of these narratives, or outside them, they invariably used dramatic dialogue, i.e. dialogue in which the speaker became each of the participants and acted out their voices through direct speech. They were using the same resources as novelists and poets frequently use, but with the powerful addition of voice quality and the rich and flexible sound system of the language. This is a 75-year-old ex-building labourer recalling his work experience:

> So one day I says to him – he calls us in a ring – he said, 'I want you all to come in a circle.' In the dinner hour that was from one to two o'clock. So we said, 'All right.' So we all went down the lobby, and er – so he said, 'Now,' he said, 'now all you,' he says, 'are here, I want to talk to you.' So he says, 'I want you – er – all down here to do a few more blocks a day, as it's not paying,' he said. 'I'm also – want to see the years come back when there's four deep on the dole, and a mile-and-a-half queue.' That's what he said. 'Well,' I said, 'governor –,' because I put my foot in it. I got so wild that I had to let it come out – I said, 'Well, governor,' I said, 'allow me to tell you, you'll never see them times again.' He said, 'I won't?' I said, 'No, you won't,' I said. 'The generation's coming up now,' I said, 'they want easy money, and they're getting easy money.' So I says, 'And on the other hand,' I said, 'the whip's finished: the masters have had their day.'
>
> (Rosen, 1974)

I am not, of course, suggesting that working-class speakers are unique in their use of dramatic dialogue; on the contrary, it is central to my argument that it is a universal resource. I want to suggest that for social and cultural reasons they use it more readily, more frequently and to fulfil functions which other speakers satisfy by discursive methods because, in Cassirer's words, their dramatic dialogues were 'built up by the consciousness according to their constitutive traits'. Far from being 'context-bound' or 'tied to the here-and-now', they were able to deliver a general significant meaning.

Finally, I was strongly influenced by Brecht. Somewhere in his poems he had said all this. I went and found it in one poem, 'On the Everyday Theatre' (Brecht, 1961, trans. Berger and Bostock), which begins:

> Actors
> You who perform plays in great houses
> Under false suns and before silent faces
> Look sometimes at
> The theatre whose stage is the street,

The everyday theatre
Common, unrewarded with honour,
But of this earth, living,
Made from the traffic of men together.

The whole poem enlarges this theme and displays for us actors in everyday life: the man at the street corner who has seen an accident and is re-enacting it, a scarf-seller who cake-walks up and down behind his stall dressed in hat, false moustache and scarf:

… the theatre of the street
Has uses
And dignity.
Not like parrot or ape
Do those men imitate for imitation's sake,
Unconcerned with what they show
Save that they themselves are imitating well.
They have their purposes in mind.

Brecht had seen this link between theatre and dramatic behaviour and also the difference between parroting and aping and having purposes in mind.

Let me now return to those student teachers and my hasty scribblings as I watched them. They had forgotten, or perhaps never knew, that spontaneous dramatic behaviour is affected by the performers having purposes in mind. Drama in schools is well established and it takes a multitude of forms – mime, 'movement', improvisation, dance-drama, dramatization of texts, dramatic texts. Do these activities have common roots? What exactly are the participants doing? What are the functions of their activities? Is drama a separate, clearly identifiable activity which needs to be marked off from other kinds of learning? As soon as we distance ourselves from younger children's dramatic activity it does seem a little odd. A little girl in a long cloak taken from the dressing-up basket ('dressing-up', there's an idea to grapple with!) stalks round the room and declares apparently to no one, 'I am a queen and I am outrageous'. It seems less odd when we remember that as adults we dramatize in our heads situations just as remote from our lives.

Inevitably, great writers have observed and used the dramatic impulse not only through the use of dialogue but by portraying someone caught in the act of dramatizing, a tertiary. Remember Trabb's boy in Dickens's *Great Expectations*, who, though he makes only a fleeting appearance on a page or two, and namelessly at that, leaves a memorable mark. Pip has been changed by the effects of his unexpected affluence and his great expectations. He returns to his home town rather full of himself and enjoying the deference and wonder of the townsfolk until Trabb's boy, the tailor's errand-boy, with his large blue bag, approaches:

> I had not got as much further down the street as the post-office, when I again beheld Trabb's boy shooting round by a back way. This time, he was entirely changed. He wore the blue bag in the manner of my great-coat, and was strutting along the pavement towards me on the opposite side of the street, attended by a company of delighted young friends to whom he from time to time exclaimed, with a wave of his hand, 'Don't know yah!' Words cannot state the amount of aggravation and injury wreaked upon me by Trabb's boy, when, passing abreast of me, he pulled up his shirt-collar, twined his side-hair, stuck an arm akimbo, and smirked extravagantly by, wriggling his elbows and body, and drawling to his attendants, 'Don't know yah!'.

What is important in this fragment of drama is that Trabb's boy is *not* being Trabb's boy. He is in the presence of Pip and *is* Pip, or rather is Pip as he has interpreted him to be; he isn't reproducing something of Pip that he has heard or seen. Through enactment he delivers the message to Pip and us that Pip is becoming a snob who will reject his humble background. The imitation of a few gestures and a single phrase can make an explicit image.

What Dickens knew was that the dramatic ends up in theatres but does not begin there. The lowly Trabb's boy has it all at his fingertips. We all have it in some degree; for as surely as we can all speak and move we can also imitate speech and movement. We can call upon this ability as a means of communicating and as a means of knowing. Representation of action and speech through the use of our own bodies and speech is the birthplace of drama.

How does this process work out in more detail? I have tried to set it out diagrammatically in Figures 1 and 2, taking the risk inherent in all attempts to schematize – neatly – complex, untidy human behaviour. To mitigate the hazard I shall attempt to explain what began as a scribbled diagram on a scrap of paper in those drama classes.

Since I see dramatic behaviour as being interwoven with all human behaviour, I begin with an interrelated triad.

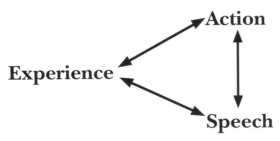

That is an absurdly simple way of inserting everything to begin with. It says no more than that we experience the world and come to develop our consciousness by acting in and upon it and that through speech we articulate our consciousness and organize it in new ways; through communication we act in a new way.

Our observable actions are very complex, for they consist not only of those which enable us to wield our bodies in order to move or come to rest but also to use them to act upon things with intent – to do. In addition, there is a whole language of meaningful gestures, some expressive (the arms thrown up in horror or welcome), controlling gestures (beckoning, waving for attention), some of them highly codified (the conductor, policeman, umpire). Finally, there are all those involuntary actions which we learn to read and use (drumming with the fingers, nodding and shaking the head), through which we interpret mood, attitude and response. We watch others closely when we wish to penetrate their innermost thoughts. To be guarded or inscrutable we attempt to reduce the gestural clues we give others so that, just as speech-flow silences are meaningful, so the absence of gesture may become a gesture. Clearly there are enormous inter-cultural differences – a great source of misunderstandings and jokes.

A person digging or threading a needle or cutting down a tree is not simply experiencing the world but acting upon it, changing it. Indeed, for Piaget (1969) this is the fountainhead of our intelligence:

> The essential functions of intelligence consist in understanding and inventing, in other words building up structures by structuring reality ... knowledge is derived from action ... to know an object is to act upon it and transform it.

Language interpenetrates with action so that often one is meaningless without the other. Language, to function at all, must be a shared system: most of our messages must get through for most of the time. But groups differ from each other in many ways and different occasions provoke different kinds of language. Each individual's language has its unique qualities. All this we observe too. That is another long story, but for present purposes I only wish to insist that we are talking, walking, doing animals. I want to consider these 'articulate mammals' at the stage when they act very competently, can use language to interact, to express ideas, feelings and attitudes, and also to form ideas about ideas, feelings and attitudes. Speech and action, I repeat, are intimately interrelated. Gesture and body language and instrumental activity are often so intimately orchestrated into the speech score that they must be considered as essential components embedded into it rather than embellishments. We may talk then of action-with-speech, bearing in mind (since I shall be getting back to dramatic action) that action can occur without speech and speech without action. You may do the washing up in miserable silence or may talk while doing it – about the washing up or anything else under the sun. Similarly, speech can occur without action in monologue or dialogue (the telephone conversation).

Now I can return to my main theme. Developmentally it begins with the representation of speech and action in play. It is often difficult to distinguish at the early stages from imitation. A small girl who often says very distinctly, 'I will not have it!', exactly reproducing her mother's speech, is not necessarily playing but rather trying out in the appropriate contexts a piece of ready-made language. She may learn later that it is not considered to be children's language except when playing. Once dramatic play is fully established, it is usually quickly recognizable. The 'rules' prescribe, as they continue to do in adult life, that we must accept what the actor-speaker is representing through the action-with-speech of another, or even of himself or herself at another time – past or future, true or fictional. We have to construe the here-and-now event as both happening and not happening. It is the imposition of design on events which makes the difference. The onlooker must pick up the signals in order to interpret aright. Sometimes they are explicit and obvious, signalled by narrative conventions, special tones of voice or even 'props'. Children withdraw to engage in dramatic play, suspending the activities of life to do so. But they also do intermittently what we do as adults, so that dramatic representation is more ubiquitous than clearly marked-off episodes would suggest.

What since classical times has been called direct speech (*oratio recta*) – that is, the citation of the actual words, real or supposed, of another – contains within it, however, faintly, the features of enactment rather than mimetic reproduction. Consider the ways in which different speakers might say: 'So quite suddenly he said to me, "Do you like classical music?"' Volosinov's recently resurrected work (1929, trans. 1973) long ago drew attention to the significance of the use of direct speech, and offers a brilliant analysis of its use in literature. He suggests that in double-voiced speech the voice of the other, the quoted one, is inevitably passive and therefore open to manipulation by the quoter. Thus the quoter's own intentions are superimposed on the speech of the quoted one, whose original goals are transformed into new ones. We could say that exactly the same applies to doubly-articulated action, in which we act the actions of another in order to present them recognizably and at the same time transform them. In both of these, double-voiced speech and doubly-articulated action, it is the tension between the two components which gives us meaning.

Once we enter the world of representation in the form of enactment we can make some further discriminations or subdivisions; these I call re-enactment, pre-enactment, and the enactment of fictions. In speech or writing, by reshaping experience through imagination, we can create what is not, what has not been and will never be, or what might have been or might be. What we can speak of and write of we can perform, using as our sources and resources our direct experience or, more indirectly, using the symbols provided by our culture (witches, *Superman*, *Dr Who*, cowboys).

Re-enactment is the presentation (highly selected, edited and patterned) of what has happened, like this:

So I started nudging him. 'I think there's something creepy about this place,' and he said, 'Don't be daft. You're always imagining things.' So I started tugging his arm. Then this big fella comes up and says, 'Remember me?'

Pre-enactment is the rehearsal of how things might happen. It may be a complete fantasy or the prelude to an ordeal or confrontation. We need to peer into the fog of the future. Like this:

He'll come round this evening all bluster and noise. 'Did you put the hose on our cat?', wagging his podgy finger in my face. 'Ah, Mr Penny,' I'll say, very polite, 'nice of you to call again. I know what you'd enjoy. Come have a look at my fuchsias. Sorry, I forgot. They're not there anymore.' You know him. He'll start mumbling. 'She didn't say nothing about ... '

The dramatic is always lurking just below the surface of the flow of interaction, ready to surface for a moment or longer. We can see this readily if we attend to the flickers of mimicry, borrowed gestures, voices, accents. The more relaxed and informal the situation, the less cautious and self-regarding the participants, the more readily the dramatic breaks through, for like all expressiveness it withers with inhibition and coldness.

If the various forms of dramatic activity are ubiquitous, long before they put on grease paint and find their way into theatres, they permeate our consciousness even more imperiously. When we do not need them for communication we learn to internalize them. We can produce our little dramas in our heads. Vygotsky's charting of the process of the development of inner speech (1962) needs to be extended to embrace this other kind of inner representation. Piaget had proposed that egocentric speech (speech without an audience or interlocutor) in young children disappeared because their language became completely socialized. Vygotsky demonstrated that it did not vanish but was internalized. The radical reduction of egocentric speech occurs at about 7 years of age when it becomes internalized as verbal thought. Dramatic play dwindles at the same time. Inner speech, internalized action and imagery merge, and the imagination can dramatize for our purposes the explorations of our minds. Inner speech does not consist solely of interior monologue in which we listen to our voices. It can consist of the voices of others. The others and their actions can be represented by inner imagery. But internalization takes for audience the self and does not have to be shaped and edited so that others can share our understanding. Inner drama, like inner speech, is not shaped by the pressures of an immediate audience. There is gain and loss. We gain in freedom, including freedom from taboo, and lose in reality-controlled discipline. In externalized drama we are obliged to deliver our thinking to others through yet another set of personae.

The ideas I have sketched up to this point could be further elaborated and refined. I have been concerned only to show how dramatic activity occurs as part of communication and thought, that it is part of the general process of representation. Like talk itself, it is in such general, daily use that mostly it goes unremarked as something unusual. Everyone does it, most of us do it well and some are highly talented. One culture or subculture may foster it more than another. It is available as a means of knowing and explaining our world. Wherever there is vitality, spontaneity and intimacy it will out.

Institutionalized drama (theatre) may become stylized and intensely conventionalized, but it draws its strength from popular performance, just as all literary art is inconceivable without speech. Indeed, we might say that organized drama is to spontaneous enactment what written language is to speech. Therefore we should ask ourselves, 'If drama occurs without any designated apparatus, why do we need to introduce it, to develop all the paraphernalia of theatre? Does some new transforming element enter in, which cannot be present in the spontaneous, fitful, unpredictable dramas of common interaction?' I have already suggested the answer, which I can put another way. As spontaneous expressive language can become poetry, so spontaneous expressive dramatic language can become a form of art. When the dramatic impulse becomes highly ordered and controlled it becomes theatre. But a theatre is a kind of social institution and is historically evolved. It will, therefore, develop its own conventions and stylized resources for delivering a meaningful virtual experience. In the course of its development it will often become sharply differentiated from its origins.

Dramatic activity thus becomes elevated by the creation of an intense focused moment of interpretation and understanding and presupposes an audience which has willingly, eagerly submitted itself to this experience. Perhaps the most significant shift is the creation of a text, which is in our theatres the supreme form of control of the actor and the performance. In spontaneous drama we 'become' somebody else. With text the actor becomes somebody else's somebody else, somebody else's way of knowing through the dramatized word. The audience must carry out, in a highly attentive and, in a sense, collective manner, an effort of understanding, of knowing what the antics signify. That capacity, perceiving how this thing means, is firmly founded on their daily experience of tendering and receiving dramatic meaning. This will remain true of theatrical forms as diverse at Peking Opera, Malayan shadow puppets, Punch and Judy, Kathakouli dance and European ballet. The distance between these forms and Everyman in his dramatic mode may be similar to the difference between gossip and *War and Peace*. It is huge but bridged. To put it differently, we trace the progress through gradations of conscious control, degrees of performance and staging. The great Russian puppet-master who directed the most elaborate and refined puppet theatre used to put a ball on each of his forefingers and develop little dramas between the two 'people' he had created. He would insist that all that was significant in puppetry was there. The rest was elaboration. He was just as insistent that the fingers were activating the performer's built-in dramatic sense of human action.

But I have jumped a step. All spontaneous drama is a collaboration between performer and onlooker, who may easily switch roles. However, they may also combine in the sense that the onlooker takes on the game and the whole interchange is an enactment. Children's dramatic play is an absorbed collaboration of this kind. This is spontaneous group enactment in which emergent meaning must be negotiated, in the main through the drama itself, although at moments of breakdown children will readily switch to the other reality in order to sort things out.

> X: Pretend you're sick
> Y: O.K.
> X: (speaks into phone) Hey Dr Wren, do you got any medicine?
> Y: Yes, I have some medicine.
> X: (to Y) No, you aren't the doctor, remember?
> Y: O.K.

(Garvey, 1976)

For the most part, though not entirely, early dramatic play disappears. I am not sure why this is so. Is it that children share each other's construction of the world more completely and compellingly than do adults? That seems unlikely. More plausible is that we are socialized into a particular view of adult dignity and composure. We must not be caught off our guard. Spontaneity and yielding to impulse have to be tamed or at least channelled. We discriminate more and more firmly between play and work and regularize play, allotting to it a safe place. Whatever the reason, it is certainly rare for a group of adults to engage in collective spontaneous drama. It does happen. Charades are (or were?) just that, and occasionally amongst groups of intimates the invention catches fire. The probability is that the occasion has to be licensed by intimacy, informality and a sense of holiday from the work-a-day world. Drink helps. An instrumental purpose may be glimpsed in serious and business-like enactments such as the practice which has grown up in some schools of rehearsing pupils for interviews for jobs and places at college, or in 'gaming' and simulation exercises.

The growth of improvised drama in schools derives its strength from the fact that it makes room for this missing link in the chain. It offers to pupils the possibility of turning the individual and sporadic into the collective, and it provides a permanent regular space for it. Even more, it can propose areas of attention that the pupils themselves would not propose. There's the rub. For in much improvised drama, intentions are imposed on pupils that are alien to them. The dilemma is familiar enough: compare the constrained speech and abortive discussions of many classrooms with the speech of pupils outside school. Speech outside the classroom does not have to grope for motivation, nor does spontaneous drama. On the other hand, since the customary communicative style of the classroom does not invite interchanges which are like those of informal daily conversation, improvised drama can be a huge liberation. If I am right and the dramatic mode, even in its slightest and most ephemeral form, is a way of communicating and understanding, then group drama is a means of moving towards collective wisdom. Every participant's insights complement and develop everyone else's and, potentially at least, an understanding can emerge which belonged to no one at the outset. This is what we hope will emerge from discussion, but so often it does not. The analytic mode we prize and which takes so long to emerge can be short-cut by selective representation in which all the analytic processes are out of sight.

At the end of my attempts to look past the bleak little dramatic exercises being amiably and perfunctorily performed in the classrooms by those children under marching orders, I felt that if we could not do better than that we should leave human dramatic language (and more-than-language) to do its own work or perhaps make classrooms places where it would easily emerge at the right moment from a story, perhaps, or a disagreement. Fortunately, there are drama teachers who do better than that, who, building on the dramatic resources developed outside their classes, take their pupils towards a co-operative enlargement of their dramatic vocabulary and towards a collective act of giving form to experience. I was more concerned, however, to explore the ways in which drama can enter into all learning by, at one and the same time, communicating experience and giving the communicator a deeper understanding of experience. For, as Vygotsky said of play, spontaneous drama is imagination in action.

We are, I hope, coming to realize that human beings have rich and varied strategies for learning and communicating. We should be cheered and delighted by the possibility of understanding a common possession with so much potentiality. Accordingly, we should not only honour it but also give it more sustained attention. The great sociolinguist Labov (1972) almost stumbled upon his discovery that vernacular speakers translating personal experience into dramatic form can evaluate behaviour in a controlled and concentrated way. At the end of his study, which is analytical and statistical, his admiration breaks through:

> When these devices [i.e. complex linguistic devices] are concentrated and embedded deeply in the dramatic action, they can succeed in making the point. Many of the narratives cited here rise to a very high level of competence ... they will command the total attention of an audience in a remarkable way, creating a deep and attentive silence that is never found in academic or political discussion.

There is still much to discover about how spontaneous drama is constructed, how it works and the functions it fulfils. I have tried to suggest why such further explorations could be rewarding.

References

Argyle, M. (1967) *The Psychology of Interpersonal Behaviour.* Harmondsworth: Penguin.

Birdwhistell, R. (1952) *Introduction to Kinesics: An annotation system for analysis of body motion and gesture.* Washington, D.C.: Department of State, Foreign Service Institute.

Boomer, G. and Spender, D. (1976) *The Spitting Image.* Adelaide: Rigby.

Brecht, B. (1961) 'On the everyday theatre', in *Poems on the Theatre* (J. Berger and A. Bostock, trans.). Northwood, Middlesex: Scorpion Press.

Bruner, J., Jolly, A. and Sylva, K. (eds.) (1976) *Play.* Harmondsworth: Penguin.

Cassirer, E. (1953) *The Philosophy of Symbolic Forms: vol. 1, language.* New Haven, CT: Yale University Press.

Cazden, C. (1976) 'Play with language and metalinguistic awareness', in J. Bruner, A. Jolly and K. Sylva (eds.), *Play.* Harmondsworth: Penguin.

Chomsky, N. (1959) Review of Skinner's *Verbal Behaviour, Language,* 35 (1).

Chukovsky, K. (1968) *From Two to Five.* Berkeley, CA: University of California Press.

Garvey, C. (1976) 'Some properties of social play', in J. Bruner, A. Jolly and K. Sylva (eds.), *Play.* Harmondsworth: Penguin.

Goffman, E. (1959) *Presentation of Self in Everyday Life.* New York: Doubleday.

Hall, E. (1959) *The Silent Language.* New York: Doubleday.

Labov, W. (1972) *Language in the Inner City.* Philadelphia: University of Pennsylvania Press.

Piaget, J. (1951) *Play, Dreams and Imitation in Childhood.* London: Routledge and Kegan Paul.

Piaget, J. (1969) *The Science of Education and the Psychology of the Child.* London: Longman.

Rosen, H. (1972) *Language and Class: A critical look at the theories of Basil Bernstein.* Bristol: Falling Wall Press.

Rosen, H. (ed.) (1974) *Language and Class Workshop 1.* London: Language and Class Workshop.

Salmon, P. (1980) *Coming to Know.* London: Routledge and Kegan Paul.

Volosinov, V. (1973 [1929]) *Marxism and the Philosophy of Language* (M. Ladislav, and I. Tutunik, trans.). New York: Seminar Press.

Vygotsky, L. (1962) *Thought and Language.* Cambridge, MA: MIT Press.

Weir, R. (1962) *Language in the Crib.* New York: Mouton.

Language Diversity as Part of the Language Curriculum

Languages and Dialects of London School Children (1980), which Harold wrote with Tony Burgess, begins:

> In September 1977 … we received a small grant from the Department of Education and Science to enable us to carry out a limited survey of linguistic diversity in inner-London schools … Nine months after the granting of the research fund, an interim report, based on the results in eighteen schools, was submitted to the DES. [The book which follows], our second and full account, is based on the results from twenty-eight schools …

> … as far as we know, our investigation is the first of its kind to be carried out in the United Kingdom, and it constitutes a pioneer study. We are confident its findings will arouse widespread serious interest and lead to further and broader investigation which will disperse national and local ignorance.

The book presents the results of the survey, carried out, its authors are at pains to say, with the willing collaboration of the teachers and pupils in the twenty-eight schools in the then Inner London Education Authority and the neighbouring London Borough of Haringey. The survey embraced 4,600 pupils (46% of whom were boys and 54% girls) in their first year at secondary school; so they were all either 11 or 12 years old. They constituted 14% of the total age group in the secondary schools of the ILEA and Haringey.

It is impossible to do justice here to the complexity and subtlety of the findings in the book, and to their analysis. The book repays re-reading, even though the linguistic situation in London schools (and in urban schools through the UK) has changed dramatically in the decades since it was published. The bare facts reported were that:

– 70% of the 4,600 pupils were 'monolingual speakers with use of a Great Britain-based dialect of English only'; this percentage was made up of 56% speakers of London dialect, 2% speakers of a non-London non-standard dialect, and 12% speakers of Standard English

> - 14% of the 4,600 pupils were 'bilingual speakers with some use both of English and a language other than English'
> - 55 languages other than English were spoken by one or more of the bi- or multilingual pupils
> - 14% of the 4,600 pupils were 'bi-dialectal speakers with some use both of a Great Britain- and overseas-based dialect of English'
> - 24 overseas-based dialects (the great majority of Caribbean origin) were spoken by one or more of the bi-dialectal pupils
>
> There is discussion in the book of the varying levels of literacy in languages other than English, and of the phenomenon of code-switching or code-sliding, whereby speakers with access to more than one dialect of English move between them depending on the context in which they are speaking.
>
> Harold wrote chapter 4 of the book, among others. Reprinted here is a section entitled 'Language Diversity as Part of the Language Curriculum', in which he proposes that the (then) new situation of rich linguistic diversity in classrooms presents a golden opportunity for the curriculum.

During our work we derived great satisfaction from the interest taken by many pupils in our enquiry. While it was our deliberate intention that they should see it in a positive light, we had not anticipated that we would be questioned so frequently about languages and dialects. Assumptions were made about our linguistic omniscience which were flattering but unjustified. A completely unforeseen by-product of our work grew out of this interest. We had made the suggestion that one way of collecting the information we needed would be to introduce some basic ideas of diversity to the selected classes and that they could then assemble the data relating to themselves. One school took up this idea with enthusiasm and it was suggested that linguistic diversity was, if handled imaginatively, a potentially rich curriculum resource, and that language diversity of all kinds could be the core of language study. Teachers were quick to point out that any sustained effort of this kind could not be improvised. It was both uneconomic and difficult for small groups of teachers to assemble materials and to shape a new curriculum. Accordingly, a working party was set up. A very short time after its inception we were able, in June 1978, to organize a conference based on documents and materials assembled by them. The working party is still actively functioning and this section of our report is very much theirs. *This work on curriculum materials for the study of linguistic diversity and the development of a rationale is a most promising development. With financial support it could make a major contribution to the reform of language study in schools and at the same time to multicultural education.*

This is no place to discuss the scope of language study in the curriculum. We shall have to content ourselves by noting the vacuum left by the widespread abandonment of traditional grammar teaching. In general, the emphasis of English teaching has been on developing a capacity to use language well by using it rather than learning about language and its structure. Much of the criticism of the study of language in school has been based on its inadequate view of what language is and how it works, on the premature introduction of abstract concepts, its lack of effect on language performance. Bearing this in mind, we can take a closer look at some new possibilities.

The working party set out to show how their pupils' languages and dialects, those too often left at the school gates, were not problems, but a rich, natural resource for learning about language and languages. Language diversity can mean something multidimensional. It can mean, for instance, varieties of English: dialects, group languages, slangs and jargons and styles, private language, anti-languages, non-verbal languages, as well as the languages associated with sex and age and class and occupation. And it can mean, most especially, languages which are not English. In this way, diversity would include all the uses of language, in which all children, for most of the time, are skilled practitioners. Partly, this would be a matter of making public and explicit what teachers are beginning to understand. If some areas of linguistic study have been helpful to teachers, then it is time, perhaps, for pupils – some of whom have broader language experiences than many of their teachers – to be let in on the act. It is a double act, really, which uses diversity as productive and important in itself, while encouraging a view of language as a system which, more than any other, unites human beings; something they most extraordinarily have in common.

This programme for language teaching would centre on activities designed to explore language in action, language as it is used, though there would be scope for reflection on the nature of language, of its written forms, its relation to thought, its first appearance in young children. Such a programme would generate its own material and subject matter, so that general features of language could be studied as it is used, in all its variety, in the shifts and combinations of styles and registers which characterize language in its communal uses, as well as in its place within individual development.

Central to such a programme are attitudes to language: ideas about correctness, appropriateness, effectiveness. Children who are to develop as successful, confident users of language have to be encouraged to look beyond habits and prejudices, too often endorsed without explanation by teachers, examinations and employers, to the nature and implications of judgments about 'good' and 'bad' language. Children need to be aware of the ways in which language can exert power or confirm weakness. By exploring the functions and effects, as well as the constraints, of forms of spoken and written language, children may be enabled to revalue their own skills, gain much needed confidence through an appreciation of their ability to make sense of language in different modes, to move between dialects, styles, accents themselves and to interpret intention and motive from the language they attend to in others. These skills, and others, for mimicry, expressiveness and organization, for instance, are ones possessed by most children already, though a constricted view of language study can disguise them. There were many teachers who felt that by concentrating on them they themselves were more likely to discover how to help the pupils do those things they could not do yet.

It can be made to sound too easy. Language may be the pivot of human culture; it is also the touchstone of divisiveness, an area which is fraught with possibilities for pain and embarrassment. In the early days of developing the materials it was found that asking a couple of Chinese children to present a version of a story in their own language to a multi-ethnic classroom met with stubborn and articulate refusal. English children, they believed, would laugh at the story's supernatural happenings; too many things needed explaining. That episode exemplified for many teachers the problems as well as the scope of the undertaking. It made it clear, above all, that before any of the work they were proposing could go on they would have to make their classrooms places where such contributions were known to be welcome. The connections between languages and the connections between stories from different places and times have to be established, not theoretically but practically. There may be common reasons for telling stories and for the presence in them of common themes and forms and values, but the people who tell them do so in the belief that they and their hearers or readers have particular purposes and particular experiences to share. 'Language diversity' must not be a Babel, but grounds for making sense and order out of what has been allowed to remain a damaging confusion for thousands of children. It is a confusion which, at one level, allows 'O level language' or a letter of application, say, to embody 'good' English, while the speech which children first acquired, first confronted the world with, and which they now use with their families and with their friends, is accounted 'bad'. It is not a matter of introducing people who have come to live in this country to 'our' cultural heritage (a complex, controversial and, at times, hazy concept), since their arrival has, in any case, altered that 'our' irrevocably. The purpose is to take an entirely fresh look at what we share and at what we need to share from now on if we are to extend the capacities of all children to understand the nature of culture and of language, and to be free of the constraints inherent in both those forces while learning how to use them for their own purposes.

Before describing in detail the materials which have been produced and used in some multi-ethnic classrooms in London schools, it is worth mentioning one other matter. There were some teachers in the group who felt initially that such work might be difficult or even irrelevant in classrooms with a relatively monolingual population. Their doubts turned out to be unnecessary. Work which took diversity as its starting point could not fail to find such diversity. The materials have been used in schools and in classes where more than half the pupils were bilingual and where, therefore, as many as a dozen languages were spoken; and in classrooms where all the children spoke English as a mother tongue, although they also possessed a variety of dialects of English, both overseas and home-grown ones.

The materials

All the teachers involved in the creating and the using of the materials started from the survey, with collecting evidence of diversity. This, in itself, generated questions and suggested distinctions and categories. What is a mother tongue, for instance? The prevalence of a range of bilingualism and bi-dialectalism made this a difficult question to answer, even as it elicited a wealth of varied experiences. What do you think of the language or the dialect you speak and what do you think other people think of it? Or, which of your two languages or dialects do you think would be more appropriate in particular situations and with particular people? Answering questions like these has led inevitably to discussion of the status of particular languages and of the reasons people have for making judgments about them.

The next stage has often been to tape speech of different sorts produced by pupils and to listen, refine and modify such judgments. Groups of children have improvised plays on tape in different languages and dialects, translating for each other, registering the ways in which a dialect of English may produce differences of accent, structure, vocabulary, behaviour and even character. There were teachers who made use of the original survey or devised modified versions of it to get the pupils themselves, in pairs or small groups, to compile information about the languages they spoke without teacher intervention, and this effectively highlighted the queries which are bound to come up in the process of deciding how to describe any individual's linguistic biography. One English department prepared for the survey by running a series of assemblies on the theme of the children's multicultural background. They displayed a chart to show the various flags of the countries represented. Another school is preparing to produce a booklet about the languages spoken by its pupils and to include in it useful information about the school and the community as well as stories written in the different languages. Display and discussion of the wealth of dialects and languages a school or class could boast, as well as the high incidence of bilingualism and multilingualism produced considerable pride, even competitiveness, and allowed for a demonstration of some consummate imitative skills.

The group has collaborated to produce a booklet called *Languages*, which uses the classroom's languages to look at the diversity of languages in the world as a whole. It proposes work on families of languages, on the history, changes and borrowings of English and other languages. There are sections on languages with written forms and ones with none, and on the implications of different alphabetic forms and on the other kinds of symbolic systems used to convey information and ideas. For some teachers this has led to a consideration of the effects of literacy on societies, to discussion of what the ability to learn and use language tells us about human beings and societies. Another section deals imaginatively with the virtues and the difficulties of insisting upon a standard spelling. This work used dialect writing and encourages activities where children will work together to invent, improve or explore spelling systems.

The materials include tapes of children and adults telling stories in dialect and in other languages, and these have been used to discuss stories and storytelling, to explore questions about veracity, narrative authority, shaping, persuasion and implicit point of view. Using these tapes again, children have been asked to translate, interpret, paraphrase and transcribe. They have been asked to speculate about a speaker's age, biography and circumstances, to match faces and houses with examples of speech and to investigate their attitudes to speakers and to the features of a speaker's performance from which they derive these attitudes.

An outstanding benefit of the work has been its collaborative nature and the scope it allows for children to teach each other. Children have been encouraged to teach other people something about their own language, for example its written form, words for numbers or colours or days of the week. Some children have brought into school newspapers and magazines in their home languages and books they have outgrown. The *Languages* booklet suggests work for whole classes as well as for individuals. A class might, for instance, make a collection of oral and written stories, and this would involve them in transcribing and translating. The formal properties of language can be looked at comparatively. What knowledge is required to produce questions or use negatives or tenses or plurals? Do other languages mark these features in the same way? The usefulness of punctuation can also be looked at through a comparison with the way other languages operate. A selection of ideas involving codes, nonsense verse, invented words, alphabets or even grammars, rhyming slang, onomatopoeic language, bowdlerisms or malapropisms are also presented in ways which would encourage a teacher to help children to discover the formal properties of language rather than lecturing them. Children are encouraged to examine jargons and kinds of rhetoric and to describe and evaluate their use by, say, sports commentators, fashion writers, politicians, teachers, disc-jockeys. This has produced some imaginative drama work; and in general drama has turned out to be an ideal way of exploring the conceptual underpinning of language, verbal as well as non-verbal, while developing confidence in using language in ways which allow us to interpret it.

This list of possible language activities inspired by this work, an account of the writing and the speech and the dialogue it has inspired, and a look at the insights produced by it in teachers and pupils, could go on forever. In many ways this approach to language teaching thrives on itself. It is not costly and it produces its own resources. Nonetheless, resources are needed, and it would be churlish to pretend that where this work has gone on it has not made use of what can be expensive books and other materials. BBC language programmes for schools have been plundered, and Thames Television's *The English Programme* with its accompanying booklet, *Language* (Goldenberg *et al.*, 1979) has been an invaluable source of ideas. The work is necessarily dependent on talk, and this means using tape, video and film at least as much as it means books, pens and paper. All the teachers involved in the project have expressed a need for dictionaries, for books (textbooks and story books) written in the languages of their pupils. There is a need for adult speakers of these languages to teach, tell stories, interpret and translate. It is not difficult to see how a teacher-initiated and teacher-run innovation of this kind could, with adequate funding, become both more ambitious and more widely disseminated.

The Australian experience, recounted in *Curriculum and Culture* (Claydon, Wright and Rado, 1977), has much to offer teachers in urban and multicultural schools in the UK, on two counts. In their School Education Materials Project, the authors have produced curriculum material based on two principles which seem fundamental for future developments. The first is that using the languages of their pupils and helping them either with English or with a flourishing or diminishing mother tongue might be much more effectively done through teaching about subjects other than language. So far their work has been confined roughly to a territory which might be described as social studies, and has concentrated on the children's experience of the demands made by the community in which they live. It is possible to see an extension of the kind of work they are engaged in into virtually every area of the curriculum. The second principle has been that of using bilingual material within the classroom. This involves the possibility for each child to learn through double texts or bilingual tapes to approach a subject area through English or through his mother tongue, or, as he becomes more confident, through a combination of both. This has seemed to the teachers involved in developing material for multicultural mixed-ability classes the necessary next step.

Finally, to charges that this way of welcoming and capitalizing on diversity is no more than 'tokenism', barely touching on the problems underlying vital aspects of language learning in our urban schools, these teachers would wish to reply that the work itself has been stimulating, productive and illuminating for teacher and learner. They would readily agree that when a Greek-speaking child teaches his class some Greek words, thereby introducing to them some skills such as translating, interpreting, comparison and transliteration, this is by no means the only way of addressing the needs of a child in need of special help with English or of another who requires encouragement to learn or maintain his mother tongue. The situation cries out for diversity of provision, not for single solutions. But the teachers who have been involved in this work would also want to insist that using linguistic diversity within the classroom has vitally important implications for education within a multicultural society. It allows for the modifying of attitudes to languages and to dialects in ways which could be central to combat racism and prejudice generally. It also proposes a study of language based on pupils' own knowledge and experience, and in so doing forges links between school and community which can only enhance the curriculum.

References

Claydon, L., Wright, T. and Rado, M. (1977) *Curriculum and Culture*. Sydney: Allen and Unwin.

Goldenberg, S., Griffiths, P., Lee, J. and Sandra, M. (1979) *Language*. London: Thames Television/Hutchinson.

Rosen, H. and Burgess, T. (1980) *Languages and Dialects of London Schoolchildren: An investigation*. London: Ward Lock.

Language across the Curriculum

A changing agenda

> Harold wrote this piece as the introductory chapter to *Teachers, Language and Learning* (1988), edited by John Hickman and Keith Kimberley. Hickman was at the time Head of English and Senior Teacher with responsibility for staff development at Forest Gate Community School in east London. Kimberley was Lecturer in the Department of English and Media Studies at the Institute of Education, University of London. The book is an account of the explorations into the relationship between language and learning undertaken by teachers at Forest Gate.
>
> In the preface to the book, Hickman and Kimberley write:
>
>> This book began when a small group of teachers working in a school to the east of London agreed to write down talks they had given to a cross-curricular committee. It grew because other teachers followed their example and because some teachers in the school undertook small-scale investigations of their classroom practice. Slowly, almost imperceptibly at times, the book has become a record of activities across a period of six to seven years, charting ideas and initiatives in the general territory of language and learning. It now ranges widely into many aspects of the school's curriculum and organization but retains at its centre a concern to understand how students learn and how teachers can best support them …
>>
>> Despite much talk about language policies since the publication of *A Language for Life* (The Bullock Report) (The Bullock Committee, 1975), there are very few examples of the long-term development of language policies and still fewer documented accounts of the processes involved.
>>
>> We have attempted to unfold this longer-term history.

Standing behind this book is an important piece of educational history. Some of it has never been written – at least in any public form. For me this history is personal since I was very close to many of the events which were central to it. How does it belong with this book? The protracted endeavours described here, warts and all, are not only a record of a unique achievement in one school, but also grew out of a decade of attempts to put life and meaning into what has now become one of those much bandied about phrases or slogans which resound through the educational world – language across the curriculum (wisely translated by the teachers at Forest Gate School to 'language and learning'). There had been conferences, courses, books, official pronouncements and local-authority promotion before the teachers who write here got down to the difficult business of realizing in one place the translation of general policies into classroom practices. There were also, as always happens, particular individuals who were the carriers of ideas from 'outside' to the discussions reported in these pages.

One more preliminary. Amongst all the publications which flood the educational market it is all too rare to find close-focus accounts of attempts to innovate in one school. It is even rarer to find accounts written by the participants themselves. This is true of language across the curriculum. It becomes clearer every day that the enthusiasm and years of sustained work which went into attempts to turn language across the curriculum from a piety into working practices is being largely ignored in the government's proposals for a national curriculum, in the terms of reference of the Kingman Committee and in proposals for national testing. All this gives this book a special importance. We will need to turn to it (and others) because the philosophy it represents will not lie down and die. Teachers will see to that. And we can take heart from the fact that alongside current central government policy we have had the National Writing Project and the beginning of the National Oracy Project. The latter offers as two of its three aims:

> to enhance the role of speech in the learning process, 3 to 19, encouraging active learning across the curriculum; to develop the teaching of oral communication skills across the curriculum.
>
> (School Curriculum Development Committee, 1987)

Thus in its very first document it declares that it will place 'particular emphasis on process materials geared to school-based teacher development'.

I think I know where the central ideas of language across the curriculum were born. Back in the 1960s the London Association for the Teaching of English (LATE) found itself breaking out of the boundaries which had usually defined the concerns of teachers of English. We stopped minding our own business and ventured into discussing language in education, language and experience, language and thought. For we had begun to realize that some goals could never be reached if we continued to regard language as something which happened only in five or so lessons each week. We turned our attention to the integrated curriculum, group work, environmental studies; beginning to scrutinize more closely the ways in which pupils encountered and used language throughout the school day.

Much of this will sound familiar and possibly commonplace today, but twenty years ago these themes were radically new and there was very little to turn to other than our small-scale investigations and explorations, a hint here and there and some powerful theory about language and learning in scholars like Vygotsky (scarcely known at that time), Piaget and Bruner. These theoretical insights would not have flavoured our sessions if it had not been for the work of James Britton, his colleagues and teachers/students at the Institute of Education. At that time his work was known to us by word of mouth for he had not yet published *Language and Learning* (Britton, 1970). Perhaps this would all have had very little impact and the excited arguments of a few dozen teachers would have evaporated. But we began on this in 1966 when the reappraisal of the curriculum and ways of learning began to climb to the top of the educational agenda and, though we were largely unaware of it at the time, a new receptive audience was coming into being.

This was the period when the tape recorder was coming into its own. Our discussions were based on tapes which we had made of children talking in different situations and some of our assumptions were rudely challenged by what we heard. In those days it was possible to write books about children's language and indeed about language in general without including a single transcript of real live talkers. We began with talk, seeing it as at the heart of learning and discovering ways in which it was managed in the classroom. The culmination of two years' activity came in May 1968. We wanted to make an impact, to achieve a wider dissemination of our ideas. We set about formulating a manifesto which would be relevant to teachers of subjects other than English. It was produced in the heat of our discussions by five groups in half a morning, typed and duplicated in a lunch hour, finally stitched together and edited by a small committee. It was a prodigious effort by forty or so teachers. To the best of my recollection it was at that weekend conference that the phrase 'language across the curriculum' was born.

How did we propose to disseminate our ideas? We were fortunate in having eagerly ready Martin Lightfoot of Penguin Books. In 1969 he published *Language, the Learner and the School* (Barnes, Britton, Rosen and the LATE, 1969) which contained a research report by Douglas Barnes on 'Twelve Lessons in the First Term of Secondary Education', a piece by James Britton called 'Talking to Learn' and a short piece which I wrote on behalf of LATE to introduce 'A Language Policy Across the Curriculum'. The success of the book in terms of its circulation, national and international, took us by surprise given the modest circumstances in which it had been born. In 1971 a new and revised version was published and I expanded the few pages introducing the language policy document to some fifty, which I more cautiously entitled 'Towards a Language Policy Across the Curriculum' [see chapter in this collection]. It included some discussion of theory and of the ideas generated by the first edition and a much revised version of the policy proposals which now concluded:

> Arising from discussion and investigation it should be possible for some
> schools to put into operation a language policy which would act as a guide

to all their teachers. Such a policy would, of course, be developed and modified in the light of the experience gathered from its formulation and application and would, therefore, be shaped to meet the needs of specific schools.

We know now, for we have learnt the hard way, that to embark on both the formulation and application of a language policy in a school is to tread a long hard road. This book from Forest Gate School takes us down that road. But we knew back there in 1971 that it would be fatal to propose a policy suited to every school, a Platonic blueprint. Here too this book shows how true this is. A warning to those assiduous compilers of guidelines, objectives and national curricula.

The Bullock Report (1975) gave its blessing to language across the curriculum. In Chapter 12 we find:

> We strongly recommend that whatever the means chosen to implement
> it a policy for language across the curriculum should be adopted by every
> secondary school.

Such a recommendation could easily be a mixed blessing. Indeed some authorities, in their eagerness to toe the line, made peremptory demands that schools hand over a language policy in short order! At Forest Gate, we can see a delicate awareness of some of the less desirable consequences of the Bullock Report's blessing. Indeed, its Language and Learning Committee went further and, from the outset, declared its intention 'to explore processes rather than write a policy'. This may well be one of the most important pointers of the book. The documents which constitute this book create a different universe from one which issues marching orders. Though our original intention of dramatizing the issues through the language policy document may have been right at the time, we should now give them a different emphasis, much more like Forest Gate's – share, discuss, investigate, report, propose. But remember that the Bullock Report gave a mere five pages of its 600 to language across the curriculum. Yet the impact of that short chapter was enormous. It stimulated discussion at all levels and set in train many initiatives in many schools.

Yet when all is said and done the results overall were disappointing. In *Bullock Revisited* (Department of Education and Science, 1982) a certain disenchantment was very evident. The Forest Gate teachers could tell you why. They would be the last to set themselves up as a model. But what they demonstrate by their evidence and their appraisal of it is that, even with their refined and principled tact, the process of working on language and learning within one school is slow and to some extent unpredictable. Success turns on the style of work which teachers settle for, not one which an authority, however benign, dictates to them. They show further that their growth of understanding was much more than hoisting themselves up by their bootstraps. They were in touch. By 1980, it was possible to link up with other activities of various kinds. They may well insist that their school is ordinary. I think that they are right. But we have to seek for those forces at work which enabled them to carry on from 1980 to 1987 and, indeed, to emerge with a serious and important publication at the end of it.

The work undertaken did not consist of individualistic fantasies nor did it exist simply within one school. It took place in relation to a back-drop of local and regional involvements, national research projects, subject associations, and, for many individual teachers, wove into their studies for award-bearing courses. The precise details of this back-drop emerge in the text again and again. There were teachers in the school who had connections with a network in which language across the curriculum was quietly being revised, expanded and rewritten. Why was that necessary?

I leave aside the fact that, in 1969, and even in the Bullock Report, the ideas were largely programmatic. To be more precise there was no living example which could be cited of a school which by one means or another had made language and learning a significant feature of its planning. In the intervening decade, new and burning issues forced themselves onto the agenda. When we set out our proposals, we were fully conscious of the fact that most schools had no agenda in the sense of a more or less democratic machinery created for the discussion and planning of the curriculum. All that changed. In this sense Forest Gate was, as the teachers insist, 'ordinary'. Documented meticulously here is the process by which the teachers fashioned an apparatus suited to the complex ideas which they wanted to pursue, shaped to enable them to teach each other and to help them 'become their own experts'. This documentation is the more important because it records frankly the stumblings, the reservations, the disagreements. We would learn less from it if it did not. The staff booklet on talking and learning never got beyond the introduction! The record of attempts to get down to some theoretical reading (ambitious, even avant-garde) reveals how an apparently splendid idea can partly founder when it meets reality.

But let me return to the new agenda of the 1970s. We know it now almost as an incantation: racism, gender, and class. These were the thundering silences in our efforts of the 1960s, which were guilty of assuming a basically benign context for innovation. It was as though we assumed that if only people could be persuaded that talk in the classroom was a liberating force, that writing for real purposes would help students to learn, that the reader was an active creator of meaning, that students could help each other to learn – then all would be well. Needless to say those ideas and others still need promoting, enriching, and modifying. They remain firmly at the heart of the enterprise and at Forest Gate we can see that process at work. But we can also see the new agenda surfacing.

As the teachers settled down to their discussions, they did so well aware that another slogan-programme was filling the air. It was called multicultural education and, like language across the curriculum, was being promoted at all levels and in various forms. Even the Department of Education and Science, in muted and cautious language, gave it currency. But the teachers would also have been conscious of the scepticism and hostility, particularly in the black community, which insisted that the core issue was racism and how to combat it in schools. Jon McGill's paper (cited in Chapter 4 of this book) shows how early in its life the Language and Learning Committee addressed the question. Racism is not a matter of language alone; yet language is installed in it whether we are looking at minority languages, the prejudices and vicious myths incorporated in the English language, or how all kinds of school texts transmit and perpetuate a white racist view of the world. The images, icons, assumptions, and references of racism stalk the pages of texts we turn every day. Jon McGill urged his colleagues to address matters of this kind:

> ... it is pointless to abdicate the responsibility of suggesting how we might better inform ourselves, how we might be more aware of the interference of our own prejudices or standards in the education of all children.
>
> (Hickman and Kimberley [eds.], 1988)

It is clear from Jon McGill's paper and many other passages in the book that the language issues linked to racism belong with an awareness of linguistic diversity. Schools were slow to come to terms with the dramatically new configurations in the language repertoire of their students. The presence of speakers of dozens of languages and dialects had of course been registered but remained unstudied and unreflected on. The drive was to teach them English as fast as possible and, in the 1970s, the ESL teacher became a familiar figure in the schools.

Slowly a change became perceptible not unconnected with the growing awareness of racism. It manifested itself as an effort to uncover the 'basic facts', to discover which languages and dialects were spoken by the school population, by how many of them, to what extent, and for what purposes. The answer to these simple questions turned out to be very complicated as we discovered when we set about the survey reported in *Languages and Dialects of London Schoolchildren* (Rosen and Burgess, 1980), to be followed by the much larger-scale investigation by the Linguistic Minorities Project reported in *The Other Languages of England* (Linguistic Minorities Project, 1985). But these investigations were much more than surveys. We set out in a final chapter the educational implications of our findings and the researchers of the Linguistic Minorities Project, through their dissemination wing, did the same. Both these projects were known to the teachers at Forest Gate through the fine web which connected them with the world of research via individuals and organizations.

The presence of large number of students of Asian and Caribbean origin would have made it almost inevitable that the teachers would address the linguistic diversity under their noses. What was by no means so inevitable was that they would do so with such high awareness. I see none of the glib assent to comfortable formulae in their deliberations. Naz Rassool epitomizes this with her insistence that the rationale of bilingualism cannot be a comfortable pluralism, but that language learning must 'challenge the predominantly monocultural and monolinguistic perspectives' (cited in Chapter 15). Forest Gate teachers were thus both exhibiting and contributing to a linguistic awareness which made the early 1970s look distant and insensitive. So we find in this book an account of a vigorous Bilingualism Working Party; and a readiness to take on a new approach to English as a Second Language, shifting it to the mainstream classroom. There is a glimpse of a first-year English programme which includes the Forest Gate Language Survey (see Document 4 in the Appendix) and of 'community' language provision in the fourth- and fifth-year curriculum.

Of course linguistic diversity is not only about readily perceived languages and dialects. Diversity is in each one of us and in apparently homogeneous communities. Nowhere is this more apparent than in social-class variation and the role of Standard English. Throughout the 1970s, the educational significance of the relationship between language and class was the battleground for a major clash. What was it all about? Fundamentally it was about the educability of working-class children, contrasted unfavourably with that of middle-class children. It was a battle between those who regarded working-class language (whatever that was – dialect? code?) as an inadequate instrument for learning and those who not only saw it as adequate but possessing its own strengths.

I oversimplify in those brief sentences and refer to the issue for one reason alone. I find very little direct attention given to it by the Forest Gate teachers. I get a sense that they had left all that behind them, had taken a stance before the Language and Learning Committee came together. Or it may be that the 'old' issue of language and class was now subsumed under wider concerns. Indeed, my feeling is that the teachers just assume their students are as capable of learning as any others. They concentrate on how best to foster that learning. If I am right, then what the teachers seem to be saying, but only implicitly, is, 'We finished that item of the agenda before we began on ours.' The issue will not, of course, go away as a matter of general concern. It haunts the pages of *English 5 to 16* (Her Majesty's Inspectorate, 1984) just as it did the Bullock Report. Linguistic deprivation, as it came to be known, seems to be a non-issue at Forest Gate, at least in the activities of the Language and Learning Committee; what the non-participants thought is another matter.

It is a tribute to the growth of feminism in the country at large, and amongst teachers in particular, that after 1970 it became almost impossible to engage in serious educational discussion without including gender. To go back before that date is to discover that gender questions had left the schools virtually untouched. A re-reading of my own, and like-minded colleagues', pre-1970 publications is embarrassing. Yet it comes as no surprise that one of the subgroups at Forest Gate concerned itself with issues of gender and race. They had at their disposal a host of reports and studies which showed beyond doubt that in the management of classroom discourse (who is listened to, what is ignored), in the selection of texts, in the texts themselves, in subtle ways of transmitting expectations, sexism was the order of the day in schools.

The ways in which the wider discourse of the educational world found its way into the Language and Learning Committee can be found in every chapter. Against their preoccupations, the priorities being put before us at this moment seem like irrelevancies but for the power which sustains them. The teachers do not spend their time debating which grammar items should figure in the curriculum nor how they might best conduct tests of language development at 11, 14 and 16. On the contrary, they look to the outside for work which gives them deeper understanding.

Let me take just one example. We know a lot more now about language in classrooms. It is true that some linguists and sociologists pursue their researches in classrooms in order to address their own disciplines and with no concern for questions of learning. On the other hand we can point to Douglas Barnes' development from the work reported in *Language, the Learner and the School* to that reported in *Communication and Learning in Small Groups* (Barnes and Todd, 1977). The titles tell all. Edwards and Furlong (1978) have argued fully on the basis of their classroom evidence in *The Language of Teaching* that:

> ... teachers can never actually transmit knowledge, for they are still dependent on the pupil undertaking his own interpretive work and making the necessary links for himself. Only by engaging in this essentially creative process can he enter the teacher's system of meanings. Only in this way can he learn.

There are echoes there of the stance taken on language and learning right from the beginning. The difference lies in the fact that Edwards and Furlong base their conclusion on the fine detail of their classroom evidence. The work continues, as we can see from the socio-psychological approach of Edwards (a different one) and Mercer in *Common Knowledge: The development of understanding in the classroom* (Edwards and Mercer, 1987). I drop these few names (many more could be cited) to indicate that we have come a long way and stand on stronger ground. The intellectual and theoretical base for work like that of the Language and Learning Committee is wide and deep and teachers should know it. I might, with more space, have shown how the same is true of our understanding of the reading process and the role of the reader, the act of writing, and advances in the understanding of the relationship between language and thought.

In spite of attempts to exile it from official pronouncements, the concern for language and learning will not go away. This account of how teachers undertake for themselves the same kinds of learning processes as those they hope to develop with their students will help us to ensure that that will be so. For we have presented here a unique compilation which gradually lays bare the intricacies of trying to convert high aspirations into working practices. It is a unique record but not a unique experience.

We need particularly strongly at this time to tell each other the stories of our lives in teaching and to remind those who propose from afar what life in schools is really like. Had we known at that weekend conference that what we were saying would make a contribution to the coming into being of this book we would have been incredulous but thrilled. And there's a moral in that.

References

Barnes, D., Britton, J. Rosen, H. and the LATE (1969 and 1971 [revised edition]) *Language, the Learner and the School.* Harmondsworth: Penguin.

Barnes, D. and Todd, F. (1977) *Communication and Learning in Small Groups.* London: Routledge and Kegan Paul.

Britton, J. (1970) *Language and Learning.* London: Allen Lane.

The Bullock Committee (1975) *A Language for Life* (the Bullock Report). London: HMSO.

Department of Education and Science (1982) *Bullock Revisited: A discussion paper by HMI.* London: HMSO.

Edwards, A. and Furlong, V. (1978) *The Language of Teaching.* London: Heinemann.

Edwards, D. and Mercer, N. (1987) *Common Knowledge: The development of understanding in the classroom.* London: Methuen.

Her Majesty's Inspectorate (1984) *English from 5 to 16.* London: HMSO.

Hickman, J. and Kimberley, K. (eds.) (1988) *Teachers, Language and Learning.* London: Routledge.

Linguistic Minorities Project (1985) *The Other Languages of England.* London: Routledge and Kegan Paul.

Rosen, H. and Burgess, T. (1980) *Languages and Dialects of London School Children: An investigation.* London: Ward Lock.

School Curriculum Development Committee (1987) *National Oracy Project Planning Brief.* London: School Curriculum Development Committee.

The Politics of Writing

Harold contributed this essay to *New Readings – Contributions to an understanding of literacy*, edited by Keith Kimberley, Margaret Meek and Jane Miller and published in 1992. He also included a version of the piece in his collection of stories and articles *Troublesome Boy* (1993). The version here is a combination of the two texts.

This essay is the prosing of a hefty fistful of notes for a lecture I gave in Detroit in 1983 to the National Council of Teachers of English. It bears the marks of a certain podium style, but I decided to let that stand. In view of the recent burgeoning of genre theory and more particularly of a pedagogy of genres, mostly Australian (see, for example, Kress 1982 and 1989, Reid 1987), it seemed to me worth making this available.

Let's begin with a story with a happy ending. On a certain day in autumn for certain, for in the Bronx or Brixton we have to wait until the harvest is in, Little Audrey begins her first day at school. The chemistry of a long-drawn-out metamorphosis is launched. Up to this point Little Audrey has relied on the mere accident of birth, the chance encounters of everyday life and on the unplanned and frequently repulsive didactics of the subculture (a euphemism for sub-groups) for her education. But now, if all goes well, our infant is going to be socialized at state expense, that is, she is going to be inducted into the mainstream culture. And if there's one thing we can be sure of it is that a central pillar of that culture is literacy. I must rush towards our happy ending – when our infant emerges at the other end, she will not only be civilized into being a good citizen but will also have acquired the very special, indeed superordinate, achievement of literacy. As numerous experts have told us, this leads to profound changes in the psyche. Little Audrey will have acquired, so they say, abstract, context-free thought, rationality, powers of criticism, detachment, in sum a totally new way of looking at the world which will change the whole cast of her cognitive processes (see Ong, 1982; Goody, 1977; Olson, 1977). And all that at the mere cost of learning to read and write. Since we are concerned today specifically with learning to write, let me cite Olson's well-known essay, 'From utterance to text' (1977), as typical.

> ... the invention of the alphabetic writing system gave to Western culture many of its predominant features including an altered conception of language and altered conception of rational man. These effects came about, in part, from the creation of explicit, autonomous statements,

> statements dependent upon an explicit writing system, the alphabet and
> an explicit form of argument, the essay.

O lucky and thrice-blessed Little Audrey!

Forgive my sceptical tone so far. But remember we are a special group, very much predisposed not to question the value of writing (we earn our living by it!) and we are anxious to learn about better ways of teaching it. I too believe in the value of writing but in nothing like the unproblematic way that Olson and others do. So let me try to disturb you a little. I will add a little to my story. Little Audrey had been introduced to the special cultural joys described by Olson and at the end of a year she was able to write the words in the blank spaces in standardized tests. She had thus 'an altered conception of rational man'. One day a gentle old French professor called Michel de Certeau was visiting her classroom and saw her engaged on a writing task. He walked up to her and whispered into her ear:

> To write ... is to be forced to march through enemy territory.

Little Audrey never forgot the professor's words even when (especially when!) she was filling in her tax from, writing assignments in freshman English and applying for research grants. She had by then of course bought a copy of de Certeau's remarkable book, *The Practice of Everyday Life* (1984). I shall come back to his disturbing and outrageous notion, but for the moment I shall assume that you find the idea a little odd (at the very least) and perhaps lunatic. Certainly it does not match the enthusiasms of Olson and others who hint at no such thing. But if you find the idea odd, I ask you to recollect having to write a piece of formal prose recently: a report, an official letter of some length, the minutes of a meeting or, better still, a letter of application for a job. My guess is that you experienced some tension between what you wanted to say and what you knew were the expectations of how you should say it. A self-censorship produces a calcified prose you would gladly disown.

There is, after all, a common way of treating socialisation, especially sociali-sation into a specific kind of literate culture. We all know that from the moment of their birth all children have to be changed from little animals into social human beings. One way (not mine) of looking at this process is to say quite simply that the complex organism we call society, heterogeneous and elusive as it may be, is sustained, confirmed and reproduced by a set of norms and rules, and that basically a child's socialisation consists in learning those rules and governing her practices in the light of them. There are obvious refinements on this model, the incorporation of some diversity of norms and rules and sub-systems; but in general, as Agnes Heller (1982) puts it:

> ... professionalism [in the social sciences] ... views society as it exists, the
> status quo as a datum ... [it] is concerned to investigate but not to change,
> at most to improve the way society works.

To put it another way, the social system is looked upon as lying in wait for us with a whole apparatus of practices, values, beliefs and so on, and we are irresistibly drawn into them. Let me say very briefly what I think is wrong with that model.

(a)   The social system always confronts us at a particular moment in history.

(b)   Because power is unequally distributed, some practices will be given high value not because of their intrinsic merit but because they are validated by the powerful.

(c)   Many of the most important practices in the culture help to keep the powerful powerful, though they are never presented that way but rather as universal or value-free or in their final state of evolution.

(d)   The model does not offer us any understanding of the conflict of values and of practices except as deviance or maladjustment, and so on.

To come down to earth from those generalisations, let me cite an instance of how the discourse of social scientists has its parallel in everyday discourse in one of its most common locations, school. I borrow the example from Henry Giroux (1983).

> Mrs Caplow is a kindergarten teacher working on a unit devoted to citizenship. The aim of the unit, she says, is to teach 'respect for the law'. As part of her scheme she appoints a 'sheriff' from among the children. The sheriff interprets this by pushing and shoving the children who step out of line. Here is the exchange conducted for the reader's benefit.
>
> Mrs Caplow: David, can you tell Mr Rist why you are wearing a star?
>
> David: 'Cause I the sheriff.
>
> Mrs C: Can you tell him how you got to be sheriff?
>
> D: By being a good citizen.
>
> Mrs C: David, what do good citizens do?
>
> D: They check up on others.
>
> Mrs C: Well that's not all they do.
>
> *(Mrs C repeats the question for Frank.)*
>
> Frank: Good citizens obey the rules.
>
> Mrs C: That's right, Frank, good citizens obey the rules, no matter what they are.

I quote that exchange because it makes brutally explicit what for most of the time is conveyed by much more oblique means: the tacit assumptions behind everyday discourse and practices which naturalise the way society works, and are familiar to us, perhaps, as the hidden curriculum. In its most extreme form the basic assumption subsumes these ideas:

(a)   Society as we know it is in a state of achieved perfection, or, if it is not, it has never been bettered and never will be.
(b)   We must play our cards right to ensure that no inferior form asserts itself.
(c)   The 'rules' are in no way problematic.
(d)   Society is not a legitimate site for conflict, since it is neutral and even-handed: the same rules apply for all.

What has all this got to do with writing? What about all those things we hear so much about like conferencing, redrafting, paragraphing, the use of journals, topic sentences, and so on? Perhaps you will have glimpsed a way of reading what I have been presenting which points in that direction. Mrs Caplow can be read in this way. A good writer (citizen) obeys the rules no matter what they are. And I don't just mean grammatical rules, spelling rules and so on, but also discourse rules. One of the very few writers to have taken a sociocultural view of writing, Gunther Kress (1982), puts the matter gloomily when discussing genres, which we might call forms of discourse or kinds of writing. These different kinds of writing, he says,

> ... are fixed, formalized and codified. Hence the learning of genres involves an increasing loss of creativity on the child's part and a subordination of the child's creative abilities to the demands of the genre.

Or, later in the book,

> ... just as there is a fixed number of sentence types so there exists a small fixed number of genres within any written tradition.

Now Kress is aware that kinds of writing are related to our social system, but he never works out satisfactorily what that relationship is. The idea that writing is fixed, formalised and codified needs examining more closely. It is only partly so. There is not a fixed number of genres. Note in passing that Kress does not reveal this magic number, although, if there are so few, it should be an easy business to do so. Moreover, the writing police – editors, employers, writers of school manuals and self-appointed controllers of other people's language – try to promote this world of fixed genres, so that discourse itself in all its heterogeneity comes under the yoke of sets of rules. For all their intimidation they never quite succeed. Kress clearly perceives that learning to write is a form of socialisation, but he sees this in a determinist way. According to him there is no escaping the iron rules.

> Learning language is one of the highly developed rule systems ... Learning genres ... represents the child's socialization into appropriate and accepted

modes of organizing knowledge. It is important to recognize that genres have this constraining effect and that they are conventions.

So we are back to the rule of law and order, with this important difference, that Kress sees the source of that law and order and does not give it his stamp of approval. One interesting remark he makes is:

> Other conventions can be imagined: indeed it is one of the main points of this book that children constantly invent their own modes of organizing and knowing which, however, do not become recognised as such but rather are categorized as errors.

It is my argument that to behave as though adult forms of writing are fixed and codified is to accept the messages which power delivers and to ignore what actually happens. The legitimised forms of writing are in fact constantly being eroded and undermined – and not just by children – just as are other powerful social norms, the family, for instance. Writing is a site of conflict, and ferocious play goes on within its boundaries. Old forms die out and new ones appear, others are in a state of flux. This is especially true if we stop thinking of typical prose and look at other forms. A few examples. First, consider obsolete and obsolescent forms. I take off the shelf beside me *A History of Leicester*, J. Throsby, 1791. It begins with the now obsolete sycophantic style of dedication complete with special layout.

To the

Right Honourable

George Townsend

Earl of the County of Leicester

Baron de Ferrars of Chartley

Lord Bourchier, Lorraine, Bassett and Compton

My Lord

As the following sheets are the first published attempt at a regular history, the writer looks up to your Lordship in particular, as Patron to his labours. Your Lordship's supereminent station in the Antiquarian Society and your illustrious descent from the renowned Earls of Leicester show the propriety of this address

He is,
  My Lord
    with due deference
    John Throsby

Dedications are now either omitted entirely or go like this:

> For Boyd, Elizabeth, Greta without whom I could not have gotten on.
>
> > (Heath, 1983)

Where is the code which specifies the rules governing those texts? What is the fixed, formalised, codified set of rules for writing a philosophical work? Would the rules (how many?) enable you to predict a passage of this next type?

> Once upon a time there was a man; we tell his story. Once upon a time there was a King, and he had three sons; we tell their miraculous stories. Once upon a time there was a hunter ...

This is taken straight from Agnes Heller's *A Theory of History* (1982). But then, Heller is not only a radical who writes but also someone who writes radically. And that is precisely my point. Of course there are many, many texts which we could group together and through analysis show to be governed by a code; but:

(a) The rules are by no means as rigid as some (for instance, dogmatic manual-writers and codifiers) would maintain.

(b) The rules are constantly being abandoned, subverted, mocked, ignored, sometimes as a deliberate act of refusal, sometimes as intuitive innovation.

(c) The rules are tightest where very direct controls operate and a certain measure of power is in the hands of certain controllers – editors, employers, teachers, who themselves came through a formation likely to make them eager rule-obeyers.

There is a long history to the evolution of this state of affairs. It has yet to be written. For the moment let us take a look at one corner of the field. Harvard Educational Review, which in practice is an enlightened journal and tolerates some diversity, informs its contributors that:

> All copy, including indented matter, footnotes and references, should be typed double-spaced and justified to the left margin only. The author should be identified only on the title page. Manuscripts should conform to the publication guidelines of the APA (for technical and research articles), the MLA Handbook (for theoretical, descriptive, or essay-style articles) or The Uniform System of Citation published by the Harvard Law Review (for legal articles). For general questions of style authors should consult The Chicago Manual of Style.

The recollection of lengthy transatlantic telephone calls from *Harvard Educational Review* reminds me just how seriously all this is taken. No wonder Enzensberger once remarked that we can see an attempt in our society to industrialise the mind. The attempt to drill students into conforming to certain supposed rules of discourse amounts to nothing less than the imposition of a code of unquestioning obedience.

It turns them and us away from asking the important questions. Eagleton (1983) puts this simply:

> The language of a legal document or scientific text may impress or even intimidate us because we do not see how the language got there in the first place. The text does not allow the reader to see how the facts it contains were selected, what was excluded, why these facts were organized in this particular way, what assumptions governed this process, what forms of work went into the making of the text and how all this might have been different.

In other words, concealed beneath the surface of the most humdrum document, which we would take for granted as a satisfactory not-to-be-tampered-with means for achieving its end, there is always a deeper social process at work. As students proceed through our schools and possibly into higher education they are unlikely to be encouraged to probe their own writing and that of others for the workings of this deeper social system. One form a writing workshop might take would be the interrogation of a set of texts like these:

(a)   Contrary to the impression we may have given in this column on 16th March, the Acme Thunder Railway Guards' Whistle marketed by Mailpost is made by J Hudson and Co. (Whistles) Ltd., a British firm which has been manufacturing whistles for more than 130 years. The whistles offered by Mailpost are replicas.

(b)   We are seeking to appoint an Officer in Charge to our Hostel for 20 emotionally and mentally distressed young adults at 15 Homerton Row, E.9. Applications are invited from mature, experienced men/women with qualities of management. The successful applicant …

(c)   Mum, Back at 11.30. Don't lock garden door. Leave caviar and champers in fridge. Chaz.

Jay Lemke, in a fascinating paper (1982), asked a set of questions which might be applied to any text and which we might use to deconsecrate them:

> Who is doing what to whom in this text?
>
> How?
>
> What other texts and doings stand in what relevant relations for the meanings made and the acts performed by this text?
>
> What social systems are maintained or altered by what relations among the set of texts to which we may assign this one?
>
> What social interests and their conflicting discourses are being served or contested in this text and through its intertextual relations?

How does the text contribute to the maintenance and change of the linguistic system and the patterns of use of that system in the community?

To ask questions of this kind is, as Lemke says, 'to strengthen our ability to dispel the sense of givenness and inevitability … and better arm us to contest them'. It might lead us to consider more carefully what we ask our students to write and how we respond to anything which is fresh and liberating. We need to look at every form of writing as a specific form of social practice embedded in our social system and impregnated with its own social history. Our kind of scientific writing, for example, is the culmination of three centuries of the development of science as an institution and is therefore likely to be thought to have attained a state of immutable perfection. When we have served an apprenticeship in any particular genre of writing we are neither inevitably nor inextricably enmeshed in its rule system. But greater awareness of that system and how it works can enable us to begin to free ourselves from some at least of its oppressive features.

Over the last fifteen years there has been a significant shift in research energies directed towards investigating language in schools. Writing has been discovered. We are in the process of redressing a strange imbalance (another piece of social history). When we began our writing research at the Institute of Education in 1966 there was available a whole library of work on reading, whereas worthwhile work on writing consisted of a mere handful of books and monographs. We now have the results of large funded projects, a proliferation of models of the writing process, analyses of students' written texts, maps of functional diversity, blueprints for patterns of development and much more. A discriminating study of this literature can teach us a great deal. But in preparing this paper I set my face against reviewing fresh material. For all the insights and useful findings there has been a consistent failure to address the issues I have been exploring. There has been no attempt to question the goal (good writing? mature writing? competent writing? genre writing? and so on). Largely, the goals have been taken for granted, no matter how elaborated they have become, and the debate has focused on the route. To put it simply, the unspoken proposition is, 'We know what good adult writing looks like: so let us research the best ways of attaining it. If we know what kinds of acceptable language are used in our society then we can devise better ways of training students to use them.' In terms of the old pieties this is part of the process of preparing children for society. Since there are many kinds of writing, we will need to establish priorities. Up pop the old favourites – the business letter, the job application, the essay. Should we add advertising copy? Kress is almost alone among those addressing writing in schools in pointing out that

To become proficient in the genre one has to become absorbed of these contents [i.e. ideological and cognitive contents] and of the institution itself. Effective teaching of genres can make the individual into an efficiently intuitive and unreflective user of the genre. The genre and its

> meanings will come to dominate the individual … and this is so whether
> he be scientist, bureaucrat or short story writer … Is that what we want?

I do not hear that question being asked by most of those engaged currently on work on writing. I grumble once again at Kress's assumption that the more we are drawn into the system the more inevitably we accept its hidden agenda. The literate culture is full of examples of writers who conduct unceasing guerrilla warfare against it. How for example do you write for an audience of educationists about writing? Easy. Follow this model. It comes from a collection of papers (Freedman and Pringle 1980). This writer slips into the mode like a homing bird.

> A common assumption shared by many rhetoricians is that the act of composing is linear. Gordon Rohman, for example, distinguishes three stages in the composing process: first the pre-writing, then the writing, and finally the re-writing. Pre-writing, like Aristotelian invention, is …
>
> (Butturf and Sommers, in Freedman and Pringle, 1980)

And so it continues. However, what we do find in this same volume in which one contribution after another obediently follows the tradition (as indeed does this essay for the most part!) is a contribution from Don Murray (1980) which begins by cheerfully defying the code, the rules and expectations.

> Emptiness. There will be no more words. Blackness. No, white without colour. Silence.

> I have not any words all day. It is late and I am tired in the bone. I sit on the edge of the bed, open the notebook, uncap the pen. Nothing. Or.

> Everything has gone well this morning. I wake from sleep, not dreams.

What follows is a set of juxtaposed stories, a collage, with none of the devices the manuals tell us are so necessary. A modernist text with the author's thumbprints all over it and the man unashamedly declaring himself.

All this leaves me in an uncomfortable position. Yes, the Don Murrays of this world, established and secure, may be able to thumb their noses at the conventions, but their ways are scarcely a credible recipe for the teaching of writing. Suppose we do have an understanding that writing is an interlocking set of social practices shaped by the context of the society we live in. What are we expected to do about it? The students eventually have to get jobs, don't they? If they don't toe the line, they are finished. And how could we possibly change our teaching to accommodate the alternative view? The first part of my answer, as I have been suggesting, is that the Kress picture insufficiently accommodates the subtle diversity of possibilities within the written language and the promiscuity of genres. These possibilities are present from the moment a child starts to write. The real issue is whether we exploit these possibilities and help students to avoid being drawn inexorably into the embrace of house styles. The one theorist who sheds a helpful light on this matter is Bakhtin. He alone provides a base which shows how every act of writing can potentially break the code within which it is operating. In his book, *The Dialogic Imagination* (1981), he argues that two forces are always at work in language use: he calls them centrifugal and centripetal. The centripetal describes all that which pulls us towards a centre of prescribed norms, genre conventions, discourse etiquettes, and so on. The counterforce is centrifugal, which pulls us away from the normative centre. Bakhtin writes:

> Every utterance serves as a point where centrifugal as well as centripetal forces are brought to bear. The processes of centralization and decentralization, of unification and disunification, intersect in the utterance.

Linked with these concepts is Bakhtin's contrast between authoritative and internally persuasive discourse.

> ... in one the authoritative word (religious, political, moral, the word of the father, of adults, of teachers, etc.) that does not know internal persuasiveness; in the other the internally persuasive word that is denied all privilege, backed up by no authority at all and is frequently not acknowledged in society (not by public opinion, nor by scholarly norm).

Authoritative discourse demands

> our unconditional allegiance – permits no play within its borders, no gradual or flexible transitions, no creative stylizing variants. It is indissolubly fused with authority. All is inertia and calcification.

Bakhtin's elaboration is much more complex than this, but I have cited enough to show that his ideas open up new possibilities for students and teachers alike. We can see in every act of writing those two forces at work. We can never totally escape the centripetal pull: we cannot jump out of the language system and its practices. On the other hand we do not have to elevate that system into an object which has achieved perfection. On the contrary, it is necessary to insist again and again on the need to disrupt the authoritative voice with the unheard voices of our students, to help them engage in the difficult struggle (so difficult for all of us) to articulate, develop, refine and advance their meanings as against the mere reproduction of the words of the textbook, the worksheet, the encyclopaedia and the guides. To insist on this involves squaring up to the oppressive power of authoritative language. Millions of notebooks, examination papers and 'essays' are crammed with words which are in essence no more than transcriptions, the forced labour of submission. The very least we can do is to emancipate ourselves from the notion that there is only one good and proper way, and that that way is quite rightly prescribed by others, because they are paying the piper or because we have bowed before their assured authority without question.

What I find cheering is that many who would not subscribe to the views I have expressed or at any rate to the idiom in which I have expressed them know all that in their bones. They are the centrifugal teachers. (See the writing in *Beat Not the Poor Desk* [Ponsot and Dean 1982].) In the early days of the National Writing Project in the UK John Richmond (1986) shrewdly set out in diagrammatic form seven 'Key Ideas' about writing and placed them tellingly against 'what often happens in schools'. I should stress that he also extends an invitation to amend, add and disagree. He does not in fact address the issue I have been trying to elaborate. Yet if we write it in as a subtext, each of the key ideas can be seen in sharper form. Let me try this with a few of them. 'Writers as Assessors' is one of his key ideas, which he enlarges on.

> The development of a critical sense, the ability to get outside your own or someone else's product, to make judgements, is an essential half of the reflexivity between creation and criticism. Writers need it.

Agreed. But what is the platform from which the criticism is to be launched? Any well-indoctrinated students – including very young ones – may have internalised a set of criteria which will lead them to place their own efforts solely against the authoritative model. Are there binding rules for the structure of a story? Or a lab report? What kind of teaching emancipates students from that punishing form of self-criticism?

'Collaboration' is another of Richmond's key ideas.

> The process of interaction, conversation, mutual support and criticism grants orientation and critical space to the writer as well as the benefits of others' ideas.

This is better still. For here is the moment when the large social processes filter into everyday exchanges, but also when the culture and values of the students have a chance to emerge, though only if teachers nurture and validate centrifugal moves. There is a huge discourse of experience which is largely censored out, and collaboration is one way to let it in. It must be added that if what is being collaborated on is itself suspect (the imitation of a piece of inflated descriptive writing, for instance) collaboration will contribute very little or nothing.

'Development' is a third of Richmond's key ideas.

> All writers come from somewhere and are going towards somewhere as long as they keep writing. Going towards somewhere else does not necessarily mean somewhere good; some developments are blind alleys or red herrings.

Nearly but not quite. It is not so much a matter of blind alleys or red herrings (I'm not sure what that's about). It is that some writers are slowly heading towards a facile capacity to churn out pieces which conform perfectly to available models.

In applying any of these key ideas it would help if we bore in mind Bakhtin's reminder:

> … language is not a neutral medium that passes freely and easily into the private property of the speaker's intentions … expropriating it, forcing it to submit to one's own intentions is a difficult and complicated process.

'We never write on a blank page but always on one that has already been written on,' says de Certeau (1984). To write is to engage with social history, the social history of discourse, but it can never be the total history, only the writer's particular links with that history. What is pre-inscribed on the page is different for each one of us. Never to have encountered the classic folk tale or blank verse is to have these forms erased from the page. There is gain and loss. On the one hand the writer is released from the tyranny of the model and on the other is more limited in choice and support. As the pen moves and pauses the writer is making choice after choice, powerfully affected by the already inscribed invisible texts. With each specific piece of writing the invisible consists of the matrices of particular genres, a selection of lexicon, formalities, mini-structures, stylistic devices and so on. What asserts its presence will be different if I am writing a fable, a pseudo-folk story, some notes for a lecture, a set of instructions, a letter to my wife. Indeed, one of the ways of forcing the writing to submit to my intentions is to call up the 'inappropriate' model or to mix one tradition with another. This is a possibility, whatever the work in hand. But there is one mode which lends itself to this tactic more than any other: narrative. Of course, we all know that there are profoundly established stereotypes; but there are two properties of narrative which leave it open to the play of infinite possibilities:

(i)   We inherit an enormous range of resources.
(ii) Within the text of any one narrative there is infinite space for play, juxtaposing strategies and tactics drawn from any kind of discourse.

Here, for instance, is Helen, aged eleven, demonstrating the use of these possibilities.

The Hero Howard

Howard was the city's most cowardly man. He had one ambition and that was to marry the King's daughter, Princess Victoria. She was a beautiful girl with silky brown hair. She said, 'Whoever kills Great Hadden, the fierce, fiery dragon, I will marry.'

On hearing this, Howard decided to kill the dragon. He went to the library and asked for books about killing dragons and marrying princesses. The librarian looked rather surprised and told him to go to the children's department, thinking he was looking for books for his children. He came out of the library with a big pile of fairy tales to read.

(Later in the story the librarian writes Howard a letter. It is couched in perfect bureaucratic prose.)

The play of language here depends on the intertwining of two sets of social meanings, which have accreted around specific genres (folk-tales, realistic short stories, farcical tales, official letters, kinds of conversation) and by these means have coaxed a new meaning out of the text. Helen has successfully refused to make the forced march through enemy territory and has set off on a jaunty discourse journey of her own.

As a last step, let me suggest – pursuing the possibilities of narrative – how all students from the youngest to the oldest might be helped to make that journey. John Scurr School is a primary school in the heart of inner-city London. Two thirds of its pupils are Bangladeshi and speakers of Sylheti. It is a school where story-telling by the teachers occupies an unchallenged place in the curriculum, and that includes bilingual story-telling. In a class of ten- and eleven-year-olds, which I now know quite well, I told an Italian folk story, 'The Land Where No One Ever Dies', which my wife Betty Rosen had given me. It is a subtle and ironic tale of time and death. I proposed that the children should re-tell the story in writing. My only suggestion was, 'Tell it which way you like. Change anything you like.' I watched the children with some misgiving as, after a generous amount of time, they had written very little, perhaps some five to ten lines. With no prompting from me they promised they would finish before my next visit. Two weeks later I returned to do some more story-telling. Joe, the teacher, put a folder in my hands. It contained all the children's re-tellings. In them you can find dozens of ways in which they have shifted the genre, frequently by filling the story with contemporary dialogue. Most striking perhaps is the very shy little girl, who changed the chief character of the story from the inevitable young man to a young woman, who, instead of setting out on her own, takes the whole family with her!

Now let me shift the context. We are still in the inner city but this time in a class of fifteen-year-olds. There is a strong contingent of students of Caribbean origin, and the rest are as ethnically diverse as they come. Here the teacher, Betty Rosen (who is also my wife, as already acknowledged) has designed a whole unit on re-telling, which includes much discussion of ways in which stories can be changed (see B. Rosen, 1988 and 1991). This unit is based on Greek legends, a surprise perhaps, given the context. At one point she tells her very lyrical version of the Orpheus story. Here too the children move outwards from the told version, using every possible ruse to shift it to their own telling, changing events, characters, language, dialogue, points of entry and exit, omitting and adding.

Narrative, but more especially re-telling, is one way of wriggling out of the coils of the quasi-official written codes, because it invites cunning. The story is given, established, approved. Within its confines it is possible, while nodding agreement, to defy it: defy it to just the extent we wish. A nice paradox then appears in the ways we all operate. The beauty of re-telling is that while it appears to desert invention (the old rhetorical term) it lets it in by the back door. At the intimate level of the classroom a micro-culture of shared discourse can assert itself.

References

Bakhtin, M. (1981) *The Dialogic Imagination.* Austin: University of Texas Press.

Butturf, O. and Sommers, N. (1980) 'Placing revision in a reinvented rhetorical tradition', in A. Freedman and I. Pringle (eds.), *Reinventing the Rhetorical Tradition.* Conway, AR: L and S Books for the Canadian Council of Teachers of English.

de Certeau, M. (1984) *The Practice of Everyday Life.* Berkeley, CA: University of California Press.

Eagleton, T. (1983) *Introduction to Literary Theory.* Oxford: Basil Blackwell.

Giroux, H. (1983) *Theory and Resistance in Education.* Westport, CT: Bergin and Garvey Press.

Goody, J. (1977) *The Domestication of the Savage Mind.* Cambridge: Cambridge University Press.

Heath, S. (1983) *Ways with Words.* Cambridge: Cambridge University Press.

Heller, A. (1982) *A Theory of History.* London: Routledge & Kegan Paul.

Kress, G. (1982) *Learning to Write.* London: Routledge & Kegan Paul.

Kress, G. (1989) 'Texture and meaning', in R. Andrews (ed.), *Narrative and Argument.* Milton Keynes: Open University.

Lemke, J. (1982) 'Thematic analysis: Systems, structures and strategies'. *Recherches Sémiotiques/ Semiotic researches,* 3.

Murray, D. (1980) 'The feel of writing – and teaching writing', in A. Freedman and I. Pringle (eds.), *Reinventing the Rhetorical Tradition.* Conway, AR: L and S Books for the Canadian Council of Teachers of English.

Olson, D. (1977) 'From utterance to text: The bias of language in speech and writing'. *Harvard Educational Review,* 47 (3).

Ong, W. (1982) *Orality and Literacy.* London: Methuen.

Ponsot, M. and Dean, R. (1982) *Beat Not the Poor Desk.* London: Heinemann.

Reid, I. (ed.) (1987) *The Place of Genre in Learning: Current debates.* Melbourne: Deakin University.

Richmond, J. (1986) 'What we need when we write', in *About Writing,* 2 (Spring 1986). London: School Curriculum Development Committee National Writing Project.

Rosen, B. (1988) *And None of It was Nonsense.* London: Mary Glasgow.

Rosen, B. (1991) *Shapers and Polishers.* London: Mary Glasgow.

Throsby, J. (1971) *A History of Leicester.*

Third Interlude

Barn Owl

The sooty plane trees in Ford Square
Shed their drips
On the grassless gravel
And on the sparrows and pigeons.
They jostle around Miriam
From the Tailors and Garment Workers,
Extended apron full of crumbs
Leftovers from the nosh
Served with lemon tea
Over there beyond the railings
And Ford Square's meagre wildlife.

My mother plucked from beneath
The roof gutter a naked nestling sparrow
Kept it in a lined shoe-box.
Somehow she knew how to
Cajole it into adolescence.
Its readiness took it
On an ambitious flight
To the kitchen window-ledge
Then over the chimney pots.
She always swore
It came back several times
And pecked on the window.

Harold Rosen

Our English teachers coming up
From the Underground in Aldgate
Sniffing the bitter air
Roses in their buttonholes
From – we surmised – open country
A green Arcadia
Way beyond Whitechapel
In fact from no further away
Than their suburban rectangles
Harrow say or Hendon.
They assiduously undertook to fill out
Our barely begun glossaries.
Naturalists to a man
They knew all the EngLit birds
That fluttered in the pages
Of the *Golden Treasury* and *Poems for Today*
Blithe spirits all.

On a fence post near Windermere
In the early morning light
A barn owl blinked
At the oncoming London train.
In a chaos of gear
Some young campers snoozed.
One wide awake
Watching the dawn
Saw a bird on a fence pole
Blinking into the early morning light …
His first live owl.

Cribs

I was sitting there so bored I could have cried. I'd finished the arithmetic paper and was waiting for Mr Powell to declare the exam over and done with. Following the order of the time, if you finished before the Head rang the bell in the hall, you sat there in total silence doing nothing. Could have let us have a book from the cupboard, I thought. Like *King of the Golden River* which we'd started reading in class, and which was nice to handle, bright red and gilt lettering. It was all good practice for something or other – the army? prison? – but an excruciating strain for a ten-year-old. All you could do was look round the room to see how the others were making out or study the flaking map of the world and the faded pictures, 'When did you last see your father?', 'The Fighting Temeraire' and 'Napoleon on the Bellerophon'. Most of the others had their arms curled round their papers and their heads almost buried inside them. This was to stop someone nearby from cheating. Bit of a laugh in Benjy's case. He would be lucky to get a couple of sums right and he would certainly not finish more than a quarter of the paper. Yet there he was like a miser over his hoard. He might not be very good at arithmetic but he had mastered the ethics of scholarly behaviour. I think he believed that if he only adopted the correct physical posture he would join the elect. Getting sums wrong shows a certain lack of fibre but cheating we all knew was a moral disorder of a much more reprehensible kind. We knew this, not because we were able to take in all that moral business but because we could tell from the scale of the outrage of our teachers when confronted by some protesting little cheat that copying an answer from someone else's paper or writing something in the palm of your hand or smuggling in a tiny scrap of paper was a crime against the social fabric itself. 'Cheating is a kind of stealing,' said Mr Powell. 'It's stealing knowledge.' Dicky Kahn thought that was funny. 'So *mein kind*,' he said later in a Yiddishe momma's voice, 'you mustn't be a knowledge *gunuf*. Same as in Woolworth's, *tatele*.'

In the morning assembly after a suitable run-up of prayers and a hymn, Mr Margolis has sketched out the ground rules.

'Tomorrow you all start your exams. This will be the most important day of the year. You will be given full instructions by your teachers but I want to say something special to you. As you all know, if you copy or even try to copy from another boy's paper, that is cheating. All your work must be your own. Never try to ask someone else for an answer and don't attempt to give one. Anyone doing any of these things will be severely punished.'

Some of us glanced at the canes in brine in the aquarium. Mr Margolis had used one of his special voices, not the more-in-sorrow-than-in-anger one, not the bespoke sarcastic one for a shaking criminal hauled to the front of the hall, but the high solemn one of an Old Testament prophet warning of a plague or the risk of God's displeasure. I can't say I was following very closely. One way to avoid getting shaky and afraid was not to listen. In any case I didn't think any of this concerned me very much. Cheating wasn't my particular line of crime. Mr Margolis was now taking one of his long pauses. His gaze went to and fro and through us to let the dire threat sink in. And then he started up again.

'Now when you're doing your exams you'll stay out of trouble if you keep your eyes on your papers and don't look to right or left. Like that idiot at the back is doing right now. Yes, you with the uncombed hair.'

And here he suddenly bellowed,

'Get out! Get out of my sight! On the landing. I'll deal with you later.'

The uncombed one, for us a hero, a martyr, slouched out.

'You see?' he went on. 'There's always one. Make sure it isn't you. Another thing. You mustn't make signs of any kind to another boy. Don't pull silly faces. Don't make lip movements. Don't signal with your hands. It's all cheating. Cheating, you understand. We are not going to tolerate any of it. Not a flicker of it. There will be no cheats in my school.'

Now that I'd finished the paper there was certainly no need for me to cheat from the arm-curlers around me. Then I noticed Dickie Kahn. He was just across the aisle from me and he too had finished. He was leaning back in his seat, arms behind his neck, and staring at the ceiling. I tried to catch his eye and failed. That was a risky thing to do. All classes in the Big Boys were examined at the same time. The classroom doors were fastened wide open so that Mr Margolis could monitor the whole exercise from the hall and prowl round the classes to root out the slightest irregularity and, in particular, cheating. The open doors were also to impress upon us that this was one of the big ritual moments of the year. They also made us feel more exposed, out in the open. Given the surveillance of our own teachers they would otherwise have seemed foolishly unnecessary. All in all, by the time we'd started examinations only wild desperation or advanced idiocy would have made anyone try it on.

I looked across at Dickie Kahn. This time I did catch his eye. Catching an eye was, I suppose, within the meaning of the act. But I did. And he let the faintest hint of a smile cross his face. There were just a few minutes to go. He silently mouthed the word, 'Finished?' I mimed the answer, 'Hours ago.' As I did so, a great terrifying shout hit my ear like a punch. It was Mr Margolis who had spied me from the open door, rushed in and bellowed into my ear, 'Cheat! You were cheating! Mr Powell, this boy was openly cheating. Now, cheat, get out and stand in front of my desk in the hall. We know what we do with cheats here.' He was dragging me from my desk and pushing me to the door, past Mr Powell who looked a bit upset. Possessively, he didn't like one of his pupils in big trouble.

Mr Margolis made short work of me. My fear and sense of huge injustice had already set me crying and I made one spluttering attempt at a protest. Much good it did me. Out came the cane and I got two fierce whacks on each hand. Mr Margolis led me back to my class and the others took in my tears and misery. He led me right up to my desk. There was the arithmetic paper I had finished with such assurance. With a red pencil he scored a punitive diagonal line across one page after another and then he wrote on the first page, '0 marks. CHEATING'. I'd been in some scrapes before but nothing like this. And there was worse to come. Every one of the papers I had already done was given a nought mark and I came bottom of the class when minutes before I had thought that Dickie and I were competing to be top. The disaster darkened my world. I had in a way bought the cheating thing and had come to believe there was something despicable about it. But now a thousand Mr Margolises would never convince me that justice had been done and been seen to be done. Mr Margolis had devoured and digested me and it had nothing to do with cheating as I had really understood it. He was the fraud and cheat.

Now there was my mother to face. As I crept home I realised there was no need to assume that she would see me as a branded outcast. She was more likely to worry about my being entered in a dossier somewhere and that the word 'cheat' against my name would dog me for the rest of my days. She had, with some reason, views about dossiers. My best hope was that her view of what she called The System would make her furious about my treatment. System or no System, she was inclined to side with teachers when I grumbled about them.

'That Powell, he never explains properly. He mumbles out of the window and you can't hear a word so I can't do my decimals and always get the dots in the wrong place.'

'You know something? Maybe he don't explain all that good or maybe someone else sometimes looks out of the window or fools around with Manny and doesn't pay attention. If I went up to the school and asked how come you don't know decimals, I might hear a thing or two wouldn't make you seem so hard done by.'

'Did I say anything about going up to school? You'll make me look like a real mummy's boy. You'll make me look like a real fool.'

'I don't have to try. You're making a good job of that without my help.'

The matter was left there and she made it very clear that there was no future in spilling out all my little grievances. But if she sniffed out some real injustice she'd be up at the school like a shot. She had already had one or two brushes with Mr Margolis and he'd learned to treat her with care, almost deference.

'Who does he think he is? God? He can make himself a *ganzer macher* with little kids but as far as I'm concerned he's just a tin-pot bully. You see, he's part of The System. He has to teach you to obey, to do what you're told, no questions asked. You know why? Because that's what you're supposed to do for the rest of your life, be a *stummer* little *tuchas-lecher*. Very nice for the bosses. Don't worry, I'll have a word or two with him.'

A word or two! I hugged myself. What I would have given to have heard her with a word or two, teaching Mr Margolis about The System? And then I had to remember that when it suited her turn the tin-pot bully was a stern wise man, a *malamed*. And then it was, 'He's got letters after his name, you know that? BSc. That's a degree from a university. It means he's a scientist. You can learn a thing or two from a man like that.'

Out tumbled my story as soon as I got home and I cried again for a bit.

'Enough, enough,' she said with her arm round me. 'Sometimes I think he's a bit touched, screaming his head off and hitting little boys. Other times I think he just pretends to go mad like that because he thinks the kids might all run wild like little gangsters. Mind you, he'd no business to hit you with the stick just for moving your lips. It's like it was for the Jews in the Tzar's army. Hurting and hitting is no way for a school. Or, come to that, for a man who's been to college.

'What about my marks and making me bottom?'

'Your marks, your marks.' She was miles away, talking to herself.

'Bottom, he's making me bottom! He's the cheat, not me!'

'I'll speak to him,' she said quietly. 'Wash your face and go make yourself a *platzel* and cream cheese.'

She spoke to him. I got all my marks, even the arithmetic. The cane she could not take back. As for cheating, I'd begun to think about it.

****

When it came to it I chose to do Latin. At the beginning of the third year we all had to start on German. They gave you a short dose, three weeks with Mr Jones and *Deutsches Leben* and then they asked you if you wanted to continue or do Latin instead. A choice! Every other subject in the curriculum had fallen upon us like acts of God. No one had asked at the beginning of the first year whether we fancied five years' worth of French or a similar sentence of doing chemistry with bloody-minded Mr Old. It was strictly *table d'hôte*. Faced with this new phenomenon, choice, we could have done with a little advice. Not a word. At other schools there would have been some parents who knew about such things, or thought they did. Our parents together could have mustered a lot of languages, Yiddish, Russian, Polish, Lithuanian and the men could all read Hebrew. It wouldn't have struck us that this qualified them to tell us about German and Latin. All their languages were part of their incurable immigrant backwardness, usually spoken because they couldn't speak English or couldn't speak it very well or just weren't comfortable with it. As for Hebrew which they didn't speak, they read it because that's how you practised your religion. That's how they learnt their prayers and were able to get to grips with the Torah and the Talmud. German and Latin we knew were something quite different, real languages with textbooks, declensions and conjugations and you could do them for Matric. The teachers could have said a word or two but they didn't. They certainly didn't compete for our custom. Our own folk-lore had it that lawyers and doctors needed Latin though no one seemed to know why. We knew that you didn't learn Latin so that you could go and speak it to the Latins. And Latin used to happen in the school stories we read. None of that mattered very much to me. I was plumping for Latin.

It was like this. English was the language spoken in my house. All the adults could speak Yiddish fluently but they only used it when they didn't want the children to understand or when people came to the house who were only at home in Yiddish

– which was most of them. The English spoken was peppered with Yiddish words, exclamations, curses, threats, proverbs. Their English had occasional touches of Yiddish grammar and was usually spoken with a distinctive Yiddish lilt. They sang Yiddish lullabies and folk songs, '*Herrt a meisser, kindele*', '*Az der rebbe Eli Meli ist gevoren sehr gefreli*'. I picked up a lot of Yiddish this way and would not have spoken it at all if it weren't for the fact that in the homes of all my friends Yiddish was the language you lived in. Simply to be civil, say 'please' and 'thank you', 'good Sabbath', 'Is Solly in?' I had to muster some working Yiddish. I was never really fluent with it but all my school friends could speak it as confidently as they spoke English and they usually spoke to their parents in it. There was even Manny's father who, as a Jewish socialist, was militant about Yiddish. 'Forget Hebrew,' he would say, 'it's for the Zionists. Yiddish is the language of the Jewish proletariat.' As a member of the Bund he sent Manny to evening classes at the Workers' Circle where a scholarly little man introduced him to the Yiddish literary canon. Sholem Aleichem, Y.L. Peretz, Sholom Asch and the rest.

Neither I nor my classmates would have known that Yiddish began as a mediaeval German dialect. It was only when we began our classes that it dawned on us that German sounded very familiar. The fluent Yiddish speakers were cock-a-hoop. If only French had been like this.

As Nat said, 'German's only posh Yiddish'. Whole sentences and dozens of words were understood immediately. They all took to German like ducks to water. Mr Jones couldn't go fast enough for them. But my nose was out of joint. I was floundering. It is Latin for me, I thought. At least we'll all start level pegging. So eight of us went down the corridor to the Sixth Form Library, all oak panels and glass-fronted book cabinets. We were an elite before we'd started.

Mr Chester, the Latin master, was a bit remote but quite a gentle man. With only eight of us to teach he relaxed all the disciplinary ploys. No one was given lines nor detentions, nor made the butt of sarcasms and savageries. We were a cosy little club. And Latin wasn't difficult at all. You didn't have to try to speak it. Once you had galloped through all the conjugations and declensions you translated simple little phony sentences about Lucius, the line of battle, centurions and Gaul. Then you progressed to concocted little paragraphs mostly military or mythological. At the beginning of the Fourth Year our happy little band were in for a bit of a shock. We had Virgil's *Aeneid*, Book Two, the Trojan Horse one, thrown at us and we suddenly felt we knew no Latin at all. You had to prepare a chunk at home the night before a lesson. It was slow work. The standard little blue edition of the time had a driblet of Virgil's text wedged between an Introduction and the Notes and Glossary. I pored over the pages, fluttering to and fro, in an effort to drag some kind of meaning from them. All very rabbinical. Back in the class the ancient method persisted. You took it in turns to translate a ration of lines. Latin had become a wearisome grind. Mr Chester, with no recriminations, would patiently help out if you got stuck but there was no joy in it at all.

Then the word went round that if you went to Foyles in the Charing Cross Road you could buy an English translation of Book Two, quite cheap as well.

'It's what's called a crib,' Simon Frumkin said with authority.

'A crib?' I asked. 'Funny word.'

'It's a book to cheat with, *schmeryl*.'

So we elected him our book buyer and he came back from Foyles with a clutch of these so-called cribs. I took my copy and went off to a quiet corner to examine it. I took an immediate dislike to it. It looked and felt as though it had been printed on thin blotting paper. There wasn't very much of it. The text had been crammed into almost all of the available space on the page and the print was microscopic and slightly fuzzy. Nothing broke up the unrelieved tedium of the pages. There was only the identification at the top of page one, Classical Translations No. 27, *Aeneid* Book 2, B L Braithwaite, BA. If ever you wanted to make a publication look like under-the-desk contraband, this was it. The translation was in an English which had been tortured to enable desperate learners to match phrase with phrase. My disgust did not prevent me from using it though I never took it into class out of a kind of squeamishness I didn't know I had in me. I certainly didn't want Mr Chester to catch me with anything so obviously grubby, without the slightest pretence of being a real book and manifestly designed as a swindle. I mustn't overdo my distaste, though. That crib saved me hours and hours of slavery. High-minded principles were not going to stand in my way.

Then one day I was in Whitechapel Library. It was one of those magnificent Carnegie libraries which the old London Boroughs prided themselves on. Its stock was as good as a university for many people in the East End. I didn't know my way around the shelves all that well. I usually headed for the novels and, less often, a book to help me with my homework. Tentatively, I had picked up *All Quiet on the Western Front* and *Brave New World* which an English teacher had suggested, and I'd toyed with Trevelyan's *History* but, glancing at a few pages, I could see it was over my head. I was wandering past some unfamiliar shelves when I spotted a large handsome collection of many books. I could see there were really two collections in the same format, one bound in green and the other in red. I went closer and read their titles. Here, I realised, were the classics, all of them, Greek in green, Latin in red. I looked along the Latin shelves and there was Virgil's *Aeneid*. I loved the feel and look of it, good paper and friendly type-face. It had class. I saw it as coming from a world where fastidious gentlemen sat in leather armchairs and read it easily and earnestly. Flicking through the pages, I realised there was something unusual about the book. I had no idea such books existed. On the right-hand page there was the Latin text and on the left an English translation. I hunted for Book Two and for the bit I had just been working on, Anchises being carried from burning Troy. The translator, I could see even then, had been free and easy, making his prose read like a real English book. I stood and read a page or two, savouring it. I had stumbled on the Loeb Classics.

I took the book out and went home. I flung Braithwaite into a corner, planning from then on to work only with my find. I wish I could say that I was a really generous-minded youth and immediately shared my find with the other founder members of the Latin club. I didn't let the thought cross my mind. It was my own discovery and besides, they were satisfied with their grimy cribs. They'd find out soon enough anyway because I was going to take my treasure quite openly to the Latin class. Mr Chester, I was sure, would be pleased and perhaps impressed.

It came my turn to translate. I took my book from my satchel, placed it on the desk and began glancing from time to time at it and my own notebook. I had scarcely translated two lines when Mr Chester stopped me.

'Rosen, what have you got there?' He sounded quite surprised.

'A translation I have been using, sir,' I said chirpily. Mr Chester was looking genuinely baffled and, I thought, a little hurt.

'You know that's a crib. You not only bring a crib into class but you open it under my very nose. Don't you think that's a bit silly?'

'But, sir, this isn't a crib. This is a Loeb Classic.' I said 'Loeb Classic' as others might have talked of the Seven Wonders of the World. Mr Chester smiled and nearly laughed.

'Rosen, if you bring a Loeb Classic to class it becomes a crib. There's no difference at all.'

He picked up my book and read a bit to himself.

'Fine translation. Don't bring it to class again, there's a good lad.'

The club members bunched round me after class. They weren't angry or jealous. They just wanted to thumb the book and enjoy it a bit. After that they always came to me to copy out the next passage. But I felt cheated.

****

Whenever I went past the Mission to the Jews in Philpot Street I thought of Gothic. I mean the Gothic language. I first encountered Gothic as soon as I went to the University. Like most people I had never heard of it before and I've heard almost nothing of it ever since. It doesn't exactly crop up. Somebody had decided that if you were to get a degree in English Language and Literature then you simply had to study Gothic. On the face of it the connection between the two was not too obvious to an eighteen-year-old. I suppose that tucked away in some dusty archive in the Senate House there is a solemn rationale for this bizarre element in our course. The main thing is that Gothic is the earliest Germanic language known to the trade and no doubt there were scholars who got very excited about this. It's a bit like those people who get quite a buzz out of tracing their ancestors back to the Normans. Perhaps there was a lot more to it than that but I had expected university English to be one long round of delight and professors talking like Quiller-Couch and Leslie Stephen and endless days reading novels and poems and plays. But here on my timetable was Gothic (to say nothing of Anglo-Saxon, Phonetics and Paleography) on Monday mornings at 10 a.m. with Dr Brookfield.

I had been far too naïve to investigate beforehand what English actually meant at university, and when I discovered it meant Gothic, that was a nasty shock. I went off to buy my Gothic textbook in a rebellious frame of mind. Page after disheartening page of Gothic grammar, which I discovered very soon was mostly invented on the basis of some identikit principles which I never fully understood. The grammar book had asterisks against the word forms they had made up. Most of the words had asterisks against them. I took it to the first class with Dr Brookfield. She was a frail-looking oldish lady with a chalky white face and wire-wool hair. She always wore a navy-blue dress with a white lace collar and round her neck was a large ornate gold cross. We soon found that she was an amiable lady though as a mentor she might have been made of steel. I remember that in her first hour with us she told us we were going to study a Gothic text by someone with the unlikely name of Ulfilas. We'd find it at the back of our text book. This Ulfilas had translated the Bible into Gothic in the fourth century AD. It turned out that only a few tiny bits and pieces of Ulfilas's mighty work had survived and some of this is what we had to prepare for translation in class. So this was going to be our dry bread and water for the year and the price we had to pay for enjoying ourselves with Chaucer and Shakespeare was a fictional grammar and old scraps of the Bible in an utterly outlandish language.

Then Dr Brookfield suggested that we should all toddle off to the British Museum just down the road to take a look at Franks Casket. That had a nice homely ring. It turned out to be a decorated box with runic inscriptions all round it. We didn't know why Dr Brookfield had told us to go and look at it. Maybe Mr Ulfilas wrote in runes. Were there quotes from him on it? Was it a casket from Gothic times made in Gothic-land? Why was it called Franks Casket? Was it made by Frank or for the Franks? I found in a corner of the display case a puzzling translation of the runes and enjoyed an indecisive bit which read, 'The whale became sad (or, The ocean became turbid)'. The scholars didn't seem too sure about their precious Gothic. After all, there's quite a difference between an ocean and a whale. Dr Brookfield never mentioned Franks Casket again. She might just as well have sent us to look at the Rosetta Stone. Perhaps she knew how baffled and dismayed we were by the prospect of the Monday Gothic hour and thought a pretty little ivory casket with carvings of the Adoration of the Magi and Wayland the Smith on it might cheer us up. Doesn't seem likely. After I'd been in the college a few months I'd got to know the very popular beadle in the cloisters in his claret frock coat and gold-braided topper. His name was Frank. I said one day, 'You know, Frank, your name's in the British Museum. They've named a box after you.'

'Have they now? A student told me that when I came here in 1928 and I said, "Listen, Sonny Jim, Frank's a very common name but you can keep your comic turns for your clever pals. I may be wearing a funny hat but I'm not a museum piece yet."'

Back in our class we were soon on the treadmill, preparing and translating the fragments of Ulfilas. The first-year English group, it must be said, consisted mostly of young women who came in from the outer suburbs each day. They were clever, very diligent and almost always unquestioning. Ulfilas was not their favourite writer. They didn't think he was a good read any more than I did. He'd given them a nasty surprise, too. But they sighed and got down to it, arriving in class with their tidy files and flawless handwriting. If you had to do Gothic to get a degree in English, so be it. They were not ones for teach-ins, sit-ins, picket lines, boycotts and protests. That came much later. Most of them were very up-front Christians and that turned out to be important for me. The bits of Gothic we had to translate were from the New Testament. I recollect that one was that passage about 'where moth doth corrupt and thieves break in and steal'. Another was the Lord's Prayer.

I had never read the New Testament. The very idea of reading it was distasteful to me. This was not a religious objection. I wasn't religious. I didn't go to synagogue except to keep my grandfather company on the few occasions when he went as an act of solidarity. My scant, rote-learnt Hebrew was disappearing fast. No, getting into the New Testament would be like going over to the other side, kissing its icons. The name Jesus I found difficult to say. He was their Man, not mine. My Christian classmates, of course, were not finding translation the least bit difficult, if you can call it translation. They scarcely had to look at the Gothic – they knew that stuff by heart. I ask you, the Lord's Prayer! At eighteen I might have heard of it but I certainly didn't know it.

Gifuns himma daga …

Give us this day …

Perhaps Dr Brookfield knew why I was having difficulty, or partly knew. If she did she gave not the slightest indication. But then, none of the lecturers ever gave a flicker of awareness that *The Jew of Malta* or *The Merchant of Venice* or *The Prioresse's Tale* might be making me resentfully uncomfortable. We were doing literature, not politics. And, as someone once said, maybe English is not a university subject for Jews.

So it was that I seethed in the first few classes and spent far too many hours preparing bloody Ulfilas while the young women could spare time mugging up Germanic sound changes, the Great Vowel Shift, Grimm's Law, Verner's Law. One of them said to me one day, 'You're a funny chap, Rosen, you really are. All you've got to do is buy yourself a copy of the New Testament.' And then she added wickedly, 'Still, you might lose a grievance that way.'

She was right. I had to get a New Testament. If translating bits of it was a kind of betrayal, imagine what a total defection buying it would be, actually walking into a shop and buying one. This was to give a home to their Book on my shelves. To hear coming out of it their words. Buy it I couldn't. Remember, no one had ever said to me that I mustn't read that book. I don't think they ever referred to it. They banned it by silence. Yet I knew how shocked they would be if they knew that my course obliged me to buy it and read it. I exaggerate, there were some people at home who would not have turned a hair and maybe even laughed. My Uncle Sam might have said, 'Comparative Religion, eh? Very advanced!'

I could go so far and no further. I was not going to buy it. Borrow one from the library maybe? Copy out chunks before returning it? Tedious. Suddenly the solution came to me and I laughed to myself at the beauty of the irony. The Mission to the Jews.

Philpot Street Synagogue was a large building disguised as a Greek temple with its fat columns and pediment. A few buildings further along the road was the Mission to the Jews. When I was young this seemed to me like a most wilful act of provocation but when I was a teenager a couple of friends and I found the Mission very funny and also enigmatic. We could not imagine any adult we knew ever going into the place. What for? What would they say? 'Good morning, I'd like to be a Christian. How long does it take, please? Does it cost?' Manny said,

'You ever heard of a Jew becoming a Christian? You couldn't make yourself into a *goy* even if you wanted to. You couldn't talk like one, you couldn't eat like one, you couldn't look like one.'

'Henriques talks like one and looks like one.'

'Oh, him. He's Sephardic, that's different. Even so, he hasn't become a Christian. He takes Jewish prayers in that boys' club of his.'

'So you tell me. That building over there. Must cost a fortune. They do it all for nothing?'

We were sitting on a low wall opposite the mission. It was about five o'clock and we'd decided to settle a problem. We'd never seen anyone going in or out, would-be convert or missionary. Who were they, these missionaries? What did they look like? How many were there? We soon found out. At their closing time, four of them came out of the front door, three men and a woman. They all wore sober clothes which we thought of as gentile and seemed to us, though I think we invented it, downcast and furtive. They certainly weren't sprightly in their step nor did they look round with good cheer. Manny said, 'And that lot think they're going to make us all Christians? Some hopes.'

'Nice job, though, being a Jew-converter. You don't lift a finger, year in, year out, and get paid for it.'

'You know, there's a woman in Varden Street married into a Jewish family A *shiksa* she is – well, was – but she converted. Learnt all the prayers and everything. And what about Rutman's presser? Speaks Yiddish better than me and he's a *goy*. Old Rutman thinks it's marvellous. He keeps saying to him for a joke, "Henry, you speak Yiddish so good you should get circumcised."'

'That's all different,' said Manny. 'There's no Mission to the Christians, is there? And there'd be a right *shemozzle* if there was. It's different, isn't it?' He didn't sound all that sure.

And now, just because of Ulfilas I was on my way to this same Mission to the Jews. The beauty of it was that I wasn't swallowing my pride and giving in to the quiet tyranny of old Ulfilas. I was going to put one over him. I pushed open the door and there in the large hall was a desk, all very neat. There were small stacks of pamphlets and a letter rack. Around the hall were posters with quotable bits of the New Testament in large black letters. And there were some in Hebrew. I hadn't expected that. I had expected lots of pictures of Jesus Christ extending his arms over little children with blond curls. Or the Crucifix. Of them not a sign. A man behind the desk looked up when I came in. I told myself that he was amazed. I had prepared my great *chutzpah* performance.

'Do sit down. Can I help?'

'Yes,' I said firmly. 'I have never read the New Testament, you see, and I'd very much like to do so.' The man brightened up.

'Do you think I could borrow one for a short while?'

'Borrow one? We'd be happy to give you one.'

He pulled open a drawer and with a touch of ceremony handed me a New Testament. I have it to this day. Soft black leather covers extending beyond the body of the book and fine rice paper made it flexible and different. I got up to go. But he wasn't going to let this occasion slip by so easily.

'Would you mind waiting just a moment? I'd like you to meet our Director.'

He edged me into a nearby room. I hadn't bargained for this. The Director, a man with a gold watch chain across a black waistcoat, in no time was asking me questions. 'Was I a student? Why did I want to read the New Testament? Would I like to know more about Christianity? Would I like to meet a group of Christian students?' I improvised feebly, almost always with a lie. When they asked for my name and address ('to keep in touch') I invented them. They pressed pamphlets on me. I fled from the place, knowing things hadn't turned out to be such a laugh after all. But I had my New Testament and when I next saw Manny I gave him a full report.

'I missed being baptised by a whisker.'

I was still sufficiently aggrieved about the Ulfilas business to be determined to be quite open with my New Testament. I went into class, smiled at the others and spread it out at the right page. When my turn came I consulted it with slow deliberation. Dr Brookfield drew up alongside me.

'Mr Rosen,' she said as quietly as ever, 'have you prepared this passage?'

'Most carefully, Dr Brookfield.'

'In that case, why do you need this crib?'

She lifted the New Testament, rather irreverently, I thought. By now I was sick of the childishness of it all.

'No, Dr Brookfield, this is not a crib, as you call it. This is your New Testament.'

She was taken aback and I instantly regretted my improvised rudeness and wished I could withdraw it.

'Well,' she said, 'in this class my New Testament is, I am afraid, a crib and using it is not fair to the others.'

'No,' I said, 'can't you see that the whole of this class is unfair to me?'
I closed my books, stood up, stumbled along the row and left the room.

Maginot Line

He was summer's man.
The straw hat, the sunglasses,
The brick-coloured trousers,
The white canvas shoes.
So overflowing with bonhomie
That he stopped to give me a lift.

The sun smiled at him
And he smiled back.
His fingers tapping the steering wheel,
Drumming to the cabaret songs and hits of the day.
We ate his peaches from a paper bag,
The juice dribbled down our shirts.
Shimmering untainted August
And I saying hello to every minute.

In every village touched
By the same hot holiday rays
Sombre knots of men gaze
At the walls by post offices and *mairies*.
Small posters topped by *tricolores*.
'Rappel sous les drapeaux'
Their heads craned to see
The crucial number in the corner.

This after all is August 1939.

My man stops again and again
To see if his number is up there.
On the dashboard his own card
Pink, I remember even now,
And the number 6.

In this blazing light
He finally meets his match,
Returns to the spectator in his car,
Still manages an easy smile.
'That's me.' Pockets his 6.
'I'm off to the Maginot Line.'
A halo of doom about his head.

The Maginot Line. Indestructible, he told me.
Tunnels, narrow-gauge railways,
Gun emplacements. Boche-proof.
Millions of francs to buy an impregnable frontier.
The Maginot Line. He utters it like a charm,
Warding off catastrophe.
'Couldn't be in a safer place'
Than in his concrete labyrinth.

The war, biding its proper time,
Duly broke out on our way to Paris.
After all it was August,
Invasion weather and the crops were harvested.
Hitler weather, the Germans called it.

So he headed north for the Maginot Line.
Gave me a smile from under his straw hat.
'Safest place in the world.'

In Paris
The buses rumbled past
Crammed with loaves of bread
For the new conscript cohorts.
At the Gare du Nord
Eerie in its dimmed blue light
The iron railings of the forecourt
Held apart thousands of men
And their womenfolk.
Some grasping the bars.
All searching for faces.

And how's my summer man?
In his safest place?
Metres of concrete thickness above his head
Between him and the sunlit world
Between him and the scream of the future.

Harold Rosen

We know what we know.
In his safest place
There is a halo of doom about his head.

Old Ladies in the Pyrenees

'When you look to the heights, hold on to your hat' —Yiddish proverb

In the eyries of the recollecting mind
Even yet they form their tableaux.
Among the headlong slopes they persist,
Across more than fifty years they gaze
From the blackness of their robes and sober headscarves,
Reanimated by a whiff of wine or wood smoke
Or a path ascending into mist-enveloped trees.
I salute you now, *mesdames*,
Defying erasure, unfaded and unforgotten.

Through the gaping door
Neither come in nor stay out
Made out an old lady knitting by the fire,
French style back to front
Unfurling a dark something as brown as her face
And beyond the partition
The snuffling and munching of big beasts,
The odour of urine and fresh dung.
Around her the pared-down detritus
Of a summer season's mountain living,
Sooty pots and pans, old boots drying on the hearth,
Second-best bedding lurking in a dark corner,
On guard a yapping terrier.

It was all going so well
This daring adventure among the peaks
Until, unnerved by a petered-out path,
Ambushed by a white wall of mist
And a sad clanking cow bell,

We surrendered to dismay, bravado gone,
The August contract broken.
Somewhere above this whiteness the sun smiled down.
Here all was dampness, drizzle and danger.
Our minds probed invisible drops,
Fearful of every next uncertain step.
And then suddenly … The front wall
Of a rough cabin huddled in its summer pasture
And there the old lady, her knitting and yapping terrier.

Unstartled she greeted us coolly,
Soon established our confused lostness.
She inspected us gravely and was not pleased.
Took in our yellow Michelin map,
State-of-the-art Bergen rucksacks and nailed boots.
'All the time it happens, all the time,
Young people especially, over-excited strangers
Doing their first mountain,
Mother's milk wet on their lips.
Up here kids from the town
Think they're ready for anything.
Soon get lost when the mist comes down.'
She stood up, sighing and tutting.
We shuffled to the fire, wriggled in our damp gear.
A wooden platter of bread and cheese appeared.
She conducted us across her patch.
Somewhere hot rays were shining on lucky *estivants*.
Here the mist and clanking cow bells still.
Shepherded us to a walkable gravel track.
She watched our wary faltering feet.
'Don't rush it. This will take you down
To the road, houses, shops. St. Bertrand it's called.
You'll feel safe again.'
She turned, waved and smiled.
'Bonne route! Bonne route!'

The well, the huge walnut tree, the deep shade,
The old lady installed in her basket chair,
Fanning herself, sipping her glass, a dish of olives.
She patted the low well wall
As though we were waited-for visitors.
'Sit down, sit down. Cool here, eh?

Harold Rosen

It'll be a bottle of *rosé* you're after.
They all stop for that.'
The path up the mountain beckoned,
Shimmering on the slope and grey rock.
'Up there at this time of day, in this heat,
Those poor boys they'll shrivel to raisins.
Stay with me. It's always fresh by the well.
What will you see up there
You can't see down here?
The same grasshoppers and lizards and dandelions.
And not a hair's breadth of shade.
You have to know when to be still.
Why rush to nowhere in particular?'
Our bottles were filled with *rosé*.
We chafed at the delay.
'Stay with me here,
We could talk the morning away.'
We reached her gate, turned to wave.
'Take care up there.'
Coming back hours later,
We passed the old grey house, the walnut tree, the well;
Would have stopped but the basket chair was empty.

An old lady, in her eighties I would guess,
Digging out from a pot dark brown honeycomb,
Pausing, scoop in the air,
Pausing to see whose footsteps
Were arriving so high up.
The stone farmstead spread out around her,
At first sight a random rock fall,
Then taking shape as a calculated clearing,
Deliberate as the gnarled table
And knotty benches on the paving slabs.
They say the Romans planted the chestnut terraces
But who decided a living was to be had
Amongst the rocks and dizzying slopes?
And who assembled chunks of unyielding stone
Sufficient to build a farmhouse and sprawling barns
So hidden that even the methodical and marauding *Wehrmacht*
Had somehow missed it or found it too menacing?
A lair for the *maquis*, perhaps.

Yet there was a crawling track
Right up to the entrance arch in the wall,
All potholes, deep ruts and hefty boulders.
The wild boar laid claim to it, she said.
'I've ferried a few loads up and down
On that old sledge.
Once they bumped me down to the hospital on it,
Down to that road.'

We stood side by side looking down on the wriggling valley road
And way beneath us a hovering smudge in the air.
'A buzzard,' she said, not shielding her eyes.
'What do you folks see in this ugly old place?'
We could find words easily enough.
'It belongs,' someone ventured. 'Grows out of the ground,
Same rock, same wood.'
Baffled, she knew, and we knew too,
It was not an answer.
We chewed on her dark sticky honeycomb,
Sipped her wine, stroked the grey stones.
'In winter now, would you live here,
When the snow comes right up to the door?
It's hard, hard. And not a soul about.
When I've gone there'll be no one else.
I'm the last. The wild boar can inherit it.
Heap of rocks again.'
Meanwhile all stands and looks eternal.

On the mountainside, overtaking us, an old lady,
Black dress from neck to heels
Impeccable silver hair brushed back.
We heard her steps approaching,
Saw her below on the u-bends to the col,
Knew she would pass us, couldn't match her strides.
The adults were humbled, the boys outraged.
She could have been Norbert Casteret's mother,
Her walnut face peering into the candlelight
To find the true source of the Garonne;
Photos of the old lady in his book.
And here was just such a one, indestructible.
She must have been heading for her spartan perch,
For her flock of nimble goats,

Harold Rosen

Cheese pats laid out on stone benches.
As she swept past she called out,
''sieur dame,'
And for the boys, *'Au 'voir, la jeunesse.'*
Goodbye, youth. Strangely abstract to our ears,
We cited it over the years.
'Au 'voir, la jeunesse.'
An old lady's words in the Pyrenees,
'Au 'voir, la jeunesse. Au 'voir, la jeunesse.'

I salute you all, *mesdames,*
Defying erasure, unfaded, unforgotten.

Part Three

3

Story

The topic which dominated the last period of Harold's intellectual life was narrative – or, put even more simply – story. Stories – factual and fictional, autobiographical and concerning the world beyond the self, traditional and contemporary, fabulous and realistic, oral and written, permanent and ephemeral – seemed to Harold a fundamental, essential element of our humanity, both as individuals and as social beings. He contended that narrative had failed to gain the recognition and acceptance within the curriculum that it deserves, and that the curriculum, learners and teachers are the poorer for that.

He wrote one full-length book on narrative, or more particularly on autobiography: *Speaking from Memory: the study of autobiographical discourse*, published in 1998. Parts of that eventual book, or drafts of those parts, are included in some of the pieces in this third part of this collection, and in the second half of 'The Whole Story?', which for reasons explained in its introduction is in Part One.

There is a fair bit of repetition in the pieces that follow. Harold quotes frequently from writers who have greatly influenced him (Dell Hymes and Mikhail Bakhtin, for example), and some examples of students' language appear more than once. Nonetheless, each piece has a majority of original material, and to have removed sections which also occur elsewhere would have been to damage each's internal argument.

Stories and Meanings

The National Association for the Teaching of English published Harold's *Stories and Meanings* as a pamphlet in 1985. The pamphlet brings together two papers on narrative, 'The Nurture of Narrative' and 'Narratology and the Teacher', and one of Harold's autobiographical stories, 'Not Yet'. Myra Barrs wrote the introduction to the pamphlet.

Introduction

These two papers centre on the subject of narrative. The first is a reflection on the role of narrative in our lives and recalls Barbara Hardy's assertion that narrative is 'a primary act of mind'. The second is in the nature of a teach-in on the new specialisms in the field of narratology. It suggests starting-points and a reading programme for teachers who want to pursue the idea that narratives can be classified, and that systems of classification can teach us more about the nature of narrative itself.

Narrative is a powerful generative concept. It crosses boundaries. In *Learning to Write* (1982) Gunther Kress points out that 'the textual structures of speech differ from those of writing in most respects with one major exception, namely narrative'. So this subject enables Rosen to bring together two large areas, and two of his own major interests: oral storytelling and the oral powers displayed in the endless story-making of everyday lives; and the written fictional narratives we know as Literature.

The other boundary that narrative dissolves is the boundary between fact and fiction. James Moffett made this point in *Teaching the Universe of Discourse* (1968) in relation to his theory of development:

> Whereas adults differentiate their thought into specialized kinds of discourse such as narrative, generalization and theory, children must for a long time make narrative do for all. They utter themselves almost entirely through stories – real or invented – and they apprehend what others say through story.

But whereas Moffett sees development as the ability gradually to put away childish things and to begin to use abstractive forms of discourse in relation to history, science and metaphysics, Rosen analyses the elitism that underlies this concept of a progression towards abstraction, and shows how narrative, given proper status and respect, may prove to be good for more than has been generally thought.

These papers then are concerned with story in all its forms, and appropriately enough Harold Rosen has included one of his own stories in this pamphlet. It is particularly relevant to 'Narratology and the Teacher', since it is referred to at some length at the end of that paper. But in its fusion of personal reminiscence and literary discourse, and its underlying themes of culture, class and classrooms, it is an especially neat way of drawing these papers and their themes together.

Myra Barrs

The nurture of narrative

'Listen children,' runs the Yiddish folk song, 'listen with your nose and eyes' and listen we did for in the very next line a cow flew over the old gossip granny's roof. What nonsense! Listen with your nose and eyes, cows flying over the roof-top. I should be ashamed to be dealing in such trivial absurdities. And I would be, were it not for the fact that our readiness to listen to and to tell stories is so universal and takes such a variety of forms and is made to serve such a range of functions that flying cows belong with fundamental processes of the human mind. For I do need to earn myself a crumb of respectability. There are, of course, canonized stories which will guarantee genuflexions even from those who have not read them – what shall we say, *War and Peace, Madame Bovary, Moby Dick, Ulysses?* They are stories for those who have put away childish things. That is a persistent message of our society and in particular our educational system: stories are for children, the gullible, the naïve. We have other kinds of discourse for the serious business of society. 'We may start by telling stories but we must end by telling the truth', including the truth *about* stories which we call literary criticism or even narratology. In the literature of language education it is often proposed that the ultimate goal for the teaching of composition is academic prose, objective exposition or some such. No one tells us why language development should not include as a central component getting better at telling and responding to stories of many different kinds. We should have been warned. We know now that every Tom, Dick and Harry is a master of infinitely delicate language skills from a very early age, rich competences of grammar and modulated language use, and that every Tess, Bess and Hannah inherits a complex linguistic semiotic, systems of meanings developed in their culture, which include modes of story-telling. We should have been warned that a common possession of humankind was not *ipso facto* of little account but rather an indicator of the functioning of the mind, a part of the deep structure of the grammar of our world.

'Ah,' my mother would say, 'the King and his diamond scarf-pin.' Just that; no more. She never told the story. From the accumulation of contexts which produced this opaque reference I composed the story. For always there was the expectation of a gift, a reward perhaps; at the very point of its being proffered, it was withdrawn; the giver retained the gift. You too can now tell the whole story of the King and his diamond scarf-pin. And you are able to do so because your knowledge of the well-formed story is such that with no more than an elliptical maxim to go on and a context to prompt you, the necessary elements waiting in the shadows can be assembled into the appropriate formation. Were there time I would give you my version. But, like yours, it would be more than a mere conformity to the formal elements. Propp's famous morphology of the Russian folktale (1928, translated into English in 1968), the great foundation stone of narratology, told us what was the same in very diverse stories, the limitation of choices in their structure, but did not attempt to explain the differences. Thus we do not know at the end of the morphology why we should prefer one tale to another when their structures are identical. Notice I have assumed throughout that my mother's cryptic utterance belonged with some fuller story-like version. What kind of knowledge permitted me, and I presume, you too, to assume that? Given the least prompting we are disposed to arrange around people and things a meaningful sequence of events. Indeed, we must do so even when reading works of literature saturated with signifiers in order to create their signification. As Barthes (1975) says:

> ... the goal of literary work (of literature as work) is to make the reader no longer a consumer, but a producer of text.

Or Genette (1980):

> ... the real author of the narrative is not only he who tells it, but also, at times even more he who hears it ...

It may be that those who wish to hustle us through the immature phase of story-making and story-thinking believe that stories are no more than a contrived solace from which we must be weaned, a comforter designed to infantilize and thus enslave us. Later, I shall argue that on the contrary 'narrative is a disposition of the mind, a valid and perhaps ineradicable mode of human experience' (Eagleton, 1981). But I am speaking as though argument itself is not backed by a thousand stories; occasionally even in the most austere and abstract debate one of them surfaces only to be told to go back to its crib with a shaming label of 'anecdote' hung round its neck.

My mother had a black trunk which she bought for the sea journey back to England from America. It became in our household a grand piece of furniture even though it was kept under her bed. I have it still. Inside, it had two layers. The top one was a deep tray one half of which had a lid. Once its travelling function was finished, the trunk was used as a storage unit for all the family photographs, hundreds of them, lying pell-mell in the lower section. The tray held an assortment of documents and mementoes, the lidded section being reserved for precious sentimental objects. From time to time my mother had some need, real or pretended, to seek out some paper or other from the trunk – a birth certificate, a letter, a membership card, a newspaper cutting. At such moments she would sit on the floor by the open trunk and my sister and I would sit by her. The ritual was unfailing. Every photo, every document, every object was inspected and for each one there was its proper story. There were relatives in Durban and Johannesburg, in Rochester and Philadelphia, in Strasbourg, and in Warsaw and Vienna. How did uncles, aunts, cousins, two brothers and a father come to be scattered over the face of the earth? Why were some of the men in uniform wearing the uniform of the wrong side? Who was alive and who was dead? Why was the ostrich feather fan so precious to her? The miniature replica of a miner's lamp, what did that signify? Who was Eugene Debs, whose bronze bust wrapped in tissue paper lodged in the covered section of the tray? Who married whom? Whose children were they? Who died young, and how? Who lived in that house? What happened, what happened, what happened? A story for every item. We knew when she would cry and when she would laugh. We sat for hours and discovered who we were, the way of our world, motives, values, beginnings, endings, a kind of cohesion, sufficient stability in our terrifyingly unstable world. This was our *Thousand and One Nights*, our *Decameron*, our *Canterbury Tales*. So it is that we can readily conceive of ourselves as deprived of all kinds of cultural resources, TV, theatres, even books, but strip us of all the accumulation of stories heard and told, reported and invented, traditional and spontaneous, and what is left of us? Fortunately, of all the catastrophes which haunt our dreams, in which our age has developed a special expertise, that particular disaster has no credibility, for the drive to represent experience as narrative is indestructible and catastrophe itself is after all a story we tell ourselves.

Walter Benjamin did not think so. In his famous essay 'The storyteller' (1970) there is an ironic tension. On the one hand he is able confidently, precisely and delicately to illuminate 'the chaste compactness' of an oral story and on the other he wrings his hands and announces its doom:

> … the art of story telling is coming to an end. Less and less frequently do we encounter people with an ability to tell a tale properly. More and more often there is embarrassment all around when a wish to tell a story is expressed. It is as if something inalienable to us, the securest among our possessions, were taken from us: the ability to exchange experiences.

The reasons for this impending death are, he tells us, that experience has fallen in value, the rise of the novel, the plausibility of newspaper reports.

> Every morning brings us news of the globe, and yet we are poor in noteworthy stories and no event any longer comes through to us without already being shot through with explanation.

But Benjamin was wrong; our possession remains inalienable. It is true, as he saw, that story telling has become an ideological industry and stories are commodities; romances, comic strips, pulp magazines, TV dramas and the like can easily be seen as competition too powerful for the story-teller who has at best only his mat to unroll. Benjamin is like the collectors of folk-song and dialectologists of the nineteenth century who hurriedly scribbled in their note-books what they earnestly believed were the last testimonies of pre-industrial societies. Folk-song and dialect were on their last legs. We know better now. And Benjamin, who wrote *The work of art in the age of mechanical reproduction*, did not have the benefit of what the tape-recorder has taught us. How we have retained 'the ability to exchange experiences'!

For the moment one example must suffice to counterpose to Benjamin's gloom. In the course of his studies of Black English Vernacular, Labov (1972) had the insight to perceive that the youngsters he was working with, supposedly verbally deprived, were expert story-tellers. He therefore set about eliciting from them what he called 'narratives of personal experience' by posing these questions:

(a)   Were you ever in a situation where you were in serious danger of being killed, where you said to yourself – 'This is it'?
(b)   Were you ever in a fight with a guy bigger than you?

For the transcripts of the stories and the detailed analysis of them you must turn to Labov's text. I am here only concerned with what he discovered. He began with a very simple definition of narrative, which would make narratologists wince:

> One method of recapitulating past experience by matching a verbal sequence of clauses to the sequence of events which (it is inferred) actually occurred.

Now if there were a neat match between experience and a sequence of clauses then we could consign to the flames whole libraries of books on the philosophy and psychology of language. As D. W. Harding (1963) showed, the move from experience into words is by no means a simple or obvious one. This is exactly what the analysis of the stories revealed. The critical addition to so-called matching is evaluation, which for Labov is

> perhaps the most important element in addition to the basic narrative clause ... the means used by the narrator to indicate the point of the narrative is its *raison d'être*, why it was told and what the narrator was getting at.

This evaluation is not merely an addition to the narrative clauses but impregnates the clauses themselves. It is 'concentrated and embedded deeply in the dramatic action'. Stories, then, become a way in which the story-teller appraises his life-experience. At the end of his analysis Labov makes this concluding comment:

> Many of the narratives cited here rise to a very high level of competence; when they are quoted in the exact words of the speaker, they will command the total attention of an audience in a remarkable way, creating a deep and attentive silence that is not found in academic or political discussion. The reaction of listeners to these narratives seems to demonstrate that the most

> highly evaluated form of language is that which translates our personal
> experience into dramatic form. The vernacular used by working-class
> speakers seems to leave a distinct advantage over more educated styles.

Bear in mind that these stories are elicited by a researcher in special circumstances, yet even these constraints do not prevent them from 'creating a deep and attentive silence'. So much for Benjamin's 'embarrassment' at the prospect of a story.

So far I have confined my remarks to everyday 'natural' storytelling, for I am keeping an eye on the point at which I shall want to relate this everyday, pervasive competence to schools and to language in education. I want now to extend this discussion in two directions: (a) to give some considerations of the scope of narrative and (b) to speculate about its cognitive significance. We might expect that the development of narratology would have yielded great insights into these matters. Genette's book has the inviting title *Narrative Discourse*. Todorov's work *The Poetics of Prose* (1977) contains promising chapter titles: 'Primitive Narrative', 'Narrative Men', 'The Grammar of Narrative', 'The Quest of Narrative', 'The Secret of Narrative'. Seymour Chatman's *Story and Discourse* (1978) proposes to construct the 'elements of narrative theory' and offers us a complex diagram of narrative structure. The expectations aroused by these titles and promises are invariably disappointed if we expect treatises which analyse all narrative, which attempt to explain the significance of narrative in its most general aspects, which offer psycho-social explorations of what narrative means to all of us. If we are disappointed it is not because narratology cannot record impressive achievements but because narratologists inhabit the world of literature, of great fiction; and, generally speaking, jostling the traditional literary critic to one side, they set out not to interpret or describe works of fiction but to consider how they are constructed, the semiotic machinery by which they work. So it turns out that although narratology promises much it stays on familiar ground, great works of fiction, to deploy its strategy. Genette's book is based on Proust's novel. The mystery remains – how did he know it to be narrative fiction in the first place? The narratologists do from time to time cast swift glances at more humble, everyday narratives. Jonathan Culler (1978) remarks:

> We still do not appreciate as fully as we ought the importance of narrative
> schemes and models in all aspects of our lives.

He goes on to propose a study of 'what is story or what are the basic models of narrative which could become for graduate students the focus for new and important enquiry'. You may observe how programmatic is that project compared with the energies which have flowed into the analyses of fiction. And Eagleton (1981), in an almost throwaway passage, tantalizes us with:

> We cannot act or desire except in narrative; it is by narrative that the
> subject forges that 'sutured' chain of signifiers that grants its real condition
> of division sufficient imaginary cohesion to enable it to act.

So we must move to another place, to an alternative and in some ways complementary
set of propositions. It is best not to plunge straight into the most sophisticated forms
of written narrative or even into written narrative at all but rather, as I did earlier, to
consider narrative in those forms which are as universal as language itself. For the
moment let us put aside even such artefacts as folk-tales. My first two propositions
then are these:

(a)   Inside every non-narrative kind of discourse there stalk the ghosts of narrative.
(b)   Inside every narrative there stalk the ghosts of non-narrative discourse.

There are always stories crying to be let out and meanings crying to be let in. As
Benjamin (1970) wrote:

> A proverb, one might say, is a ruin which stands on the site of an old story
> and in which a moral twines about a happening like ivy round a wall.

All abstractions and generalizations are, at however great a remove, rooted in a tissue
of experience and every tale invites judgements and reasoning, and enfolded in its
particularities are seductive invitations to penetrate its secret, to lure us into values.
People like us are predisposed to see stories as autonomous islands, becalmed in books
or perhaps, like Benjamin's story-teller's tales, reserved for special occasions around
camp-fires, in family gatherings, at the child's bedside. But more characteristically
they came to life in the ebb and flow of leisurely talk and most of all in the mind with
its eternal rummaging in the past and its daring, scandalous rehearsal of scripts of the
future. We might be disposed to take stories much more seriously if we perceived them
first and foremost as a product of the predisposition of the human mind to narratize
experience and to transform it into findings which as social beings we may share and
compare with those of others. We must expect then that narrative will always be there
or thereabouts, surfacing in the daily business of living and less obviously framed as
a test than *Alice in Wonderland* or *The Three Little Pigs*. So it is that we are always in a
high state of readiness to transform into story not only what we experience directly
but also what we hear and read – a cross on a mountainside, graffiti, 'Accident Black
Spot', a row of empty whisky bottles, a limp, a scar, a dog howling in the night, a
headline, a cryptic note.

One of the boldest attempts to see narrative in this very fundamental way is
Barbara Hardy's (1968). Forthrightly she says:

> My argument is that narrative, like lyric or dance, is not to be regarded
> as an aesthetic invention used by artists to control, manipulate, and
> order experience, but as a primary act of mind transferred to art from

> life … What concerns me here are the qualities which fictional narrative shares with that inner and outer story-telling that plays a major role in our sleeping and waking lives. For we dream in narrative, remember, anticipate, hope, despair, believe, doubt, plan, revise, criticise, construct, gossip, learn, hate and love by narrative. In order really to live, we make up stories about ourselves and others, about the personal as well as the social past and future.

In Hardy's inventory of the functions of this primary act of mind we could find dozens of research projects which would tell us a good deal more about cognition and perhaps about culture than we know at present, for experimental psychologists have been very reluctant to meddle with such insubstantial things as narrative or, when they have done so, it has been of course to discover the cognitive processes of understanding the formal elements of story structure rather than taking narrative itself as a cognitive resource – a meaning-making strategy. Barbara Hardy herself does not pursue her pronouncement any further, for she too is concerned primarily with the analysis of prose fiction. However, if we take her recital seriously (as indeed we should) it would lead us to look at our educational programmes in all areas of the curriculum in quite a different way. But Hardy busies herself with the functions of narrative and assumes that we all know what narrative is. It is more than time that I got round to that.

We have come to the point then when we can locate narrative in human actions and the events which surround them, and in our capacity to perceive the world as consisting of (amongst other things or predominantly) actions and events sequentially ordered. The story is always *out there* but the important step has still to be taken. The unremitting flow of events must first be selectively attended to, interpreted as holding relationships, causes, motives, feelings, consequences – in a word, *meanings*. To give an order to this otherwise unmanageable flux we must take another step and invent, yes, invent, beginnings and ends, for out there are no such things. Even so stark an ending as death is only an ending when we have made a story out of a life. This is the axiomatic element of narrative: it is the outcome of a mental process which enables us to excise from our experience a meaningful sequence, to place it within boundaries, to set around it the frontiers of the story, to make it resonate in the contrived silences with which we may precede it and end it. But to perceive it and invent the story is not enough. It must be verbalized; it must be told. There must be a telling which delivers it as a narrative discourse. This is why the narratologists have always drawn the important distinctions between

(i)   the story – the events (real or imaginary) being referred to
(ii) the narrative – those events verbalized
(iii) the narrating – the act of producing the narrative.

The narrative is the making. The narrative edits ruthlessly the raw tape. I like the little story cited by Harvey Sachs (1972) in his paper 'On the analysability of stories by children':

> The baby cried. The mommy picked it up.

All the processes I have attempted to describe must have been involved in that little novel. As Sachs emphasizes, the telling is a social act, a recognisable kind of performance called telling a story. We must, therefore, add briefly but essentially two other features of story-telling.

It may be that the disposition to narrative is a universal more potent than any of those proposed by Chomsky. This is certainly a plausible hypothesis: remember Hardy's 'primary act of mind'. However, if we are programmed to learn a language, we must still be exposed to a language in order to learn it and its socially constituted use. In the same way, however universal our human bent for narratizing experience, we encounter our own society's modes of doing this. There is no one way of telling stories; we learn the story grammars of our society, our culture. Since there are irreconcilable divisions in our society of sex, class, ethnicity, we should expect very diverse, but not mutually exclusive, ways of telling stories. The composer of a story is not a completely free agent. As Macherey (1978) puts it:

> The author certainly makes decisions, but, as we know, his decisions are determined; it would be astonishing if the hero were to vanish after the first few pages, unless by way of parody. To a great extent the author also encounters the solutions and resigns himself to handing them on.

It is 'playing the game of free choice according to the rules'. The speed with which children learn the story grammars of their culture is demonstrated by the ease with which a seven-year-old will launch into them.

> Once upon a time there was a wicked witch ...

Stories are as they are only because others exist; they are 'intertextual'. This intertextuality must include the circumstances and the style of the telling. A visitor to an African school noted:

> The teacher is telling a story, but not in the way I, an Englishman, would tell it. She is dancing it, singing it, acting it. She tells it with her face, her voice, her whole body. The class is completely caught up in the action; toes and shoulders wriggling in sympathy. There is a song involved; the whole class joins in without invitation.

(Hawes, 1979)

It may have struck you that my speculative account of the nature of narrative contains one glaring omission. That is fiction narrative. We do not after all pluck our stories

391

only from direct experience. We invent the experience, the actors, the action, the circumstances, the provocations and the outcomes. I have already suggested that the simplest narrative, which would seem to be a report of recent events (yesterday's quarrel, losing and finding the front-door key, buying a suit), is itself an invention, an act of imagination. But this kind of narrative, rich enough in its autobiographical potential, undergoes vast extension when we once surrender all intentions to constrain what we say by its faithfulness to, as we say, 'the facts'. We are familiar with this in the world of dreams, day-dreams and in the play of childhood. The 'facts' are reorganised so that what happened becomes what might happen; in this way fiction encompasses and extends the *possibilities* of human experience.

> The ends achieved by fiction and drama are not fundamentally different from those of a great deal of gossip and everyday narrative. Between true narrative and fiction there exist, in fact, transitional techniques such as the traveller's tale and the funny anecdote in which the audience's tacit permission is assumed for embellishments and simplifications … True or fictional, all these forms of narrative invite us to be onlookers joining in the evaluation of some possibility of experience.
>
> (Harding, 1962)

With these few naked simplicities I must leave the matter at the point where written fiction enters. We certainly do not lack a wealth of literature on that subject.

Instead let me turn to an aspect of narrative which has received far less attention and which might offer a glimpse of some educational possibilities. We are in error if we believe that narrative is restricted to the kind of activities I have been discussing and that it stands in complete contrast to other kinds of discourse. In fact, it is an explicit resource in all intellectual activity. A few days ago my son Brian passed on to me a paper of his (Rosen, 1982). It was sufficiently specialist for the title itself to be, for me, completely opaque. If I have understood the drift of one part of his argument, it is that if you aspire to becoming an invertebrate palaeontologist you must be someone given to story-telling. What is geology but a vast story which geologists have been composing and revising throughout the existence of their subject? Indeed, what has the recent brouhaha about evolution been but two stories competing for the right to be the authorized version, the authentic story, a macro-narrative? There are stories wherever we turn. How do we understand foetal development except as a fundamental story in which sperm and ovum triumph at the denouement of parturition? Every chemical reaction is a story compressed into the straitjacket of an equation. Every car speeds down the road by virtue of that well-known engineer's yarn called the Otto cycle. In linguistics there are the adventures of Chomsky's LAD, in which by the age of three our hero achieves competence, deep structures, surface structures and more besides. But I am being a shade too flippant. There are two sober questions we might well ask.

(i) To what extent do scientists (amongst others) come to understand the principles and processes of their particular science through coming to master its particular set of current stories?

(ii) To go further still, to what extent have the discoveries of science been made possible by the innovator constructing a plausible story?

I do not know the answers to these questions, but they seem worth asking if only because we can observe that when children are attempting to construct their own explanations (as distinct from learning answers) this is precisely what they do. It turns out that an eminent neuropsychologist, R. L. Gregory, has interested himself in these questions. He suggests (1974) that it is time for psychology 'to take fiction seriously'. His argument is highly suggestive. I can only give you a taste of it here:

> By neither being tied to fact nor quite separate, fiction is a tool, necessary for thought and intelligence, and for considering and planning possibilities. Fiction is vitally important – indeed we may live more by fiction than by fact. It is living by fiction which makes the higher organisms special. By recognising the importance of 'brain fiction' for perception and intelligent behaviour, we might make psychology a science.

To repeat: ' … we may live more by fiction than by fact. It is living by fiction which makes the higher organisms special.' And:

> The success of science shows the power of hypotheses as fictions of limited truth.

The sheer ubiquity, pervasiveness, functional diversity and multiplicity of forms of narrative make any discussion and analysis an awesome and intimidating undertaking. That is why I have limited myself to certain themes and forgone others. I have tried to concentrate on oral narrative because it is neglected yet significant. I have also tried briefly to examine its relationship to thinking and communicating. There is time, perhaps, for me to set out schematically a grid by means of which we can build a bridge into the educational context, a bridge between narrative and learning. I propose four scales on which we might place any oral narrative:

(a) *the scale of spontaneity* or degree of improvisation
(b) *the scale of fictiveness* or degree to which the events are invented
(c) *the scale of embeddedness* or the degree to which the story stands on its own
(d) *the scale of economy* or how much is left to the hearer.

Thus on the scale of spontaneity at one pole (least spontaneous) we can place the traditional tale or the joke or the ballad, and at the other the spur of the moment blurting out of events which at the time press to be told. The scale of fictiveness ranges from the fantasy in which the characters and events seem to defy all natural occurrence to the true story. On the scale of embeddedness we range from the story which is told because it is story-telling time (or the teller is making it so) to the story which crops up when and because other business is afoot. The scale of economy ranges from the sparsest elements of story (remember 'The baby cried. The mommy picked it up.') to the most fully elaborated. These are not a comprehensive set of possibilities; we might add a dimension of cultural specificity, of structured organisation and so forth. I have selected those dimensions which most clearly hold some important implications for schools.

Unfortunately we know from numerous studies of classroom language (Bellack, 1966; Sinclair and Coulthard, 1975; Barnes and Todd, 1977; Stubbs and Delamont, 1976) that as a communicative context the classroom is subject, normally speaking, to rules for speaking which constitute massive constraints on the pupils. Very few contexts which purport to be allocated to interaction so effectively close down the options on the right to speak, to stay silent, to initiate a topic, to interrupt, to evaluate, to censor, to interpret, to ask questions. The further up the school system we go the less likely is it that spontaneous, pupil-made narrative will be able to insert itself comfortably and naturally into the flow of talk. For in most classrooms the chief and privileged story-teller (stories of any kind) is the teacher. The right to tell stories of any kind is invisibly conferred on her and the exploitation of that right is itself very limited. If my general contentions have any validity, they are a plea for making major shifts in that style and conferring full story rights on the pupils, so that the heuristic of narrative can come into its own and the narrative mode of meaning which runs so freely in the veins of the vernacular can be heard in the classroom.

You will not expect me to spell out here and now the dimensions I have proposed (there is nothing sacred about them), because in truth it calls for a huge collaboration. Let me instead select some icons which for the moment must serve.

First there is Brian (a different Brian) who is about seven years of age. He is in an infant class and has been patiently listening while the rest of the class excitedly tell their latest stories about a bird's nest under the school roof where chicks have been hatching. Other stories of birds (some, I suspect, imaginary) have been woven in. At the very end of this multiple narrative session, Brian comes in with a contribution amazingly sustained for a seven-year-old. He begins like this:

> When I was look … leaning against the pole I saw the two … three baby
> birds, and they all put their wings out and tried to fly, and when I made
> a noise, the mother noise, they all put their heads up and flapped their
> wings and started to fly. And I saw the mother come back. She had a worm
> in her mouth … and then she gave it to them.

He continues in this vein for some time and then, speaking of the recently hatched chicks, he says:

> ... they all went down off each other and put their heads down ... so I
> couldn't see them except for their wings. They had all like stripes going
> down them ... and they are black, brown and white ... and they had only
> little wings about this big ...

At this point the teacher intervenes.

> Teacher: How big's that?
>
> Brian: Ooh about ... em ... don't know really
>
> T: Can you say how many inches?
>
> B: I can't remember how big they were
>
> T: How many inches would that be ?
>
> B: Er about ... about ... on top of their head they had all fur sticking up.

And miraculously his narrative drive is so strong that the derailment never occurs and
after those shudders he picks up his mode again.

I chose this snippet of a transcript because as I have indicated this is a classroom
where children are given every encouragement to seize upon the spontaneous,
where stories are embedded in learning, where the sparse traditional tale is told
and children read books not 'readers'. Yet in so favourable an atmosphere as this, a
teacher positively talented at releasing the children's narrative competence still has
flowing in her veins the last dregs of conventional pedagogic necessity. 'How many
inches?' displaces her customary eager complicity.

My second icon. A teacher in an east London dockland secondary school,
Richard Andrews, has evolved a complete system for basing his English work on oral
story-telling, using taped versions for reworking or transposing into written form.
The spontaneous stories eventually become audio-taped programmes or booklets
or video. Stories are transcribed, edited, typed up, rehearsed, revised and become
a centre of responsible, serious activity. Andrews' document (no date) is rich with
suggestions; just one of many is

> ... a game in which the audience listens to stories told by members of the
> class. The audience has to guess whether a story is true or 'made up' and
> the tellers learn to pitch a story so that it is hard to judge.

The activities are many-layered, reaching out into the community when the pupils retell the stories of their parents and grandparents. One parent of gipsy origin comes
to the class and, with his own daughter sitting there, tells in the most accomplished
manner traditional tales. He is not Benjamin's story-teller come back from the dead.
Whenever schools have looked outside themselves they find him.

When the pie was opened the birds began to sing. How to open the pie, that's the problem, for what is needed is nothing less than the project of looking at the whole school curriculum from the point of view of its narrative possibilities, a liberation of the narrative genius of humankind. We must do more than ransack the libraries to find the fictions to put before children, the fables, the folk-stories, the novels. Narrative must become a more acceptable way of saying, writing, thinking and presenting. I am not proposing that anecdote should drive out analysis but that narrative should be allowed its honourable place in the analysis of everything, that stories-in-the-head should be given their chance to be heard.

The project then is to re-examine all practice in this light. I have suggested some dimensions along which we could carry out this scrutiny and make our propositions. What better time to do it than now, when throughout the world we hear reiterated the same tune: close down the options, limit school time to the production of measurable, marketable merchandise. We must make the claim for the narrative mind over the spurious claims of the market.

Narratology and the teacher

> Every genuinely important step forward is accompanied by a return to the beginning … more precisely, to a renewal of the beginning. Only memory can go forward.
>
> (Medvedev and Bakhtin, 1978)

In the attempt to go forward I shall follow Bakhtin's suggestion and begin with memory, coming at narrative in a different way from that in the first paper. The huge and cloudy obscurity of my title points in the direction of the aspirant science of narratology, which amongst its preoccupations gives close attention to *hermeneutics* or what we might call the secrets of the text. You can serve your apprenticeship with my title. It's all right. The secret will out.

So, to renew the beginning and go forward with memory, I had to seek out in my head occasions in my life when a story was repeated. It came out like this.

> We would stand by the edge of the grubby old public swimming pool drying ourselves, my *zeider* and I. As likely as not he would tell me once again about how he would go swimming back in *der heim* somewhere in Poland. I would listen to this fragment of his boyhood. Always I saw him in some Arcadian setting of endless pine trees and velvet grass sloping down to a still lake. It was always early morning. He would emerge from a log cabin, run to the water and fracture its stillness with strong strokes. He would go on swimming till he was lost to view. There were no other people, no other houses, no other movements. It was an idyll I clung to from which I had banished pogroms and poverty and the fearful little community

huddled over their prayers and sewing machines. That was my story not his. And when we went on day trips to Southend, east London's seaside, in his sixties he would set out to swim the length of the pier and back, a mile or so each way. My *booba* without fail went through the identical torments of anxiety. 'The *meshiggenah!* He's gone out too far again.' I was free from all such fears. For he was always the intrepid boy swimmer in the pure lake who always came back. And he did. And even in death still does.

So I have told you a story enfolding the story of a story or rather the story of a set of stories about a set of stories. It is a story, I now realize, which is not only dependent on *intertextuality* but is actually *about* intertextuality, which is to say that a story only exists as a story by virtue of the existence of other stories. I did not in narrating shape into narrative discourse a unique sequence of events, such as:

(i) My grandfather (*zeider*) spoke of repeated swimmings ('how he would go swimming')
(ii) As an old man he would tell me many times about the many swimmings ('As likely as not he would tell me')
(iii) I saw him swim the length of the pier many times ('he would set out … ') provoking the same responses in my grandmother ('without fail')
(iv) When this happened, it always evoked in me the other stories, mine and my *zeider*'s.

Narratology, as we shall see, illuminates such things. As Genette (1980), a narratologist par excellence, says:

> Schematically we can say that a narrative … may tell once what happened once, *n* times what happened *n* times, *n* times what happened once, once what happened *n* times.

Very arithmetic! And it takes us no further than the identification of an elusive apparatus of one set of choices. Given the choices, why should one be made rather than another? However, bear in mind that all of the possibilities proposed by Genette, and refinements of them, may be taken up in a single narrative; and you need to read his analyses of the dance performed by them in Proust's *Remembrance of things past* to appreciate what complexities are revealed by it. Nevertheless whatever possibilities we reveal in narrative theory, we should never forget what Barthes (1976) called the 'pleasure' and 'ecstasy' of the text, not meaning, I hasten to add, amorphous hedonism. We shall, I hope, only momentarily lose sight of them. But there is for us another, usually unasked, question. Who is there to speak for the pleasure and *meaning* of the *making* of the text? The why rather than the how of that making. Dominating the analysis of narrative is the attempt to reveal the physiology and anatomy of the text. This is always to the forefront in one way or another of a reader's, a consumer's, a processor's activity. The writer or author, the darling of the traditionalists, is either disappeared through silence or condemned in open court as an irrelevance. At best the author becomes an 'authorial voice' or 'pseudo-author'. For teachers this is monstrous, for we call upon pupils not only to engage with texts but to be the makers of them, to make writing and reading, like speaking and listening, genuinely complementary activities. We cannot evade the question, 'What are our pupils doing when they take up for themselves the role of narrator?' And my story about my *zeider* and his swimming is a brief celebration of part of myself, but it is just as much a less than importunate invitation not only to share that celebration, but at the same time to enter into dialogue with it, to place a value on its value. So we collaborate in the possibilities of pleasure in the meaning and meaning in the pleasure.

In the making of meaning from stories of any kind, and their diversity is vast, we are engaging in what is at the very least one of the most pervasive activities of human beings and possibly a kind of engagement which is an essential component of our humanness. We neglect it at our peril. We have to reinstate it to its proper place in the discourse of the classroom. Once we embark on that project we shall discover, if we haven't already, that others have been there before us.

Always behind us, half in shadow, stand the licensed scholars. What do we make of their granite severity? We cannot simply shrink back and clutch the old superannuated gods. There is always the promise of a new and penetrating light which will transform our daily struggle to make sense of making sense. As never before we are made to face the possibility that new scholarship has rendered obsolete and routine our past practices. We are sent scurrying anxiously to libraries and rush from one section to another – New Rhetoric, New Criticism, Anthropology, Cognitive Science, Psychometry and Linguistics, always Linguistics. And now Narratology. You may not have heard of it yet but sooner or later it will have designs on you.

Never was it more necessary to look to what nourishes us, soberly to cherish and champion all those things which give us the right (pupils and teachers alike) to speak and know in the teeth of those who would reduce us to hypnotised purveyors of technocratic idiocies. We are in the midst of the most direct assault we have ever known on the best intentions of English teaching. If we delve deeply enough into our resources we shall find half-buried the abundant disposition to make stories and receive them (as Labov [1972] pointed out) with special attention. Chomsky's ideal speaker-listener, a somewhat battered figure of late, is not a narrator-narratee. He may know an NP from a VP but can't tell a folk-tale from an anecdote nor make judgements about when and how to tell one. The relationship between story-teller and story-listener, always interchangeable, always a collaboration, should be the place where we focus our attention. The great works of prose fiction, though not excluded, are not for present purposes in the sharpest focus in spite of our training directing us towards them as the supreme realisation of narrative intent. It takes nothing from them to suggest that we should search for their origins, indeed their life-support systems, in what appear to be basic, constantly renewed processes of the human mind. Together we inscribe upon the flow of daily discourse a chain of intertextual narratives and no standardised test can devise a means to assess our optimum spontaneous performances.

Stories break the surface of our discourse not as great edifices but as spontaneously constructed coherences – cheap as dirt, common currency, a popular possession. You will not need reminding that in our society common property is suspect. What everyone possesses is scarcely worth possessing. Stories are not an optional extra of everyday conversation, but rather conversation is inconceivable without them; in embryo perhaps, incomplete, or faltering.

> One might say that human consciousness possesses a series of inner genres
> for seeing and conceptualising reality ...
>
> (Medvedev and Bakhtin, 1978)

The story genre is undoubtedly one of them. But much more, it challenges for a pre-eminent position. Hayden White (1980), discussing Roland Barthes's claim that narrative 'is translatable without fundamental damage', suggests

> ... that far from being one code among many that a culture may utilize
> for endowing human experience with meaning, narrative is a metacode,
> a human universal on the basis of which transcultural messages about
> the nature of a shared reality can be transmitted. Arising, as Barthes says,
> between our experience of the world and our efforts to describe that
> experience in language, narrative 'ceaselessly substitutes meanings for the
> straightforward copy of the events to be recounted'. And it would follow,
> on this view, that the absence of narrative capacity or a refusal of narrative
> indicates a refusal of meaning itself.

The resolute insistence on narrative in education in defiance of other priorities is then at the very heart of the attempt to keep meaning itself at the centre of language education. And we must not forget that narrative takes a thousand diverse forms even in formal settings. If we examine the proliferation of narratives we can perceive beyond my old grandad's unportentous anecdotes (you all have your own anthologies) that to compose and receive stories is transformed into *diversity of form* and coaxed into serving a *diversity of functions*. We are talking then not only of the heard tale and the written story but also of tales-in-the-head which as you know are about everything and are skilled at slipping past the censor and can make the future into the present or the past. I suggested once (Rosen, 1980) that we need to amplify Vygotsky's inner speech to include inner drama. [This essay, 'The Dramatic Mode', is reprinted in this collection.] It should also be extended to include inner narrative. There is probably no way of depriving us completely of our story-telling rights. If there were, it would be like taking away speech itself. If we take storytelling rights from children in the classroom – all classrooms – what have they left to say in that rule-governed setting? We know the answer. We have heard the constrained exchanges and have seen the written evidence.

Childhood toys are superseded and put away or we hand them over to the younger ones. We are told that something called expository prose (who invented that curious and inaccurate term?) is nothing less than the greatest intellectual achievement of Western civilization. It is in a state of achieved perfection called the Essay (remember the Essay? voted most likely to succeed in the heyday of 'O' level English). It is cleansed of ideology, purged of concreteness and the encumbrance of context. It soars into the high intellectual realm because, so it is said, it is 'decontextualised' (as if that could be true of any kind of discourse). It is so autonomous that, if you interrogate it, it will speak for itself: Speech without the imprint of the speaker! It is, as Barthes would say, 'white writing'. It is to this achievement and no other that we must ask our students to aspire. Literacy, they say, made the Essay possible but it did not supersede the story: it embraced it, made love to it and still does.

I was delighted to come across, somewhat belatedly, Dell Hymes, in a piece called 'Language in education: Forward to fundamentals' (1979), writing:

> And what is the fate of narrative skill in our society? There is some reason to believe, I think, that the expressivity of traditional narrative styles has often been disapproved of by the upwardly mobile persons and the middle-class more generally.

We should treat seriously such a warning from one of the world's greatest sociolinguists, who has such a record of scholarly analysis of oral culture, and moreover an honourable record of participation in the critical debate about the linguistic rights of children in school. Indeed, Hymes went further in a joint paper with Courtney Cazden (Cazden and Hymes, 1978) and argued that in American education there is a widespread denigration of narrative as a communicative medium. They go on to argue that this denigration, since it bears most heavily on those for whom narrative is a vital component of communicative style, can constitute a pseudo-objective ground for discrimination. If the culture of the community is to enter the culture of the school, its stories must come too and, more profoundly perhaps, its oral story-telling traditions must become an acknowledged form of making meaning.

Let me be clear. I am in favour of literacy. As Eliza Doolittle said of gin, I've taken so much of it myself I know the good of it. But we should listen to the warning voices. Jack Goody (1982), whose life's work has been devoted to the study of literacy and its impact on oral societies, asks us soberly to appraise the impact of schools on oral tradition. I must quote at some length.

> When the bulk of knowledge, true knowledge, is defined as coming from some outside, impersonal source (a book) and acquired largely

in the context of some outside, decontextualised institution such as the school, there is bound to be a difference in intrafamilial roles, roles with the elders, than in societies where the bulk of knowledge is passed down orally, in face-to-face context, between members of the same household, kin-groups, or village. There the elders are the embodiment of wisdom: they have the largest memory stores and their experience reaches back to the most distant points. With book cultures, particularly with mass cultures of the printed word, the elders are by-passed; they are those who have not 'kept up'.

Mass literate cultures are the product, even in the developed nations, of the last hundred years. This is the point where attempts were made to generalize school education. The result is a generalization of the devaluation, including the devaluation of knowledge and tasks that are not gained through the book but by experience. It is not my intention to take this analysis into the realm of sociopolitical action, although the implications are obvious ... But intrinsic to bringing effort to change the situation is a revaluation of forms of knowledge that are not derived from books. Not a return to 'savagery' but a modification of one's concessions to the civilization of the book.

The testimony of those closest to narrative cultures, be it in oral societies, minority cultures or the culture of childhood, is unambiguous. The 'elders' with their memory stores are the sources of wisdom. Memory stores of story stores. We know too that in recent years the study of language acquisition has gone far beyond the description of an emergent grammatical competence in young children to reveal a competence in language use, an intricate semiotic, systems of meaning-making developed in dialogue and active participation, a partnership of mind and society. The narrative mode, acquired early, is an intrinsic part of language acquisition. But we do not put stories away with the discarded toys of childhood. As with language itself we get better at using them and broadening their functional range. Some of us may end up writing novels.

So let us look to our resources knowing that others have been here before us – the narratologists. I should explain that I have taken liberties with this term and made it sufficiently elastic to embrace all those working on narrative, though it is usually confined to those working in French structuralist poetics and their followers. They don't talk to one another very much. Thus the cognitive scientists don't seem to have heard of Barthes or Genette, and more understandably vice versa. As usual those of us in education have our own homework to do. For it turns out that, though we might have been unmindful of narrative, others for a variety of reasons have not and in an astonishingly short space of time scholars have converged on narrative from the most diverse corners of the academic world. We should take note of their work, weigh it critically and possibly use it. For our part we need to do two things:

(a) deepen our own understanding of the educational power of narrative
(b) use this understanding to resist menacing efforts to install Gradgrind's progeny in the classroom with their thin gruel of drills based on floating bits of language. (Goody's realm of 'sociopolitical action', above.)

The task is not a simple one but no-one can do it for us. It should be a collective one and I look forward to the day when we organize an international conference on this theme alone. There was indeed a great conference on narrative in 1979 (see *Critical Inquiry, Vol. 7, No. 1 Autumn, 1980*, which contains the papers). It was an 'interdisciplinary compendium' of some of the most important recent thinking on narrative, attended by literary critics, philosophers, psychologists, theologians, historians, novelists, but not by us. No-one to speak from the point of view of teachers and learners. The truth is that we were so busy with other things (standardised language tests?) we hadn't earned the right to be there. And yet it was here that the debate raged about 'the value and nature of narrative as a means by which human beings represent and structure their world'. Does that sound familiar? Insert the word language instead of narrative and it could have been a quotation straight from the work of James Britton. It was there that Ursula Le Guin, challenging the others' expository mode, told a cunning woven sequence of tales ending with one told to her as a child. She then concluded like this,

> There may be some truth in that story, that tale, that discourse, but there's no reliability in the telling of it. It was told you forty years later by the ten-year old who heard it, along with her great-aunt, by the campfire, on a dark and starry night in California; and though it is, I believe, a Plains Indian story, she heard it told in English by an anthropologist of German antecedents. But by remembering it he made the story his; and insofar as I have remembered it, it is mine; and now, if you like, it's yours. In the tale, in the telling, we are all one blood. Take the tale in your teeth, then, bite till the blood runs, hoping it's not poison; and we will all come to the end together, and even to the beginning: living, as we do, in the middle.
>
> (Le Guin, 1980)

We need a map, though I am aware that some of us, like the soldiers in Miroslav Holub's poem, have found our way to the right place with the wrong map. I shall try to sketch in some of the features bearing in mind that I haven't the space, nor possibly the competence, to do more. So we'll start with three features:

1. work on discourse processes
2. cognitive approaches
3. structuralism and post-structuralism.

1. Discourse Processes

Here is a rich series of investigations, long overdue, of all forms of multi-sentence or multi-utterance framed discourses – kinds of written prose, text 'grammars' and their construction, cross-cultural comparisons of communicative competence, informal conversation etc., etc. It turns out, almost it looks by accident, though I believe it is not, that one of its repeated concerns is the production of and reception of different kinds of oral narrative ranging from the most traditional to the most casual. The strength of these studies, many of which English teachers would respond to warmly, lies in their intimate presentation of specific groups of speakers – tellers, audiences and contexts, some remote from us, some straight from our own kind of culture. They are grounded not in idealizations of competence but in what people actually do. Some examples:

(A) THE PEAR STORIES: COGNITIVE, CULTURAL AND LINGUISTIC ASPECTS OF NARRATIVE PRODUCTION (CHAFE, 1980)

All these studies by some seven researchers examine the responses in different settings and different cultures to a film, with sound but no dialogue, of the stealing of some pears. The elicitation took the form of requests to retell the story ('What happened in the movie?'). One study (Tannen, 1980), for example, compared retold stories from English-speaking students in California and Greek students in Athens. Here are the results.

Greek: Construct stories round a theme and omit details from film which don't contribute. *American:* Include as many details as possible as though performing a memory task: very anxious to get temporal sequence right.

Greek: Make comments on behaviour and philosophize about events. *American:* Confine judgements to film's technique.

Greek: Try to present themselves as good story-tellers and judges of behaviour. *American:* Try to present themselves as good recallers with critical objectivity.

For the Greeks it was a matter of interpersonal involvement. To the Americans it was a school-like task.

(B) SPOKEN AND WRITTEN LANGUAGE: EXPLORING ORALITY AND LITERACY (TANNEN, 1982A)

In one of the papers in this collection (1982b), Deborah Tannen examines the oral story-telling of New York Jews, all highly literate. She shows that contrary to confident assertions in the existing literature, it *is* possible for speakers steeped in literacy to use story-telling strategies which are inherently oral, provided that those strategies are within their cultural traditions. It is true, however, that other story-tellers are profoundly influenced by literacy.

Harold Rosen

(c) Narrative, literacy and face in inter-ethnic communication (Scollon and Scollon, 1981)

This is a study of interpersonal communication amongst the Athabaskan Indians of Northern Canada and Alaska. It includes the transcription and analysis of the telling of the life-story of Chief Henry of Huslia. The Scollons' analysis is more than an evocation of another way of life and its interwoven stories.

> We see the bush consciousness as organising knowledge, through the use of themes. This form of organization is highly metonymic. The world is known as situations, processes and events which are characterized parsimoniously. It is possible in this way to integrate a wide range of personal experience into the experience of tradition while retaining a feeling of individual control of knowledge and understanding ... In the best telling little more than the themes are suggested and the audience is able to interpret those themes as highly contextualised in their own experience ... patterns of discourse differ from the modern consciousness and essayist literacy.

I have been able to do no more than point you in the direction of work on discourse processes and suggest what they have to offer. What they have begun to do is to give the same serious and, yes, loving attention to stories embedded in daily life that most of us have given only to literary texts. They have been able to show that these stories are complex in structure, layered with a multiplicity of social meanings and that they deploy resources which have hitherto been treated as the prerogatives of literary style. The converse is also true, for literary language conducts an everlasting flirtation with everyday spoken language.

> ... merely narrative collisions, but on concrete social speech diversity ... it is a historical and concrete plenitude of actual social-historical languages that in a given era have entered into interaction, and belong to a single evolving contradictory unity.

> (Bakhtin, 1981)

It is sadly true that most of these studies would have been enriched and deepened if their authors had paid any attention to the work of the structuralists. You will look in vain in their compendious bibliographies for Todorov, Barthes, Genette, Ricoeur and others. We shall come to them later. On the other hand, unlike the structuralists, you will find in them a world view of narrative. For the structuralists remain firmly anchored in the familiar territory of European high literary art and more serenely amongst the 'privileged' great works.

2. Cognitive approaches

In this tradition the approach is more narrowly psychological. Stories, it is contended, have story grammars, schemata, basic patterns; to comprehend them or produce them presumes certain cognitive processes at work. We can learn about these processes by studying how children and others use archetypal patterns. Stories are considered in terms of their constituents – setting, characters, plan of action, action, final outcome. The approach is strongly experimental. Characteristically 'subjects' (often children) are regarded as processors of stories. I have little sympathy with this approach and draw attention to it because, as we know, what begins as a particular kind of method of investigation today turns up tomorrow as a form of instruction and the day after tomorrow as a form of testing. If I shrink from all of this it is because I have read some of the contrived little stories which are used for some of this work. The 'story grammars' used for these purposes are as limited as the grammar of an utterance which, as we know, cannot deliver to us the significance of the utterance. Neither can it tell us about the motives and history of teller or listener. They wrench the story-telling situation into a special experimental context. They show us what is remembered but not why it is remembered. They are preoccupied with 'information'. Most of the studies have a deafness, if not actual antipathy to, the achievements of millennia of literary and rhetorical scholarship. There is almost nothing here for those of you who want to know, need to know, 'What is a story-teller doing and why?' (For examples of this 'school' see Bower, 1976; Glenn, 1978; Stein and Glenn, 1978; Thorndyke, 1977.)

3. Structuralism and post-structuralism

For sheer verve, imagination and creative theory the contributions of the structuralists at their best are most rewarding, even dazzling. It is only with some effort one can remind oneself of their limitations. You can, if you wish, trace the development of structuralism from Saussure (Bally and Sechehaye [eds.], 1916, translated by Harris, 1983) and his working out of the relationship between signifier and signified, and from Propp's great breakthrough in *The Morphology of Folk Tale* (1928, translated by Scott, 1968). I must necessarily skip the intervening history (see Todorov, 1977 and Hawkes, 1977). Structuralist work on narrative began as an attempt to create a poetics of the novel or fiction story, to unravel the *sameness* in its strategies, in its ordering of signifiers. But this left a problem. What we do not know at the end of Propp's innovative analysis of the seven spheres of action and thirty-one elements, which he claims *all* folk tales must deploy in one way or another in various combinations, is why we should prefer one to another, or indeed why a given combination should ever be embodied in two different stories. We need a theory of difference as well as of sameness, something which brings together the specification of structural communality and the specificity of the exploitation of resources within a particular narrative. Consider for example how a skilled oral narrator does improvised repair-work to cope with interruptions, lapses of memory, etc.

The two structuralist virtuosi, the narratologists par excellence, who have attempted to handle the specificities of complex texts, pitting themselves against the most challenging refinement of prose fiction are Barthes in *S/Z* (1975) and Genette in *Narrative Discourse* (1980). The first is a study of Balzac's 'Sarrasine' and the second of Proust's *Remembrance of things past*. Before we glance at them we can note that what structuralism has contributed to the development of the study of narrative is the development of the distinctions between *story, narrative discourse* and *narrating*. The story is the actual sequence of events, real or supposed; the narrative discourse is the framed text in which these events are reported; and the narrating refers to the actual process of fashioning the discourse, the act of telling. Finally a repeated theme is *intertextuality*. Any story presupposes the existence of other stories. For both reader and listener threads of connection exist, threads of many different kinds – shapes, devices, signals, echoes, explicit references and, more generally, a sense of how a story belongs with others as a verbal act.

Barthes's *S/Z* is itself a unique kind of text, defying summary by virtue of its method. In a difficult but challenging passage he states his ambition to bridge at last the general theory of all narrative and the detailed analysis, almost phrase by phrase, of a complex work:

> … the single text is valid for all texts of literature, not in that it represents them (abstracts and equalizes them) but in that literature itself is never anything but a single text: the one text is not an (inductive) access to a model but entrance into a network with a thousand entrances: to take this entrance is to aim, ultimately, not at a legal structure of norms and departures but at a perspective (of fragments, of voices from other texts, other codes) … each (single) text is the very theory of this difference.

This shift from structuralism, i.e. 'a legal structure of norms', leads Barthes to develop his famous five codes and put them to work in fictive discourse. He pursues this through the words, phrases, sentences and passages of Balzac's short story. They cross and recross, coincide, come to the fore or recede. Here they are:

(a) *the hermeneutic code* – which formulates questions, hints at secrets and enigmas
(b) *the semic code* – which delivers multiple or connate meaning
(c) *the symbolic code* – which through concrete elements points to generalized significance and is developed through antitheses
(d) *the proaeretic code* – the actions as represented in the text
(e) *the cultural code* – which is the presence in the text of the accepted knowledge of our culture.

In one respect the whole exercise is an act of terrorism through display, for few or none of us could bring to a text the iconoclastic erudition of Barthes. Yet I suggest we cannot refuse the invitation to look at any text in this manner even though we may not use all of the Barthes apparatus to do so. As he says,

> Alongside each utterance, one might say that off-stage voices can be
> heard: they are the codes; ... the convergence of the voices ... becomes
> stereographic space.

To listen for off-stage voices is an enticement and to regard a story as stereographic space is a liberation from the tendency to regard it as simply linear, however serpentine or meandering – the story line, as we say.

Genette's project is to demonstrate that all fiction stories share the same resources but that each separate work deploys these resources in a unique way. Quite unlike the simple story grammars of the cognitive school, which only work at best for the barest of little tales, his analysis has to work for nothing less than the labyrinthine intricacies of Proust. It is that which challenges him to achieve both theoretical depth and perceptive delicacy in the development and use of his apparatus. The earlier structuralists made their choice – the development of a theory of narrative – and they turned away from attempts to reach a deeper understanding or 'interpretation' of a given work.

Genette refuses to make this choice and integrates the two objectives. He sets out a three-fold division of the problems of the narrative:

tense – the relationship between the treatment of time in the discourse and time in the 'story'
mood – the ways in which a narrative takes on a particular perspective and establishes a particular distance, i.e. the *modes* of regulating information
voice – the relations between the narrator and the story he tells.

Let me give one example of how this system is refined and developed by Genette. When he elaborates on *voice* he has a sub-section which deals with the *functions* of the narrator, which we might have been forgiven for thinking consisted solely of telling the story. That is there, of course, as the *narrative function*; but there are also the *directing function*, the purpose of which is to direct attention to aspects of the narrative, 'stage directions' so to speak, calling attention to its own organization; the *communicating function*, the narrator's relationship to her/himself, the part she/he takes in the story, possibly affective, moral or intellectual; the *testimonial function*, which accounts for the part the narrator plays in the story she/he tells; the *ideological function*, which operates when the testimonial function becomes didactic. That display of just one of Genette's systems may give a glimpse of a narratologist preparing the tools of his craft before getting down to work, but as Genette notes:

> These five functions are not to be put in watertight compartments; none of
> the categories is completely unadulterated and free from complicity with
> others; none except the first is indispensable, and at the same time none,
> however carefully an author tries, can be completely avoided.

I said at the outset that we must weigh all that with care and perhaps scepticism. I justify my acting as a roughly functioning digestive tract because as teachers of English we have been slow to come to terms with developments in the study of narrative, much less to participate in them, adding our distinctive voice. For narratology inhabits its own kind of stereographic space in which our questions go unanswered. One is 'What does a narrator learn in the art of narrating?' I pointed towards some possibilities in the first paper. I want now to set out for you how in the very process of story-telling the teller can make surprising even shocking discoveries. Story-telling may be discovery learning.

I am asked to tell stories to a class of 13-year-old boys for a regular story-telling session in an inner-London multi-ethnic comprehensive secondary school. The session, nicely placed on Friday afternoons, has been given over by the teacher to story-telling by the boys, herself and the occasional outsider. The formula for outsiders is: one fiction story, one true story (autobiographical). I select Oscar Wilde's *The Happy Prince* as my fiction story and then search the attic of my childhood memories. Amongst the dust and cobwebs I catch sight of something glinting a little. I pull it out, brush it down, polish it. It will do. It tells of events which lasted an hour but, as the structuralists taught us a long time ago, narrative time is tricky and is not the same as chronological time. I can tell it to you in a few seconds.

> When I was about fourteen some six of us were kept behind in school, the ritual 'detention' of English schools. One boy, a newcomer to the class, set off the fire-extinguisher when the master in charge was out of the classroom. The master, a very ineffectual man, came rushing in and managed to direct the fire extinguisher out of the window, at which point it managed its last feeble spurt.

That's it. Not much to it. I felt it right, I suppose, because I remembered that at the time we found it hilarious and perhaps because it was one more skirmish in the non-stop guerrilla warfare between teachers and kids and therefore mildly scandalous and subversive. That's what I thought. As I rehearsed it with some care I had a strong urge to write it out and that I did. I give you one more detail to aid the hermeneutic process. All the boys of that class were Jewish and all the teachers Gentile. I take up the story at the point early in the written version when the boys had selected their seats in the detention room. Hoffman, the new boy, is choosing his.

> Hoffman hadn't moved yet. He slowly gave the room the once-over, his inspection drifting past us. He made his fastidious choice and sauntered over to the desk nearest to the door under the baize notice-board, next to the fire-extinguisher. We watched him and his almost adult ways. Not our kind of adults though. Ours overfilled their clothes and spilled schmalz on them, they walked with their feet close to the ground, toes outward,

heads bent forward and turned towards each other, and they poked fingers into each other's shoulders. They were cocooned in communal noise, did not know about Private Persons. They all talked at once, shouted as they slapped down their dominoes at the Workers' Circle or slurped their lemon tea or bitterly cursed the tailoring trade in noisy knots at the corner of Great Garden Street. No, the adult Hoffman was shaping up for was more like those occasional figures you saw stalking down the Whitechapel Road who came from Outside and made your mind shuffle uneasily at the faint whiff of power they gave off. They dealt with others, haunted offices or inspected something and never looked to right or left to catch sight of a relative or someone from the same stettel back in the East. Up there in the Sixth Form where they put on white coats to do Zoology there were one or two who were beginning to get the knack and might soon pass themselves off as the real thing. Golly Gottlieb came to school with a rolled umbrella and he was going to study at the London School of Economics, whatever that was. Gluckstein, whose father owned the big furniture shop opposite the Jewish Reading Room, had taken to wearing a fine light grey suit which clearly had not come out of the tailoring dens off the Commercial Road. A lawyer he was going to be and he had already closed his face to get into that part. Had they stopped eating pickled herring and latkes?

You will see that at this point the events of the story are absolutely minimal or, in Genette's terms, the narrative function is in one sense temporarily suspended while the testimonial and ideological functions take over. Hoffman takes his seat. We watch him. Then off I go, much to my surprise later, on a digression about two different kinds of adult. At one time we would have labelled it that way and left it but that won't do now. It is, in fact, a series of embedded and minimal stories. Some other time any one of them may grow into a story: but as they stand the micro-stories are delivering meaning to the macro-story, they hang about in its shadows, step forward and retire. There are embryo narratives of the spilling of schmalz, talking and shouting, playing dominoes, drinking lemon tea, strangers walking down the main street, Sixth Formers and their posh gear etc., etc. This is a kind of seeding. Each potential tale which never happens is, however, a signifier not only to you the hearer but also to me the writer. I have given you one example, but I discovered as the story uncurled that a pattern I had never 'intended', and quite different from the story I told, became exposed. As each spare event related to the central fire extinguisher episode was presented, it had attached to it another story or other stories much more overtly and assertively foregrounded and very didactic – a whole way of thinking. So there are stories of previous detentions, of an occasion when I was sent to the staff-room to get a dictionary, an earlier encounter between the new boy and a feared sarcastic teacher, and so on. As Calvino writes, in his role of fictive narrator in *If On a Winter's Night a Traveller* (1982), a novel about writing novels:

> I am producing too many stories at once because what I want is for you to feel, around the story, a saturation of other stories that I could tell or maybe will tell or who knows may have already told on some other occasion, a space full of stories that perhaps is simply my lifetime, where you can move in all directions, as in space, always finding stories that cannot be told until other stories are told first.

Genette, I suppose, would have pointed out that there are six sections in my story, some relatively lengthy, which take us back to time *before* the fire extinguisher story; and one to a time *after* it. Only three sections carry the interrupted central narrative. They embrace it with an ideological past and hesitate in front of an ideological future. As Kermode says, 'Secrets are at odds with sequence'. What I saw happening as I wrote was that the hilarious little episode was becoming a serious joke. Every digression pointed up an almost irreconcilable opposition between 'their way' and 'our way', the Gentile teachers and the Jewish boys. Almost. Because Hoffman is an ethnic transvestite. And anyway the bribery of schooling is beginning to exert its pull and all the boys are hovering on the brink of ambivalence. For me the writing of the story was a startling discovery of the ambiguities of ethnic confrontation. I am convinced that if I had not spent many years now looking at the consequences of class, ethnic and cultural diversity which play themselves out through linguistic diversity, then perhaps the story would never have been written or, if it had been, it would have been a very different one. Yet nothing could have been further from my mind when I began it. This is how it ends – just when the teacher, nicknamed Queenie, has been mocked and ridiculed by the boys as he demonstrates his incompetence.

> Suddenly Queenie turned on us, hugging the gleaming fire extinguisher. Yes, I was sure now, his eyes were brimming with tears. The cheers died into silence. He came a step nearer and out of his anguish he yelled.
>
> – What do you people come here for? What do you want of us?
>
> As if we knew. Perhaps Hoffman did. But we didn't. Not for sure. Not yet.

Let the story grammarians beware. Sentences end with full stops. Stories do not. That is the guarantee that not only do we learn from the making but that the process continues beyond the end as the seed of another story readies itself for germination.

Not yet

Detention. Just six of us; the usual crimes, the usual criminals – me, Solly, Berko, Saxy, Mo (of course) and the unknown quantity, Hoffman. The crime sheet was so routine you could have run it off for the whole term on the old Gestetner. Talking in class, calling out, passing notes, homework not in on time, lying – conduct prejudicial to good order and discipline. All down in Brock's flawless hand. So flawless, so durable and ineradicable, it turned our follies and foibles into everlasting wickedness so that we despaired of ever going straight. But Hoffman was new, only two months with us. His clothes were more expensive than ours, dapper men's, not youth's, shoes and silk shirts, I do believe. He was more pink than us, his hair was straight and fine and sandy. He was more suave too. We thought him, I hesitate, almost – well, Gentile. He was in for cheek rather than chutzpah. To Gobby with whom we had long since learned not to trifle. Gobby had been pursuing an earnest enquiry about nouns in apposition and drawn Hoffman into the quest. 'I've never been taught that – er, Sir.' Harmless enough, but this Hoffman could languidly imply that, if he hadn't been taught such things, they weren't worth knowing or at any rate he shouldn't be pestered about them. Gobby did his eye-flicker for a second or so and then struck, as we knew he would. He was suddenly affable, even solicitous.

– Ah yes. It has crossed my mind that your last school left you a little – er – unfinished. We can help a little. May I suggest you present yourself in Room 23 at 4 o'clock?

Hoffman tried to get out a word …

– No need to thank me. You'll find it all works out best if you arrive strictly on time. Now take this example, 'Albert, the Prince Regent … ' And we were back on course. Meanwhile Hoffman had smiled gratefully at the unlooked for chance to study the detention system.

So here he was with the old lags looking less cast down and aggrieved than us and less tousled by the wear and tear of a school day. No ink on his hands, tie and collar fit for a studio photograph, no marks of brawling or chesting a wet football. We mooched to the empty desks, sullen and grumpy but resigned, dumped ourselves down and dropped our satchels on the floor. We spread ourselves around like strangers, knowing if we didn't we'd only be separated in a minute or two. Hoffman hadn't moved yet. He slowly gave the whole room the once-over, his inspection drifting past us. He made his fastidious choice and sauntered over to the desk nearest to the door under the baize notice-board, next to the fire-extinguisher. We watched him and his almost adult ways. Not our kind of adults though. Ours overfilled their clothes and spilled schmalz on them, they walked with their feet close to the ground, toes outward, heads bent forward and turned towards each other, and they poked fingers into each other's shoulders. They were cocooned in communal noise, did not know about Private Persons. They all talked at once, shouted as they slapped down their dominoes at the Workers' Circle or slurped their lemon tea or bitterly cursed the tailoring trade in noisy knots at the corner of Great Garden Street. No, what the adult Hoffman was shaping up for was more like those occasional figures you saw stalking down the Whitechapel Road who came from Outside and made your mind shuffle uneasily at the faint whiff of power they gave off. They dealt with others, haunted offices or inspected something and never looked to right or left to catch sight of a relative or someone from the same stettel back in the East. Up there in the Sixth Form where they put on white coats to do Zoology there were one or two who were beginning to get the knack and might soon pass themselves off as the real thing. Golly Gottlieb came to school with a rolled umbrella and he was going to study at the London School of Economics, whatever that was. Gluckstein, whose father owned the big furniture shop opposite the Jewish Reading Room, had taken to wearing a fine light grey suit which clearly had not come out of the tailoring dens off the Commercial Road. A lawyer he was going to be and he had already closed his face to get into that part. Had they stopped eating pickled herring and latkes? Maybe you could learn how to do it. But then they couldn't have been the sort who had landed up regularly in detention when they were in the third year. Hoffman's kind of adult we saw in the pictures at the Rivoli or Palaseum, poised possessors of occasions, velvet public movers, who knew how to stand, walk or confer the benefit of themselves on a chair, always affable but always inviolable. But this Hoffman wasn't out of a film and was no Sixth Former. New he might be, but his lot was cast in with ours, a Third Former with an essay to do on Henry IV Part One, trying to get the hang of simultaneous equations, chanting defective Latin verbs for next Friday's test, listening to forty minutes uninterrupted droning on the Factory Acts and scribbling the notes from the board. What's more we'd noticed he wasn't too good at that kind of thing. As if that mattered. For the moment we were not competing furtively for B pluses and As but studying his glide over to the desk by the fire extinguisher and his so English manner of gracing the seat. It was already said by the know-all yuchners that he'd never been to cheder classes and, though this was beyond belief, that he'd not been barmitzvah-ed. Was that how you did it and got to be a Sixth Former before your time?

So we sat and endured the minutes. Mo was gently rattling coins in his pockets, Solly was drawing on the little pad he carried around, Saxy was whistling pianissimo through his teeth and drawn back lips, Berko cheated of his football was torturing himself by listening to the sound of the ball being thumped about outside. I was looking at Hoffman. He was leaning back in his seat and waiting, it seemed from the beginnings of a rosy smile, for a performance to begin.

If anything stirred beneath our torpor it was speculation about who would be the master in charge of this detention. And it mattered. If it was going to be Burroughs, he would give out dictionaries, select an arbitrary page and you copied out entries for an hour. 'Wouldn't want to be wasting your precious time,' he would say. Leggy would make us sit in total silence, arms folded, eyes front. (All of them had been in the army.) Then he'd read his paper or savagely mark books. He once crossed a page of my futile maths with such ferocity that his red pencil slashed the page open. He had to be watched for he had a filthy temper and we had just enough prudence to be wary of him. In detentions he would glance up often enough to take a good shufti at us and spot a backslider who would be made to stand facing the wall with his nose touching it. O'Shea on the other hand made it clear that he was bored out of his mind himself and he just used to chat with us and encourage us to be ever so slightly cheeky. We'd ask about his rural peat-brown Harris tweed, the like of which we'd never clapped eyes on.

– Where d'you buy suits like that?

– Buy 'em? You don't buy 'em. They get handed down as heirlooms.

– Did you really play hockey for your university?

– Yes, he'd say, we didn't win a ghost of a match that year. And don't be prying so much.

– Which football team do you support?

– And why should I be supporting a football team? Haven't I got my work cut out supporting meself and me aged mother? I won't be taking on a football team till I'm a Headmaster and mebbe not even then, the money won't run to it.

We had just begun to detect the Celtic fringe amongst our teachers and had a dim and wildly inaccurate notion of what it all amounted to. But a kind of humour came into it somewhere and anyway O'Shea was good value especially in the deserts of detentions. Imagine trying to talk to Gobby like that. No, that would be like trying to imagine him with his trousers down or doing a Highland fling. When Gobby took detention you stayed on the alert every second. No Yiddish obscenities and curses meant to be just heard but not understood, no deaf-and-dumb signals across the spaces, no scamping of chores, no ostentatious shufflings and coughings, no slumping from mock exhaustion as the clock dragged towards five, no cross-legged squirmings and asking to be excused and staying for five minutes to watch the football. No nothings with Gobby. You could forget the whole repertoire of diversions from tedium and illicit resistances. Gobby never raised his voice, never gave a sign of teacherly outrage or distress, just that sinister flicker of the eyelids, a slight pursing of the lips, a sniff or two, the handkerchief drawn from the sleeve, dab, dab, then a stiletto sentence. With him it was all heads down and not a whimper of rebellion.

It turned out in a minute or two that it was Mr King's stint for the detention shift. We called him Queenie not just to turn the world verbally upside down nor even because we saw him as a homosexual. We knew neither the word nor the idea. It was just that he moved, talked and engaged with us in ways we knew only from women. Even his public school speech was the soft caressing variety you hear in some artists and writers – all the same sounds but articulated in a different place and with a different music coaxed out of them. Poor old Queenie! He might just as well have presented his jugular to ravening wolves as come amongst us with his alien kind of chivalry, gentleness and vulnerability, his inability to disguise his hurt at rejection and mockery. Easy enough to recognise years later that there was a man it would have been perfectly good to know and learn from, but then he was nothing more than a perfect prey, a goy with a difference. He belonged to that little band of folk who are not made for this wicked world, should not be let out alone. They must be protected, taken round ambushes, have their tickets bought for them and be put on trains while they are freed to go on thinking about Baudelaire. He was certainly no person to send into the lair of Yiddisher knuckers, coarse clever-dicks ever on the look-out for a rare sacrificial victim. We'd never run into his like, someone both clever and easily wounded, articulate but without a repertoire of put-downs, humiliated but not a humiliator, knowledgeable about books but not about boys. Poor fellow, he paid for it all. We sacrificed him without remorse. Such a schmeryl! Strange revenges for our own hurts which we could not have put in words flowed against him. Without personal animosity we demolished him and scored it up as a little victory against all the nameless defeats. What a misfortune to be a nice man without a shell amongst such frustrated predators.

Queenie came bouncing into the room with all the simulated energy of the fearful. Insubordination flickered into life immediately and Queenie was saying, through the escalating disorder:

– Now, look chaps. Do something sensible, eh. You can start on your homework. It'll save you time later. Read a book. The hour will go more quickly. Or why don't you …

We orchestrated a huge clatter with our satchels, complained about empty ink-wells, chuntered to each other mimicking and mocking his speech, turning it into foppish silliness. We half-began a bit of reading or set about an exercise. Queenie teetered on the edge of total impotence and we teetered on the edge of open defiance and worse. I do not like to think about it now. It's not only a squeamish recoil from the cruelties. Nor is it that a mere eight years later I was on the receiving end, having gone over to the enemy. It is because I know now why we were pitted against one another in the detention room and that poor Queenie could never have known where it had all gone wrong for him. He had his first-class French degree (Cantab.) and a gown. Why had he been set down amongst these pitiless torturers, with their outlandish names and outlandish noises?

We were all in it except Hoffman. He was eyeing Queenie in his long black gown, and was leaning back in his seat, not joining in with the rest of us, just steadily watching the fluttering and flappings of the wounded bird – in a nicely restrained sort of way, a well-balanced spectator in the better part of the house.

We simmered and simmered towards five o'clock. If it had been a whole class we would have erupted, but a scattered handful we kept an eye on the boundaries. Solly's thumb and forefinger had a frozen hold on the top of a page of a textbook.

Berko had written a few scratchy lines in an exercise book. If Queenie's glance lighted on him, he advertised himself as someone grappling with difficult ideas. In between foghorn yawns Saxy was fiddling with his maths homework. He loved the damn stuff really. And Mo was keeping up a grumbling mutter, looking up occasionally to the ceiling with his eyes shut and then down to an open book: this was his regular learning-something-by-heart performance. Oh yes. We each had our little fail-safe system on the go. We didn't overdo it. The work was at best sporadic but just enough. Between whiles there was a good laugh. Berko could belch at will and control the volume and texture to suit the occasion or his fancy. He chose his moments to crackle and rumble knowing his virtuosity and variety always had us in fits.

– Ach, such a filthy chuzza! We applauded.

The rule book laid down the iron laws of a well-run detention but some teachers worked their own little variations. If you were in luck, at about half-time, they'd leave you to it and nip up to the staff room. A teacher would look round at the class, assure himself we were moderately cowed, walk up and down the rows a couple of times to uncover any illicit goings-on. (A comic, I remember, was a very illicit going-on or any kind of sweet-popping.) Then he'd make slowly for the door and turn for a last quelling stare. We'd listen with good behaviour and pray. And he'd be gone. A calculated brief silence just in case. And then …

– All right for him. I'm busting for a piss

–Gone for a quick drag

– A quick drag! With that pipe. It'll take him till five to get it going

– Doing his betting slips

– Chaim Schmerl went to the races, Lost his gutgas and his braces …

– Such a voice! A chazan we should make of him

Then we'd shush each other up and drop to whispers while the detention master took his ease in the Staff Room. None of us had ever been into that secret lair. At most you got a glimpse of billowing tobacco smoke, dusty tomes, tatty old leather armchairs, huge heaps of grimy exercise books and a flickering coal fire. Where else in the world could there be a room like it? Gobby once sent me up to get Funk and Wagnell's Dictionary on a dull winter's evening. The gaunt joyless Brock stood in the doorway without his gown, the keeper of Hell's Gate. Behind him I caught a glimpse of the other masters floating eerily in the smoke touched by the light of the fire. They seemed dead and doomed.

    No point in Queenie waiting for a lull. He took his chance, left us to our bogus work and bolted out of the door.

Hoffman said, It's 4.27, and crossed off another minute. Then he swung his legs out from under the desk and stretched them out over the top. There were sharp creases in his trousers. Berko moved over to the window to watch the footballers who were doing without him. Someone behind me was patiently picking a hole in the thick oak desk top with his geometry compass. Suddenly Hoffman said in a loud voice, How does this thing work? He was lightly tapping the fire-extinguisher above his head. It didn't sound like a serious question. All the same we all turned towards him. Berko turned his head from the window and the woodpecker behind me stopped tap-tapping.

– Tells you on the side.

The fire-extinguisher we all knew. Amongst all the battered wood, splintered parquet, scratched brown varnish, pock-marked tiles and flaking distemper its gorgeous red, black and gold looked like a mistake. In every classroom they were untouched and untouchable. We'd all read the instructions 'In case of fire … ' and so forth. Please God, we'd never need to use it. Enough trouble without emergencies. Emergency exits; in emergency use hammer to break windows; the coiled hose; life-belts; high voltage; electrified rails, do not cross the lines. Emergencies we could do without.

– Don't you know then? said Hoffman.

Mo couldn't resist.

– There's a sort of hammer fixed to the side. And there's that pin. Stops you moving the hammer. When you pull the pin out, you can move the hammer up and down. You just lift the hammer up and bash it down on the side and that …

Mo stopped as he realized Hoffman was listening seriously and taking note.

But Hoffman said, That sounds really stupid. Don't believe a word of it pins and hammers. You don't expect me to swallow that, do you?

– He's *meshiggah*, Solly whispered to me. We were uneasy. We had our sense of things getting out of hand.

Hoffman was on his feet. A panicky voice said, Leave it, Hoffman, But Hoffman already had the pin out and was looking contemptuously at us. He lifted the hammer and let it drop onto the side of the extinguisher. Clonk! Nothing happened.

– You see, said Hoffman, you're so stupid. It doesn't work like that.

We were getting desperate. Little wickednesses were one thing but sin on this scale was beyond us. There would be some terrible retribution. Grand audacity was for others.

– You're right, you're right, we told him. Only leave the bloody thing alone. You'll damage it. Just leave it alone, leave it alone.

Hoffman fingered the hammer again. We were squeaking with cowardly anxiety.

– We'll all cop it. God knows what they'll do to us.

Hoffman found our performance distasteful. Swiftly he turned his back on us, lifted the hammer and smashed it down against the fire extinguisher. White foam came gushing out of the nozzle and hit the front of the classroom, a gorgeous white froth, unstoppable and wondrous. We fell into a bewitched silence. Hoffman grabbed the thing from the wall and sprayed it nonchalantly about, having the time of his life.

– Should be put away, the schmendrik

– Certified

– Locked up

We palpitated with shock and delight. The foam began to spread over the floor, over the desks and around our feet. It was irresistible. We started kicking it about, romping in it, shouting with abandon. White flecks spattered on trousers and jackets.

– Get it out of here! Shove it in the corridor! Stick it in the book cupboard!

We hoped he wouldn't. Hoffman's posture had become heroic. He pointed the nozzle like a fixed bayonet. He would hold out till the last round. There should have been a camera.

The foam still gushed. Somewhere beyond our jolly paddling and splashing a nerve of panic still throbbed.

– Get Queenie, Saxy said.

We laughed our heads off at such a delicious possibility. Queenie in this madhouse. Saxy wasn't joking. He paddled out of the room and was back in no time with a flushed Queenie struggling to look masterful and cool. He was on the edge of tears. He rushed madly at Hero Hoffman to grab the extinguisher. Hoffman somehow didn't time his release too well. By the time Queenie was in full possession after the badly-managed transfer there were gobbets of foam down the front of Queenie's suit. He steadied himself and adjusted his grip while the extinguisher sprayed around wildly. We faked terror, ducking and side-stepping.

Queenie shouted, Open a window, open a window. That one.

Two of us wrestled for the window pole. The winner waved it around the catch, found it and tugged. We egged him on, choking on our laughter. And while the foam still sprayed Queenie hopped up and down with the fire extinguisher as though he were holding a bomb. He wanted none of it, having no taste for emergencies himself. His face was bright red and creased with anxiety.

At last the window squeaked open and Queenie rushed up to it. With his only touch of masterly control he directed the nozzle out of the window. At his first go the jet hit a window pane but he adjusted his aim and got on target. The creases dropped from his face. But at the very moment of his triumph the stream of foam curled into a weak arc. Queenie stood his ground as though hoping for better things. And then a last feeble dribble splashed onto the floor. Queenie's shoulders dropped and he let the extinguisher hang from his hands.

To a man we burst into cheers and jumped up and down beside ourselves. All caution gone we let rip mounting a huge din.

– You silly, silly man, I heard Hoffman saying while clapping appreciatively.

Suddenly, Queenie turned on us hugging the gleaming red extinguisher, his legs apart. Yes, I was sure now, his eyes were brimming with tears. The cheers died slowly into a silence. Queenie came a step nearer. Out of his anguish he yelled.

– What do you people come here for? What do you want of us?

As if we knew. Perhaps Hoffman did. But we didn't. Not for sure. Not yet.

References

Andrews, R. (no date) *Storytelling in School.* Mimeo.

Bakhtin, M. (1981) *The Dialogic Imagination: Four essays* (C. Emerson and M. Holquist, trans.). Austin: University of Texas Press.

Bally, C. and Sechehaye, A. (eds.) (1916) *Saussure: Cours de linguistique générale.* Lausanne: Librairie Payot. *Saussure: Course in general linguistics* (1983) (R. Harris, trans.). La Salle, IL: Open Court Publishing Company.

Barnes, D. and Todd, F. (1977) *Communication and Learning in Small Groups.* London: Routledge and Kegan Paul.

Barthes, R. (1975) (R. Miller, trans.) *S/Z.* London: Jonathan Cape.

Barthes, R. (1976) (R. Miller, trans.) *The Pleasure of the Text.* London: Jonathan Cape.

Bellack, A. (1966) *The Language of the Classroom.* New York: Teachers College Press.

Benjamin, W. (1970) 'The storyteller', in H. Arendt (ed.) *Illuminations.* London: Fontana.

Bower, G. (1976) 'Experiments on story understanding and recall'. *Quarterly Journal of Experimental Psychology,* 28.

Calvino, I. (1982) (W. Weaver, trans.) *If on a Winter's Night a Traveller.* London: Picador.

Cazden, C. and Hymes, D. (1978) 'Narrative thinking and story-telling rights: A folklorist's clue to a critique of education'. *Keystone Folklore,* 22 (1–2).

Chafe, W. (ed.) (1980) *The Pear Stories: Cognitive, cultural, and linguistic aspects of narrative production.* Norwood, NJ: Ablex.

Chatman, S. (1978) *Story and Discourse.* Ithaca, NY: Cornell University Press.

Culler, J. (1978) *The Pursuit of Signs.* London: Routledge and Kegan Paul.

Eagleton, T. (1981) *Walter Benjamin or Towards a Revolutionary Criticism.* London: Verso.

Garnica, O. and King, M. (eds.) (1979) *Language, Children and Society*. Oxford: Pergamon Press.

Genette, G. (1980) *Narrative Discourse* (J. Lewin, trans.). Oxford: Basil Blackwell.

Glenn, C. (1978) 'The recall of episodic structure and of story length in children's recall of simple stories'. *Journal of Verbal Learning and Verbal Behaviour*, 17.

Goody, J. (1982) 'Alternative paths to knowledge in oral and literate cultures', in D. Tannen (ed.) *Spoken and Written Language*. Norwood, NJ: Ablex.

Gregory, R. (1974) 'Psychology: Towards a science of fiction'. *New Society*, 23 May.

Harding, D. (1962) 'Psychological processes in the reading of fiction'. *British Journal of Aesthetics*, 2 (2).

Harding, D. (1963) *Experience into Words*. London: Chatto and Windus.

Hardy, B. (1968) 'Towards a poetic of fiction: An approach through narrative', in *Novel: A forum on fiction, Fall 1968*. Providence, RI: Brown University.

Hawes, H. (1979) *Curriculum and Reality in African Primary Schools*. London: Longman.

Hawkes, T. (1977) *Structuralism and Semiotics*. London: Methuen.

Hymes, D. (1979) 'Language in education: Forward to fundamentals', in O. Garnica and M. King (eds.), *Language, Children and Society*. Oxford: Pergamon Press.

Kress, G. (1982) *Learning to Write*. London: Routledge and Kegan Paul.

Labov, W. (1972) *Language in the Inner City*. Philadelphia: University of Pennsylvania Press.

Le Guin, U. (1980) 'It was a dark and stormy night'. *Critical Enquiry*, 7 (1).

Macherey, P. (1978) *A Theory of Literary Production*. London: Routledge and Kegan Paul.

Medvedev, P. and Bakhtin, M. (1978) *The Formal Method in Literary Scholarship: A critical introduction to sociological poetics* (A. Wehrle, trans.). Baltimore, MD: Johns Hopkins University Press.

Moffett, J. *Teaching the Universe of Discourse*. Boston, MA: Houghton Mifflin.

Propp, V. (1928) (1968) *The Morphology of the Folktale* (L. Scott, trans.). Columbus, OH: American Folklore Society and Bloomington, IN: Indiana University.

Rosen, B. (1982) 'Review of vicariance biogeography: A critique'. *The Palaeontological Association Circular 107*.

Rosen, H. (1980) 'The dramatic mode', in P. Salmon (ed.), *Coming to Know*. London: Routledge and Kegan Paul [reprinted here].

Sachs, H. (1972) 'On the analysability of stories by children', in J. Gumperz and D. Hymes (eds.), *Directions in Sociolinguistics*. New York: Holt, Rinehart and Winston.

Scollon, R. and Scollon, S. (1981) *Narrative, Literacy and Face in Inter-ethnic Communication*. Norwood, NJ: Ablex.

Sinclair, J. and Coulthard, M. (1975) *Towards an Analysis of Discourse: The English used by teachers and pupils*. Oxford: Oxford University Press.

Stein, N. and Glenn, C. (1978) 'An analysis of story comprehension in elementary school children', in R. Freedle (ed.), *Discourse Processing: Multidisciplinary perspectives, vol. 2*. Norwood, NJ: Ablex.

Stubbs, M. and Delamont, S. (1976) *Explorations in Classroom Language*. Chichester: John Wiley.

Tannen, D. (1980) 'A comparative study of oral narrative strategies: Athenian Greek and American English', in W. Chafe (ed.), *The Pear Stories: Cognitive, cultural, and linguistic aspects of narrative production*. Norwood, NJ: Ablex.

Tannen, D. (ed.) (1982a) *Spoken and Written Language: Exploring orality and literacy*. Norwood, NJ: Ablex.

Tannen, D. (1982b) 'The oral literate continuum in discourse', in Tannen (ed.) (1982a).

Harold Rosen

Thorndyke, P. (1977) 'Cognitive structures in comprehension and memory of narrative discourse'. *Cognitive Psychology*, 9.

Todorov, T. (1977) *The Poetics of Prose* (R. Howard, trans.). Oxford: Basil Blackwell.

White, H. (1980) 'The value of narrativity in the representation of reality'. *Critical Enquiry*, 7 (1).

The Importance of Story

Harold first gave this paper at the annual conference of the UK National Association for the Teaching of English in Nottingham, England, on 12 April 1985. It was published in March 1986 in *Language Arts*, 63 (3), the journal of the National Council of Teachers of English in the USA.

A month or so ago I found myself immersed in a very lengthy work by Dell Hymes (1983), the great sociolinguist, in which he elaborates the notion now familiar to many of us – communicative competence. He first developed this concept as a sharply combative response to Chomsky's concept of competence (an internalized set of rules, to simplify or vulgarize). Rest assured I am not going to drag you through a replay of that important polemic, because I want to get on with my story. I did not find the Dell Hymes an easy read. It was both dense and microscopic, pursuing its argument down every theoretical byway and subjecting every concept to critical scrutiny, a kind of intellectual war of attrition. However, I persisted over several days and reached a point in the argument where Dell Hymes, having taken us step-by-step through a demonstration of the inadequacy of Chomsky's model, says that given the complexity of language we should be able to do better than that. What happened next? Just this:

> Let me mention here Mrs. Blanche Tohet, who in the summer of 1951 had David and Kay French and myself wait for a story until she had finished fixing eels. A tub of them had been caught the night before near Oregon City. Each had to be slit, the white cord within removed, and the spread skin cut in each of its four corners, held apart by sticks. The lot were then strung up on a line between poles, like so many shrunken infants' overalls to dry. Mrs. Tohet stepped back, hands on hips, looking at the line of eels, and said, 'Ain't that beautiful.' (The sentence has been a touchstone for aesthetic theory for me ever since.) All then went in, and she told us the story of Skunk, when his musk sac was stolen and carried down river, how he travelled down river in search of his 'golden thing', asking each shrub, plant and tree in turn, and being answered civilly or curtly; how down the river he found boys playing shinny-ball with his sac, entered the game, got the 'ball', popped it back in, headed back up river; how, returning, he rewarded and punished, appointing those that had been nice to him a useful role for those who were soon to come into the land, denying usefulness to those who had been rude. All this in detail with voices for

different actors, gestures for the actions, and always animation. For that, as people will be glad to tell you, is what makes a good narrator; the ability to make the story come alive, to involve you as in a play. Despite the efforts of white schools and churches, there are people in whom such style lives today. Knowing them, it's impossible to think of them as tacit grammarians; each is a voice.

This brief diversion in the onward march of academic prose was for me much more than a respite. It probed backwards and forwards in the whole text, giving it a new dimension of validity. And Dell Hymes chooses a pivot, a fulcrum in his text as the moment to code-switch, marshalling for his purpose language which could scarcely survive in the withering abstractions of his other prose. His opening phrase, 'Let me mention here', underplays the weight given to the story. I take it to be pseudo-apologetic, pseudo-casual. Now Dell Hymes has spent a lifetime in the study of Amerindian languages out of which he has plucked this single instance. It is, of course, a narrative. No – more than that. It is the story of the occurrence of a story as well as that story itself (or rather a retold compressed version of it). Finally, it comes with a coda, which stresses in a non-narrative mode why he is telling the tale of a tale ('it's impossible to think of them as tacit grammarians'), though this is much more overt, committed, and passionate than any other part of his text. This is a reminder that narrative is multifunctional. Dell Hymes uses his two-layered narration to give persuasive power to his general theme, whereas Blanche Tohet has no such readily construed designs on us. Rather she is handing on from her culture a composition of events in such a way that it constitutes in its own right 'an experimentation with life' (Bakhtin) and its moral weight is inextricably enfolded in the tale and its telling. Though she is retelling a traditional tale, she imposes on it her own intonation which is only another way of saying that her own experience makes its unique contribution to the communal one. 'Animation,' Dell Hymes calls it. I would take that in its French sense of the driving force or prime mover of an enterprise. 'Each is a voice.' That is why retailing is not retelling. Retelling requires imagination and wisdom. A reanimator must not refuse her own learned life. Finally, Dell Hymes' story strikes out at that reductiveness and schematism which picks away at narrative until we are left with the bare bones. There is an obsession with plot structure both in structuralism and cognitive science. It is still plot even when it's called narrative programmes or schema or some such. There is no denying this essential feature of narrative; the danger consists in stopping there or, as Derrida puts it, 'stifling the force under the form'.

The educational abuse of narrative

We could as teachers happily leave such matters to the theoreticians, since a long apprenticeship has taught us not to treat stories like games of chess (as Shklovski did) because the identical plot moves in two different stories take on different meanings, meanings constructed from everything else which is there. All the complex formulations of narrative structure and the interesting notion of narrative competence have their vulgar, drab, and ominous counterpart in the world of English teaching. A recent British government set of objectives for English from 5 to 16 (Her Majesty's Inspectorate, 1984) cravenly refused to address questions of culture and imagination. However, notice the way the authors handled narrative. An objective for eleven-year-olds is that they should be able to give 'the gist of a story'. So narrative dwindles to this mundane object. Derrida (1978) confronted this tendency without compromise:

> Thus the relief and design of structure appears more clearly when content, which is the living energy of meaning, is neutralized. Somewhat like the architecture of an uninhabited island or deserted city, reduced to its skeleton by some catastrophe of nature or art. A city no longer inhabited but haunted by meaning and culture.

Yet this is just what Her Majesty's Inspectorate was inviting us to – 'an uninhabited or deserted city'. We are, God knows, all too familiar with whole atlases of deserted cities in education and English teaching: Logopolis, Drillville, Skillville … To take up narrative is to refuse that atlas and firmly concentrate on 'the living energy of meaning'. It is all too easy to let it elude us. Here is how it's done.

Hilyard and Olson (1982) set out to conduct an experiment, through the advanced techniques of cognitive science, you understand, on the memory and comprehension of stories. In particular they wanted to know whether children who heard a story remembered and comprehended it better than those who had read it. These are interesting matters for reasons which I have no need to spell out and the results of such an enquiry might point in certain directions for our own practice. (At this point let me pause and ask how you would go about it.)

I shall not give you a full account of the so-called experiment but shall limit myself to certain features of it, enough, I hope, to show how some eminent people in renowned educational institutions do research into narrative on behalf of teachers. The children (eight-year-olds, don't forget) were to offer 'responses' to four stories. It is assumed without demonstration or discussion that stories contain four kinds of information, structurally important (explicit or implicit), structurally incidental or irrelevant (explicit or implicit). Now you might think it quite a difficult matter to analyse a story using nothing but those categories. But there are ways of solving such problems. The experimenters avoided the messiness of a real story and wrote four stories, twelve to fourteen lines long, making sure they contained only the four classes of statements. I quote:

> Each story was accompanied by [they mean 'contained'] 12 statements, such that across the four stories 12 examples of each item type were

prepared. It was not possible to present equal numbers of each statement with each story since to do so would result in the stories being stilted and awkward.

Here is one of the stories, purged of stiltedness and awkwardness by the cognitive science story-writing cooperative.

> Susan and Jonathon lived in a house in the middle of a city. At the end of the backyard there was a large maple tree. Susan and Jonathon often played under the maple tree in their sandbox.
>
> One morning they found something in the sand. It was tiny and white. Susan went into the house to find a container to put it in. She went up to her bedroom and came back carrying a black and white box. It's too big, said Jonathon.
>
> So Susan found a handkerchief and some kleenex. They put the handkerchief on the bottom of the box and laid the tissues on top of the handkerchief. Jonathon carefully laid the strange thing on the tissues. Next morning their teacher was interested in what they had found and gave the whole class a lesson on how birds' eggs hatch.

I confess that I don't find that a gripping yarn – no pictures and no dialogue, but let that go. How are we going to compare listeners to readers? First you read the stories to one group and let the other group read it for themselves. Then you administer a test, of course, which consisted of a set of alternative statements from which the children had to select the correct alternative, thus:

A Susan and Jonathon found a bird egg.
B Susan and Jonathon found a stone.

(If you are already perceiving some promising lesson material here, you might like to know that the whole procedure took about forty minutes. Perfect!) More seriously, it would be possible, wouldn't it, to produce both objectives and curriculum material from such research? Imagine if HM Inspectorate were to respond to the criticism that their objectives for English are vague. They could produce a toughened-up version on narrative. For eleven-year-olds:

> to be able to recognize and distinguish between the structurally explicit and the structurally implicit
> to be able to recognize and distinguish between the incidental explicit and the incidental implicit
> … and so on.

The 'basics' of narrative

What work of this kind (and there is much more) should do for us is to harden in us the intention to keep our eyes firmly fixed on principles:

1. that it matters which stories we work with and that remembering and comprehending are especially related to the power of a story to engage with the world of feeling and thought in the listener;
2. that receiving a story is an exploration by the receiver(s), not a set of responses to someone else's questions in right/wrong format;
3. that we should ask why we should remember a story and not simply what we remember;
4. that the most constructive way of examining the hold a story has is for it to be presented in a propitious context and to be retold in an equally propitious one.

Sorry to have detained you so long on this drab and misguided work. But we know now how vigilantly we must scan the horizon for every sign of impending menace. These 'scientific' ineptitudes are only made possible by virtue of ignoring all that we need to attend to in examining narrative. I'll set it out in general terms.

1. Narrative is multifunctional. It can be pressed into service by anyone for almost any purpose, good or bad.
2. Compared with other kinds of discourse (say, petitionary prayer), narrative is always of necessity taken up by everyone everywhere. Its very diversity and universality is a guarantee of both its use and abuse. Children take it on very soon after the earliest stage of language acquisition and all get better and better at it. In some cultural settings it is more fostered than in others.
3. It is frequently embedded in other kinds of discourse.
4. The less constrained the discourse, i.e., censored by power, the more likely it is to have recourse to narrative. Spontaneous speech narrative is the most difficult kind of language to censor.
5. Since we dream in narrative and speak to ourselves in narrative (inner narrative speech), these are pointers to its profound relationship to thought. The narrative forms we master provide genres for thinking with.
6. A basic form of narrative is not only telling but also *re*telling and this includes our willingness to hear some stories retold.
7. Narrative is oral in the sense that we can engage fully with it without encountering it in written form and always *before* that encounter.

These are some but by no means all of the features which have led so many to suggest that narrative has an importance much deeper and broader than the purely literary values we customarily give to it and that it has a pre-eminence among the discourse options open to us. Thus it has been said that:

it is a mode of knowledge emerging from action;

it is the imposition of formal coherence on a virtual chaos of human events;

it is a primary and irreducible form of human comprehension;

it is the central instance or function of human mind.

The making of narrative

What all these well-argued claims emphasize is a positive, productive, universal function of narrative for the narrator. What they do not bring out sufficiently is the process of the making of narrative; nor do they stress its communicative aspect. We tell ourselves stories, of course, all the time, some we wouldn't dare to tell to others. But we *do* tell them to others. John Berger (1984) says, 'Events are always to hand. But the coherence of these events is an imaginative construction.' And it is just that coherence which we want to offer and share with others. The internalized, private story is itself an impossibility without a prior sharing, a prior discourse, without social memory and social action. There is a central distinction firmly established in the study of narrative derived from the Russian formalists, that is between what they called *sujhet* and *fabula*, now confusingly 'story' and 'discourse'. That is, the actual events, real or supposed, and their transformation into a narration. (Genette's *Narrative Discourse* [1980] and Barthes' *S/Z* [1975] are supreme examples of studies of this transformation.) Even the simplest, most trivial, and ephemeral little anecdote (How I took the wrong exit off the motorway or the simplicities of *Little Miss Muffet*) deploy this same process of transforming events into narrative. For all narration proposes an ever-alert scrutiny of a never-ceasing, unstoppable infinity of events without beginning or end and the rigorous selection from them of a meaningful and significant sequence impregnated with social values. The selection itself is value-laden and the narrating heightens this with every word it uses, for every word is a social microcosm. The most 'realistic' story is thus never reality itself. As Umberto Eco (1981) reminded us recently, to tell a story is to take a stance towards events and, rather than reflect a world, to create a world. To begin a story is to make a choice from an infinity of possibilities, selecting one set rather than another. That is why it is not just fiction which is an exercise of the imagination, it is any construction of narrative coherence. From this all else flows:

1. The creation of this coherence never starts from cold because it always draws on culturally inherited complexities, ways of telling, archetypal ideologies of narration. (Who lives happily ever after? And why?)
2. If a story is to be communicated, it must engage the willing attention of others, which is why it must always go beyond structure. Let's see how this goes. We'll start with Chomsky's famous story:

    NP + VP + NP

If you find that somewhat bare, I'll liven it up:

Somebody did a something to a something.

Not a lot better. Try again:

My uncle won the war.

Suppose it to be the first sentence of a story, and I think you can say that my three examples are steps up the enticement ladder. They constitute improved attempts to engage your willing attention. To recruit your willing attention is an invitation to a learning process because it is an invitation to a totally motivated search for significance. To tell a story is to formulate an interlocking set of meanings; to listen to one is in its turn an active search for the teller's meaning via one's own; to retell a story is also to do just that because listening is a kind of retelling.

A story is a communication. Its selective sequencing beckons towards somebody rather than anybody. This is very clear in the oral story. This is an Irish storyteller recorded by Michael Murphy (1975).

> Were you ever up at the Long Woman's Grave ... in the mountains between here and Omeath? Well, this was supposed to happen up there. But it must be donkey's years and years ago, for there's not a track of a horse there now.
>
> Anyhow this old woman lived up there, her and her man called John, their two selves by their lone. And this day anyhow she was herding a cow or a calf and they had sheep of course. When who comes walking up the road but this student – damn me if I can say for truth now whether he was going on for a priest or a parson, but one or the other. He got to talking to this old woman anyhow and says she: 'Would you be a hatter from County Down come to buy wool?'
>
> He said not; he said he was going on for a clergyman. Damn, but I mind now he was going on for a priest.

Now this recruitment of present listeners is so deep in the tradition of narrative that writers of stories are always resorting to it. Here's a twelve-year-old boy beginning on a written story:

> I really can't think of anyone who I'd like to be less than Jossy Phent. To begin with, what about the name? And his Dad – oh yes his Dad! ... Even so I like Jossy. He's one of nature's bad examples, a warning to humankind. He was quite illiterate. He went to school once – not that that proves anything though. Anyway, it all happened ...

The written story plunders the oral story. Frederic Jameson (1981) sees a wider significance in this:

> The gestures and signals of the story-teller symbolically attempt to restore the co-ordinates of a face-to-face story-telling institution which has been effectively disintegrated by the printed book and even more by the commodification of literature and culture.

That is the familiar voice of radical 'pessimism of the intellect', which I won't stop to quarrel with partly because, interpreted aright, I would find much to agree with. But what Jameson calls the 'co-ordinates of story-telling' are worth attending to. I take these to be the basic shifts in the narrative (not necessarily linear in presentation), non-narrative intertwining in narrative space, the maintenance of relationship via the narration between teller and audience – personae who both *are* and *act* – and the relationship between narrative codes and creativity.

The conventions of narration

We don't need reminding that narrative is suffused with conventions, of structure, of 'character', of language, of authorial voice, and even conventions of subverting conventions. And we know many stories which consist of nothing else. The confident grasp of these conventions and free play within them ('Freedom,' Marx said, 'is the recognition of necessity') is amazingly managed by young pupils – Jeremy aged eleven:

> Reagen the raven was like any other raven. Nice, kind, showed interest and also an awful singer. He had black feathers with a hint of brown in his wings. He had pleasant attitudes and a nice approach to life. At parties he would joke, laugh and have a great time. Now, Reagen had a different sense of humour than other ravens. He liked boring jokes, not original ones. Ravens didn't like him for that and prevented him from going to parties by locking their doors when he came. He lived in Liptons in Harlesden.
>
> His life began to build up with problems. He was thrown out of Liptons and had to live on the streets. Soon he found an empty bird house so he made himself comfie. There was food for him every day. The other problem was that he felt lonely. One fine evening he went out to explore, partly because there was nothing else exciting to do. Then suddenly he had an idea. He flew to Ealing and even into a shop called Athena. There he bought a joke book. He learnt all the jokes by heart even though there was a thousand. When he went to parties he was accepted and all the ravens loved his jokes. Then his jokes, the ones that he knew, ran out and the ravens didn't accept him ...

Let me draw attention to just one convention being followed here among many: that is, to begin a story by *generalizing* the past, which is another way of saying that this story begins with a set of stories which are not told. A familiar device. But 'One fine evening … ' moves by another convention into the mainstream story. A general measure of its conventional mastery is that we might easily assume that it was written by an adult.

Conventionality has its obverse side. This is explored in Bakhtin's remarkable book *The Dialogic Imagination* (1981). He argues that two forces are at work in language; he calls them *centrifugal* and the *centripetal*. The centripetal constitutes all which pull us towards a centre of linguistic norms, the pressure to conform to a single set of rules, to genre conventions, to discourse etiquettes, all of which he says 'unite and centralize verbal ideological thought'. The counterforce is centrifugal, which pulls away from the normative centre.

> Every utterance of a speaking subject serves as a point where centrifugal as well as centripetal forces are brought to bear. The processes of centralization and decentralization, of unification and disunification, intersect in the utterance … [which] is in fact an active participant in speech diversity.

Bakhtin then goes on to show how the centrifugal force operates in parody, many other kinds of 'verbal masquerades', and ultimately in the novel. Reagen the raven was in the tradition of that kind of verbal masquerade which we know from Aesop's fables, Lafontaine and Krylov, Thurber and many others. We catch the centrifugal at work in Michael (age fourteen) engaged in autobiographical narrative. Double-voiced – the infant and the fourteen-year-old:

> There was nothing.
>
> And I was two. Rabbit is my very best friend. I sat in the corner and we were playing with a thing and then there were reds and yellows and browns. My brother is called Gonofan and he told Mummy (whose real name is also Mummy) to come and see the pretty colours. Mummy did not like them and hit the reds and yellows and browns.
>
> The deers in the park are brown. I like deers and I touched a deer and it ran away and I ran after it into the woods but she did not have a broomstick. She wanted to eat me so I ran back to Mummy. I ran and ran like Johnny Rabbit ran from the farmers gun …
>
> I ran up the stairs with Rabbit. My bottom hurt and I needed the potty. But I cannot run as fast as Rabbit and I had to leave the brown gunge on the stairs and I wet my eyes but I started to read and so was happy.

Mummy made me some red and blue shoes and he played nic nac
on my shoe
And I was three
He played nic nac on my knee

My Daddy (whose real name is also Daddy) is a good wizard. He did magic
on the house and made it change. I went for a ride in the car and when I
came back it had changed, but there was no room for Daddy in our new
house. He should have made it bigger.

And I was four
He played nic nac on my door.

I was with Rabbit on the pavement and we were waiting for Daddy to make
us be on holiday and a young man, really the Giant up the beanstalk, made
the door sing like Penny Penguin. She sings 'Michael row the boat ashore'.
I was taken to be mended in hospital.

The centrifugal, I think.

Narrative as curriculum

Let me indicate briefly how Bakhtin moves on to consider authoritative discourse, and
I think you will readily perceive without my dotting the i's and crossing the t's that this
all implies a view of the curriculum. Authoritative discourse has as its natural home all
institutions of formal learning. You will recognize it from Bakhtin's description. He
begins with the process ('the ideological becoming of a human being') of selectively
assimilating the words of others. There are two modes for doing this, 'reciting by
heart' and 'retelling in one's own words'.

> Retelling a text in one's own words is to a certain extent a double-voiced
> narration of another's words, for indeed 'one's own words' must not
> completely dilute the quality that makes another's words unique; a retelling
> in one's own words should have a mixed character, able when necessary to
> reproduce the style and expression of the transmitted text.

However, retelling in our own words is quite another mode if it becomes 'internally
persuasive discourse'. The two forms may coexist but that is rare. More often there
is 'a sharp gap':

> … in one, the authoritative word (religious, political, moral, the word
> of a father, of adults, of teachers, etc.) that does not know internal
> persuasiveness, in the other the internally persuasive word that is denied
> all privilege, backed up by no authority at all and is frequently not

acknowledged in society (not by public opinion nor by scholarly norms, nor by criticism).

Authoritative discourse demands 'our unconditional allegiance':

> [It] permits no play with the context framing it, no play with its borders, no gradual and flexible transitions, no creative stylizing variants on it.

It is indissolubly fused with its authority. It is all inertia and 'calcification'. Meanwhile:

> Internally persuasive discourse is … tightly interwoven with one's own word … [It] is half ours and half someone else's. [Its] semantic structure is not finite, it is open … this discourse is able to reveal newer ways to mean.

This is the totally different means of taking on the words of another, of retelling.

I have, of course, not done justice to Bakhtin's complex elaboration of these ideas. Enough, I hope, to make you want to seek it out yourselves. But why have I introduced it?

1. Because we can detect calcified, inert, authoritative discourse dominating learning.
2. Because it is within the narrative zone that there exists most promise for the alternative. Not that narrative is without its inert texts. It is only that in the making of narrative we can most easily elude the magisterial, and engage in the 'play of boundaries'.
3. Because when we are striving to retell, this is 'no simple act of reproduction but rather a further creative development of another's discourse in a new context and under new conditions'.

The whole curriculum might, could, should have as its simple quintessential rubric 'retelling in one's own words' and the replacing of authoritative discourse with internally persuasive discourse. And for that segment of the curriculum we claim as our own, English, we should find generous space for the retelling of stories.

People like us have come to value within that danger zone we call creativity a special feature – originality. It's not difficult to see why it was and still is necessary to insist again and again on the need to shatter the authority of recitation with the unheard voices of our pupils, to help them to engage in the difficult struggle to articulate, develop, refine, advance their meanings as against the mere reproduction of the words of the textbook, the blackboard, the handout, the encyclopedia, the dictionary, the crammers' guides. Set in the context of Bakhtin's analysis, English teachers' insistence on the working through of students' own imaginings and thinking is seen to be a necessarily rebellious squaring up to the oppressive power of authoritative language. We all know that there are millions of notebook and examination papers crammed with words which are in essence transcriptions of the forced labour of submission. There is no need to dwell on this. We unearthed this slave society long ago in the samples collected by the Writing Research Unit (Britton, Burgess, Martin, McLeod and Rosen, 1975 – [see 'Sense of Audience' in this collection]).

But all that is quite different from retelling, from the ways in which we at one and the same time repeat the words and stories of others and also transform them. We even repeat our own words and stories as the context changes and new meaning potential asserts itself. We elaborate, compress, innovate, and discard, take shocking liberties, delicately shift nuances. In some cultures there are privileged tales (authoritative, again) which must be retold; but every authentic teller must turn them into internally persuasive discourse or be reduced to a mere reciter, an inflexible mimic.

There should be no need to plead for more retelling. We accept without question Shakespeare as a reteller of Plutarch and Holinshed, Chaucer of Boccaccio, Chapman of Homer. We are all translators in the basic sense of that word, carrying over and changing one discourse into another. And it all begins at a very early age. Carol Fox (1983) in her fascinating recordings demonstrates this to perfection. Here is Jack (aged five):

> Now as you know there was some bears who lived – um – at the very edge
> of the forest and they would hunt for rabbits … but as you know – who
> lived in the forest? Well, shall I tell you? Well it was a great big wicked wolf
> *(pause)* and so – so – so how to get away from this forest? Cos if he saw
> them he would surely follow them up …

Carol Fox comments that her study shows that 'children can transform their literary experiences to their own narrative purposes'; or, as Bakhtin would put it, these children are setting themselves on the path of liberating themselves from the authority of another's discourse while not rejecting the discourse itself. What will they encounter in their schooling? A programme to re-establish the authority ('that's not what it says') or a continuation of the self-liberating process seen in Carol Fox's very young children?

In the broadest sense every story is a kind of retelling only comprehensible in the light of other texts or bits of them. Every text, says Barthes (1975), is a mirror of citations (*déjà lu*). We are all a plurality of other stories, including our own. We are our stories. Wayne Booth, whose *Rhetoric of Fiction* you may know, said in a lecture last summer (1984):

> Who am I now is best shown by the stories I can tell and who I am to
> become is best determined by the stories I can learn to tell.

A warning – and a promise

You will have noticed that I have come full circle. I began with Dell Hymes and Blanche Tohet caught in the act of retelling and with Dell Hymes' insistence that each reteller is a voice. I have tried to show something of what that 'voice' might mean by giving pride of place to retelling. There is, of course, much that I have left unsaid but I am conscious of one particular omission which a recent book, Ross Chambers' *Story and Situation* (1984), develops cogently. I did refer earlier to enticement in narrative. This is Ross Chambers' theme; he calls it seduction. How is it that others let the storyteller go on? Seduction is the means by which the storyteller acquires the right to narrate, displaying a capacity to occupy the conversational space of others without possessing it. It recruits the desires of the other in the interests of maintaining narrative authority. Chambers ultimately sees this as political.

> Seduction, producing authority where there is no power, is a means of converting historical weakness into discursive strength. As such it appears as a major weapon against alienation … an oppositional practice of considerable significance.

I hope, in one respect at least, that I will not be misunderstood. I think I know very well that stories are not innocent, that there are many which have the kind of designs on me which I recognize as sinister and destructive. The very universality of narrative contains its own surreptitious menace. Stories are used to manipulate, advertise, control, above all to soothe, to massage us into forgetfulness and passivity. They are, in the original sense of the word, diversions.

Recollect now how the nineteenth century drew the teeth out of folk and fairy tales. Brecht (1976) knew this and the alternative, when he advised his actors, as they performed, not to 'let the Now blot out the / Previously and Afterwards':

So you should simply make the instant
Stand out, without in the process hiding
What you are making it stand out from …

          In this way
You will show the flow of events and also the course
Of your work, permitting the spectator
To experience this Now on many levels, coming from
      Previously and
Merging into Afterwards, and also having much else now
Alongside it. He is sitting not only
In your theatre but also
In the world.

I offer *that* as a realistic, practical pedagogic programme.

References

Bakhtin, M. (1981) *The Dialogic Imagination: Four essays* (C. Emerson and M. Holquist, trans.). Austin: University of Texas Press.

Barthes, R. (1975) *S/Z* (R. Miller, trans.). London: Jonathan Cape.

Berger, J. (1984) *And Our Faces, My Heart, Brief as Photos.* London: Writers and Readers Coop Publishing Society,

Booth, W. (1984) 'Narrative as the mold of character', in *A Telling Exchange: Report of the Seventeenth Conference on Language in Inner-City Schools.* London: Institute of Education, University of London.

Brecht, B. (1976) 'Portrayal of past and present in one', in *Poems 1913–1956.* London: Eyre Methuen.

Britton, J., Burgess, T., Martin, N., McLeod, A. and Rosen, H. (1975) *The Development of Writing Abilities (11–18).* London: Macmillan Education.

Chambers, R. (1984) *Story and Situation.* Minneapolis: University of Minnesota Press.

Derrida, J. (1978) *Writing and Difference.* London: Routledge and Kegan Paul.

Eco, U. (1979) *The Role of the Reader.* Bloomington: Indiana University Press.

Fox, C. (1983) 'Talking like a book: Young children's oral monologues', in M. Meek (ed.), *Opening Moves* (Bedford Way Papers 17). London: Institute of Education, University of London.

Genette, G. (1980) *Narrative Discourse.* Oxford: Basil Blackwell.

Her Majesty's Inspectorate (1984) *English from 5 to 16.* London: HMSO.

Hilyard, A. and Olson, D. (1982) 'On the comprehension and memory of oral vs written discourse', in D. Tannen (ed.), *Spoken and Written Language: Exploring orality and literacy.* Norwood, NJ: Ablex.

Hymes, D. (1982 [1973]) *Toward Linguistic Competence* (Texas Working Papers in Sociolinguistics, No. 16). Austin, TX: University of Texas.

Hymes, D. (1982) *Ethnolinguistic Study of Classroom Discourse. Final report to the National Institute for Education.* Philadelphia: University of Pennsylvania Graduate School of Education.

Jameson, F. (1981) *The Political Unconscious: Narrative as a socially symbolic act.* London: Methuen.

Murphy, M.J. (1975) *Now You're Talking.* Belfast: Blackstaff Press.

The Autobiographical Impulse

Harold first gave this paper as a lecture in summer 1985 at Georgetown University, Washington DC. The lecture was part of a National Endowment for the Humanities Institute, 'Humanistic Approaches to Linguistic Analysis'. The paper was published in 1988 in *Linguistics in Context: Connecting observation and understanding*, edited by Deborah Tannen. In 1993, Harold included it in his collection of stories and articles, *Troublesome Boy*.

To begin somewhat autobiographically: in April of this year I was preparing a paper for the National Association for the Teaching of English and was casting about for a short exemplar of my opening point. I think I found it. I want to return to it now because I think my nugget contained more than I realized at the time.

Some time last year I found myself immersed in three very long mimeographed volumes by Dell Hymes (1973 and 1982). He had pushed them into my hands with typical generosity when he noticed that I was ploughing my way through them in his outer office at the University of Pennsylvania. They constituted a vast elaboration of the now very familiar notion of communicative competence, and it could be described as an unremitting polemic against Chomsky's concept of competence. I did not find it an easy read. It was both dense and microscopic, pursuing its argument through every possible theoretical twist and turn; every concept was subjected to critical scrutiny. It was a kind of intellectual war of attrition. However, I persisted over several days for all the reasons you can guess at. For as they used to say in my family – draughts is draughts and chess is chess and there's no point in getting the two confused. I reached a point in the argument where Dell Hymes, having taken us step by step through a demonstration of the inadequacy of Chomsky's model, says with seductive simplicity, ' ... a fair request would be to do better'. What happened next? Just this. I cite the text verbatim:

> Let me mention here Mrs. Blanche Tohet, who in the summer of 1951 had David and Kay French and myself wait for a story until she had finished fixing eels. A tub of them had been caught the night before near Oregon City. Each had to be slit, the white cord within removed, and the spread skin cut in each of its four corners, held apart by sticks. The lot were then strung up on a line between poles, like so many shrunken infants' overalls, to dry. Mrs. Tohet stepped back, hands on hips, looking at the line of eels, and said: 'Ain't that beautiful!' (The sentence in its setting has been a touchstone for aesthetic theory for me ever since.)

All then went in, and she told the story of Skunk, when his musk sac was stolen and carried down river, how he travelled down river in search of his 'golden thing', asking each shrub, plant and tree in turn, and being answered civilly or curtly; how down the river he found boys playing shinny-ball with his sac, entered the game, got to the 'ball', popped it back in, and headed back up river; how, returning, he rewarded and punished, appointing those that had been nice to a useful role for the people who were soon to come into the land, denying usefulness to those who had been rude. All this in detail, with voices for different actors, gestures for the actions, and always, animation. For that, as people will be glad to tell you, is what makes a good narrator: the ability to make the story come alive, to involve you as in a play. Despite the efforts of white schools and churches, there are people in whom such style lives today. Knowing them, it is impossible to think of them just as tacit grammarians; each is a voice.

(pp. 14–15)

For me that passage was much more than a respite or rest in the onward march of academic prose. It brought into the sharpest focus some key questions about narrative in general and autobiographical narrative in particular. What impulse drives a world-renowned scholar at the critical shift in his text, at its pivot or fulcrum, to scan his own past, to demand imperatively from it the recall of a few hours of experience, and cast them into this story about a story? How can he justify chatter about fixing eels amidst the interwoven propositions and abstractions of the rest of the text? It must be a reminder to us that his vast erudition is a superstructure erected on and motivated by meanings which had their beginnings and verifications in a past rich with encounters of this kind. I can do no more than surmise that in the process of the construction of many kinds of texts, spoken and written, the memories of the past are in constant play flashing beneath the still surface like gleaming fish in a still lake. We could enlarge Vygotsky's notion of the subtext of every utterance to include this clandestine presence of memory. This dramatic shift in rhetoric in Dell Hymes declares that the autobiographer locked away in a closet is for an instant coming out to propose another way of meaning and to recruit its persuasive power. Narrative, Chambers (1984) insists, is about desire and seduction. And autobiography permeates the seductive strategies of ordinary people. They are always at it with their damned anecdotes and what an impatient nineteenth-century judge once called their 'dangerous confabulations'.

Hymes begins with an intriguing phrase to handle his transition: 'Let me mention here … ' It is the storyteller's throwaway guile which advertises as a parenthesis what turns out to be a central and bold effort to enlist your assent. The whole business of fixing eels could be written off as mere embroidery or even cheap bait. I think not. To tell the tale of one's own experiences is to trust what memory offers, not in the sense of indiscriminate use of what it transmits, but rather in rendering oneself hospitable to surprises both in the what and in the how. If Hymes is right and each one is a voice, it is a voice coming from a situated person. This kind of autobiography is memory verbalized into art – common, popular, unprivileged – that is to say, without a sanctioned locus in time and space. It marshals the ruses of discourse. Mrs. Tohet's story, for all I know, may already have figured in a collection of folk-tales, where it would sit bereft of voice, bereft of the story of one particular telling.

We are looking at the story of a story. This is by no means a rare feature of autobiographical speech. It not only provokes responses in the same mode, chains of narrative, but provokes other tales in the teller. If we tell of other people, we recollect too the tales they told.

Memory again. We remember what others tell us they remember. That familiar device of narrative fiction, the story-within-the-story, has like so much else been borrowed from the oral story teller. Take the opening of Eco's *The Name of the Rose* (1983). We are to suppose that we are hearing a diligent contemporary scholar pursuing a manuscript across Europe which turns out to be the autobiography of a medieval monk and constitutes the main text of the novel. Thus we begin with the contemporary scholar's tale:

> … as I was browsing among the bookshelves of a little antiquarian bookseller on Comentes … I came upon a little work by Milos Temsvar …

And the tale of the monk begins.

> I prepare to leave on parchment my testimony as to the wondrous and terrible events that I happened to observe in my youth.

From a lifetime spent in the study of American Indian languages, Hymes has plucked this single instance. It comes with these components:

1. the eel-fixing
2. Mrs. Tohet's traditional tale; more exactly a stylized summary (a sequence of 'how … how … etc.') which omits the represented speech of the actors
3. a coda which shifts back to a non-narrative model in which Hymes makes clear his motive for telling the story but with a certain mockery ('It's impossible to think of them as tacit grammarians') which never figures in his main text.

Thus the whole of this three-layered narration is intended to give power to his argument and general theme. And that is just how it is with us when spontaneous autobiography is inserted into the flow of conversation. Mrs. Tohet herself has no such readily construed designs on us. She is handing on from her culture a composition of events in such a manner that it constitutes 'an experimentation with life' and moral weight is enfolded in the tale. Here you might say that we have arrived at the opposite of autobiographical narrative. But that would be too easy. Though she is retelling a traditional tale which belongs with countless others, in its composition she imposes on it, literally and metaphorically, her own intonation, which is only another way of saying that her own experience makes its unique contribution to the communal one. A reanimator must not refuse her own learned life. This is not to propose that her tale is autobiographical; but I do want to suggest at this point no more than that autobiography is not easily tidied away into its most recognizable forms, nor are our autobiographical moments simply micro-versions or primitive versions of the classic volumes of Gorki, Boswell or Rousseau.

(Dell Hymes's awareness of these issues is put powerfully and delicately in a joint paper [Hymes and Cazden, 1980]:

> In sum, our cultural stereotypes predispose us to dichotomize forms and functions of language use … And one side of the dichotomy tends to be identified with cognitive superiority. In point of fact, however, none of the usual elements of conventional dichotomies are certain guides to level of cognitive activity. In particular, narrative may be a complementary, or alternative mode of thinking.
>
> [p. 130]

Just to leave us in no doubt, he concludes with what he calls Warm Springs Interlude, rich with his own autobiographical narrative and observations of narrative in the lives of the Indian people he knows:

> It is the grounding of performance and text in a narrative view of life. That is to say, a view of life as a potential source of narrative. Incidents, even apparently slight incidents, have pervasively the potentiality of an interest that is worth retelling … A certain potentiality, of shared narrative form, on the one hand, of consequentiality, on the other. [p. 135])

Let me put alongside Hymes an analogue taken from a very animated spontaneous conversation. The occasion, to put it briefly, is a small gathering of five people in an Afro-Caribbean club, four of them black, one a white researcher, David Sutcliffe. They are discussing their feelings about and attitudes to white people. One of them, Miriam, a night-shift worker, at one point dominates the discussion.

> Now I've got five children, all born here, between the ages of 18½ and 23. I've got three sons. And I would rather see them come through my door with a coloured girl. Admittedly, a whole lot of coloured girls, born in England, they are only coloured *outside*. They are everything white like you people. They've got white minds. But I would still prefer that colour coming through my door.

We move through (a) autobiographical data – which establishes her speaking rights (compare Dell Hymes locating himself with his friends outside Oregon City), (b) explicit statement of attitude (which Hymes held back to the end), (c) analysis, (d) restatement of attitude ('coloured on the outside') – in stronger form.

The discussion then becomes noisy and heated as the group members try to decide whether they too are prejudiced. At this point Miriam intervenes again with, 'Well, there's a lot you could say about this sort of thing', which turns out to be a signal that she is about to capture conversational space. There follows what constitutes by far the longest turn in the whole lengthy discussion. The discussion itself is the equivalent of Hymes's general text. It surrounds this narrative moment.

> M: Well, there's a lot you could say about this sort of thing. Because, I mean, for instance, this, em, boy who seems to be very unlucky with his chosen white girl, he's been going out with a girl, an English girl, for three years. He's been going to the girl's parents' home and they accept him.
>
> Oh well it was all right – they were only young. But when they got to eighteen … of course I didn't even care to know the parents, did I? *(ironic?)* When they got to eighteen, one morning there was a knock on my door; [I had] just got into bed. And, mm, by the time I got downstairs, there was this woman turning back from the door. So I called to her and she turned back. And she introduced herself. She was of course my son's girlfriend's mother. And she called to get to know me, because she didn't know me after going out with … her daughter going out with my son for three years. She just lived round the corner to me anyway. And what she called to say to me: *(mimics)* 'Did Andy tell you anything this morning?' I said: 'Anything about what?' Well I was at work the night before, and when I got home Boy had gone to work. So I said no. And she was crying tears, and she said: 'Well, we had such a row at home last night because my husband and I, we just can't get on with each other any more. Because mm – my husband is annoyed with our daughter going out with your son. Because they are getting older and they might decide to get married. And if they have children the children are going to be half-castes.' I say *(hard voice)* 'And you wait three years to say that? You didn't see what colour my son was when he was coming to your home over *three years*?!' And if they have children and they don't want half-caste children – I say, 'Listen love, your daughter is going to have them, and you don't want them – I don't want them either. *(laughter)* I've already warned my son not to come home pregnant.' *(laughter)*
>
> I: *(over the din)*: I think it's on both sides. Now we tell them at work: 'You are prejudiced, *I* am prejudiced.'

The whole of that would bear closer analysis. I must confine myself to a few points:

1. Miriam's conversational move shifts to her own life story which she trusts as a powerful form of argument.
2. It incorporates a fragment of the other woman's life story (I'll call it tip-of-the-iceberg autobiographical speech): 'we had such a row at home last night'.
3. To sustain the invasion of conversational space Miriam must deploy the ruses of the storyteller or forfeit it – thus her distribution of irony, especially in dialogue. But above all to maintain shape, a shape that has to be generated in the very act of utterance. The triumphal final joke seals the ending.
4. Unlike the momentary (but not insignificant) self-reference like:

> But my kids are English by birth because they were born in King Street Hospital and Paul was born in Whippendale Road – you can't get more bloody English than that.

– when Miriam says, 'one morning there was a knock at my door', the group will hear that as an announcement of the probability that a complete story is to follow and their listening posture will change accordingly.

To invoke autobiography is to take chances. One problem is how to avoid yet another excursion into liberal individualism. Another is how to avoid using autobiography as mere case history fodder and nothing more. There is the difficulty too that, in a sense, all utterances in day-to-day conversation, however generated, however self-protective, however deceitful, however self-censored, constitute, as Goffman showed, a presentation of the self, but they are also a contribution to that never-finished business, the construction of a socially-constituted self. Both of these processes invoke the earlier phases of the operation. Quite young children can be heard saying, 'When I was little … ' To participate in conversation means among other things staying alert to autobiographic clues and traces, however oblique. Even the stereotype is a clumsy, but sometimes necessary, effort to do this. Thus the autobiographical impulse is a way of listening as well as a way of telling: it is essentially dialogic.

The autobiographical impulse in institutional discourse

Attentive examination of everyday discourse reveals that narrative surfaces easily and inevitably and without inhibition when the conversation is among intimates and no obvious and fateful judgments turn on the encounter (a job, jail, health, divorce). Oppressive power distorts and muffles it. de Certeau (1980), in a remarkable paper, suggests that memory emerging as narrative is one means available to us for asserting our authority against institutionalized power, more precisely the discourses of power.

> Memory ... produces at the opportune moment a break which also inaugurates something new. It is the strangeness, the alien dynamic, of memory which gives it the power to transgress the law of the local space in question; from out of the unfathomable and ever-shifting secrets, there comes a sudden 'strike' ... details, intense singularities, which already function in memory as they do when circumstances give them an opportunity to intervene: the same timing in both occasions, the same artful relation between a concrete detail and a conjuncture, the latter figuring alternately as the trace of a past event, or as the production of some new harmony.

He goes on to link 'intense singularities' with story-telling. Scientific discourse, he says, exerts a careful maintenance over space which 'eliminates time's scandals'.

> Nonetheless, they return over and over again, noiselessly and surreptitiously, and not least within the scientific activity itself: not merely in the form of the practices of everyday life which go on even without their own discourse, but also in the sly and gossipy practices of everyday storytelling ... a practical know-how is at work in these stories, where all the features of the 'art of memory' itself can be detected ... the art of daily life can be witnessed in the tales told about it.

And, I would add, inevitably they are nearly always autobiographical.

To point this out does not necessarily mean that we must hasten to justify it by allocating the interest to some already established terrain and refer it, let us say, to the certain micro-features of texts like deixis or cohesion (Halliday and Hasan, 1976), or in a semiotic vein to explore the deep semantic structure of narrative (Greimas, as discussed by Hawkes, 1977), or in a narratological vein to look for signs of the implied or pseudo-narrator. These are in themselves far from trivial enterprises. However you may know everything about the anatomy and physiology of a horse but that will tell you little or nothing about the horse as a commodity, or as a totem, or its obsolescence as a form of transport and beast of burden. My concern here lies in the periphery of the well-established discourses about narrative. The reason is simple. We need to understand, no matter how speculative and partial our efforts at this stage, the full significance of something which in our culture and in many (all?) others is a resource drawn on so heavily by everyone. Beyond that there is the need to understand why the autobiographical impulse is so constantly thwarted, put down, and often explicitly outlawed in our educational system and in 'high' discourse.

Ronald Fraser's (1984) autobiography uniquely combines his own recollections with the testimony, collected in interviews, of all those he knew in his childhood; it is thus a many-voiced work. All the voices speak of the same past. At the very end, in a two-sided conversation, he attempts to fix the impulse behind this exacting task:

> – I've always thought history served one purpose at least. By discovering the major factors of change one can learn from them. The same ought to be true of an individual's history.
>
> – Yes … you want to be the subject of your history instead of the object you felt yourself to be …
>
> – The subject, yes, but also the object. It's the synthesis of the two, isn't it.
>
> – The author of your childhood then, the historian of your past.
>
> (p. 187)

To be the subject and object, both author and historian of one's own past, is asking a lot, but in this case justified by the book which precedes it. Come down the scale, or should I say across to another scale, to all those little anecdotes, recollections, episodes, and reminiscences which we all trade in, and we might say that a modest version of Fraser's aspiration asserts itself. Some can be the autobiographers of whole epochs of their lives and, using written language, control it judiciously to keep subject and object always harmoniously in harness. But the impulse is the same whether we know it or not. Bakhtin (Volosinov, 1976) says:

> In becoming aware of myself I attempt to look at myself through the eyes of another person … Here we have the objective roots of even the most personal and intimate reactions.
>
> (p. 87)

I know of someone who wrote about her childhood, setting out to recount the games and inventive pastimes which seemed to her both inexhaustible and full of meaning. At the end of it she said thoughtfully, 'It's about a lonely childhood.' Thus in the art of articulating autobiography we do not simply unmask ourselves for others, we too await to know the face under the mask.

Genre

Once the autobiographical impulse makes enough space for itself, the tactics for which have been learned in many interactions, the archaeological practices of memory come under a minimum control of *genre* – the loose rules of which have been acquired through use, observation and the lessons of success and failure. The impulse is kept on a loose rein but a rein nonetheless. I am using the word 'genre' in Bakhtin's sense. He proposes that speech genres are an essential part of language acquisition and have important consequences for thought.

> ... to learn to speak means to learn to construct utterances ... we learn to construct our speech in generic forms and when we hear the speech of others we deduce its genre from the first words; we anticipate in advance a certain volume ... as well as a certain compositional structure; we foresee the end; that is from the very beginning we have a sense of the speech whole.
>
> (cited in Holquist, 1983, p. 314)

As utterance moves towards monologue, it is possible to perceive these genres much more clearly (a plan of action is proposed, a lay sermon delivered, such a one is denounced, a case is argued, etc.), though of course the monologue is always dialogic even when the other is silent. The autobiographical spoken narrative is so distinctive as to be swiftly recognized and identified. Bakhtin attributes to it certain features. For him (Medvedev and Bakhtin, 1978) all speech genres constitute a way of thinking and learning.

> Every significant genre is a complex system of means and methods for the conscious control and finalization of reality.

and

> A particular aspect of reality can only be understood in connection with a particular means of representing it.

This is to take all those discussions about the relationship between thought and language on to a different plane and suggest that we think in the genres we have been furnished with through our experience of discourse. What Bakhtin calls 'the anecdote' requires the speaker to find and grasp the unity of an anecdotal event in life but it also 'presupposes an orientation towards the *means* for the development of narrative'.

> Every genre has its methods and means of seeing and conceptualising reality which are accessible to it alone.

These methods and means have been analyzed with great finesse by structuralists like Genette (1980), Barthes (1982) and others, but I am not aware of their having applied them to an autobiography or more particularly to autobiographical speech when the speaker already shares the past of his/her autobiography with those spoken to. These methods and means make the narrative of personal experience an essentially social activity. Such narratives are an interplay of concern for the material and a concern for the reception of it by others. But this is not to juxtapose the private and the public. The episodes of life past were already shaped by their social content and they are articulated in a socially constructed genre (i.e. methods and means socially created) and they are proffered as part of a social interchange.

However, these methods and means may well conceal from us, if we examine the text only, what is in the awareness of the participants and is shaping the narrative. Dunning (1985), working with oral narrative in her own classroom, elicited hospital stories from three of her students, aged fourteen. These stories do not arise from a sociolinguistic experiment. They were told in a regular story-telling session conducted with the whole class. Dunning is able to show how certain features of the story can be accounted for by the fact that all three story-tellers are negotiating their standing in the class.

David's standing at the time of his story-telling is fragile. He is back in school after a minor operation and, as Dunning says, 'suffering from the familiar re-entry pangs … after an absence'. Thus in his story there are methods and means used to enable him to build up a tough, defiant, comic, slightly risqué character for himself and to suppress the anxiety he almost certainly felt at the time. This is an extract from David's story, with the response of the listeners:

> D: I didn't go to sleep [the] last night. I was mucking around late. Nurse came in and 'it us 'cause we were mucking around in there.
>
> Pupil: Might've known.
>
> D: Night of the operation, we was reading comics. *Beano* … We 'ad the lights on and we 'eard the nurse say, 'Get that light out' and we didn't take no notice, just kept on reading. Then she came in next minute and hit us, just about, so I turned it out.
>
> Teacher: Hit us 'just about'. Did she hit you or just threaten to hit you?
>
> D: She said, 'Get into bed like this' (illustrates with a cuffing gesture) and I were just sitting there looking at 'er.
>
> P: Yeah David.
>
> P: Hard David.

David is receiving, and continues to receive beyond this point, the message from the class that his renegotiation of his standing is going quite well. This kind of narrative event is an inter-animation of production and reception. The narrators, no longer invisible authors, have known or partly known motivations and aspirations. Here there is shared history. The personal narratives enter into a disclosure already begun which will continue beyond the ends of stories. In this respect written autobiographical discourse is quite different. It must enter the silent unknown.

Some while ago I began a written autobiographical narrative which would contrast sharply with an improvised narrative of the same events.

Of course she thought of it. It wouldn't have crossed my mind.

– It would be nice, she said, a nice thing to do.

– Course, said my sister, you shouldn't get too big for your boots.

– You don't remember, said my mother, why should you remember? *I* remember.

– What'll I say to him? Remember me? The corner near the window, your favourite pupil. Turns out I am a genius. My mother thinks you ought to know. How's the little school going? Punishment Book filling up nicely?

– Such a clever-dick don't need a rehearsal, said my sister.

– Have a bit of heart, said my mother. You knock your *kishkas* out for twenty years teaching a bunch of snotty nosed *momzeirim* and in the finish what you got to show for it? Felling-hands, pressers, cutters, machinists, button-hole makers, market boys. Why shouldn't he know, now and then, that one of them won his matric?

– Passed, I said, not won, passed, together with thirty other future Nobel prize winners.

– Two a penny, said my sister. Pish, pish. It's a nothing.

– He'll go, he'll go, said my mother. A thank-you costs nothing.

– Did I say I wouldn't?

– My mother brushed the crumbs off the table into the palm of her hand and stood looking at them. She was so full of pride. She didn't know where to put it all.

[This became the beginning of the story 'Troublesome Boy', in Rosen, 1993 and 1999; reprinted in this collection.]

Imagine a live telling of that story to the younger members of my family and you will know at once that the means and methods would have to be radically different. Nor, I hasten to add, would it be allowed to become a monologue. (I must leave it to you to work how it might go in different settings and why).

It must be clear that I am in certain respects privileging the autobiographical genre. If I do so, it is because some genres offer greater possibilities than others for certain purposes, are more dialogic, deploy a wider range of resources, are more open to individual working. The genre of parade ground language offers no play at all (though Yossarian had a try). In spontaneous conversation among intimates, self-imposed controls are at their lightest. In that setting the autobiographical impulse is likely to be strong and following it leaves the greatest room for manoeuvre; authorship asserts itself in everyone. Holquist (1983) puts it well.

> ... so that we may be understood, so that the work of the social world may
> continue, we must all, perforce, become authors. To use the shift of signs
> to represent the world is to use language for social relations ... Insofar as
> we wrest particular meanings out of general systems, we are all creators; a
> speaker is to his utterance what an author is to his text.
>
> (p. 314)

In the *now* of our speaking our efforts to find meaning in the world have as their
richest resources the *then* of our past, perceived as events saturated with values and
feelings. We do not, as we often say, relive the experience; we rework it to fashion it
into a sense which we need to discover for its validity now and to share with others.
We do not put on a rerun of the past; there is no switch we can throw and let the
cameras run. To tell of the past is to negotiate it, sometimes with love, sometimes
with hate, but always with respect. The existence of a genre, learned in thousands
of tellings, offers us a framework which promises order and control. I have only to
begin, as I did very recently, like this:

> My mother, who was always in a state of near paupery, always gave money
> to beggars in the street.

– and I know that that sentence emerges from a long apprenticeship in the genre and
that it is no sooner uttered than a set of choices beckons me which are all narrative
choices, some of which will be so imperative that they might betray me into a loss of
meaning or, as Derrida (1978) puts it, to stifle the force under the form.

Authenticity

Labov (1972) noted that oral accounts of personal experience command a unique
attention from listeners.

> Many of the narratives cited here rise to a very high level of competence;
> … they will command the total attention of an audience in a remarkable
> way, certainly a deep and attentive silence that is never found in academic
> and political discussion.
>
> (p. 396)

But in spite of his interesting analysis he does not attempt to account for that 'deep
and attentive silence'. I have been suggesting that the particular kind of attention we
give arises because

1. the power of narrative in general corresponds to a way of thinking and imagining
2. it speaks with the voice of 'common sense'
3. it invites us to consider not only the results of understanding but to live through
   the processes of reaching it

4. it never tears asunder ideas and feelings; it moves us by permitting us to enter the living space of another: it is perceived as testimony
5. it specifically provides for the complicit engagement of the listener.

To try to put all this in one word I suggest *authenticity*. Let's explore this a little further.

Barthes (1982) said that narrative is present at all times and in all places and that all human groups have their stories. So do individuals. But narrative is certainly not present in all places. In fact, there are places which are tacitly declared to be 'no-go' areas where, as Foucault (1970, 1977) suggests, both space and the discourse which belong with it are closely policed.

Autobiographical stories often lie completely concealed beneath the genres which come to be defined precisely by their omission of personal stories. We are actually taught in the education system how to cover our narrative tracks and even to be ashamed of them.

Gilbert and Mulkay (1984), two sociologists, in a wicked book, tell us how they discovered that a very sharp controversy was going on in an area of biochemistry called oxidative phosphorylation. They go on to conduct research which would reveal how the dispute was played out, how scientists speak about such things. They interviewed those involved in Britain and the United States and examined the published papers. You can guess what emerged. In the interviews stories came tumbling out, like this one.

> He came running into the seminar, pulled me out with one of his other post-docs and took us to the back of the room and explained this idea that he had … He was very excited. He was really high. He said, 'What if I told you that it didn't take any energy to make ATP *at* a catalytic site, it took energy to kick it *off* the catalytic site?' It took him about 30 seconds. But I was particularly predisposed to this idea. Everything I had been thinking, 12, 14, 16 different pieces of literature that could not be explained and then all of a sudden the simple explanation became clear … And so we sat down and designed some experiments to prove, to test this.
>
> It took him about 30 seconds to sell it to me. It was really like a bolt. I felt, 'Oh my God, this must be right! Look at all the things it explains.'

The authors' comment reveals what happens to such stories in the academic culture:

> In the formal paper we are told that the experimental results suggested a model which seemed an improvement on previous assumptions and which was, accordingly, put to the test. In the interview we hear of a dramatic revelation of the central idea which was immediately seen to be right … and which led to the design of new experiments.

Bakhtin would perhaps say, 'There you have the difference between *internally persuasive discourse* and *authoritative discourse*.' Standing behind them are two great forces always at work in language, the *centripetal* and the *centrifugal*. The centripetal is constituted from everything which pulls us towards a centre of linguistic norms at every level, the pressures to conform to one language, one dialect, one set of rules, the order of certain discourse etiquettes, and indeed genre conventions. The counterforce is centrifugal, which is constituted from everything which pulls away from the normative centre, the mixing of dialects, lexical and syntactical innovation, play with language, defiance of the genre conventions, use of a genre considered to be inappropriate, persistence of stigmatized language, phonological mockery. According to Bakhtin (1981):

> Every concrete utterance of a speaking subject serves as a point where centrifugal as well as centripetal forces are brought to bear. The processes of centralization and decentralization, of unification and disunification, intersect in the utterance; ... it is in fact an active participant in such speech diversity.
>
> (p. 272)

There is no escaping centripetal forces; the question is what kind of discourse offers the greatest possibility to the play of centrifugal forces. For it must be clear that centripetal forces control or even suppress that crucial attempt which we all make to struggle against the given and already determined in language, a struggle which is an attempt to assert our own meanings against the matrix of ready-codified meanings lying in wait for us.

For Bakhtin, the medium with most promise is the novel. I think there is a case for suggesting that autobiographical utterance is the folk novel. It is almost impossible to police and springs up unpredictably outside the surveillance of the grammar book and the style manual. de Certeau (1980) argues that it is one of the means of outwitting established order, what he calls 'tactics'.

> Where dominating powers exploit the order of things, where ideological discourse represses or ignores, tactics fool this order and make it the field of their art. Thereby, the institution one is called to serve finds itself infiltrated by a style of social exchange, a style of technical invention, and a style of moral resistance – that is, by an economy of the 'gift' (generosities which are also ways of asking for something in return), by an aesthetic of 'moves', 'triumphs' or 'strikes' … and by an ethic of tenacity … This is what 'popular culture' really is and not some alien corpus, anatomised for the purposes of exhibit …

Bakhtin saw the centrifugal in operation in parody, verbal masquerades, and in the folk buffoonery of local fairs. However, the centrifugal can be attempted by anyone, the young included. By, for instance, Michael, aged 14, writing of his infant days:

> There was nothing.
>
> And I was two. Rabbit is my very best friend. I sat in a corner and we were playing with a thing and then there were reds and yellows and browns. My brother is Gonofan and he told Mummy (whose real name is also Mummy) to come and see the pretty colours. Mummy did not like them and hit the pretty colours.
>
> The deers in the park are brown. I like deers and I touched a deer and it ran away and I ran after it into the woods but she did not have a broomstick. She wanted to eat me so I ran back to Mummy. I ran and ran like Johnny Rabbit ran from the farmer's gun …
>
> I ran up the stairs with Rabbit. My bottom hurt and I needed the potty. But I cannot run as fast as Rabbit and I had to leave the brown gunge on the stairs and I wet my eyes but I started to read and so was happy.
>
> Mummy made me some red and blue shoes and he played nic nac on my shoe
> And I was three
> He played nic nac on my knee
>
> My Daddy (whose real name is also Daddy) is a good wizard. He did magic on the house and made it change. I went for a ride in the car and when I came back it had changed but there was no room for Daddy in our new house. He should have made it bigger
>
> And I was four
> He played nic nac on my door
>
> I was with Rabbit on the pavement and we were waiting for Daddy to make us be on holiday and a young man, really the Giant up the beanstalk, made the door sing like Penny Penguin. She says, 'Michael row the boat ashore.' I was taken to be mended in hospital.

I think of all those who have laboured to discover the essence of the 'well-formed story' and wonder what they would make of that. The story eludes the centripetal tug by being double-voiced; its surface texture is the voice of the infant from two to four years (a changing voice in that time, you may have noticed) but it is produced by a fourteen-year-old modernist who knows how to manage the juxtaposition of images, abrupt transitions, montage. The opening words defy centripetal narrative: 'There was nothing.'

Deborah Tannen (1979) noted the widespread use of terms in many disciplines to deal with patterns of expectations (frames, scripts, schemata, scenes and so forth). There are two ways in which this pattern of expectations can enter narrative activity: (a) the recognition of an experience as a scene or several scenes with narrative potential; (b) conforming to a pattern of expectations in the composition of actual narrative which tells the story of the scene. Now suppose we separate (a) and (b) by – a day, a month, twenty years. We now complicate the notion of frame enormously. Instead of a structure of expectation derived from past experience (i.e. a form of memory) and related to the presenting experience, we now have the intervention of memory in a different way. The *form* of presentation (narrative) fits the frame notion comfortably. But what does this telling filtered by memory and intervening experience do to the original experience? I suggest we now have a fascinating complexity – a new and bigger frame is placed around the original one which is at the same time definitely not discarded. It is this which constitutes the double-voice of autobiography. It is both how it was and how it is fused together. It may well account for the legitimate fictions of autobiography (perfectly 'remembered' conversations, for example). To sum up, a recognizable narrative is both constructed by and understood by a frame derived from past experience *but* the experience was originally understood by one frame and is now understood by a new one which includes understanding of the original frame.

Bakhtin was concerned to identify the essential differences between discourses which are, so to speak, compulsory and those which satisfy us by their feel of authenticity. He writes (1981) of 'two categories':

> … in one, the authoritative word (religious, political, moral; the word of a father, of adults and of teachers, etc.) that does not know internal persuasiveness, in the other the internally persuasive word that is denied all privilege, backed up by no authority at all, and is frequently not even acknowledged in society (not by public opinion, not by scholarly norms, nor by criticism) …

(p. 342)

Authoritative discourse, he goes on to say, demands our unconditional allegiance – permits no play with its borders, no gradual and flexible transitions, no creative stylizing variants on it. It is indissolubly fused with its authority. It is all inertia and 'calcification', whereas

> Internally persuasive discourse … is … tightly interwoven with 'one's own word' … [It] is half-ours and half-someone else's … [Its] semantic structure … is *not finite*, it is *open* … this discourse is able to reveal ever newer *ways to mean*. (italics in original)

Internally persuasive discourse is the arena in which autobiographical speech finds its scope and its diversity of intentions. Narratology has had a good run for its money but is not permitted to speak of such things (no authors, no intentions!). We must increasingly turn our attention to narrative as a form of participation in interaction when the narration is embedded in dialogue. We know that the story-teller can acquire or be offered the right to narrate, the chance to recruit the desires of the others, to achieve a moment's authority without being authoritative. We also have accumulating evidence that speakers can transform a turn in dialogue into a personal narrative which is a contribution to the goals of the dialogue. Erickson (1984) has shown how within a particular culture this is the prevailing mode and very disconcerting for those who do not share it. Halligan (1984), in studying over a long period the small-group discussions of 12/13-year-old students in a black working-class inner-city area, found a very similar pattern. In one analysis of a discussion (which turned on whether stealing is a result of poverty) he isolated five major personal anecdotes and demonstrated that

> These anecdotes are the main structural members upon which the fabric of the discussion is erected, both because the discussion which intervenes is in reaction to them, and because they embody the logical structure of the discussion …

You will not suppose that I am under the delusion that stories of personal experience will set the world to rights. I do, however, believe that from the top to the bottom of the educational system, authoritative discourse holds sway but that inroads into it can be made by giving students genuine fuller speaking rights in the classroom. An inevitable consequence will be the emergence of a much greater role for personal narrative. For most students this would constitute a liberation. In the end, stories about the past are also about the future. On the other hand, we have only to remind ourselves of the way in which folk story was domesticated into coziness, to remember that stories themselves can kow-tow with subservience. Their very universality contains its own surreptitious menace. They can be used to manipulate, control, create a market, and above all to massage us into forgetfulness and passivity. Nor do I wish to forget that alongside the autobiographical impulse there is the autobiographical *compulse* of the courtroom, of the government inspector, of the attitude tests, of the curriculum vitae, of the torture chamber. There are some very sinister people engaged in hermeneutics! We are not left free to limit our pasts to unpoliced crannies and congenial moments. Stand and deliver. There are many ways in which power attempts to wrest from us our past and use it for its own ends. Our autobiographies also figure in dossiers wrung from us as surely as were confessions by the Inquisition. Such invitations do not coax and tempt memory, for they surround it with caution, fear and even terror.

Yet in spite of the inquisitors, indeed, in stark defiance of them, we have no alternative. We must persist with archaeological expeditions into the substrata of our

Harold Rosen

memories so that, returning, we may look the present in the eye and even dare to peer into the future.

References

Bakhtin, M. (1981) *The Dialogic Imagination* (C. Emerson and M. Holquist, trans.). Austin: University of Texas Press.

Barthes, R. (1982) 'Introduction to the structural analysis of narrative', in S. Sontag (ed.), *Barthes: Selected writings.* London: Fontana.

de Certeau, M. (1980) 'On the oppositional practices of everyday life'. *Social Text,* 1.

Chambers, R. (1984) *Story and Situation.* Minneapolis: University of Minnesota Press.

Derrida, J. (1978) *Writing and Difference* (A. Bass, trans.). London: Routledge and Kegan Paul.

Dunning, J. (1985) 'Reluctant and willing story-tellers in the classroom.' *English in Education,* 19 (1).

Eco, U. (1983) *The Name of the Rose.* San Diego: Harcourt Brace Jovanovich.

Erickson, F. (1984) 'Rhetoric, anecdote, and rhapsody: Coherence strategies in a conversation among Black American adolescents.', in D. Tannen (ed.) *Coherence in Spoken and Written Discourse.* Norwood, NJ: Ablex.

Fraser, R. (1984) *In search of a Past.* London: Verso.

Foucault, M. (1970) *The Order of Things: An archaeology of the human sciences.* London: Tavistock.

Foucault, M. (1977) *Discipline and Punish: The birth of the prison.* New York: Pantheon.

Genette, G. (1980) *Narrative Discourse* (J. Lewin, trans.). London: Basil Blackwell.

Gilbert, G. and Mulkay, M. (1984) *Opening Pandora's Box.* Cambridge: University Press.

Halliday, M. and Hasan, R. (1976) *Cohesion in English.* London: Longman.

Halligan, D. (1984) 'Social context, discourse, and learning in small group discussion'. PhD dissertation, University of London.

Hawkes, T. (1977) *Structuralism and Semiotics.* London: Methuen.

Holquist, M. (1983) 'Answering as authoring: Mikhail Bakhtin's translinguistics.' *Critical Inquiry,* 10 (2).

Hymes, D. (1982 [1973]) *Toward Linguistic Competence, Texas Working Papers in Sociolinguistics, No. 16.* Austin, TX: University of Texas.

Hymes, D. and Cazden, C. (1980) 'Narrative thinking and storytelling rights: A folklorist's clue to a critique of education', in D. Hymes (ed.) *Language in Education: Ethnolinguistic essays.* Washington, D.C.: Center for Applied Linguistics.

Labov, W. (1972) *Language in the Inner City.* Philadelphia: University of Pennsylvania Press.

Medvedev, P./Bakhtin, M. (1978) *The Formal Method in Literary Scholarship: A critical introduction to sociological poetics.* Baltimore: Johns Hopkins University Press.

Rosen, H. (1993) *Troublesome Boy.* London: English and Media Centre.

Rosen, H. (1999) *Are you still Circumcised?* Bristol: Five Leaves Publications.

Tannen, D. (1979) 'What's in a frame? Surface evidence for underlying expectations', in R. Freedle (ed.) *New Directions in Discourse Processing.* Norwood, NJ: Ablex.

Volosinov, V. [Bakhtin, M.] (1976) *Freudianism: A Marxist critique* (I. Titunik, trans.) New York: Academic Press.

Troublesome Boy

Of course, she thought of it. It wouldn't have crossed my mind.

'It would be nice,' she said, 'a nice thing to do.'

'Course,' said my sister, 'you shouldn't get too big for your boots.'

'You don't remember,' said my mother. 'Why should you remember? *I* remember.'

'What'll I say to him? "Remember me? The corner near the window. Your favourite pupil. Turns out I'm a genius. My mother thinks you ought to know. How's the little school going? Punishment book filling up nicely?"'

'Such a clever-dick don't need a rehearsal,' said my sister.

'Do me a favour,' said my mother. 'You have to have a bit of consideration. You knock your *kishkas* out for twenty years for a bunch of snotty-nosed *momzeirim* and in the finish what you got to show for it? Pressers, cutters, button-hole makers, market boys. Why shouldn't he know now and then that one of them won his Matric?'

'Passed,' I said, 'together with thirty other future Nobel prize-winners. Passed. You don't win anything. They give you a nice piece of paper you can nail to the wall.'

'Pish, pish,' said my sister. 'Pish, pish. Two a penny. It's a nothing.'

'He'll go. He'll go,' said my mother. 'A thank you costs nothing, and you got plenty to thank him for.'

'Did I say I wouldn't go?'

My mother brushed the crumbs off the table into the palm of her hand and stood looking at them. She was so full of pride she didn't know where to put it all.

So next day I was off to see Mr Margolis, the Headteacher of the elementary school I'd attended until I was eleven. After five years Mr Margolis had not faded. I had forgotten nothing about him and even now decades and decades later he is more vivid than all my other teachers who are now just fuzzy masks. I don't think there are teachers like that any more, mostly because, thank God, they don't want to be like that and in any case the kids won't let them. Margolis was a monster. A single stony glance from him could set your heart quaking. What am I saying? A glance? Just being there was enough. That silent figure in a classroom doorway could freeze the marrows of forty or more case-hardened little hooligans just by being there. That awesome man could beam his terror across the full width of the Whitechapel Road or from the far end of the playground. If I saw that black trilby a hundred yards away I'd seek out a shop doorway or alleyway to press myself into rather than face the ordeal of simply saying, 'Good morning, sir' and raising my cap (a little ritual drilled to a nicety when you went into the Big Boys at seven). He dressed the part, too. No one I knew wore a black jacket and waistcoat, striped trousers, wing collar and spats. Spats, yes, spats. I used to stare at them, hypnotised, under the iron bar of the oak desk. Little felt-like, ankle-high gaiters with an elastic strap which went under his shoe. I wondered what they were for. My mother said it was to keep his feet warm. Though I believed she knew everything, right down to the functions of men's clothing, I felt they were some kind of badge of office. He was the Head and no other teacher wore them. The others wore peat-coloured Harris tweeds, all hairy and pouchy, except for Mr Solomons who wore an immaculate double-breasted blazer and dark grey, pure wool flannels with sharp creases. Very smart, yes, but not what you would call headmasterly. And another thing, the pince-nez. The last exquisite refinement of terror, they enlarged his grey eyes, still and unblinking, to a predatory, basilisk, scrutinising goggle. He haunted my dreams, stalking across vast halls, swishing his cane to winkle me out from a hidey-hole in the cloakroom, contrite and guilty, not of any identifiable crime but of having committed the sin of being. He may have had a wife, and children even. Somewhere, sometime, his face must have thawed into a smile and his voice must have melted into laughter. My fluttering mind could not entertain such an outlandish fiction. Immaculate, he inhabited the brown chipped-tile world of Myrdle Street Elementary School, ruled over it and, at nights, roosted immobile in a gruesome eerie, eyes open, probing the darkness for cowering sinners and backsliders.

In those days, the Head sat at one end of the hall, up on a dais, his desk covered in green baize, backed by the Union Jack and portraits of the King and Queen. It seems to me now that he never left that chair behind the desk from which he could hear and see everything. No chance of his not knowing you were late or had managed to persuade a teacher to let you go to the toilet before playtime. Always you had to run the gauntlet of the Gorgon in the chair. On his desk were the cane, the Punishment Book and a large brass handbell. The cane saw regular service and he had a reserve supply pickling in brine in an aquarium under the window. We tried not to look at it during assemblies. All of us would have admitted to anything, served any penance, had he so much as ruffled his brow with a frown. I suppose it was because we would not have paid the price and the bite of pain would not have delivered its moral message. And the Punishment Book would not have recorded your sins for posterity. Turn to any page and you'd have discovered the Moral Order of Myrdle Street School – the crime, the punishment, the executioner's signature:

Disobedience 4 strokes
Lateness 2 strokes
Impertinence 4 strokes
Damage to school property 6 strokes
Talking in class 2 strokes
Foul Language 6 strokes
Obscene Behaviour 6 strokes

It was Obscene Behaviour when Kossoff pissed over the toilet wall.

I still marvel in a dazed sort of way at how much he could achieve through pure, unsullied fear. He taught us for music lessons and we were assembled in rows in front of the piano in the hall. Someone once told me he was a fine musician and he did teach us some good songs. But at that time I had only one musical ambition. I was ten but there were older boys in Standard Seven, some, of course, with breaking voices. Mr Margolis would prowl up and down the rows once he had launched us into 'From the Cotswolds and the Chilterns' (where, for God's sake, were they?) or 'Charlie is my Darling' (Charlie? Could that be right?). Up and down the rows he went, his back bent and his ear cocked, all in the holy cause of hunting down what he called grunters. It was a personal crusade from which he never relaxed. 'Please God,' I used to pray to myself, 'let me not be a grunter. Let me get all my sums wrong, have too many blotty scratchings-out in my compositions, be caught sniggering and whispering, or even trying and failing to piss over the toilet wall.' Yes, even that, rather than being singled out by Mr Margolis, hand-picked inches from his pince-nez and spats and damned as an incurable grunter. Why? In heaven's name, why? All that happened to grunters was that they were sent to the back of the hall where, provided they did not bat an eyelid, they could indulge themselves to their heart's content, listening to the non-grunters' palpitating voices doing 'Nymphs and Shepherds, Come Away'. It was enough for Mr Margolis to indicate that a grunter was a despicable worm and deservedly an outcast for me to dread ending up on the pariahs' bench at the back of the hall. In the army during rifle inspection when the officer of the day fetched up in front of me, about to give my Lee-Enfield the once-over, I caught a whiff of that same kind of dread. But only a whiff.

It was this same terrifying man who pulled about eight or nine of us out of class to prepare us for the scholarship. A couple of boys a year passed and went on to grammar schools. It was a heavy price to pay to have to sit with Mr Margolis and make our mistakes under his very nose. We were supposed to think it a dazzling privilege to be selected and groomed for stardom. My mother, for instance, couldn't contain her delight.

'The Headmaster teaching you. Personally. Better than that *shikker*, O'Carroll.'

Mr O'Carroll was in her bad books because it was known that he went to a pub at midday where he probably had a modest pint and a sandwich, so that he became in her eyes that gentile reprobate, a *shikker*, a drunk. He certainly smelled of beer in the afternoons and we used to sing in the playground to the tune of 'Hey Ho Come to the Fair':

Where there's a barrel
There's Jimmy O'Carroll
So hey ho come to the pub.

In fact we quite liked him. But for my mother, the austere and awesome Mr Margolis seemed a much more suitable tutor. I don't know whether he was or wasn't. Perhaps she was very impressed when I told her of one surprising ploy of his. He would give us Latin words and have us try to think up English words derived from them. He'd write up '*scribere, scriptum*' and if we were lucky we'd make a list of scribe, inscribe, describe, subscribe, script, scripture. Someone suggested scribble and he didn't seem quite sure. When it came to the exam there was none of this in it at all. Perhaps my mother hadn't got it right but I passed and that vindicated her completely.

'Without him,' she said, 'you'd be sitting in Standard Seven for another three years like those other wooden heads.'

So I left for the Grammar School and glory and five years later passed the Matriculation exams. To be honest, I didn't think to myself, on hearing my results read out, good old Margolis. If it weren't for him, etc, etc. In fact at that particular joyous moment I didn't think about him at all. It was only when my mother started nagging me to go and see him that Mr Margolis came to mind. The truth is I wasn't keen because I just couldn't see us exchanging pleasantries and having a friendly laugh about the good old days and him telling me he knew all along what a brilliant scholar I was and would I remember him to my mother. I knew it wasn't going to be like that but I also couldn't imagine what it would be like. So I felt at best dutiful and distinctly sulky. The thing to do was to get it over as quickly as possible.

Mooching along the road to the school I'd forgotten that I had to get into the place. Those old London three-deckers loomed over the area like Bastilles, designed to resist the barbarian natives who surrounded them. What's more, once they'd got you in you couldn't get out because they locked you in. After the second late bell the caretaker did his rounds and turned his key in the narrow single gates pierced in the high walls. Carved in the stone lintels were the words Infants or Girls or Boys. The iron bars of the gates were covered with a sheet of metal to seal you off from the world outside. To get in after the late bell you had to ring and bring the caretaker from his lair, all wheezes, grumbles and frowns. It was the perfect system for making you tremble with guilt, even before you confronted Mr Margolis' glare. When I had the perfect excuse for being late, like a trip to the dentist's, I couldn't shake off the feeling that I'd done something wrong.

So I walked down Myrdle Street, passed the sweetshop, to the Boys' entrance, a bit disappointed that the turbaned Indian man with his strange little barrow wasn't there any more to sell his tiger nuts, black locust pods, liquorice root, Polish nuts and Indian toffee. I'd have bought some tiger nuts and had a nibble for old time's sake. How quiet that huge school sounded. Somewhere pens were scratching, a child was being ticked off, pages were rustling, chalk was tapping and squealing on a blackboard. A bored boy was probably sitting in my old desk, shuffling his feet. Perhaps Mr Margolis was padding from one classroom door to another, peering through the glass panes. Perhaps a monitor was distributing inkwells or paint pots and was making chinking music. But the great hulk of the school was as quiet as a convent.

I rang the bell. I could hear the lock being fidgeted with and there was the caretaker, looking older and more tired but just as disapproving and testy as ever.

'What do you want?'

'I've come to see Mr Margolis.'

'What for?'

Not an easy question really. Words didn't come easily to the triumphant Matriculated scholar, paying his condescending visit. I cursed my mother's insistence.

'I've come to tell him about my exam results.'

He looked at me without moving and stayed silent. It was as though I'd said nothing at all.

'Well, I used to be here, in Mr O'Carroll's class.'

He made an impatient noise somewhere at the back of his throat.

'Up the stairs, over there. Top floor.'

And he was on his way. I couldn't resist saying loudly enough to his back, 'I should know. Went up them often enough, didn't I?'

Some of my cockiness restored, I went up the staircase, passed the Infants on the ground floor (was the beautiful Miss Gwyllym still there, with all that heaped auburn hair?), past the Girls on the first floor where I had never been. Last lap. Might as well be honest. My mind for a second or two toyed with the notion of turning back. The whole enterprise now seemed ludicrous and distasteful. I was even sketching out a tale to tell my mother. 'He wasn't there. Out on business.' or 'He was teaching a class for an absent teacher.'

By now I was at the double doors to the hall. I went through and there he was, at the end of the baize-covered desk, all his accoutrements in their old places, the cane, of course, neatly set out on the table. To the left of him was the glass-fronted cupboard which someone with a nice sense of humour had named The Science Cupboard. The same mangy old bird wing, grey dusty fossils, knobbles of nondescript rock, some bottles with coloured liquids in them, a sloughed snake-skin, a little stuffed rodent, threadbare beyond identification.

The whole length of the hall between him and me. I hadn't got half way and was already out of countenance. I fetched up in front of the dais and the desk, and steeled myself to cope with the pince-nez. Who makes the first move, I wondered. Him, surely. He must greet me in some way or another, if only to ask me my business. By now I didn't quite know what to do with myself. I wanted to put my hands in my pockets and look at the tips of my shoes. I wanted to lean against something or sit down but I knew I shouldn't and couldn't. A silence came down on us and I had no choice throughout but to clench my fists and, unbearably, to look him in the eye. And so I waited and waited and waited. Mr Margolis moved his head very slowly from side to side. Finally he spoke.

'Don't remember the name but a troublesome boy, a troublesome boy.'

All the old terrors gripped my guts. I shrivelled to ten-year-old size. Had he ordered me at that moment to put out my hand, mesmerised, I'd have done it. Such is my memory of that moment that I can tell you absolutely nothing about what followed – all totally erased from the record.

Stories of Stories

Footnotes on sly gossipy practices

This essay appeared in *The Word for Teaching is Learning: Language and learning today – essays for James Britton*, edited by Martin Lightfoot and Nancy Martin and published in 1988.

> Going over past events in our minds must occupy us for a great deal of our spare time, and might be called the typical form of mental activity for many old people. It has been pointed out that 'memory', as we usually think of it, takes a narrative form. It may well be that the stage at which narrative speech becomes possible to a child is the point at which memory in this sense begins …
>
> (Britton, 1970, p. 71)

James Britton touches here on an aspect of narrative largely neglected in the literature. And the literature is huge. It is not as though, when looking at narrative, we find that the field is undeveloped or that studies are sporadic or that they are conducted largely within one discipline. On the contrary, scholars from almost every humanistic and social science discipline (psychology, psychiatry, cognitive sciences, sociolinguistics, history, anthropology, discourse analysis and, above all, literary theory) have turned to examine narrative. We have a name for the study of narrative on which so many diverse endeavours converge – narratology. Gerard Prince, whose book (1982), a kind of users' manual, is called just that, set about outlining its goals.

> Narratology examines what all narratives have in common – narratively speaking – and what allows them to be narratively different. It is therefore not so much concerned with the history of particular novels or tales or with their meaning, or with their aesthetic value, but with the traits which distinguish narrative from other signifying systems and with the modalities of these traits. Its corpus consists of not only all extant, but also all possible ones.

These goals are ambitious but yet extraordinarily narrow, for they exclude concerns which any educator would regard as central – meaning, narrative thinking, the motives of narrators, culturally specific narrative styles, narrative within spoken discourse and, of course, memory, which for James Britton is a starting point. Prince's examples, liberally scattered throughout his text, are all drawn from written narrative, though he claims that 'much of what I say is applicable to any narrative regardless of the medium of representation'. The reader will look in vain for any reference to narrative memory or the slightest concern for the thought processes of the narrator. The same is true for many others who attempt comprehensive studies of narrative (see, for example, Chatman, 1978). For James Britton narrative is best looked at, first and foremost, as an act of the mind, the remembering mind, the mind which is for ever sifting the past in order to celebrate, to mourn, to confront its riddles, to rewrite it – in a phrase, to wrest meanings from it. We transform raw events and actions into causes, consequences and point.

If memory does receive attention, it is not at all in the way James Britton had in mind. For, as we might have guessed, it is based above all on short-term recall of stories which have been read or heard. The tradition goes back to Bartlett's classic (1932) study of retelling. But whereas Bartlett was interested in how narrators interpreted and changed stories, current work puts its main emphasis on how close children and others can come to the original or retain what the investigator believes to be its essential features (plot or 'story grammar'). This has nothing to do with memory as art, our capacity to transform past experience and thus to make our own stories or, like Chaucer and Shakespeare, to make new stories from old ones. I have met people who were shocked at the suggestion that children might be encouraged to change stories in whatever way they wished. They were steeped in curriculum practices which confront the student with the unremitting demand to hand back what has been handed out in the teacher's words, the textbook's words, the blackboard's words. Success is measured by how close the student comes to the original. More sophisticated methods of judging recall have developed within cognitive science, in particular within schema theory (Mandler, 1984):

> From this program has emerged the insight that in addition to knowledge about concrete plots and actions people have a more abstract understanding of what happens in stories. From an early age people develop expectations about the overall form of traditional stories: they learn that these stories involve protagonists who have goals and who engage in attempts to achieve these goals, and that goals and events cause other goals and events in predictable ways.

The work is full of interest, yet it is flawed both by the experimental conditions under which it is carried out and by a total disregard for how people, including of course school students, change stories when they retell them, not because of faulty memory of either form or content or specific narrative features, but because that is what creative storytellers, strictly retellers, do everywhere, reworking what is given in the light of other memories of other experiences, of other stories, of other language. The reteller works to his/her own double sense of goodness of fit, that is, both to the original and to his/her own sense of rightness. To read the studies described in

Mandler is to be informed by some discoveries but also to be strongly aware of how the self-imposed limitations have taken us a long way away from really motivated storytellers, what they do and why they do it.

Nowhere are memory and narrative more closely intertwined than in the autobiographical story, par excellence in the story which insinuates itself into conversation, which is tendered as a fully valid contribution to that conversation, in pursuit of its evident intents. Indeed, once we are alerted to the presence of autobiographical narrative in everyday conversation, we cannot avoid the impression that it is a powerful and often dominant feature of all such encounters, that we cannot talk freely and informally without drawing on our narrative competence. For we are always testing ideas and motives against our memories. Such narrative, significantly, tends to be eliminated only by special social constraints which announce, 'No stories here', in the seminar room, for instance, or certain religious gatherings. On the other hand in many cultural settings conversation would be defined by the stories which bind it together, the tales of personal experience, the anecdotes. Conversation without stories is impossible to imagine: it would be the banishment of life itself.

It makes sense therefore when we come to look at narrative in school to begin by turning to a careful examination of its most modest and ephemeral moments, performed without benefit of clergy, sanctioned by no hierarchical authority, uncanonized, even despised as some low-order activity. We should beware of dismissing 'anecdotes' (e.g. Stahl, 1983) simply because anybody can compose one, which would be like dismissing speech because we can all talk. We need to turn away from those narratives which have won themselves a comfortable and secure place in the curriculum, the great novels, children's literature and even traditional tales, the latter transformed, as Zipes (1983) has shown, into sanitized printed versions in the nineteenth century. We should do this not ultimately to ignore them but so that in returning to them we should do so with a deeper understanding of the narrative impulse. More than this, we would come to respect the skills and complex competences of the everyday storyteller. By that means we come to perceive some new possibilities for the classroom by liberating and extending children's narrative powers to enrich classroom discourse. This is simply to extend what we learned a long time ago from James Britton when he made us think again about that simple activity, talk.

Conversational storytelling fuses memory and autobiography. Michel de Certeau (1980) goes so far as to assert that memory, emerging as oral narrative, is a special resource enabling us to resist institutionalized power and its oppressive discourse:

> It is the strangeness, the alien dynamic of memory which gives it the power
> to transgress the law of the local space in question.

What de Certeau calls 'the intense singularities' of storytelling he counterposes to scientific discourse, which, he says, 'eliminates time's scandals'.

> Nevertheless, they return over and over again, noiselessly and surreptitiously, and not least within the scientific activity itself: not merely in the practices of everyday life which go on without their own discourse, but also in the sly and gossipy practices of everyday story-telling … a practical know-how is at work in these stories, where all the features of the 'art of memory' itself can be detected … *the art of a daily life can be witnessed in the tales told about it.* (italics added)

The idea that everyday anecdotal storytelling is an oppositional practice occurs too in Ross Chambers's book (1984), where he argues that the storyteller gains authority without power and thus is able to convert '(historical) weakness into (discursive) strength' and become 'a major weapon against alienation, an instrument of self-assertion'. Everyday storytelling then derives its power from being outside the legitimized operation of institutions and wriggles its way into the interstices of those same institutions.

The extensive literature on narrative has its rewards and frustrations. The adventurous search by scholars for invariant taxonomies is seductive. To read Barthes's *S/Z* (1975) or Genette's *Narrative Discourse* (1980) is to be challenged and enriched. Yet all the time, with the eye fixed on storytellers who are not thin and elusive spectres hovering behind written text (always scrutinized strictly within its pure white frame), one is conscious that stories are communicative acts committed in particular situations by known and knowable people. Although we might look at certain texts in the classroom in this way ('reading', 'literature', 'comprehension'), it is quite impossible to participate in storytelling as tellers and listeners and not be intensely aware of who is telling, who is listening, the shared history of the group and the particular circumstances of the telling. This is only to do with narrative what we have learned to do with all discourse – put it in context. It is anthropologists and ethnographers to whom we have to turn for a thoroughly contextual approach, for it is they who have shown the significance of *performance*, the very act of storytelling, which is

> a way of speaking, the essence of which resides in the assumption of responsibility to an audience for a display of communicative skill, highlighting the way in which communication is carried out … From the point of view of the audience, the act of expression on the part of the performer is thus laid open to evaluation for the way it is done, the relative skill and effectiveness of the performer's display. It is also offered for the enhancement of experience, through the present appreciation of the intrinsic qualities of the act of expression itself. Performance thus calls

forth special attention to and heightened awareness of both the act of expression and the performer.

(Bauman, 1986)

Here at last I begin to recognize the storytellings in which I have participated, from the unexpected tale which captures conversational space and is readily accorded a larger than usual measure of it to the recognizable storytelling event where by tacit or overt agreement storytelling is the business in hand. For storytelling belongs with conviviality and trust and flourishes when people are comfortable with one another. It both arises from a sense of social ease and also creates it. It confirms and extends social relationships, in the renewal of acquaintanceships, in intervals at work, at street corners, wherever knots of people gather to become spectators of their own lives, as Britton has put it. The stories exchanged on these occasions not only emerge from memory of others but are available for retelling. Memories of the memories of others. It is Bauman who seems to have the keenest sense of what the anecdotal tissue of conversation means.

> Because these stories are about known and familiar people and constitute part of their social biographies, they are deeply indexical in a concrete social sense. That is, part of their meaning derives from the indexical associations they evoke – the people portrayed, other known aspects of their lives and characters, including those present at the storytelling event, with whom they are linked by the kinds of social and communicative ties that give cohesion to the conversations in which the stories are told.

(*ibid.*)

After examining in great detail different kinds of Texan oral narratives, he concludes:

> When one looks to the social practices by which social life is accomplished one finds with surprising frequency people telling stories to each other as a means of giving cognitive and emotional coherence to experience, constructing and negotiating social identity ... investing the experiential landscape with moral significance.

(*ibid.*)

We are very familiar with the great claims made for the value of studying works of fiction in the classroom and can hear echoes of them in Bauman's analysis of the functions of storytelling. It makes good sense to see in both activities similar forces at work. Fiction writers certainly have always drawn on the resources of the oral storyteller and an unbreakable thread has always linked the two together. But what is being said here is that the oral storytelling has particular potency because the human disposition to narrative experience makes available unique methods and means for creating by themselves ways of achieving in one and the same act the most ambitious of acts – cognitive, emotional, social and moral. Storytelling, then, taken in all its forms, is a curriculum. To isolate a single anecdote by a child and invest it with such huge significance would be to invite ridicule, though closer scrutiny usually reveals a richer meaning than a hasty glance. It is the web of narratives, the storytelling culture, which must be weighed. Narrative both in and out of school is best regarded as a complex set of social practices rather than as isolated texts to be appraised in isolation from each other. It is the narrative culture of classrooms which we should be debating, what it is and what it might be.

I am making no attempt in this paper to draw on all the diverse literature on narrative from which we might derive illumination and develop a full educational theory and practice. I have started on that agenda and some sketches of the possibilities I have expressed in other papers (see Rosen, 1985; [reprinted in this collection]). Suffice it to say at this point that my own explorations have led me to conclude that we have most to learn from those scholars who have rejected the notion of the autonomy of the text and those who do not see narrative as simply a cultural mirror but rather as a means of actively re-creating and changing culture (see, in addition to Bauman, Hymes, 1981; Polanyi, 1982; Smith, 1981; Stahl, 1977 and 1983; Tannen 1982 and 1984; Heath, 1983).

Wherever we turn in the literature, no matter what its stance, sooner or later we encounter a phrase which suggests an awareness of the deep meaning of narrative in human life and in the human psyche: 'the central function or instance of the human mind' (Frederic Jameson); 'the interpretation of reality is radically implicated in the narrative process from the very beginning' (Jeremy Hawthorn); 'a primary and irreducible form of human comprehension, and article in the constitution of common sense' (Louis Mink).

These ideas (there are many similar ones) are usually proposed almost parenthetically when other business is in hand or as an aphoristic reflection generated by a particular study. They are never elaborated, developed or lingered over. For mere writers never seem to ask the question, 'What do I have to do to read a story?' (in Wolfgang Iser, for example). It is an axiom of narratology, which we owe to the Russian formalists, that one must distinguish between actual events which have or might have happened and the discourse which presents them (*histoire* and *récit*), the actual street accident I witnessed and the story I tell about it. This crucial distinction has made it possible to create very refined analyses of the transformations made by narrators of all kinds. Genette (1980) shows with great subtlety the differences between real time and story time. We need, however, to show what exactly even the humblest, youngest storyteller does which reveals the process of the narrative act. Suppose I were to tell you about my frustrated endeavours to fix to the garden door a hook for holding it back in the wind and how I broke two drills in carrying out this simple task. Actually it is quite a long story. For the door-hook events to be rendered into a story, I must do at least the following:

(i)   I must confront the unceasing flow of events and actions and, by cutting into them, create 'a beginning', which need not be either an event or an action but might be a way of signalling that I am about to begin a story or a general comment on my life as a handyman or many other opening gambits. This will be my first step in constructing a verbalized demarcation of the events. I am building boundaries with my words.

(ii)   I must then proceed with my boundary building so that what was inchoate, interpenetrated with a multitude of other events, is foregrounded by a process of selection, emphases, silences, evaluations, indications of causality, digressions, reflections, accommodation of the listener.

(iii) The boundary must be completed with an 'ending' which in reality was no such thing. Life, as we say, goes on. The ending-ness of the final comment or event has to be composed.

(iv)   In telling the story of the door-hook I must draw on all those resources which I have learned from encountering the narrative events of my culture.

That is but the bare bones, sufficient, I hope, to indicate that storytelling calls for an active, exacting attention to the world, the very kind of attention which should be at the heart of learning. An invitation to narrate should be seen in the classroom as a call for this high-order attention. Since narrative draws on any language resource that suits its turn, plundering every kind of discourse, especially through representing the speech of its protagonists, it digs deep into the linguistic resources of the narrator. Indeed, the teachers with whom I am working are persuaded that narrative, more than any other mode, produces the highest levels of linguistic performance.

Deborah Tannen uses the idea of frame in one of her papers on narrative ('What's in a frame?', 1979). She notes the widespread use of terms in many disciplines to deal with patterns of expectation (frames, scripts, schemata, scenes and so forth), such as the typical buyer–seller exchange in a shop. There are two ways in which patterns of expectation can enter narrative activity.

The first would make it necessary to modify Tannen's description. Because we develop a rich experience of hearing and telling stories we see one experience rather than another as having narrative potential. Thus an experience in a shop when the normal frame operates, that is, the purchase is effected without a hitch, is scarcely worth the telling. But if I have suffered because of incompetence and incivility, I find myself telling the story. The story will still be framed by the conventions of the buying-selling episode, though I am free to disrupt them both in the actual event and in the telling. But beginnings and endings are naturalized by the culture. Football matches begin with the kick-off and end with the final whistle, but a storyteller, who might be one of the players, is under no obligation to be constrained by that frame. He might begin with a quarrel in the changing room or his thoughts while packing his kit. Nevertheless it would be interesting to know more about events in which we immediately perceive a compelling and dramatic story, ready made. This is the stuff of journalism, good and bad.

A second refinement which I would add to the narrative-composing process I have outlined above is particularly relevant to the account of personal experience. I was writing briefly the other day about my grandfather handling a piece of cloth from which I wanted a suit made [see '*Zeider* and the Suit' in this collection]. At the time the scene was, as Tannen suggests, framed by recognition of it as having narrative potential, of matching other scenes in which the craft expert carries out his inspection techniques and uses his judgement. A half century later around this frame another is constructed. Instead of a structure of expectation derived from similar experiences and relating to a present experience (i.e. a form of memory), we now have the intervention of memory in a different way. The form of presentation (narrative) still conforms to the notion of frame, but this distant scene is now filtered through intervening relevant experience represented in my memory and in particular by the frequent and increasing evocation of my grandfather in my thoughts.

This gives autobiographical narrative a fascinating complexity – a new and bigger frame is placed around the original one, which at the same time is definitely not discarded. The autobiographical narrative speaks with a double voice, the voice of then and the voice of now indissolubly fused together. At this point the frame metaphor becomes an encumbrance. I linger over this speculative point not only because of its intrinsic interest, which I could have lingered on (perfectly 'remembered' conversations, for example), but also because it reminds us once again of how complex are the processes by which some stories, easily taken for granted, are composed.

Jerome Bruner has for a long time been a leading participant in seminars on narrative theory and practice at the New School for Social Research in New York. In his most recent book, *Actual Minds, Possible Worlds* (1986), there is a chapter called 'Two Models of Thought' which is a bold attempt to assess the role of narrative in human thought. Bruner starts without compromise by proposing that when we speak or write we have two quite distinct ways of thinking which each give rise to their own kind of discourse.

> There are two modes of cognitive functioning, two modes of thought, each providing distinctive ways of ordering experience, of constructing reality. The two (though complementary) are irreducible to one another. Efforts to ignore one at the expense of the other inevitably fail to capture the rich diversity of thought.

Note first that Bruner is talking about language as a way of 'ordering experience'. One of the two modes is narrative; the other is 'paradigmatic', epitomized in argument, of which scientific thought and discourse are kinds. I immediately find myself objecting. Why are there only two modes of thought, not three or ten? To be sure, Bruner wittily explains that scientists have their stories to aid invention and discovery but these are under-the-counter, non-legitimated ways of going on.

That is surely beside the point, for formal scientific discourse abounds in narrative of processes, descriptions of experiments and case studies. Indeed, it is these narratives which, once freed from the constraints of conventional language and policed style, point the way to a wider role for narrative right across the curriculum – the stories of all kinds of learning experience. Bruner's apparent neglect here is more easily understood if we notice that, although he begins by talking about all narrative, the kind of narrative he has in mind is essentially literary narrative. Herein lies the essential weakness of the argument, for he cannot by this approach show us what links all narrators. It also absolves him from the necessity of giving close attention to the ways in which everyday stories enter the fabric of society and would do so if not a single written story existed. He tells us:

> I shall want to concentrate on narrative … at its far reach as an art form … The great works of fiction that transform narrative as an art form come closest to revealing 'purely' the deep structure of the narrative mode in expression.

and

> One does well to study the work of trained and gifted writers if one is to understand what it is that makes good stories powerful and counselling.

None of this is argued, and it certainly does not bear close inspection, coloured as it is by cultural snobbery. It takes nothing away from the great works of fiction to note that they are a particular narrative phenomenon arising from a European historical context, that narrative also exists as a highly developed oral art and, finally, that it is necessary to demonstrate rather than assert that great works of fiction come closest to revealing 'purely' the deep structure of the narrative mode. This would be like saying that the Royal Ballet Company would best reveal to us the deep structure of dance throughout human culture. Bruner writes: 'Anybody (at almost any age) can tell a story.' Any young child can speak but that did not lead Bruner in his studies of early language development to choose star performers. Nor is it any surprise that he chooses to apply his analysis to a classic short story, James Joyce's 'Clay'.

Flawed though this chapter is, we would not expect so profound and adventurous a scholar to fail to provide us with many insights into narrative, though even here he concentrates on the quality of written texts, not on the narrative mode of thought we were promised at the outset. The most promising set of ideas deals with what he calls the subjunctivization of a narrative text, an elaboration of some ideas in Todorov's work. This enables us to see precisely what features in a story change it from a set of mere assertions of fact to an engagement with psychological process, transform 'pure information' to a world of presuppositions, possibilities and predicaments. The whole chapter is richly informed by every strand of narrative scholarship; a better introduction to it could hardly be found. For all my reservations it puts narrative in a context which makes for immediate educational relevance.

Take retelling. Bruner sees how much can be learned from a student's retelling of a short story. His focus is on how the student picks up the subjunctivization of the original story and also strives to preserve its point and maintain its genre.

> Genre seems to be a way of both organising the structure of events and organising the telling of them – a way that can be used for one's own story telling, or, indeed, for placing the stories one is reading or hearing.

All stories feed greedily on other stories in many different ways. Children can soon learn how to compose a particular kind of story. From the retellings I have elicited and examined it is clear that we can go beyond Bruner and say that, given the encouragement of a teacher, pupils can switch in a retelling from one story genre to another. Betty Rosen's book on storytelling in the secondary school (1988) contains many examples of students doing just this. If one thing stands out in that text it is that retelling is a profoundly creative activity. For stories do not offer single isolable meanings. They formulate interlocking sets of meanings, and listening to a story is a search for these meanings through the meanings we already possess. In retelling we both repeat the words of others and also change them. Even in the retelling of our own personal intimate stories (for we do retell them!) we change them in new contexts, carrying forward some of the old and with certain reworkings shifting however slightly the meanings of the story. We are incorrigible reworkers of our own and other people's stories. I tell not only my own stories but reworkings of my family's and my friend's stories.

It is worth lingering on this point. We have come to believe that creativity in language consists in the creation of a novel text as distinct from the reproduction of an existing one. And what higher praise can we offer than to say a story is original? Such a view runs counter to all we know about narrative practices. To retell with changes a story we have received is only to continue what we did as little children. The teacher can put richer resources at the disposal of pupils, other stories which propose new strategies, and can provoke students into taking liberties with the original. We might say that this is to turn time-honoured practices over their heads. The schoolboys in Betty Rosen's book are liberty-takers of this kind. They elaborate, compress, innovate, discard. None of them is a mindless mimic. They act as all good storytellers do, taking what they want, shifting nuances, even turning the story upside down. These changes repay study for they reveal the creativity of retelling and the delicate tension between reproduction and invention. The traditional storyteller was never a mere echo of an accepted version but a creative performer putting his personal stamp on a traditional tale. The role of the teacher emerges clearly. It is first to emancipate students from the incessant demand for recall and then to set them free to take over the story and bend it to their purposes.

An American teacher, Valerie Polakov, one of the few who believe totally in stories, including the teacher's stories, argues (1985) that the teacher's stories are a valid kind of research.

> On every story there exists a dialectic between teller and listener and at some moment the horizons of listening and telling fuse … and as our lived worlds merge, engagement begets reciprocity and participation in the world of the other and evokes from us a call to act. The educator-researcher as storyteller is a metaphor for engagement, a call to action.

For narrative truly to penetrate school culture, teachers will need to tell each other the stories of their stories. From that repertoire of metanarrative the best narrative practices will emerge.

References

Barthes, R. (1975) *S/Z* (R. Miller, trans.). London: Jonathan Cape.

Bartlett, F. (1932) *Remembering.* Cambridge: Cambridge University Press.

Bauman, R. (1986) *Story, Performance and Event.* Cambridge: Cambridge University Press.

Britton, J. (1970) *Language and Learning.* London: Allen Lane.

Bruner, J. (1986) *Actual Minds, Possible Worlds.* Cambridge, MA: Harvard University Press.

de Certeau, M. (1980) 'On the oppositional practices of everyday life'. *Social Text,* 1.

Chambers, R. (1984) *Story and Situation.* Minneapolis: University of Minnesota Press.

Chatman, S. (1978) *Story and Discourse.* Ithaca, NY: Cornell University Press.

Genette, G. (1980) *Narrative Discourse* (J. Lewin, trans.). Oxford: Basil Blackwell.

Heath, S. (1983) *Ways with Words.* Cambridge: Cambridge University Press.

Hymes, D. (1981) *In Vain I Tried to Tell You.* Philadelphia: University of Pennsylvania Press.

Mandler, J. (1984) *Stories, Scripts and Scenes: Aspects of schema theory.* Hillsdale, NJ: Erlbaum.

Polakov, V. (1985) 'Whose stories should we tell? A call to action'. *Language Arts,* 62 (6).

Polanyi, L. (1982) 'Literary complexity in everyday storytelling', in D. Tannen (ed.), *Spoken and Written Language.* Norwood, NJ: Ablex.

Prince, G. (1982) *Narratology.* Berlin: Mouton.

Rosen, B. (1988) *And None of It Was Nonsense.* London: Mary Glasgow.

Rosen, H. (1985) *Stories and Meanings.* Sheffield: National Association for the Teaching of English (reprinted in this collection).

Smith, B. (1981) 'Afterthoughts on narrative', in W. Mitchell (ed.), *On Narrative.* Chicago: Chicago University Press.

Stahl, S. (1977) 'The oral personal narrative in its generic context'. *Fabula,* 18.

Tannen, D. (ed.) (1982) *Spoken and Written Language.* Norwood, NJ: Ablex.

Tannen, D. (1979) 'What's in a frame? Surface evidence for underlying expectations', in R. Freedle (ed.), *New Directions in Discourse Processing.* Norwood, NJ: Ablex.

Zipes, J. (1983) *Fairy Tales and the Art of Subversion.* London: Heinemann.

Talk as Autobiography

Harold gave this paper at a conference in Toronto in May 1991. It was published in *Troublesome Boy* (Rosen, 1993).

Thereby always hangs a tale. For instance, the two-inch scar just below my left ankle which is sixty-two or sixty-three years old. Or the battered photo of my older brother Laurie in the uniform of the 11th Hussars who ran away from home when he was sixteen and who I never saw again. Or the story that explains how it was that I became a teacher even though when I was sixteen I was sure I was going to become a lawyer. These are tales (and at my age there are many, many of them) which are, to use Gorky's phrase, fragments of my autobiography. They are not very long and if I tell one of them yet again, it will usually be in the midst of a conversation. If I could bring them all together I would be content to say, 'There you are, that's me'. Which is what Jean-Jacques Rousseau said at the beginning of *The Confessions* (1953 [1781]). There's nothing special in that. Everyone has a similar repertoire, an invisible autobiography. We are at it all the time. So are our pupils, even when their pasts amount to very few years.

The trouble is that, like most words of Greek origin invented by the educated, 'autobiography' is a heavy word. We didn't, it would seem, even have the word until shortly after 1800. Yet when we think of the kinds of activities meant by it we are comfortable enough. We've read an autobiography or two and probably quite a few novels which are written as though they are autobiographies and of course sometimes are. For instance:

> 'You must not tell anyone,' my mother said, 'what I am about to tell you. In China your father had a sister who killed herself. She jumped into the family well. We say that your father has all brothers because it is as if she had never been born ... '
>
> (from *The Woman Warrior*, Maxine Hong Kingston, 1975)

I suppose that if I asked you what sort of thing autobiography is, you'd answer, 'It's someone telling his or her life-story', which sounds like an ambitious project, not one a person would undertake lightly. Listen to the opening words of Rousseau's *The Confessions*:

> I have resolved on an enterprise which has no precedents and which, once complete, will have no imitator. My purpose is to display to my kind a portrait in every way true to nature. The man I portray will be myself.

'Portrait' is a kind of metaphor, of course. *The Confessions* turns out to be a long story within which are dozens of other stories. Rousseau's claim to uniqueness at that time was certainly justified but only if we discount such things as journals, diaries, letters, traveller's tales and personal stories interpolated into almost any kind of work. We can go back as far as Bede's *Ecclesiastical History of the English People* (1990, modern edition) and we find in the eighth century Bede writing about his religious and scholarly life in the monastery. And of course we have Pepys's seventeenth-century diary (2003, modern edition). Nowadays we take for granted that everyone has a life story even if they never get round to telling it. Perhaps we do not notice how much of it they do tell when they just sit and chat. Nor do we notice how much the culture has taught them how to do it, how it licenses self-revelation. They do not learn this complex and delicate art from literature, linguists or psychology classes but in the very process of talking and listening to one another. That is why we should shift our attention away from the portentous sense of autobiography in the printed tome to the verbal world where, I believe, such works have their roots (i.e. the day-to-day world of common interchange) but also where we would learn something important about all autobiographical activity and the role it plays in everyone's life. But it requires a special effort. Just as it is difficult to pay attention to the very air we breathe or to observe what makes up our culture, so it is difficult to notice what goes on in conversation. If we listen carefully to intimate, friendly, relaxed talk (or eavesdrop, I might almost say) or better still attend closely to tape and transcript of such talk, we shall always find that the participants offer each other moments of their pasts, recent or distant. They are not only saying 'This is how it was' and 'This is the way I am' but also 'This is the way the world goes'. Some conversations consist of almost nothing else: they are little anthologies about, let us say, domestic disasters, recollections of schooldays, holiday episodes, our children, incidents at work, inexplicable mysterious events and so on. We make these offerings as fully fledged stories or as very brief utterances. Take the former. We recognise the initiating signals:

That reminds me of the time …

Did I ever tell you about …

… and usually we accord more than the average ration of space given to a speaker and surrender our turns as a small price to pay for what we expect to be a proper story. Context, of course, makes a huge difference. Suppose I tell my teacher friends how I came to leave a job unexpectedly and then I have to tell the same story when I am asked about it at a formal interview for the next job. Those would be rather different tellings and I think we can safely say that the second would be carefully censored and hedged about with much more verbal caution than the first. Though all stories of personal experience share underlying characteristics, there are important differences. They may be no more than the briefest intimation of past events:

I never questioned or challenged my parents' views until I was nineteen …

That party was a real washout, a flop …

At a different time and given more propitious circumstances, they might have blossomed into full stories. After all, I haven't told you the full story of the scar under my ankle or of my brother Laurie's photo. Or take this snippet:

A. Do you know that since I've lived here four kids have died in that damned canal?

B. Yeah. When I was twelve I fell in …

But the conversation is about putting pressure on the local council to organise better safety precautions and it sweeps on, leaving only the trace of what might have been the full tale. Some other time perhaps. At the other pole is that repertoire of stories which, as far as I can tell, everyone has tucked away in the pouch. Given the right moment in the conversation – encouragement, provocation, rivalry, the need to establish identity, etc. – the fully-fledged personal experience story emerges. Or it may be that an episode which has never been put in words before will be trawled from memory and given an airing. By contrast, repertoires often contain stories which have been polished over many tellings, like the one I tell about visiting an old manor house in Devon. After looking over the house we settled down in a corner of the lawn to eat our lunch. Major what-ever-he-was came charging out and said, 'Do you usually eat your meals on other people's lawns?' and we crawled away: that was only the *coup de grace* after a series of devastating put-downs. Stories like that often achieve an almost canonical form and change very little from one telling to another, many wordings remaining intact, although there will always be some adjustments as we shall see later.

We can take it, then, that there is a spectrum of autobiographical talk, from a remark like:

I came to England when I was three years old.

… to a full version of how I sat an algebra exam and half-way through decided I couldn't pass. In despair I put my pen down and listened to a barrel organ playing a waltz I associated with my mother. Somehow soothed, I picked up my pen again … Of course there's more to it than a simple continuum from short to long, for on any point on that continuum we can distinguish differences. Let me take the extremes.

A. The brief utterance: why is it brief?

(i)   It is brief because that's all the speaker wants to say at that moment.
(ii) It is brief because that's all the speaker gets a chance to say.
(iii) It is brief because the speaker hoped for encouragement which did not come.

(iv) It is brief because the speaker is not yet ready to develop the story or is unsure about how to develop it. Perhaps memory has not thrown up the detail.

B. The fully-fledged story: why is it being told?

(i) It is being told because it's a serious contribution to a discussion, an alternative to other ways of making a point, where opinions are being exchanged, explored, reshaped.

(ii) An anecdote can itself initiate a discussion, e.g. indignation events (a student tells a group how a teacher has unjustly accused him of cheating and not allowed him to defend himself. The others then launch into a discussion of the vagaries and mysteries of teacher behaviour).

(iii) The story is being told in its own right, i.e. its only justification is that it is calculated to command full attention and interest. The implication is that 'you're going to enjoy this'. A sub-genre is when the whole group moves into the storytelling mode, e.g. hospital stories, supernatural episodes, dreams, etc. That at any rate is the surface phenomenon. Such story sequences are often, in fact, alternative ways of conducting a discussion. We know that conversation involves the skilled art of turn-taking and a special form of this is turn-taking at storytelling.

(iv) Those who have shared a significant set of experiences will engage in collective reminiscences, e.g. those who were at school together ten or twenty years ago; parents and their now adult children looking back at their earlier shared life.

(v) A story is told in response to some form of invitation, e.g. 'Tell me what happened' or 'Tell them about the time when … ' This, of course, could be sinister because some responses to invitations are made under the duress of interrogation.

To the best of my knowledge no one has made a thoroughgoing attempt to produce a taxonomy of the forms of autobiographical talk looked at linguistically, psychologically and socially. [This is what Harold attempts in 'The Whole Story?' – see piece in this collection – and in *Speaking from Memory: The study of autobiographical discourse* (1998).] However, Sandra Stahl in three carefully worked papers (1977a, 1977b and 1983) has attempted to take an analytical look at stories of personal experience. I will not attempt to summarise them but I want simply to draw attention here to the two broad categories into which she divides those stories:

(i) The self-oriented, in which the tellers emphasise their own involvement, their own self-image, the motives and values behind the actions.

(ii) The other-oriented, in which the tellers underplay or eliminate entirely their own personal role. They become witnesses much more than participants.

That's just a two-category system along one dimension. For the rest, notice that all we have instead of a taxonomy is simply a collection of terms, some used by scholars, some by ordinary folk and some by both. Here's my collection: personal-experience stories, oral personal narrative, autobiographical speech, chronicates, secular chronicates, true oral stories, recollections, reminiscences, eye-witness accounts, anecdotes, case histories, gossip, rumour. What most of these terms indicate is that there is a strong and diffuse folk-awareness of the mode.

To understand the personal-experience narrative, it is necessary to say an all too brief word or two about narrative in general. There has been, as many of you will know, a huge surge of interest in narrative over the last twenty years which has gone far beyond literary criticism. A new discipline has been created, narratology, though it limits its territory very narrowly. Gerald Prince, a major exponent, tells us that it concerns itself with what all narratives have in common and what distinguishes them from other forms of discourse. What Prince's statement omits is a profound socio-psychological idea, namely that narrative is a major activity of the human mind. Or, as some have said, a primary and irreducible form of human comprehension, an article in the constitution of human common sense, the central function or instance of the human mind. These are massive claims, aren't they? Those who say such things are not only talking about vast and renowned narratives like Tolstoy's *War and Peace*, Proust's *Remembrance of Things Past* or Gibbon's *Decline and Fall of the Roman Empire* but are also linking them to the sort of thing any one of us might say at any moment about which I was speaking earlier.

> I couldn't get to sleep last night. There was a hell of a noise from cars in the street. So I went to the window.

> Sorry I couldn't get over last Tuesday. A miserable two inches of snow and the whole of this area came to a standstill (from a Canadian in England!).

What embraces all narratives is what they reveal about the working of the human mind. For our purposes just now I shall give a very simple definition of narrative. Narrative is the representation in a text, written or spoken, of a sequence of interconnected events. We shall see that to produce or respond to that representation calls for complex thinking and verbalization. More of that later.

Side by side with feverish academic activity there has been the revival of storytelling. No need, I understand, to tell you that in Toronto. There are now professional storytellers; local virtuosi have been winkled out from their rural backwoods; there are storytelling clubs; there are storytelling festivals. Mostly the stories told are traditional but there are also occasions which elicit autobiography, in community projects, oral history sessions and the reservoir tapped by folklorists. Moreover, autobiography is often threaded into both the telling of and the listening to a traditional story.

So, from the renowned scholar in his study speculating about story grammar to an eighty-year-old remembering his first day at work, there has developed a new world of narrative consciousness and narrative activity. However, as always happens when a new field opens up, the distribution of attention is very uneven. Autobiographical talk has until now received very little attention. Perhaps that is going to change because a scholar with a world reputation, Jerome Bruner, is making it the central object of study. I give a mere summary of his ideas on the subject, though they will appear in a forthcoming book. In 1986, in his book *Actual Minds, Possible Worlds*, he signalled or registered a major shift in his interests as a psychologist and educationist. In it there is one chapter in particular entitled 'Two Modes of Thought' in which he sets out a radical view. The telling of stories, he maintains, is not merely a discourse choice we make from time to time among all sorts of options, but rather one of only two ways of telling and thinking. Here is the crucial passage:

> There are two modes of cognitive functioning, two modes of thought, each providing distinctive ways of ordering experience. The two (though complementary) are irreducible to one another. Efforts to ignore one at the expense of another inevitably fail to capture the rich diversity of human thought.

The two ways are paradigmatic (i.e. logical and scientific) and narrative. This is a bold, challenging, novel proposition and places narrative firmly in the cognitive domain, as a way of ordering experience. To elaborate on this idea, Bruner's analysis concentrates on the fiction story, though clearly he must have in mind also stories of personal experience. Now, although one would never have guessed it from his first sally into narrative, this is exactly the next move he made. He was good enough to send me the series of papers he had written. They are: 'Life as narrative' (1987); 'Culture and human development: A new look' (1990a)'; 'The narrative construction of reality' (1990b); 'Self-making and world making' (2001); 'The autobiographical process' (1993). Moreover, we are promised a book (a collaboration with Susan Weisser) which will document his investigations, *Autobiography and the Construction of Self* (Bruner and Weisser, 1992).

At the heart of Bruner's thinking on autobiographical stories is a challenge to us. For he says the way we know about the physical world is not the same as the way in which we develop and refine our knowledge of ourselves and others and the way in which we construct and represent human interaction. We learn about people and the social world differently from how we learn about things – how a car works or the structure of the atom. We do the former, he says, mainly narratively. That is the meaning of all those gossipy little stories which as our education proceeds are so frequently dismissed as a trivial, low-level activity which needs to be cured. We might almost say that in higher education the guiding principle is 'Forget the stories, learn to generalize, learnt to be theoretical, be impersonal'. If Bruner is even halfway right then I think he is saying, 'Sacrifice your autobiographical thinking and telling and you sacrifice a major form of learning'.

The next step Bruner takes is to test his speculations empirically by asking a number of people to tell their life stories in half an hour. You must seek out the details and dramatic surprises for yourselves. At the moment Bruner's conclusion runs like this:

> My life as a student of mind has taught me one incontrovertible lesson. Mind is never free of pre-commitment. There is no innocent eye, nor is there one that penetrates aboriginality. There are instead hypotheses, versions, expected scenarios. Our pre-commitment about the nature of life is that it is a story, some narrative, however incoherently put together … the only life worth living is the well-examined one.

That is just a whiff of the excitements to be found in Bruner. In the London Narrative Group we have tried to replicate Bruner's work with the half-hour life story. No one seems to have difficulty in taking it on, no matter what their age, education, kind of social life. But unlike Bruner's people, ours find it impossible to limit themselves to half an hour. My own victim, a twenty-nine-year-old, used up the complete hour of tape and he had only reached the age of eighteen! 'That was the turning point,' he told me. 'What changed then?' I asked him. 'My parents told me that as I was eighteen I was now a man. I took them at their word and started to behave like one.' We have also noticed that some of our people go about the task in a different way from Bruner's. They do not deliver their half-hour life histories in a single trajectory. They offer them more as objective testimony, evidence of how life was or as dredged up separate memory images. This is what Sandra Stahl calls other-directed. An old lady in her nineties, totally *compos mentis*, remembers a whole universe of social life but she keeps her own feelings very much in the background.

Bruner until now has not turned his attention to those fleeting autobiographical glints which illuminate every conversation, to which I have already referred and which I see as the starting point for all autobiographical activity. We have to speculate about what precisely it is in interaction which fans a small red glow into the blaze of a full story. Certainly the teller must chance his or her arm and rely on an intuition that the story will either clinch an argument or be savoured as verbal art, as oral literature. What sort of judgement was involved when my son, returning from field work on a coral reef in the Indian Ocean, told us about the Moray eel? He had been snorkelling along a reef and prising off small pieces of coral with a crowbar. At one point he said he felt a sudden and juddering clonk on the crowbar. It was a snapping bite from the Moray eel, which lurks in the fissures of the coral. A bite from it could take your arm off. Why was it he chose to tell that little tale when he came back, and not in one of his many storyful letters?

Reminiscences are about remembering, but the literature on narrative pays little attention to the role of memory. Prince's *A Dictionary of Narratology* (1988) does not even have an entry under memory. It takes a James Britton (1970) to remind us that

> going over past events must occupy us for a great deal of our spare time ...
> Memory, as we usually think of it, takes a narrative form.

Memory is implicated in personal-experience stories in different ways. We begin with how we actually experience events and the recall of those events in short-term memory. That is, what we remember and how we remember it, let us say an hour later. And then there is the long-term memory, possibly decades after the event. Further, there is the construction of the memory in words, the telling of the memory. Lastly, in order to tell it we must remember the appropriate forms for telling which we have learned from others since our earliest years as surely as we have learned 'Once upon a time ... ' The goals and intentions of many remarkably perceptive scholars, Genette, Chapman, Prince and others, do not include considerations which any teacher, indeed any participant, would take for granted: the motives of the teller (why is she telling me this?); the personal point of a story (was the tale of the Moray eel to show the dangers to be faced when working on the reef? was it a sort of rite of passage?); more broadly, what does a story tell us about the teller? what do I now know about the teller which I didn't know before? Our interest in the person who is engaged in the act of remembering includes an interest in how that person's memory is working. For James Britton, autobiographical stories are first and foremost an act of the remembering mind. For me that means a mind ceaselessly reviewing the past to confront its riddles, to rework it, to resavour it, to celebrate it, to mourn it. In a word, to wrest a huge array of meanings from it. Raw events and actions, lingering images of places and people, are transformed by memory into causes, motives, consequences and point.

The story of personal experience might almost be called the making of memory. We do not easily perceive that such a story cannot be a straight reproduction of past events, the plain unvarnished truth, as we say. We do not, in spite of our strong belief that this is often so, re-live an experience. We cannot put on a re-run of the past. We have to create beginnings, select some details and ignore others, we must adapt to an audience and our telling is likely to be suffused with our present feelings. To tell the tale of how I didn't become a lawyer I must confront what was a non-stop flow of events and cut right into them to create a beginning, which need not be either an event or an action but simply a way of signalling that I am about to begin a story. The choice is mine. I could make a general comment on my life and on the theme of the story.

> You know how it is. I was sixteen and didn't have the faintest idea about what I would do or what I wanted to be. That is until Cousin Leslie paid us one of his rare condescending visits.

This is my first step in the demarcation of the events of my story, where I choose to put the entrance door. I must then proceed with my construction work so that what was inchoate, interpenetrated with what now seems to me irrelevant other events, is now given shape by a process of selection, by systems of emphasis, silences, evaluations, indications of causality, cunning digressions, reflections, accommodation of the listener. I may even take to invention. For example:

> So I picked up the phone. I was nervous, very nervous. 'Can I speak to Mr Sunshine, please?' They put me through. 'It's me, Leslie, Harold. My exams … You know, well … I passed!'

Now that memory, which I would swear to, is that I DID phone cousin Leslie from the call box outside the Sussex Laundry in New Road. I am equally certain that I gave him my exam results on which I thought, wrongly as it turned out, my future as a lawyer depended. But how could I remember at fifty-four years' distance the actual words I spoke over the telephone? So the words I use telling the story are fabricated but very faithful to the events. [Harold's story 'Not Becoming a Lawyer' is in Rosen, 1993 and 1999.]

The boundary must finally be drawn with an ending which in reality was no such thing. Life, as we keep telling ourselves, must go on. Stories must end and end appropriately. The endingness of the final event in some way or another must constitute a comment and be composed.

> So I stood there waiting, waiting for the silence at the other end of the line to be broken. Nothing. Was he still there? So I said again, 'Leslie, I passed; I passed my Matric.' 'Ah, your Matric … You did, did you? Congratulations.'

> And he put down the phone.

In telling that story it's not only my memory of the events and their penumbras on which I draw but also on an infinity of models learnt unawares from those around me.

Because we develop a rich experience of hearing and recounting stories from life, we see one experience rather than another as being story-worthy. So the experience of changing a tyre without the least difficulty is not worth the telling. But suppose everything goes wrong: the spare is flat, I've mislaid the pump, I've broken a spanner and cut my finger, it rains throughout. My son comes out and, in the midst of my despair and anger, asks, 'Why didn't you say you were changing a tyre? I'd have given you a hand.' I do not kill him. Now we have the possibility of a story. Despite what I have already said about beginnings and endings, they are to some extent naturalized in the culture and are therefore clearly perceived as ready to be appropriated. Football matches begin with the kick-off and end with the final whistle. But a storyteller who might be one of the players need not be constrained by that pattern. He might begin with a quarrel in the dressing-room or his thoughts while packing his kit. It would be interesting to know more about those sets of events in which we perceive a compelling story apparently ready-made.

A further point about the composing process. A personal story about the distant past is subject to important changes over the years. I told a story about how my grandfather, a tailor all his life, handled and tested a piece of cloth from which he was going to make me a suit. I first told the story, I imagine, because it was an intimate experience of the skills of a craftsman: judgement and expertise in action. Donkey's years later the story changed fairly subtly because of the frequent and increasing evocation of my grandfather in my thoughts as an object of admiration and love. [See '*Zeider* and the Suit' in this collection] The distant memory is filtered through intervening relevant experience which is also represented in my memory; then and now are indissolubly fused together. de Certeau (1980) speaks of 'the sly, gossipy practices of storytelling'.

> … In these stories all the features of the art of memory can be detected …
> The art of daily life can be witnessed in the tales told about it.

So memory is not simply a function of the mind; it is also an art. The oral storyteller is not like the ghosts who haunt the shadows behind written texts, those we call authors. Oral storytellers' presentations are communicative acts performed in the presence of known or knowable people. It is quite impossible to participate in storytelling and not be intensely aware of who is telling, who is listening and, very often, the shared history of the group. The invitation to share a memory is usually a convivial act or, at the very least, the invitation to some kind of assent. To share a memory with someone you know is to advance your relationship even if it is only by the tiniest step.

The working of memory into a story is not by itself enough, for orality demands performance. The storyteller has to accept a certain responsibility for the display of culturally learned skills: use of voice, variations in speed, pitch, volume, voice quality, intonation and silence. Add to that facial expression, gesture, direction of gaze and all kinds of body language.

Listeners are ruthless judges. They not only weigh what they are told – a story of courage or cowardice, as it might be – but also the performance itself, the level of skills of the storyteller, the totality of his or her expressive powers. As Bauman (1986) puts it:

> performance thus calls forth special attention to and heightened awareness
> of both the act of expression and the performer.

However, should the teller exert too much effort in drawing attention to the performance rather than the tale ('look how good I am at this') we resist, shift uneasily and become a little embarrassed. He's going over the top, we say. Personal storytelling then calls for an active, exacting attention both to the world and the word, the very kind of attention which should be at the heart of all learning. In the classroom an invitation to tell that kind of story should be seen as a call for attention of a very high order which will also dig deep into the linguistic resources of the narrator. Ask yourselves now what it is which is most likely to lure someone into offering a story of personal experience. For there are, after all, hazards in such revelations. Such a one is a show-off. The classroom is not thought to be the appropriate place: it's before total strangers, or it's a particular cultural milieu which does not approve of such things. But if we know what enables a teller nimbly to elude such frosty condemnation then we have in our possession a powerful intimation of how to foster such stories in the classroom.

Autobiographical storytelling belongs with trust, informality and conviviality and most easily comes into its own when people are comfortable with each other and do not feel constrained to be on their best behaviour. It not only emerges from a sense of ease but helps to create it. It confirms and extends social relationships – in the renewal of acquaintanceships, in those precious intervals on the job, at street corners, on long journeys, wherever knots of people gather together to become spectators of their own lives, uncensored by social anxiety. Memories exchanged on these occasions not only emerge from our own pasts but from the pasts told by others which have become available for retelling by us. Grandma's stories are also our stories. To make a space for students to tell their personal stories is above all to affirm the worth of their own culture and at the same time to enable them to make discoveries about it.

It has been a hard struggle over the years to convince others that common-or-garden talk, everyday, messy, interminable chatter, easily engaged in by everyone, navvies as well as Nobel Prize winners, needed to be given full scope. The battle is far from won. We need, nevertheless, to extend the argument and to create an awareness of the significance of the anecdotal tissue of conversation. Bauman, after a detailed analysis of different kinds of Texan storytellers, says:

> When one looks at the social practices by which social life is accomplished, one finds with surprising frequency people telling stories to each other as a means of giving cognitive coherence to experience, constructing and negotiating social identity; investing the experiential landscape with moral significance … Narrative here is not merely a reflection of the culture … but is constitutive of social life.

Bauman only makes these strong claims after his analysis of the stories. We are all familiar with the claims made for the value of studying works of fiction. I think it makes good sense to see in both activities some of the same forces at work. Indeed, fiction writers have always drawn on the resources of oral personal recollection. A strong thread has always linked them together. Here, for example, is a snippet from my most recent novel reading:

> ... My father, as well as being a superstitious man, had a knack for telling stories. Made up stories; soothing stories; warning stories; stories with a moral or no point at all; believable stories and unbelievable stories; stories which were neither one thing or another. It was a knack which ran in the family.

Graham Swift, Waterland (1980)

The power of oral storytelling which novelists plunder so freely derives from the human disposition to narratise experience using our own unique methods to create a cognitive, emotional, moral, social world.

So personal stories in all their forms could be said to be a kind of self-made curriculum. To take one simple anecdote by a child and invest it with such huge potential would be to invite ridicule, but it is not the single isolated tale we must examine. It is the intricate web of narratives. Autobiographical stories, both in and out of school, are best regarded as a set of social practices which belong inside the larger set of narratives in general. They should find an honourable place in the narrative culture of the classroom.

References

Bauman, R. (1986) *Story, Performance and Event.* Cambridge: Cambridge University Press.

Bede (1990) *Ecclesiastical History of the English People* (D. Farmer, ed.; L. Sherley-Price, trans.) (modern edition). London: Penguin.

Britton, J. (1970) *Language and Learning.* London: Allen Lane.

Bruner, J. (1986) *Actual Minds, Possible Worlds.* Cambridge, MA: Harvard University Press.

Bruner, J. (1987) 'Life as narrative'. *Social Research,* 54 (1).

Bruner, J. (1990a) 'Culture and human development: A new look'. *Human Development,* 43.

Bruner, J. (1990b) 'The narrative construction of reality'. *Critical Inquiry,* 18.

Bruner, J. (1993) 'The autobiographical process', in R. Folkenflik (ed.) *The Culture of Autobiography: Constructions of self-representation.* Stanford, CA: Stanford University Press.

Bruner, J. (2001) 'Self-making and world making', in J. Brockmeier and D. Carbaugh (eds.), *Narrative and Identity: Studies in autobiography, self and culture.* Philadelphia: John Benjamins Publishing Company.

Bruner, J. and Weisser, S. (1992) *Autobiography and the Construction of Self.* Cambridge, MA: Harvard University Press.

de Certeau, M. (1980) 'On the oppositional practices of everyday life'. *Social Texts,* 1 (3).

Chapman, S. (1978) *Story and Discourse.* Ithaca, NY: Cornell University Press.

Kingston, M. (1975) *The Woman Warrior: Memories of a girlhood among ghosts.* London: Vintage Books.

Genette, G. (1980) *Narrative Discourse* (J. Lewin, trans.). Oxford: Basil Blackwell.

Pepys, S. (2003) *The Diaries of Samuel Pepys – A Selection* (modern edition). London: Penguin.

Prince, G. (1988) *A Dictionary of Narratology.* Aldershot: Scolar Press.

Rosen, H. (1993) *Troublesome Boy*. London: English and Media Centre.

Rosen, H. (1999) *Are You Still Circumcised?* Bristol: Five Leaves Publications.

Rousseau J-J. (1953 [1781]) *The Confessions* (J. Cohen, trans.). Harmondsworth: Penguin.

Stahl, S. (1977a) 'The oral personal narrative in its generic context'. *Fabula*, 18.

Stahl, S. (1977b) 'The personal narrative as folklore'. *Journal of the Folklore Institute*, XIV (1–2).

Stahl, S. (1983) 'Personal experience stories as folklore', in R. Dorson (ed.), *Handbook of American Folklore*. Bloomington, IN: Indiana University Press.

Swift, G. (1980) *Waterland*. London: Picador.

Zeider and the Suit

When he was seventy-two my grandfather, my *zeider*, that is – fell down in my auntie's garden and never got up again. Poor little Helen, my cousin, ran crying for help because there was no adult in the house. I imagined him crashing heavily into the flower bed, his nicotine-stained walrus moustache burying itself among the pot marigolds and the scared bees. My cousin, showing me later, said, 'He liked those goldy ones best. I found his glasses under the leaves.'

He liked dahlias, too. Why else would he have raised them in our tiny unpromising back-yard year after year, a dozen plants at most with their heavy, purplish-red blooms as big as the palm of your hand? Every autumn he lifted the tubers as carefully as a suburban gardener would and put them in the left-hand drawer of the kitchen dresser. I used to sneak a look at them from time to time and wonder how these grimy bunches of little potatoes would throw up strong shoots and produce flowers. When the milkman's or coalman's horse obliged I would dash out with the fire-side coal shovel and a stick to collect the steaming dung. Another miracle: horse-poo was going to provoke the opening-out of those multi-petalled flower-heads.

Why did he grow nothing but dahlias? More to the point, where did he learn to do it? And where did he get his first tubers from? I invented a gift from one of his *chaveirim* at the Tailors and Garment Workers Union club in Ford Square. A little brown paper bag was handed over like contraband and the occult mysteries of dahlia culture handed over, too. Pure invention, of course. I couldn't imagine that *Zeider* had brought gardening know-how from the muddy alley of a *shtetl* in Poland. Yet only a few days ago I read a poem, a sentimental hymn to the archetypal *shtetl* where there were

> … old Jews in orchards in the shade of cherry trees.

On the other hand, Isaak Babel tells us that, when he played truant from his violin lessons and wandered out of the Odessa ghetto into the docks, a sailor who befriended him discovered he wanted to be a writer but didn't know the names of common trees and birds. 'You can't be a writer,' he told him, 'if you don't know the names of the trees and the birds.' I think *Zeider* was more like Babel than old Jews with their orchards and cherry trees.

Why did he grow nothing but dahlias? Why not marigolds, for instance? My sister Sylvia said he helped her grow pansies from a packet of seeds. Nothing in my memory delivers anything other than his lonely dahlias. Indeed, as I remember it, in the Jewish East End no one knew the names of the trees and the birds. It was a flowerless world. I cannot recall a flower shop in the Commercial Road or the

Whitechapel Road. I can't recall a flower stall in Hessel Street Market wedged in amongst the barrels of pickled herring, *heimisha* cucumbers and sacks of bagels. I can't find in my images of the jostle of Petticoat Lane, with its *schleppers* and barkers, a single bunch of flowers. There were no vases of flowers on front room tables nor amidst the biscuit barrels, brass candlesticks and silver *menorrahs* on sideboards. Sylvia said flowers were for hospital visits and you could buy a bunch from a kind of kiosk outside the London Hospital. Yes, and there were white carnations in men's lapels at weddings, a concession to anglo wedding regalia. If I had thought about that at all, and I don't think I did, I would have attributed it to benighted immigrant-ness like the weird mixture of English and Yiddish or the inability to understand why their teenage children wanted to go camping in muddy fields with only a bit of white *schmutter* over their heads. *Liegen afen drerd*, they would say, lie on the ground when you've got a warm bed with a *daunendecker*? Only for madmen and poor tramps. In one night you could catch your death. *Zeider*'s dahlias were in a small way an act of defiance, a rejection of the old taboos and fears.

So I've decided he was a town Jew not a *shtetl* Jew. Not from Kratchikrak, that impoverished spot in folk legend, but from Warsaw perhaps, or Lvov or even scholarly Vilna. Back then I hadn't an inkling of what bit of the map he had emerged from to take a long-distance train and a North Sea boat and deliver himself to a lifetime bent over a sewing machine, working the treadle and pushing a million yards of cloth into the rag trade. I never once asked him, *Zeider*, where do you come from? Show me on the map. And tell me about your mother and father. Have you got any brothers and sisters? But at the time they weren't my kind of question. Anyway, my *zeider*'s earlier life had gone missing. He seemed unencumbered with a pre-marriage past. No relative, close or distant, ever turned up at the street door or sent a letter. To me it was all the more strange because my *booba*'s past was a fat story book in which there appeared every grade of kinship extending to in-laws of all sorts, cousins, first, second and beyond, greats, great-greats into the distant past, and there were her sisters, my great aunts Sarah, Ray and Bella, my great-grandmother Miriam who had catered for weddings and *barmitzvahs* in Newcastle. There were the gold and diamond seekers in Durban and Johannesburg whom we never saw, except for the one who arrived in a fat white car, had all the kids gawping and never came again. They all stood behind her and animated her talk, reached across the globe and back into the Nineteenth Century. But *Zeider* had not a single forebear. Not a single name crossed his lips, not a single tale about one. So how would I know where his dahlias came from? Or, come to that, what were the beginnings of his talk about class struggle and the dictatorship of the proletariat?

It's not as though he was a taciturn man and I had reason to know. I spent a lot of time with him and it always bubbled with talk which I treasured. We went out together. He took me to play clumsy two-man football in Victoria Park. Anyone could see he hadn't an idea of how to kick a ball and his legs were already giving him trouble. Near the park gate was a little dairy where we had a glass of milk and a huge biscuit. I went with him to the Yiddish Theatre to watch Shakespeare. It was *Macbeth* which he knew I'd done at school. We went up the Mile End Waste together and fingered junk on the stalls. Sometimes he'd get me weighed on a huge balance with a chair on one side and weights on the other. We ended up having sarsparilla from a barrel surrounded with ice. We went to Speakers' Corner in Hyde Park with its bizarre collection of orators and ritualized heckling. Only when I got a bit older did I realise it was an entertainment, street theatre spiced with politics. It was always followed by tea and pastries at Marble Arch Corner House where he patiently explained the speakers' jokes and obscure debates. Why, for instance, did a heckler keep shouting out, 'What was the role of Borodin in the Chinese Revolution?'

A regular trip was to the Tower of London gardens to admire the famous dahlia border. I too was dazzled by it. It was several yards deep and about fifty yards long. The dahlias from the huge cactus sort to the little pom-poms were graded from front to back.

'Such a sight,' he said, '*es geht in aller glieder* – it flows through all your limbs.'

He'd stand and breathe in deeply as though he could inhale all his pleasure and hold it inside himself. The border ranged along the edge of the huge moat which ran round the grey stones of the Tower. We'd turn and watch a phalanx of soldiers marching meaninglessly to and fro. A sergeant was barking orders. The moment one order was given it was followed by a different one.

'What are they doing that for?' I asked.

'For nothing. It's pack drill. Punishments. With armies, is always punishments. *Oi*, armies. We shouldn't know of such things.'

'What are they punishing them for?'

'Breathing, or laughing, mebbe.' We turned back to his adored dahlias.

There were four of us kids in the house – me, my sister and two cousins. *Zeider* singled me out to be his Reader as someone else might be appointed an amanuensis. I'm not sure why unless it was because my mother, the eldest of his six daughters, was his favourite. They marched in demos together, went to rallies which they talked about for days and they spent hours together planning The Revolution. As a seven-year-old I stood between the two of them, holding their hands during the General Strike of 1926, watching grimly the troops and armoured cars going down the Commercial Road on the way to the Docks. The bond between them must have begun long before they worked together to topple The State. The story goes that my mother taught him to read and write English when she was a very little girl. My Aunt Lallie liked to tell it as though she'd been there. It worked like this. When my mother was learning to read and write at school at about four or five years old, she came home each day and gave *Zeider* a version of what she'd learned. The fact that he was literate in Hebrew and Yiddish would have helped, of course, but it must have been tough going because he was still learning to speak English. For how long this went on nobody said but eventually it did the trick. To this day I am deeply moved by the picture I construct of the little girl coaching her father and his ready acceptance of being for once the taught rather than the teacher. Far from being a humiliation it must have filled him with pride and love. No wonder they became good comrades.

So it came about that my *zeider* could eventually read English and I rejoiced in it all those years later just as I did in the fact that he didn't have a straggle beard of wire wool, go around with his head covered all the time, nor spend hours rocking to and fro at his prayers. I see him seated among his heraldic dahlias with his *Daily Worker* almost at arm's-length, specs at the end of his nose, lips moving. And not just the *Daily Worker* but also *Plebs* and *Labour Monthly*. He would get tired, though, or perhaps he just liked being read to, re-living all those hours of apprenticeship. That's where I came in.

'*Boychik*,' he would say, '*sei a mensch*. Read me a *bissel*. Here, this. The bit about the Polikoff strike. You know Polikoff's, that barrack in Curtain Road. Old Polikoff, the *momser*, wants to cut their wages. Read. Read.'

So I read, ploughing through the indignation of the *Daily Worker* and beginning to assemble the glossary which I came to assume was obligatory – solidarity, scabs, picket lines. There was also a blurred photograph of the picket line and you would make out in it some mounted police.

'See, a capitalist boss is a capitalist boss. The leopard can't change its spots. Old Lipschitz over the road thinks because Polikoff is a *yiddel* and his workers are *yiddelech*, he'll treat them good. There's no difference. A *yiddisher* capitalist like Polikoff, the bloodsucker, or Henry Ford, the *anti-semeet*. You think there's such a thing as a *yiddisher* wage cut? See those cossacks.' He stabbed at the photo. 'They'll always be there for the bosses. They don't inspect them first to see if they've been circumcised.'

'*Zeider*,' I said anxiously, 'suppose they lose?'

He picked up his paper and specs again and looked up at the sky for a moment or two.

'On the way is a lot of defeats. We've had worse. Before 1917 was 1905.'

I knew more about 1066 than 1905. I also knew when to stop questioning and leave it at that. So in my sittings as Reader-to-*Zeider* there was slowly emerging an elaborate syllabus which never appeared between covers but would have made them have a fit at the Board of Education.

There drifted in and out of *Zeider*'s talk references to all sorts of left-wing organisations, many of them long since defunct or moribund. They were like a secret code because they occurred mostly as sets of initials – S.D.F., B.S.P., S.P.G.B., W.S.F., I.L.P. and, of course, the C.P.G.B. There was also something called the Bund and the Workers' Circle. Needless to say I couldn't crack this code and made very little of the bitter hatreds and acrimony which surrounded it. From the smoke of battle there emerged the banner of the Communist Party which to me was not a set of pre-1914 initials but what my mother and *Zeider* busied themselves with. Listening to my *zeider*

I learned that his intonation alone would tell me whether a given organisation was damned beyond redemption or given the seal of approval. It was, and still is, the dialect of the Left. Up from the depths came Lucifer, the fallen angel, Trotsky. The venom injected into his name was almost frightening especially as I didn't know what he'd done to deserve it, and why he seemed so much more sinister than the Polikoffs and their like. Once *Zeider* slipped in the fact that before the First World War his party had been the Social Democratic Federation. The niceties of doctrinal polemic left me lost and I was amazed when he spat out the name H.M. Hyndman, an S.D.F. leader. *Zeider*, in a frenzy of anger, denounced him for supporting the war.

'A class traitor, I crap on him.'

How could he burn with such emotion so long after the event? He might have been speaking of someone who had done him a grave injury the day before rather than an obscure time-server twenty years earlier. That was how he annotated for me the political world, complementing my mother's little lectures which were even more didactic than his.

Still, when a session was finished he'd give me a ha'penny.

'A servant I've got. Doesn't even get the rate for the job.'

It was the nearest I had to having a father since my own was not about.

For all the solemnities of the class struggle he was good at laughing and would bring a very meaty fist down on the table to enjoy his own and other people's jokes. His own jokes baffled me at first and I would have to put on a phoney laugh at stories I wasn't ready for. He once told me the story of the great sage Rabbi Nachman. I've heard it in dozens of versions since. The old rabbi was on his deathbed and his devoted disciples gathered round and took their last chance to ask him the great question, 'Rabbi Nachman, tell us what is life.'

They waited for a long time, fearful that they would not hear a reply. At long last the rabbi gasped out, 'Life – is like a fish.'

Baffled, they hastily conferred and came back to his bedside.

'Rabbi Nachman, why is life like a fish?'

The old man looked at them.

'So – it's not like a fish.'

Zeider gave the rabbi's reply the tone of impatient irritation. How was this a joke? The adults loved it. Relished it and would repeat, 'So – it's not like a fish' and fall about. In due course I came to laugh too. There were also his favourite bits from books he had read. He knew he spoke with a strong Jewish accent and had trouble sorting out the English spoken sounds for 'w' and 'v'. He saw this as very funny so he loved to quote old Mr Weller in *The Pickwick Papers* or rather, his version: 'Spell it with a wee, Samivil, spell it with a wee.'

Then there were his practical jokes. He'd choose the most unsuspecting child in the room.

'Stand outside the door. Stand any way you like. Give a shout when you're ready and I'll tell you how you're standing.'

Out the child would go and adopt the most contorted posture, arms twisted round the neck, bent double and a fearful grimace on the face.

'Ready, *Zeider*. How am I standing?'

'Like a bloody fool,' he would shout.

And for him it was always as funny as the first time.

I warmed myself in his warmth. *Booba* was different. She was stern and tough. Never embraced me or kissed me, never said a warm or loving word. When I saw other *boobas* drowning their grandchildren with affection, noisily declaring their love, I was consumed with jealousy, especially as they so overflowed with love a little of it came my way. Some nosh was pressed on me, most likely almond biscuits or a slice of strudel. I was told what a nice boy I was, patted and my cheek pinched. It was only-to-be-expected *booba*-ness. That's what *boobas* did, didn't they? Why couldn't I have a real *booba*? My wife doesn't like me to speak this way of the old lady. All the cooking for a house of twelve people, the shopping, the washing. You couldn't manage it without being tough. And only just enough money to get by, if that. And didn't you say she would buy just for you pieces of expensive halibut because you didn't like the other fish? That must have been her way of saying something.

But I had my *zeider*. He believed in treats. One day he promised to take me to the *schvitzig*, the Russian steam baths in Brick Lane.

'You know what is the *schvitzig*?' I knew the building from the outside but didn't really know what went on in it. I imagined a room full of steam which didn't seem all that alluring and I also knew that by our family's standards it was not cheap and that *Zeider* would have to dig deep.

'Well, yes. It's a steam bath.'

'Listen to him. Steam bath he says, steam bath. It's paradise. Another world.'

So we set off together for paradise. And he was right. Calling it a steam bath just wouldn't do.

We entered the lobby and stripped off our clothes in a cubicle. Then we joined the other naked bodies in the first room. The steam swirled round us but I could make out a set of high marble steps. The higher you went the hotter you got and the more sweat streamed off your body.

'Good, eh?' said *Zeider*, to make sure I was enjoying paradise. 'You get cleaner in here in ten minutes than if you had ten thousand baths. Is only the beginning.'

The naked men with big bellies were chattering in Yiddish, stretched out on the marble shelves. Some business deals were being done. The state of the tailoring trade was as ever being lamented and old friendships were being cemented. For a short while the tired tailors became Roman decadents while getting pinker and pinker.

We moved on to the next steam room, a replica of the first but much hotter. I was a bit scared and couldn't manage the top shelf.

'By the finish there won't be a speck of dirt left in you. Like a blessing it feels, don't it?'

And there was the rest of paradise still to come. You left the steam room and passed through a pair of cold sprays coming from the sides like a miniature car wash. Here you picked up bay tree twigs to rub yourself with.

'*Schmekt gut*, and is healthy, too. Helps my rheumatism.'

He was pummelling his chest, twirling his arms and marching on the spot in the perfume of the bay leaves. From there we went into the plunge bath, alive with thrashing bodies. Supplied with huge white towels we went back to our cubicles, each of which was big enough to house a narrow couch. An attendant in a white jacket brought tea and biscuits and after that you were expected to sleep. I had not dreamt of such self-indulgence. Definitely more than a steam bath. It was very, very posh. *Zeider* put his head round the door.

'*Schlaf*,' he said, '*schlaf*. Sleep.'

I didn't really feel like sleeping, wanting to go on being a lord, but as he stood there wrapped in his towel I dozed off. After a while we woke up, got dressed and left. '*Nu*, what did I say? Another world.'

When I got to the grammar school *Zeider* treated it as a personal triumph, even though it didn't seem to match his egalitarian principles.

'We made it, we made it, you *lobbus*.'

He pored over my textbooks, stroked the pile of brand-new exercise books, colour-coded for each subject and looking splendid with the school's coat of arms and motto. He'd flick through the textbooks and very occasionally stop to read a sentence or two. I think he liked my Latin books best because their utter impenetrability assured him that the best of higher learning was taking place. He would watch me doing homework while he was pretending to read the paper. I knew he *kvelled* at the sight of what he took to be scholarly activity. He once came over when I was doing some geometry. I had spread out my geometry set on the living room table – brass compass, protractor and set square. He rubbed his thumb along them.

'Lovely little tools. Like a watchmaker's.'

He glanced at the very elementary work I had just done and I guessed he wanted to ask me what exactly the instruments were for and what my homework meant. I was glad when he didn't because I could not have explained. You did geometry because you did geometry.

'Tell me,' he asked one day when he'd come to meet me at the school gate to take me to the pictures at the Rivoli, and saw some teachers crossing the school yard in their gowns, 'why do those teachers wear black cloaks, like a funeral?'

I could tell he was a bit disappointed that they didn't wear something grander and more striking.

'*Zeider*,' I said, 'it shows they've got letters after their names like Bee-Ay and Bee-Ess-See.'

'Funny way to show it.'

'We say it's only to keep the chalk dust off their suits.'

And I didn't dare tell him that Mr Lee, the History master, used the long sleeves of his MA gown to clean the board and store chalk in. *Zeider*, after all, was in the tailoring and had views about clothes. It always astonished me when for weddings and the like he dug out of his wardrobe an impeccable morning suit and topper.

'You see, I'm a capitalist really. All I need is a cigar and a £ sign on my weskit and you could put me in a cartoon.'

When my cousin Bernie was getting near to his *barmitzvah*, he let me know, a little too smugly, I thought, that he was going to get his first long-trouser suit as was the custom. *Zeider* knew my nose was out of joint. He announced to me one day, 'You know what. I'm going to make you a suit. Long trousers, of course.'

I should have been unreservedly overjoyed but I worried how he could afford it and how a mere machinist was going to do the work of a full-blown tailor. Carefully I asked, '*Zeider*, how will you do all the marking out, the cutting, basting and hand-stitching?'

'Do you think I haven't got that all worked out? We'll go down The Lane and get a really good cloth. And you're going to choose it. Trousers is easy, a weskit is easy. But like you say, a jacket is work for a master tailor. I'm going to ask Uncle Jack. He could do it with his eyes shut.'

Uncle Jack was a master tailor all right. I'd seen him cutting suits, working along his careful fine chalk lines with giant shears which made a beautiful crisp krerch- krerch sound and had a bite like a long-billed bird. All very well but Uncle Jack and I had never hit it off. When I got the scholarship it was in his eyes almost an offence, for his daughter, my cousin, did not make it. Sure enough, one day soon after the suit project was announced, *Zeider* told me with a long face, 'Uncle Jack won't do it. Give a guess what he said. "You ask me in the middle of the busy? If you'd asked me in the slack … " And then he says, "You know what costs a fully tailored jacket?" Like I don't know. I could price one to a farthing.'

My spirits plummeted. Come Bernie's *barmitzvah* I'd still be in shorts.

'*Kvetch nisht*,' said *Zeider*. He shook my shoulder. 'We'll go up The Lane this Sunday and buy the cloth. Remember what I said? You choose and I stay *shtumm* and we'll get the trimmings same time, buttons, lining, canvas – everything. That suit, I promised it. You'll have it, my life so sure.'

And I did. We went up The Lane and stood before dozens of bolts of cloth on a big stall. I could see that *Zeider* knew the stallholder.

'For my grandson, here, Ben. So none of your left-over bits and pieces. A first-class worsted.'

'For such a boy,' said the stallholder, 'nothing but the best.'

'Leave off the *schmooze*, Ben, and no fancy prices. I'm not spending hours here beating you down.'

'*Tit mir a toiver*, Joe. Have I ever sold you anything which wasn't a *metzeer*? And how's that wonderful wife of yours? Such an English she speaks and walks like a queen.'

'More *schmooze*. Instead take me a bit more off the price. What's the good of being *mishpucha* if we don't help each other out a bit?'

They finished their spoof haggling and I had the makings of a suit. I chose dark blue with a faint grey stripe. Soon I saw some of it gliding under the needle of *Zeider*'s sewing machine. And the jacket? All I can tell you is that somehow the master tailoring got done and in the busy at that. Not by benign mice in a fairy tale but I guess by a *chaver* from the Tailors and Garment Workers Union. The dahlia man, perhaps?

When Bernie came round after the suit was finished and it lay in its long flat cardboard box in tissue paper, I spilled out the whole story. We were good friends and he was pleased for me.

'Put it on, put it on and I'll see if its swanky enough for my *barmitzvah*.'

I got it out of its box and swiftly changed into it.

'I wish you health to wear it. You could be the *barmitzvah* boy, if you weren't too young.'

I had a year to go and wasn't going to be *barmitzvahed* anyway. Those two canny atheists, my *zeider* and my mother, had seen to that.

'So,' said *Zeider*, 'what did I say? A long trouser suit you said you wanted, a long trouser suit you got. Not so bad, eh? I wish you health to wear it.'

There was another great treat for me coming up. *Zeider* was going to take me to Highbury to watch Arsenal. We never made it. Instead, I found myself in a Daimler watching the trees flash by in Epping Forest on the way to the Jewish Cemetery. My first death, my first funeral. I didn't cry. I just wondered what I'd be doing at reading time and who would take me to the *schvitzig* again and what would happen to his dahlias.

Isaak Babel and the Bird

Now there was a rum friendship
Isaak Babel nipping out of the Odessa ghetto
And skipping violin lessons –
Didn't want to be another Yasha Heifetz.
Palled up with a sailor in the docks
Who failed to teach him to swim
(His hydrophobic ancestors
Dragged him down, he said).
When he'd extracted from him
His wild ambition to become a writer
Asked him to name a passing bird
Some hopes!
The sailor knew for sure
That the writing trade demands
Swift bird recognition
Maybe other fauna, and flora too.
Did he go off and mug up
Observer Books and Field Manuals
Or haunt old booksellers
For a *Natural History of the Ukraine?*
Of course he didn't,
What he truly needed was
The Universal Observers' Guide
To Homo Sapiens.
He managed well enough without it
Which is why he slipped out of sight
In the days of the vanishings.

Isaak Babel (1894–1940), one of the greatest writers of the Soviet era, was murdered by Stalin's secret police. Yasha (Jascha) Heifetz (1900–1987), a child prodigy and later world-famous violinist, was born in Vilna, emigrating to New York in 1917.

How many Genres in Narrative?

During the 1980s and into the 1990s there was an academic debate, sometimes fiercely conducted, about how explicitly teachers should teach the characteristic structures of kinds of writing. 'Genre theory', associated with a group of Australian academics whose early work is most concisely represented in *The Place of Genre in Learning: Current debates* (Reid [ed.], 1987), started from the proposition that an over-free emphasis on personal expression in English teaching, favouring imaginative and personal kinds of writing (for example fictional narratives, poetry and autobiography) over factual and impersonal kinds of writing (for example argument, report and critical essay) had sold learners short.

The argument ran that students will not learn how to write across a range of kinds of writing unless they are shown how to do so. These kinds of writing have recognizable and teachable characteristics. High-status jobs in society require control over factual and impersonal kinds of writing much more than over imaginative and personal kinds, and it is a disservice, particularly to students whose home backgrounds mean that they are not easily familiar with the use of factual and impersonal kinds of writing, not to show them how to handle them. In this sense, genre theory was politically radical; it wished to empower the disempowered.

In 'Social processes in education' (1987), Martin, Christie and Rothery write:

> The whole movement toward child-centred education has foundered on the idea that children can understand and undertake history, geography and other subject areas 'in their own words'. That this is a necessary starting point, none would deny, especially those not interested in genre-based approaches to writing development. But that children should be stranded there, writing stories for example as their only genre in infant and primary school, is impossible to accept.

In the same paper, the authors attack 'process writing', an approach particularly associated with the work of Donald Murray (1982 and 1984) and Donald Graves (1983), which attaches great importance to giving students choice in subject matter. The teacher is seen in this approach principally as a sympathetic mentor to students when the latter run into difficulties in their writing.

The genre theorists' position was open to a number of criticisms. First, it is of course true that a classroom where students only write personal stories, day after day, week after week, term after term, never trying other kinds of writing, is offering them a narrow and impoverished experience of the landscape of writing. It is equally true that teachers who only *tell* students to write, repeatedly, and give them no guidance as to how to do it, are selling them short. However, there was sparse evidence, at least in the United Kingdom, for the claim that too many opportunities for personal writing represented a major barrier to students' educational success, although it is always possible to find extreme examples of practice in support of a generalisation. Some English teachers and teachers of language in primary schools gave their students plenty of opportunities for personal and imaginative kinds of writing because they knew that, overall, the students' experience of writing across the curriculum was overwhelmingly dominated by the factual; and within the factual, overwhelmingly by low-level factual report and the generalised re-presentation of previously given information, as typified by the ubiquity of the worksheet and the comprehension exercise. Without some opportunity to express themselves in personal and imaginative ways, the students' capacity to do these vital things would atrophy for want of use. So while it was true that many students' experience of writing was narrow, it was not true, on the whole, that the guilty party was too much personal and imaginative writing. The guilty party was the poverty of the kind of factual writing which dominated students' experience.

Secondly, early and dogmatic versions of genre theory claimed that any written language contains a small number of easily identifiable genres. Gunther Kress, in *Learning to Write* (1982), says as much:

> There exists a small and fixed number of genres in any written tradition.

Thirdly, these early versions of the theory were unhelpful in that they approached the study of whole texts in the same way that the imposition of synthetic phonics or of long lists of spelling rules or of heavy loads of decontextualised grammatical terminology approaches those fields of learning. It is tempting for those with an adult and analytical understanding of a field of learning to suppose that the understanding they have is also the way in which a learner comes to apprehend that field. It is not; to yield to that temptation is to show a failure of educational imagination. (In England, the Department for Education and Skills later adopted the 'teach the rules of discourse' approach to kinds of writing in its National Literacy Strategy for England [Department for Education and Skills, 2002]. The result in many schools was the literary equivalent of painting by numbers: 'just follow these instructions and you will have an effective piece of argument'.)

Fourthly, early versions of genre theory were impatient with the notion of development in writers. They claimed that no-nonsense direct teaching would bring about competence. In fact, we know that apprentice writers need to find their way towards full control of the characteristics of a particular kind of writing by trial and error, and that transitional efforts at factual genres such as advocacy, discussion, instruction or report may include, for example, awkward mixtures of the personal and impersonal, switchings between present and past tense, and comings and goings of the active and passive voice. Only by allowing these awkward mixtures to present themselves and to be commented on will students move toward consistent control of the characteristics of a particular factual genre.

Later, genre theorists offered more subtle versions of their position, admitting that kinds of writing are not confined in watertight containers, that there is substantial overlap between genres, and that there is more than one way to produce a successful example of a kind of writing. By 1992, for example, Kress had changed his mind about the number of genres in any written tradition, and their fixity. The three bullet points in the following quotation (Kress and Knapp, 1992) are from a list of eight. The first seems to confirm Kress's earlier position; the remaining two significantly modify it:

> In our approach we would like to focus on making available at least the following knowledge about genres:
>
> - an understanding by teachers and by children that nearly all our speaking and writing is guided to a greater or lesser extent by conventions of generic form …
> - an understanding that while generic conventions provide certain dimensions of constraint, generic form is never totally fixed, but is always in the process of change …
> - an understanding … of the possibilities for change, innovation and creativity …

That was the context for Harold's paper. He first gave it at an international conference entitled Domains of Literacy, held at the Institute of Education, University of London on 9 and 10 September 1992. It then appeared in the first issue of the journal *Changing English*, 1 (1) in 1994. Harold begins the printed version by referring to his conference presentation.

I began with a warm-up – an extract from a review by Anthony Burgess in *The Observer* (6.9.92) of Edelman's *Bright Air, Brilliant Fire: On the matter of the mind* (1992).

It is good to hear a joke, like the one of the two Jewish tourists who visited Israel for the first time. In a Tel Aviv nightclub a comedian told one-liners in Hebrew. One of the two tourists fell off his chair laughing uncontrollably. His companion said, 'What are you laughing at? You don't even understand Hebrew.' The man on the floor clutched his sides and said, 'I trust these people.' As Edelman comments: 'formal semantics cannot account for such richness'.

Clearly here is a little narrative (what constitutes narrative we'll leave on one side for the moment). Does it drop nicely into one genre or sub-genre or sub-sub-genre? Are jokes one genre or many? Is there a sub-genre called Jewish jokes? Are there several genres of Jewish jokes? How do we determine such genres and sub-genres, if they exist? By purely internal features or what? Can we be certain it is a joke (apart from Burgess's labelling)? Could it not be a tragic tale?

The punch line – 'trust these people' – requires interpretation. What do we need to know to perceive it as funny, as everyone in the workshop seemed to do? All the answers pointed in the direction of knowledge about Jews and their complicated, often ambivalent attitudes to Zionism and Israel. Nothing in the text will give us that. The joke warns us that apparently simple little fiction narratives can be complex and that schematic structures often do not capture the heart of them (see for example Labov's scheme used by Martin *et al.*, 1987). A final point. What would one need to know textually speaking to compose a joke like this? Or to understand one? Certainly one would need to know how to create/understand a quintessentially narrative text; but that would not be nearly enough. The knowledge would be derived from two main interacting elements: location of the teller/hearer in historical and cultural space and location in the universe of narratives.

Though it goes without saying that many narratives drop into stereotypes, it is a mistake to believe that traditional tales are always very sparse and moralistic or that their structure always leads to perfect closure (resolution). In an Italian folk-story, in which a poor peasant is turned into a frog for not saying 'God willing' and, having served his penance of seven years in a pond, repeats his sacrilege, the ending ('And not for the life of him would he say another word') is always given the most diverse of interpretations by groups of teachers.

One other warm-up example. It is sometimes thought that traditional tales carry a light cognitive load compared with certain non-narrative genres. As John Frow (1986) remarks, it is ' ... not possible to assign cognitive privilege' to any universe of discourse. Take a Dervish story, or 'recital', as Idries Shah (1968) calls it. The first few paragraphs must suffice.

The Man, the Snake and the Stone

One day a man who had not a care in the world was walking along a road. An unusual object to one side of him caught his eye. 'I must find out what this is,' he said to himself.

As he came up to it, he saw that it was a very large flat stone. 'I must find out what is underneath this,' he told himself as he lifted the stone.

No sooner had he done so than he heard a loud hissing sound, and a large snake came gliding out from under the stone. The man dropped the stone in alarm. The snake wound itself into a coil, and said to him:

'Now I am going to kill you, for I am a venomous snake.'

'But I have released you,' said the man. 'How can you repay good with evil? Such an action would not accord with reasonable behaviour.'

'In the first place,' said the snake, 'you lifted the stone from curiosity and in ignorance of possible consequences. How can this suddenly become "I have released you"?'

'We must always try to return to reasonable behaviour, when we stop to think,' murmured the man.

'Return to it when you think invoking it might suit your interests,' said the snake.

'Yes,' said the man. 'I was a fool to expect reasonable behaviour from a snake.'

'From a snake, expect snake behaviour,' said the snake. 'To a snake, snake behaviour is what can be regarded as reasonable.'

The story continues in the vein, basing itself on intellectual disputations and once again showing that narrative will defy being tied down to a set of genres with firmly distinctive characteristics. Why should this be? One suggestion has been that narrative is central to our cognitive activities (Ricoeur, 1981; Bruner, 1986; and others), is 'the central function or instance of the human mind' (Jameson, 1981), and that it is a universal method of giving meaning to experience. 'Like life itself, it is there, international, transhistorical, transcultural' (Barthes, 1982). However, narrative, like other kinds of discourse, reveals 'the impossibility of ... closed taxonomic systems'. Derrida (1980) sounds this warning:

> … as soon as the word 'genre' is sounded, as soon as it is heard, as soon as one attempts to conceive it, a limit is drawn. And when a limit is established, norms and interdictions are not far behind.

> (cited in Frow, 1986)

Derrida goes on to propose that the law of genre is a taboo on miscegenation but the counter law is the impossibility of *not* mixing genres. We'll return to that.

For my purposes here I must avoid being lured into interminable discussions on those two slippery terms *narrative* and *genre*. However, since I shall continue to put on the table diverse narratives and relate them to some prevailing and recent developments of the very long established notion of genre, I presume we can take for granted some propositions on which we would agree:

(i)   In the language of a given society there is a vast diversity of discursive practices, some of which are clearly marked by certain characteristics (legal documents, petitionary prayers, football commentary, cookery book recipes). Others are much more fluid and unpredictable (graffiti, advertisements, election speeches).

(ii) A major means (Bruner thinks it is one of two ways) of representing the world is through narrative, that is to say by representing verbally an interconnected set of events through the selective use of traditions and conventions. To the narratologist narrative is 'the representation of *at least two* real or fictive events or situations in a time sequence, neither of which presupposes or entails the other' (Prince, 1982).

Now the problem is how to relate these two, and we shall attempt to do so. But first let me say that in the literature on genre by some of its main Australian exponents there is a tendency to be uncomfortable with narrative, and their attempt to bring it within the fold is not very happy. Take Martin, Christie and Rothery (no date). In 'A note on teaching narrative' they tell us they use the term to refer to one particular type of story, that is, one which they find they can analyse by using Labov's five-stage structure. It is by no means clear why this structure is privileged over, let us say, the well-known Propp morphology (1928) or Barthes' five codes (1982) or Genette's story grammar (1980) or Hymes' breakdown for which he uses the mnemonic SPEAKING (setting, participants, ends, act sequences, keys, instrumentalities, norms, genres). It soon becomes clear that Martin *et al.* need to take account of other kinds of narrative (recount, thematic narrative, moral tale, myth, spoof, serial). They then tell us that 'genre theory would have to classify narrative as a wide range of genres'.

A second tendency is the disparagement of narrative as inferior to other genres. Frances Christie in a recent document spoke of children being encouraged to write stories, 'even autobiography', rather than reports. Martin *et al.* tell us that their analysis of the writing of certain bilingual children shows that 'every one of their texts is a recount – simple sequential retelling of events'. What is 'retelling' of events? This is as though events tell themselves first and someone retells them afterwards. No wonder they can be dismissed as simple. Moreover, the children 'fall back on oral genres'. Why is the written genre privileged over the oral? No genre, oral or written, can have more powerful meanings than an author is motivated and competent to put in it.

A third tendency is to treat narrative as though it is synonymous with fiction, with possibly the addition of the story of personal experience (autobiography). Yet any attempt to categorize narrative must inevitably lead us to show that it embraces a very wide range of functions and forms. In 1866 the rhetorician Alexander Bain wrote that narrative form occurs in history, biography and science.

The growth of a plant or animal has to be recounted according to the rules of narrative method. It is the fact that narrative is highly varied in function and form which points to its being both uncomfortable and problematic for genre theory. Only recognition that it constitutes a superordinate category can begin to resolve some of this difficulty.

The three characteristics proposed by certain genre theories to identify genres are that they are *staged, goal directed* and *socio-cultural.* They are also supposed to be relatively *stable.* The development of the mass media has in fact led to rapid changes in, for example, journalism and the language of disc jockeys, and some genres are quite simply not staged at all: for example, all kinds of lists (shopping lists, lists of bye-laws at the entrance to a park, dictionaries, etc.). But from the literature I have read there is scarcely any attention given to one important feature of genres, which is *their capacity to absorb one another.* Genres cannibalise other genres. They have strong digestive systems. This absorptive power is at its greatest in fiction narrative, in the historical development of which it has shown itself capable of incorporating any kind of genre. The first answer then to my title, 'How many genres in narrative?' is 'As many as exist'. It is Bakhtin above all who perceived this development. He saw that in the novel all the forms and all the genres are mixed and interwoven and that the principal mass is furnished by prose more diverse than that of any genre (Todorov, 1984). So let's now look at a passage in which Bakhtin gives the essence of his 'polyphonic' view of the fiction narrative.

Passage one, from Bakhtin, *The Dialogic Imagination* (1981)

> The novel can be defined as a diversity of social speech types (sometimes even diversity of languages) and a diversity of individual voices, artistically organized. The internal stratification of any single national language into social dialects, characteristic group behaviour, professional jargons, generic language, languages of generations and age groups, tendentious languages, languages of the authorities, of various circles and of passing

fashions, languages that serve the specific socio-political purposes of the day, even of the hour (each day has its own slogan, its own vocabulary, its own emphases) – this internal stratification present in every language at any given moment of its historical existence is the indispensible prerequisite for the novel as a genre. The novel orchestrates all its themes, the totality of the world of objects and ideas depicted and expressed in it, by means of the social diversity of speech types [*raznorecie*] and by the differing individual voices that flourish under such conditions. Authorial speech, the speeches of narrators, inserted genres, the speech of characters are merely those fundamental compositional unities with whose help heteroglossia [*raznojazycnie*] can enter the novel; each of them permits a multiplicity of social voices and a wide variety of their links and interrelationships (always more or less dialogized). These distinctive links and interrelationships between utterances and languages, this movement of the theme through different languages and speech types, its dispersion into the rivulets and droplets of social heteroglossia, its dialogization – this is the basic distinguishing feature of the stylistics of the novel.

Bakhtin in this piece speaks of 'inserted genres', but the 'diversity of social speech types' and the 'diversity of individual voices' suggests that genres enter the novel in many different ways and that he has in mind something closer to what we now mean by *intertextuality*. For other genres, including speech genres, assert their presence in quite different ways: firmly framed and complete (e.g. in an official letter), through the speech of the characters (e.g. a judge in a court case), through the narrative voice of a pseudo-narrator, through a single word or phrase which is heard as a 'question' from a specific genre, and so on. So genre may jump at us from the page or flicker in or out of the text.

All this is true not only of the novel, which plays the game in ever new and surprising ways, but also of the oral storyteller, who has the additional resource of voice and physical movement to represent shifts in genre. Volosinov (1973) pointed out a long time ago that any citation of the words of another will always change its meaning, however slightly, by the new context which surrounds it.

Let's take a look now at multi-voiced narrative in some extracts from one particular text.

Passage 2(a), from Julian Barnes, *A History of the World in 10½ Chapters* (1989)

Source: The Archives Municipales de Besançon (section CG, boîte 377a). The following case, hitherto unpublished, is of particular interest to legal historians in that the procureur pour les insectes *was the distinguished jurist Bartholomé Chassenée (also Chassanée and Chasseneux), later first president of the Parlement de Provence. Born in 1480, Chassenée made his name before the ecclesiastical court of Autun defending rats which had been accused of feloniously destroying a crop of barley. The following documents, from the opening* pétition des habitans *to the final judgement of the court, do not represent the entire proceedings – for instance, the testimony of witnesses, who might be anything from local peasants to distinguished experts on the behavioural patterns of the defendants, has not been recorded – but the legal submissions embody and often specifically refer to the evidence and thus there is nothing absent from the essential structure and argument of the case. As was normal at the time, the pleas and the conclusions* du procureur épiscopal *were made in French, while the sentence of the court was solemnly delivered in Latin.*

(Translator's note: The manuscript is continuous and all in the same hand. Thus we are not dealing with the original submissions as penned by each lawyer's clerk, but with the work of a third party, perhaps an official of the court, who may have omitted sections of the pleas. Comparison with the contents of boîtes *371–379 suggests that the case as it exists in this form was perhaps part of a set of exemplary or typical proceedings used in the training of jurists. This conjecture is supported by the fact that only Chassenée among the participants is identified by name, as if students were being directed to examine the instructive dexterity of a distinguished defence counsel, regardless of the result of the case. The handwriting belongs to the first half of the sixteenth century, so that if, as may be, the document is a copy of someone ...)*

Here the novelist disguises himself as a researcher-scholar presenting an important set of documents for, in particular, 'legal historians'. The 'source' and the 'translator's note' are presented in language which makes them an example of a scholarly genre. The reader at this point is caught in a not unpleasing dilemma. Is Barnes using genuine archive material to insert in his novel, where it would speak with a new voice? Or has he made the whole thing up? Or part of it? At the end of the book is an author's note which tells us that 'Chapter 3 is based on legal procedures and actual cases described in *The Criminal Prosecution and Capital Punishment of Animals* by E. P. Evans, 1906'. Which at best only partly answers our questions. What is undeniable is that the whole chapter has an aura of authenticity derived from faithfulness (as far as a lay reader can tell) to *two* genres. The second is exemplified by what follows the italicised scholarly genre, in a sequence of what are apparently seven depositions in a fifteenth-century French religious court.

Here is the final page of Barnes' book.

Harold Rosen

Passage 2(b), from Barnes (1989)

Sentence du juge d'Église

In the name and by virtue of God, the omnipotent, Father, Son and Holy Spirit, and of Mary, the most blessed Mother of our Lord Jesus Christ, and by the authority of the Holy Apostles Peter and Paul, as well as by that which has made us a functionary is this case, having fortified ourselves with the Holy Cross, and having before our eyes the fear of God, we admonish the aforesaid woodworm as detestable vermin and command them, under pain of malediction, anathema and excommunication, to quit within seven days the church of Saint-Michel in the village of Mamirolle in the diocese of Besançon and to proceed without delay or hindrance to the pasture offered them by the habitans, there to have their habitation and never again to infest the church of Saint-Michel. In order to make lawful this sentence, and to render effective any malediction, anathema and excommunication that may at any time be pronounced, the habitans of Mamirolle are hereby instructed to pay heedful attention to the duty of charity, to yield up their tithes as commanded by the Holy Church, to refrain from any frivolity in the House of the Lord, and once a year, on the anniversary of that hateful day when Hugo, Bishop of Besançon, was cast down into the darkness of imbecility …

Here the manuscript in the Archives Municipales de Besançon breaks off, without giving details of the annual penance or remembrance imposed by the court. It appears from the condition of the parchment that in the course of the last four and a half centuries it has been attacked, perhaps on more than one occasion, by some species of termite, which has devoured the closing words of the juge d'Église.

Barnes shifts his genre to the legal record of the case which is concerned with the infestation of the bishop's throne by woodworms and with a plea by inhabitants of Mamirolle to the Church to cast them out. The extract here comes at the end of the chapter. It concludes by a return to the scholarly discourse of the opening. The detail could be examined at great length (e.g. the cross-headings untranslated from mediaeval legal French) but suffice it to say that it's a display of exactly what Bakhtin was talking about. For not only is this one chapter in an unusual and provocative novel, but that one chapter constitutes a narrative within a narrative. We can assemble that story, of the events surrounding the bishop's throne, the legal case and its outcome, solely through the documents. Here the method is that of collage, the juxtaposition of different voices, that of the scholar and the various mediaeval litigants whose lawyers deploy a particular kind of rhetoric. What is left open at the end is why Barnes chose to tell his woodworm story through supposed genuine documents rather than as a straight narrative. Only an examination of the whole book can begin to answer that question. In fact the whole novel is a generic playground – and the toys are the genres.

Here, without attribution, is a third passage.

Passage three

> To understand a message is to decode it. Language is a code. *But every decoding is another encoding.* If you say something to me I check that I have understood your message by saying it back to you in my own words, that is, different words from the ones you used, for if I repeat your own words exactly you will doubt whether I have really understood you. But if I use *my* words it follows that I have changed *your* meaning, however slightly; and even if I were, deviantly, to indicate my comprehension by repeating back to you your own unaltered words, that is no guarantee that I have duplicated your meaning in my head, because I bring a different experience of language, literature and non-verbal reality to those words, therefore they mean something different to me from what they mean to you. And if you think I have not understood the meaning of your message, you do not simply repeat it in the same words, you try to explain it in different words, different from the ones you used originally; but then the *it* is no longer the *it* that you start with. Time has moved on since you opened your mouth to speak, the molecules in your body have changed, what you intended to say has been superseded by what you did say, and that has already become part of your personal history, imperfectly remembered.

Where does this come from? Some will recognize it, but for the rest I think I can take it that you will assume it comes from a lecture on the nature of language from an academic expert. Just possibly it could be a written text written in an unbuttoned style. There is nothing here which would beyond all question identify it as a passage from a novel. In fact it is from David Lodge's *Small World* (1984). Whereas Julian Barnes, above, ingests fifteenth-century discourse for the purposes of his novel and uses a sequence of juxtaposed 'documents' to tell an embedded story, Lodge gives us the voice of a contemporary genre – the academic lecture – of a kind he himself, I suppose, might easily give to his students. Indeed, in order to place this text within the text of the whole novel we need to follow its argument and ask ourselves, among other questions, whether we are supposed to take it straight or not.

Narrative may crop up in any kind of discourse. So many writers seem to be intuitively aware of the power of stories to make a point. Often at the very moment when a text is at its most abstract and theoretical a story is told. (See my account [Rosen, 1986, and reprinted here in 'The Importance of Story'] of the use by

Dell Hymes of the story of the telling of a folk story in the midst of a theoretical critique of Chomsky.) An excellent book which explores these matters is *Narrative in Culture: The uses of storytelling in the sciences, philosophy and literature*, edited by Cristopher Nash (1990).

A writer will often resort to a story not because what he is writing can be represented by a sequence of events, but rather because a story will do what another kind of discourse will not do so graphically or dramatically. This is achieved in many different ways. I recollect a very avant-garde school textbook on the theme of time and its measurement which began with the story of an old retired sea captain who fired a little gun every evening at precisely the same time. Other set their watches and clocks by it. The story seeks to find out how the captain was sure of the correct time, and thus poses the central question of the book.

Passage four

> There was once a man who aspired to be the author of the general theory of holes. When asked, 'What kind of hole – holes dug by children in the sand for amusement, holes dug by gardeners to plant lettuce seedlings, tank traps, holes made by road makers?', he would reply indignantly that he wished for a general theory of holes which would explain all these. He rejected *ab initio* the – as he saw it – pathetically commonplace point of view that of the digging of holes there are quite different explanations to be given; why then, he would ask, do we have the concept of hole?

The passage is from Trevor Pateman's *Language in Mind and Language in Society* (1987), a difficult work located in the boundary between philosophy and linguistics. The story is borrowed from Alisdair MacIntyre and the discussion which surrounds it is about the problems of establishing 'an exploratory historical linguistics'. Why a story at this point? I am not quite sure, but the effort must at least be due to the fact that it is with a story you can most easily turn a thorny point into a sort of joke. Moreover, it permits the teller to do things which the genre 'rules' of this larger discourse would not permit. Thus the philosophical opponent who by name would have to be treated with the customary academic respect becomes an anonymous fellow who 'aspired to be … ' and whose rejection of particularism is put down by '*ab initio*' and the almost innocuous 'as he saw it'. The invisible narrator's sceptical mockery is legitimised by the story form and its indirectness. The resolution of the story is only a valid resolution if you perceive that the man has got it wrong or is being philosophically misguided if not actually ridiculous. If the story does not do this by itself the context leaves you in no doubt.

Narrative in non-narrative discourse can be somewhat more elusive than in the neat clearly marked examples I have given. It can link in the sub-text or can depend on a way of reading a text not immediately perceived as a narrative. Leith and Myerson (1989) analyse a philosophical work which functions through the classical device of dialogue. They come to the conclusion that it is both story and philosophy.

****

I have attempted to set out *some* of a huge range of possibilities within narrative and to show that narrative cannot possibly be regarded as yet another genre. To show what this implies for the curriculum would require another paper. However, let me at least turn in that direction, since genre theory is closely linked to pedagogic prescriptions.

Narrative is now installed at the heart of thinking about how we function as social beings and users of representation. There is a huge and ever-proliferating literature which remains relatively little known even by those who write about narrative in education, including genre theorists. Richard Bauman, in *Story, Performance and Event* (1986), concluded:

> When one looks to social practices by which social life is accomplished one finds with surprising frequency people telling stories to each other as a means of giving cognitive and emotional coherence to experience, constructing and negotiating social identity … investing the experiential landscape with moral significance.

This places story-telling, broadly conceived, at the very centre of the curriculum, installed as it is in both the thinking and discursive competence of pupils – not simply as fiction but as the form of discourse most readily available and responded to. It is a point of entry for all and it offers not only functional diversity but also initiation into every form of discourse. What this proposes is that the narrative possibilities of the whole curriculum should be explored. I have tried to show that narrative offers a space in which a student can without risk experiment with any kind of genre. I have also tried to show that narrative can be used in diverse ways in many different kinds of discourse, either as the complete text or with it. We should take every opportunity to let the narrative possibilities of learning and teaching be on offer. Perhaps it would help if teachers took note of how many scholars are saying just this. Take Oliver Sacks, the neurologist, in his preface to that collection of his case studies called *The Man Who Mistook his Wife for a Hat* (1985):

> The is no 'subject' in a modern case-history; modern case-histories allude to the subject in a cursory phrase ('a trisomic albino female of 21'), which could as well apply to a rat as to a human being. To restore the human subject at the centre – the human, affected, fighting, human subject – we must deepen a case-history to a narrative or tale: only then do we have a 'who' as well as a 'what', a real person, a patient …

Harold Rosen

It was said some years ago that we need to put the knower back into the known. The construction of much of the language we encounter in education involves exactly the opposite process. It is, as Rom Harré (1990) remarks, 'untouched by human hand' and presented 'as if it were context-free, relative to nothing'. Students as apprentice scientists are trained in this rhetoric, from school days on. Everything that is personal is left out of the discourse.

It looks as though there are now some educators who would like to polish and refine training in that kind of rhetoric. Against that I am saying that we must first and foremost make it possible for students to see and use the vast potential of narrative.

I hope no one will assume that I believe that narrative is by itself a road to power, some kind of emancipator almost by definition. I said this as long ago as 1985 [in a lecture later published as 'The Autobiographical Impulse' (1988), reprinted in this collection]:

> You will not suppose that I am under the delusion that stories of personal experience will set the world to rights. I do, however, believe that from the top to the bottom of the educational system, authoritative discourse holds sway but that inroads into it can be made by giving students genuine fuller speaking rights in the classroom. An inevitable consequence will be the emergence of a much greater role for personal narrative. For most students this would constitute a liberation. In the end, stories about the past are also about the future. On the other hand, we have only to remind ourselves of the way in which folk story was domesticated into coziness, to remember that stories themselves can kow-tow with subservience. Their very universality contains its own surreptitious menace. They can be used to manipulate, control, create a market, and above all to massage us into forgetfulness and passivity. Nor do I wish to forget that alongside the autobiographical impulse there is the autobiographical *compulse* of the courtroom, of the government inspector, of the attitude tests, of the curriculum vitae, of the torture chamber. There are some very sinister people engaged in hermeneutics! We are not left free to limit our pasts to unpoliced crannies and congenial moments. Stand and deliver. There are many ways in which power attempts to wrest from us our past and use it for its own ends.

What I said then about the autobiographical impulse is relevant to a wide range of narrative endeavours. Only the collective critical mediation of narrative in the classroom will rescue it from domestication and liberate students from presentations in which they must speak about their knowledge, not as it is but how they are told it should be: in Rom Harré's words again, 'a "smiling face" presentation. All has gone well.'

References

Bain, A. (1866) *English Composition*. London: Longmans Green.

Bakhtin, M. (1981) *The Dialogic Imagination* (C. Emerson and M. Holquist, trans.). Austin: University of Texas Press.

Barnes, J. (1989) *A History of the World in 10½ Chapters*. London: Picador.

Barthes, R. (1982) 'Introduction to the structural analysis of narrative', in S. Sontag (ed.), *Barthes: Selected writings*. London: Fontana.

Bauman, R. (1986) *Story, Performance and Event*. Cambridge: Cambridge University Press.

Bruner, J. (1986) *Actual Minds, Possible Worlds*. Cambridge, MA: Harvard University Press.

Department for Education and Skills (2002) *Implementing the National Literacy Strategy*. London: Department for Education and Skills.

Derrida, J. (1980) 'The law of genre'. *Critical Enquiry*, 7 (1).

Edelman, G. (1992) *Bright Air, Brilliant Fire: On the matter of the mind*. New York: Basic Books.

Frow, J. (1986) *Marxism and Literary History*. Oxford: Basil Blackwell.

Genette, G. (1980) *Narrative Discourse* (J. Lewin, trans.). Oxford: Basil Blackwell.

Graves, D. (1983) *Writing: Teachers and children at work*. Exeter, NH: Heinemann.

Harré, R. (1990) 'Some narrative conventions of scientific Discourse', in C. Nash (ed.) (1990).

Hymes, D. (1972) 'Models of the interaction of language and social life', in J. Gumperz and D. Hymes (eds.), *Directions in Sociolinguistics*. New York: Holt, Reinhart and Winston.

Hymes, D. (1982 [1973]) *Toward Linguistic Competence, Texas Working Papers in Sociolinguistics, No. 16*. Austin, TX: University of Texas.

Jameson, F. (1981) *The Political Unconscious: Narrative as a socially symbolic act*. London: Methuen.

Kress, G. (1982) *Learning to Write*. London: Routledge and Kegan Paul.

Kress, G. and Knapp, P. (1992) 'Genre in a social theory of language'. *English in Education*, 26 (2).

Leith, D. and Myerson, G. (1989) *The Power of Address*. London: Routledge and Kegan Paul.

Lodge, D. (1984) *Small World*. London: Secker and Warburg.

Martin, J., Christie, F. and Rothery, J. (1987) 'Social processes in education: A reply to Sawyer and Watson (and others)', in I. Reid (ed.) (1987).

Murray, D. (1982) 'Give your students the five writing experiences', in *Learning by Teaching: Selected articles on writing and teaching*. Montclair, NJ: Boynton Cook.

Murray, D. (1984) *Write to Learn*. New York: Holt, Reinhart and Winston.

Nash, C. (ed.) (1990) *Narrative in Culture: The uses of storytelling in the sciences, philosophy and literature*. London: Routledge and Kegan Paul.

Pateman, T. (1987) *Language in Mind and Society*. Oxford: Oxford University Press.

Prince, G. (1982) *Narratology*. The Hague: Mouton.

Propp, V. (1928) (L. Scott, trans., 1968) *The Morphology of the Folktale*. Columbus, OH: American Folklore Society and Bloomington, IN: Indiana University.

Reid, I. (ed.) (1987) *The Place of Genre in Learning: Current debates*. (Typereader Publications No 1). Geelong, Victoria: Centre for Studies in Literary Education, Deakin University.

Ricoeur, P. (1981) *Hermeneutics and the Human Sciences*. Cambridge: Cambridge University Press.

Rosen, H. (1988) 'The autobiographical impulse', in D. Tannen (ed.), *Linguistics in Context: Connecting observation and understanding*. Norwood, NJ: Ablex [reprinted in this collection].

Sacks, O. (1985) *The Man Who Mistook his Wife for a Hat*. London: Picador.

Harold Rosen

Shah, I. (1973) *Caravan of Dreams*. London: The Octagon Press.

Todorov, T. (1984) *Mikhail Bakhtin: The dialogic principle*. Manchester: Manchester University Press.

Volosinov, V. [Bakhtin, M.] (1973) *Marxism and the Philosophy of Language* (L. Mateyka and I. Titunik, trans.). New York: Seminar Press.

We are our Stories

This short paper was published in *Troublesome Boy* (Rosen, 1993).

Oral tradition encompasses all kinds of stories from riddles and jokes to folk-stories and legends. In a living tradition, all these can be valued and have their place. But what happens in societies where folktales and myths are rarely told?

Stories are everywhere: lined up on bookshelves (we call them novels), on television, in the theatre, in the cinema. All over the world in every culture there are traditional tales, thousands and thousands of them, retold again and again, reworked, transformed and changed. Story jokes travel at great speed from place to place. Listen in to any group of people chatting in a relaxed, intimate way and you will hear another kind of story – the story of personal experience or the story of hearsay. And so on and so on.

As different as they all are, we call them all stories. In some intuitive way we know that *Great Expectations* is in certain important respects the same in kind as *Cinderella*, or the one about the dog who went into a pub and ordered a beer, or my wife telling about the time when she took a moose skull wrapped in brown paper through Canadian customs. Stories are as common as dirt and therefore easily dismissed or at any rate not taken very seriously. There was a time when novel reading was thought of as a trivial activity fit only for light-headed young ladies. Stories are suitable for little children, we think, but in due course they will get round to more serious and important uses of language. Oral stories, the kind we find ourselves telling all the time (what happened to us this morning, last week, last year, when I was little), are so much part of the fabric of our everyday lives that, just like our conversation, gossip and chatter, we are not likely to think of them as very significant or important. Yet that's where storytelling begins and the very fact that we do so much of it points to its importance.

So let's take a closer look. First, let's notice that relating the simplest anecdote is quite a complex business, requiring the mind to be fully active and creative. I could tell you the story about how, many years ago, my son and I were canoeing in the pouring rain on a tiny river on the Welsh border, dressed in shorts and plastic bags, and how we frightened the life out of some villagers as we appeared suddenly from behind a hedge. Where does that story begin? Nowhere. Stories don't begin. We make them begin. We decide to start here rather than there. I could, for instance, start with the two of us staring out of the tent into the rain or with the sound of the Land Rover coming up the farm lane with the canoe, or in a hundred other ways.

The same applies to endings. Our lives just go on happening. They can't stop and say they'll start another story tomorrow. But in stories we, the storytellers, make endings.

– And I never saw him again.
– She went over to him, spat into his face and slowly walked out of the room.
– 'I can't speak German,' I lied.

Between the beginning and the ending we choose to mention this, but not that, to digress for a few moments perhaps, to describe something or someone, to put in dialogue or compress it into a few phrases ('an argument broke out'), all the time selecting, sorting, ordering. It happens that my son has told the story of that canoe trip in a published poem. It's totally different from the way I would tell it. I keep wanting to say, 'But you left out the bit where … ' Of course he didn't leave it out. He was telling a different story. What all this choosing, selecting, omitting, shaping amounts to is that these are the ways in which we make our stories meaningful. So it turns out that even our most gossipy, apparently trivial stories are ways of making meaning of our lives. Stories make organised sense out of very chaotic experiences. The process of constructing them is first and foremost a process we need to use for ourselves. After all, there are many stories we tell which never see the light of day. We tell countless numbers of them to ourselves in our heads. Good stories do not make sense because they have a tidy hidden moral or because you can summarize their meaning neatly in a sentence. Meaning is distributed right through them, though we may feel that one meaning is more dominant than others.

However, there's much more to it than that. After all, we do tell our stories to others. We invite them to agree to our meanings. So storytelling is a basic form of communicating meaning. Many of the devices of storytellers (suspense is the one most often mentioned) are part of the act of seduction of the audience so that their attention is won for the real point and purpose of the tale. Every personal anecdote is a fragment of autobiography and to set about a full autobiography is to propose a meaning of life itself, to offer it to others. To engage intimately with others is to invite their stories, for it is via our stories that we present ourselves to each other. It is an interesting feature of personal storytelling that it usually sets in motion a sequence of stories. Tell a hospital story and you will provoke others, just as jokes beget jokes. If you analyse a sequence of this kind you will almost always discover that, far from being a random collection, they constitute an endeavour to reach a collective understanding of some important theme like fear, courage, loss, or eccentricity.

So then, all storytelling is an essential part of the functioning of the human mind. It is a major means of thinking and communicating our thoughts. That is why room must always be found for it in schools, for pupils of all ages, and why adults will listen entranced to old folktales. Many people would be surprised to learn that scholars of many different kinds, psychologists, linguists, sociologists, literary theorists, anthropologists, theologians, historians and folklorists, have all insisted that narrative is not an optional extra – froth on the surface of human behaviour – but 'the central function or *instance* of the human mind' (Fredric Jameson, 1981). Richard Bauman, who has studied both folk stories and personal tales, has come to the conclusion (1986) that an essential feature of managing our social lives is

> people telling stories to each other as a means of giving cognitive and emotional coherence to experience, constructing and negotiating social identity ... investing the experiential landscape with moral significance.

Not only do we have storytelling minds; we become social beings through storytelling. It is good to be reminded that not only the great novels but modest little tales too can lay claim to profound functions. Great debate has waged for millennia on what constitutes the essence of being human. We can now propose as a candidate the disposition to narrate experience.

I have deliberately started at the humblest end of the narrative spectrum – the oral personal tale – but I want to move along it to take in traditional tales of all kinds, not as we find them in books but as they are retold by storytellers. We can notice in passing that there has been a vigorous revival of public storytelling, which you might think wouldn't stand a chance against the glamour of TV and cinema. I invite readers to work out why this is. Meanwhile, we can consider why the spoken story has such power. Compare reading a folktale in one of the many magnificent collections now available with a telling of the same story. You would soon notice that all tellers make the story their own. They are not mesmerised by the original but take a path somewhere between being faithful to it and adapting it to their own sense of the story's meaning. Even another telling by the same teller is different, for the time and place change and the audience changes and the teller subtly adjusts to the mood and context of the moment, affected by visible reactions in the audience. Storytellers have available to them a repertoire of effects which writers, poor folk, do not possess: the tone of voice, the variations of pitch, pace, volume, the use of silence and body language.

So the written version (these days we mostly encounter folk tales in written form) is utterly transmogrified by the fact that it becomes a performance, not in the theatrical sense but rather as a direct doing and making and a collaboration with listeners. Thus the traditional tale is constantly being renewed and refreshed. With the traditional tale we enter the realm of fiction, fantasy and magic, of talking beasts, magic rings, little people, of play with the passing of time, cleverness where it's least expected, tricks and riddles. Have we left the world of experience behind? Not a bit. For it is a feature of our humanness that we can not only represent experience directly but also work on the representation and thus deal with experience obliquely. A fiction story tells of events which, however improbable, are spoken of as though they actually occurred. The folk tale, worked over and polished by generations of tellers, embodies communal ways of making sense of experience, operating through symbolic fictions. I have recently retold the Irish folk story about an osier cutter who, sadly, cannot tell stories. He is magically whisked away to a wake where, in spite of his protests about his incompetence, he plays the fiddle superbly, becomes a dignified officiating priest at a mass, and carries out a skilful and improbable piece of surgery. When he returns he has now, of course, a wonderful story to tell. He has become a storyteller. All the major episodes of the story are symbols of the human experience of diffidence and confidence.

We are beginning to discover that the act of storytelling raises the level of the language of the storyteller. Storytellers display a competence and power which is not present in their other uses of language. Charles Parker, who collaborated in those famous *Radio Ballads* like 'Singing the Fishing' and 'John Axon', always used to stress that the working-class speakers whom he taped telling stories did so with amazing eloquence. Teachers are finding that students retelling stories are far more inventive and creative than when they are asked to 'make one up'. We need to understand this more fully. But it seems that the teller, no longer burdened with the need to invent the basic elements, is free to allow the imagination to play inventively. Surprising dormant resources come into action. A stereotypical character takes on a particular idiom and voice, a new episode is introduced, or an old one elaborated. This is the very opposite of repeating a rote-learned story. Retelling is a creative act.

A final word. Stories live off stories. Of all the genres learned through language, that is to say, ways of saying things – how to set out an argument, compose a letter of complaint, propose a toast, offer an explanation – narrative is the genre we are most comfortable with. From a very early age we gather a rich experience of stories and we learn more and more how they work, their methods and devices. So in our tellings, without our realising it, we use this hidden repertoire. We have a much more limited experience of the other genres but in storytelling we are comfortably at home. We are all storytellers, if only we are given the chance.

References

Bauman, R. (1986) *Story, Performance and Event*. Cambridge: Cambridge University Press.

Jameson, F. (1981) *The Political Unconscious: Narrative as a socially symbolic act*. Ithaca, NY: Cornell University Press.

Rosen, H. (1993) *Troublesome Boy*. London: English and Media Centre.

The Two Frogs

Here's a purloined story
Or, if you prefer, let's say
I've borrowed it,
Which is after all common practice
With stories, that is.

You'll find the original version
Buried in the last few pages
Of Ghada Karmi's book *In Search of Fatima*.
To save you a chase I can pinpoint it.
It's on page four hundred and forty six,
The last twelve lines of chapter fourteen.
You couldn't ask fairer than that.
Twelve lines, that's all.
The bare bones of a story.
As it turns out it's not even a story.
She borrowed it
Which is after all common practice.
Borrowed it from Akiva
Whose father had plucked it
From his repertoire for his son to borrow
Which is after all common practice.
Where Akiva's father borrowed it from
I can't say.
Judge for yourselves.

Akiva's story was spoken to Ghada
To her inconsolable bitter Palestinian despair.
Page four hundred and forty six
As I said, and I quote.
'Might as well accept it. We're finished.
The new Armenians, doomed to be fragmented,
Dispersed for ever.'
How was that again? Did she say Armenians?
Was that a slip of the tongue?
Or a sly knowing thing to say,
To say to her friend Akiva the Jew,
Akiva the Israeli,

Harold Rosen

Who knew a thing or two
About dispersals and fragments?
That's why Akiva the Jew
Reached for his borrowed story
To tell to his dispossessed friend
Ghada the Palestinian.

'There was once an old frog and a young frog.'
As bald as that. No more.
Had they just met, perhaps,
Bumped into each other in a puddle?
Needed a roomier wet place to confer in?
Or more likely they were father and son
Wallowing in the shallows …
'A lovely damp day like this
We should take a little stroll.'
'Your little strolls I know already.
To my worst enemies they shouldn't happen.'

They hopped together all the same,
The young one, all sprightly and jaunty,
Bounced along.
'What can be wrong with a bit of exercise?
Take deep breaths.'
'A joker. Deep breaths he says.'

And then from nowhere and nothing
The story says they fell into a jug of milk.
As though frogs fall into jugs of milk
All the time.
What sort of *shmerels* were they?
Weren't they always told
Don't go near milk jugs?
Milk is frog-unfriendly
Nothing like lake water, pond water,
Dirty ditch water.

It was the young one, ready for anything
Who spotted the large white pitcher
(It was a pitcher of course not a jug)
The big belly of the pitcher he couldn't say no to.
'Let's get up there and take a look.'
'Little stroll you said, remember.

Turns out now it's mountaineering
With my old legs.'
With that the young frog
Took an easy leap, croaking joyously.
The old frog swallowing his misgivings
Somehow scrambled in.
And there they were up to their necks
Confronted by the concave walls,
The old one saying his prayers.
The *shema* – you know how it goes.
Together they floundered
Tried to keep afloat.
'Keep going,' said the young one.
'See where your *mishegas* has taken us?
It's no use. I can't go on.'
He managed a last four-legged scramble
Against the curve of the pitcher wall.
'We're done for. Nothing we can do.
I give up.'
And he closed his eyes and slowly sank.
And the milk closed over his head.
Scarcely knowing why, the young one
Went on with his frenzied battle,
His froggy limbs beating the milk
Into a froth.
Until – you're not going to believe this
But it's in the story –
His wild thrashing went on and on
And churned the milk
And turned it into butter,
Gave him a platform
To vault out of the pitcher.

Leaping through the long grass,
He survived to – I don't know what.
It doesn't say.

No moral?
A moral you want
For your money?
It's just a sad-happy tale
About a couple of frogs.

Harold Rosen

You can't add a moral.
Pin it on like a medal.
Where there's life, etc. etc.
As if Ghada needed one.
If you're short of one,
Feel deprived without one,
Make one up.
Some people can trot them out
Just like that …
Akiva had a go.
Should have known better.

Choose your frog.

Autobiographical Memory

This piece appeared in *Changing English*, 3 (1), in 1996.

This paper is an extract from a work in progress, *Speaking from Memory: The study of autobiographical discourse* (Rosen, 1998). Autobiography is used by many teachers in many different branches and levels of education. However, the literature about it comes from so many different fields of study and so much of it is very recent that I set out to offer a guide to major theoretical studies and to give an airing to the questions which arise when we write, read and speak life stories. This led me to explore autobiographical memory, which I deal with here. In the history of ideas it is by no means uncommon for innovative thinking to lie quiescent like a hibernating bear and to be roused after a great lapse of time into vibrant new life. The work of Gramsci is an example, as it burst into the discourse of new-look Marxists after almost half a century of neglect in Britain. And this is how it was with the work of Frederick Bartlett, whose *Remembering: A study in experimental and social psychology* (1932) broke new ground on memory and then was ignored by all but a few scholars until the Eighties. But then Bartlett was complicit in the long sleep of his early ideas, for, as Mary Douglas (1980) wryly remarks:

> The author of the best book on remembering forgot his own first convictions. He became absorbed in the institutional framework of Cambridge University psychology, and restricted to the conditions of the experimental laboratory.

Given the appearance in the 1980s of a new and serious preoccupation with autobiographical memory, it was inevitable that Bartlett's early work should be dusted down, freshly scrutinised and used as a launching pad for new kinds of exploration. It makes sense, therefore, at this point to take a look at his creative investigations and what he concluded from them.

Bartlett was determined to study memory in ways which were as close as possible to the ways it functions when people actually do their remembering for life purposes and then express it in words. This means that he restored to the study of memory the significance of the context in which remembering is done. Where and when we remember affects how we remember. From what socio-cultural location do we speak? The original events and everything which surrounded them are now perceived by the rememberer in the micro- and macro-world in which he or she is now speaking, and which determined the form and content of the articulated memory.

517

Bartlett's work, now highly valued, is often represented by summaries of his 'The War of the Ghosts' experiment, which is a landmark in the study of memory (see, for example, Fentress and Wickham, 1992). It is a parlour game adroitly lifted to the level of a *locus classicus.* In one form, the game consisted of his asking a group of people to retell a story following his instructions. Only one person was given the story, who then told it to one other and in this way it travelled round the whole group. As every party-goer knows, the final version is very different from the first. In another form of the experiment, one person retold the story at various intervals of time. What adds special significance to the retellings is that Bartlett had chosen his story with particular care: it was a Native American folk story, which followed the conventions of such narratives, conventions very different from those in the European tradition, so much so that it would seem to Bartlett's storytellers to be permeated by ambiguities and discontinuities to such a degree as to make it baffling. The outcome was that the retellers 'obliged' the story to make sense, that is, they changed it in different ways but always so as to give it their kind of intelligibility. They reculturalised the story, making it cross the boundary between the Native American narrative world and the British one.

Maintaining his naturalistic stance, Bartlett asked his collaborators to discuss their ways of remembering and in the process discovered that some of them used as a mnemonic the very vivid images of the original. However, he held to the view that such actual traces of the past become woven into reconstructions of memory. For this is what stands at the heart of his contribution – that memory functions by interpreting the past in order to give it meaning. Moreover, that interpretation and meaning, conscious and unconscious, emerged from the culture of the person retelling the past.

If the import of Bartlett's work were restricted to a demonstration of how people remember stories, its interest would be limited, perhaps, to folklorists, ethnographers and narratologists, but it has relevance for students of autobiography, too. Remembering a story you have been told is, of course, a kind of autobiographical memory. For example, I first encountered the Yiddish story of Bontshe Schweig (Bontshe the Meek) when my grandfather told it to me. Only much later did I discover that it was a classic Yiddish short story by Isaak Peretz. It remains for me an essential part of the way my grandfather figures in my autobiographical memory as a teller of stories both fictional and autobiographical. The stories we remember do not float in mid-air; they exist firmly anchored in the context of part of our lives. Somewhere in the labyrinth of their memories Bartlett's subjects would not only have a version of 'The War of the Ghosts' but also of the intriguing events surrounding their acquisition of it.

Bartlett's emphasis on the reconstructive nature of memory adds to the views coming from other commentators who have looked at autobiographical discourse and found it an inventive reconstruction. Perhaps that reconstruction reaches its most challenging form in autobiographical fiction. However, his work, which he saw as a social-psychological study, is criticised by Middleton and Edwards (1990) for not being whole-heartedly social. They had replicated his serial reproduction experiment with 'The War of the Ghosts' in which each storyteller, they say, passes on his version to the next in line in a kind of one-way traffic. What this eliminates is the possibility of conversational interaction and therefore of witnessing the social creation of memory.

> There are no conversations: the 'subjects' have no opportunity to engage with each other communicatively. It occurred to us that, however messy the data might get, there might be an advantage in allowing the participants to talk to each other, and to create together a joint version of remembered events. This might get us closer to the social creation of memory, which Bartlett himself sought.

The social act of remembering I shall be returning to shortly. For the moment, note that the above citation not only reinserts the social and the collective into autobiographical memory, where they had been lying low since the Twenties, but also brings into view what is virtually absent from recent studies of autobiographical memory: its occurrence and meaning in conversation, which in general has been passed over. This is hardly surprising when we see how much energy is poured into experiments which, in spite of differences in design, share an almost obsessive preoccupation with having participants (usually students, of course) make records which yield the number of memories they have logged or the dating of particular memories (see Conway, 1990). Conway in his introductory text, which is for me the best and most comprehensive account of the state of the art seen from a cognitive psychologist's point of view, comments at the outset of his book:

> Autobiographical memory constitutes one of the areas where cognitive psychologists have no choice but to confront aspects of human cognition which are often set aside in mainstream cognitive research.

and later:

> Unfortunately, however, the concepts of 'emotion' and the 'self' are not sufficiently well-developed in psychology ... One further problem is that there are no generally agreed models of either emotion or the self. In fact, both these areas ... [are] currently undergoing something of a research revival.

And about time too! For it is something to marvel at that there could be a credible psychology which by-passed emotion and the self.

Conway, like Middleton and Edwards, does give some attention, albeit very brief, to the possibility that 'autobiographical memory is taught within a culture in the form of explicit instructions provided in, say, mother/child interactions'. If memory is culture-specific, then we must wonder how it comes about that the analysis of autobiography scarcely acknowledges the existence of autobiographical discourse in non-'Western' cultures. It has needed the vigorous intrusion of feminists, 'other' ethnicities and a rare scholar like Michael Fischer (1994) to turn our gaze away from the confident allocation of the beginnings of true autobiography, which places them quite unconditionally in Europe. Fischer's programme attempts to install an entirely new agenda.

> I have been making a plea for the cross-cultural, the comparative, the critique of the categories we use and for cross-disciplinary conversation on uses of life-histories to rebuild social theory, to rebuild the technical polity, to rebuild theories of psychology and to refashion the world we live in. That seems to me a not unambitious project for the study of autobiography to undertake.

Behind his plea is a complex, even elusive, view of memory, of which we catch more than a glimpse or two in other writers. This is memory structured somewhat like geological strata, each with its own characteristics and fractures but 'collaged together in consciousness and in unconscious manoeuvrings' and therefore posing a hermeneutical challenge to anyone attempting to dissect and anatomise it.

To read Fischer is to experience a kind of embarrassment as his horizon is so wide as to render our own views parochial. All the same, the stirrings of the 'research revival' which Conway speaks of are giving rise to some new preoccupations. There are two recurrent themes which are worth dwelling on – flashbulb/significant memories and involuntary memories – the very names of which seem to propose a willingness to investigate the kind of memories with which we are all very familiar and hitherto have looked for in vain in the literature. Anyone can offer you memories which in the mind are as bright and sharp as a film even after huge intervals of time, while others are fuzzy and elusive. Are the very vivid memories in a special class of their own? Brown and Kulik (1977) certainly thought so, so much so, in fact, that they invented the term 'flashbulb memories' for them. It comes as something of a surprise that their research concentrated upon memories in which people heard of a dramatically important event (typically, the assassination of John Kennedy). These are memories logged within circumstances of exceptional national importance. The choice may be convenient for the researcher, but for many the circumstances of the death of a close relative may be much more momentous than that of a national or international figure. The flashbulb term was adapted because it is as though a memory of an event which has caught someone off guard and is, as we say, sensational, lights up the contextual details, however trivial they may be. Brown and Kulik suggested that these autobiographical memories constituted a special category, because they were encoded in a different way owing to their special biological meaning, i.e. a response to a particular threat which generates a special awareness and a need to file away the record. Moreover, they noted that flashbulb memories frequently illustrated such aspects of the moment as the who, what, when, where and why.

Seductive though the flashbulb metaphor is, it has been dismantled thoroughly by other scholars who have been able to show that the perfectly remembered moment in time is often wrongly remembered, often endowed with significance after the event, or even before it. Further, the structure given to the remembered event is derived not from a unique encoding but conformity to well-known conventions of narration which even unsophisticated narrators deploy and which is likely to have been through many repetitions. A much more modest view of flashbulb memories has now been established. It is readily acknowledged and supported by copious evidence that there exists a class of memories which are peculiarly vivid; such memories, however, are not uniquely recorded. What makes them different, as we might guess, is the high level of emotion which saturated the original experience and its meaning in the life of the rememberer. In spite of the frequent mis-remembering demonstrably contained in many of them, they prove to be peculiarly resistant to change; they achieve a canonical form which seems to render them proof against amnesiac loss.

Conway, pursuing the decline of memory in the elderly, turns to Salaman's book, *A Collection of Moments: A study of involuntary memories* (1970). The respectful and lengthy attention he gives to this book constitutes an intriguing intellectual event. The research psychologist places before us the testimony of someone who is doing no more than inspecting and analysing, with healthy intellectual curiosity, her own memories and those of some famous writers. Conway quotes substantial passages from her work and he listens respectfully to what many would dismiss as anecdotage from a lay source. My appetite whetted by Conway citations, I could do no less than turn to Salaman's book.

Salaman was a research physicist who worked with the celebrated scientist, Rutherford; but she was also a novelist and autobiographer. Her sensitivity to autobiographical memory must, I believe, be seen as related to the fact that she is an inter-cultural, multi-lingual woman, one of those many people who embody in one person two or more cultures, several languages and a changing, adjusting identity and for whom memory not only reaches back into the past but into another place where it speaks another language and operates with other codes. Memory for them must travel past frontier posts, literal and psychological. Although memory for them does not enter a totally alien world it is rather the extreme form of all memory. For the past, as L.P. Hartley told us, is a foreign country. Salaman says:

> It was years before I realised that my home sickness in Berlin had been for the past, that people who have never left their country have similar experience: we are all exiles from our past.

Nevertheless, hybrids like her are propelled more irresistibly towards their lost lands. She spent childhood and adolescence in Russia in a Jewish family, left in 1919, studied physics and mathematics in Berlin and, on Einstein's advice, went on to study under Rutherford in Cambridge.

> After three years at the Cavendish I realised I had clung to science as to a raft, and by the time my scientific papers appeared I had had a child and begun a novel.

Her book proved to be compelling, for it assembled coherently an unusual interweaving of materials which constitute her resources for pursuing the theme of involuntary memories. The chief nodes of her book are her own substantial autobiographical moments. They are buttressed by citations from the work of writers of autobiographies, some of them with massive reputations like Goethe, Tolstoy and Proust, and others far less well-known like William Hutton and Harriet Martineau. Around these materials she constructs her speculations and reflections. It is impossible to do justice here to the richness and originality of this book and I will have to be content with giving some inkling of its methods and ideas.

Let me begin with Salaman's discussion of the way experiences came into her mind after fifty years and, once there, how they drew towards her a constellation of connected memories. She goes on to say that our understanding of memory would be deeper if people gave, when they were able to do so, the history of involuntary memories. This would be particularly true of writers who are for the most part too busy getting on with the job of writing their memories to linger over how they got there and how they disinterred them. That is why she is at pains to gather together those occasions when a few writers like Proust and Dostoevsky make their comments on the working of their memory. However,

> ... often a writer does not himself remember when one of his early memories came back involuntarily, and we, his readers, cannot tell whether he is recording a memory a few minutes old, or is writing the memory of a memory a few years later. Sometimes it happens that the revival of a memory is itself fixed in sensations, space and time.

She has already shown us this happening to De Quincey. He has a vivid and joyous memory of looking from a window at a country-town market when he was three years old. He then in adulthood remembers remembering this moment of intense pleasure when wretchedly he is running away from school at the age of seventeen.

Salaman herself in her fifties remembers remembering, at the age of thirteen, stealing a piece of soap when she was five years old. She offers us her earliest memory as an example of this memory-of-a-memory phenomenon. I must quote it at some length, not only because of the interest in the points she is making but also to reveal her characteristic use of her own memories.

I was playing one fine morning outside our house, the one we left when I was eight; Mother was talking to a friend when suddenly I rushed and told her excitedly that I remembered going with her in the diligence. There may have been something about a journey in a diligence in what she had been saying, or the diligence may have just appeared (it was the hour when it usually arrived from Kiev) drawn by many horses – always a fascinating sight, or both may have happened simultaneously. I began to tell Mother that she was wearing her rotonde (a cape lined with fur) and that I was inside it. She said: 'But you can't remember. You were too young.' Her friend must have suggested that I was mixing up that journey with some other because I remember Mother telling me that the only time she had taken me by diligence to Kiev was on the occasion of her brother's wedding. I gave her more details but I am certain that I did not tell her the heart of my memory; I could not have, even if I had wanted to.

The diligence used to start on its return journey to Kiev at about four, but on a short winter day it was dark when it passed our house. The moment I had remembered was this: we had settled in the dimly lit diligence in the left corner by the door, but it had not yet moved. I am on my Mother's lap, inside her rotonde. Her large smooth black fur collar was standing up round her head; on her head she had a black lace scarf. As she saw me looking at her, a smile of happiness lit up her broad fair lovely face and she gave that smile to me.

There is the heart of Salaman's strategy. Having led us into the complexities of these multiple involuntary memories, she implicitly invites us to examine our own. But the detail of this highly treasured memory also invites us to look into much more than the single point she appears to be making – the way others negotiate and question our memories. Her book is full of them and they often tell us more than her comments do, perceptive though they often are. She does grapple with them, egged on by her keen sense that very little is known about involuntary memories.

Trying to find an image for the particular characteristics of involuntary memories, especially of childhood, she wrote in *The Fertile Plain* (1956), an autobiography she wrote after the failure of much earlier attempts:

My memories of childhood are like scenes lit up by sheets of summer lightning as one speeds in a train through the night.

She notes that this image – which recalls the flashbulb metaphor – is very close to Harriet Martineau's, who wrote that her memories ' ... were revived in an inexplicable way as by a flash of lightning over a far horizon'. Involuntary memories are those which come without warning and bring back a past suffused with emotion. They have a particular quality which gives a sensation of once again living in that moment, whether it be joyous or distressful. As an autobiographer, writing at a period in life when maturity generates many new involuntary memories, Salaman is confident that autobiography cannot be constructed from conscious memories alone but that room must be made for what has surfaced from the unconscious mind while the conscious mind diligently takes pains in doing its own work. Failure to make this accommodation leaves an autobiography constructed from 'rationalising and invented sentiments' alone and therefore impoverished.

She goes on to make discriminations which are suggestive rather than fully argued. A feature of involuntary memories is what she calls the difference between 'the background' and the central event in the memory. The terms are not really helpful. What she is discussing is what I would call the setting or precise location of the memory and the core of the moment. One of her examples, as always, makes the distinction very clear.

> One day, while working on some early memories, and living in one of the 1905 Revolution, when I was five, I was terribly taken aback. I was looking out of the window when I was five, with my eyes on two women running past, just underneath, each frightened in her own way. They had neither hats nor kerchiefs and their hair was bobbed. 'The Revolutionaries,' Mother said, close behind me: I turned my head to her. To my amazement I realised that the room I was looking at was the sitting-room to which we moved when I was thirteen.

Which puts a different gloss on flashbulb memories as they were first proposed and when the assumption was that what made them unique was their total reliability. For Salaman there is what she calls an 'island' and this is inviolable, whereas the rest is expendable. On the other hand the sitting-room, post-thirteen years of age, she admits as a totally reliable memory. What is left unresolved is why the relocation of the 1905 event takes place. Salaman makes the proposal that we need to remember the setting of the core moment but, if we are removed from our environment in early childhood, we have to 'borrow a background' for our early memories. Perhaps or perhaps not: but what Salaman has helpfully done, and she has other examples, is to draw attention to a neglected aspect of involuntary memories recalled in old age. The scene-shifting could well have a significance in its own right.

As against this *mis-en-scène* (the past moment relived in the present) Salaman has memories which she calls 'fragments', which seem to float in the mind, devoid of setting, not fixed in time or space or even sensations. Her hypothesis is that although they recapture powerful feelings, they have lost the sense of shock or, as a Freudian would say, have been repressed.

Ultimately, Salaman's book is a kind of celebration of involuntary memories which, even when they are painful or poignant or tragic, can in a certain sense be cherished. Why should this be? She feels that they yield meanings of great importance and that these meanings help us to live. The older we get, the more they contribute to an appraisal of an entire life. The book is also a plea for us to examine closely the history of our involuntary memories, for there remains much about them which is still not clearly understood, and her own book does not pretend to be more than a meticulous reconnaissance. It is, I hardly need say at this point, yet another outstanding example of a contribution to the study of autobiographical memory from outside the world of appointed experts.

Let me enter here a note which I value partly because it sheds light on how this book is getting itself written. I was, having written the last few sentences, impatient to turn to very recent developments in the study of memory which I was very much in tune with. A day or two elapsed before I did so, during which I received as a gift Oliver Sacks's *An Anthropologist on Mars* (1995). It had some important things to say on autobiographical memory, including a special insight into what I had just been writing about Salaman's description of fragments or floating memories. Sacks is writing about an extraordinary autistic woman called Temple Grandin, who had become an expert on animal behaviour and a teacher at the University of Colorado. He is impelled to visit her not only because of her rare achievements as an autistic person but also because she had written an autobiography, *Emergence: Labelled autistic* (Grandin and Scariano, 1986). How, he wondered, could an autistic person write an autobiography? It was a contradiction in terms. The outcome of his visit I shall leave to his own characteristic case-study narrative, but I select one moment in it when Temple Grandin tells him of the time when a slaughterhouse manager spied on her in order to watch how she calmed excited animals. Sacks writes:

> I was struck by the vividness of the re-experience, the memory, for her
> – it seemed to play itself in her mind with extraordinary detail – and by
> its unwavering quality. It was as if the original scene, its perception (with
> all its attendant feelings) was reproduced with virtually no modification.
> This quality of memory seemed to me both prodigious in its detail and
> pathological in its fixity.

Grandin herself says her mind is like a quick-access computer; she has to play the whole scene and cannot access separate parts of it. To this phenomenon, which she so clearly explained, Sacks adds a fascinating footnote, in which he comments that her memories are not reconstructed, as Bartlett had argued. On the other hand, he instances Damasio's *Descartes' Error* (1994):

> Images are *not* stored as facsimile pictures of things, or events, or words,
> or sentences. The brain does not file Polaroid pictures of people, objects,
> landscapes; nor does it store audiotapes of music and speech; it does
> not store films of scenes in our lives … In brief, there seems to be no

permanently held pictures of anything, even miniaturized, no microfiches
or microfilms, no hard copies.

(cited in Sacks)

What is Grandin doing then? Just deceiving herself that she has perfect recall,
something we all do from time to time? Perhaps, Sacks wonders, Bruner is right when
he suggests, in Sacks's paraphrase, that:

> there may be in [unusual people like Grandin] some failure of integration
> of perceptual systems with higher integrative ones, and with concepts of
> self, so that *relatively* unprocessed, uninterpreted, unrevised images persist.

In another chapter, called 'The Landscape of Dreams', Sacks elaborates ideas about
memory provoked by a painter, Franco Magnani, who spends decades painting
hundreds of pictures from memory of the native village in Italy he had known in
childhood. By the time Sacks meets him, Franco has achieved recognition in the
USA, where his works were displayed in an exhibition called 'A Memory Artist'.

> ... he indeed possessed a prodigious memory – a memory that would
> seemingly reproduce with almost photographic accuracy every building,
> every street, every stone of Pontito ... It was as if Magnani held in his head
> an infinitely detailed, three-dimensional model of his village, which he
> could turn around and examine or explore mentally, and then reproduce
> on canvas with total fidelity.

In 1965 at the age of thirty-one Franco settled in San Francisco, where he had a
strange illness, during which he began to have vivid dreams of his beloved Pontito.
Having scarcely painted before, in twenty or so years he painted thousands of pictures,
every one of which was a view of Pontito. You may get a good idea of his work from
Sacks's book, for there are illustrations in colour of Franco's paintings placed side
by side with same-view photographs of Pontito. Sacks's story of Franco is not only
utterly compelling, by virtue of what it narrates, but also touches the imagination
because it is told with infinite wisdom and empathy. Sacks meditates on the subject
of autobiographical memory provoked by his experiences of meeting Franco and his
paintings.

He is moved to observe that Franco's amazing visual autobiographical
productivity is the work of an exile. As I have suggested, this cross-over from one
kind of life to another gives a potent thrust to recollection which is a particularly
poignant form of mutability, separation and loss. Discontinuity and nostalgia, suggests
Sacks, are at their most profound when the expatriate or exile loses the very site of
childhood, though like Salaman he acknowledges that we are all exiles from our past.

We have already seen how much the recollection of the past undergoes a
constant re-editing which alters, forgets, adds, elaborates afresh in what Bartlett

called an imaginative reconstruction. Sacks, however, is disposed to speculate on whether there are not unusual forms of which this is not true. He instances not only Luria's celebrated 'mnemonist' (*The Mind of a Mnemonist* [1967]), but also rote memories of long epic poems in oral cultures and the formidable memories of 'idiots savants' and the compulsive replaying of traumatic memories, all of which he sees as 'a fixation or fossilization at work' which differ from the dynamic, constantly revised memory. He never completely resolves the riddle of the perfectly reproductive memory as against the creative one, but tentatively suggests that any view of autobiographical memory must include both concepts. Franco's pictures are 'minutely accurate in the tiniest details' but are also 'serene and idyllic' and highly edited to leave a picture of a kind of paradise. They are a myth of happy childhood. There is no question that both the autistic Temple and the compulsive Franco are rare and remarkable people, but it is something of a surprise that so diligent and eagle-eyed a writer as Sacks does not give greater attention to his own words. Grandin, he says, replays a scene 'with virtually no modification'; Bruner speaks of images which are 'relatively unrevised'. This is scarcely 'fixation' and 'fossilization', however closely it approaches them. What all this suggests is that even in memories of such reproductive and prodigious accuracy as those which Sacks reports, there is a reconstructive process at work, albeit minimal. So much is not changed, however, that it seems right to argue that we are observing a different phenomenon from the proven reconstructions of flashbulb memories.

Autobiographical memory, then, is not a single kind of monolithic process which delivers an equally monolithic kind of text. It grows out of different kinds of images, which in their turn, when they are verbalised, are shaped by a diversity of textual resources and social contexts.

****

Up to this point I have been concerned to look at the ideas of scholars who, however powerful their insights, have taken memory to be a psychological phenomenon which functions within the individual. From time to time, another viewpoint can be glimpsed in my account, notably Bartlett's attempt to put the social into any discussion of remembering and to make room for the role played by culture and context. I now want to return to that theme; for very recent work not only proposes a social view of memory, but takes that notion much further than Bartlett ever did.

There are those who set in sharp opposition the private and the public, the self and the other, the individual and the communal, and for whom memory is perhaps the greatest and most powerful instance of the functioning of the private individual self. To use a word like individual, let alone the more overtly ideological word individualism, is to pluck one of the most resonant chords in Western aesthetics, ethics, economics and politics: chords which can be heard loudly sounding in the dominant appraisals of autobiography, as, for instance, in the extraordinary claim that it was invented in Europe and in its true form is derived from the Romantics. To challenge this view is 'to be engaged in a struggle with a single dominant text: the centrality and sovereignty of the individual and the problems to which it gives rise' (Shotter and Gergen, 1989). In fact, this struggle is well under way, and memory itself is now seen as something different from the view powerfully represented in individual psychology and in most of the principal students of autobiography over a long period. There are now others who counterpose vigorously to that view the concepts of social memory and collective memory (see, for example, Middleton and Edwards, 1990 and Fentress and Wickham, 1992). Some feminists in particular, scenting a patriarchal component in the dominant view, have also challenged it (see Stanley, 1994). There is a sparse but highly valuable legacy here. Innovators, however iconoclastic, look to their forebears and it is in just this spirit that the work of Maurice Halbwachs has only recently surfaced. *Collective Memory* (1992) is assembled from two publications in French: one of 1941 and a posthumous volume of 1952. He was the pre-eminent pioneer of the notion of collective memory. For him this was not a special kind of memory, but rather it described all memory which arises from our most telling experience in social groups: the family, the neighbourhood, our working lives and a host of other formally or informally constituted institutions. Autobiographical memory for Halbwachs always arises from our interactions with others with whom we share a group membership. The remembering 'I' remembers by virtue of interactions with 'you', 'she/he' and 'they', who are in some sense always fellow members of a group. Stated baldly in this way, without Halbwachs's supporting text, collective memory can be perceived as a daring and total reversal of the prevailing view. But he went much further than this and showed how all societies are involved in building an elaborate superstructure of commemoration.

There is an imperative which comes from the dominant culture, sometimes operating with overt compulsion but more often by incorporation, which says to its members, 'Remember this'. There are rituals, statues, inscriptions, ceremonies, centenaries, symbols, icons, traditions (some recently invented!) which foreground selected events, especially wars and battles, and haloed individuals. There is no need to elaborate, except to add that commemoration can be contested and alternative icons and ceremonies installed (think of the Tolpuddle Martyrs). Indeed, commemoration can reach into the micro-structure of our lives – families' annual visits, wedding anniversaries, and so on. In other words, there is often a social struggle to gain ascendency over our memories, and those who feel the pull of two different cultures, ethnic, religious, linguistic, national, class-based, will experience the dilemmas and often the pain of this battle, fought out within their social consciousness.

To attach 'collective' to memory requires us to scrutinize its meanings more closely. It is easy to understand the ways in which there is a public, closely-observable collection of activities which we can properly label collective. Yet can we properly allot them to autobiographical memory? There is always the danger that public memory-making can become so routinist that it scarcely impinges on some individuals' memories. For others it may be momentous and move from autobiographical memory into autobiographical text, because in one way or another it represents peak experiences, as I shall try to show in a moment. The intensely personal and the publicly acknowledged may merge to make them indelibly recorded – a funeral, a prestigious award. There is, nevertheless, a much deeper and more direct way in which we should see autobiographical memory as social, even if it is somewhat elusive for being overlaid by individualist concepts and because the most vivid memories are so rich in fine detail.

It was the family first of all where Halbwachs saw social memory being constructed. Apart from the few home-based formalities, religious holy days and anniversaries, there is always an informal process at work, in which there are not only shared rememberings but highly memorable shared events. Nor are they necessarily separate from the official and quasi-official. A family involved in one way or another in the Second World War will represent it to each other in a very different manner from the approved version. Members of families collaborate in teaching each other what is memorable. Children are taught to remember and taught what is to be valued in their remembering. They overhear memories being talked about. 'Do you remember when … ?' is common currency in every family. A memory becomes collective because it emerges from the constant negotiation of conversation.

There is more to it than that. Memories must be saturated with social meanings as soon as they are turned into texts, spoken or written. They may have been formulated already in inner speech, but when they are externalised they must draw on memories of existing texts. These resources can be seen at every linguistic level and they are all a social creation. Every text is a complex intertwining of social meanings encoded in language. This can be seen in the central device of autobiography – narrative, with its own strategies, tactics and conventions, many of which are available to everybody. Autobiography can and does draw on other social linguistic legacies: any discursive model may be followed. Bakhtin (1981) shows how in the novel one kind of genre can be set alongside another and be given a particular tone. This kind of generic insertion takes on a new meaning by being played off against another, usually the mainstream text. In autobiography too, there is often generic diversity, when the writer or the speaker shifts the mode of discourse to philosophize, analyse, draw on relevant expertise or offer quotation. All text, as Bakhtin says, is dialogic and this, too, makes it social. For Halbwachs, memory is collective because it is structured by language, by teaching and by observing, by collectively held ideas and shared experience.

Some autobiographers may be highly aware that their tellings of life-stories are intensely social acts but, whether they are so or not, they cannot exempt themselves from the social worlds inscribed in their texts. This does not mean that a kind of autobiographical determinism totally controls the writer, who becomes no more than a channel through which one or other social voice is speaking or a mere pen being inexorably pushed by social forces. We all incorporate within ourselves many voices, loud and soft. Each one of us becomes a unique assemblage in a constant and dynamic state: the meeting place, the intersection point of innumerable forces. Like every individual in the social world, the autobiographer is not a free soul, rising above it but, as Marx said, social being determines consciousness. He or she is not, however, a zombie scribe; for there are degrees of choice and intensely personal experiences, which cannot easily or totally be attributed to social origins. Moreover, we can say that the degree of socialness is highly variable.

I have a vivid memory of my very first sortie, in somewhat bizarre circumstances, into the world of the upper middle class, for instance. I was invited or sent to visit a most unlikely new friend of my mother's, in her flat in Belsize Park in north London. Her person, the furnishings and what transpired on that occasion, turned out to be overwhelming, embarrassing and disastrous for me. I was eleven or twelve, I can't say for certain. Something good and special, was, I imagine, supposed to emerge from this encounter. At one point on that winter's evening, after crumpets and tea, the woman in question showed me some of her large abstract paintings, and I knew with utter certainty that I was expected to make some intelligent and sensitive response, and I knew with the same certainty that I had absolutely nothing to say. When I left I was miserable with a sense of failure. [See 'For Beatrice Hastings', in Rosen, 1999; and reprinted in this collection.]

Now it is not difficult to see that occasion as saturated with social meanings – a social-class encounter, a Jewish/gentile encounter, a generational boy-and-fiftyish-woman encounter, a gender encounter, a low-culture/high-culture encounter. All this came to be realised in fine details – the carpeted room, the pools of light from shaded lamps, the walls hung with pictures, the tea tray and Beatrice Hastings herself, with her upper-class speech, her straight, clipped grey hair, long blood-red earrings and loose clothes in shades of brown. There is a social template we can place over all this which would reveal that this occasion matches to perfection all of those millions of other collisions with which it shares so much and which make it inescapably social. But in the end, though that template would tell us so much, it can only do so by covering up many features which make the occasion unique to me. Every fraught, baffling meeting of this kind has its specificities, which are not trivial. Only someone absolutely bent on a comprehensive social tidy-up would brush away the fact that in the sub-text is my mother's capacity for making unlikely friendships or the little mystery of why I remember the street name painted on a wall, flaking black and white. We have need of a new term. My memory of that moment is both individual/social and social/individual and we have as yet no word for that particular inter-animation.

I wrote one story a few years ago called 'Comrade Rosie Rosen' (in Rosen, 1993 and 1999 [and reprinted in this collection]) which, I think, shows several aspects of social memory at work. The last section of the story tells of the time when I was sent to school on Empire Day without a Union Jack, an unheard-of and provocative and outrageous act, engineered by my communist mother when I was eight years old. The story registers three different forces at work. First is the very loud noise of official, national, imperial, military remembering, embodied in a nationwide ritual, sanctioned, promoted, embellished by the State, reinforced in patterned rituals in which The Flag is made the central icon. The schools were allocated and took on willingly the role allotted to them. And each individual child was incorporated into the fête-like construction of the day by being called upon to declare an act of allegiance, the bringing and brandishing of a flag and dressing in best clothes. Everyone was being enjoined to remember both the day and a certain version of the history of Empire. Secondly, and against this, there is my mother's mode of countering this commemorative strategy. In one way it is anti-memory, in another it is counter-memory, a contestation in which I am given a particular role. The third component of the memory is a struggle between being faithful to my mother's powerful ideas, which I believed in totally, and having to endure a kind of martyrdom as the only child without a flag. In the end I succumb to a teacher's kind gesture. She buys me a halfpenny pasteboard flag. This is for me both a massive relief and an appalling betrayal. The autobiographical story, then, recalls a public commemorative act which recruits children to the idea of Empire and attempts to implant the day, its icons and its rituals at the very core of their social memories. My mother, on the other hand, is challenging for the same memory space. In fact she had almost totally encamped in it, especially as she could promote a rival symbolic day, May Day, which also occurs in the story. But this struggle to construct social memory is not as simple as that, at least not within me. I attempted to play all this out in the story.

> On this fine summer's morning I turned grumpily into Myrdle Street, passing the other children flaunting their finery and flags at each other. Not me. I was in my usual old jersey and scuffed shoes and no flag. My mother was not going to have me tainted with the iniquity of Empire and at least one person was going to crack the enamelled surface of unanimity – me. Carefully she had lectured me on what the Empire really meant. She had lots of pamphlets on the subject with appalling pictures in them, of floggings, shootings and hangings presided over by men in pith helmets. They haunt me to this post-holocaust day. As ever, I only partly understood what she was saying, but I approved of all of it. It was my mother saying all this and she knew. She knew the truth about Empire as she knew about everything else … which was all very well, but she had made it quite clear that there was going to be no flag for me and no poshing-up. It was one thing to be dazzled by her inside knowledge but quite another to be

selected as the representative of her principles, defying the British Empire all by myself.

Elsewhere in the story I wrote:

> I knew she had to be right. The trouble was, I was dazzled by the Lord Mayor's Show and that golden coach. As for soldiers, I wouldn't have dared to admit to her that I tingled when they marched by with their shining bands.

For many, collective memory is shot through with conflicts, contradictions, ambiguities and doubts. Wars, battles and skirmishes are fought out in their heads and may emerge into the light of day through their autobiographical acts.

References

Bakhtin, M. (1981) *The Dialogic Imagination: Four essays.* (C. Emerson and M. Holquist, trans.). Austin: University of Texas Press.

Bartlett, F. (1932) *Remembering: A study in experimental and social psychology.* Cambridge: Cambridge University Press.

Brown, R. and Kulik, J. (1977) 'Flashbulb memories'. *Cognition*, 5.

Conway, M. (1990) *Autobiographical Memory: An introduction.* Milton Keynes: Open University Press.

Damasio, A. (1994) *Descartes' Error: Emotion, reason and the human brain.* New York: Putnam.

Douglas, M. (1980) *Evans-Pritchard.* London: Fontana.

Fentress, J. and Wickham, C. (1992) *Social Memory.* Oxford: Basil Blackwell.

Fischer, M. (1994) 'Autobiographical voices and mosaic memory', in K. Ashley *et al.* (eds.), *Autobiography and Post-modernism.* Amherst: University of Massachusetts Press.

Grandin, T. and Scariano, M. (1986) *Emergence: Labelled autistic.* Tunbridge Wells: Costello.

Halbwachs, M. (1992) *Collective Memory* (L. Coser, trans.). Chicago: University of Chicago Press.

Luria, A. (1967) *The Mind of a Mnemonist.* Cambridge, MA: Harvard University Press.

Middleton, D. and Edwards, D. (1990) 'Conversational remembering', in D. Middleton and D. Edwards (eds.), *Collective Remembering.* London: Sage.

Rosen, H. (1993) *Troublesome Boy.* London: English and Media Centre.

Rosen, H. (1998) *Speaking from Memory: The study of autobiographical discourse.* Stoke-on-Trent: Trentham Books.

Rosen, H. (1999) *Are You Still Circumcised?* Bristol: Five Leaves Publications.

Sacks, O. (1995) *An Anthropologist on Mars.* London: Picador.

Salaman, E. (1956) *The Fertile Plain.* London: The Hogarth Press.

Salaman, E. (1970) *A Collection of Moments: A study of involuntary memories.* London: Longman.

Shotter, J. and Gergen, K. (1989) *Texts of Identity.* London, Sage.

Stanley, L. (1994) *The Autobiographical I.* Manchester: Manchester University Press.

For Beatrice Hastings

It was a most unlikely assignation with a lady at her flat in Belsize Park. I was twelve, perhaps a bit more, and she must have been fiftyish. I was not relishing this encounter mostly because I did not understand why it was happening, not for sure anyway. She wore long blood-red earrings which were never still. Beatrice. A very gentile name. I didn't at the time know anyone called Beatrice. There was Great-aunt Beatty who may have been Beatrice on her birth certificate but I didn't know about that. Just like there were Aunt Addie who was really Adelaide and Aunt Lallie who was Sarah and Aunt Millie who was Amelia and my *booba* Betsy who was Betsy. It seemed to us at home that Beatrice Hastings was properly so-called and her name alone kept her at arm's length in spite of her not infrequent appearances to eat and talk with us in our sombre brown kitchen.

'Beatrice Hastings said she liked my *borsht*,' booba said. 'I don't believe it. Like Bella Stern saying she liked my cheesecake. She'd say she liked it if I gave her poison. That's their way.'

'Borsht or no borsht,' said my *zeider*, 'Beatrice Hastings is a comrade. To be a comrade you're not obliged to like *borsht*.'

But even I knew it would have helped.

'Beatrice Hastings,' he went on, 'has … has … well … come over.'

Like the rest of us, his classification system couldn't quite place her. I think if it hadn't been for the comrade bit he could have sorted it out. But then, if it hadn't been for the comrade bit he wouldn't have needed to.

I surfaced at Belsize Park underground station on the Northern Line. I'd never got out there before. It all looked alien, perhaps hostile, and on that November late afternoon it was slightly foggy and dampish. The shops were too smart for my liking, none of them spilling onto the pavement, not a *schlepper* in sight, and the passers-by far too well-dressed. They weren't hanging about in twos or threes to have a *muttel*, shaking and nodding their heads, expecting people to edge their way round them. They were going about their affairs in a very direct eyes-ahead sort of way.

'Your petit-bourgeois,' said my Uncle Sam (who knew his Marxist alphabet from *Anti-Duhring* to *Zinoviev*), 'doesn't like the streets, too unpredictable and teeming with proletarians with bombs in their pockets.'

The petit-bourgeois on Haverstock Hill didn't seem the least bit bothered by all that. Inside their thick overcoats and fur collars they looked very much at home. I wasn't. I slouched towards Beatrice Hastings's flat, baffled by this sortie over the border not of my choosing. Somehow I found my way across the main road and along Belsize Avenue, then into Belsize Park Gardens. Did I have a map? Had I learned the name and route by heart? No *A to Z*, that's for sure. Since that moment now tastes of uncertainty and timidity I wonder about such things. Perhaps I was less of a *nebbich* than I have imagined.

Belsize Park Gardens was a street of sudden quiet gentility, huge stuccoed Victorian fortresses with great windows, porticoes with columns, barred basements and substantial walls. I found the house. I found the right bell-push next to a handwritten 'Beatrice Hastings'. There was nothing for it. I rang the bell and waited shakily. Ring a doorbell, rap a knocker, rattle a letterbox, bang on the woodwork and always there will be that second or two of anxiety or hope before you cross the threshold from everyone's street to the private indoors. Sure, I could have fled and told my mother I couldn't find the house or something, but for all my unwillingness and resentful spirit there was also, lurking deep down, a smatch of excitement and promise. It was just possible that, in spite of the inevitable torment of the coming *tête-à-tête*, something special and good for me would emerge.

I suppose I'd better go back a bit before I go up into the flat and tell about what happened. The thing is, if I were speaking the story this would be the moment when I would say 'Half a minute. I forgot to tell you … ' Nobody would mind. They'd let you mend and patch as you go. They'd even help you out if need be. 'Great Uncle Schmul,' someone will say, telling the tale once more of how he got to England and thought it was America, 'used to live in the Portobello Road after the Boer War. Master tailor he was.' 'Great Uncle Schmul? No, no,' says Aunt Millie. 'A tailor? Just a little furrier in Ladbroke Grove. After the Boer War, like you say. How come he lived up West?' Just putting the record straight. No hard feelings. So I'll go back.

My *zeider* began it. He was given to bringing home out of the blue people he'd run into, we never knew how. They were always in our eyes exotics, collectors' items, you might say, real finds. There was the improbable Hedley, for instance, whom *Zeider* had met down in the docks. And what was *Zeider* doing in that dangerous and hostile territory? Something political, we guessed vaguely. Hedley was a black seaman from Jamaica, I think. This was the Thirties, remember. Not many Hedleys about then. I marvelled at my *booba* who always kept a watchful eye on the food supply. To my surprise and her credit she didn't bat an eyelid. She was a stern and judgmental woman and didn't exactly smother Hedley with hospitality. He was not in her *gast-in-shtetl* class but she always found him a place and a plate at the kitchen table. The neighbours monitored his toings and froings, wild with curiosity and churning with suspicions.

'*Gottinue!* A *schvartzer!* That Betsy Hyams, don't I know she doesn't keep *kashrus*? So what do you expect? And that Joe Hyams (my *zeider*) he's always *kreerching* round meetings. On *shabbas* even. Meetings, meetings. Where else would he find a *schvartzer*? In *schul*, I suppose.'

They prophesied disaster. 'They're all *gonovim*. He'll take everything one day.'

From time to time, when Hedley's ship was in dock, he'd show up at the house bringing with him food, mostly big root crops we could not recognise, never seen in Hessel Street market. I think the family relished their display of comradely broadmindedness, but food they did not know put this to the severest of tests.

Booba turned over a big turnipish-potatoish lump in her hands, frowned and put it away on the dresser. Hedley laughed his head off, knowing exactly what was going on. He peeled and scraped and chopped, beamed over a saucepan and brewed until a dark brown liquid swirled round his gift. We all knew that we could do no less than give it a try. It tasted worse than the most punitive medicine. We did what we always did thereafter, gritted our teeth, gulped and did not gag. After all, Hedley had to do the same when he bravely tackled pickled herring. The thing is that we, the kids that is, liked Hedley because he laughed more than all the grown-ups put together. He could make it seem as though he had pulled off the top joint of his thumb and he taught me how to do it. *Zeider* loved these occasions. He hugged himself,

'He's a *mensch*, a real *mensch*,' and we agreed.

Of course he was proving something. No harm in that.

When Hedley left, Mrs Hamburger, prompt on her doorstep, sourly saw him off the street and the Kromlechs, crammed goggle-eyed in their doorway, waited till he came abreast to slam the door, surprised, I suppose, that we had not yet been murdered in our beds.

'Who's that blackie who comes round your house?' Herbie next door asked. I laughed in his face.

'A captain. A pirate captain. My *zeider*'s been on his ship and seen the skull and crossbones.'

Herbie wasn't laughing but he stopped asking me about Hedley.

My mother easily caught the habit of bringing home non-ghetto strangers, mostly *goyim*. One day she arrived with a tall blonde sailor from Hamburg who was a member of the German Communist Party, the KPD. He wasn't her own find but had been passed on by comrades. I was excited by a little transaction which used to take place in the hallway when he came, a transaction which I realized or imagined was illicit. My mother either collected from him, or gave him, I can't remember which, a batch of contraband copies of a journal which she called *In-Pre-Core*, a name so impenetrable that it made me even more sure that there was something very risky and subversive afoot, especially as it was printed on very thin slippery paper like the pages of the *Concise Oxford*. It was years before I found out that it was *International Press Correspondence*, one of the Comintern's enterprises, no less. Kurt came from time to time for his pick-ups or drops. He was quiet and uneasy and not having much English didn't help but the grown-ups managed fairly well with transmogrified Yiddish and there was a certain amount of sport as they sorted out who meant what. From time to time Kurt looked utterly baffled but Lallie wasn't to know that *'machatonim'* wasn't a German word. Sometimes Kurt went off for furtive mutterings with my mother which must have stretched her Yiddish-German to the limit. *Booba* fed him but eyed him sternly and warily. Still, she always tried to find him a bit of wurst to put on the table, believing this would console him for being away from home. His visits became less and less frequent and then he stopped coming altogether. Hitler had come to power. We did not dare say to each other what we thought. I imagined that *In-Pre-Core* had done for him and I saw him being manhandled by a uniformed thug during which *In-Pre-Core* tumbled onto the pavement from under his arm. One day somebody mentioned Kurt's name and my mother wept.

There were others, too, until we were almost used to these arrivals, so unlike those uncles and aunts and cousins who sat for hours over tea and *kichelech* or the excitable tailors with their talk of the impending doom of capitalism and the next demo. But I wasn't ready for Beatrice Hastings. As outlandish as Hedley and Kurt were, they slid into the cramped kitchen in Nelson Street and installed themselves around the old wooden table quite easily. *Booba* handled Hedley's roots with aplomb compared with her dismay at Beatrice Hastings's little oval tins of vegetarian something-or-another and her nut cutlets. Beatrice Hastings was our first vegetarian but she didn't win a single convert in our house. The tins contained pastes of unspeakable mid-brown or yellow colours and unidentifiable odours and tastes. Our courtesies didn't rise to this. Only my mother made a bold pretence of feeding happily with her guest. When Beatrice Hastings nodded away *Booba's kreplech* soup, a legend in the family, we scored this up as a black mark.

'She's only a high class *shiksa*,' *Booba* said. 'Never done a hand's turn for herself. Surrounded by *tuchas lechers* and low-lives. And she brings me those tins of *dreck*. And I'll tell you something else. Been through a few men in her day. She's probably got one hanging around somewhere right now.'

My mother and *Zeider* looked at each other like conspirators and *Zeider* mouthed '*shtumm*'.

I watched those blood red earrings jiggling to the vibrations of her voice. And what a voice! I may have heard one or two like it on the wireless or in the newsreels but I had never had one aimed straight at me from a yard away, emerging from a totally organised face. It wasn't just posh. Miss Drysdale, one of my teachers, talked posh and Henriques, boss of the Jewish boys' club, talked posh but this was born-to-rule super-posh, Bloomsbury posh, Roedean posh. It was the voice of someone who never expected to be gainsaid. Her hair was steely grey, straight, fringed over the forehead and clipped sharply below the ears. It was a style which my son, decades later, spotting certain older anti-nuclear women on the march, called Aldermaston hair. East End ladies of this era had their own notions of decent middle-aged style and they didn't run to minimalism. As for Beatrice Hastings's clothes, they seemed to us neither tailored nor dress-made, essential requirements at the hub of the rag trade. We couldn't place these garments which hung loosely and were made from rough folky fabrics with shaky stripes in dark browns, purples and deep reds. She never wore a hat. We did eventually break bread together but I fancy she was not quite ready for seeded rye and black bread. Give her her due, she managed well enough.

No doubt she came from a long line of ladies who took free soup to poor cottagers and expected to venture into quarters utterly remote from their own and, if need be, in any part of the world. Don't misunderstand me, there wasn't a whiff of this in her demeanour. On the contrary, she believed she could learn something from my mother and *Zeider*. I'm only saying that part of her inheritance had taught her to be quite unabashed by our alien ways and our outside lavatory.

There was always a certain twitchiness in the room, not out of nervous deference but because we just didn't know what we had to do to reach across the gulf between us, even though she was a comrade. *Zeider* talked much less and his bonhomie evaporated. He fidgeted when she looked at him and he rolled a lot of cigarettes. *Booba* was totally silent and I was suddenly very aware of her little gold earrings and the tigerclaw brooch with its gold mounting and her white hair stretched tautly in a bun (no *sheitel*) and her dark workaday pinafore. She resisted conversation.

'Were you born here, Mrs Hyams?'

'No.'

'Really? Where then?'

'Newcastle.'

Newcastle! I didn't expect that. Some of my father's people lived in Gosforth. *Booba* looked very slightly cross.

My mother, knowing that all was not going well, tried to salvage something from the afternoon.

'Beatrice,' she said, 'have you always been a journalist?'

'Good God, no! I'm not a real one now. Don't think I've ever actually done an honest job in my life. Honest jobs don't run in the family. Too much money about. Once did a bit of auxiliary nursing until I realized I was acting the lady bountiful.'

I was taking notice now. Journalist. Clever woman. My first real writer. What did she write? Would we see some of her stuff? My mother surely must have read some of it.

Things got better between us so we saw a lot more of her, against all the odds, almost taking her into the family with her veggie tins. *Booba* stopped glowering. Where could my mother possibly have found her? It turned out they had found themselves on a march to Hyde Park and got talking, as happens. There was ragged slogan shouting, of course – hands off this, smash that, free somebody, fight something and Beatrice Hastings confessed she felt embarrassed marching through the West End with the *sans-culottes*. Bellowing slogans was completely beyond her because bellowing of any kind just wasn't in her repertoire.

'How do you do it without feeling a bit of an ass?' she had asked.

'I've been doing it for so long I don't know,' said my mother who then patiently explained about party discipline. 'Don't worry about it. You're here, aren't you? That's the big thing. It'll come. I used to think I'd never work up the nerve to sell the

Daily Worker at Aldgate East station. Even for Lenin it must have been embarrassing at first. Anyway, it's harder for us women.'

They ended up taking tea in Lyons Corner House at Marble Arch. Eventually my mother lured her onto a committee which organised women's conferences on birth control.

Undoubtedly they hit it off. Beatrice Hastings had been swept to the Communist Party like others in the thirties who moved across from good causes. She was now not only a comrade and fellow reader of the Daily Worker but also a catch. For all my mother's impeccable communist credentials and her hammer and sickle red star badge, I have to say she bathed in Beatrice Hastings's aura of confidence, education and (need I say it?) wealth. She was in this light a superior woman to be paraded before the family as my mother's social achievement.

Beatrice Hastings was full of books and papers, some of which she would leave on the kitchen table as she left. I tried to read one of them, Samuel Butler's *The Way of All Flesh* and the joke is that my mother already had a copy with a broken spine and dog-eared pages, tucked away in her little bookcase. Beatrice knew a lot of people whose names were in the papers. When she spoke about the Royal Family her opinions seemed to have been formed when dining with them.

'Them,' she once snorted, 'dogs and horses, the only things they know about.'

And then it turned out she had been the mistress, as they used to say, of a well-known editor of a radical journal, who still has a modest niche in encyclopaedias. She herself started a little lefty weekly as if there weren't enough already to go round. My mother showed me an issue or two.

'She writes every line herself,' she said, keeping a straight face.

It had about four grey pages of double columns. I don't think she made much of an effort to sell it. It was more of a kind of accessory, like a good-quality handbag. I don't mean to mock her, for the truth is I was dazzled by this *grande dame* who, I had to admit reluctantly, knew more than my mother about some things. Once, finding me doing my French homework and discovering that my pronunciation was barbaric, she set about improving it. Caught in such august attention, I prayed she would soon give up for my words stuck in my throat. She did. On the other hand, when foreign place names came up in all the political talk, she made me look them up in an atlas – Brest-Litovsk, Locarno, Manchukuo, Amritsar. I felt noticed.

I might have simply added Beatrice Hastings to my collection of folk who, for a few precious hours, made the kitchen exciting and provided us with endless gossip. I might have been left with no more than a few bright tableaux of Beatrice Hastings, looking, for instance, incredulously at a Yiddish newspaper while *Zeider* translated the hieroglyphics and coming near to permitting herself to look surprised, shocked even, when she discovered that we, atheists all, not only did the complete *seder* night at the beginning of Passover and relished it but even stopped eating bread. She wasn't ready for the dozens of boxes of *matzos* and trays of eggs piled high on the landing.

'If this is what atheist Jews do, what's left for the orthodox ones?'

'The synagogue,' said *Zeider*.

A few bright images, no more, if that's all there had been to it. But then there came the day when my mother, after a few obscure hints, let me understand that I was going to visit Beatrice Hastings at her flat in Belsize Park. Perhaps I had been invited. Perhaps my mother had fished for it. Perhaps they had concocted the idea together, each thinking in her own way it would do me some good. Some of the cultured life would brush off and I'd stop dropping aitches forever, be given an improving book or two and – who knows? – be taken out.

'Beatrice says four o'clock. For tea. You take the Underground to Belsize Park.'

And then she added very slowly, 'She wouldn't do this for anybody, you know.'

More than my mother's words, it was her demeanour which told me she had high hopes for my *tête-à-tête*. It signalled weighty expectation. I was full of foreboding. Tea! Mustn't use my own teaspoon to take sugar from the bowl, mustn't put my helping of jam straight on the bread. Don't slurp, don't make munching noises. There must have been something I didn't yet know which would shame me. What would we talk about? I bet she'll ask me about school and I'll have to tell a few lies. How long must I stay? It was going to be an ordeal, without doubt, but all the same Beatrice Hastings might become my patron and I her *protégé*. It was frightening and thrilling.

I followed Beatrice up the carpeted stairs and after her, brushed past the green baize draught curtain into a very large room.

I didn't know one even faintly like it. Even Dr Abrams's, though it was big, was comfy and battered with a leaking sofa and lots of higgledy-piggledy books. My school friend, Harry Mintz, had a big sitting room over his parents' shop. It was crammed with furniture from side to side, all looking brand new. I never saw it in use. In our own house, apart from the kitchen, there was a small semi-basement living room almost filled by a large table, a dozen hard chairs and a basket armchair next to the kitchen for my *booba*'s sole use. In Beatrice Hastings's room the heavy curtains, already drawn, hung from floor to ceiling. Several standard lamps cast pools of light on a thick, mostly red, carpet. The rest of the room was, to my eyes, in semi-darkness. In this tasteful cave I could see items of furniture and none of them matched. I could just make out that the walls were lined with bookcases and somewhere there were shelves with a dinner service on display. I stepped into the room carefully. I was given a seat by a little table under one of the lamps.

'Tea would be good,' said Beatrice Hastings, 'don't you think? Do you like muffins? Better than crumpets, lighter. Dripping with butter, eh?'

'Yes, yes,' I said. 'Yes, please.'

Any other time I would have been licking my chops at the thought of it. Dripping with butter? Where will the drips go?

She left the room and came back holding a tray with curvy edges and on it frighteningly delicate china. I prepared to take my test. But you lose marks for trying too hard, don't you? And I didn't know what to do about my buttery lips. I can't remember what we talked about but it wasn't about school. At one point she asked me if I'd ever been to Whitechapel Art Gallery. I hadn't but knew that I should have been. She nursed the conversation along, apparently not the least dismayed by my minimal responses, filling in with little stories about her childhood somewhere in the green shires, and rebel escapades in her hated boarding school. Sitting close by this completely composed lady and trying to find responses which wouldn't come while managing my tea-cup and muffin plate, I knew I had failed the conversation test. And me from a family where everyone, myself included, competed noisily for conversational space. I was, as the Australians say, duchessed. I imagined that my patron-elect could hardly wait to send me on my way back to Belsize Park station, Whitechapel and her good friend, my mother.

Not a bit of it. When the tea things were cleared she turned to me.

'I'd like to show you some of my paintings. I've been trying out some new ideas. Would you like that?'

Well, you can't really refuse, can you? She permitted herself a tiny laugh from far down her throat. Another test now, I thought.

She brought into the room one of those huge artists' folders, untied the bows and began turning over the poster-size paintings one by one, very slowly. They were all on bright red matt paper and consisted of very avant-garde black whirls and twirls, twists and turns. I began slowly to realize that incorporated into each one and only just detectable was a black, very stylised, hammer and sickle. She sat there coolly turning the sheets and glancing up at me from time to time. I knew, of course, that some kind of bright perceptive remark was expected of me and I knew just as certainly that I had absolutely nothing to say. If she had been turning over the Mona Lisa, the Laughing Cavalier or the Stag at Bay I wouldn't have had anything to say either because I had no painting talk whatsoever. My silence was the more total because I actually thought in a kind of philistine way that the paintings were indecipherable rubbish and no more than the self-indulgence of an eccentric with too much time on her hands. This phase of the visit reduced me to such dumb misery that I had no thought but to count the minutes before I would be able to go.

So I failed. I know that, and that all my far-fetched hopes had dissolved over those silly paintings. But why do I recall that occasion so vividly that with the greatest of ease I can summon up that room and my excruciations in it? Humiliations bite deep and are terribly durable. But that's not it. I don't think I've mentioned that Beatrice Hastings was a very handsome woman and must have been a real beauty in her day. But when I had recovered from that wretched tea, young as I was, I realized that she was on her way down to join the has-beens. I admired her, might have loved her if she had been more accessible and, as *Zeider* had said, she was a comrade. So I was sad for her and even mourned her better times which I knew nothing about.

Beatrice Hastings was, however, no stranger to the Jewish world, having lived with the artist Amadeo Modigliani. She was also a model for him. She committed suicide in 1943.

A Necessary Myth

Cable Street revisited

This piece appeared in *Changing English,* 5 (1) in 1998.

> Nothing is more fully agreed than the certainty that memory fails. Memory
> fails, leaving blanks, and fails by filling blanks mistakenly … But memory
> also succeeds. It succeeds enormously and profoundly; for it is fundamental
> to human life, not to say synonymous with it.
>
> (Fields, 1989)

In an earlier issue of this journal I discussed autobiographical memory [the piece
is reprinted in this collection], a neglected topic, only recently given sustained
attention by a few psychologists (Rubin, 1986; Conway, 1990). By a happy accident
of sorts I can now supplement that with what I hope will be a useful addendum.
Before I do so, here is a reminder of the main propositions I advanced.

– Where and when we remember, the socio-cultural location, affects how we
remember.
– A so-called 'flashbulb' memory, supposedly the bright, perfectly remembered
moment, often turns out to be wrongly remembered and endowed with significance
after the event or even before it.

I wrote then:

> It is readily acknowledged and supported by copious evidence that there
> exists a class of memories which are particularly vivid; such memories,
> however, are not uniquely recorded. What makes them different is the high
> level of emotion which saturated the original experience and its meaning
> in the life of the rememberer … they prove to be peculiarly resistant to
> change; they achieve a canonical form which seems to render them proof
> against amnesiac loss.

Halbwachs (1992) argued that all memory is in various ways collective memory, and
he was counterposing this to the prevailing view that autobiography is essentially
personal, emerging from the individual's psyche.

I was invited by Marxism 1997, an extensive programme of lectures and
discussions, to fill a slot entitled 'I was there', in which someone who had participated
in an event which the left perceives to be a significant part of its history gives his or her
testimony, brushing history against the grain, perhaps. The topic proposed for me was

Cable Street, or perhaps I should say 'Cable Street', for reasons which will emerge. I agreed without hesitation. I had lived with Cable Street buzzing in some corner of my head for 60 years. More than that, I had let it take flight on innumerable occasions in conversations of all kinds in which I used my story to make a political point, to polish my credentials, perhaps, or quite simply to put into words an experience which is encircled by a particular aura. There was, too, the fact that I had for years been interested in all kinds of autobiographical practices and in autobiographical memory. Here was an instance which was in many ways a paradigm case – a memory which had been verbalised by me up to this point only in spontaneous speech, which I was about to revisit in a particular form, an address in an auditorium, certainly spoken, but this time supported by very full notes. Lastly the Cable Street event is one which I cherish, though I am aware that it has undergone transformation over the years and that it is, supremely, a kind of memory that has been and still is shared by others. The intensely personal and the publicly acknowledged merge to make something that is indelibly recorded.

Cable Street is a red-letter day in the left-wing almanac that could teach us a lot about, first, how such occasions enter the consciousness as oppositional memory; second, what happens to such memories over time as intervening history puts a different gloss on them; third, what, if anything, we do with them. A short while before I gave my talk I read a newly published book, *Children of the Revolution* (Cohen, 1997), which is a compilation of autobiographical pieces. These were recollections of growing up in communist families. The title of the book itself tells us something about how the lexicon of the left requires its own little dictionary. None of the families in the book were, in fact, involved in a revolution, but, as they would have seen it, they were part of The Revolution: a very different matter, indeed, a sustained process which would ultimately lead to a radical transformation of society. One of the writers, Pat Divine, says, 'My father was the East London organiser of the party at the time of Cable Street'. Another, Jude Bloomfield, says, 'My father was a steward on the famous Cable Street march'. Neither of these writers thinks it necessary to explain what Cable Street was. Each confidently assumes that half a century after the event most readers of the book will get the reference which is enough to confer militant credentials on their fathers, especially as these comments are made *en passant*. One of them gets it a bit wrong: Cable Street was not a march but a blockade.

In the year before the 'I was there' talk I went to a commemoration of the Cable Street events at Gardiners Corner, because it was there on 4 October 1936 that a huge crowd had assembled to bar the way to Mosley's British Union of Fascists, who were proposing to march along the Jewish East End's major thoroughfare, Whitechapel Road: a blatant provocation. Gardiners Corner, therefore, was the proper assembly point for a commemoration meeting and march, 60 years after the event. Strangely, I remember asking myself for the very first time what should have been an obvious question. Why do we call it Cable Street? After all, the decisive happening was the gathering of a vast crowd at Gardiners Corner, where they solidly blocked five important roads which converged on a large open space. The answer seemed obvious to me once I had asked the question. It was in Cable Street that a barricade was constructed. A barricade! That potent icon of urban revolution: 1848 across Europe, the Parisian Communards in 1871, the Russian Revolution. So then, the very choice of name was a crucial part of the creation of a myth in the particular sense that I am giving to that word.

I went to the 60th anniversary of Cable Street and joined the damp little gathering. After a few speeches, off we went and I retraced some of the topography of my childhood and adolescence – Commercial Road, Cannon Street Road and, yes, Cable Street. We passed the end of New Road, a hundred or so yards from what had been my home in Nelson Street. Sadly, but I suppose inevitably, it was a thin turn-out. Any little rave-up could attract a larger gathering. Those who had 'been there' were invited to take a place of honour at the head of the demo. It turned out to be a dozen of us at most. I know, just from my own circle, it could easily have been more. That's the way of it. Memories of events which are not nurtured by state panoply (army units, top clergy, establishment dignitaries, cathedral services) struggle for a niche in people's consciousness. Yet, as I've indicated, Cable Street is still a name to conjure with. Oral historians sometimes warn that if someone does not hurry along with a microphone in hand and interview a certain octogenarian a piece of history will die, which may well be true. But Cable Street still lives in the heads not only of people like me but of my relatively young audience. It has even found its way into the written record, into photos and film.

If you are lucky, there are moments in your life which are especially and uniquely illuminated. They stand out from the rest of your life as bright icons, huge representative symbols, which give meaning to how you have lived. This is why we purify such moments, polish them and, in our heads, play them over again and again. Cable Street was one of those moments for the left in the 1930s. We gave it a mythological and heroic dimension. Because we are short of such out-and-out victories, we badly needed those dynamic images.

I was 16 at the time and thoroughly demo-hardened from a very early age because I had grown up in a Jewish communist/socialist family. By Cable Street time I'd been on so many demos they were almost a way of life. Sometimes they were what they call these days 'a peaceful protest' and sometimes they were bloody confrontations. You could read from the faces of the police when you started out which would be which. Cable Street was bloody. I have wondered many times since precisely what demos are for. Do they make converts? When do they actually make a difference? Who takes notice? How do you measure success or failure? No doubt someone has analysed demos, done a sociology Ph.D. on the subject – 'The demonstration as a form of political action'. I have felt for a long time that whatever the declared function, the most important one is what it does for the participants –

showing the flag, enjoying the collectivity, savouring in a particular way the solidarity of the occasion. Solidarity, of course, was always a key word in the lexicon.

Cable Street was, however, intended to be a demo with a difference. We were not going to plod through the streets to demand something or other. Quite simply, we told ourselves, we were going to stop the Fascists. How? With our bodies, as it turned out. There had to be enough of us to cram the huge space at Gardiners Corner and the streets that converged on it to ensure that Mosley's Black Shirts would not be able to pass. '*No pasaran!*' they were saying in Spain.

As I remember it – have always remembered it – there were four of us, two couples, in fact, all close friends at 16, all at grammar schools, all Jewish. Two of that foursome still survive. Ask me by what precise social mechanism we arrived on the scene and I don't know the answer. Leaflets and posters perhaps, talk at home in my case, words exchanged in daily encounters. What I want, and perhaps need, to believe in order to keep the grandeur of the myth alive is that the East End was agog with it, that on everyone's lips was the news that Mosley was going to march and that we were going to stop him. Even the dozy Jewish authorities has roused themselves from their torpor, but only to pronounce that the Jewish people should stay at home and rebuff the Fascists with silent dignity. How often had we heard that from the old folk? 'Don't draw attention to yourselves. Don't make trouble. *Shtumm.*' This time they were only a bleat in the background.

By the time we arrived, a seething crowd had already assembled, packed more and more tightly in all five roads. Right in the very centre was a tram whose driver had deliberately abandoned it. We knew we weren't going to a picnic but we weren't sure what exactly we were going to. There were police everywhere. I paint them for myself now as all grim-faced and menacing. Demo participants know that strange amalgam of emotions on such occasions. At the beginning we were caught up in a wild sense of excitement laced with naïve optimism. This was going to be an instant victory. Kids that we were, we thought we were freely enrolled in a spontaneous uprising. We shouted slogans and raised our clenched fists. A carnivalesque moment.

Hardly more than a moment, though, for the police had decided they could batter a way through for Mosley with baton charge after baton charge. This ceaseless onslaught went on for what seems now like hours. The pattern was unchanging: mounted police hitting out indiscriminately and the foot police following up to arrest the wounded, some bloody-headed. My little group was not in the front line. We were – less heroically – some 20 rows back on the Aldgate East side, swept to and fro by the unpredictable surges in the crowd. The police were operating from a space they had cleared right in the middle of Gardiners Corner. I suspect I know that only from photos I've seen since. I want to believe now that there was not a moment in the confrontation when we thought the police would succeed in smashing a way through. Finally, they must have recognised this when they negotiated with Mosley and he agreed to drop his original grandiose plan. He accepted a humbling alternative – a march along a back-street route – Cable Street, in fact. Of course, we didn't know about that at the time.

Somehow the word got round, 'All to Cable Street'. For those interested in the texture of everyday political action or, as I am sure some would put it, 'mob behaviour', how does that happen? Who breathed it into our ears and how did they know? I have no visual or auditory memory of getting the message, but I know that I did because of what followed. When I tried to answer those questions, looking back over so many years, I have to answer that it was not, as I thought, some radical magic at work conjuring up a brilliant inexplicable communication system (spontaneity again), but that the Communist Party had mounted a flexible military operation, a predetermined strategy. What mattered to us then was that we knew if we wanted to be where the action was we had to get to Cable Street, and then the word had it that in Cable Street there was a barricade, the barricade that later became famous. If that can still intoxicate the left today, imagine how it drove us on with wild imaginings. There might even be someone with a red flag and a blood-stained bandage round his forehead. If this wasn't The Revolution, it was the next best thing. A rare glorious victory was unfolding. So we were off.

Our *naïveté* now strikes me as comic. We didn't even ask ourselves the crucial question: how do you make sure you're on the right side of the barricade? Being on the wrong side of the barricades is an old metaphor snatched from revolutionary history and used less glamorously to mean siding with the class enemy in contemporary disputes. That the old metaphor should take on a literal significance on the day is what strikes me as comic. Well, you can't stop a fellow demonstrator and ask, 'What's the best way to our side of the barricade, comrade?', even if you perceived it as a problem, which we didn't. Remember, I knew Cable Street very well, ever since my communist mother had dragged me as a very small boy to branch meetings in a shabby room reached across a dank yard in Cable Street.

Two of us, my girlfriend and I, made our way to the barricade. And there it was, on our left. We hugged ourselves. An alien historic structure had become naturalised. Once again, we assumed that the righteous indignation of the masses had conjured it into being. Some folk had even overturned a lorry and consolidated the barricade with assorted junk. Intoxicated by the wonder of it, it took us a moment or two to realise that we were indeed in an absurd predicament. We had just enough time to take in the fact that to our right a row of mounted police filled the street from side to side and were just starting to trot, as a preliminary to the actual charge. We were stranded in front of some very small terraced houses which gave straight on to the pavement. Terrified, we pressed ourselves into a shallow doorway, hoping that the charge would sweep past us. The heroic version wasn't supposed to be like this. Suddenly the door behind us opened, hands grabbed us and pulled us inside.

That's really the end of my story because I recall nothing of what happened after that. The rescuing hands inscribed the last line, the perfect closure, my sense of an ending. I remember nothing of our talk with our rescuers, nothing of how and when we emerged, nothing of how we finally learned that we had won or what we did to celebrate.

That is how Cable Street took shape in my head through numerous informal tellings. Now it was being re-formed in a talk to a large and totally left-wing audience, whose presence, needless to say, was reshaping my story. Finally, there is this written prose version.

Let me now stand back from those versions and the satisfactions and perhaps self-indulgent pleasures that I have derived from them and see whether there is something to learn from them. All memory is inherently revisionist, as Freud put it, and, as Samuel and Thompson (1990) write:

> Memory requires a radical simplification of its subject matter. All recollections are told from a standpoint in the present. In telling they need to make sense of the past. That demands a selecting, ordering, and simplifying, a construction of a coherent narrative whose logic works to draw the life story towards the fable.

A short while after I had given my talk, I met one of the foursome who, in my version, went together to Gardiners Corner, and she told me very firmly that I was wrong. She and her boyfriend (later her husband) were indeed there but not with us. This accounts for the fact that by the time of the barricade episode there were only two of us. It seems a trivial error now, but I do not think it was. The foursome for me is an important part of the myth. We remained life-long socialist friends, and our mythic presence is about the shared excitements of being young and collectively enrolled in the purity of the Good Old Cause. I needed to insert that enduring foursome as a significant little group, separate from, but part of, that epic gathering. As I have noted, my memory tells me that at the time I was euphoric with what I felt was the spontaneity of the coming together of that vast crowd. I did not have an inkling that it was a highly organised affair and that the Communist Party had set up a command post from which it did its best to conduct the battle. It even had its own intelligence service. Years and years later I learned that a certain Hugh Faulkner was a plant in Mosley's HQ and that he was able to channel vital information as the day unfolded. I met him as a fellow student at University College London, and naturally he never breathed a word about his dangerous mission. The tram at a standstill in the midst of the battle has become, inevitably, a glittering object in most accounts, both in its bright specificity and in the elevation of the driver's bold act of solidarity. Dave Renton, who has researched these events, tells me that he has met numerous people, each of whom claims to be the one who persuaded the driver to leave the tram!

Whatever else in my story changed over the years, it always stopped at the identical point: the anonymous hands pulling us into the shelter of the little terraced house. A constructed narrative is designed to deliver meaning, and a dramatic closure is a crucial part of the process. My podium telling, which is very much what I have written here, was a new version. It embodies for the first time post-event awarenesses, which have not hitherto been incorporated and which derive from some years of study of autobiographical memory and its mythological propensities. I must stress that I do not mean by this that I have so far transformed, rearranged and inflated Cable Street as to have distorted it out of its real significance and in defiance of what is now well-established knowledge of what happened on that day. However, what it used to be in my settled canonical form was a tale from a mythical golden age of antifascist militancy, untarnished by shabbiness and opportunism. The rescuing hands, my own story, were my own symbol of solidarity, but they belonged beyond doubt alongside the tram driver, who was everybody's story. Cable Street happened, and thousands of ordinary folk did actually stop a fascist march from taking place in an unprecedented manner: the East End was never the same again. It was a time when the shadow of fascism hung over the whole of Europe.

Jean Peneff (1990), studying myth in life-stories, warns oral historians to be highly sceptical:

> The life-story can be a way of excusing ourselves in public, an effective means of building an enhanced self-image.

and

> ... by concentrating the story on the occupation of a factory, the celebration, or the meeting, the narrators turn their eyes away from what goes on behind the scenes.

Peneff is at the extreme pole of scepticism (for instance, 'We all to a greater or lesser extent falsify our social origins'!). She does not acknowledge that the storyteller may in fact not know what went on behind the scenes, which was the case in my story. She goes on to say that autobiography is one way in which we convince ourselves

> ... that the commitment, with all that lost time and energy, had a meaning, either individual – in the building of an interesting life – or collective; that history has a meaning. In the myth the trials are reversed: lost strikes become victories, failures only temporary and meaningful for the future.

I find it strange that Peneff does not see that mythical versions have their own kind of truth and that past commitments may indeed have the meaning which tellers believe them to have. Elizabeth Tonkin (1990), writing in the same volume, looks at the mythical element in our stories of personal experience in a quite different, even opposed, manner.

> Myth is a representation of the past which historians recognise, but generally as an alternative to proper history. All understandings of the past

affect the present. Literate or illiterate, we are our memories. We try to shape our futures in the light of past experiences – or what we understand to have been past experiences – and representing how things were, we draw a social portrait which is a reference list of what to follow and what to avoid. The model is part of the processes we live in and call 'groups', 'institutions' and 'society' and it helps to reproduce or modify them.

One of the key turning points in my thinking about autobiography was provided by *The Myths We Live By* (Samuel and Thompson [eds.], 1990), and in particular by the editors' introduction. I owe much of my present understanding of the Cable Street story to their volume. It taught me the many ways in which stories of our pasts are to a greater or lesser extent myths. It also represented a turning point for oral historians in the way they regarded the materials they collected.

> When we listen now to a life-story, the manner of its telling seems to us as important as what is told … it has also brought a new and much broader potential. As soon as we recognise the value of the subjective in individual testimonies we challenge the accepted categories of history. We reintroduce the emotionality, the fears and fantasies carried by the metaphors of memory, which historians have been so anxious to write out of their accounts … each individual story draws on a common culture: a defiance of the rigid categorisation of private and public, just as of memory and reality.

All students of autobiography draw attention to its fictive features, but Samuel and Thompson, in presenting a rich and challenging way of looking at oral memory, are at pains to insist that they are not working with memories of a false past, that much of what is delivered in oral testimony, especially its rich detail, 'remains objectively valid, sometimes demonstrably so from other sources'. Oral memory, they go on to claim, has a double validity, in which 'myth was embedded in real experience: both growing from it and helping to shape its perception'. I now see the Cable Street story in this light. I am sure that there have been and still are thousands of stories of Cable Street in circulation which each express a participant's necessary myth. Put them together, and collectively they express a larger necessary myth, magnifying an event which was a speck on the political map of 1936 into a decisive turning-point which, in a modest way, it was.

I have only this to add. Autobiographical practices in various guises have found their way into the curriculum at every level of education, chiefly through forms of 'changing English' from the 1960s onwards. The most innovative element has been the involvement of students in recording their own, their families' and their communities' memories. All this activity could now include considerations of the mythical elements in these stories. Everywhere there are Cable Streets in local memory, which need to be evoked, valued and scrutinised thoughtfully and positively.

References

Cohen, P. (1997) *Children of the Revolution*. London: Lawrence and Wishart.

Conway, M. (1990) *Autobiographical Memory*. Buckingham: Open University Press.

Fields, K. (1989) 'What one cannot remember mistakenly'. *Oral History Journal*, 17 (1).

Halbwachs, M. (1992) *Collective Memory*. Chicago: University of Chicago Press.

Peneff, J. (1990) 'Myths in life-stories', in R. Samuel and P. Thompson (eds.), *The Myths We Live By*. London: Routledge.

Rosen, H. (1996) 'Autobiographical memory'. *Changing English*, 3 (1).

Rubin, D. (1986) (ed.) *Autobiographical Memory*. Cambridge: Cambridge University Press.

Samuel, R. and Thompson, P. (eds.) (1990) *The Myths We Live By*. London: Routledge.

Tonkin, E. (1990) 'History and the myth of realism', in Samuel, R. and Thompson, P. (eds.), *The Myths We Live By*. London: Routledge.

Narrative in Intercultural Education

This paper appeared in the *European Journal of Cultural Studies,* 10 (3) in 1999.

1. Stories and intercultural awareness

When did you last hear a story? When did you last tell a story? Don't struggle to recollect. For if you stretch the concept of story wide enough to include any narrative, you will realise that it was a very short while ago indeed that you were involved with narrative. For we cannot engage in spontaneous conversation without resorting to some kind of narrative. Why?

Two white young men who had refused to pay their fares attacked a friend of ours, who is a black London bus conductor, on his bus. In our kitchen he told us, very calmly, what had happened. It is not a rare event for him. He did not rage against racism and prejudice; he did not make a speech about justice. He just told the story. Why that mode and not another?

An American professor friend of mine can, with the greatest of ease, tell dozens and dozens of Jewish stories. He tells them in English. Why are they Jewish stories? Bengali children in our schools can tell many stories of the evil and terrible Rakoshni or the savage Kuskur. Caribbean children can tell you stories of the clever and rascally monkey spider Anansi or of the frightening spirits called Duppies. Do white children have a living repertoire like that? Are the surviving remnants of that vast thesaurus of European folk tales a real equivalent? What's the difference?

Wherever we turn to examine narrative in its numerous forms, question after question will be thrown up. Apparently simple tales, anecdotes and personal accounts all belong in a narrative universe, which interrogates our assumptions about culture, cognition, language, communication, learning and teaching. I want to argue that stories have much greater significance in learning and teaching than we usually accord them in educational literature and programmes. It follows that we should appraise them as a potential resource in intercultural education. I am talking, you understand, of stories as a universal human practice. This takes us far away from canonised, officially approved prose fiction, which has for so long occupied a secure place in school curricula. It also takes us far away from sanitised, emasculated, safe versions of folk tales, which fill little books for infant classes. Dickens, Balzac and Thomas Mann must, of course, be included in any account of narrative. So must school versions of *Red Riding Hood* or *Beauty and the Beast.* But to understand narrative, it makes sense to begin with its most universal, commonplace, everyday manifestations. We are all storytellers and story-listeners and, in a flash, can be transformed from one into another. Stories would continue their flourishing lives if schools ignored them, if there were no university departments of literary studies, no publishers, or no species called novelist.

That wise and tantalising scholar, Michel de Certeau (1984), wrote: 'What the map cuts up, the story cuts across.'

Like illicit travellers, stories, it seems, ignore national and regional boundaries, by slipping across frontiers. The invitation seems irresistible. Such material appears perfectly designed for any programme of intercultural education. But, as we have learned to our cost, the crossing of cultural frontiers is not a painless and untroubled journey. Yes, it is true that many stories are citizens of the world, and they laugh at customs barriers, border police, passport regulations and the immigration authorities. *Cinderella, Cendrillon, Aschenputtel* provide the classic case. Researchers have found a written Chinese version dating back to the ninth century AD, though the extreme smallness of foot, which is made such a point of in the story, clearly has lost its significance. Small wonder then that Roland Barthes (1983) could write:

> All classes, all human groups, have their narratives, enjoyment of which is very often shared by men [sic] with different and opposing cultural backgrounds. Caring nothing for the difference between good and bad literature, narrative is international, transhistorical, and transcultural: it is simply there, like life itself.

We can all cite a thousand examples to confirm that picture. But that is too simple. We need to understand better what happens to stories when they travel, when a story from one culture finds itself in another. What do the new receivers make of it? What makes the diffusion of many folk stories an apparently easy process is firstly the common narrative structure shared by many stories of quite different provenance. Propp's (1928, trans. 1968) famous study, *Morphology of the Russian Folk Tale*, can be used to demonstrate this. Some would claim that such tales express universal themes, but we should be careful about drawing such a conclusion. For our purposes, we could acknowledge that the confrontation between the weak and the strong has been such an abiding force in human history that this common theme of folk tale comes very close to universality. There are others. But notice that the characteristics I have been pointing to, so far from suggesting that narrative is ready-made material for introducing other cultures, suggest quite the opposite. A few days ago, I told an African story to a class of primary-school children. I told it partly because it ends with a moral-riddle, which I knew they would want to solve. I repeat, it was an African story, set in a timeless African village on the edge of a desert. I can say with confidence that it added nothing to the children's awareness of African culture. We tell stories from *The Thousand and One Nights* to children and, at best, they give only fleeting glimpses of Persian or Arabian culture. At worst, they contribute to a stereotype of the Middle Eastern world. Because stories travel so well, they are easily incorporated into children's narrative culture, filled as it is with exotic images, characters from other times, other worlds or no worlds at all, and all the trappings of demonology and magic. The djinns, sultans, emirs can be set alongside princes, witches and fairies with no tension at all. Suppose a story told to a class begins, 'A long time ago in a city on the coast of China there was a rich merchant … ' Suppose further that in that class there are several children whose parents come from Hong Kong. There is no reason to suppose that those children necessarily perceive this to be part of their culture, nor for anyone else in the room to do so, including the teacher. Stories do not arrive in a package complete with their cultural context and ethnic origins. Another context slides easily into place. Unless stories are mediated in particular ways, there may be nothing intercultural about transcultural stories. I shall return to the question of mediation later. For the moment, to summarise, let me put this axiomatically: *Transcultural narrative is not* ipso facto *intercultural narrative.*

There is another difficulty from the opposite direction. There are stories which, in one way or another, do not travel well. Firstly, they may be culturally incomprehensible or obscure, being too dependent on specific cultural meanings or on narrative traditions different from our own. The two anthropologists Scollon and Scollon (1981) analyse in great detail Athabaskan (i.e. Alaskan and North Canadian) stories, and they demonstrate why they are incomprehensible or simply irritating for an English speaker. Whereas in English (perhaps European?) narrative tradition:

> actions are explained, evaluated and motivated by the text in advance of their description, and follow as the logical implications of pre-existing values and ideas, in Athabaskan, narrative actions are presented directly and as much as possible without interpretation. Further explanation and motivation are added where called for by the audience.

Translation, say the Scollons, is therefore particularly difficult. In many stories, we may not know what cultural features are eluding us. Here is an extract from an oral story collected by Michael Murphy (1975) in Ireland. The whole story consists of verbal duelling between a peasant woman and a student priest in which the woman comes out on top.

> … who comes walking up this road but this student – damn me if I can say for truth now whether he was going on for a priest or a parson, but one or the other. He got to talkin' to this old woman anyhow and says she: 'Would you be a hatter from County Down come to buy wool?' Damn but I mind now he was going on for a priest. For he smelt bacon frying above in her house. Says he to her: 'Do you know what day it is?' 'Why,' says she, 'what day do you make it?' 'Friday,' says he, 'and yous are frying. Do you

> not know that Christ died for you on a Friday?' 'And do you tell me,' says
> she, 'that that man is dead? Sure up here John or me never hears a thing.'

It is possible to enjoy the story and take delight in the uneducated woman verbally outwitting the student priest, but for those outside the Catholic and, more particularly, the Irish-Catholic culture it must inevitably lose much of its force. Remember Cinderella's tiny feet. My second axiom is then: *Many narratives will not cross cultural boundaries without some negotiation* (perhaps not even then!).

I recall a Nigerian storyteller pausing in his narration to tell his English listeners what gourds are and how they are used.

Cultural dissonance can be experienced in many ways. I myself encountered this repeatedly in my school and university days. In my teens, I had chosen naively to study English language and literature. Until the age of 19, I lived in London's Jewish ghetto. Perhaps my choice of study was one way of indicating that I would go quietly and give no trouble to the police and quote Shakespeare rather than Sholom Aleichem. At school, I was repeatedly confused, baffled and alienated by a totally opaque Anglo-Christian universe. A pervasive allusiveness – references, images, assumptions, citations and the taken-for-granted of a Christian world – permeated the literature we studied. This was not only a matter of my ignorance; the very attempt to overcome it filled me with a sense of betrayal. Worse, much, much worse, was meeting the thread of anti-Semitism which weaves its way through the literature. I sat in a class where we were studying Chaucer's *The Prioress's Tale*, the story of little Hugh innocently walking through the Jewish ghetto of Lincoln singing *'O alma redemptoris mater'*. He is subsequently ritually murdered by the Jews. Our teacher inducted us into an awareness of the literary perfection of the story. He was oblivious to (or at least silent about) the seething rage inside me. More significant perhaps was my silence, for there was much that I could have said. There are classes today which are full of children who are Muslims, Hindus, Buddhists, etc. and who must be undergoing very similar experiences as they encounter the assumptions and racism which disfigure the narrative repertoire of our schools. The very universality of the narrative mode is ironically a guarantee that this will be so. Therefore my third axiom is: *While narratives may cross cultural boundaries, they may at the same time be culturally oppressive, offensive and threatening.*

I should add at this point that, even across communities sharing the same religion, there might be an unsuspected clash of cultural values. Shirley Brice Heath's book *Ways with Words* (1983) is an ethnographic study of two working-class communities in Carolina, USA; one is white, the other black, and they are only a few miles apart. She observes that in both communities people spend a lot of time telling stories, but that the judgement of what makes a good story is quite different. In Roadville (white), stories must be explicitly didactic with a clear moral. Children offering accounts of personal experience must be very scrupulous with the facts and again draw a moral from that experience. In Trackton (black), the expectation is that the storyteller will be highly creative when recounting real events. He or she must above all be entertaining, by presenting life in an exaggerated form. In Trackton, what they call a 'true story' would seem to a Roadville resident to be anything but true. In contrast, neither Roadville's factual accounts, nor tales from the Bible, would be thought of as stories in Trackton … Heath concludes: 'In short, for Roadville, Trackton's stories would be lies: for Trackton, Roadville's stories would not even count as stories.' [Harold's review of the book in reprinted in this collection.]

2. Narrative and its potential for intercultural communication

I have been trying to emphasise, as must be obvious by now, that an intercultural approach to narrative must be created with a full awareness that it is more than a simple matter of ensuring that there is a rich provision in schools of stories of diverse cultural origins. I want now to shift the focus entirely in order to make clear why narrative has the potential to be the supreme mode for intercultural communication. Whatever cultural obstacles we may find in specific stories, it is helpful to begin by thinking of narrative as a function of the mind; indeed, a central, persistent, ineradicable function. It is nothing less than a universal cognitive resource, a means by which we endow experience with meaning. For every story that we actually tell, there are thousands that are articulated only in our heads. We tell ourselves, and perhaps no one else, what has happened, what might happen, what our desires would like to have happen. We retell what others have told us. We dream in narrative.

Vygotsky (1962) taught us to take account of inner speech as a major cognitive resource. We could elaborate this by adding that much inner speech is conducted through dramatic narrative. Just as he suggests that inner speech can only develop after the development of socialised speech, so we can say that inner narrative can only be developed after the experience of participating in socialised narrative. In wider terms, Bakhtin (1981) proposed that we think in the genres we have learned in spoken social interaction. I suspect that most of us make meaningful for ourselves the high abstractions we encounter by converting them into inner narrative. And as Bruner (1986) writes,

> Scientists … rely on familiar stories to fill gaps in their knowledge. But their salvation is to wash the stories away when causes can be substituted for them.

We might remind those disposed to relegate narrative to some lower order of thinking and discourse that the composition of even the simplest story is a complex matter. Suppose I compose a brief anecdote, the spoken recollection of a recent personal experience. In the telling, I must transform the raw material; the events will not tell themselves. From the continuous and unstoppable flow of events, I must construct a story. I must seize hold of just that sequence of events that is right for my story. It must be dissected out of life itself. Something must be transformed into a beginning; something else into an end. Personae must be inscribed by some means, endowed with purposes – all by means of a selective process, which cuts away from the original experience everything that does not serve my end. I must give point to this framing and controlling process. The irrelevant must drop away like chips from a sculptor's chisel. I must do more than this. I must adopt a stance towards events. I must win the attention of my audience and keep it. The Russian Formalists set us on the road to these considerations when they began to analyse the difference between what they called *sujhet* (the actual events covered in a story) and *fabula* (the way the events are enunciated in the story or the actual process of narration). The simple truth is that we can all do this. We can all cooperate these complex principles and, what is more, can start to do so when we are very young. What principle is at work here? Oliver Sachs (1986), the eminent neurologist, assembled in *The Man who Mistook his Wife for a Hat* a set of 'human clinical tales'. 'What facts! What fables!' he says. One of them concerns Rebecca, a declared moron with an IQ of 60 and with gross perceptual and spatio-temporal problems. Sachs notices her frequent use of poetic language and her love of stories.

> But what was the composing principle that could allow her composure (clearly it was something other than schematic). I found myself thinking of her fondness for tales, for narrative composition and coherence. Is it possible, I wondered, that this being before me – at once a charming girl and a moron, a cognitive mishap – can *use* a narrative … to compose and integrate a coherent world?

The goal of composing and integrating a coherent world seems to me a high aspiration for intercultural education, though this does not mean a harmonious or idyllic world that is free from conflict, from contradictions and every form of violence. The power of narrative to give coherence to the world as it is lived and by implication how it might be lived is, as far as we can tell, universal. It is by virtue of its deep roots in human thought *the most accessible genre*. Let me mention here the London Narrative Group, a group of teachers who worked together from the mid-1980s until the early 1990s in schools, most of which had a multi-ethnic population. The pupils' narratives, both spoken and written, which we analysed and discussed, revealed in dramatic ways that, when a narrative culture is created in the classroom and children are accorded genuine speaking rights, they demonstrate and deploy linguistic resources which their teachers did not dream they possessed. Let me list certain observations made by the group.

1. The retelling of stories is a creative act of learning. This emerges with particular force when two languages are involved, e.g. when a story which a pupil knows in Greek is told by him or her in English.

2. Children can collaborate in the translation of stories and the production of dual texts.
3. Children change stories so that their own values and cultural standpoint can be incorporated.
4. Children bring into the classroom stories told to them by parents and grandparents.
5. A dramatic recent experience reveals new possibilities. A severely deaf child with (naturally) severe learning problems followed with pleasure and success the telling of a story and retold it to her mother at home.

It is becoming increasingly clear to us that, in multi-ethnic classes, the retelling of stories by pupils and teachers is multifunctional. Members of the group see it as central to all language development, including at the secondary-school phase. Teachers and pupils have become storytellers. One member has found all this to be true of adult second-language learners (see below).

3. Narrative as a mode of thought

I have digressed somewhat because I wish to indicate some relationship between narrative and our intercultural theme. I want to return to the idea that narrative is a mode of thought. Jerome Bruner (1986), in his book *Actual Minds, Possible Worlds*, devotes a chapter to this very idea and summarises his position like this:

> There are two modes of cognitive functioning, two modes of thought, each providing distinctive ways of ordering experience, of constructing reality. The two (though complementary) are irreducible to one another. Efforts to reduce one mode to the other or to ignore one at the expense of the other fail to capture the rich diversity of human thought.

These two modes he calls paradigmatic (i.e. logico-scientific) and narrative. Although Bruner seems largely concerned with great prose fiction, much of what he says applies to all narrative, including oral narrative. For instance, when talking of the reader, he proposes a kind of active engagement with the text. We can easily substitute 'listeners' for 'readers' in the following passage.

> As our readers read, as they begin to construct a virtual text of their own, it is as if they were embarking on a journey without maps – and yet they possess a stock of maps that might give hints, and besides, they know a lot about journeys and map-making. First impressions of the new terrain are, of course, based on older journeys already taken.

In narrative theory, this is known as *intertextuality*, which not only accounts for why stories are as they are, but also why readers and listeners construe their meanings in the ways they do. Standing behind each story is a huge collection of stories already encountered. When Bruner speaks of a stock of narrative maps, we should recollect that, though we all have such a stock, the stock differs from culture to culture. Storytellers from an Afro-Caribbean culture have a stock of oral narrative maps available to them when they are telling stories which are not traditional. Later in his book, when dealing with what he calls the language of education, Bruner puts forward some propositions about culture, and it is a great pity that he did not integrate his ideas about narrative with his idea about culture. Culture, he says,

> … is constantly in process of being recreated as it is interpreted and renegotiated by its members. In this view a culture is as much a forum for negotiating meaning and explicating action as it is a set of rules or specifications for action … It is the forum aspect of a culture that gives its participants a role in constantly making and remaking the culture – an active role as participants.

Therefore, he argues, schools must be part of this forum-like culture-creating, and the language of schools must not be the so-called 'uncontaminated language of fact and objectivity'. This is exactly the point! And we know too well how many classrooms bear not the slightest resemblance to a forum. Narrative culture in the classroom can be made such a forum, NOT by a simple recitation of the time-honoured tales, NOR by poring over hallowed masterpieces with all the archaeological practices borrowed from classical studies, NOR by embalming stories in the oil of bogus moral values. There is a quite different, time-honoured practice which we can take from the secular world outside schools: that is, the reworking of narratives by pupils who can refashion them to their own meanings, influenced by the mobile and diverse culture which they are both making and living. The narratives of the classroom must not be fossils or holy relics of the past presented as inviolable or represented as *the* culture of the pupils, who may not recognise it as their own. All narrative is there to be hotly debated, perhaps by means of another narrative; the context may have to be unearthed. When do you tell these stories in Nigeria? In Iran? In Trinidad? All stories are there to be challenged and changed. What does a little Indian girl make of the Ramayana here and now? How does a story about then become a story about now? I had some little Bangladeshi boys and girls retell a folk story from Italo Calvino's collection. Two shy little girls in their versions changed the heroic central figure from a young man to a resourceful young woman. What do we make of that?

> The operational models of popular culture cannot be confined to the past, the countryside or primitive peoples. They exist in the heart of the strongholds of contemporary culture.

> (de Certeau, 1954)

4. Children and adults as storytellers

It remains to be emphasised that though most children, if given the chance, can become highly competent storytellers, some are now the inheritors of a still-living oral tradition: in their newly established communities, the practice of oral storytelling either in or outside the home still goes on. It is clear from the ease with which it is possible to collect Anansi stories from pupils of Caribbean origin or Nasreddin stories from pupils from the Arab Mediterranean that, for the time being at least, the oral tradition survives in its new setting. Such stories do carry a direct intercultural meaning, for the tellers often adopt an ethnic style in the retelling. Caribbean stories, for example, cry out for the use of patois and an amazing repertoire of paralinguistic devices, which declare unambiguously the cultural identity of the storytellers. A pupil bringing into the classroom a story which he or she has acquired at home, and also bringing the story of its acquisition, constitutes a qualitatively different act from plucking the same story off the printed page.

By implication at least, I have been talking about stories that are acquired by storytellers from books, oral retellings, reminiscences by members of their families. To confine ourselves to such stories would be to miss the significance of narrative in our lives. Narrative does not only arrive ready made or immediately perceived as a fiction. Narratives of that kind grow from the soil of everyday interactions in which they constitute communicative acts of different kinds. Some are merely embryonic and others become transformed into stories in their own right when a speaker captures conversational space, and by his or her narrative authority is permitted more than the usual ration of time. The stories that insinuate themselves into the practices of everyday talk are a means by which people transmit (or partly conceal) their identity; they show how people understand the world; they display their values and feelings. Taken all together, we are the stories we tell and could tell. By telling stories, we offer our identities to one another. In interethnic communication, stories take on a special significance.

Let us look at one such spontaneous narrative. The occasion, to put it briefly, is a small gathering of five people in an Afro-Caribbean club. Four of them are black and one is a white researcher, David Sutcliffe. The black people are talking about their attitudes to white people and the conversation becomes very heated and noisy. They are trying to decide whether they too are prejudiced. At this point Miriam intervenes as follows: 'Well there's a lot you could say about this sort of thing.'

This is her way of signalling that she is about to challenge for conversational space, and she succeeds. Notice that this narrative is her mode of contributing to the debate. She utilises her story as a powerful form of argument.

Well, there's a lot you could say about this sort of thing. Because, I mean, for instance, this, em, boy who seems to be very unlucky with his chosen white girl, he's been going out with a girl, an English girl, for three years. He's been going to the girl's parents' home and they accept him.

Oh well it was all right – they were only young. But when they got to eighteen – of course I didn't even care to know the parents, did I? *(ironic?)* When they got to eighteen, one morning there was a knock on my door; (I had) just got into bed. And, mm, by the time I got downstairs, there was this woman turning back from the door. So I called to her and she turned back. And she introduced herself. She was of course my son's girlfriend's mother. And she called to get to know me, because she didn't know me after going out with – her daughter going out with my son for three years. She just lived round the corner to me anyway. And what she called to say to me: *(mimics)* 'Did Andy tell you anything this morning?' I said: 'Anything about what?' Well I was at work the night before, and when I got home Boy had gone to work. So I said no. And she was crying tears, and she said: 'Well, we had such a row at home last night because my husband and I, we just can't get on with each other any more. Because mm – my husband is annoyed with our daughter going out with your son. Because they are getting older and they might decide to get married. And if they have children the children are going to be half-castes.' I say *(hard voice)* 'And you wait three years to say that? You didn't see what colour my son was when he was coming to your home over *three years*?!' And if they have children and they don't want half-caste children – I say, 'Listen love, your daughter is going to have them, and you don't want them – I don't want them either (laughter). I've already warned my son not to come home pregnant (laughter).'

That should give us a glimpse of the potentiality of personal testimony in the classroom where racism can be talked about and confronted.

5. Bilingualism and intercultural narrative

The most fertile ground for intercultural narrative is the bilingual situation. Mike Baynham (1986), who works with adult second-language learners, found that the most promising learning resource was a bilingual use of different kinds of narrative. In his paper he has given a detailed account of a protracted sequence of work with one class. I can only give a compressed version of one portion of it.

The teacher began by having the class read a story by Stephen Leacock in which the hero attempts to open a bank account. At first he is treated by the bank manager as someone of importance but, when it turns out that he has only a very small sum to deposit, he is humiliated by being sent off contemptuously to a counter clerk. The students then discussed their own experiences of embarrassment and humiliation and how people are judged by appearances. At one point Manejieh, as a contribution to the discussion, told the story of Mullah Nasreddin at the party. The teacher suggested that she should write down the story. This is her version.

> One day Molla-Nasraddin was invited to a party, he went to the party without changing his ordinary clothes, but the receptionist stopped him to go there, and told him he couldn't go while he is wearing ragged clothes but he rushed back home and changed his clothes to the best clothes ever he had.
>
> He came backed to the party everyone bowed at him, and offered him nice place to sit down.
>
> It was time for dinner; they served best food, but Molla instead of eating the food he was putting the food in his sleeves.
>
> Everyone was astonished, what he was doing, probably they thought he was mad. Somebody asked him why is feeding his clothes.
>
> He said I am hear because of my clothes.

The teacher then photocopied the text and worked with the class at improving it, not only the grammar and spelling but also more elusive things such as the punch line. A second version by the whole class then emerged.

Mullah Nasreddin and the Party

> One day Mullah Nasreddin was invited to a party. He went to the party without changing out of his ordinary clothes. When he arrived at the party the doorman stopped him from going in.
>
> 'You can't come in here wearing ragged clothes like that,' he said. So Mullah Nasreddin rushed back home and changed his clothes. He put on the smartest clothes he had. Then he hurried back to the party. Everyone bowed at him when he arrived and offered him a nice place to sit down.
>
> It was time for dinner. They served the best food. But Mullah, instead of eating the food, started putting the food in his sleeves. Everyone was astonished. What was he doing? They thought he was mad.
>
> Then somebody asked him: 'Why are you putting food in your sleeves?'
>
> And Mullah said: 'My clothes have been invited to the party, not me. So I am feeding them.'

Manejieh was satisfied with this version. It had by now gone through a number of transformations: out of its original context of the Iranian language and culture, to be told orally to a mixed audience of English, Spanish and Iranian people; into its first written form; and thence to its final written form. I felt that there might be one more stage: a bilingual version for use with newly arrived Iranian students. Manejieh wrote a Farsi version and, finally, the two versions were put together in a booklet.

One classroom, one story, one story of a story. An epitome of how a narrative, springing spontaneously into the give-and-take of discussion, can serve as a model, infinitely adaptable, of the intercultural possibilities of many kinds of narrative.

References

Bakhtin, M. (1981) *The Dialogic Imagination: Four essays* (C. Emerson and M. Holquist, trans.). Austin: University of Texas Press.

Barthes, R. (1983) 'Introduction to the structural analysis of narratives', in S. Sontag (ed.), *Barthes*. London: Fontana.

Baynham, M. (1986) 'Bilingual folk stories in the ESL classroom'. *ELT Journal*, 40 (2).

Bruner, J. (1986) *Actual Minds, Possible Worlds*. Cambridge, MA: Harvard University Press.

de Certeau, M. (1984) *The Practice of Everyday Life*. Berkeley, CA: University of California Press.

Heath, S. (1983) *Ways with Words*. Cambridge: Cambridge University Press.

Murphy. M. (1975) *Now You're Talking*. Dundonald: Blackstaff Press.

Propp, V. (1928) (L. Scott, trans., 1968) *The Morphology of the Folktale*. Columbus, OH: American Folklore Society and Bloomington, IN: Indiana University.

Sachs, O. (1986) *The Man who Mistook his Wife for a Hat*. London: Picador.

Scollon, R. and Scollon, S. (1981) *Narrative, Literacy and Face in Interethnic Communication*. Norwood, NJ: Ablex.

Vygotsky, L. (1962) *Thought and Language*. Cambridge, MA: MIT Press.

Ending

Harold in the uniform of the U.S. Army

Bell-pulls at The Adlon

I stayed in a hotel in Berlin, the remains after bombing of what I discovered had been a famous international hotel, The Adlon, all marble and *fin-de-siècle*. The bathroom was vast and had a row of curlicue gilt and porcelain bell-handles each with its label. In theory you could summon any specialized flunkey you wished. I thought the most practical was *Dienstmädchen* ('serving maid' or 'wench', perhaps). Tried it – no one came. Life is full of such irritating little disappointments. Wasn't prepared to scrub my back without help so I abandoned all plans to bathe and went back to the preserve-the-natural-oils routine. In fact, the team capable of responding to bell-pulls consisted of tired old waiters left over from before the war – thin grey Pinter-men who wouldn't and couldn't drag themselves upstairs. So I looked out of the window at the shattered gun-emplacements in the rubble and the Russian soldiers stroking their automatics at the Brandenburger Tor, and wondered yet again how the hell I'd ended up there.

In a letter to Betty, February 1977

The Dinosaur and the Professor

Some little girls were making daisy chains, smiling their way amongst the gravelly graves of Russian soldiers hastily buried in the thin strip of park close by Irmgard Strasse where I had just been stationed. The graves, scattered to the point of randomness, were those of the very last casualties of the battle of Berlin. Over each was a wooden red star nailed to a short wooden stake with a name painted on it. In that first post-war late summer the paint was already flaking. The little girls danced away, carefully skirting the graves. I stopped on the path.

Frau Somebody stopped on the path beside me. Suddenly she burst out, 'Barbarians! Barbarians! No crosses. What a way to bury the dead!'

I looked at the indignant German woman. So much I might have said. About barbarians, for instance, or ways of disposing of the dead, but I took my words and my anger away with me through the once genteel suburb of Zehlendorf, past the tank turrets sunk at crossroads, taking in the acrid smell of brown coal from thousands of improvised stoves somewhere in the rubble.

Once on an overcrowded underground train (they had started up again) I stood strap-hanging and a middle-aged man, seeing my uniform, stood up and deferentially offered me his seat. He seemed baffled by my impatient refusal. The others in the carriage watched and then looked at their feet.

And then there was that day when you could feel the arrival of winter and you started turning up your greatcoat collar. I stood on the platform of an underground station on the edge of the city. The line had taken Berliners out to the woods and lakes. It was crammed with people who had been collecting wood and had strapped bundles of logs and branches to their backs. The stronger ones carried prodigious quantities which jutted above their heads. They stood there silently waiting for the train. A little old man stood near me. He was bent double under his load, his grey pointed beard stuck out in front of him. He could have been a figure from a folk story, a woodcutter returning home from fuel gathering, but with one startling difference. His face was a strange yellowy-grey and his eyes were fixed in an unnatural gaze. He's going, I thought. At that moment he fell. I stepped forward and knelt beside him to unhitch his load and loosen his collar. His eyes rolled and he made a dry sound in his throat. 'He's finished,' I was sure. Not one of the other wood-gatherers moved or looked down. And the train came in. As though we were nothing more than an obstacle, they stepped over us and crammed into the train. Twenty minutes later the two of us caught the next one for by then the old man had struggled to his feet.

Later that year the first snows came. I had found my way to Invaliden Strasse in the Russian Sector and was making my way to the *Geologische und Palaeontologische Museum.* At least that's what my memory tells me it was called. The museum, with its huge Greek-column facade and pediment, you could recognise immediately as one of those European buildings which look like replicas of each other. It had taken some direct hits from bombs or shells but was still unmistakably what it was. All its columns were still standing but it was cocooned in silence. Not a soul was about even in Invaliden Strasse. I went slowly up the broad flight of steps, hugging my big brown paper parcel, and moved through powdery snow, two inches deep perhaps, towards the great doors. There was not a footprint in the snow but chunks of masonry showed through. The museum was defunct.

My mission with the parcel seemed so absurd, so improbable that I was inclined to turn round and make my way back to my billet. But I had a promise to keep and would at least be able to tell Nan that I had tried, even while cutting a ludicrous figure entering the dead *Museum* to look for Herr Professor Dietrich, an aged academic who might be anywhere in Germany or even long since dead and was certainly not going to be found in amongst the rubble and debris. Nan was the mother of David, my closest university friend, and I had over several years visited the house. His father was a university teacher, grimly dying of a brain tumour, in an armchair. In spite of this cloud the house was to me an exciting revelation. David's younger brother, later a brilliant physicist, sat like a sinister conspirator in the cellarage twiddling with his ham radio transmitter and conducting improbable conversations with fellow hams in unlikely places like Brazil and Hawaii. David himself kept snakes in cages in the garden and raved about their beauty. Of the feeding of them I will not speak. The house dazzled me with its books, Cooper's marmalade, Bath Olivers, and assorted university lefties who came there to talk soberly of the coming war or listen to classical music on the acoustic EMG gramophone. Nan herself was an historian and, despite her personal tragedy, had time to be very hospitable in her brusque way to two egocentric students. I had not met before a woman who'd been to Cambridge. What's more, that had been at the end of the First World War. One day, talking of Nazism, she told me that some time before Hitler took over she had spent a wonderful year in Berlin perfecting her German and pursuing her abiding interest in the Peasants' War. She had lived with a family who'd been very good to her, treated her like a daughter. Herr Professor Dietrich, the head of the household, was a gentle scholarly figure who always found time to help put some polish on her German. He took her round the museum where he worked and introduced her to Kathe Kollwitz's Peasants' War drawings.

And now there was Nan's letter. There was no exchange of pleasantries; just that she'd heard I was now stationed in Berlin and she knew that the order had gone out that Allied soldiers were not to fraternise (that was the word they used) with the Germans. In particular there was a ban on making gifts of any kind. Did I remember, she asked, her talking of Professor Dietrich? She would send a parcel of warm clothing directly to me. Would I seek out the old man and give it to him? There was just a chance that I might find him in the museum. Unlikely, she knew, but I must try.

Had she gone off her rocker? I wondered. She must have seen the newsreels of devastated Berlin. And what had the Professor been up to during the war? All the same, wasn't it just like Nan to send that parcel in defiance of officialdom and against all the odds to hope it would reach him? It was all of a piece with her collecting for an ambulance for the Republican side in the Spanish Civil War and running concerts for Basque orphan children.

Had the request come from anyone else I might have demurred. At the very least I might have checked out Professor Dietrich first. When the parcel arrived, in spite of some inner truculence, I set out for the museum. A lifetime of film-watching has made me see these moments as the opening shots of a continental film – the battered museum, the muffling layer of snow, the solitary uniformed figure ascending the steps clutching a shapeless parcel tied with string. Who is he? Where is everybody? What's in the parcel? When is this? Where is this? Does the body language suggest reluctance? And the building; was it a college? A seat of government? *Rathaus?* Museum? Will the young soldier go in or turn back?

No, I didn't turn back but went up to the big doors, pushed and entered what was a great exhibition hall. In the midst, defying probability, stood a vast, heroic dinosaur, its length stretching from one end to the other. The glass roof dome over it had shattered and scattered thousands of pieces of broken glass around its feet, mingling with the snow which had drifted in. Its head still craned forward but its vertebrae had collapsed and littered the ground beneath. I thought of its sibling in the Natural History Museum in London, still intact and with which I had been on friendly terms since childhood. The Germans in their miseries were still not ready to do the housework, sweep up and ready the poor dinosaur for restoration. Maybe the Professor somewhere was planning to collect the vertebrae into a neat pile, number them, protect them under sheeting and submit a meticulous report on work in progress. Meanwhile the broken-backed creature towered over me and I picked my way around it and headed for a staircase at the end of the hall. I wasn't quite sure why I was doing that. I went up the stairs, turned at a landing and was suddenly confronted by a huge grinning gorilla. I confess it terrified me, for by now I was taut in every nerve. Then I realised that the gorilla's glass case had been blasted away, leaving him standing there like a living creature shouting, 'I've survived! I've survived!'

The staircase continued but suddenly came to a jagged end, jutting out into empty air. I turned and descended warily and, as I did so, I heard, or thought I heard, sounds coming from somewhere, scrapings, a muffled thump or two, a door closing and even voices – nothing very distinct, but the subdued signals of human presence. That film again. I was assembling a soundtrack. All imagination. I listened intently nonetheless, and it seemed to me then beyond doubt that the sounds were coming from somewhere deep in the basement. From the ground floor there was another staircase going downwards. I followed it. At the bottom there was a row of dim light bulbs burning which showed a long vaulted passage. Slowly I realized that all along one side was an improvised plywood partition and in it, at regular intervals, doors with numbers and labels on them. I moved along the tidy debris-free passage and started to read the labels. They told me one thing: scholarship had survived in the catacombs. The dinosaur might be terribly maimed but the lectors, the *dozents* and the professors were still in business and hard at it … I remained sceptical about my mission but there it was, on a door: 'Herr Professor Hans Dietrich'. I wasn't quite ready. I hadn't fully prepared my head for this encounter. As I stopped before the door I tried to imagine how I would look to the Professor in the uniform of an occupying power and with an unmilitary, inexplicable bundle under my arm. I rehearsed my opening gambits and then knocked on the door. A voice gave me permission to enter.

The Professor was seated at his desk, around him the paraphernalia of scholarship – books, files, papers, some beautiful small fossil specimens and a microscope. There was a separate pile of what looked like to me student essays. It was all cramped, gloomy and uncomfortable. Behind the Professor's head was a black framed photograph. Anyone in Europe and well beyond would have recognised it at once: an icon of our times. It was a photo of a young German officer, head and shoulders, serious face, peaked cap, immaculate tunic and all the insignia, as well as, in this case, an Iron Cross at the throat. The Professor himself was as old as I thought he would be and looked very weary and apathetic. He was clearly bewildered by his visitor. He frowned and asked my business. As soon as I mentioned Nan's name he rose to his feet.

'Nan, Nan,' he repeated. 'I never thought to hear from her again. Especially now. A very clever young woman she was. Did she ever write her history of the Peasants' War?'

'No,' I said, and provocatively took the plunge. 'She was too busy with anti-Fascist political activities.'

A blatant oversimplification, in fact, but I needed the phrase at that moment. His face closed up and he looked away and said nothing. I had so far not mentioned the brown paper parcel simply because I hadn't worked out how to carry out the awkward manoeuvre of handing it to him. Meanwhile I found myself looking at that photo, the icon. The Professor swivelled and looked at it with me.

'My son,' he said, struggling to speak. 'You cannot know what it is like to lose a son. Very hard. Very hard.'

Leave it, leave it, I thought. A man is mourning his son. But I couldn't leave it.

'No, not a son.'

And I should have left it at that.

'Killed,' he managed to get out. 'A very promising biochemist.'

Again, I thought, leave it now. But again I didn't leave it.

'Where was that?'

'On the Russian front, somewhere near Smolensk.'

'A long way away, in another country,' I said, 'and what was he doing there?'

'Doing? Doing?' he said sternly. 'His duty, what else?'

I could have told him.

'Smolensk, on the Russian front,' I repeated. 'Doing his duty. What else? And your famous museum is in ruins and you're down here in the cellars. And the dinosaur's back is broken.'

'We shall repair it,' he said with his first smile. 'We must. We have our duty too. That's why I'm still here.'

I picked up the brown paper bundle.

'Nan sent these warm clothes for the winter.'

The Professor stood up again. I could see now how frail he was. I dropped the bundle on the table. In the shock-surprise of our encounter we had omitted some of the basic formalities.

'My name,' I said, 'my name is Rosen,' and I left.

Upstairs I crunched past the sad dinosaur, down the steps into the Invaliden Strasse, knowing I would not return to fraternise.

The dinosaur in Berlin was, in a sense, the sibling of the dinosaur in the Natural History Museum. Copies of the original fossil were distributed to prestigious museums all over the world.

Professor Dietrich continued to work at the museum and was much honoured in the German Democratic Republic.

In the SS barracks, 1945

Wir sind die Moorsoldaten was written by prisoners in Nazi moorland labour camps in Lower Saxony, Germany. The *Emslandlager* – 'Emsland camps', as they were known – were for political opponents of the Third Reich. In 1933, one camp, Börgermoor, held about 1,000 socialist and communist internees. They were banned from singing existing political songs so they wrote and composed their own.

In the SS barracks in Frankfurt-am-Main
(home of IG Farben, makers of holocaust gas)
I lie in one of the beds allocated to the Occupying Power.

In the dormitory in the dark in 1945
I hear an anonymous hummer in the bed beside me
Wir sind die Moorsoldaten
The song of the concentration camps
I hum along with this master-ironist

In this army bed only a few killings ago
A fine young man stretched himself out
He had not yet heard the guns in the south
Not a speck of mud or blood on his uniform
His black uniform folded tidily beside him
Nor on his lovely black boots
Standing to attention by his locker.

My hummer has stopped now.
Comrade in the dark, in your SS bed,
Are you too asking yourself
Why is there no blood on these sheets?
And how can we sleep with ghosts?